LANGUAGE ACTS

Language Acts

ANGLO-QUÉBEC POETRY
1976 to the 21st Century

Edited by
Jason Camlot & Todd Swift

Véhicule Press

Published with the generous assistance of The Canada Council for the Arts, the Book Publishing Industry Development Program of the Department of Canadian Heritage and the Société de développement des entreprises culturelles du Québec (SODEC).

The editors and publishers also express their appreciation for the support of David Graham, Dean, Arts and Science, Concordia University.

Cover design: J.W. Stewart
Set in Adobe Minion and Futura Book by Simon Garamond
Printed by Marquis Book Printing Inc.

LIBRARY AND ARCHIVES CANADA CATALOGUING IN PUBLICATION

Language acts : Anglo-Québec poetry, 1976 to the 21st century / Jason Camlot and Todd Swift, editors.

ISBN 978-1-55065-225-3

1. Canadian poetry (English)—Québec (Province)—History and criticism.
2. Canadian poetry (English)—20th century—History and criticism.
3. Canadian poetry (English)—21st century—History and criticism.
I. Camlot, Jason, 1967-
II. Swift, Todd, 1966-

PS8159.5.Q8L35 2007   C811'.54099714   C2007-900643-4

Published by Véhicule Press, Montréal, Québec, Canada
www.vehiculepress.com

Distribution in Canada by LitDistCo
orders@litdistco.ca

Distribution in U.S. by Independent Publishers Group
www.ipgbook.com

Printed in Canada on 100% post-consumer recycled paper.

Dedicated to the memory of
Louis Dudek (1918-2001)
Irving Layton (1912-2006)
and to our dear friend and teacher
Robert Allen (1946-2006)

Contents

Acknowledgments

This book began as an idea shared between the editors back in 2001and has been pursued as a labour of love since then. It has been developed with the hard work and assistance of numerous individuals.

For discussions which led to useful ideas and advice about what such a book about Anglo-Quebec poetry might become we are grateful to Robert Allen, Howard Fink, Bertrand Klein, Linda Leith, Steve Luxton, Aurèle Parisien, Bryan Sentes, Vincent Tinguely, Monique Tschofen, Derek Webster, and each and every one of the contributors to this collection.

Alessandro Porco and Fiona Foster provided thorough editorial readings of the manuscript at various stages, Darcy Ballantyne was a helpful researcher at the start, and Christopher Dilworth provided key technical assistance. Karen Emily Suurtamm's archival work in compiling information about Anglo-Quebec little magazines was indispensable, and Adrian King-Edwards generously allowed Jason Camlot to consult his private collection of periodicals for those titles that could not be found in either Montreal or National library collections.

A shortened version of Jason Camlot's introduction to this collection was presented May 16, 2006 at the 74ᵉ Congrès de l'ACFAS, Université McGill, on a panel co-organized by Lianne Moyes and Gillian Lane Mercier, entitled "Textes, territoires, traduction: (dé)locatisations/dislocations de la littérature anglo-québécoise." Thanks go to Martine-Emmanuelle Lapointe, Catherine Leclerc, Richard Cassidy, Gillian Lane-Mercier and Lianne Moyes for their useful questions and comments.

We are grateful for financial assistance that has been provided by the Concordia University Faculty of Arts and Science, and to Simon Dardick for taking on this formidable project.

We wish to acknowledge the loss of several great Anglo-Quebec poets during the period it took for this book to come into print. Ruth Taylor and Artie Gold were exciting and innovative poets. Louis Dudek and Irving Layton were key mentors for the generations of poets covered in this book. Robert Allen, too, taught and influenced hundreds of young writers. He was a dear friend and teacher of both editors and we feel blessed to have known him.

Finally, we are most grateful to our families—the ones who make the poetry possible—for their constant love and support: Todd, to his beloved wife Sara, mother Margaret, brother Jordan and father Thomas (d. 2006), Jason, to the loves of his life, Cory Garfinkle, Oscar and Nava.

Introduction: Anglo-Québec Poetry (b. 1976-)

JASON CAMLOT

English Poetry in Quebec/Anglo-Québec Poetry

There has not been a collection of essays taking account of English-language poetry in Quebec in forty years. Back in 1965, McGill University Press published the proceedings of the Foster Poetry Conference, held two years earlier in Quebec's Eastern Townships. John Glassco, who edited the proceedings under the title *English Poetry in Quebec*, remarks that the discussions at the gathering were characterized by "a constant sense of clash and conflict, not only between arrière-garde and avant-garde, between the forces of tradition and revolution, between the elders still presumably stumbling around in post-war darkness and the clear-sighted children of a putative post-nuclear dawn, but between sharply differing conceptions of the role of the poet in society and even of the nature of poetry itself."[1] In the mid-1950s Louis Dudek could write with confidence about "the dominant role of Montreal as a center of activity and a source of new poetry" in Canada.[2] By the early 1970s, most Anglo-Quebec poets who ventured to speculate about their relative significance on the national (let alone, international) stage, were developing theories that underscored the special importance of their place on the cultural margins. The essays in the present collection explore the cultural contexts, venues, forms, and politics of poetry written in English in Quebec during a period of great demographic and cultural change, starting from the moment when the Parti Québécois was first elected into power and when Montreal was in the international spotlight as host to the Summer Olympics, to a post-millennial period that has been marked by new vocabularies and modes of self-definition for Quebecers and Québécois, alike.

The idea of a coherent post-1970s Anglo-Quebec poetry community and tradition is mediated by a series of public language acts and events, words I intend to use in a sense that combines (1) the historical idea of an event that has involved linguistic conflict, (2) the legislation of linguistic practice, and (3) philosopher J. L. Austin's idea of language as functioning according to syntactical structures that make things happen.[3] The language acts and events that mediate and inform Anglo-Quebec poetry since 1976 include the tabling of several "official language" bills and their amendments, and two referenda (1980 and 1995) concerning the place of Quebec within (or without) the rest of Canada. The idea of Anglo-Quebec poetry is mediated further by the loaded terminology used to characterize Quebec society: if it is not multicultural (a Trudeau-era catchphrase that would not be embraced by Quebec nationalists) then how can the idea of a Québécois *peuple* with national aspirations that are defined by cultural, political, linguistic and geographical territory, be reconciled with a newer Québécois vision that makes gestures towards certain idealized visions of cultural pluralism? Discussion of Anglo-Quebec poetry activities is mediated even further by issues surrounding the status of English-speakers in Quebec, and consequently must address the relative usefulness of the idea of a "minority culture" in this context. Just what does "minority" mean when one can speak of the Francophone minority in English Canada, as well as the Anglophone minority in French Quebec? What is minor and what is major (what marginal and what central) in a late twentieth-century context that has us cabled, wired, and wirelessly connected across great divides and at breakneck speed?

The very idea of "Anglo" poetry, as opposed to "English" poetry of Quebec, suggests a significant shift since the 1970s in ideas about Englishness and linguistic identity in Quebec. The acute accent that appears in the title of this English-language book is there to emblemize the fact that our present, local use of *Anglo* is related in substantial ways to the francization of Quebec. *Anglo*, the Canadian colloquialism initially used within a Canadian context as a noun to distinguish between "English-speaking" as opposed to "French-speaking" Canadians, increasingly refers more specifically to the Anglophone as opposed to the Francophone Quebecer. Now a cultural icon of its own, with an array of stereotypical characteristics that have been developed by both the French-language press and English-speaking satirists and comedians, the Quebec Anglo is arguably a product of the aforementioned language events and the establishment of French as Quebec's one official language. There is a specific resonance to the word "Anglo" when used in the Quebec context. From the perspective of 1977, say—the year of the Parti-Québécois's successful initiative to adopt The Charter of the French Language—Bill 101—one understands the idea of Anglo-Quebec as originating in a newly designated community's *feelings* about a lost *past*, a new sense of its *separation* from Canada, the *francization* of its immediate society, and the *restriction* of venues for learning and using the English language which would apply to newer, non-French-speakers arriving to the province.

But even more recently, this version of the Quebec Anglo has been qualified as dated and dubbed "The Old Anglo"—the argument being that twenty years after the Parti-Québécois came into power, "a very different breed of English speakers...has emerged as many of Quebec's more traditional, longer-established Anglophones die off or leave the province."[4] A series of articles titled "The New Anglo" written by Alexander Norris for the Montreal *Gazette* in 1999 explores this idea in some detail. Norris's investigation develops the image of a new kind of Quebec Anglophone, one who is not of Anglo-Saxon origin, has had extensive education in French, speaks English, French and often a third language without angst, lives east of Boulevard St-Laurent (the traditional divider of Montreal's "two solitudes"), and is less interested in "language rights" than in the right to be a full, employable equal "within the new cultural linguistic regime of Quebec society."[5] As Le *Devoir* columnist Josée Blanchette, in her own response to Norris's series, titled "L'Anglo Tout Nouveau, Tout Beau," ["The Anglo Brand New, All Right"] remarked: "The atavistic quarrels of long ago are the common fact of the last generation of separatists and federalists who are balancing their accounts with history, as, all the while, reality follows its own cross purpose."[6] While Anglo-Quebec poetry as a self-conscious possibility may have been born with the election of the Parti-Québécois, it remains to be seen what a "New Anglo"-Quebec poetry might look like.

The solidly identifiable geographical locus of Anglo-Quebec as the originator and center of cosmopolitan modernism in the history of Canadian English-language poetry had dissolved into a postmodern "replica" (in scare quotes) of that original, both drawing upon its grounding aura, but resisting the solidity of it, as well. The Foster Poetry Conference, in this sense, came at a time of dislocation and doubt as far as the formulation of a workable mythology for Anglo-Quebec poetry goes. In other words, rather than functioning as *the* place where Canadian poetry happens, and identifying itself as a concrete, international "modernist" city, Montreal has become the *no place* or *elsewhere* of some of Canada's, North America's, the English-speaking world's most cosmopolitan writers. The past resides in the present imaginations of many of these contemporary poets as an impossibility, and that sense of the impossibility of place results in a special kind of interrogation of naturalized links between geography, language and culture. While this sort of interrogation may well be a phenomenon apparent in all literary environments that are subject to an established literary canon experienced by living writers as a territorial *nulle part*, the essays in this collection argue that it has an interesting resonance of its own for writers of Quebec who continue to work in English, given the specific literary and linguistic history of the province, and the substantial transformation of Quebec society over the past forty years.

This cosmopolitan, anti-regionalist, de-territorializing stance is discerned by the essayists of the present volume in a great variety of poetic themes, techniques, linguistic opportunities and cultural practices. It is there, first and foremost, in Tony Tremblay's account of Louis Dudek's Pound-influenced anti-provincialism and Dudek's pragmatic conception of culture as an activity of small presses and aesthetic constellations alive in relation to each other, and in conflict. It is discernible in assertions as diverse as Ken Norris's idea of a "second generation postmodernism" that conceived of poetic environment in terms of "*locale*" rather than "*nation*", and in Corey Frost's observation that the non-verbal performance elements of spoken word poetry are especially suitable to "the unique linguistic minorities-within-minorities situation" of Montreal. Accounts of the particularities informing an Anglo-Quebec post-regionalist conception of culture are present in Dean Irvine's take on Ann Carson's "neither here nor there-ness" within the international publishing market, Zachariah Wells's description of Peter Van Toorn as a tradition-translating "cosmopolite… alien in a strange land", and in Nick LoLordo's conception of David McGimpsey's poetic travels "Abroad" through cultural regions that are simultaneously American and multi-national. This idea of cultural passage is also conceived by the contributors to this book as something that happens at home, in the mind, and especially in language, as in Philip Lanthier's account of D. G. Jones's poetic praxis of living and "imagining in two languages," Carmine Starnino's examination of Michael Harris's microcosmic explorations of vernacular musicality, and Lianne Moyes's "recognition of the global dimensions of

Quebec culture" in the work of writers as diverse as Robyn Sarah, Mary di Michele and Erin Mouré. With the ambivalent sense of being deeply attached to a home that isn't quite there anymore—this ambivalence arising from a particular demographic situation—Anglo-Quebec poets, as David Solway puts it, find themselves at liberty "to build their home *in the domain of language itself*."[7] Such are some of the manifestations of the new mythologies of marginality, mobility and cultural hybridity informing the Anglo-Quebec poet's sense of self.

The Arguments of Anthologies

In his introduction to *4 Montreal Poets* (1973), Solway offered a kind of retort to Dudek's assertion of Montreal's centrality in stating that, "over the last ten years"—that is, since the Foster Poetry Conference, which took place in 1963—"Montreal has been a kind of deadwater sump, the literary boondocks of the nation."[8] A little later in the essay Solway describes Montreal as a "small and ingrown" town.[9] Such assertions are not meant to incite the city of poets into a program of urban renewal, but rather form the keystone of a series of new arguments characterizing the Anglo-Quebec poet that were developed in the 1970s. Like A. M. Klein in his "Portrait of the Poet as Landscape" (1948), only with greater polemical purpose, and in prose, *one* new argument about the Anglo-Quebec poet says, "The truth is he's not dead, but only ignored."[10] Or, as Solway puts it: "[T]he English-speaking poet in Montreal labours under the greatest disadvantage of all poets in Canada. His position is a lonely and untenable one: on the one hand he finds himself rejected by the French in Quebec, and on the other, neglected by the English in the rest of the country."[11] This represents another, and probably the most repeated, new argument about the Anglo-Quebec poet, that which is defined by Solway in its most recent manifestation, in his essay that appears in this collection, as the English Quebec (or, more specifically, Montreal) poet's unique position of "double exile" in which these poets "form the literary wing of a twofold hostage community."[12]

The opening note of Michael Harris's anthology *Poets Reading: 10 Montreal Poets at the CEGEPs* (1975) explains the occasion for his publication of "the first representative anthology to come out of Montreal in the last twenty years"[13] in terms that match Solway's comment about "far away" poets being promoted at the expense of many fine local ones, due to the recent Montreal tradition "in the local colleges and universities…to bring into the city poets from elsewhere in Canada and America."[14] *Poets Reading* would function as a handbook to a reading tour of about fifty readings scheduled as a corrective to the underexposure of Montreal poets within their own city.[15]

It is worth pausing for a moment to comment on the significance for Anglo-Quebec poetry of Quebec's English institutions of higher education. Canadian poetry since the 1940s has been generated, in great part, from academic venues. Louis Dudek commented upon this phenomenon in the mid-1940s, remarking that "a considerable part of our [Canadian] literature is being written in the universities, by professors and teachers," and noting that the same "does not hold true for the Major writers in English or American literature."[16] A reason for this, Dudek argues, is the "essentially commercial" nature of Canada: "it is a conventional, narrow, and materialistic country; and in such a country, where there is no public, there can be no people's poets or artists."[17] A similar kind of argument was revived by Farkas and Norris in their introduction to *Montreal: English Poetry of the Seventies*, when they state that the Montreal poet is isolated not only from the majority of (French-speaking) readers in his province, and from the rest of English Canada, but because "the isolated Anglophone community [of Quebec], unlike the Francophone, does not consider its arts as necessary for survival; rather, the modus operandi has been economic dominance."[18]

The Quiet Revolution, and its renovation of the Quebec system of higher education to include (since 1967) two years of CEGEP (Collège d'enseignement general et professionnel) education, created a new employment venue for Anglo-Quebec poets, and supplied a new kind of academic public for poetry. Where McGill University continued to be the primary campus of English Quebec Poets into the mid-1960s, with the likes of F. R. Scott and, especially, Louis Dudek on the McGill faculty, many of the McGill students who studied with Dudek would go on to have teaching careers in the CEGEPs. Further, given that most CEGEP instructors teaching in the humanities were not required to have doctorates, and thus have not been trained to define themselves as academic scholars subject to the institutional prescriptions of refereed journals and research societies, the CEGEP became a space that encouraged the cultivation of a more proactive, self-defining (as opposed to institutionally-defined) idea of the poet/critic, modeled upon a variety of conceptions of the public intellectual, some of them more in tune with the realities of their immediate cultural forum, than others. The significance of Concordia University's creative writing program in producing young Quebec and Canadian poets is also worth noting.[19] The degree to which these educational institutions function as a primary locus of Anglo-Quebec poetry activity may indicate, to some extent, the limitation of other institutions and venues through which English-language poetry might be disseminated in Quebec.[20]

Andre (later known as Endre) Farkas and Ken Norris pick up Solway's "double exile" argument in their introduction to the next anthology of note, *Montreal: English Poetry of the Seventies* (1978).[21] Following an epigraph from Louis Dudek stating "[i]t is the destiny of Montreal from time to time to show Canada what poetry is,"[22] Farkas and Norris identify the Quebec Anglo poet's doubly-exiled status as a linguistic issue, primarily: "English poetry in Montreal has always been written under the most unique conditions. Being a member of a minority culture within the bounds of a dominant Francophone community has made the English poet in Montreal intensely aware of his own language as well as informing him of the problem inherent in the use of language as an agent of communication."[23] Craft becomes a chief concern for these poets writing "in a language that is, in many ways, under siege."[24] It is in his sensitivity to "the potential volatility of the misuse of the language" that the political stance of the Anglo-Quebec poet is most manifest.[25] Their argument suggests that the political content of the poems in their collection is largely latent, registered at the level of a refined attention to language that has been cultivated in a linguistic hothouse. Attention is paid to how a simple idea of truth based upon correspondence (the correspondence of words with a "happening" reality), is undermined by a constant focus upon the contextual and cultural sense of language.

The first poem to appear in the next significant anthology, *Cross/cut: Contemporary English Quebec Poetry* (1982), is entitled "Bill 101". Peter Van Toorn's introduction to *Cross/cut* describes the anthology's historical moment as one of transition from an idealized period of visionary flux, characterized by meditations upon aesthetic, social and political possibility (the period of Émile Nelligan, Saint-Denys Garneau and A. M. Klein), to a period of positional conflict, practical responsibility and poetic isolation, all triggered, one assumes, by that specific language bill. For Van Toorn, the idea of Quebec as a "pluralist mosaic" defines the literary climate in which the Anglo poet (circa 1982) stirs, and his Anglo-Quebec poets (like those of

Solway, Farkas and Norris) are perceived to be in an "alienated position" because this "gypsy group" receives "the congenial reception of neither Canada nor Québec."[26]

The idea of a literature emergent in an historically confirmed exilic situation has strong precedents in Québécois literary history. With the more recent Anglo-Quebec arguments of double exile and alienation in mind, it is not so much embarrassing as strange and suggestive to note that Gilles Marcotte first used the formula in 1955, in his essay, "Le Double exil d'Octave Crémazie," to explore the situation informing the literary work of a mid-nineteenth-century poet of French Canada. In writing about Crémazie, Marcotte remarks that the desire of "le Mouvement littéraire de 1860", of which Crémazie was a part, was defined largely by a patriotism "of the *Ancien Régime*, fully nourished by regret and nostalgia. We live in Canada, and here we will stay, we belong here; but at the same time we do not stop dreaming of France as a lost country."[27] Crémazie's ideal, while he lived in Quebec, was that of an idealized, lost homeland. That is the first exile. Crémazie's second sense of exile arose when he was forced (in order to avoid prison) to return to France for the remaining seventeen years of his life.[28] Writing from this situation, the poet expressed a burdensome sense of loss for "Le Canada." Marcotte concluded that Crémazie's human drama served as an apt symbol for the French Canadian writer, a symbol that captured a personal drama of division, of being torn between two necessary identifications. Marcotte's final comment about Crémazie states that he did not become a major poet because he was unable to fuse these two conflicting identifications, and because "he lacked the basic unity of consciousness that is absolutely needed for poetic creation."[29] In drawing this conclusion, Marcotte did for Québécois literary history what T. S. Eliot did for British literary history (with his idea of "a dissociation of sensibility" articulated in the essay "The Metaphysical Poets"[30]), that is, he identified a key, historically specific experience with which to define a national corpus of literature—and that defining experience was, as summed up neatly by Pierre Nepveu, "estrangement from life, a sense of separation from the world, and an alienated consciousness", in a word, total exile.[31] More recent French-language criticism—for instance, Françine Bordeleau's article in *Lettres Québécoises* (hiver 2006)—has made use of this exilic model as a comparative frame for understanding connections, rather than disjunctions, between Anglo and Franco literatures of Quebec. While it is probably worth exploring further the fact that Marcotte's idea of double

20

exile is one of "either/or" demanding a fusion of both, and the Anglo-Quebec poet's conception of double exile is more of a "neither/nor" one ("neither Canada nor Québec," as Van Toorn puts it), the one point I will stress here is that of a common definition of the poet's sense of self as one that is thoroughly alienated.

Whatever one might think about the poetical potential of this "alienated position"—and even if the idea of the Anglo-Quebecer's double alienation or minority status must, certainly to my mind, be qualified significantly by the fact that Quebec-Anglophones possess far more opportunities to identify with (a) Quebec-Francophones and (b) the rest of English-speaking North America, than this "double exile" argument wants to allow—there is a strong (generational) basis for this description of the Anglo-Quebecer's position if one considers it in relation to the official linguistic and social policies of Quebec and Canada since 1976.

Language Events and National Pluralism(s)

In 1969 the Canadian Official Languages Act established English and French as the two national languages of Canada. And in 1971 the government of Canada proclaimed its policy of Canadian Multiculturalism, which would support the cultural efforts of non-official linguistic and cultural groups throughout Canada. These policies, which would become the basis for the continued Canadian advocacy of ethnic and cultural multiplicity within a bilingual frame, would come to seem inadequate in the context of a Quebec that was working towards its own linguistically-conceived national self-definition. For example, in 1974, the Quebec Liberal government adopted Bill 22, making French Quebec's official language, and requiring new immigrants to the province to pass an English language exam to verify that they were eligible for education in English. More language laws, and heightened efforts of a newly elected separatist party, the Parti Québécois (PQ), to establish Quebec as a sovereign nation would inform the sense of place and identity of Quebec Anglophones into the next century. The first legislative act of the PQ was the adoption of Bill 101.[32]

One important narrative about English-speakers in Quebec since the adoption of Bill 101 is that they gradually developed a community-identity that altered their sense of place in relation to Canada, with its bilingual, multicultural federalist vision, on the one hand, and to Quebec, with its sometimes nationalist, sometimes more pluralist conception of francization, on the other.[33] As Anglo advocate Reed Scowen describes it, prior to the election of the PQ "the English 'community' of Quebec was not really aware of its own existence."[34] While it had several unifying elements, like its two daily newspapers (the *Gazette* and the now defunct *Star*), and its local television and radio stations, it did not recognize itself as a distinct, homogenous group. English-speaking residents of Quebec saw themselves more as "Canadians living in Quebec." But with the PQ's political program that highlighted the link between language and social identity, and worked to promote a more exclusive use of French in Quebec society, Scowen argues,

> The English discovered that they did exist as a group, at least in the minds and the hearts of the French majority. It might be said that the English "community" in Quebec was invented by the French, and the invention was not a pretty thing to see. It was in many ways a caricature.[35]

What was invented, Scowen goes on to say, was the Quebec Anglophone's conception of himself as the member of a minority community. Prior to the 1970s, Anglophones in Quebec had been acting as a majority despite their actual numbers in the province. Now, the Francophone majority, through its support of a nationalist political party, "insisted that the English awaken to their own existence and then transform their understanding of themselves into that of a minority."[36] This idea would form the basis of Scowen's "different vision" for the future of Quebec, which calls for a new kind of cooperation between the province's Francophone majority and Anglophone minority, characterized by the removal of language legislation (because "no government can guarantee linguistic security"[37]), and the relaxation of the persistent call for "linguistic and cultural distinctiveness."[38] Scowen bases his call for cooperation and legislative relaxation upon a distinction between language and culture ("a language...is finally only a means of communication"[39]), and (occasionally) on a vision of cultural hybridity rather than cultural homogeneity.[40]

From the perspective of the popular Québécoise political analyst Josée Legault, Scowen's vision represents a sneaky power grab: a radicalization of Anglophone political discourse, with the ultimate objective of reestablishing bilingualism and cultural parity between the Anglophones and the Francophones in Quebec.

He aims to convince the Francophones that the Anglophones are a minority "like the rest", that their language, spoken by close to 300 million North Americans, is in danger, that they are menaced and mistreated, and above all, that their "rights" should be extended, and not reduced. He aims, further, to have us believe that an Anglophone community could not live in a Quebec in which the principal language of communication is not its own. He aims, finally, to obtain the "maximum", bilingualism, whether in an independent Quebec, or not. This duality, destined to fail in the rest of Canada, will thus be transposed into a "reborn" Quebec.[41]

Legault contests the idea that Anglo-Quebecers are a minority "like the rest," pointing out that they are actually part of an English-speaking majority in North America. Her book, titled *L'invention d'une minorité: Les Anglo-Québécois*, stresses the inventedness (i.e., the fictionality) of this representation of Quebec's Anglophones as a community of victims under siege, and the strategic purposes it serves, namely, the reestablishment of bilingualism in Quebec, and the refusal (which is "inavouable", shameful, according to Legault) of Quebec Anglos to accept their social responsibility as members of a political and linguistic minority within Quebec.[42]

Scowen and Legault provide two opposing visions of a pluralist Quebec. Scowen's vision deploys a Trudeauist argument for bilingualism and cultural diversity within a legally protected "just society" (Trudeau's catch-phrase for civic nationalism) as a safeguard against the governmental decree of any one "official" culture, and the dangers of cultural or linguistic isolation.[43] Legault, on the other hand, sees Scowen's Trudeauist approach to Quebec society as shamefully disrespectful of Quebec's more recent vision of integration nationalism, which attempts to combine a support for pluralism with a stress on the necessary "affirmation of the francophone collectivity and institutions as a pole of integration for immigrants...in order to guarantee the survival of the French fact in Quebec."[44]

For the most part, the Anglo-Quebec poets of this period are not, like Legault, obvious advocates of a normative pluralism that stresses the integrative role of Quebec's majority language and culture. Nor are they Scowen-like Anglo-activists, pitting their identities as artists and citizens upon a politicized Anglophone community identity. Still, one thing that these writers do have in common is that they are all, in one way or another, working, writing and living within a local political and media din that scrutinizes, debates and reports upon Quebec language events on a regular basis. In Quebec, the programming of language-event-radio may come in and out, depending on seasonal reception, but the radio itself is never turned off. While I will not venture to attribute a single political vision to the diverse group of poets who fall under our rubric *Anglo-Quebec poet*, I do believe that the constant exposure to the loud, partisan political discourses I have just alluded to tends to develop in many Anglos (and many Francophones, as well) a sympathy with an advanced (and perhaps, idealistic or impractical) version of extreme pluralism that sociologists and political scientists call "interculturalism" and cultural theorists refer to as "cultural hybridity."

As Dimitrios Karmis describes it, interculturalism surpasses multi-cultural and multinational visions of society by asserting "that most individuals have multiple identities" and "that none of these identities is dominant enough to subordinate the others."[45] In *Hybridité Culturelle*, Sherry Simon argues that recent inhabitants of Montreal's Mile End district have consciously capitalized upon an existent sociological heterogeneity in order to live according to a hybrid conception of culture that they value in the abstract, as an alternative to the two dominant political modes of discourse (bilingual multiculturalism and French integration nationalism) that have character-ized language debates in Quebec over the past several decades.

Simon notes the difficulty in conceiving of Québécois culture in terms that promote the heritage and history of French Canadians in Quebec and yet are simultaneously multifarious and inclusive. Is the ideal of a unified national culture still desirable, let alone realizable, she asks? One of her responses to this question states, "It is the artists, as much as the politicians, who will find answers to these questions."[46] And she goes on to find an artist's answer to this question about the desirability of Québécois cultural homogeneity in the fact that most Quebec writers, whether Anglophone or Francophone, bear signs in their work of what she calls "l'écriture hybride"— a mode of writing marked by the dissonant effects of unrealized translation, unusual syntax, disparate vocabulary, and a general interrogation of naturalizing tropes of linguistic mastery and cultural belonging.[47]

Hybrid Writing/Local Reading

There are all kinds of examples of hybrid writing to be found in Anglo-Quebec poetry, from A. M. Klein's *franglais* neologisms ("erablic", "maisonry", "Bilinguefact") in his much-anthologized poem "Montreal"[48] to Peter Van Toorn's "Mountain" translations of poems from their original languages he does not know.[49] As in a "minor literature" which Gilles Deleuze and Félix Guattari say "a minority constructs within a major language," Anglo-Quebec poetry often deploys its "own" language "like a 'paper language' or an artificial language," that is, as a language aware of its own idiom in relation to more dominant and naturalized kinds of usage.[50] Erín Mouré's *O Cidadán* (2002), for example, which intersects a word (citizen) with an Othered semblance of itself so that it becomes "[a] word we recognize though we know not its language," creates an unsettled "semantic pandemonium" out of a concept that official discourse (whether Canadian or Québécois political discourse) wants to settle, to *mean* harmoniously and quietly.[51] The language acts Mouré dreams of in this book are not prescriptive official bills to be enforced, but rather the quixotic and rich activities of an ongoing process: "It is citizenship's *acts* I dream of, acts not constrained or dilated by *nation*, especially as *nation-state* and its 19thc. model of sovereignty. Rather, *acts* as movements or gestures across a differential plane, not tied solely to ideology's (history's) rank function. But how to articulate this without invoking transcendent 'citizens' as if Platonic 'ideas'?"[52] Carmine Starnino's *With English Subtitles* (2004), although a very different kind of poetry book than *O Cidadán*, is equally concerned with the complexities of personal idiom and intimate usage as it relates to officialese. In the poem, "On the Obsolescence of Caphone," for example, the poet of "careful, English talk" harvests his sounds from the likes of Italian roofers and his Uncle Louie in order to "urge his poems to unschool themselves."[53]

The very idea of un-schooling one's English, in order to make oneself less *femminiello* (less "faggoty") by using a "tough-vowelled and fierce" language, a language with more "gots" in it, raises other, more public Quebec-specific language questions that are simultaneously central and marginal to the concerns of Starnino's poem. "Caphone,"[54] the opening stanzas tell us, was, to the speaker's ears,

> Last heard—with a lovely hiss on the "ph"—
> August 1982 during an afternoon game of *scopa*

25

turned nasty. And now, missing alongside it,
are hundreds of slogans, shibboleths, small

depth charges of phrasing. Like an island-colony
of sea-birds screeching our own special cry,
I recall words all backwater squawk, recall
the curmudgeonly clunk and jump of their song,

a language dying out but always, someplace,
going on...[55]

While Montreal is never mentioned in this poem—and in that sense it is a
poem reporting upon an inadvertent progress of linguicide and glottophagie
that might be happening anywhere[56]—the simile used to describe the
material that is recollected is rich with local significance. The screeching
"island-colony/ of sea-birds" evokes both the actual gulls that can be heard
on the island of Montreal (say, the north-central part of the island, which
borders Rivière des Prairies, where Starnino attended elementary and high
school[57]), and, through the analogy at work, the Italian community that
made this part of the island of Montreal its own, that re-colonized it, so to
speak. The slippage between the screeching that is recalled by the speaker as
something separate from himself—the way Wordsworth recalls the "Cry"
of the cuckoo that he heard in "schoolboy days"[58]—and the simultaneous
identification of that same screeching as "our own," captures nicely the
trouble that a local, linguistic inheritance can cause to any supposedly
autonomous lyric self, speaking any supposedly straightforward utterance,
spoken in what is supposedly his "own" language.

The very fact that Starnino is writing about his specific Italian community's missing "shibboleths"—test-words of pronunciation and cultural
distinction, inclusion and exclusion—in *English*, locates his argument about
the loss and preservation of his familial culture within Quebec's larger
debates about cultural loss and preservation as they relate to language
education, to the system originating in the BNA Act which guaranteed the
two "originary" national groups of Quebec (Catholics and Protestants) the
right to study in schools organized according to their respective religions,
and which had attached to it the added right (argued for by religious leaders)
to study in their respective language (Protestants—English, Catholics—
French).

As Marc Shell has pointed out, "[o]ne way to understand the nationalist workings of such states as Quebec is to ask, What happens to these 'immigrants' to Quebec who are, by racial or linguistic generation, neither French-speaking nor English-speaking, or neither 'English' nor 'French'?"[59] A poem like "On the Obsolescence of Caphone" is one of the things that happens as a result of such workings.[60] The very "obsolete" word that sparks Starnino's meditation upon the status of his family's "buckaroo"[61] Italian dialect within his own lyric English, points to this issue of the relationship between education, linguistic refinement, and one's inclusion in or exclusion from a self-constituting community. While "Caphone" is not as extreme an exclusionary term as the Greek word "Barbarian", which signifies enemy, stutterer, and in an even earlier meaning, "a people who cannot speak 'our' language properly,"[62] it is still a strong, pejorative designation for someone perceived to be boorish and ill-mannered. Its earliest meaning seems to have been "peasant" or "uneducated person."[63] Education—school—is both what enables this rich, lyric meditation upon the losses that school has entailed, and what leaves the speaker thinking that "*futtiti*" is "a good word for the situation/…that might one day leave my poems illiterate."[64] There is no real equivalent for "*futtiti*", and in revealing as much, Starnino also reveals that when we settle in a new place and learn a new tongue, we find that language isn't just about language. It is about belonging, about personal identity, and national identity, and about ideological boundaries of various kinds. Further, language is (in the words of Alan Liu, here speaking of Wordsworth) "about the raw elsewhereness of the sense of history," about the "elsewhereness" of the immigrant "whose tongue cuts him off from the new, and of his descendant whose tongue cuts him off from the old."[65]

The speaker of "On the Obsolescence of Caphone," comes to the realization that "I'm whatever comes across in the translation,"[66] or, to put it another way, that he is not so much here in the language of his poems, as he is elsewhere, in the pregnant silences that surround them. When Starnino refers to the "immigrant jabber" the vigour of which he now tries to match in a tough-sounding English, and then again, when he questions what he even means by "immigrant"—"I say 'immigrant'/but, really, what the hell do I know?"[67]—he is packing a long history of Italian-Quebec language events into idiomatically dense quatrains. And these language events, with their controversial public mandates and proud and private familial motives, hopes and expectations, are there in the quatrains to be unpacked. (See footnote 60 of this essay for more details.)

The confrontation of private motive with public mandate is a key trope of much recent Anglo-Quebec poetry. In one stanza from a poem in Carolyn Marie Souaid's *October* (1999), for instance, the speaker addresses her Québécois lover and the various forces of distance that accumulate between them as he drives off with their son:

> In case you're interested, my tea's down to the cold dregs
> And I'm reading stuff in the paper—
> 17,436 8,947 10,420 11,325
> 8,642 7,618 4,129.
> Quebecers coming, Quebecers going. By the planeload.[68]

Lists of numbers cataloguing the results in the most recent election appear in this stanza without the charged, political choices attached to them, making us see the abstract demographic clusters calculating political positions that inundate Quebec newspaper-readers on a weekly basis (and we, significantly, have no idea *what* paper is being read here—the *Gazette*, *La Presse*, *Le Devoir*?[69]) as a formal, abstract and conditional, rather than politically meaningful reality. Quebecers are coming and going both literally (people are leaving by the planeload), and figuratively in the sense of being bewildered by the effects of having to answer such official, public questions about the future of Quebec society. Consequently, the poems in *October* suggest, Quebecers often find themselves not knowing whether they are coming or going.

If they are going, chances are (at least according to the separatist slogan "101 or 401"—what had been a Hobson's choice for rigidly unilingual Anglophones) they are going to Toronto, where they will find themselves wandering the streets and feeling a new kind of exaltation, or alienation, as the case may be. In David McGimpsey's *Hamburger Valley, California* (2001), a book far less explicitly Quebec-focused than Souaid's *October*, but rather "about" California as a rich and imaginative everyplace, such a scenario is richly explored. The poem "Où Est Queen Street?" figures Grade-Nine detention time spent in the library as a *Bildung* story that leads through the (natively Can-Lit) backwoods, where the English-educated teen of the late seventies eventually grows up to be a man who thinks he may be too old to "crawl under desks," too old, in short, not to prepare for a final departure from ambivalence and a cold, unwelcoming place that had been home.[70] School in Quebec is the place where one learns "careful, English talk" (recall the phrase from Starnino's poem), if you have the legal right to go to an English school, and your parents chose to send you there. In McGimpsey's poem, English school is where official national policy could be disobeyed, ignored, spit-balled like the back of the geography teacher's head. School is where detention was served in the library,

> ...while the class was patiently dedicated
> to continuing its macaroni salute
> to Canadian Unity.
> *Quebec On Vous Aime.*
> *Ensemble Nous Restons Fort.*[71]

Library detention here is that safe refuge where *Oui* isn't the choice Anglo-Quebecers fear most, but a Québécois porn magazine hidden behind the bulrushes, poplars, the shade of triplexes, in the Ville d'Anjou backwoods past the school yard. It is where Greek is a perplexing refuge from more immediate language skirmishes.[72] And, insofar as it fails to teach you enough French to be employable in the new reality of Québec Français, it is the gateway to the path that leads to other Canadian cities and American ones, to Ottawa, Ontario, to "a gazebo/ behind the parliament buildings" where assurance is sought "that there really is a little difference/ between Dada and Surrealism,/ between B- and C+", between Montreal and any other place one might live, like Toronto, for instance. Out from under the protective desk, out of the "boondocks of the nation" (recall the phrase from Solway's essay), the English-educated Quebec poet grown-up asks himself: "[A]m I preparing for the final departure...?"[73] The final departure is indeed imagined (both humorously and sweetly) by McGimpsey as a liberating move westwards, to an ever-shining sun, and a fresh start:

> Through the backwoods,
> through wilted maple and discarded Frigidaires,
> I'm sure I'll come to that sunlit clearing
> where I'll finally see the palm trees of the Don Valley,
> the GTO convertibles cruising the Danforth;
> the carpark view of the avacado groves of Etobicoke;
> the Big Kahunas of Ryerson who dump school
> and head to The Beaches with their boogie boards;
> the light-drenched promenades off Bathurst...
> I'll meet you and your freckles there.[74]

Toronto, California, is, finally, a dreamscape both lamented and mocked by McGimpsey who has, in reality, like many English-educated poets of the seventies, decided to stay (or return) home, and, further, in a certain sense, to stay in school, and enjoy the continued refuge that comes with the significant Anglophone institutions of higher education that still thrive in Quebec in the twenty-first century.

Introductory Conclusion, or, On Local Reading in General

The last few pages have rehearsed local readings of poems that have much more to them than the Anglo-Quebec interpretations I have given them. Still, one argument of this collection is that it is interesting, enlightening and important to engage in particularizing readings of books that will most commonly be taken to be about more general issues: national versus global citizenship (Mouré's *O Cidadán*), the post-immigrant experience (Starnino's *With English Subtitles*), or a Canadian poet abroad in America (McGimpsey's *Hamburger Valley, California*). In exploring possible interpretive connections between place (or conceptions of place) and poetic practice, and in generating readings of actual poems in light of an array of linguistic and geo-political realities that shape life in Quebec, the essays in this book inform the reader of English-language poetry activities in Quebec, and collectively develop cases for their significance in relation to broader social, political, linguistic and literary transformations that have occurred in Quebec, Canada and abroad over the past forty years. Still, local readings of the kind I am advocating here come with their own set of critical pitfalls and rhetorical formulae of which we should be aware. As Leah Marcus, whose *Puzzling Shakespeare: Local Reading and Its Discontents* represents a key early example of this kind of criticism, has remarked: "The project for localization sets itself resolutely against the general and universal, but has its own ways of creating generalities, leaping over difference in order to construct an alternative order of 'essences' out of the materials of history."[75] Alan Liu has called this critical tendency the inadvertent assertion of "local transcendence." In a lengthy essay of that title ("Local Transcendence") Liu argues strongly that many modes of cultural criticism (from cultural anthropology, to the "new" historicism, pragmatism and Marxism) follow a directional argumentative formula that moves from a major premise of material reality, through a "minor," detailed account of that reality 'in practice', towards a conclusion in aesthetics—the close reading of a poem, for instance, which is approached as an artifact that contains, and accounts for symbolically, the great cultural complexities that also informed its production.[76]

While this is a formula the reader will recognize in some of the essays in this book—it is manifest, to some degree, in my own introduction—*Language Acts: Anglo-Québec Poetry, 1976 to the 21st Century* has been organized in such a way that no single argument about a particular poet, or school of poets, functions as *the* unifying, essentializing conception of Anglo-Quebec poetry-ness. On the contrary, one of the rewarding lessons that emerges from this collection is how differing abstract claims arising from the analysis of particular historically-located scenes, poetry collectives, and poems, can emerge in simultaneity. This fact is made especially clear in this collection as a result of its containing essays by poet-critic "practitioners" alongside articles by scholars who work in the academy. The academic scholar writes out of a different set of concerns than the Anglo-Quebec poet who is writing to make sense of his own significance within his local setting, and the import of his local setting within a national and international frame.

The book opens with a series of reprinted essays spanning the late 1950s to the 1990s. These pieces, some of them articles from literary journals, others the introductions to key anthologies that I have already discussed above, are all written with the aim of assessing the place of English language writing in Quebec, and represent acts of literary account-taking from specific historical moments along the continuum of the period in question. Louis Dudek's confident essay "The Montreal Poets" (1957) locates the origin of contemporary poetry in three graduates of McGill University, and then, listing Phyllis Webb, Leonard Cohen, Eli Mandel, Gael Turnbull, Daryl Hine and Al Purdy as more recent keepers of Montreal's literary exuberance, goes on to argue for Montreal poets as the cornerstone of a national movement that will materialize in the very near future, in the early 1960s. One thing that Dudek could not foresee was a shift in Canadian poetry towards an American Black Mountain and experimental aesthetic, which would be perceived by the natural, local heirs of Layton and Cohen—figures like Seymour Mayne and K.V. Hertz, for example—as neglectful of the Canadian tradition and obfuscating of its important poetic past.[77] Most of the remaining essays in this first section—those of Farkas, Norris, Van Toorn, Hancock and Solway—develop narratives that attempt to explain, from a variety of aesthetic positions, what happened during that interim period between 1958 and the early 1970s, in order to assess what Anglo-Quebec poetry means in each of their own particular moments.

If the first section of this book offers polemics and self-assessments from localized instances in the recent history of Anglo-Quebec writing, the concerns of the essays in the second section of the book examine similar materials and concerns, but with the benefit of hindsight. Tony Tremblay's article on Louis Dudek provides us with as thorough an account as has been written of Dudek's great importance for contemporary writing in Montreal, and, in doing so, also delivers a compelling account of what it meant for a devout internationalist like Dudek to promote English-language writing in Quebec. Norman Ravvin's essay on the legacy of Layton and Cohen represents another key retrospective account of the meaning for present local writers of these two formidable father figures. Rounding off this section is a frank and elegant account of the literary geo-politics informing the city of Montreal from the perspective of a scholar and poet, David McGimpsey, who continues to work and write in this city, and to think about the implications of his doing so.

The third section of the book contains essays that examine the cultural and aesthetic significance of specific sites of literary collectivity, whether it be an actual arts collective like the Vehicle Poets of the late 1970s, an important venue for the publication of English-language poetry in Quebec as *Zymergy* magazine was, the important scenes of the oral performance of poetry in Montreal during its thriving spoken-word period in the 1990s (to the present, really), or an actual geographical site, in this case the Eastern Townships, a region of Quebec 100+ kilometers out of Montreal, where some of the province's most important Anglophone writers wrote and lived for an extended period. The essays in this section provide the insights of individuals who were directly involved in the sites of collectivity they are writing about: Sonja Skarstedt was the editor of *Zymergy*, Michael Benazon was a Townships writer, Ken Norris, Artie Gold, Stephen Morrissey, Claudia Lapp, Endre Farkas, Tom Konyves, and John McAuley were all Vehicle poets, and Corey Frost is a spoken word artist. But in addition to having personal investment in their subject matter, the writers in this section are also teachers and scholars of literature, and their examination of their topics reveal a rich combination of implication and critical distance.

The fourth and longest section of the collection provides the reader with detailed accounts of the strengths, pleasures and significance of the poetry of a rich selection of English-language poets who have been active in

Quebec since 1976. Some written by Canadian literature scholars and others by fellow contemporary writers, all of these essays will instill in the reader a new sense of appreciation and understanding of what adds up to a rich corpus of English-language poetry from Quebec. Some of the poets written about here—Robert Allen, Michael Harris, Robyn Sarah, and possibly even D. G. Jones and Peter Van Toorn—may be discovered by readers for the first time, while others who may have a more developed national or international profile—writers like Ann Carson, Mary di Michele, and Erin Mouré, for instance—will be rediscovered by readers for having been placed in the context of their important, local scenes of writing. All of the authors featured here are worth learning about, and are profiled and examined with great critical insight by the authors who are either appreciating or analyzing them. As in any anthology, exclusions are inevitable. To my mind, the exclusions of the present collection are felt most strongly in this section of essays on individual writers. There are many other Anglo-Quebec poets who might have been featured here, both for their unique poetic voices, and for the possibility of identifying their work within the context of Quebec. Among only the most obvious candidates who are not fully covered here, and who would be interesting to write about, at length, from an Anglo-Quebec perspective, I would include, Mark Abley, Fortner Anderson, Raymond Filip, Bill Furey, Ralph Gustafson, Charlotte Hussey, Catherine Kidd, Steve Luxton, David Manicom, Eric Ormsby, Norm Sibum, David Solway[78], Carolyn Marie Souaid, Andrew Steinmetz and Ruth Taylor, as well as more recently transplanted poets, like Stephanie Bolster, Jon Paul Fiorentino and Susan Gillis. I mention these names not so much in apology as to incite the interest of the poetry reader and scholar to build upon the work offered here and to remind readers of the actual richness and diversity of contemporary Anglo-Quebec poetry even beyond the bounds of this already wide-ranging collection. Selected titles by some of these authors can be found in the appendix to this book that lists past nominees and winners of the Quebec Writer's Federation's annual A. M. Klein prize for poetry.

As a coda to the essays in this collection, we have provided other appendices, as well. These additional informational lists and bibliographies will be of interest to readers who want to have a sense of the variety of names and publications that together make up the Anglo-Quebec writing scene of the last forty years. One substantial element of this series of appendices is an annotated bibliography of Anglo-Quebec poetry periodicals. This bibliography provides a series of informal, descriptive entries for over fifty different little magazines—ranging from internationally known poetry journals to mimeographed, stapled pamphlets. This list of poetry magazines, each one developed, edited, assembled, and printed by its own team of individuals who cared deeply about English-language poetry in Quebec, emblemizes the rich, eclectic, often ephemeral, but always interesting and enthusiastic field of poetic activity in the province since 1976.

I. Foundational Polemics and Self-Assessments

The Montreal Poets[1]

LOUIS DUDEK

To the envy of less happy cities—Toronto, Halifax, Victoria—one of the particularities in the development of English poetry in Canada over the past thirty years has been the dominant role of Montreal as a center of activity and a source of new poetry. Of the poets who have taken up residence in Montreal for an important phase of their career, or who have been bred here from the start, the list includes the principal names in the modernist school. The main literary magazines, also, containing the programs of modern poetry in Canada, have come from Montreal. Work along the same lines elsewhere has often taken its rise from the example of Montreal. Not that Montreal invariably turns out the best poetry; far from it. E. J. Pratt (Newfoundland and Toronto) is still the most accomplished poet we have, with the most solid body of work behind him; Earle Birney is a dominant figure in B.C.; James Reaney, Anne Wilkinson, and Jay Macpherson have appeared at other outposts, although Miss Macpherson has felt a touch of Montreal's magic wand (by work and study in McGill's Redpath Library): these hold their own beside the best poets from Montreal. But Montreal poets include the key figures in the development of modern poetry as a definite tradition in Canada, opposed to the sentimental-genteel poetry of the old culture. The reasons for Montreal's special role in poetry has often been a matter for speculation—not that the problem is a very momentous one, it is no doubt only a form of self-congratulation—yet a few further self-indulgent reflections on the subject may be entertaining, or even useful.

Although it is the largest city in Canada, Montreal is not a central metropolis in relation to this country in the way that Paris or London are cultural capitals of their countries. The thin ribbon of Canadian life stretching along the border of the U.S. from Pacific to Atlantic could hardly have a physical center of any kind. The bow of the ribbon is really in southern Ontario, and Toronto is the economic knot that keeps it neatly tied. Montreal, moreover, is predominantly French in population, so that poetry in English would hardly be expected to find its natural home here. The English-reading audience for poetry in this city is veritably non-existent, and the newspapers habitually ignore poetry in their review pages. How does it happen, then, that Montreal has sprung forth a whole branch of twentieth-century poetry in English within the last three decades?

The scope of this achievement is worth noting. Contemporary poetry in Canada takes its origin from the work of three poets beginning in the late 1920s, A. J. M. Smith, F. R. Scott, and A. M. Klein, all three of them graduates of McGill University. Their work developed through the thirties, appearing in the *McGill Fortnightly* and in the collection *New Provinces* (1936), the latter edited by F. R. Scott in Montreal; the movement then went through a sudden expansion in the early 1940s, stimulated by the Montreal magazines *Preview*, *First Statement*, and *Northern Review*, bringing out the poets P. K. Page, Patrick Anderson, Irving Layton, and a half-dozen others. It was in *First Statement* that I first appeared, and I was for a time one of the editors of this magazine. The publication of a score of important books, anthologies, and studies of Canadian poetry mark this major phase of the movement. Since then, Montreal poetry has brought into prominence other poets, notably Phyllis Webb, Eli Mandel, and at present Leonard Cohen and Daryl Hine. Other names decorate, or have decorated, the way of advance, among them Leo Kennedy, Bruce Ruddick, Patrick Waddington and Miriam Waddington.

At its best—and a good anthology of Modern Canadian Poetry has not yet been compiled—this poetry ranks on a par with work from England and the U.S. since 1930. (We have nothing near or equal to Auden, true; as to Dylan Thomas, I think he is a much smaller figure than most people have imagined.) The comparison for Canadian poets would be with Spender, MacNeice, Barker, Karl Shapiro, Jarrell, etc., excellent poets in their kind, but not over-shadowing presences. We have individual poems to match the best of theirs: an achievement that most Canadian readers and reviewers seem to know nothing about. This modern poetry in Canada amounts to a complete body of literature; it is the third sizeable harvest of poetry we have produced, the first being that of Carman, Roberts, D. C. Scott, and Lampman, the second that of Service, Drummond, and E. J. Pratt.

One way to guess at the possible reasons why Montreal has played so important a part in this development is a look at the nature of the poetry coming from this city. Taking Klein, Anderson, and Layton as exhibits for one theme, we can see in their poetry a sense of place, of a real city that has an odd, ugly vitality of its own. (Like Souster's Toronto, the city may be seen by the poet in terms of rejection, yet provide a grand subject for poetry.) These poets give us images of Montreal from various point of vision: Klein with a nostalgic Jewish *Gemut*; Anderson with a visual and verbal imaginative idealism; Layton with a tortured and distorting passion; yet it is a recognizable city, this exasperating, "cosmopolitan," superficial, rigid yet loosely-jointed Montreal—Westmount and the East End separated by the barricades of Main street and its adjoining blind lanes. I do not say that Montreal poets have on the whole done a very thorough job of depicting or projecting their city in poetry, nor that this is the main source of their strength; but a certain advantage has come to Montreal poetry from the physical tumult and discords of this great city, and from the impulse of the poets, sometimes as a modernist program, to get it down on the page. So here is Klein's Montreal:

> the full birdseye circle to the river
> its singsong bridges, its mapmaker curves, its
> island with the two shades of green, meadow and wood;
> and circles round that water-tower'd coast...

And the Montreal of Patrick Anderson:

> Lonely, hauling down rain,
> or full of summer birds untying the air,
> carrying the ribbons of air away in their beaks,
> mountain, volcanic mound and mindlessness,
> central, empty, and windswept giddy crown,...

And here that of Irving Layton:

> At the explosion of Peel and St. Catherine
> O under the green neon signs I saw
> the ruined corpses of corpulent singers
> arise from their tight mounds, sigh and
> stumble upon each other dragging
> their tattered shadows in their arms...

The mixture of races—French Canadian, Jewish, English, Irish, Scotch, with several communities of other nationalities (10 per cent)—has given Montreal poets a social kaleidoscope of diverse interest which they have occasionally exploited. Klein has made a definite program of it, one would think, in *The Rocking Chair*. Elsewhere it lies scattered in a fragmentary form, or as background, in the books of the poets; a vein never sufficiently worked, but offering a perpetual stimulus as variety of experience to anyone living in Montreal.

With the mixture or superposition of races, the exact degree of development, or rather lack of development, in our cultural relations is just enough to make the poets feel the lack bitterly, and want to supply it, or curse their fate for failure to do so. The intellectual stagnation of Canada as a whole has a special tang for the poets in Montreal, because here the possibilities of a rich cultural growth are frustrated by ignorance, laziness, hollow tradition, and immovable conservatism. The poets P. K. Page and Phyllis Webb blend subtle feminine potions of dissatisfaction; other poets take theirs straight. So Miss Webb writes, both out of time and timelessness—

Sense of loss
across
my hand—
it droops
to my side—
I stand
wilting
like some poor
summer flower
of tradition...

Montreal poetry, in fact, has been characteristically satirical. F. R. Scott is of course the chief wit; but not one of the fifteen or so poets of the last three decades has omitted to make his sardonic social comment. Where the rest of the country is either settled into traditional conformity or wastes in a bookless and mindless semiliteracy, Montreal has produced poets who are social critics and poets of protest (Layton, Anderson, Scott, etc.), because our "cosmopolitan culture" is forever in that state of simmering, power of boil, that is just enough to exasperate an active mind.

In his recent book *The Eye of the Needle*, F. R. Scott has this bilingual bit of wit:

> It was a big parade.
> The floats were big.
> Such lovely old costumes!
> There were big bands.
> And delegates in top hats
> From St. Hyppolyte de Kilkenny
> And Ste. Suzanne de Boundary Line.
> In front were all the leaders
> Leading,
> While behind came all the followers
> Following,
> And the cheery crowds gave cheers
> Content with all their yesteryears.

Having said this much, one remembers that poetry in Canada, in the period since 1925 when Montreal became the stage foremost of the new work, has undergone a transition from a late-Romantic poetry, rooted in a Loyalist genteel culture and in moral-religious optimism and puritanism, to the cosmopolitan and exploratory poetry of American modernism. In this transition, Toronto could hardly serve. Fredericton, Kingston, Ottawa might catch on later, but could not possibly begin the break-up. Montreal, having the advantages of a loose miscellaneous society, has therefore provided the setting for a radical change in taste which has since passed, or is passing, to the rest of the country.

But all these reasons for our poetic vitality are obvious enough; they are the first that would come to mind in any discussion—and they are still not the right ones. One might say that it is all simply a matter of chance, the lucky occurrence at one time in one place (McGill of course) of three poets: A. M. Klein, A. J. M. Smith, and F. R. Scott in 1927. Before these poets set to work, a Torontonion [sic], W. W. E. Ross, had already written poems for Marianne Moore's *Dial*, clean speedy modern poems that had learned a diction and form from Miss Moore, from William Carlos Williams, and from Cummings. Ross had anticipated our Montrealers; but he had no assistants.

What makes a literature is the contact between one poet and another, between one generation and another. Poets breed by scission. Even when they disagree, they learn, and stimulate one another. Nothing stimulates a beginning poet more than the irritating activity of another poet in his vicinity. And once this local decoction has been started, it perpetuates itself—it can hardly be stopped.

What happened in Montreal is that the first three modernists passed on their impulse—to Leo Kennedy, to Bruce Ruddick, to P. K. Page; they were joined by Patrick Anderson from Oxford, England, and that period is a whole story in itself; this joint activity roused John Sutherland into competitive emulation (as the literary war between *First Statement* and *Preview* clearly showed); the magazines brought out many poets, among them myself, Layton, and the Waddingtons (who came to Montreal from Toronto, during the literary storm); and since then other poets, Phyllis Webb, Leonard Cohen, Eli Mandel, Gael Turnbull, Daryl Hine, Al Purdy, have been drawn into the Montreal cycle. All this may seem very simple, but it is, in brief, the outline of a complete literary evolution, with about fifty volumes of poetry to make it monumental. It is still open territory for a good critic.

The theory of literature here would be that there is no "school" of single principle that unites the poets who have written in Montreal; nor is there any real sociological influence that we could not dispense with to produce this poetry. Its law is one of chance occurrence and of conditions favouring continuity, like a forest fire. It will no doubt continue for some time, perhaps to be fanned to a mighty blaze before "Canada's century" is over. But by that time—in fact, very soon—the Montreal movement will have to become a national movement, and more; as in fact it must do if it is to prove itself really successful, that is, a genuine new branch of English literature.

[1957]

41

Introduction to
Montreal: English Poetry of the Seventies[1]

ANDRE FARKAS* & KEN NORRIS

> It is the destiny of Montreal to show the country
> from time to time what poetry is.[2]
> –Louis Dudek

English poetry in Montreal has always been written under the most unique conditions. Being a member of a minority culture within the bounds of a dominant Francophone community has made the English poet in Montreal intensely aware of his own language as well as informing him of the problem inherent in the use of language as an agent of communication. When he writes, the Montreal poet knows that the vast majority of people living in his city have no interest whatsoever in what he has to say because what he is saying is in a language that has no relevance to their cultural life. He also recognizes that, because he is Québécois, he is isolated from English Canada. The third disadvantage he experiences is that the isolated Anglophone community, unlike the Francophone, does not consider its arts as necessary for survival; rather, the modus operandi has been economic dominance. Yet, despite these somewhat sobering facts, or perhaps because of them, Montreal has been one of the important centers of English poetry in Canada for most of this century and is now, once again, after the lull of the sixties, beginning to assert itself.

Montreal poets take their craft seriously, writing as they do in a language that is, in many ways, under siege. The tradition of English poetry in Montreal is a long one, and it is one that shows no signs of terminating.

In November of 1925 F. R. Scott and A. J. M. Smith took part in the founding of *The McGill Fortnightly Review* and, in so doing, launched the McGill Movement which played a major part in bringing modernism to Canada. The spirit of modernism which they infused into Canadian poetry in the 1920s tentatively continued to manifest itself throughout the Depression years when poetry publication was sparse and there was not a significant little magazine dedicated to the cause of modernism in all of Canada. The political, social, and economic reality of the 30s created a consciousness that led to the writing of a poetry of social realism in the early forties. In Montreal, during this time, two magazines, *Preview* and *First Statement*, waged a literary feud in regard to the poetics of how social realist poetry was to be written. The *Preview* group, headed by Patrick Anderson, argued for a cosmopolitan and politically militant approach to poetry. The writings of W. H. Auden and Stephen Spender served as their models. The *First Statement* group, with John Sutherland, Louis Dudek, and Irving Layton as their major spokesmen, advocated the position that poetry should be the direct expression of first-hand experience. They denounced the *Preview* group for the artificiality of their language and their bourgeois leftist sentiments. The *First Statement*-ers found their literary models in the democratic American poetry of Walt Whitman, Carl Sandburg, and Hart Crane. This feud, if nothing else, established a poetic movement that was politically and poetically mature. When this movement faltered after *Preview* and *First Statement* had merged into *Northern Review*, edited by an increasingly conservative John Sutherland, there ensued a lull of several years until Layton and Dudek helped to start *CIV/n* and encouraged Souster in his publication of *Contact*, both magazines making further inroads in the modernist movement; these publications worked counter to what *Northern Review* was doing at the time, guided by Sutherland's increasingly Catholic tastes. One can see that there was a substantial tradition established in Montreal by the late 1950s, a working tradition of social realism which many of the Montreal poets of the sixties were quite willing to embrace.

During this time two of Canada's most important poetry personalities emerged in Montreal. In the fifties Irving Layton developed a truly confident poetic voice and found acceptance with critics who had earlier panned his work. Almost simultaneously, Leonard Cohen's first book, *Let Us Compare Mythologies*, was published by Louis Dudek in the McGill Poetry Series. These two poets headed in the direction of a Jewish romantic lyricism while Dudek, influenced by Ezra Pound, sought larger poetic structures in which to explore Western philosophy and aesthetics. Dudek's rationalist constructions served as an Apollonian counterpoint to the Dionysian element in Layton and Cohen's work. These were the two diverse influences working

43

upon the Montreal poets of the sixties.

There were many young poets writing in Montreal as the sixties began and, by number alone, seemed to suggest that yet another vital movement was about to evolve. This was not to be the case. Although certain poets (Al Purdy, Milton Acorn, Seymour Mayne, and David Solway) produced significant work, the movement as a whole failed. This was for several reasons. The first of these was that, by and large, it had nothing new to offer in terms of poetics and poetic techniques. At a time when the rest of Canada was being influenced by an influx of various new ideas and experiments in poetry, ranging from Black Mountain to Dada to North American Indian rituals, the Montreal poets, ironically, chose to conservatively work within an established Canadian poetic tradition. Much of what they wrote was an echoing and pale imitation of Dudek, Layton, and Cohen; none of the poets could eclipse their lyrical mastery or come close to cultivating more engaging poetic personalities. Montreal, in the sixties, clung too rigidly to the poetic values of the past. Poets writing in the West simply had more to offer.

The beginnings of the current Montreal poetry scene can be seen to originate in 1967 when New Wave Canada made its official entrance into Montreal with George Bowering taking up a writer-in-residence post at Sir George Williams University. Bowering brought with him a new orientation towards poetry based on what he had learned from the Black Mountain poets Charles Olson, Robert Creeley, and Robert Duncan; now, as creative writing instructor, he passed on to his students these teachings. However, his most important contribution to the new generation of Montreal poets was the institution of a series of readings at Sir George which exposed them to the diverse experimentation that was taking place across Canada and the U.S. Although immediate results were not visible, by the time Bowering returned to Vancouver in the spring of 1971, the energies of the current movement were beginning to coalesce; this would result in numerous local readings and the establishment of a number of little magazines and small presses.

The current Montreal English poetry movement is not one that has risen out of the ashes of the failed movement of the sixties, but rather has taken its impetus from the diversification of and experimentation in poetry that has occurred in Canada and the United States over the past fifteen years. The rigid approach to what a poem is that characterized Montreal poetry in the sixties has been rendered invalid; the poem has been established as an open and plastic form. This openness and plasticity, however, is tempered by an absolute precision in the use of language. Because of the politics of language in Quebec, the Montreal English poet recognizes the potential volatility of the misuse of the language in which he is writing.

On first reading these poems, one may be surprised at the lack of what one would expect to find in a current English anthology coming out of Quebec—poems dealing with political realities. It would seem that political and social events are not their main concern. But a careful re-reading will show that the degree and area of political and social awareness are there but appear in a different guise—that of language. Language is the most powerful of all political realities in Quebec. To write in English is to take a political stand. That political stand is for the survival of an Anglophone culture in Quebec, a culture that, inevitably, must benefit both Anglophone and Francophone.

For Montreal poets poetry must still contain "the music." The Montreal poem is, by nature, lyrical in quality; in this it is different from the prosaic vignettes indigenous to Toronto and the loose serial poems of Vancouver. In this anthology there are beautiful sonnets that take a traditional form and make it vital again. There are also innovative visual and sound poems that resonate with excitement. The music and the language and the sounds of Montreal poetry retain a melodic hint and powerfully infuse it into excellent verse.

In these ultra-modern times it is usually difficult to distinguish one city from another without a program; not just because they all have the same smell about them and are dying in the same fashion but because they seek to have a common series of tourist and cultural attractions—Montreal has its "French" style as its lure. However, through this anthology, it is hoped that something else is made clear—that there is a sacred geography of Montreal (as there is of all places). This sacred geography is the true terrain, and in this anthology its contours, rhythms, invocations and spirit are celebrated.

[1978]

*Andre Farkas later changed his given name to "Endre."

Introduction to
Cross/cut: Contemporary English Quebec Poetry[1]

PETER VAN TOORN

> Gentlemen, there are too many of us.
> −Yeats

When Yeats opened his address to the Rhymers Club at the turn of the present [twentieth] century with the above remark, he may have been commenting acidly upon a hiatus in some members' social vision— suspicious, perhaps, of increasing material restrictions imposed on their swelling numbers—but he could not have been disparaging the main company. They were too hugely original and brilliant: Moore, AE, Morris— just for starters—or Johnson, Davidson, Dowson, Symons, and Beardsley (even Wilde, once). Two decades later, Yeats extended his circuit from Dublin to London. At that time Pound, Eliot, and Frost were there. London in 1914 might still have hosted a convention of brilliant delegates from the arts, but they hailed from small ravaged areas. Most of England's literary resources were from the outlying colonies, principally Ireland, Scotland, and Wales. If we add to the list cited the names of Shaw, Synge, O'Casey, Joyce, Beckett, and others in anticipation (such as Thomas and McDiarmid), we obtain a depressing picture of intense imaginative activity imported from areas characterized by political and economical squalor. Perhaps there is something inflammatory about the disclosure of statistics in a literary discussion; perhaps poets, anthologists anyway, tend to be too extravagant in their claims. This anthologist, for instance, presumes in cooperation with another to survey some of the most significant poetry to appear in the English-speaking world in recent decades—in Québec*, Canada. In consideration of the demography of English speaking people, this claim to significance on the part of a gypsy Anglophone group seems extravagant—there are over three hundred and fifty million English speaking people east, west, and south of Québec, but only half a million in Québec, and those mainly in its harbour metropolis, Montreal.

2

That so many poets exiled from their native home in the clouds to an area which historians envisage as a colony within a colony have such variety to offer within the brief span of a decade is impressive. The energy, abundance, and scope of their productions, within the last half dozen years especially, suggest that usufruct may no longer be an issue in Québec now that a change in consciousness is struggling to articulate itself in a mode of expression whose very subject is consciousness itself. At once a philosophical and historical mode, poetry refines our most public and private—and, therefore, our most elusive—currency. When it succeeds in providing a symbolic form for significant states of mind, poetry restores a balance and radiance not only to language, our spiritual currency, but to the imagination in charge of it, the human spirit invested with the awesome task of employing that currency with dignity. So in one sense, poetry is a beautiful worm with its head and tail in its middle—the place of the heart—where things are cut, healed, and made new. Poetry, therefore, is a redemptive mode whose lyric rhythms aspire to reach into primitive and civilized areas of consciousness simultaneously, especially at times of change or upheaval, in order to surface as a dramatic celebration of sacred intervals of space and time, between the airports and the stars, and between the ruby vibrations of men, women, and children of all nations. Perhaps that is why its genuine representatives have been described by one poet and critic (Ezra Pound) as the "antennae of the race."

Prophecies are never only of their own time and people, of course, but of all time and people, so it is not surprising that prophets have usually been to some degree exiled from their native home in the clouds. Many poets have transcended the temporal order during periods of social and political upheaval; many have succumbed to its distractions. Yet when the hoped-for change in consciousness establishes itself and the confusion settles, works embodying an imaginative synthesis will be discovered, much to the delight of the mind burdened by the imbalance which social conflict engenders, because the mind craves art. And the mind craves art because the mind is a work of art. Specimens of such poetic achievement can occur at any time, and although periods of intense change and distress may even contribute to their conception, they are more likely to achieve an imaginative radiance in epochs exuding peace and ease. During just such an epoch, the second half of the seventies, which fluctuated between points of intense change and stress and points of relaxation and ease, Canada witnessed a renewed flow of poetic energy. That these brief stretches of respite resembled a dotted line to which so many Canadian poets affixed their poetic signatures is a coincidence worth noting.

The flow experienced by poets in Québec, moreover, was not prim or neatly channelled. The variety, abundance, and intensity of their activity may reflect a cultural phenomenon, namely, that "La Belle Province" periodically fosters more poets, certainly more of the authentic and indigenous ones—French and English—than the rest of Canada combined. Naturally, Québec's predominantly French speaking population is more warmly appreciative of its "native" poets than of those included in this selection. An edition of poems by an original Québécois poet is sold out within months in Québec; a collection by a figure with popular stature, such as Gilles Vigneault, achieves the same result with a first run of ten thousand copies. Even the endorsement of Canada's most conspicuous literary prize, the Governor General's award, cannot attract half that many readers from all the provinces of Canada for an English book of poems. This situation has not altered profoundly since the precedent set by Lampman in 1895 when he finally found a publisher for his second volume in Boston through the efforts of his influential friend, Thomson: *Lyrics of Earth* appeared, after being rejected in both Canada and the States, in an edition full of blunders. Canada fosters many more poets now, of course, than it did in Lampman's time, hundreds more—of minor and major stature—but to the same degree of wholeheartedness. So it may be that Canada is still waiting for its poet. The obverse is true for Québec. Here is a description by Rejean Ducharme, in an article called "le Nez Qui Voque," of a Québécois poet already famous at the turn of the century, who adopted the culture and language of his pianist Québécoise mother instead of his Irish father:

Chateaugué le trouve beau, dit qu'il a les cheveux comme en feu, un nez de lion et les yeux doux comme des ailes de papillon. La photo que nous avons volée le represente avec un lavallière autour du cou. La photo aurait pu la representer avec un lavallière autour du front. Alors, il aurait eu l'air arable. Les cheveux ardents, les yeux de femme, un nez de bête, les lèvres douces, la bouche dure; il est tout à fait comme nous nous l'imaginions: c'est cela qui nous a le plus frappés quand nous l'avons rencontré entre deux pages...[2]

These are lover's terms, describing the Québécois poet Emile Nelligan.

The gypsy group of Canadian poets represented here, therefore, are at a serious disadvantage: for while they contribute significantly to Canadian literature, they enjoy the congenial reception of neither Canada nor Québec. This alienated position becomes more grievous when it is considered that Québec's poets constitute not only the bulwark of Canadian poetry (for up till recently Canadian poets from Québec, whether Québécois or English, accounted for eighty per cent of the contents in major anthologies) but that they also constitute, along with the novelists of Québec, the main body of writers who effect the translating of Québec's imaginative contours. From a serious point of view, these observations about poetic currents based on sales figures are subject to dispute and proclaim little more than the indices of popular vagary, the market's response to what's in fashion. A further objection to these observations could be made. Excellence has always involved more hard work than Utopians allow for. And it may be that Québec's indigenous population feels inclined to dreaming. Encumbered by its Cartesian heritage—its predilection for metaphysical introspection, revolutionary reform, egalitarian fervour, love of *pays*, and consuming passion for political debate—Québec is, moreover, out of touch with an English host who is saddled with foreign traditions—with British empiricism in science and philosophy, and with American pragmatism in commerce and politics. Nevertheless, Québec has provided the concerted support needed to elect the party and prime minister piloting Canada through its difficult passage to nationhood in the seventies and early eighties. So from a visionary perspective (and it is the visionary perspective with which we are concerned here, the sympathies and reflections which guide us into the future and past simultaneously, and which make our present source resonate with unity and clarity, not sad separateness or violent opposition), the renascence of poetic life across Canada, if that phrase does not exaggerate the phenomenon of recent small press activity, indicates that something besides oil is being found: namely, that the identities of Canada and Québec are simultaneously undergoing radical metamorphosis.

3

Québec's role in Canada's evolution has been largely heuristic. Its capacity for "negative capability" (to stretch Keats' definition of poetic capacity a little and apply it more generally to the creative mood in politics and economics) is not well understood. If Québec's participation in the economic sphere of Canada has been limited, its influence on policies affecting the imaginative dimensions and directions of Canada has been as inspirational and decisive as the silence and desultory eruptions of Canada's aboriginals. By its mere presence, Québec has positioned the visionary template of Canada, on which Canadians count and build. Perhaps in this respect Québec's traditional heritage, although once considered its weakness, has really proved to be its strength. (Mark Twain is reported as having made a crack about Québec's traditional loyalty to the church. During his visit to Montreal, a city which has retained much of its old architecture despite the rapid growth of skyscrapers and industry in the past two decades, Twain remarked: "Montreal is the only city in North America where you can't throw a brick without breaking a church window.") A capacity for enlightened endurance, vivacious celebration, and irreverence assists a people in facing long, snowbound winters: it assuages irritation and dispels the proclivity to scepticism and mortification which a society imbued with predominantly Catholic and agrarian values feels when making the transition to a predominantly industrial and Protestant way of life, especially those segments of the population for whom such a radical transition entails massive urbanization. Take away Québec's tendency to fervent introspection and its subsequent aspiration to political autonomy, and it resembles its stoic neighbour to the south, New England.

Sometimes in indigence, sometimes in brusque self assertion, sometimes in quest of a discrete spiritual synthesis, Québec has endeavoured to embody a conception of existence which stands in stark contrast to the dominant mode of industrial and mercantile efficiency characteristic of the more North American style of operation. Québec's Anglophones have had some role in the shaping of this new mode of existence, especially those who have stimulated a vision of man as the measure of all things—"La personne avant toutes choses"—a vision which Canada's political institutions accommodate with increasing accuracy and *élan*; thus, by its imaginative contrast, its silence as well as its unique philosophical development, Québec has contributed something precious to the Canadian identity. If this contribution has been gradual, inspissatory, and unacknowledged, Québec remonstrates Canada for the degree to which the latter has still to diffuse a block in its imaginative flow: paradoxically, the way Canada treats Québec reflects the way it treats its aborigines, its origins, and itself.

The recent drive for independence issuing from Québec is paradoxically a renewed invitation to Canada, a way of inviting it to reinterpret its history. To reinterpret the history of Canada means to reinterpret the original settling motives and to reinterpret the history of Europe and the States vis-à-vis Canadian history. Although this invitation has all the clamour of an infant struggling for nourishment and growth, it is a cordial one, with all the promise of dividends which the metaphor implies. And it is an urgent invitation to revision, for if Canada is to avoid the species of civil strife which has erupted in the United States from time to time, it must revise its conception of origins and original purposes, about which the States and Europe have brooded and struggled much longer. In a sense, Québec's remonstrative behaviour is an appeal to Canada's historical conscience. Canada has still to revise its conception of a viable democracy. To accept or emulate solutions the United States has stumbled on is to accept American history instead of creating a Canadian one; to accept a foreign solution is to stay under a foreign thumb. If Canada accepts Québec's cordial invitation to a symposium on the subject, with intentions to act on its findings and, more importantly, with intentions of sharing in decision making, it will begin to consider the implications of policies which at present oppress a third of its population conveniently concentrated in a small area of its enormous domains. These policies, which are both cultural and economical, are policies which Canada has not created in full consciousness but which it passively accepted for itself. These are policies which are restrictive rather than expansive; they discourage rather than initiate self motivation, and they attempt sporadically to relieve symptoms rather than consistently and respectfully deal with their causes.

To such policies Québec's only option until recently has been cultural genocide or radical Anglicization. That these policies are colonial, that they are historically myopic, that they are congestive rather than carminative is obvious. That such policies do not enucleate the favourable sense which Aesop and Keats decree they might in their aphorisms, "A good deed lives forever" and "A thing of beauty is a joy forever"—that such policies contain seeds which will, in the future, be a cause of embarrassment or rue—is not so obvious. The dilemma invokes the Muse.

4

Three areas of endeavour in which Québec has supplied Canada a model for a novel and imaginative approach to itself are aesthetic philosophy, political debate, and social consciousness. The first needs no elaboration. (Figures who illustrate the application of aesthetic principles to several areas of our life are numerous—from Nelligan to Vigneault, from Trudeau to Lafleur.) It is only logical that Québec should be keenly interested in contributing to the second area of endeavour. Québec inherits from its founders and cultural antecedents a passion for political debate with a revolutionary orientation. From its humanist tradition, from the savants and founders of the Enlightenment down to the existentialist philosophers of recent times, Québec inherits a faculty for rational analysis and intro-spection (annoying as that faculty may be when it ministers to an obsession with classification). Québec inherits from its language, moreover, an instrument of extraordinary precision and subtlety, tailored by the Academie Française through the centuries for the purpose of exploring what Pascal termed "la raison du coeur." To this sensitive tongue, capable of expressing subtle nuances of feeling, Québec has contributed its own rhythms and vocabulary. Québec has restored to French some of its original Medieval vibrancy: the intestinal twang and scouring plangency of Villon surfaces in contemporary Québécois, which at its best is richly demotic, with a jazzy scat patter whose Anglicisms are a sad but comic parody of the current attitude which outsiders hold to the French tongue. Finally, from its legal matrix, from its Code Napoleon, and from its experience of subjugation, Québec has come to be imbued with a resilience to the numerical, military, and economic superiority of its English neighbours. In response to these historical experiences, Québec has developed not only an aspiration to autonomy but a unique twist of flavour for debate. For whatever it has con-tributed to the debate of Canada's identity and the configuration of its democratic ideals, Québec has, by its insistence on self -parody and on the repudiation of colony status, for itself as well as for all Canadians, infused Canada's parliamentary style with panache.

The third area in which Québec has provided a model for a novel and imaginative approach to Canadian history is social consciousness, the very fabric out of which some kind of poetry is made. Comments on this aspect must be limited and brief; a fuller exploration of the substance and value of Québec's social consciousness should be made by a ripe Québecer. Let it be said, however, that Québec's "rainbow vision" of society, its cultural catholicity, its ethnic pluralism, is difficult to understand. Why, for example, should Québec, struggling for its own survival as an ethnic group, exhibit a cordial welcome to a confluence of alien groups—the people immigrating from the States, Europe, the U.K., Asia, South America, the Middle and Far East, and from other parts of Canada? One possible explanation is that Québecers extend their hospitality to small groups from other parts of the globe because most immigrants tend, or have tended, until recently to flow into English life and so they do not strain the economic or psychic tolerance of the Québécois (that is, in any way oppose Québec's aspiration to freedom, being too preoccupied with their own survival and acculturization). Other explanations may be tried. But whether the cosmopolitan mosaic of Québec, Montreal's pluralist mosaic especially, owes its existence to an enlightened Protestant English minority or to a charitable Catholic French majority is difficult to determine. Ethnic and cultural pluralism, however, seems more conspicuously vital in Québec than elsewhere in Canada. So perhaps Québec's enlightened social consciousness is more developed than has been supposed.

5

If the preceding remarks err on the side of truth, it follows that the much debated topic of Canada's identity has a great deal in common with the endemic political fermentation and the aspiration to independence issuing from Québec. Perhaps it is, or has been, Québec's directives to secession that have roused the provinces horizontally, for economically the vertical pull to the States appears more compelling. Given Québec's increasingly articulate provocations, Canada has become more imaginatively agonized over its unity and direction: it has started to repudiate its image of itself as an attic of the United States and as an unrepatriated colony of England. It has proceeded to accept a mode of becoming at the pace of a native Indian dithyramb and dilated its "democratic vistas" proportionately.

Historians might reasonably argue that assigning Québec a major role in the drama of Canadian maturation is a fond but foolish judgement. They would probably aver that an interpretation of the causes behind any renewal in self-confidence, any renascence in the Canadian vision, which did not focus on economic issues, and largely on American ones, would be simplistic.

And they could muster a number of events, and the absence of events, to support a more pragmatic point of view. They might claim that Canada's relative freedom from involvement in any international crisis since the last world war has left it with energy to devote to domestic affairs; or that, rather than any resurgence of separatism, the influx of American idealism in protest of the war in Vietnam supplied Canada with extra confidence and heightened its momentum in the seventies. But an indigenous Québécois poetry, one that does not consciously strive to emulate an American or European poetics, or to find acclaim outside of Québec, does not seem to bear this inference out.

6

What such an indigenous Québécois poetry (as distinct from a colonial or derivative poetry) does seem to bear out is a commitment to becoming adjusted to origins. This commitment to locating a source, an original starting point, a free slate, redeemed from history, is a commitment to a particular experience, one of defeat, resignation, containment, endurance, ascesis, and faith rooted in social vision. This attention to origins, to an authentic point of arrival, is also an attention to final things, to a radiant point of departure. Such an apocalyptic attention must arrange itself in metaphors of becoming to match the unconscious ambivalence of the Canadian imagination to history itself. The Canadian imagination is confused about its origins, which lie about in another time and space, either entangled in the history of Western civilization, European civilization in particular, or buried alive in the Canadian past, in the encounter with Canada's original inhabitants, its Inuit and Indian aboriginals, and later, in its encounter with the French settlers. Much of the European stuff is not actively part of most Canadians' cultural apparatus; much of the Canadian past isn't either, consisting of obscure records of violence, of a series of con-quests rather than original discoveries. Wherever the historical record depicts a contact made with authentic origins—the paintings of Emily Carr, for example, whose contact with the lustral realm of the West Coast Indians registers an unmistakeable shock of discovery, by a European on a spiritually equal footing with her aboriginal neighbours—the artistic result has been rich and impressive. This tradition of the voyage is an eminently French tradition (Carr and some of the Group of Seven painters started developing only after returning from France, fresh from their discovery of Impressionism), and accounts of this spiritual voyage are to be found in the *Essaies* of Montaigne as well as in the Journal of Saint-Denys-Garneau, they are to be found in the poems of Rimbaud, who prescribed a program for himself which involved "the derangement of all the senses" (*"le poète se fait 'voyant' par un long, immense et raisonné dérèglement de tous les sens"*) and a conviction in the belief of the poet as *voyant*, seer; similar records of authentic contact with an indigenous Canadian imagination are to be found in the paintings of Tom Thomson, whose lonely searching in the North led to the first imaginative use of oil.

That Québécois poetry exhibits a peculiar mode of assimilating experience, one which focusses its attention on origins and arranges its findings in metaphors of becoming, is not surprising. Insofar as Québécois poetry is not resigned, it is a poetry of high achievement. The Québécois have, after all, settled in one place; they have, like the aboriginals on their reservations, chosen a spiritual rather than a secular expansion. Their poetry shows it: it is marked by a tendency to manifest containment, introspection, declaration, evocation, meditation, transformation, and celebration with central figures of Christian suffering as protagonists, comic as well as earthy. True, the commitment of the Québécois to origins and to authentic vision has been made for them as well as by them. Their commitment is a redemptive one, less clearly stained by the blood of conquest, the lurching rhythms of imperial expansion, the violent confrontations which epitomize the drama of frontier consciousness. Thomas Gray's "Elegy," said to have been recited by Wolfe on the eve of the fateful battle, contains two cautionary lines which apply to the Québécois in their commitment: "nor circumscribed alone. Their growing virtues, but their crimes confined...". Nevertheless, much Québécois artistic endeavour has the flavour of original discovery rather than of conquest. In short, Québec has provided the ambience in which a new consciousness might develop.

7

Québec has thus nourished a Canadian poetry into a youthful identity of its own. Canadian poets have experienced this stance partly by choice, by choosing to remain in Québec rather than adopt a more established literary centre, and partly by luck, by finding themselves immersed in a French cultural framework and by absorbing the aspirations and achievements of the French imagination in literature and philosophy in the past and present. Even poets born and raised in other parts of Canada, the United States, and elsewhere, when they have experienced some of their crucially formative years in Québec, have subsequently imaginatively identified their experience of Québec with the impulse to artistic autonomy, decolonization, and to originality—to reaching more deeply into their own roots upon returning to their adopted region or native home. Much of what they made of Québec and its experience, much of what subsequently informed their imaginative commitment, had to do with the fact that an accelerated dispossession of ethnic pluralism was not mandatory in Québec as elsewhere. Whether you were from Paris, St. John's, Calgary, Athens, Melbourne, Bombay, Tokyo, San Francisco, Prague, or Amsterdam, in Montreal you were at home.

8

If one wishes to know what it has meant to be a poet in Canada until recently, whether in or out of Québec or, for that matter, what it has meant to be a visionary in Canada in any role, one has only to remember that Lampman died after finally finding a reluctant publisher for his work through a New York agent—and Lampman was one of Canada's first, and still one of its finest; that Klein abruptly curtailed his meteoric career with twenty years of silence; that Nelligan suffered a premature abrogation of sanity and a lapse into more than forty years of silence; and that Saint-Denys-Garneau exposed himself increasingly to a metaphysical mortification which would frighten a Carmelite monk. Each of these poets ended life in a terrible isolation whose cause is not to be conveniently extrapolated from the facts of biography by some fashionable paradigm from sociology, psychology, or economics: for each of these poets was crushed in his imaginative hopes and poetic endeavours by the relentless inertia of historical progress. The price of their vision was dereliction, not economic and social, but imaginative dereliction.

There is something about imaginative dereliction, if we are familiar with the lives of artists such as Smart, Baudelaire, and Van Gogh, which suggests that their madness was the kind which society, had it had the perspicacity and enlightened self-interest to cherish these artists before their demise, could have drawn strength from, namely the apocalyptic sanity which it sadly lacked—our continued devotion to these artists is proof of that. Lampman, to return to a Canadian artist of this stamp, died inwardly of stultification long before he contracted the heart ailment that led to his death. Like some coco-chewing mountain porter of the Andes, squeezed out of the more congenial, temperate valleys by the aggressively mercantile Spanish hacienda élite, Lampman had no alternative. There was probably no escape for him into a world more congenial to the imagination. Such a world did not exist in Canada at the time, if it ever did, anywhere, except, perhaps, for brief accidental moments, and where least expected: Emily Carr looked for it later in the rainforests of the West Coast Indians. And Canada has had to pay for its colonial folly: for if an artist cannot altogether escape the conditions of his own time except at moments of creation, it is equally true that men and women collectively cannot escape them at all when they are deaf to the imaginative exertions around them. So if Lampman suffers the conditions of colonialism in his less favourable productions, but transforms them, or transcends them, in his best, then the imaginative conditions of society must have been very indigent generally. Take a look at the price of colonialism in his work. In his best work, and that usually meagerly anthologized—there is currently almost a Canadian embarrassment about Lampman in vogue—he is finding a uniquely personal and Canadian idiom, and working out of local landscapes and portraits toward a prophetic vision, of the sort we find in "Heat", his great Canadian pastoral lyric, with its intensely apocalyptic solar vision, its scientific objectivity, meditative ecstasy, and imagist congeniality.

His straining in the vein of *fin-de-siècle* Hellenism, his emulation of classical subjects and models, or his imitation of the then popular strokes of transcendentalist fatuity by Carman at his worst, are now all but unreadable. Like Tom Thomson, the painter, Lampman tried to escape his essentially colonial situation almost physically; like Thomson (or Rimbaud, whose ascetic travels and feats of physical endurance Enid Starkie describes in her vivid account of the French *voyant*), Lampman travelled back into a spiritually vital, emblematic, neglected area of our consciousness, into the terrain buried under the abstraction of dominion.

Neither Lampman nor Thomson wholly integrated the connection with mythic time in the bush and secular time in the community, indigenous and colonial time respectively. They were not able to integrate the consciousness which they were after and which they wanted to share imaginatively with us—to succeed in that aim they would have had to succeed in projecting a vision not only on an imaginative, artistic scale, but to succeed in living with it among people in a community; and such a community did not exist.

Lampman and Thomson lived their visions in solitude and in art. Emily Carr, the painter, perhaps more than either of these two great Canadian artists, accomplished a blazing identification with an indigenous vision, the symbolic, totemic, lustral realm of the West Coast aboriginals. Both Thomson and Lampman were reclaimed by the wilderness: Lampman contracted a heart ailment during an over-strenuous hike (the ailment was further strained by the difficulties he experienced getting his second book of poems published), and Thomson died mysteriously, in a way that is legend by now. And if "Nature never betrayed the heart that loved her" then her reclamations were, hopefully, merciful.

But that part of our heritage which has been forgotten, overlooked, or insidiously repudiated—not a Romantic version of it by Drummond, Service, or Carman, but the real thing—still lies waiting. It is a door the immigrant in his deepest moments swings open. It is a vision of the unexpected. It is a vision of becoming. It is a vision, moreover, which the early governors of European courts intent on colonizing Canada could not find reference to in their mandates, and which leaders of the white race have been incapable of acculturating to. It is a vision which the Indians were in touch with, and which made them in turn fierce, and then, after their defeat and losses, sad and demoralized. The voyageurs may have kept a nomadic trace of it in their stream of consciousness; such a transmission would account for the residual difference in the vision issuing from Québec. But it is not a vision of man with a supernatural relation to man and nature, of man going in and out of sync with his awareness of the numinous—man as the measure of all things. And wherever this vision has been neglected by men driven against men and nature in a Faustian hurry, there is an incompleteness to be found. This incompleteness is one of the conditions which Wilgar, in his classic essay, "The Divided Mind" claims as the cause for the lack of any truly first-rate Canadian poetry.

Sometimes a Québec poet, a poet having passed through the experience of which Québec is a metaphor, hints hugely at this vision of Canada. Certain monumental, lyric, never totally achieved poems come to mind from the Canadian bestiary: Nowlan's "The Bull Moose", with its Christian archetype embedded in its pastoral Maritime matrix; Layton's "The Bull Calf", with its elegiac Marxism and funerary catharsis; and especially Acorn's lament for the cosmic circus, "The Natural History of Elephants", with its pan-Canadian Gnosticism. To the degree which each of these poems laments the death of the poet, the Canadian imagination laments the loss of its aboriginal past. The loss of this vision is what Klein compassionately laments in his "Portrait of the Poet as Landscape" and which he invokes in his "Montreal". The abeyance of this vision within Canada's institutions is a discovery which Atwood too makes in her sardonic "The Landlady" poem. This vision includes a world which Purdy bravely assembles in his unique selection of Canadian poetry, *Fifteen Winds*; which Cohen evokes in his warm collection of lyrics, *The Spice Box of Earth*; which Lee commemorates in his *Civil Elegies*; and which Pratt parodies into possibility against the rollicking pageant of a mechanistic cosmos. There are huge, warm doses of it in the plum blossom poems of Souster, in the scientifically observed ecstasies of Lampman, and in the poems of several other Canadian poets. But generally this vision is rendered with a more local and certain passion by Québécois poets.

In the last decade a change in stance on the part of Canadian poets to this incompleteness of the Canadian imagination has become more evident. There are still no Canadian happenings like the Québécois "La Nuit de Poesie," but there has grown a kind of deeper, sometimes aggressively obsessive, preoccupation with Canadian identity, resulting in the attempt to shake off vestiges of colonial conditions. The recent reluctance to reach out to creative influences from outside, whether from the States, Europe, Asia, or Russia (the reluctance diminishes when its scope approaches third-world countries) stems from a distaste for the Faustian thrust of the European Enlightenment. A look for something here and now, a kind of antidote to the perpetual threat of holocaust, is what Jones and Layton posit as the central preoccupation of the younger poets. A brief digression on the technical features which this approach appears to entail for most Canadian poets may be useful. Three features (paraphrased from an excellent essay by Paul West) seem to dominate contemporary Canadian poetry: 1) a one-side-of-a-pinetree look, a ragged stichic mode of verse assimilation; 2) a tendency to a discursive, rapidly discontinuous epic of daily life; and 3) an aspiration to vocal imagism, the verbal representation of the shape of sound. And these technical characteristics appear not so much in a satiric vein, for we have produced little satire of great permanence (unless Scott's and Smith's anthology of satire, *The Blasted Pine*, argues otherwise), not so much in satiric, as in elegiac form. The loon crowds out our best moments.

9

If current poetry from Québec, Francophone especially, but Anglophone as well, shows less tendency to emulate the trends of foreign literary movements, and despite whatever loss in artistic possibility this hermetic stance may entail, whatever it does emulate or reflect is not a Québec as it has conventionally been viewed by outsiders, but a human condition for which Québec has provided a working political metaphor: a motion of becoming. This "hermeneutic motion" (Steiner's phrase for the process of all translation) is a fragile mode of growth, as fragile as the grip which the flora and fauna of the Arctic have upon life during their brief summer existence, yet entirely appropriate to Canada. And if Québec, in its slow ascension, reverses the spiritual tailspin which characterizes the fate of Canada's most completely indigenous peoples, its Inuit and Indians, it has certainly exhibited an easy tolerance for the pluralist society which has constituted the buffer between the traditionally Cartesian way of Québécois life, with its rigours, mortifications, and assertions of political belief, and between the way of life prevalent on all sides. Québec's tolerance for a plurality of values, despite some few recent signs of xenophobia, is not easy to grasp. In the compulsive and acquisitive traffic towards an abstract state of well being which appears to be the consuming goal of a half-hearted democracy, the small and the politically weak are often ignored. But Québec, with a shrug of the shoulders, has adopted a confluence of native and alien civilizations: it has been a sanctuary and a watershed for the refugees and the dispossessed seeking inner clarification, in Cohen's phrase, via "all the languages of Montreal." It has provided this hospitality and asylum in a spirit free of condescension, and in a mood of increasing independence from what Frye has called "the garrison mentality" that a protracted colonialism settled in Canada's imaginative life, whether in poetry or in politics.

That the search for Canadian identity, a quest which, for better or worse, now informs the somewhat nationalist movement of the Canadian literary scene, is further advanced in Québec is not surprising; that this momentum is readily converted into a specific economic metaphor outside of Québec is a feature of our empiricism. The history of English poetry, science, and philosophy is to some degree a history of unacknowledged appropriation from extraneous sources, especially French ones. England's application of the French Revolution is a case in point. England was the first to industrialize and establish colonies in various continents after it investigated the positive scientific and philosophic method developed in France. America followed suit. And their language served them well. English borrows easily, and more readily from French because of their common classical heritage. But it refuses—and this refusal, which extends into American and Canadian history in different forms, is paradoxically a logical feature of empiricism—to express a debt of gratitude in any terms which would help resolve the tension we now find ourselves in. As Canada has begun to crystallize in response to Québec's rigorous introspection and subsequent metamorphosis, successive generations of Canadian poets in Québec have endeavoured to mediate the gap. Where Québec has provided the atmosphere of integrity, the unique aesthetic philosophy, and the political motivation to enshrine a new conception of man, various Québécois ethnic writers have supplied the creative *élan vital*.

10

The revamping of colonial attitudes in art represents the catabolic phase in the chemistry of the Canadian vision; it indicates what artists and thinkers in the Nuclear Era have been trying not to do. Their repudiation has come to mean trying to be at home in the wilderness, not of trees, though that too, but of faces, varieties of speech, sensibility, ways of being—at home with historic pluralism, with a global specimen of humanity threatened, in the face of plenty, by the chaos resulting from a desire to impose a political identity derived from past models on what is a state of natural flux. Québec is a small community, smaller in population than many communities which occupy a tenth of its area, a community, moreover, which is still trying to find itself in a situation of bewildering complexity caused by its having to assimilate the confluence of radically diverse values and histories, while having to confront the blandishments of the most industrialized and competitive nations in the world. Québec is much in difficulty: but it is exceptionally brave and witty in its view of its giant neighbours. Québec has, of course, no experience with the consequences of nationalism and fascism, since it participated very little in the disasters which Canadians and Americans confronted in Europe; and Québec's ingenuousness may cause it much distress in the future. But insofar as it has asserted itself in bringing about a new state of societal being, a new, richer, more democratic life, Québec has demonstrated something valuably Canadian.

The Anglophone poet remaining in Québec is just as witty as the Québécois poet, in at least one sense, for he now faces what Québec has long faced, but he faces it entirely alone. Sensitive to the wastefulness of conflict, even a little envious of his Québécois counterpart's more congenial environment, and despite all the affection and sympathy he feels for the new Québec (and doubts, reservations, fears, and antipathies too), the Anglophone poet now finds himself in a situation which was evident all along, but which he closed his eyes to: cultural dereliction. For his community, language, and identity have abandoned him. The fate of dereliction is implicit in the situation: a fragile mode of becoming surrenders to laws other than those which the parties of empiricism and rationalism engage in. His marginal status was never very secure, as Klein in his "Portrait of the Poet as Landscape" sadly points out, and which the lives of Nelligan, Saint-Denys-Garneau, Klein, Lampman, and Thomson illustrate. But the erosion of even his marginal status now brings up the spectre of exile on an imaginative scale.

Up to very recently the Anglophone poet rooted in Québec was able to observe with imaginative perspicacity the hopes, aspirations, and struggles for self-determination of the Québécois and its minorities: he was able to accomplish this much commitment by immersing himself in all the cultures and by contributing to a vision of Québec and Canada simultaneously. His very pluralist identity, his passionate complexity, and his detachment from merely political solutions were in themselves a source of strength and insight. The sometimes bohemian ambiance, even intolerant arrogance, when it did not polarize into mordant trenchancy and terrorism, was amniotic and propulsive: it fostered a metaphor of becoming.

Now a new vision, if that term is appropriate to a description of recent events, is being increasingly shaped by the conflicting groups whose positions will for some time isolate the poet. For the heat of the debate will assure each side of an increasing resemblance, without room for the diversity which lubricated the once visionary *élan*. That is the fate of historical conflict: we become what we unthoughtfully reject, fail for too long to try to understand, or exploit for profane ends. So that amazing period of flux, of hovering at the brink of a vision of man, is about to be embodied or rejected in Québec. To the *poète Anglais* (a term which must sound faintly risible to the *poète Québécois*) the numinous period of transition, of vibrant trance, for better or worse, is over. Dreams are becoming responsibilities. The enormous potential of what the poet has always dreamed of must now slip out of his being into the hands of those who claim to be more practical.

11

In a purely literary context, it seems inevitable that a poet from an area such as Québec, containing several dozen peoples attempting mutual translation, should adopt a more densely textured vernacular than has been common for a poetic medium. Such a philosophic and linguistic strain seems implicit in the practice of a poet working the grain of his native speech against the rhythms and perspectives of two kinds of English, two kinds of French, and the *mélange* of sonorities provided by dozens of European, Asian, and Eastern tongues. The fusion of French and English sensibilities in particular, has been one of the concerns of English poetry for seven centuries. D'Orléans, after all, wrote fluently in both languages and is represented in the anthologies of English and French speaking peoples. An interest in French civilization has been a characteristic of writers as diverse as Dostoyevski, Goethe, Wordsworth, and Pien Chih-Lin. In Québec, this same interest in French civilization has been extended to include an interest in contemporary Québécois literature. This interest has long been manifested by poets and translators such as Dudek, Klein, Scott, Smith, Jones, and Glassco; some of the younger poets included in this selection, such as Brockwell, Harris, Plourde, McGee, and Filip are continuing the patterns set by their seniors.

The reasons for the interest which English writers exhibit in French literature, its poetry and critical prose especially, are obvious. English shares with French and the Romance languages a common classical heritage—the mythology, philosophy, science, and literature of Ancient Rome and Greece. Moreover, after the Norman invasion, the courts of England practised French language and general culture for centuries to come, a custom which became widely adopted throughout Europe. But the attraction that French civilization, its literature in particular, exercises upon English minds is best explained by the aphorism, *les extrèmes se touchent*. For there is a body of literature which the English mind finds necessary to its imaginative diet, but which it has to locate outside its own tradition, to locate it at all: this is the stream of gentle scepticism and radical introspection which is represented by a Montaigne, Pascal, Descartes, Baudelaire, Rimbaud, Nelligan, or Saint-Denys-Garneau. Rooted in religious dogma or secular revolt, this tradition of gentle scepticism and subtle introspection is never out of touch with the fluid humanism and resigned humour which epitomizes a Montaigne, the sublime pathos but austere devotion typical of a Saint-Denys-Garneau, the visionary rompings which radiate from the utterances of a Rimbaud, or the tender and exalting lyrics of a Vigneault. The tendency in English, American, and Canadian literature, however, has been to investigate this tradition cautiously, and to react negatively to its findings—a tendency which sometimes betrays a degree of covert arrogation, for a steady empiricism and flexible pragmatism has been pervasive in the English enterprise since the Industrial Revolution. This tendency becomes clearer if the direction of Western technology and science is considered as the historic application of the principles of Judeo-Christian democracy in material form. From this perspective, modern capitalist democracy is partly the result of the French Revolution and of the principles emanating from the European Enlightenment.

English poets and critics have been signally reticent about their French sources (Arnold, Eliot, Pound, and, in this selection, Dudek, Glassco, Jones, and Scott are among the exceptions which prove the rule; that is, they are truly exceptions) because the majority have felt a need for insulation against the leavening influence which a study of French civilization induces. A bridge between French and English sensibilities involves more than the identity which Wallace Stevens claimed for them in his wily aphorism, "French and English constitute one language." Contact with French civilization involves contact with more than French values alone, if that contact is to be at least as inspired as French democratic ideals declare it should be. The goddess of Reason, like the angel of Liberty in New York Harbour, shines her lamp of freedom ubiquitously on the sombre mysticism of the Spanish; the dazzling fluidity of the Arabic and Moorish; the psychological subtlety of the French ironists mentioned earlier; the airy abandon and refinement of the Italian; the penchant for delicate reverie and truculent vituperation possessed by the Scots, Welsh, and Irish; the vitality and serpentine wisdom which the Greeks continue to manifest in their unifying myths and pastoral lamentations; the passion for justice, tender eroticism, and ironic empathy which illuminates the Jewish spirit; and the still largely esoteric principle of excluded middle (whose concomitants are moderately henotheism, ritual incantation, and fluid osmosis) which Asian and Eastern philosophy and poetry evince, and which various intuitive forms such as yoga, Zen, astrology, meditation, and the use of oracles have popularly applied to practical purposes such as the regulating and synchronizing of body and mind. These are a few of the patterns which a study of French civilization involve, and which will, in time to come, emblazon the pluralist mosaic of Canadian poetry.

12

That Québec's English writers, recently labouring in an ambiance of mass exodus, manifest signs of willingness to be influenced by these various strains, or to endeavour a voluntary incursion into the realms of visionary idiolect or private language, an aspiration which goes back to Klein's poetry and prose and to Saint-Denys-Garneau's poetry and philosophic investigations— suggests that something is stirring in Canada's literary climate. The synoptic task of determining its relevance to a wider imaginative context remains with the qualified critic. The pleasure of discovery, after all, remains the primary objective of a selection of contemporary poetry.

[1982]

*For this reprint, the editors have retained the spelling of Québec with the acute accent (aigu) as it appeared in Peter Van Toorn's original essay.

What Now, Montreal?[1]

GEOFF HANCOCK

Montreal: an exotic site seeking ritual invocation. All the discoveries of Canadian history and the whole of contemporary Canadian poetry have historic roots in Montreal. Someone should write an epic poem on the heights of Mont-Royal and recover a poetic time and place as Neruda did for Machu Pichu. The English poets of Montreal should be bonded to the site that nourishes their imagination.

Yet this is a divided city. Instead of a centre, Montreal is built around a mountain on an island in the middle of a river. Likewise the poets are divided into small groups. Montreal is all periphery, all villages: Westmount, Outremont, NDG, "east of the Main", the South shore. All these groups insist on their separateness. The endless miles of corridors beneath the somewhat seedy Place Bonaventure and the middle-class trendiness of Place Ville Marie don't lead us to the English poets of Montreal. As Henry Aubin points out in *City For Sale*, the underground city is not even owned by Montrealers, but by Belgians and other international financiers. Poetically at least, there is no single place called Montreal.

Like New York, what we can find of Montreal has texture, detail, and the carnality necessary for a great city. Yet those late night spots are easier to find than a candid poet. Unlike New York, it is hard to find the best of contemporary creative writing. You can't easily look up the answer. Montreal has no equal to the *Village Voice* or the *New York Times* or *Le Monde*. While art and music and some readings are listed in *Virus* (and even the occasional profile of a poet such as Yolande Villemaire) the magazine mostly highlights fun spots. Despite the efforts of Louis Dudek twisting the arm of the book page editor, the Montreal *Gazette* remains largely indifferent to poetic activities in the second largest French-speaking city in the world. CBC Radio's FM network has a late night program, *Brave New Waves*, hosted by Augusta Lapaix, which often interviews members of the artistic community over pizza and drinks. National radio, coast to coast, poetry and theatre at 3:00 a.m. An excellent program, with obvious disadvantages. Again, through the efforts of Louis Dudek, Ben's Restaurant has a poetry corner. Among portraits of faded hockey stars and professional wrestlers are a dozen portraits of some of Montreal's poets. A sensuous touch if you like smoked meat, happen to be in that part of town and know a Layton from a Hard Boiled Haggerty.

But if you start looking for the poetry scene in Montreal, you first feel pinched, repressed, muddled. Bits and pieces of the past come at you, but instead of feeling enriched by discovery, you sense a literary loss. The modern tradition in Canadian poetry started here. But where is it now? The more we approach, the more it recedes. It is not easy to find a focus, as poet Gary Geddes says, because of all the contrary forces operating. What happened to the old days of reading the classics, and all night poetry readings? With the exception of the *Double Hook* and *The Word* bookstores, no other bookstore has a reputation that even reaches the 350 short miles to Toronto. How comprehensive can a searcher be when there seems hardly a place to begin?

Because Montreal is a city of villages, the poets have their own individual geographic displacements. Someone said toss a stone in any Canadian city and you'll hit a poet. That's true for Montreal as well, though Mark Twain commented you're just as likely to break a church window. Montreal poets have the same concerns as other Canadian poets. They write of sex and the seasons, politics and human rights, religion and metaphysics, the problems of writing a poem and the emotional upheavals of living with an artist. They muse on strangers walking by and the absence of close friends. These examples are from a key anthology of English Quebec poetry called *Cross/cut*. To add to this obvious matrix of imagery and theme, English poets have the added dilemma of English/French relationships with its historical polarization and the evocative possibilities of another tradition.

Yet to write in English in Montreal today is no longer a political stance. Montreal poets are proud of their tradition, but not necessarily bound by it. They love political debate (when it doesn't interrupt their work), and they follow international political developments. In some cases, this even means turning their backs on Canada and looking to the U.S.A. or Europe for both inspiration and audience. But to generalize, all the cultural cross currents of contemporary poetry meet somewhere, in some stage and manner of development, in the creative writing produced by the English poets of Montreal.

We all know Montreal has a distinguished past. The McGill *Fortnightly Review* ushered in Modernism in 1925. T. S. Eliot had only just published *The Waste Land* in 1922, and Frank Scott, A. J. M. Smith and others were right up to date. The post-war vision of life as a wasteland was a manifesto that shaped the literary imagination of a generation. Montreal intellectuals separated from the past at this point; hence the Montreal literary tradition is central to our understanding of Canadian literature. The late Frank Scott was power broker of the age: poet, editor, lawyer, author of *The Regina Manifesto* for the CCF. He made headlines when he took the infamous Padlock Law to the Supreme Court and won his case. The entire story of this period is well documented in Louis Dudek and Michael Gnarowski's *The Making of Modern Poetry in Canada*. Later, Dudek was to say, "It is the destiny of Montreal to show the country from time to time what poetry is." From time to time, Montreal did.

The modernist wave from 1925 to the 1950s was centred in Montreal. Irving Layton, Louis Dudek, and Leonard Cohen evolved along their various poetic paths during the later years of this time. Montreal was the starting point of what has been called the first authentic poetic tradition in Canada. Poets turned, at least somewhat, from British and American models into what we now call the Canadian mainstream. Every Canadian poet is close to Montreal. The whole beginning of our intellectual life is rooted in the poetic activities of that city. It's so new to us and so well documented we can chart the influences, changes, trends, and overlaps on a calendar. We can argue whether Montreal developed movements or schools or important individuals producing significant work. Most likely, most members of a significant group don't know they are that until someone shows them their significance. So Gertrude Stein explained the Lost Generation, Evelyn Waugh defined the Bright Young People, and is not that what Louis Dudek did for the 1950s and Ken Norris did for the 1970s?

Montreal poetry went through several stages. The McGill movement was the first, with A. J. M. Smith, A. M. Klein, and Frank Scott at the centre. Later, there was John Sutherland and First Statement Press. This was followed by Louis Dudek and the Contact Press, with Raymond Souster in Toronto.

Around this time, the 35-year-old Al Purdy found himself on the floor at Irving Layton's house in October, 1955. Purdy was on his way to Europe.

He noted Layton, Acorn, and Dudek were all working at cross purposes from each other, but even in their quarrels, they formed a community. Purdy said at this time he felt like "a male Cinderella kicked out of the party before the dancing started." Layton mentioned "he might be eligible for cleaning blackboards after Dudek's class." But he added that to get into such arguments was a measure of the passion they felt for poetry. Purdy was, as one critic described him, "a great man without being influential."

The passion for poetry continued through the 1960s. The centre of influence had shifted from the conservative McGill and Loyola to Sir George Williams University, now Concordia. A faculty committee, which included Vancouver poet George Bowering, invited as guests the Americans Gary Snyder, Ted Berrigan, Robert Creeley, Robert Duncan, and others. They were a major influence on the creative writing students who eventually became associated with the Véhicule Art Gallery: John McAuley, Tom Konyves, and Artie Gold.

By now the older generation of poets had drifted apart, and with it, some essential energy. As Wayne Grady noted in a 1976 review, "The community of older poets had disbanded, and the younger poets were drifting about in the resultant vacuum hardly aware of each other's existence, let alone their poetry."

In a poem on the subject of Montreal poets, George Bowering complained, "The lonely Montreal poets / stand without community at social / functions eyeing one another / like a younger brother." Bowering would write in his introduction to Artie Gold's *Cityflowers*, "I found lots of poets, but no community of poets … they were not of the world." He meant what Gold had described as "the world of poetry … that MexCity-SF-Vancouver-Toronto-Detroit-NY complex … the energy centres of Canadian and American poetry." Montreal was clearly in a transitional phase.

The situation continued through the 1970s. Though the poets were aware of Montreal's distinguished past, they seemed not to want to reach for their own equally high pedestals. Although Véhicule Press published a laudatory anthology of twenty-two English language poets, the collection did not prove that Montreal was asserting itself as a centre of English language poets. As editor Ken Norris said in his assessment of the period, "Montreal lost the poetic spotlight to Vancouver's Tish and the other manifestations of New Wave Canada." Other critics noted the poems were weak, derivative, and sodden with images borrowed from Creeley, Spicer,

69

Olsen, or O'Hara. Because the anthology was self-serving, it lost credibility. David O'Rourke, writing in *CV/II*, thought the anthology cliquish, lacking in critical vision, and a decade late in its endorsement of Black Mountain and TISH. While Norris complained that the younger poets ignored new ideas and experiments, he also ignored the fact that Layton, Cohen, Dudek, and Scott were still writing. O'Rourke even suggested that many of the younger poets in fact had nothing to say.

English language poetry in Montreal had a failed moment for many reasons. The pressure of Quebec nationalism was certainly not sympathetic to English writers. Layton had already moved to Toronto. Groups of poets became a community of the present without looking to the future. As one poet said to me, "The personal politics of poetry doesn't interest me. I couldn't get any writing done if I socialized." Often, poetic criticism from peers had a sharpness that verged on vindictiveness.

CanLit had come of age across the nation in the 1970s. But many English poets in Quebec felt left out, passed by in the emergent literary history. One poet said to me that she felt editors in other provinces, especially the West, think they all speak and write in French, so they don't connect them with the contemporary English writing scene. To which another critic added that if Montreal writers are ignored outside their own city perhaps it's because their work is not any good. Other poets deliberately kept a low profile. They went to only a few readings, had sparse chapbook publications. Some clearly suffered from an inferiority complex, some really were inferior, and others built a garrison mentality in self-defence.

The two major anthologies published during this time are *Montreal: English Language Poets of the Seventies*, edited by Ken Norris and Andre Farkas, and *Cross/cut*, edited by Ken Norris and Peter Van Toorn. Both collections are edited with cheerleading zeal. They submerge the reader under too much information, not to mention biases, weakness of argument, and excessive emphasis in the wrong places. Still, they have the strengths of names, places, dates, as well as an analysis of why the poets felt apart from the Quebec literary tradition. For someone keen on Montreal poetry, these are the best places for one-stop shopping, despite, as David O'Rourke notes in his *CV/II*, article "A Second Look at English Poetry in Montreal," the elements of favouritism and bias, especially towards the Vehicle poets and against those associated with New Delta Press.[2] Montreal poetry in the 1970s ended on those exclamations of competitive fireworks and competitive natures.

What of the 1980s? Montreal is a multilingual city in a French-speaking province of Canada. But while this spirit of place is praised, too many poets, so I was told, seek inspiration from Toronto's example. Those dollars from the Ontario Arts Council, weekly book launchings, all those readings—too many even to attend regularly. Instead of seeing Montreal as an enchanted place—the Paris of North America—the poets were semi-paranoid (their term) about the ghetto mentality that afflicted the English poets of greater Montreal.

Complaints, oh, they had complaints. No poetry in the schools program, despite good teachers in the CEGEPs. They complained about the obvious difficulties of two languages (or more), the lack of grants from the Quebec arts councils, the suspicious feeling that too many of their fellow writers were passed over by important Canadian poetry anthologists. They complained that staying in touch with each other in Montreal, especially during the winter when most people don't take off heavy coats until spring, was in itself a full time profession. Some writers appeared to have given up on Canada, looking to Europe or the U.S.A. to publish their work. As Gary Geddes says, Canada has no impact on Montreal poetry for some writers. They see themselves as a minority under siege. Instead of banding together, which they tried for a short time, they dispersed.

Not that this is altogether a bad thing. As Geddes says, people can do their own work. But worst of all is a lack of any sense of a real audience. Without feedback in the positive sense (and how can a distant audience provide feedback), one has no sense of getting better. "You do more singing when you have an audience to hear your song," Geddes says, "Lack of audience is the biggest failure in Montreal today. I straddle the country, but I'm hardly known in Montreal. I have no readership here, except for other writers, compared with my Vancouver or prairie audience."

So there is a pessimistic mood. Raymond Filip, poet and literary impresario, puts it this way: "Montreal calls itself a city with a heart. The slogan is on licence plates and billboards. But read the poetry—there's no heart in it." Antonio D'Alfonso, poet and publisher, wrote in *Poetry Canada Review* that English Canadian poetry is lacking in audacity. "I'm not too enchanted by the cultural life in this part of town. The view is bleak."

The current generation of poets no longer sees Montreal as central to the Canadian poetry scene. Montreal poets have reached that junction in the road of literary progress: they can choose a route based on right-wing conservatism. Or they can take a more positive constructive route which includes what has been called "a quiet renaissance." Clearly the competitive approach still has a place in Montreal poetics.

The destructive side is the bleakness of conservativism. Perhaps even poets are affected by the world-wide swing to the right that has changed the political face of the western hemisphere. Bottom line accountability. Respectability. Preppies that grow into Yuppies. Free enterprise, profit motives, and artists bound for cutbacks too afraid to show their anger, let alone disrupt the status quo. Neither language nor content is challenged. Instead, the poets have their eye on publication and promotion, with little concern about the future of their art. Too many poets are so eager to get into print that they don't enter into any kind of artistic debate, or write lines that make a reader think. They just want to get into print and they sound old and derivative at nineteen.

Passion is the key to the magic of Montreal poetry. Passion and humour. Not just romantic passion, Filip says, but political passion as well. A passion for knowledge, for a cause, as a reaction against social ills or aesthetic limitations, or psychic evils. The literary documents collected in *The Making of Modern Poetry in Canada* are ripe with passion, as are the lines of Layton, Dudek, Cohen, Purdy, Acorn. In the words of Filip, "Passion kept the heart of Montreal poetry beating. But the new conservative hearts lack passion. Now it's Hush Puppies and dabblers with no heart, just cosmic conservativism. Magazine editors aren't interested in political or experimental poetry. They publish dribble-drabble, the work of obscurantists, everything under the sun except poems with humour and passion."

Perhaps the most positive trend in Montreal poetry in the 1980s is the "quiet renaissance." In the 1950s John Glassco, Louis Dudek, Frank Scott and others read and translated the work of French poets in Quebec. A similar interest has again appeared. Possibly the poets are trying to ease the guilt of a generation that ignored the work of writers on the French side of town. Possibly it's because the Quebec poets have ended their terrorist idiom. Jacques Brault once divided Quebec poets into three groups: *formalistes*, *nationalistes*, and *spontanistes*. The new Quebec poets (who prefer to call themselves textologists) profess no political or social ideology. They prefer the pleasure of the text as a ground for games and questioning. A poem is a place for experimenting with form. The English poets still seem to insist on traditional, patriarchal, hierarchical writing when the French have moved back to variations on "je," lyric writing, legibility, and the romantic discovery of the commonplace.

That passion for knowledge may return in full force when the English poets completely discover their counterparts east of the Main. Passion and humour, after all, are found in French poetry as well. In the 1960s Michèle Lalonde could bring down a full house at the Montreal Forum with her reading of "Speak White". Now the trend might be called "Speak Easy." Poets talk whenever they meet, in cafés, in the street, or at one of the seven Salon des Livres that take place around Quebec during the year. The Quebec poets are still waiting to see who comes to them. They are not that sure about reaching out. But at least they are receptive. The terminology of the new criticism is certainly one factor that allows French and English poets to explore each other's work. Derrida, Lacan, Foucault, Merleau-Ponty, Blanchot, Kristeva, and Culler among many contemporary critics who explore the multiplicity of meanings in language and society have provided a common language for subtextual theory.

In the 1970s, Quebec was described by Peter Van Toorn as being in contact with "the rhythms and sonorities of two kinds of English, two kinds of French, and the *mélange* of sonorities provided by dozens of European, Asian, and Eastern tongues." The creative directions were all mixed up. But by 1980 the Quebec review *La Nouvelle Barre du Jour* would describe writing in Quebec as if in a laboratory of creative writing and theory. Poet Claude Beausoleil said, "C'est un laboratoire oú s'agitent la fiction et la theorie." Some future literary historian might also want to note the influence of fifteen years of Federal Liberalism with its twin platforms of bilingualism and multiculturalism. Creative writing in Canada reflects the diversity of idea, opinion, language, and aesthetic. Eventually these ideas filter down through the literary psyche. The ideas of translation, ideas in transition, and intellectual questions raised by change are part of Montreal's real culture.

This future literary historian would also note that Quebec changed after the referendum debates in May 1980. Quebecers voted to remain part of Canada. The PQ government took upon itself the task of describing what it meant to be a Quebecer with such vigour that writers were freed to discuss whatever they wanted. As a result of this shift, Quebecers were suddenly criticising themselves, writing personal essays, questioning the nature and shape of poetry with prose poems, fragments, and diary forms. Radical political poetry moved into deconstructive formalism and then into new forms of legibility.

Historical changes happened in English Montreal as well. After the PQ election in 1976, theatre took over from poetry as the dominant literary form. People crowded into theatres to see new work such as Rick Salutin's *Les Canadiens* and David Fennario's *Balconville*. Over at Le Théâtre du Nouveau Monde, new plays by Michel Tremblay, Denise Boucher, and Jovette Marchessault attracted receptive audiences. The poets were drowned out by the excitement of the new and powerful French- and English-language theatres.

Some critics complained that few new voices were heard in Montreal's poetry scene after Leonard Cohen took his band on the road. But the scene was still there. Perhaps smaller, more esoteric, decidedly experimental. But the poetry continued. Under the direction of Claudia Lapp and Michael Harris, Véhicule Art Gallery initiated a reading series in 1973. With the aid of LIP grants and an old 14 X 20 Chief printing press, Véhicule began publishing Alan Bealey's broadsides as well as poetry titles by Bob McGee and Claudia Lapp. In 1978, Véhicule published *Montreal: English Language Poets of the Seventies*, edited by Norris and Farkas. No matter what the criticism, this was the first collection of Montreal poetry to be published since John Sutherland's *Other Canadians* in 1947. Montreal seemed on the comeback. In addition, Tom Konyves experimented with video poetry and Sharon Nelson lobbied for a feminist caucus in the League of Canadian Poets.

Some writers found that transition easier through the newly formed creative writing program at Concordia. In 1974, the Jesuit Loyola College merged with Sir George Williams University to form Concordia. Remedial and occasional writing courses under the direction of fiction writer Clark Blaise became one of five creative writing programs in Canada offering credit to the master's level. (The others are the University of British Columbia, University of Victoria, York, and Windsor.) The program now includes 400 students in one course or another, with forty degree students studying under any of twenty novelists, poets, and playwrights.

The impact of all this activity? The university emphasis has shifted from McGill to Concordia. Certainly many younger writers have shortened their apprentice years through the width and depth of the program. Fiction writers especially have profited, with published books from alumni such as Ken Decker, Sandy Wing, Sharon Sparling, and chapbooks and literary magazine publication from others such as Brian Bartlett and Jim Smith. The anthology, *The Inner Ear*, includes many Concordia graduates, several of whom are now residents of Toronto. Michael Harris did an M.A. in the writing program, and story writer Ray Smith of the Maritimes is now doing an M.A. With a staff that includes four poetry instructors, Richard Sommer, Robert Allen, Gary Geddes, and Henry Beissel, Concordia certainly creates optimism, energy, and pride in its studio courses.

Some quick notes on English poets in Montreal in the mid-1980s do not turn up clear trends or nicely organized schools of poetic thought. The concept of the Canadian mosaic has made way for distinction and individuality. Yet Montreal has no one single dominant poetic voice. There are many groups, each with distinctive antithetic splinters of the individuals within the group. There's the CEGEP poets at Vanier or John Abbott College (with the Lakeshore poets as a subgroup); the Eastern Township poets; several groups together form the Black Rock Writers' Group (named after a monument placed on the common grave of 6,000 Irish immigrant victims of the great typhus epidemic of the 1840s.) "The aim of the Black Rock is to provide a centre for working class, English-speaking Verduners. Our goal is to develop an independent voice for our community, working with other community groups in southwest Montreal." So regionalism has been replaced with neighbourhoodism, and many of these groups are talking only to themselves. Add to the street or raw verse poets, academic talents like David Solway, and the remains of the Vehicle poets of the 1970s, and the city does show some poetic liveliness, however diffusive. The city has practically no concrete poets (Richard Sommer does the occasional piece), no sound poets, and no video poets (although Guernica editions has just introduced its computer disc series for writers who own an Apple II personal computer and would like to see one of two programs on their computer screen: the first a bilingual poem by Marco Fraticelli, the second a novel for computer, *Rice Wine* by Richard O'Donnell).

The 1980s might be known as the Mystic Moment in Canadian writing. Creative writers have shifted over to an investigation of religion and mysticism in their poems and stories. Leonard Cohen's *Book of Mercy*, Morley Callaghan's *A Time For Judas* and Timothy Findley's *Not Wanted On The Voyage* are just a few of many Canadian and Quebec books with an emphasis on religious or psychic life. Marxists such as Jacques Renaud and Paul Chamberland have shifted their literary stance towards an examination of the mystic.

Why? Some reasons are obvious. If poetry has reached a limit of language, are there modes of thinking beyond language which might lead to the ultimate answers about existence? We have been conditioned to think in terms of words. Now sensitive poets might realize words alone may deny vast realms of experience that surround us. Lucien Francoeur's *Les Rockers Sanctifiés* is not about rock and roll, but the spirituality of ancient and mystical times, from Egypt of the Pharoahs to more contemporary doors of perception. Out of the rigid shell of a conservative time may come a groundswell of philosophical poetry.

With so many poetry groups, reading series can be found throughout Montreal. If you missed some of them, you can get an album of Montreal poetry, *Sounds Like*. Unfortunately, the poetry is as flat as the album. You will have better luck at The Word Bookstore, the proving ground for young poets. The owners screen the poets before presenting them, so aside from the fumblings of the inexperienced, the audience is at least spared the hit and miss of open readings.

Poetry readings are also held at McGill, Concordia, Laval, and Loyola, the CEGEPs, the Jewish Public Library, Librairie l'Androgyne, the Simone de Beauvoir Institute, the Double Hook Bookstore, and even sometimes at noon in the Royal Bank auditorium at Place Ville Marie. Despite critics who say the group is filled with hacks who speak loose left rhetoric, Monday nights the Black Rock Café with David Fennario, "the bard of Balconville" in charge, hosts readings for their members.

West of the Main, at the corner of Milton and Ste. Famille is Ray Filip's Café Commune where the Pluriel series brings together a wide range of poetic voices. Pluriel includes many factions and different cultures, often presenting Spanish, Lithuanian, Greek, or Chilean poets among the guests, as well as pairs of English and French poets. Among the pairings: Al Purdy / Gaston Miron; Dennis Lee / Paul Chamberland; Joy Kogawa / Sylvie Sicotte; Michael Ondaatje / Michel Savard (almost unknown before he won the Governor-General's Award); and Robyn Sarah / Michel Beaulieu .

The Oboro Gallery is joining with Powerhouse as one of the leading feminist reading centres. The feminist lobby, especially among the Quebec women poets like Nicole Brossard, Suzanne Lamy, France Theoret, Madeleine Gagnon, Michele Proulx, and Yolande Villemaire is comprised of strong women of letters. Most are preoccupied with the concept of body/text and with the creation of *l'écriture feminine/feministe*. As one woman said to me, the English feminist poets tend to put the emphasis on content, not language, because they feel that certain content is expected of them. Because content presides, they tend to sound the same. The English feminist poets have not formed a strong formal community despite overlapping concerns and even collaborative anthologies such as *Women and Words / Les Femmes et les Mots*.

Montreal is a poor city for English poetry magazines. Though in years gone past, magazines have existed as "survival outlets" for Montreal writers, including such classics as *Blast and Booster* [sic][3], *Contact*, *Delta*, *Direction*, *CIV/n*, *Yes*, *First Statement*, and *Cataract*, the current years have not been so lucky. Alternative newspapers such as *Logos*, *Le Voyage*, and *The Local Rag* came and went. Now, McGill University sponsors two literary magazines, *Scrivener* and *Rubicon*. The first has published nine numbers, the latter has published four. They both have student zeal behind them, with *Rubicon* the more professional in appearance and concerns. Issues have featured Quebec poets in translation, the "new" Montreal poets (which were actually student writings), and an issue of Montreal short fiction introduced by Hugh Hood and presented as a book anthology by Véhicule Press.

Still, the magazine scene is skimpy. *Athanor* had a short lifespan. A little magazine called *Short Poems* went under. Fred Louder and Robyn Sarah have published three numbers of *4 x 4*. Andre Farkas publishes a poetry magazine called *Montreal Now*. Each issue features six French and six English writers, with an emphasis on the avant garde. A newsletter called *Poetry Montreal* (modelled on the successful *Poetry Toronto*) publishes younger poets, but serves a more important function as billboard of coming events on the Montreal poetry scene. But in the 1980s, the little magazines of Montreal are not at the forefront of any battle for a mature literature of our time. Perhaps the end of the decade will see more boldness and brilliance for the literary magazines.

Certainly, the English poets of Montreal have much to learn from the examples of their French counterparts. Established magazines like *Liberté*, *Les Herbes Rouges* (recently merged with *Parti Pris* and *l'Hexagone*), and *La Nouvelle Barre du Jour* share shelves with newer magazines such as Claude Beausoleil's *Lèvres Urbaines*; a new six-page pamphlet called *Terminus*; a feminist magazine, *Arcade*; science fiction publications like *Solaris* and *Imagine*; multidisciplinary magazines such as *Dérives*, *Spirale*, *Intervention*, and *Moebius*; and review magazines such as *Nuit Blanche* and *Lettres*

Québécoises. If English Canadian poets want to be cosmopolitan, they will have to keep up to date with their contemporaries in French.

Montreal's small presses have always played a crucial role in the development of English Quebec poetry. John Sutherland's First Statement Press and Louis Dudek's Contact Press are an essential part of Canadian literary history. More recently, in the 1980s, a group of twelve Montreal English language publishers organized themselves as The Roundtable with the intention of exchanging information and knowledge and publicizing their literary activities. Their members include a scholarly publisher, a university press, a children's publisher, as well as the leading literary presses. These include Harvest House, which specializes in 19th- and 20th-century Quebec fiction in translation, as well as Guernica Editions and Véhicule Press.

Guernica Editions has an aggressive French and Italian translation program featuring the work of writers such as Gilbert Langevin, Eloi de Grandmont, Phillippe Haeck, Yolande Villemaire, and Claude Beausoleil, as well as an anthology of Italian-Quebec poets called *Quêtes*. Publisher Antonio D'Alfonso is not currently optimistic about English language publishing in Montreal and so has turned his attention to other communities.

Véhicule Press by comparison, under the direction of publisher Simon Dardick, has published the two leading anthologies of Montreal English poets. And as a companion volume to *Cross/cut*, he published a stimulating, though at times bombastic collection of essays entitled *The Insecurities of Art*. Since 1981, Véhicule has a sideline called the Signal Editions under the direction of Michael Harris. Titles in this series include work by David Solway, Susan Glickman, Bill Furey, Louis Dudek, and Ann McLean. Véhicule also has literary criticism and literary history titles in their list, with studies of Margaret Atwood, a reprinting of the 1950s magazine *CIV/n*, and a history of the Montreal Storytellers.

More recent small presses include Fred Louder and Robyn Sarah's Villeneuve Press chapbook series. Though the editions are in runs of 100 copies (or less) the handsome handset broadsides and chapbooks feature the work of some of the most promising poets such as Jack Homer, Brian Bartlett, Bruce Taylor, and Stephen Brockwell.

Another unique press in Montreal is Quadrant Editions, run by Andy Wheatley as Canada's first subscription order press. With a mailing address in the English Department of Concordia, Quadrant is quick to publish the most promising of the authors that pass through the creative writing program. Quadrant has published two poetry anthologies: *The Inner Ear* (which some critics were quick to call the Tin Ear), and *Full Moon: An Anthology of Women's Writing*. If there is an economic crisis in publishing, no one mentions it. But a quick count shows the number of poetry titles has dwindled in recent years.

What now, Montreal? At one time, the English poets of Montreal would fill a large portion of any poetry anthology in Canada. Now that Canadian poetry has matured in all the cities, and in all regions, the energy of any one city can no longer dominate Canadian poetics. But Montreal poets will continue to make their contribution. "Montreal needs to forge stronger links with the rest of the country," says Gary Geddes when asked about the future. Perhaps it is not possible for Montreal poets to write the single national epic. But in the multicultural flow of energy between Quebec and Canada, Montreal poets can still teach some new directions.

[1985]

Double Exile and Montreal English-Language Poetry[1]

DAVID SOLWAY

> And what's the news you carry—if you know?
> And tell me where you're off for—Montreal?
> —Robert Frost, "An Encounter"

It is no accident that some of the best writing in English Canada is to be found in Montreal and that some of the finest poets in the entire country reside and work within a radius of a few blocks of one another. Michael Harris, Carmine Starnino, Robyn Sarah and Peter Van Toorn have lived "in town" from the very beginning of their literary careers. Eric Ormsby moved to Montreal from the U.S. in 1986 to take up the post of Director of Libraries at McGill University and Norm Sibum, a longtime resident of Vancouver (via Germany and Alaska), arrived only a few years past but has since become an integral contributor to the poetic revival fermenting in the city. Stephanie Bolster, another recent arrival, has settled in nicely. Charlotte Hussey is associated with the very streets of Montreal—an earlier collection is entitled *Rue Sainte Famille*—and Robert Allen appeared on the scene in the mid-seventies via Cornell to join the teaching staff at Concordia University and eventually to assume the editorship of the literary magazine *Matrix*. Bruce Taylor arrived in 1978 and, although he has recently moved to the country-side, continues to regard himself, in his own words, as "a Montreal poet if I am anything."

The reason for so dense a concentration of virtuosity has to do with a civic and municipal condition that I call the "double exile," a function of our peculiar demography. I refer to the fact that the small cadre of Anglophone poets in Montreal is doubly cut off from an appreciative, or at least available, readership since it constitutes only a tiny insular minority in the midst of a sea of five million French speakers (who pay little attention to works in the "other" language). At the same time French literature is itself a minority phenomenon surrounded on every side by a nation of twenty-five million English speakers (who, for political reasons, will subsidize its token presence but without understanding or familiarity—while ignoring the Anglophone remnant almost completely). What this means for English Montreal poets, distinct from both their franco-Québécois as well as anglo-Canadian counterparts, is that they form the literary wing of a twofold hostage community. Their voices are heard neither in Quebec City nor in Toronto, a twin-barrelled neglect which leaves them in their various cummings and Gioia, whether solitary or gregarious by nature, talking pretty much to themselves, to their predecessors, to posterity or to the Lord.

The odd thing is that this relative segregation has by no means been an unmitigated disaster. Quite the contrary. For some time now it has brought along with it certain inestimable advantages from which these poets have profited as *writers* though obviously not as celebrities. Unlike their peers in the rest of the country whose work is publicized and aggressively circulated and who group together to safeguard the perks they enjoy and collect ideological pogey, these Montreal writers have worked in substantial isolation not only from the various nationally syndicated poetries at large—the West Coast school, the Prairie School, the Southern Ontario school, the Toronto-centric school, and so on—but also *from one another*. Especially with regard to diction and prosody, the private shaping of a public medium has led to genuine originality.

In other words, this state of binary preterition has created an environment in which individual poets are free to choose their own sources, influences, usage, directions and identities, reaping what we might call benefit of ostracism to build their home *in the domain of language itself*, each in his or her own special manner. Lack of public attention has liberated them from the need or the tendency to affiliate themselves with political and regional ideologies in order to further their (nonexistent) careers, a providential disregard which has sponsored a renewed sense of the printed voice and kept its possessors in touch with the free vagrancies of mind that consolidate a signature.

In this way place has been displaced into language, which becomes not simply an agency of communication but both a patrimony and an embodiment. To live in Montreal is now tantamount, for the best of these poets, to moving about fully and jubilantly in the language they explore, construct, reassemble and ultimately dwell in. Where you live has in their case become what you say and how you say it: locality disappears and re-condenses as a dialect of thought. Having absorbed the reality of exile into their inmost selves and consequent practice—having had, so to speak, autonomy thrust upon them—each of these poets has developed a distinctive style and idiolect that resists co-optation by a collective. Language has become a house with many mansions.

I give several titles as evidence for my claim. Peter Van Toorn's *Mountain Tea* is in a class by itself; the sizzling pyrolalia of a master wordsmith in his element, nothing like it has ever been published in this country. Michael Harris's *Grace* and *In Transit* represent the kind of work that Ted Hughes would have wanted to write had he been able to. (I have long maintained that Harris is a better poet than his beloved mentor.) *For a Modest God*, as has been noted by more than one reviewer, displays the verbal gemminess of Hart Crane and the meditative sweep of Wallace Stevens, but is entirely Eric Ormsby: it stands as one of the major poetic achievements of the decade in English-language poetry. His latest book, *Araby*, is perhaps even more impressive. *Questions About the Stars* by Robyn Sarah and *The November Propertius* by Norm Sibum share few thematic and prosodic features, yet the former in its technical self-assurance and the latter in its elegiac harkening are equally *classical* productions. Robert Allen's best book of poetry might well be his novel *Napoleon's Retreat*, a veritable *tour de force* of poetic prose, and Charlotte Hussey's latest divan of versicles, *Sonnets for Zöe*, improves on her already fine, partly *Montréalais* collection. Stephanie Bolster was honoured with a Governor General's Award for *White Stone: The Alice Poems* and Bruce Taylor won the QSPELL Poetry Prize for *Cold Rubber Feet* and again for his most recent collection, *Facts*. Finally, *Credo*, Carmine Starnino's second book, with its innovative sixteen-part sequence "Cornage," has brought him early and justifiable acclaim: "He may in fact be the true heir to the Montreal tradition of poetic excellence," writes one critic in a recent review.

The work, then, is *uniformly* accomplished, and yet nothing can be more *different* one from the other than the verses of Ormsby, Harris, Sarah, Sibum, Van Toorn, Allen, Hussey, Taylor and Starnino, all of whom *as poets* could just as well be living on different planets (although some of them, it must be admitted, are fellows of the *Jubilate Circle*). They will meet often, of course, to discuss, argue, compare and disagree, as a talented and amicable community of independent poets whose mutual influence, while occasionally technical or prosodic, is emphatically social and personal. That is, they reinforce each other in their reciprocal and productive solitudes but stay resolutely clear of the schools and movements, the topographical identities, cultic franchises and power politics that constrain and obviate the work of the scribbling classes in the other parts of the country. While they may, as I have said, engage occasionally in mutual critique, they stay pretty well out of one another's work. The result is that the imaginative flora and fauna are different here and in some instances almost wholly singular, so that what we are seeing is the literary equivalent of Australian evolution. This is just another way of saying that these poets are not, properly speaking, Canadian (or Australian). They are merely unique.

But English Montreal, as we have seen, is in many respects a small and lonely city despite its exotic aura, "over four centuries of cobblestones / sequined with bottle caps," as Hussey puts it. Besieged by two generations of neglect, it has thus forced its writers in upon themselves in a kind of literary quarantine. This state of affairs, as I have argued, has compelled a number of the poets to shape their own distinctive and indelible styles, which of course does not necessarily alleviate a feeling of oppression or misprision. Opportunity permitting, there is always the temptation either to leave the premises entirely for a distant arboretum, as did Leonard Cohen in the late sixties, or to establish a defensive huddle in order to create a "culture of belonging," a doctrinal and theoretical shelter from the storm of indifference and rejection impacting from the rest of the country.

Indeed this latter option was adopted in the seventies by the first Vehicle school of pseudo-demotic poets. Affecting the open-ended poetics of the Black Mountain bunch as it filtered through the West Coast anagrammatic Tish movement, a byke of these early Vehiculists unleashed what seemed to many observers a veritable hemorrhage of forgettable books. The bleeding stopped in time to save these poets for other careers as pedagogues, editors and Canadianists. Finally, after a brief interregnum, an abused Véhicule Press was brought under more enlightened editorship, restored to health and reinvented, in part under the Signal Editions imprint, to be what it is today: a home for a select group of poets who have nothing in common except an abiding passion for a rigorous Muse and a refusal to share an aggregate, homogenizing poetics. The lesson, long in the learning, had been well learned.

Regrettably, but perhaps inevitably, the managerial sensibility of the initial Vehicule movement still carries on as the Blue Metropolis annual literary symposium, in which some of the same old names tend to resurface administratively or to orbit those of the invitees, putting in effect the wrong Montreal on the map—the one that hankers for international vetting and cachet. (When Michael Harris was improbably invited to give a brief reading, he was plaided among the clan of visiting Scottish poets.) The festival is in the business of borrowing prestige which it repays in the usual provincial fashion with adulation and cash—a superannuated Norman Mailer receives $10,000 to make an appearance (accompanied by a wife with literary ambitions of her own) and local media types are dewy-eyed over the prospect of interviewing Margaret Drabble, of all people. As of this writing, the news is that John Ashbery, whose reputation is in strictly inverse proportion to his means, will shortly become a little more affluent too, as will a wizened Susan Sontag, a writer long past her best days. Put a Yank or a Brit in their midst—even if, to cite a line of Rob Allen's, they are "played out, done in, defunct"—and the festival organizers and fellow travellers circle round and round in noisy excitement like fourteen doves spooked by a Cabbage White. The spectacle of so much spurious activity and obsequious gratitude is truly chastening.

The occasional quality writer who does turn up, resident or foreign (like Mavis Gallant, for example), merely accentuates the general lack of spark and animation. Obviously one never gets any of this from local media outlets, which have united in touting the festival as unfailingly exciting, glitzy and *avant-garde*—the typical boosterism of the parochial mindset unaware of where its real strength lies. Thus it makes some sense to say that there are really two Montreals in competition with one another: the burgravial, agenda-dominated camarilla of movers and shakers connected with Blue Metropolis as well as with a cliquish outfit misnomered as the Quebec Writers Federation and the party of excellence associated with Signal Editions and the *Jubilate Circle*, the one denying the condition of exile and the other exploiting it. But it is to be expected that the former will continue to attract more attention from the media and to promote its version of what passes for a literary event for some considerable time to come.

Yet such is merely the institutional form of a cultural mediocrity whose half-life is at least as long as literature itself and must be regarded as an ineluctable feature of any literary landscape where, as Bruce Taylor writes in "The Slough," "all poor beasts that flit or thud / lie down with the frogs in the lathered mud." After all, it is only natural that Montreal, like any other place, should harbour its complement of mavens and speculators as it does its quota of weak and even catastrophic poets, but this is an unavoidable deficit in the creative budget of the race as a whole. And certainly it needs to be acknowledged that the city even at its best does not enjoy an absolute monopoly on good poetry. One will find a sprinkling of first-rate poets here and there beyond the gates of what Cohen once called "a holy city [...] the Jerusalem of the North."[2]

But the fact nevertheless persists. Canadian poetry has been flashing 18:88 for a long time now, probably since 1888 if not before, with brief but timely and providential returns to the world in the Montreal twenties with the *McGill Fortnightly Review*, in the forties with *Preview* and *First Statement* and now again at the turn of the century, the city enjoying perhaps an even greater distribution of genuine talent than before. The power is there, if we only knew where to look. Thus, as I have not scrupled to stress and reiterate, there is little doubt that in Canada at the present time, most poetry of value, interest and consequence is being written and/or published in Montreal, which thanks to the cohort of brilliant poets and editors who have gathered here is experiencing the spirit of renewal and invigoration once again, as it did when A. M. Klein, Louis Dudek, P. K. Page, Frank Scott, Irving Layton, A. J. M. Smith, John Sutherland, Patrick Anderson and John Glassco commanded the stage.[3]

Liberated from the trammels of program, region and coalition, our best editors are both stringent and encyclopedic while the poets writing here and now in the "tradition of excellence" are those who have expanded the linguistic and architectonic spectrum, permitting themselves to use all the crayons in the box instead of just a few favourite colours like narrative yellow or confessional rust, the mainstays of what we might call the Group of Seven Million in this country. While remaining members of the larger community, the Montreal poets have gone their own way with astonishing originality. Perhaps what we are seeing at work is, *mutatis mutandis*, a specialized instance of what Charles Taylor means by "deep diversity," each of these poets being "a bearer of individual rights in a multicultural mosaic," that is, belonging to a common entity while hewing to a heteronymous sense of his or her own specific identity.

The poets I have Magic Markered are the real thing, writers whose work, like Ormsby's garden snake, "silvers the whole attention of the mind," or like Van Toorn's mountain heron, refuses to be deflected from its purpose, "Still fishing the lake, / same spot—after all that rain". These are writers who can hold their own with and even surpass the achievement of their more celebrated contemporaries anywhere in the world—though it may take yet another generation before the truth comes to light. We will then have to figure out some way of expiating our lack of acumen and maturity and rendering due justice.

Meanwhile, the state of double exile—a paradoxical condition of twice solitary yet richly communal productivity—has unexpectedly turned out to be a creative godsend for which the more cuddled poets in Victoria and Calgary and Toronto, if they had an eye to permanence and an ear for Promethean language, might well envy their Montreal counterparts.

[2002]

II. Retrospectives

Louis Dudek and the Question of Quebec

TONY TREMBLAY

> If I now seem to carp and cavil, it is because the truth demands it, and because monuments are for the birds. To make [poets] live we must see [them] as problematic and we must quarrel as to [their] meaning, for only by asking searching questions can men and poetry be brought to life.
>
> —Louis Dudek, "The Monument"

While critics will forever disagree about the energies that converged to give impetus and shape to what we now call literary modernism, critics generally agree that Montreal was the locus of modernist fervour in Canada in the early and middle part of the twentieth century. First- and second-generation literary modernism evolved as form and practice in the city's cafés and reading rooms, in the literary magazines and small presses associated with McGill University's faculty and students, and in the works of key Montreal poets, literary activists, and theorists.

Louis Dudek was one of those key poets, activists, and theorists. He was a figure equal in influence to the two great pioneering Canadian modernists in Montreal a generation before him, A. J. M. Smith and F. R. Scott, founding editors of *The McGill Fortnightly Review*, the magazine that ushered a new spirit of daring and freedom into Canadian poetry. And though Dudek's contributions to Canada's evolving literary sense of itself in mid-century were sometimes overshadowed by the louder and more colourful figures in his circle—I am thinking specifically of the bombast of Irving Layton and the zealous conservatism of John Sutherland—there is little disagreement today about the importance of Dudek at the heart of the modernist program in Canada in the 1950s and '60s. Scott may have been more ambitious in his literary politics a generation earlier, but he was no more successful than Dudek in using anthologies and polemics to loosen the grip of archaism in literary language and opinions. Similarly, Layton's barbaric yawp and Raymond Souster's crystalline social realism may have found readier readership than Dudek's ponderous, sometimes Romanesque, lines, but their poetry is no more representative than his of modernist efforts to liberate the artist from constrictive forms and traditions. Nor was their cultural work more ambitious. While Layton, A. M. Klein, P. K. Page, Leonard Cohen, and other highly regarded Montreal poets focused the bulk of their creative energies on their own artistic development, Dudek pursued a more inclusive activist agenda that saw him publish the works of many other poets, most of the major English-language voices, in fact, of Quebec and Canada in the 1960s and '70s. As publisher, literary critic, editor, translator, professor, anthologist, and tireless cultural worker—with all of these roles carried out in Montreal from the time of his involvement in *First Statement* in 1942 to his retirement from publishing (and the sale of DC Books to Steve Luxton) in 1986—Dudek is unsurpassed as Quebec's pre-eminent English-language modernist, theorist, and poet. None of his contemporaries left a body of work to rival his own in terms of the range of its address to the social and political tensions of being an English-speaking poet/writer in Quebec. Dudek is, therefore, the ideal writer against which to examine the historical conditions faced by the Anglophone writer in Quebec in the last fifty years. More specifically, because the scale of his artistic ambitions demanded that he engage with the literature and cultural politics of both of the dominant linguistic communities in Quebec, his negotiations and quarrels, especially in the decade of the 1960s, reflect the diminishing authority of English-language writers in this turbulent era of political change. Spanning the period from Duplessis and Lesage to Lévesque and Parizeau, his fifty-year literary career in Quebec reveals much about the collision of ideology and art in this country.

My intentions in this essay are twofold: first, to reiterate the importance of Dudek's stewardship in encouraging, promoting, and shaping English Canada's modernist poetic voice in mid-century (a stewardship that laid much of the foundation upon which English poets in Quebec would build in the post-1976 period); and, second, to explore his own negotiations, as an English-language poet in Montreal, with the emergent Francophone activism that was coincident with his fifty-year literary career in Quebec.

Some biographical detail is necessary at the outset to establish the context within which Dudek lived and worked. Dudek was a second-generation Canadian of Polish-Lithuanian descent born in east-end Montreal in 1918. His early years were both crowded and sheltered by an extended multi-generational family of aunts, uncles, and grandparents who showered the young boy with concern over his weak constitution. So frail was his health that his grandmother didn't expect him to live beyond childhood. Dudek's many documented remembrances of his youth recount those early experiences of illness and insecurity, and, as importantly, equate his own poor health with that of his province. His reference to Quebec in the 1920s as "a narrow and bigoted society which wreaks irreparable psychological damage on little children without being half aware of the harm done" is, on the surface, a criticism of the parochiality of the Catholic schooling that he and his sisters tried so hard to escape, but a wider reading of Dudek's thoughts on his youth reveal the broader sentiment: namely, that his early experience of Quebec was one of smothering constriction wrought by social and economic systems that were near-feudal in design and application.[1]

So how did he develop? Dudek responded to living in a closed society by largely withdrawing from it, an instinct entirely in keeping with the action of other young artists and intellectuals of his time. He found solace in books, chess, music, philosophy, and classical languages, knowing that developing his mind was both his passport out and a counterpoint to the staid, regimental politics of old Quebec. His withdrawal, however, including his formal renunciation of the Catholicism he had once observed faithfully, was from a social and ideological infrastructure in Quebec, and certainly not from Francophone culture, for he admired tremendously the *élan* and spirit of the *gens du pays*. Entries from his *1941 Diary* reveal a love of French theatre, folk music, and art;[2] a complete fluency in the French language (including an early mastery of the written form); and a preference for French-speaking friends, whose sensibilities were more artistic and whose *joual* was the neighbourhood speech of his childhood. In "On Getting to Know Nelligan," an essay published in the Montreal *Gazette* on July 5, 1980, Dudek remembers the French-Canadian friends of his youth and the importance of their similar enthusiasms for writing and "talk[ing] literature."[3] He recalls, especially, the Francophone poets they introduced to him: Perrault's introduction of Émile Nelligan, "the greatest of all our poets,"[4] and Maurice Watier's introduction of Jean Narrache (Émile Coderre). From those first introductions, Dudek would develop life-long interests in Nelligan and Narrache, translating them into English for *First Statement*, CBC, *Ellipse*, and *Tamarack Review*, and, in the case of Narrache, assembling his work for reprinting. (One of the last projects Dudek worked on before his death in March 2001 was the Narrache selection, a project handed over to his trusted friend and publisher Sonja Skarstedt.) As a young man in the 1930s, Dudek also became close to Yves Thériault, who had not yet published a novel, but whose literary ambitions were revealed in an in-house magazine that he and Dudek edited at their place of business. He also came to know and respect Maurice Hébert, father of Anne Hébert, whose early work was just beginning to appear. These "contacts with poets and writers," wrote Dudek many years later, "[were] few, too few, but they [were] important for my own literary experience, and they have left some trace in the form of translations."[5] What the contacts do reveal is Dudek's attraction to a spirited life of the mind and to like-minded brethren, regardless of the language of their conveyance.

Further evidence of Dudek's early love of the spirit and creative energies of the Québécois—and of his corresponding anger with big business and the state for its systemic repression of that spirit—is to be found in his first collection of poems, *East of the City* (1946). The collection enumerates the struggles of working-class Francophones and brings into focus Dudek's belief in a democracy that liberates rather than diminishes common people. Expressed in the title poem, the quarrel he begins to formulate publicly with Quebec involves the totality of its impress on the lives of its most vulnerable citizens. In these early poems, Dudek is content to survey the damage from ground level, leaving his more pointed political pronouncements for later. Two passages from "East of the City" illustrate the point; the first describes, in Lawrentian terms, the dehumanization of men at their factory work,

Where in a crimson doorway like a sour red rind—
A round of citrus sucked in the mouth—
The haggard labourers gather, muster together;
Dwarfed by the dark, they shrink in showers
Of light spat from the walls by the welders,

Then club-footed, hunched, they shoulder through
A cloud of golden atoms, shredded fireworks. [6]

With growing despondency, the second passage shows how deeply ingrained and habitual is the institutionalization that labourers carry with them even away from work. For Dudek, it is this habit that is the tragic imprint of high-Church Quebec ideology:

Ah, here over their lager, thick and throaty,
Maudlin with pleasure, or sucking strong cigars,
They turn in phalanx against their bosses
Like impotent rats in cages, or gnawing at curtains.
Free with their money, knocking the metal on tables,
Their eyes boast of terrible strength, and wrestle
With tree roots, in the thunder of their imaginations:
They handle rough nuggets that might buy them
    freedom,
But lose them in the loam of prejudice, tired and
    ignorant. [7]

The weight of this tyranny—and particularly of the stifling conditions it created in Quebec for artists, liberals, and intellectuals—spurred the reactionary in Dudek, energizing his editorial work with fellow Montrealers John Sutherland and Irving Layton on the new literary magazine *First Statement*. Dudek's descriptions of the intellectual fervour of the debates that enlivened the first days of the magazine in the early 1940s are particularly revealing. While much of the impetus for this excitement was associated with, as Dudek describes it, "the simple idea that modernism was primarily a housecleaning, a sweep-out of sentimental propriety and moral hypocrisy," the often-overlooked context for the excitement was Sutherland, Layton, and Dudek's discomfort with the old Quebec.[8] The energy they put into *First Statement*'s avant-garde, including the way they chose to think about the rival Montreal magazine *Preview*—Dudek wrote that "*Preview* was associated with what I think of, historically, as the colonial attachment of Canadian literature"[9]—reflected their determination to do something about that discomfort. Was it coincidence, then, that the two great waves of literary modernism in Canada (those generated first by Smith and Scott and twenty years later by Sutherland, Layton and Dudek) hit the shore in Montreal, the Protestant and Jewish (i.e., non-Catholic) centre of the old Quebec? I think it unlikely, for conditions in Quebec in the 1920s and again in the 1940s were ripe for cultural overthrow and renewal. I am therefore suggesting that rather than looking at the frenzied work of our pioneering modernists as challenging either a staid Victorianism in Canadian literature or as perpetuating the "academic" socialism of the time, we should also consider the possibility that the intensity of their activism was fed by and addressed ideological concerns much broader than literature. The inhospitable climate of anti-intellectualism and insularity in the ecclesiastical culture of old Quebec made our pioneering modernists fiercer cultural warriors than they might otherwise have been.

For Dudek, however, *First Statement*'s tepid bohemianism and exhortations against "unreal" language, "pedantic absorption," and socio-political ideas were not enough to counterbalance years of borrowed idioms and ingrown ideas.[10] Put simply, he had outgrown Montreal by the 1940s. His independent reading of history and philosophy had already accelerated his leanings to the wider world, further diminishing the small arena of provincial and nationalist concerns in Quebec. His departure from Montreal for New York in 1944 was thus not surprising. Nor is it surprising in hindsight that Dudek opted for the study of history at Columbia University, the study of that discipline whose temporal range allowed him to examine broadly the question of why some cultures preferred the ephemera of aphorism to the more lasting qualities of genuine art. As he described it, the program of study he undertook to answer this question was "part of a desire to find a sound basis for understanding poetry and its history."[11] Key to it was breadth, a breadth that Dudek always embraced as an antidote to the surface textures of the popular. Detectable also in the range of inquiry, and duplicated in the restlessness of Klein, Scott, Page and Layton—Dudek's Montreal contemporaries—this desire for breadth is another rear-guard action, a reaction of sorts to an earlier intellectual enervation. I do not wish to make too much of this, except to say that the varied flights of imagination and inquiry of Dudek and his Montreal contemporaries during Duplessis's reign are disproportionate to that of other poets in Canada at the time.

While at Columbia, Dudek was aided in his study by association with the most worldly and unsettled of all modern poets, Ezra Pound, who, in the latter half of the 1940s (during a twelve-year stay from December 1945 to May 1958), was incarcerated for treason at St. Elizabeth's Hospital for the Criminally Insane in Washington, D.C. Dudek wrote a letter to Pound in 1949 to convey his admiration for the older poet's "honest and reckless" courage, hoping that Pound, only a short train ride away, would invite him to visit. He did, thereby initiating a long association that led, Dudek wrote, "to my higher education in the reality of modern poetry."[12] By "higher education" Dudek meant the characteristic Poundian dicta for cultural renewal: little magazine and small press publishing, polemical writing and editing, reading against history and canon, and social activism through the civilizing effects of poetry. The similarities between Pound's world at St. Elizabeth's and the early days of *First Statement* would have been immediately apparent to Dudek. Both spaces were vortices of creative energy and cultural subversion bent on the overthrow of outmoded ideas. The differences were two: first, the scale of Pound's project was immense (he was taking on the entire western tradition of what he called myopic philology—essentially, the denial that art is political) and, second, the fact that the universe of Pound's propaganda machine was mostly underground, a consequence of his caution not to appear to be organizing publicly—war-time treason carried a sentence of death, from which Pound had been exempted for reasons of an "unsound mind."[13] Regardless of the size and subterranean nature of Pound's program, Dudek enlisted enthusiastically. He became a foot soldier for Pound, familiarizing himself with the terrain and covertly doing the older poet's bidding. He made contact with Pound's inner circle of "serious characters" in and around New York,[14] visiting like-minded artists and radicals intent on a cultural anarchism that was grounded in republican modernism; that is, a top-down renewal engineered by historically minded intellectuals who are averse to institutionalized solutions to social problems. To properly nuance this republican modernism, Dudek read voraciously under Pound's tutelage, absorbing an international curriculum that included the sweep of his mentor's intellectual cache: obscure and censored economists, fascists, and political thinkers. The result was a sharpening of Dudek's activist instincts (particularly in the use of networked intellectual resources to effect cultural change) and a much more informed intolerance of small-minded provincialism. Earlier inclinations that Dudek had to socialist renewal evaporated. After Pound, Dudek's models were more likely to be top-down philosopher-kings such as Erasmus and Arnold than bottom-up emancipators like Marx and Engels or Auden and Spender.

Especially influential on Dudek were Pound's own cultural tracts, few more important than the 1917 essay "Provincialism the Enemy," which Dudek probably encountered around the time of his soldiering for Pound in 1950. In that essay, Pound defines provincialism as "[a] desire to coerce others into uniformity"[15] and he accuses the clergy of being an agent of this coercion: "A clergy, any clergy, is an organized set of men using these arbitrary statements to further their own designs. There is no room for such among people of any enlightenment."[16] Pound continues, writing that "[m]odern civilisation comes out of [...] renaissance Italy, the first nation which broke away from Aquinian dogmatism, and proclaimed the individual; respected the personality."[17] Throwing off dogma for civilization is the necessary first step that frees the individual to the possibility of achieving enlightenment, thereby creating a society of contented workers, exactly the opposite of the indentured labourers in Dudek's "East of the City." Pound writes the formula as follows: "Civilisation means the enrichment of life and the abolition of violence; the man with this before him can indubitably make steel rails, and, in doing so, be alive. The man who makes steel rails in order that steel rails shall be made is little better than the mechanism he works with."[18]

I summarize the argument of Pound's essay to illustrate how opportune was Dudek's association with the older poet. The uncanny appropriateness of Pound's ideas and the practical apparatus of his propaganda machine powerfully affirmed Dudek's own experiences of growing up underground in ultramontane Quebec. But affirmation was just the start. The Poundian combination of aims and means to counter regimes "which protect [their] bigotry by the propagation of ignorance" would also arm Dudek to face his own brand of provincialism at home, restore his faith in subversive action, and renew his energy to wage cultural battle.[19] Ultimately, Pound's practical poetics for civilization building ceded Dudek's larger vision: that "[i]t was not just for myself that I was going to do this work, but for this city [Montreal] and this country."[20] That rare combination of ideas, tactics, and energy was vitally important in what Dudek was to accomplish upon his return to Quebec, and also, ironically, the probable reason for his break from Pound in the late 1950s. Localizing Pound's program by consciously dissociating it from the older poet was the only way Dudek could make it uniquely his own. He admitted as much in a January 4, 1955 letter to Pound, one of the last pieces of correspondence they exchanged:

Note that the difference in Canada is, we don't mess with preten-
tious revivals of the Renaissance [...] nor catalogues of world literature. We're hitting at the particulars right here: The Shearer Mansion
on Mt. Royal; Premier Duplessis (Quebec, benighted licker of Fr.
Canadian sentimental prejudices & religiosity); the Canadian
Legion and tourist trade; Toronto puritanism; commercialism;
advertising; importation of Oxford accents to Can universities, to
spout cultured inanities, tradition & Eliotism.

Dudek's activist apprenticeship in New York is important for an understanding of his address to the political situation in his own province. When
he returned to Montreal in 1951 to teach permanently at McGill, he was
trained and ready for battle, his battleground *la grande noirceur* ("the great
darkness") that years of pious conservatism had cast over Quebec.

He got right to work. He immediately mounted a course in practical
poetics at McGill—what he called "a study [...] of the subversive currents
in modern thought"[21]—and began organizing with Layton and Souster to
publish poets ignored by the academically conservative presses. Aileen
Collins' *CIV/n* and Dudek's own *Delta*, the first of many Montreal-based
literary magazines that bore Dudek's stamp, were founded in the 1950s, as
were Contact Press and the McGill Poetry Series, which launched many
important young poets, among them the McGill students Leonard Cohen,
Daryl Hine, Seymour Mayne, and David Solway. In addition to implementing
grassroots means to literary production, something that the first-generation
modernists never did, Dudek also went out on the hustings, seeking
opportunities to speak and write publicly about the importance of aesthetics
to the life of the mind and the health of the polis. Though his essays of this
period such as "The State of Canadian Poetry: 1954" (1954) and "The Montreal
Poets" (1957) do not explicitly mention the work of Francophone writers,
his subsequent considerations of the complexity of Canadian poetry illustrate a correction of this oversight. By 1958, his essay "Patterns of Recent
Canadian Poetry" contains the following aside that would be front and centre
in all his subsequent work: "I suspect that [the sense of aimless enervation]
of the young English-Canadian poets may apply in part also to the young
French Canadians published in the Éditions Hexagone and Erta, providing
a first connecting link with our French-speaking compatriots."[22] As he
thought more about the mutualities facing "compatriots" on both sides of

the language divide in Montreal, he found he could not ignore the political situation in Quebec, for that situation, in his mind, was exacerbating the unreading public's contempt for the arts, whether the Westmount intolerance of young French dilettantes or the widening chasm between former allies in Anglophone Mount Royal and Francophone west-end Ville Émard. Dudek equated these biases with a social malaise that "enclosed [poets] in a prison of limitation and denial."[23]

As before, he pointed a finger at the old guard. Duplessis was nearing the end of his second term at the time, dealing tyrannically with striking unions in the remote mining villages of northern Quebec while his patronage machine was handing out millions to those ridings that had voted Union Nationale. Tribal nationalism was on low boil and the moderates in Quebec were demoralized. Even the clergy was being mistreated, their work in schools and hospitals amounting to a kind of neo-colonialism (what Le Devoir's editor-in-chief André Laurendeau termed le roi-nègre) that used them as low-wage cannibal-kings devouring their own people to serve the interests of the moneyed overlords. As Dudek wrote many years later, "The Québec people were easily exploited by English industrial interests in league with the government. It is here that the seeds of present-day troubles were planted."[24] After attending to his courses and initiating contact with poets and editors to begin his program of cultural renewal, Dudek began his public involvement in addressing the problems that faced Quebec.

His first address of lasting importance was nothing less than a manifesto. Written in 1961 at the start of the Quiet Revolution, "The Two Traditions: Literature and the ferment in Quebec" contains a depth of analysis and cultural bombast which suggest that Dudek initially saw the secessionist impulse among Francophone liberals as a genuine opportunity for socio-cultural renewal. Moreover, because many of the French intellectuals he admired were instrumental in the movement—his old friend Yves Thériault and the parallel group of publishing "compatriots" at Les Éditions de l'Hexagone such as Gaston Miron and Jean-Guy Pilon—Dudek felt (perhaps as his old mentor Pound did of Mussolini's early idea statale notion) that as long as artists and intellectuals were in charge of the revolution the outcomes would be positive, at the very least dismantling the bourgeois literary establishment. In his early support of the young Quebec nationalists, Dudek even went as far as pointing an accusing finger at the English, which further suggests that he saw in his compatriots' ferment and maîtres chez nous philosophy a momentum that might also carry his own cultural aspirations. The clear support for Francophone resistance in the following quotation is indicative of the hopes that Dudek placed in not only Jean Lesage's new Liberal government, but also, more generally, in the mood of reform overtaking Quebec:

> This progressive movement, which would seem to be everything that critics of Québec have always hoped for, as the much needed reform movement here, is capable at the same time of showing a nationalistic will to autonomy and a hostility to English Canada that may be hard to understand. But this is the inevitable result of the failure of English-speaking Canada—and I am thinking of the most literate and conscious part of it—to come to terms with French culture or to create a truly bilingual nation.[25]

As one of the leading bilingual Anglophones in Quebec in the early '60s, Dudek could make this argument and expect that others would listen. He therefore took the opportunity that the occasion of "The Two Traditions" manifesto provided to lay out his whole cultural blueprint for a dual-cultures nationality in Canada. First in that blueprint was bilingualism, which Dudek insisted "should be a requirement of every college teacher of the humanities."[26] Without it, he warned that "cultural division and antagonism" would continue to rule.[27] Though Dudek's ideas of civil liberty through linguistic dualism were not radically new at the time—his friends Frank Scott and Gael Turnbull had translated the work of Anne Hébert and Roland Giguère throughout the 1950s, and Ryerson Press had recently released *Twelve Modern French-Canadian Poets* in facing translation in 1958, thereby fulfilling the "duty to make each race known to the other"[28]—Dudek's particular obsession with what he termed "a minimum literacy in two languages throughout Canada"[29] was timely in its anticipation of the language and spirit of both the Royal Commission on Bilingualism and Biculturalism (1963-69) and the Official Languages Act (1969) that were to follow. Especially prescient were his views on the complementarity between pluralism and the enrichment of our nationality, not for any political end, mind you, but for social justice and greater individual freedom. Repeatedly, Dudek stressed the benefits of exchange, both to erase the more regressive "inbred cultural habit[s]"[30] of the two founding nations and to ensure our nationhood its only means of survival:

This can be done. It does not mean the assimilation of cultures one to another [...]. But to build our literature, the literati must work to become thoroughly versed both in the mother-literature of the other language and in the current literature of both parts of contemporary Canada. Is it asking too much? It is merely the minimum, if we want to survive very long as a nation [...]. We must conceive of it in this large, dramatic frame, if we are to escape from provincialism and if we are to create a new complex civilization in the north. This, and nothing less, must be our aim.[31]

Coming a full five years before Jean Marchand, Gérard Pelletier, and Pierre Elliott Trudeau—the Francophone architects of official bilingualism—were elected to federal politics, Dudek's manifesto is far-thinking indeed. It also echoes the tone and historical metaphors that Trudeau and the Committee for Political Realism evoked in *Cité libre* to explore their own budding vision of an enriched, dual-language Canadian federalism, one that also saw Canada as having outgrown its adolescent impulse toward the absolutes of unanimity or balkanization. (This parallel is not meant to suggest that Dudek had political affinities with Trudeau, even if both shared a close friendship with Frank Scott, were admirers of Pound's *Cantos*, and had similar feelings about the absurdity of the nation-state. In fact, though Dudek supported Trudeau's use of the War Measures Act in 1970, he found much to quarrel with in what he considered Trudeau's often-wistful panegyric surrounding state-legislated federalism.)

Most remarkable of all in Dudek's manifesto is the note of caution it sounds at the end, for in that note reverberates the next forty years of our political future. Only a poet with a knowledge of both world history and local affairs could be so accurate, and Dudek's flight from (and return to) Quebec qualified him to see what was ahead. I quote the penultimate paragraph of the manifesto in its entirety for reasons that will be evident:

This constructive and progressive intellectual ferment in French Canada is a precious and admirable movement of liberation and betterment. It has only one danger. In its prickly aggressiveness and self-assertion, it has shown that it can turn against the old English strawman-chauvinist as much as against the real forces of reaction at home. And the attack on English Canada as the source of all troubles can bring a possible derailing of all these fine energies, since that is an old escape-valve with all the ignorant passions still behind it. The massive majority of Québec have the necessary prejudices, and the rebellious *élite* have the spark that can set off the proverbial powder keg again.[32]

If nothing else, this passage supports Pound's contention that poets are the unheralded "antennae of the race," able to pick up signals long before others can.[33] When considered against the mounting tensions Dudek saw around him, however, not to mention his insider's assessment of the percolating resentments among artists in both language groups, his caution amounts to much more than the vapid guessing that passes for enlightened conjecture today. Rather, he saw in social history the seeds of our demise, and long before terms such as separatism, Parti Québécois, and sovereignty-association appeared in the national vocabulary. He also saw in the cultural catalysis that produced the best of Chaucer and Shakespeare a way to accommodate pluralism for the betterment of civilization. The catalysis he saw was certainly not that of the melting pot or the third space of hybridity, but of "the more promising course" of co-existence, the path of which leads "to a greater Canada that is literary in two languages."[34] It is this message of the necessity of dual-language co-existence that Dudek would carry with him as teacher, publisher, anthologist, translator, and mentor for the remainder of his days in Montreal. With it came the warning that, if unheeded, the cultural and creative aspirations of Quebec will find a way to express themselves, even, if necessary, through assimilationist and revolutionary means, thereby reflecting the habits of the colonial rule of mother France. Dudek knew from the larger world that the hijacking of art by ideology was a feature of decolonization, and thus something to guard against. The mailbox bombs that started going off in Westmount shortly after Dudek's manifesto was released would have been clear evidence of the urgency of his warning.

Seeking to bridge the gulf that he identified in Canadian/Quebec society (and with revolutionary passions intensifying), Dudek began bringing Francophone writers to the attention of "illiterate" (that is, unilingual[35]) Anglophone readers, especially in his regular columns in the *Gazette*. He introduced Gérald Robitaille's *The Book of Knowledge* as "an amazing breakthrough for Canada"[36]; he praised Gilles Vigneault as "the most gifted poet to appear in Canada since Émile Nelligan, whether in English or French"[37];

he wrote of the criticism of Jean Éthier-Blais that "these essays could only appear in French Canada, and they are living proof of the superior literary sense of the French tradition"[38]; and he repeatedly acknowledged the contributions of Saint-Denys Garneau, Alain Grandbois, and Anne Hébert in pioneering a French-language "modern poetry in Canada."[39] However, even though he admitted "feeling the greatest sympathy and good will toward the new poets of French Canada," Dudek did not pull his critical punches.[40] He offered advice and opposition when so moved, such as his recurring criticism that French Canadian poets were too inward in their "tragic submergence in the unconscious."[41] "More consciousness," he counselled, "not less, in poetry."[42]

The open-mindedness evident here—support for poetry that was independent of the poem—is essential to an understanding of what Dudek brought to Canadian and Quebec poetry in the 1960s and '70s: he could champion the artist and find the art wanting. Most important for him was the artist and the discussions surrounding art. Only by enabling production and acknowledging art as something worthy of table talk would creative endeavour ever hope to rival the vulgar modernism of commercial society. Dudek framed this idea years earlier in a letter to John Sutherland:

Maybe the way to put some life in things is to start a controversy [...]. I began to think that magazines should not publish the results of thought (which are usually static and undramatic) but the activity and the controversy which lead to new ideas. For example, my article on Scott ["F. R. Scott and the Modern Poets"] was less interesting than the exchange of letters we had about the bourgeoisie. I think it should be so to the reader. The same applies to poetry: not the hardened wisdom, but the activity that makes the poem, reflected in the poem, interests us. That is what we need.

Dudek's forays into translation, publishing, and literary journalism in the 1960s reflected these beliefs. While working on his own translations of Émile Nelligan and Jean Narrache, he wrote columns and editorials supporting Peter Miller, F. R. Scott, and John Glassco's translations of Alain Grandbois, Anne Hébert, and Gaston Miron. He also publicly challenged other bilingual writers to translate Roland Giguère, Gilles Hénault, Alfred Desrochers, Jean-Paul Desbien, Yvon Deschamps, and Claude Péloquin, among others. (When

Péloquin's work was finally made available to English readers, Dudek wrote the preface.) Commenting on "the immense possibilities" in this type of cross-pollinating exchange, he concluded that a dual-language culture is "far more interesting than any single strain of preserved mediocrity."[43] Even into the 1980s, Dudek felt it necessary to scold Margaret Atwood for her careless editorial stewardship of the *New Oxford Book of Canadian Verse in English*, for despite the qualifier in the title, he felt "the French half of the anthology [had] been wiped out."[44]

Dudek was equally energetic in bringing Montreal and Quebec poets into print in the 1960s and '70s. While his McGill Poetry Series was publishing the first collections of young McGill students (see above), his more ambitious presses, Delta Canada and DC Books, were publishing poets in great numbers. Under the Delta Canada imprint (1965-71), Dudek published over 40 titles, among them the work of little-known Montrealers such as Eldon Grier, Gerald Robitaille, Richard Sommer, and Peter Van Toorn; while, through DC Books (1971-81), he published a dozen other Quebec poets, some of the early work of Avi Boxer, John Glassco, Marc Plourde, and Henry Beissel. In addition, he encouraged the Vehicule Poets; was especially helpful to Raymond Filip and John Asfour; met countless other young writers for informal poetry tutorials over coffee at his favourite delis and *boulangeries* around University and Milton Streets; and maintained regular correspondence with a vast number of French-speaking poets and writers, among them Pierre DesRuisseaux, whose *Graffites ou le rasoir d'Occam* was another of Dudek's last translation projects (two years earlier, DesRuisseaux had translated *Dudek, l'essentiel*). The one piece of unvarying advice he gave apprentice writers was of the necessity of reading poets in other languages in order to stretch the mind.[45] In Bronwyn Chester's estimation, he became nothing less than the great McGill teacher of the middle four decades of the century, attracting, inspiring, and educating poets of the '50s (Cohen and Doug Jones), the '60s (George Bowering and Frank Davey), the '70s (Ken Norris and Andre Farkas), and the '80s (Sonja Skarstedt and Peter Van Toorn).[46] His attempt to conduct the business of civilization through poetry, publishing, teaching, and polemical criticism involved a practical poetics that required him to be indefatigable. As importantly, he felt that understanding the literature of the other founding nation in Canada would deepen the sympathies for that nation, thus enabling both dominant linguistic communities—*les autres* and *les nationalistes québécois*—to live in harmony. Like

Pound, he believed that civilization could be built with art and literacy.

The demands of Dudek's program of practical criticism never seemed to diminish him, even when the political climate in Quebec in the mid-1960s became increasingly uncomfortable for Montreal Anglophones. As French dissension became separatist demands, thus changing the debate, in Dudek's mind, from civil liberties for the many to a nativist utopia *pour les Québécois pure laine*, he waded in with characteristic zeal, using culture, again, as his ground. In a review widely circulated in the *Gazette* of Hubert Aquin's heretofore lavishly praised *Prochain Épisode* (Jean Éthier-Blais and Pierre Vadeboncoeur had been excessive in their admiration for the book in *Le Devoir*), Dudek took on the darling of the impending revolution: Aquin had written the book while in the Albert-Prévost Psychiatric Institute after being arrested for carrying an illegal firearm (his public declaration weeks earlier that he was going underground to effect independence through terrorism had led to the trumped-up charge). Commenting first on the quality of Aquin's style and aesthetics, then musing positively on the premise of the novel's dark anguish, Dudek finally dismisses the book as literature because of its "spurious vision," its lack of "moral truth" and "wisdom."[47]

The dismissal on these grounds—with the salvo that "Perhaps that doesn't matter, to some who are more concerned with revolution than with poetry"[48]—is more, if subtler, corroboration of what had been Dudek's position from the start: namely, that art should advance civilization, not inflame tribal passions. Whereas civilization-building was an emancipatory impulse, thus standing outside of ideology, tribal nationalism was proprietorial, therefore requiring initiates to capitulate to simply another doctrine of "transferred religious fanaticism."[49] "There should be no nationalistic passions involved," he said later, for "nationalism is a very strong passion, it turns you away from your real interests, the mother interest. It unbalances the poetic personality."[50] Dudek felt that politics had compromised Aquin's art. Of paramount importance in this and similar criticisms that Dudek starts to make of the tribal-nationalistic passions of the Québécois is that they are not new, nor are they altered to address the special circumstances of the 1960s. Dudek's break with his close friend John Sutherland in 1952 had been for the same reasons: Sutherland's withdrawal into fundament, the result of which was the narrowing of, and therefore increasingly "spurious," vision. As Dudek explained in a gloss to a letter to Pound (31 October 1953), "John Sutherland was gradually turning away from modern poetry, and he had become a convert to Roman Catholicism. I didn't mind the Catholicism, but I resented the literary conservatism."[51]

When applied to the question of Quebec, Dudek's criticism is remarkably consistent. Politics infantilizes art, stunts its growth, and renders its artists susceptible to the cultural cringe:

> The cultural quarrel in French Canada is often side-tracked into the anti-English or anti-federal obsession, with the result that the dynamic of French culture is prevented from generating its own powerful dialectic of growth. This is why Frère Untel and other self-critical features of the Quiet Revolution are so important a turning-point in French Canadian life and literature. Only since 1960 has the Quebec poet begun to look with anger at his own mirror-image.[52]

In the fall of 1967, four months after Dudek wrote the above, he contributed a rare non-literary polemic to the *Gazette*. It would be his last. Entitled "Too Many Controls Spoil the Show," his final parry addressed the question of control, particularly whether the tax-sponsored CBC in Quebec should be allowed to remain in the hands of an élite minority group who were using the airwaves for "pro-separatist opinion-moulding."[53] Dudek's answer did not surprise: he vehemently opposed control, even if that meant leaving the propagandists in charge. Rather than suggest they be stripped of their privilege, he countered with an appeal to a higher moral sanction, one he knew would be understood by nationalists and federalists alike. The higher morality was freedom, the condition over which the revolution was being waged in the first place. His broader suggestion, impossible to miss, was that French-language rights were but the first steps to a greater pluralism in Canada, certainly not an end in themselves. I stress again that Dudek's appeal for freedom in the passage below (written during the emotional debate preceding Bill 63, Loi pour promouvoir la langue française au Québec) is identical to his appeal years earlier in "The Two Traditions" manifesto. Though the heat had been turned up by extremists who were eroding the good will of like-minded Anglophones, not to mention the sense of personal security of Montrealers, Dudek's final polemic was a reasoned appeal to the first principles he began with:

> I may begin to sound like a moralist, but this problem is not imaginary. Wherever you turn nowadays someone seems to be say-

ing that this or that has to be controlled, something or other has to be obtained "by force, if necessary." A week ago, Marcel Masse, minister without portfolio in the Quebec government, was reported as saying that "the Quebec government will have to take steps forcing immigrants to integrate with Quebec's French-speaking population." At the same time, M. Jean-Noël Tremblay, Minister of Cultural Affairs, tells us that if persuasion does not succeed, legislation will be brought in to enforce French as the language of use in business in Quebec. And this week we have the declaration signed by over 150 Quebec intellectuals to make French the sole legal and official language of Quebec. To me, these statements are rather terrifying, though I love French, both as the language of literature and of conversation [...]. Some years ago we would have protested vigorously any interference by the state in the process of education [...]. We would have resented any suggestion that private affairs can be legislated for us; now we seem to take even this without a murmur of protest.

The political issue between Quebec and Ottawa, provincial and federal power, has the effect of reducing private freedom to a pawn in the political struggle [...]. "A plague on both your houses!" is what we ought to say.[54]

"Too Many Controls" effectively ended Dudek's public involvement in the political debate in Quebec. His intimate understanding of Quebec, his knowledge of world history and republican-styled insurrection, and the respect he had earned as a bilingual Montreal Anglophone had contributed purposefully to Quebec's self-actualization. He had participated openly, publicly sharing his views. To his credit, he had done nothing covertly. By the beginning of 1968, though, he was starting to tire: the activity of the past seventeen years had nearly exhausted him. On top of the primary demands of large classes and building an academic as well as literary career (he had become a prolific poet in these years, with ten books of his own), he had become the unrivalled dean of small-magazine and small-press publishing in the 1950s and '60s, publishing the early (in some cases, the first) works of the now best-known poets in Canada. On top of that, he had taken on the political situation in Quebec, both by introducing French writers to an English readership and calling for more social justice and liberties for Quebec's Francophones. Agreeing with poets like Jean Narrache, who wrote of "the sacred eyes of the race-power cliques" ("les saints yeux des Champions d'la Race"), Dudek wrote that "like [Narrache], I am for justice and for understanding."[55] His sense of disappointment over the failure of reasoned debate to effect change beneficial to the many rather than the few—a failure manifest in the ugly defilement of revolutionary principles that was the October Crisis—must have been profound. Knowing history, he would have recognized as spurious, again, the logic that used nationalism to counter nationalism. He could do little but support Trudeau's heavy-handedness. In the surrender of reason and moral truth to violence, murder, and extortion, what other choice did he have? Mindful of Pound's error, he hereafter ceased to lower himself to political debate, seeking in the 1970s and '80s to write about art and literature as countermands to what had become a one-issue obsession in Quebec: separation. Art replaced rhetoric as his firmament. Out of "affection and gratitude," he started by translating Narrache, who had died only months before the dark days of *Les événements d'octobre 1970*.[56]

In the last ten years of his career, though he increasingly sought "Atlantis" (that place of perfection at the intersection of poetic language and insight), he did not abandon his critique of what he had earlier called "barbarism": the vulgarity of the popular, the coarseness of commercialism, and the reductionist theories that delimited the human. Though some have misread his humanism as elitist and undemocratic, particularly in its opposition to Frye's myth criticism and McLuhan's technological determinism, his criticisms of systemization hearkened back each time to first principles. He simply did not accept any reading of humanity that treated the individual as an extension of another instrument. Nor did he accept any creation that coarsened subjectivity. His quarrels and eventual breaks with McLuhan and Frye during this period (and his break with Layton years before) parallel his quarrel and break with Québécois *indépendentistes* and *souverainistes*. His élitism must be understood in these terms: not as a condemnation of the folk, but of those agents who seek to enslave them, whether within the religious dictates of myth (Frye), the gears of technique (McLuhan), or the governing ambitions of politicos (Duplessis, Hubert Aquin, and René Lévesque). That Dudek became an élitist because of the intellectual freedom it promised is ironic only on the surface: "I say—let's not insult democracy. Democracy was not achieved to make us all mediocre, but to make us free and superior, each in his own way. Élitism is a good thing, and highly democratic, if rightly used, on behalf of the majority."[57]

Though he withdrew from public debate after the October Crisis, Dudek certainly did not abandon his larger work of advancing civilization through poetry, nor did he abandon the next generation of young Montreal/Quebec poets. Montrealers Michael Gnarowski and Glen Siebrasse especially benefited from Dudek's counsel, joining with him to publish Delta Canada Books from 1971 to 1981. (Siebrasse also became instrumental in the important Montreal magazine *Booster & Blaster* [1972], the first magazine to react to French militantism by adopting a Montreal English-speaking-poets-only policy.) As well, the principals of the Vehicle group of Montreal poets (Ken Norris, Andre Farkas, and Artie Gold) garnered much support from Dudek in their visual and performance productions (they performed, among other things, Pound's "In a Station of the Metro" in Montreal's Berri-de Montigny subway station), in the running of their gallery and reading series, and in their small press publishing. Dudek encouraged their energy, for in energy there was freshness, renewal, and hope. "I like the way you fellows descend into the chaos of the actual," he wrote. "I like your spontaneity. I like your experimental attitudes. I think the new *Postcards* demonstrates a very consistent poetics. Casualness, colloquial speech. The shaping of the ephemeral moment into a significance. They are poems."[58]

Whether they agreed with him or not, and regardless of what side of the Dudek/Layton faultline they were on, the English-language poets of the 1970s and '80s in Quebec could not but acknowledge the pioneering poetics of Dudek. Though he would refer to himself in 1980 as one of the "oldies,"[59] he was still one of the strong poets whose output, energy, contacts, and innovations had to be grappled with. As David Solway admits of the teacher/mentor whom he had broken with some years before, Dudek was the *primus inter pares*, regardless of which side of the faultline one inhabited:

Whether quoting whole passages from memory or lashing us with anecdotes, he made the poets and their work seem real, even irresistible. A sizeable number of his students decided they were intended by fate to become Dante or at least Baudelaire. Nearly everyone began to write [...]. He made us feel *chosen*, as if we belonged to the circle of the elect, to Wallace Stevens' "poetic solidarity." We felt masonic, revolutionary, indomitable. I sometimes think that I owe my present unenviable condition to Dudek for it was he, in his dual capacity of mentor and editor, who first convinced me that I had the wherewithal and stamina to become a poet.[160]

On a larger scale, Frank Davey agrees with Solway, suggesting that it was Dudek who patented the small press publishing formula for how poetry would be disseminated in a post-national world: "The general acceptance of [this formula] has caused not only the establishment of numerous writer-owned presses in the past decade [...] but also a distinct preference on the part of many writers to have a small press serve as their principal publisher."[61] It is indeed hard to imagine the existence of *Yes, Cataract, Catapult, The Bloody Horse, The Page*, Guernica, Véhicule, The Muses' Company, Pulp, *Ingluvin*, Signal, *Matrix*, Conundrum, *Anthol, CrossCountry, Zymergy*, Empyreal, and numerous other Montreal small magazines and presses— not to mention their de-institutionalized poetics—without the influence of Dudek.

2

After his retirement from McGill in 1984 and the sale of DC Books to Luxton in 1986, Dudek went underground again. More of his own poetry would come in the last fifteen years, as would honorary degrees, the Order of Canada, and many other awards and acknowledgements. He would continue to be a respected and generous mentor to poets and scholars alike. But as teacher, publisher, editor, and public intellectual, he had done his work. His lasting influence on the English-speaking poets of Quebec after 1976 was his work in the two-and-a-half decades prior, his work as publishing pioneer, literary scholar, creative conduit, and, lest it be forgotten, champion of his beloved Quebec, a province and people of two languages. Though a few other Montreal writers may have been better known for their poetry and fiction—Klein, Scott, Layton, Cohen, and Richler are the obvious examples— no other writer came close to Dudek in promoting the worth, enabling the production, and establishing the tone of mid-century Canadian poetry. And none of those better-known writers, with the possible exception of Scott, participated as intimately as Dudek in Quebec's often-painful process of self-definition. His involvement not only spanned fifty years (the most turbulent years of Quebec's partnership in Anglophone federalism), but it covered the gamut of attachments, from outright sympathy and support to reasoned criticism to exasperated withdrawal. Though statements like the following invite disagreement, I think there is more than sufficient evidence to conclude that much of what was possible for English-speaking poets in Quebec after 1976 was achieved because of Dudek. He is to them what Smith and Scott were to him a generation earlier. He is, as Brian Trehearne concurs, the strong poet of their past.[62] The isolation and neglect he endured at the end of his life were a consequence of the public stands he took for poetry and civilization, not a result of error. Without doubt, his contributions were monumental, his (sometimes stubborn and quarrelsome) integrity undeniable. Few other Canadians lived the drama of Quebec as fully as Louis Dudek. It was a drama in which revolutionary principles were co-opted by old prejudices and resentments, just as he had predicted. But Dudek's point was to make it new, not make it over. This is what the revolutionaries lost sight of in their passion. In his own words, "A revolution is a good thing as long as it doesn't succeed."[63]

Imaginary Traditions: Irving Layton, Leonard Cohen and the Rest of the Montreal Poets

NORMAN RAVVIN

B elmont Avenue and St. Elisabeth Street are not more than fifteen minutes apart by car, though they exist as opposite poles in Montreal's mythic twentieth-century Jewish geography. From his bedroom at the back of his parents' Belmont Avenue home, Leonard Cohen meditated on the green preserve of Westmount's Murray Hill Park. The park is a key lyrical presence in his first novel, *The Favorite Game*, which offers it, unnamed, as a kind of public imaginative space where a young poet's dreams of independence and love incubate:

> The park nourished all the sleepers in the surrounding houses. It was the green heart. It gave the children dangerous bushes and heroic landscapes so they could imagine bravery. ... It gave the retired brokers vignettes of Scottish lanes where loving couples walked, so they could lean on their canes and imagine poetry.[1]

At the other end of Jewish Montreal, east of the Main, Irving Layton was raised on St. Elisabeth Street, an immigrant street par excellence, not far from where writers as different as Saul Bellow and A. M. Klein confronted themselves, their inheritance, and the babel of languages on Montreal's narrow downtown thoroughfares. (When the children in Cohen's *The Favorite Game* fantasize about danger, they conjure a whore on De Bullion Street, the street where Layton's father took him to synagogue).[2] Montreal's once-Jewish downtown, with its potpourri of walk-ups, frilly mansard roofs, corner *dépanneurs*, and granite rowhouses on more venerable blocks, had its own distinct charm. But for Layton, childhood on St. Elisabeth Street in the late '10s and early '20s included its fair share of pauperized immigrant struggle, a youthful abandonment of his parents' orthodoxy, and low-grade street war with the neighbourhood's non-Jewish kids: "If someone had said the words anti-Semitism to me," he writes in his memoir *Waiting for the Messiah*, "I would not have understood. But it was in the streets and alleyways. It blanketed us like a fog. *Maudits Juifs!*"[3] Both Belmont and St. Elisabeth are interesting places to come from, but they are, in many ways, as distant from one another as two continents. Still, Layton and Cohen became companions and inspired one another. Although Layton's seniority suggests a role as mentor (born in 1912, he is twenty-two years the elder) it becomes clear with further attention to the two poets' progress that their artistic entanglement and friendship cannot be characterized simply as the attention paid by an elder, street-smart mentor to a younger, well-heeled and formally educated protégé. It is worth questioning the commonly held view regarding a line of inheritance shared among Montreal Jewish poets of the 1950s and after. Such a line begins, we are told, with A. M. Klein, who is dubbed, depending on who is doing the dubbing, the father or the grandfather of Canadian Jewish literature. Klein's mantle is said to have passed to Layton, to be taken up by Cohen. In a 1945 review of Layton's first collection, *Here and Now*, Klein's approval is not unqualified, but it is strong:

> *Here and Now* reveals an unmistakable talent, a power of expression which is unique and personal, and social awareness which endows poetic utterance with base and substance. Layton can certainly take his place in the Canadian pleiad, not like a twinkling little star, but as one of unquestioned brightness and constancy.[4]

Still, the time-line behind an orderly inheritance is not borne out by the facts. Klein went entirely silent in the middle 1950s, just as Layton's work and public persona broke into popular view. Cohen's first volume of poetry, *Let Us Compare Mythologies*, appears in 1956, a precocious debut under the sponsorship of Louis Dudek's McGill Poetry Series. Though Layton had been bringing out largely self-published books since 1945, it was his 1956 collection, *The Improved Binoculars*, with its prefatory note by William Carlos Williams, that marked a turning point in his career. The three poets' progress overlap in surprising ways: Layton's early books appear as Klein is still seeking a mainstream audience, and Cohen's breakthrough coincided with Layton's arrival as a controversial figure.

The notion of an orderly line of poetic inheritance is challenged, too, by the poets' own claims. In *Waiting for the Messiah*, Layton depicts Klein as a father figure and as an articulate bearer of polyglot knowledge, but not necessarily as a poetic model. Klein tutored Layton in Latin for school exams; he expounded, over coffee at Murray's restaurant, on Talmud and "events of the day."[5] Still, Layton goes out of his way to deny overt poetic influence: "He had little intellectual influence on me. His Zionism and conventionality left me cold. I couldn't reconcile the passionate poet I knew him to be with the paterfamilias and practising lawyer he had become."[6] Of Klein's visits to the group of young modernist poets associated with *First Statement* magazine, Layton opines, "I'd say it was we who influenced his style of writing rather than the other way around."[7]

In interviews, Cohen is equally willing to abandon Layton as a would-be mentor. In 1969 he told poet and interviewer Michael Harris:

> Well I think I became *friends* with Irving Layton, we became close friends.... There were many people who sat at his feet, I wasn't one of them. We very rarely discussed poetry or art. We discussed other things.[8]

We might hear, in each of these denials of influence, the poet's necessary overthrow of a precursor in order to assert the primacy of his own voice, alongside the myth of his own self- creation free of precursors. But there are undeniable differences in orientation, style and persona between these three. The differences include their formation in radically different poetic milieus: Klein in the English tradition of Milton and Shakespeare, along with the Yiddish writers of his youth; Layton among his modernist compatriots of the 1940s and the aggressively nativist writing of Americans such as Robert Creeley and William Carlos Williams; and Cohen's early imagistic writing developed under the tutelage of Dudek, but which then gave way to something more unpredictable, informed as much by American folk songs as Chassidic legend. As early as 1953, alongside his contributions to the poetry journal *CIV/n*, Cohen's biography informed readers that he "compose[d] poetry to the guitar."[9] When Klein, Layton and Cohen are viewed in this light, they comprise no poetic line at all. Rather, they appear as three diverse and, one might add, highly unusual personalities, whose Jewish identity was one component in their make-up as postwar Montreal poets. Klein and

Layton shared a neighbourhood and the experience of growing up in an orthodox home, but Cohen is an outsider to such experience.

In the past four decades, however, the mythology of a Montreal Jewish poetic royalty (overseen by a kingpin who pronounces on inheritance) has taken hold. These developments have been furthered by, among other things, the resurgence of interest in A. M. Klein and his role as a strong precursor to later poets. Another defining issue has been the absence, in the rest of Canada, of figures as dynamic as Layton, Cohen and Klein, which has tended to increase the attention paid to their influence. The acceptance of a Montreal line of poetic succession has done much to support the belief in the presence, within Canadian literature, of a fully-formed tradition of Jewish writing. Whether such a belief is reliable or not is beyond the scope of this essay. What is intended here, via a careful exploration of Layton and Cohen's work, as well as through an examination of their life in art, is a portrait of the two poets' impact on English-language poetry in Montreal.

The other essays in this volume point to 1976 as a watershed year in any consideration of Montreal's English-language poetic production. That year was, in fact, an interesting one for both poets. Layton published his then-notorious *For My Brother Jesus*, a collection that combined strident Holocaust-related poems with repeated denunciations of what he called the "anti-sexuality, anti-life bias at the heart of Christianity."[10] He was living in Toronto, having left Montreal in 1969 to accept a teaching post in York University's English Department. Upon departing for what would be a nine-year sojourn, Layton bemoaned the deterioration of Montreal's Jewish downtown, complaining, in an uncharacteristically sentimental tone, that the "Hanukkah candles were going out."[11] In the 1970s, Cohen was far busier with song writing and concert tours than with the pursuit of literary success. His increasing interest in Zen led him to spend time near Los Angeles at the Mount Baldy retreat, under the tutelage of his Zen teacher, Roshi. In an unpublished manuscript from this period called "The Final Revision of My Life in Art," Cohen cites, among other plans, to undertake his responsibilities as "street father to the young writers in Montreal, using the harsh style."[12]

How did two poets who are most commonly associated with Montreal's Jewish milieu, arrive at such circumstances, ensconced far from the city, thinking rather darkly of its possibilities? And what can we glean from these circumstances that helps us recognize the impact of their work on post-1976 Montreal poetry? To answer these questions (to steal a line from another

113

songwriter steeped in folk poetry) we have to go all the way back to the civil war.[13]

The Poetry Wars

The postwar Montreal literary scene, though the most important in the country, was small and divided between academics and those who denigrated university-based poetry. Poets tended to gravitate toward coteries, which were prone to infighting. A few senior figures such as F. R. Scott, A. J. M. Smith, Dudek and Klein represented a kind of generational authority and order, but their influence (whether through university posts, editorial power, or, in the case of Klein, his formal and traditional poetic rigour) was never dominant. Small press and little magazine activity presented young writers with independent outlets and a model by which to create new venues for their work. Here Layton asserted himself diligently and took up the role of cultural guide and worker alongside his pursuits as a poet. His early poems appeared in *First Statement,* and his first collections were either self-published or brought out by bare bones outfits like Raymond Souster's Contact Press in Toronto. The revolutionary stance taken up by the young writers who moved in these circles was the abandonment of Canadian (or British) poetic models in favour of American ones. And though Layton would later deny the influence of this milieu and its poetic inclinations, his early work profited from what Eli Mandel calls a "measured pro-American stand."[14] This included publishing in such influential American journals as *Black Mountain Review, Jargon,* and *Origin,* and receiving the enthusiastic embrace of Robert Creeley and William Carlos Williams. The latter famously affirmed Layton's arrival in his preface to the 1956 collection *The Improved Binoculars:* "When I first clapped eyes on the poems of Irving Layton, two years ago, I let out a yell of joy.... I believe this poet to be capable, to be capable of anything."[15]

In his excellent study of Layton's work, Eli Mandel notes that the "voice that endeared Layton to William Carlos Williams spoke an authentic North American speech. It was vulgar and therefore poetic."[16] Layton's American reception, according to poet and critic Seymour Mayne, can be contrasted with what Mayne forcefully calls a "perennial distaste" and "hostility" among Canadian reviewers and academics. These detractors, among whom Mayne includes Northrop Frye, rejected Layton's aggressive views regarding a "Canadian sensibility [and] . . . colonial gentility."[17] In addition, Mayne adds, most early reviews of Layton's poetry paid "scant attention" to the role of Jewishness in his work. "It is obvious," Mayne wrote in 1978, that "the American critics did not have the same prejudices toward Layton's work as the Canadians did."[18]

The absence of critical appreciation did not limit Layton's influence and involvement with a broad variety of Canadian poets and critics. Though Layton's poetic preferences may have been different, he maintained energetic dialogues, both private and public, with Louis Dudek, Ralph Gustafson, Desmond Pacey, and in later years, Earle Birney, Al Purdy, Milton Acorn, Barry Callaghan, Rienzi Crusz, Ken Sherman, David Solway, and Mayne himself. Leonard Cohen, however, emerges as the most interesting recipient of Layton's poetic and personal attention.

At the height of his popularity as a poet in the late 1960s, Cohen customarily downplayed his ambition to be "in the world of letters." In his 1969 interview with Harris, Cohen is at once emphatic and ambiguous on this matter. On the subject of poetic mentorship he acknowledges that if Layton had offered instruction, he'd done "it in a most subtle and beautiful way." Louis Dudek and Frank Scott were, he says, good teachers "who set out to teach [him] things in more direct ways" when he attended their classes at McGill.[19] More interesting, however, are Cohen's comments on his literary ambitions: "I wanted very much to be a poet in Montreal.... You know, to have to put out my work somehow and have it stand for a certain kind of life in the city of Montreal."[20] This suggests a fierce bond with the city itself, built upon the camaraderie, venues and reception that would follow from a writing life in Montreal. But shortly thereafter, Cohen tells Harris,

> I never sent things out to little magazines, poems, or anything like that. I never wanted to be in a world of letters. I wanted to be in the marketplace on a different level. I suppose I always wanted to be a pop singer.
>
> When I say pop singer I mean somehow that the things I put down would have music and lots of people would sing them.[21]

A sampling of Cohen's early poems can in fact be found in a 1953 number of *CIV/n*, a Montreal-based mimeographed "little magazine" whose editorial advisors included Layton and Dudek. Alongside other young poets based in the city, such as Avi Boxer and Phyllis Webb, Cohen contributed rather sketchy work that offers some presentiment of the kind of lyrical, intimate writing that would appear in *Let Us Compare Mythologies* and *The Favorite Game*. He reappears in a 1955 number with "The Sparrows," in which there are suggestions of his later more successful lyrics:

> Catching winter in their carved nostrils
> the traitor birds have deserted us,
> leaving only the dullest brown sparrows
> for spring negotiations.
>
> I told you we were fools
> to have them in our games,
> but you replied:
> > They are only wind-up birds
> who strut on scarlet feet
> so hopelessly far
> from our curled fingers.[22]

Writing retrospectively of *CIV/n* in 1965, Dudek acknowledges that "a good deal" of the journal's submissions came "from young poets who were gathering around" himself and Layton.[23] Though it is reasonable to assume that Layton attracted Cohen to the pages of *CIV/n*, there is nothing Layton-esque about Cohen's contributions at this early point in his career. Layton's contributions to the journal are declamatory, lean of line, aggressively proclaiming the stance a poet ought to take while dismissing his lessers ("I'll say nothing about E. J. Pratt: / The rhyme's too easy—blat or flat").[24] Cohen's work, by comparison, is introverted, cryptic and disengaged, offering a private voice where Layton exercises what would become his characteristic prophetic tone.

By the late 1960s, Cohen (the would-be protégé) had developed an international career based on his music, while Layton's success was largely a Canadian phenomenon. The divergence in the two poets' artistic progress can be seen by juxtaposing photographs representing the mid-1950s and the mid-1960s. Included in a volume devoted to *CIV/n* is a set of photos taken at a 1954 gathering at Layton's home (a poets' night out attended by Avi Boxer, Eli Mandel, F. R. Scott and Phyllis Webb, among others).

Representing old guard and young, Jewish and not, Montreal-born or just visiting, these photos depict a literary group for which Layton was, in its early stages, a kind of spokesman-provocateur. Cohen's interest in something other than this movement is revealed by a 1958 photo, which appears in Ira Nadel's *Various Positions: A Life of Leonard Cohen*. In it, Cohen is perched on a stool at Dunn's Progressive Jazz Parlour, performing his poetry with midnight jazz accompaniment, as he did repeatedly in 1958. According to Layton's report at the time, "Cohen is really laying them in the aisles. A new development in the Montreal School?"[25] Morley Callaghan, who took in one of these shows, was not alone in recognizing that if this was a new direction in the "Montreal School" it was one guided by the "nightclub poets of San Francisco and Greenwich Village."[26] Another photograph, taken in 1966, confirms Cohen's creative distance from what might be seen as a more traditional "Montreal School." In it, Cohen sits on the floor of a New York City apartment with such American folk luminaries as Dave Van Ronk, Joan Baez and Judy Collins, the youthful inheritors of another poetic line of inheritance, which included Hank Williams, Woody Guthrie and Bob Dylan.

Regardless of Cohen's drift from the Montreal scene, his eclipse of Layton and his increasing focus on songwriting, his reputation as an important poet in the city, as well as the inheritor of Layton's mantle, persisted. The notion of a "Montreal School," or, better, "Montreal Schools," was well entrenched. A characteristic description of the situation from the point of view of an influential outsider appears in George Bowering's "On Not Teaching the Vehicule Poets." Bowering suggests that Montreal's post-1950s poets coalesced around two traditions, or schools: "the Anglo line of Scott, Smith, Kennedy, Jones" whose work was in competition with the "Jewish mob led by Layton, but including Cohen (sort of) and the Layton-ettes, Boxer, Hertz, Mayne, etc. Neither crowd was particularly noted for keeping up with what was happening in the U.S. or Canada. The Montreal world, self-inflated, was sufficient to itself."[27] Bowering's views are suggestive for a number of reasons. The need to abbreviate Cohen's role in the "tradition" to a "sort of," and the absence of any obvious inheritor after Cohen, makes one question whether the "Jewish mob" was as influential as is typically thought. Beyond this, Bowering points toward a third line of influence in Canadian poetry (the experimental and locally grounded work of Americans like Charles Olson, the Black Mountain Poets, and the Beats, including Allen Ginsberg and Gregory Corso). Layton's rise was clearly influenced by postwar developments in the United States, including some of those who drew Bowering to an American-based poetics. However, writing at a generation's distance in 1993, thousands of miles away in Vancouver, Bowering downplays the variety and unpredictability of Layton's influences.[28]

Bowering's views come into sharper focus when read alongside the introduction to the 1977 anthology *Montreal: English Poetry of the Seventies*. In their co-written introduction, editors Andre Farkas and Ken Norris sketch what might be viewed as an accepted, though largely revisionist history of poetry production in Montreal since the 1950s. Citing the importance of *First Statement* and *CIV/n*, they characterize the 1950s as notable for the rise of Layton, and for the appearance of Cohen's first collection, *Let Us Compare Mythologies*, which together contributed to a move toward "Jewish romantic lyricism." What followed, they argue, was the failure of "a sustained movement of Montreal poetry" in the 1960s, as young writers were bent on "echoing and pale imitation of Dudek, Layton, and Cohen."[29] The local revival, according to Farkas and Norris, originated:

> … in 1967 when New Wave Canada made its official entrance into Montreal with George Bowering taking up a writer-in-residence post at Sir George Williams University. Bowering brought with him a new orientation towards poetry based on what he had learned from the Black Mountain poets Charles Olson, Robert Creeley, and Robert Duncan; now, as creative writing instructor, he passed on to his students these teachings. However, his most important contribution to the new generation of Montreal poets was the institution of a series of readings at Sir George which exposed them to the diverse experimentation that was taking place across Canada and the U.S. Although immediate results were not visible, by the time Bowering returned to Vancouver in the spring of 1971, the energies of the current movement were beginning to coalesce; this would result in numerous local readings and the establishment of a number of little magazines and small presses.[30]

Notable alongside this celebration of new developments in Montreal poetry is the list of contributors included in *Montreal: English Poetry of the Seventies*. Cohen and Layton are absent, while many of those included (Stephen Morissey, Artie Gold, Marc Plourde, Tom Konyves, Claudia Lapp, as well as

Farkas and Norris) came to be associated with a group dubbed the Vehicle Poets. The anthology's account of this group's coalescence has generated its share of controversy, but what is clear in the editors' strategy is their urge to write against (or even to erase) the influence of Layton, Cohen, and any would-be "Laytonettes." The new Montreal School is depicted as American-informed, Bowering-begotten, and thankfully free of the failed decades-old experiment of "Jewish romantic lyricism."[31]

An alternative view of the key lines of influence in Montreal poetry is offered by Michael Harris. Glasgow-born, and like many Montreal poets, a long-time teacher in the CEGEP system, Harris' career ran parallel to that of many of the Vehicle Poets: with Claudia Lapp he initiated a set of poetry readings in 1973 at the St. Catherine Street Véhicule Gallery. Yet, Harris is dubious about any claim that these gatherings marked a reorientation of poetry in the city. They included poets he felt deserved a hearing (Peter Van Toorn, David Solway and others) and once done, he felt:

> ... we should not do this again for another five years, because there were no other poets in town. I mean there weren't any other real poets in town, you know, who had published well, had interesting stuff, had some kind of profile outside the city. And yet, six months later, all of a sudden, there were the so-called Vehicle poets, who ... began to draw in crowds of each other ... audiences of six to eight, ten people max, and I had had a couple of hundred.... I mean the whole horror of what has happened to poetry in this country is that it's all being subsidized. The League of Poets is a joke. This is Groucho Marx territory. You know, Cohen never belonged, Layton never belonged, Solway never belonged.[32]

Harris suggests that some of what Farkas and Norris celebrate in *Montreal: English Poetry of the Seventies* was supported by Louis Dudek at a time when "his own star had somewhat fallen"; [33] thus, linking a figure who was among Cohen's first editorial supporters with a movement that saw its goal as writing away from the work of Cohen and Layton. (Farkas and Norris begin their introduction with a rather portentous quote from Dudek: "It is the destiny of Montreal to show the country from time to time what poetry is.")[34]

When asked whether the figures associated with the Vehicle school of the mid-1970s and after wielded substantial influence over later generations,

119

Harris is brutally direct: "Zero. No. It was a blip on the radar, collectable by university archives."[35] Cohen and Layton, on the other hand (regardless of their long absences from the city, their tendency to publish with Toronto-based McClelland & Stewart, and the lack of a clear follower in their footsteps) remain, in Harris's view, "indistinguishable from the fabric and spirit of Montreal."[36] For Harris (and here he echoes a view often asserted by others) Layton and Cohen exist as iconic figures:

> [It] was a very peculiar thing to be a poet, very strange, not a vocation that one's father for example could offer approval for. So Cohen himself was iconic… here was a man who seemed to do no work, didn't have a day job, I mean, I had no idea of his inheritance…. He simply seemed to be somebody who got up and either got laid or wrote poems.[37]

Harris recalls seeing Cohen and a companion on the Main on their way to breakfast, Cohen in a "wonderful black suit," the woman with him in a "white shift," creating a "little parade of perfectly dressed people, seven o'clock in the morning. I thought this was splendid." Of Layton, who taught Harris when he was an undergraduate and graduate student, he adds:

> I thought he was iconic also, in the sense that every time he put pen to paper, he actually created something that looked or felt like a poem…. It's the presence of that particular person, as a poet, in town, that was an inspiration. I mean, no poet is going to write well every day. So really, it's the phenomenon of the real thing that is inspirational.[38]

An ongoing discussion, which was propelled in part by Layton himself, centred on who would be the next "real thing." In his letters, Layton muses often about who will inherit his poetic mantle. In letters dating from the late 1970s, Montrealer David Solway is said to be "the real thing, a genuine poet who gets stronger with every step he takes."[39] In a 1985 interview with Michael Benazon, Layton is asked if a "Jewish Montreal tradition of poetry" could be seen to pass from Klein, through himself and Cohen to Solway. A little half-heartedly Layton agrees, adding that he "would also include Seymour Mayne, who is perhaps more Jewish than Solway."[40] In a 1984 letter to Toronto poet Ken Sherman, Layton writes,

I used to think my mantle would fall on David Solway. Regrettably, he, like Leonard Cohen, is entirely wrapped up in himself and like him too he's a narcissist who doesn't love himself.... You can only go from strength to strength, scaling ever more daunting heights with your pinions of beauty and terror. At those heights, may my mantle keep you warm.[41]

While Layton juggled this handful of would-be protégés, he maintained a large number of important relationships with younger poets. Among these, one of the longest-lasting and constructive was with Ken Sherman. Though Sherman remembers first meeting Layton "in a friend's basement," where Layton had agreed to address a Zionist youth group, he came to know him as a writing teacher in the early years of Layton's tenure at York University's English department. Sherman has high praise for Layton's refusal to comfort his students and for his willingness to "shake you up." Sherman catches some of the high comedy and pathos of creative writing taught Layton-style:

Whenever he came upon an image or turn of phrase that he liked he read it aloud in that marvelous voice that could make a shopping list sound impressive. I don't know what he saw in those pseudo-poems but he invited me to join his writing workshop.... Like most writing workshops, it was a strange mix. "Honest Ed" Mirvish's wife was in it (Layton called her, simply, "Mirvish"). A John Lennon look-alike told us that he buried his poems late at night in different parts of the city. A girl who had worked as a prostitute before attending university wrote rhyming couplets about her experience.[42]

Throughout Layton's years at York, Sherman feels that he:

... never took to Toronto. As for York, he found it a cold environment. I was amused to note that in four years he never unpacked the boxes he brought from Montreal to his York office. They remained piled up, as if he were ready to make his escape. All he unpacked were two framed photos: one of D. H. Lawrence and the other of Nietzsche. They were on the wall behind his desk.[43]

And to this, Sherman adds an impression regarding Layton's influence, which is echoed by numerous poets. He was "a daunting mountain peak. The sheer number of poems, their vividness and energy, were imposing."[44]

David Solway presents a similar sense of Layton's dominating influence in his lively essay "Framing Layton." The first poem he "committed *voluntarily* to memory," Solway writes, was Layton's "The Cold Green Element," and he refers to the older poet as a "friend, mentor, benefactor, example, and, at times … monumental Bloomian impediment…. honesty compels me to acknowledge those disturbing moments when I could wish that Layton's shadow were not quite so long and so encompassing."[45] Then, to complicate things, Solway writes in the same essay, that he "was never a student, a disciple, or a protégé of Layton's, but I benefitted enormously from the mere generosity of his presence."[46] Recently, Solway politely rejected the line of poetic influence that might be seen to run through Layton:

> There's no doubt that Layton is the *magister*. His work was in some way the culmination of Klein's. And after him Leonard Cohen was influential to many of us as a figure, as a charismatic individual on the scene, who wrote one or two extraordinary books of poetry, for instance *The Spice Box of Earth*, but then went off into other fields and became a very mediocre poet. Had he remained a poet he would have become the major poet of this country. But he didn't remain a poet. That's a fact. That's why Layton withdrew the mantle, which he'd conferred on Cohen, and gave it to me, as the next in the succession: Klein, Layton, then was supposed to be Cohen. I rejected it, because I don't see myself as a Jewish poet.[47]

Solway does acknowledge the importance of Greece in his life and work, a country that both Cohen and Layton found hospitable:

> The country has had an enormous impact on Canadian, especially Canadian Jewish writing. Cohen went to Greece in the fifties, and that's one of the ways I got there, through Leonard, or through his woman at the time, Marianne. She offered me her house on Hydra, because she was living in Leonard's house, if I would agree to tutor her son…. I went and I never recovered from that experience. The impact of the light, the sun, the Retsina, the Greek language, which changed my life.[48]

One does hear, however, a certain Laytonesque rancour (that familiar urge to outrage and foment a more heightened discussion of the country's literature) in an interview Solway gave in 2003:

> [Some] years ago I made a pact with myself to try to say what I see with as much candour and forthrightness as I could muster, and damn the consequences. You might say that the motto I adopted was: *fork out or fuck off,* which I applied equally to myself as to anyone else. The problem is that I don't have a tolerance organ in my psychical make-up for literary fast-food, for mediocrity, pretentiousness, sloppiness and self-aggrandizement.[49]

Clearly, these are the same goals that Layton set himself throughout his turbulent career, the outcome of which, according to Ken Sherman, "was to be turned into a clown by the media and eventually disregarded by the literati. His literary stock has already plummeted and no one can say if it will rise again."[50] Solway has managed to sidestep such dire outcomes in his pursuit of "candour and forthrightness."

Some of Layton's students, however, found his influence neither benign nor inspirational. Lazer Lederhendler, who enrolled in an M.A. poetry workshop at Concordia in 1989, encountered Layton near the end of his teaching career. Though Lederhendler approached his would-be mentor as "the author of some good poems," which he'd "read in undergraduate CanLit courses," his experience of being under Layton's tutelage was one of frustration and aimlessness. Lederhendler doesn't recall anything being said in the workshop relating to the existence of a "Montreal School," to the impact of the city on local writers, nor did the issue of Jewishness figure in workshop discussions. The dominant touchstones, he says, were the modernist canon and the murderous quality of twentieth-century life.[51]

The variety of Layton's friendships, his years spent teaching, the mountains of his correspondence with colleagues and enemies, and his often-reported generosity with younger poets created a long-standing, far-reaching and intimate network. Sherman recalls a time when he and Layton were neighbours in midtown Toronto, and the elder poet found the younger bereft of wine.

> The next day there was a knock at our door. By the time I opened it whoever knocked had vanished; I looked down to find a case

with twelve assorted bottles of wine (Italian, Spanish, French) and a note that read, "One of the saddest spectacles is a poet with no bottles of wine." It was signed Irving.[52]

In the same vein, the American poet Steven Osterlund, who lived for a time in Canada, published a pamphlet called *Fumigator: An Outsider's View of Irving Layton* (1975). A good part of it is devoted to describing Layton's willingness to instruct the younger poet in the ways of the artist, as well as to depicting Layton's tendency to drop a cheque in the mail when Osterlund was in tight circumstances.[53]

Cohen's career did not produce the same kind of intimate relationships with younger poets, nor do we have an archival portrait of such things as Layton's collected letters offer. Part of the reason for this is Cohen's movement away from regular publication and fully into a career as a songwriter and performer. This movement is confirmed as a conscious strategy in a 1969 piece on Cohen in *Saturday Night* magazine. Here Cohen explains that he has:

> ...always felt very different from other poets I've met....I've always felt that somehow they've made a decision against life. I don't want to put any poets down, but most of them have closed a lot of doors. I always felt more at home with musicians.[54]

The middle-sixties, the point at which Cohen threw himself most ambitiously into a musical career, also heralded a twenty-year period in which his published work appeared at roughly six year gaps: *Parasites of Heaven* in 1966, *The Energy of Slaves* in 1972, *Death of a Lady's Man* in 1978, followed by *Book of Mercy* in 1984, which could be considered the endpoint of an active public literary career. Although *Beautiful Losers* retains a critical readership, and the reissue of his selected poems in 1993 introduced his work to a younger audience, it is safe to say that Cohen's artistic longevity and increasing celebrity is based not on his literary accomplishments but on the impact of his music and persona on pop cultural taste and creative trends.[55] Proof of this can be found in two relatively recent books, which aim to take the measure of Cohen's full career. Ira Nadel's *Various Positions: A Life of Leonard Cohen* devotes its early chapters to a discussion of a writer's life, while the back half of the biography is largely a portrait of a songwriter and performer whose musical accomplishments have turned him into a cultural icon. Nadel does not downplay the early literary influences, and a reader interested only in Cohen's music must either put up with or thumb quickly through accounts of the influence of Layton, Dudek, and Scott, among others. There is, however, no detailed account in the later chapters of *Various Positions* regarding Cohen's sense of himself as a Montreal poet, nor is there a sustained discussion of his impact upon a younger generation of writers. The reader must decide whether this reflects a negligible impact or whether poetic influence in Montreal is simply too tame a subject in the shadow of questions associated with pop stardom, the recording industry and Zen. Nadel, in fact, suggests that the tendency of Cohen's music to overshadow his writing was entrenched by 1978, when *Death of a Lady's Man* was entirely ignored by reviewers in the United States, where "he had been identified as a singer and songwriter rather than a poet for too long."[56] In the collection *Intricate Preparations: Writing Leonard Cohen*, edited by West Coast poet and critic Stephen Scobie and based on a 1999 issue of *Essays on Canadian Writing* devoted to Cohen, one gets an even more aggressive sense of Cohen's role as a cultural phenomenon and musical icon above that of a poet. Scobie, who was among the first serious critics of Cohen's writing, informs us in his introduction that Cohen is:

> ... a poet who hasn't published a new collection for sixteen years, and a novelist who hasn't written a new novel for thirty-four years. Yet he remains a vital presence not only in Canadian literature but also on the international stage constituted by the virtual phenomenon of the Internet. Scarcely a day goes by on alt.music.Leonard-cohen without a plaintive inquiry, from somewhere in the world, about a new book, a new record, a new concert tour. Indeed, Cohen is acquiring a new generation of fans who have never seen him perform live (but who are nonetheless fanatical).[57]

It must be said, then, that the record of Cohen's influence on younger poets has been obscured by the tremendous success of his musical output and the celebrity associated with it. There is no difficulty in following Cohen's influence on generations of songwriters. This can be seen by a cursory look at the high calibre of contributors to the best album dedicated to celebrating

Cohen's songs. *I'm Your Fan*, released in 1991, presents artfully reworked cover versions of Cohen's songs by the likes of Lloyd Cole, Nick Cave and the Bad Seeds, John Cale, and the Pixies. In the case, for instance, of Nick Cave's raucous, over-the-top version of "Tower of Song," one can't help but recognize how aspects of Cohen's stance, his voice, his laconic humour and idiosyncratic way with a popular song have influenced the younger musician's output. (On Cave's recent recordings he often puts the best aspects of Cohen's style, musical arrangement, and even the thematic mix of gloom and religion to excellent use.)

It is more difficult to get a clear sense of Cohen's impact on younger poets. But if asked, some will give an accounting. Asa Boxer, a Montreal poet in his early thirties, and a recent winner of the CBC Literary Awards for his long poem "The Workshop," has an uncommon view of Cohen's influence. His father, Avi Boxer, was a part of Layton's poetic generation, though he was not prolific and died young. Not unlike Michael Harris, Asa Boxer speaks of Cohen as proof to the uninitiated that becoming a successful poet in Canada is not an impossibility: "He was very quiet and stuck to his own thing and got bad reviews in the *Montreal Star* for God knows how long."[58] Boxer is as emphatic as Harris about Cohen's unique impact (what he refers to as an almost spiritual influence) on Canadian culture:

> He has poems that I think have actually penetrated the conscious-
> ness. There is one very short one ("With Annie gone, whose eyes
> did compare with the morning sun, not that I did compare, but I
> do compare, now that she's gone.") I heard that around town....
> Cohen has several magnificent pieces. They're not just Canadian
> standards, they seem to be world class, international stuff.... He's
> written folk songs for us. We haven't had folk songs....And that's why
> I think Cohen, in the end, is going to be the survivor poet for us.[59]

On a more personal note, Boxer credits an afternoon chat with Cohen for helping him refine his notion of the workshop, as it relates to the creative act. His poem "The Workshop" took as its guiding image a farmhouse base- ment in the Laurentians belonging to a cousin. The hoard of things on hand was inspiring, Boxer says, but Cohen turned the poem in a new direction with the casual remark that the workshop should itself be viewed as "a work of art."[60]

Jason Camlot, another Montreal poet who has, like Boxer, lived away from the city and returned to establish a writing life, offers a different view of the impact of Cohen's work on writers who came of age in the last two decades. For Camlot, Cohen's work (and Klein's before it) framed familiar Jewish material, whether canonical stories or the Holocaust, in striking ways that were not otherwise heard as part of a Jewish Day School education in suburban enclaves. Camlot points, in particular, to Cohen's *Flowers for Hitler*, whose tone, in relation to the Holocaust, was aggressively ironic when such subject matter was "typically dealt with as sacred." [61] He argues that Cohen's "great impact on young poets is through his song writing." And he notes that one of Cohen's early accomplishments was the success with which he brought "to the identity of the poet the allure of the pop singer." Cohen's author photos and book cover copy presented the kind of attraction generally reserved for album notes and artwork. Camlot attributes Cohen's early genius on this front to his attraction to a great variety of poetic models, and to an aggressive willingness to transcend the limitations of the Montreal poetry scene as well as those associated with a Canadian national literature. [62]

Language: English, French and Jewish

A recent trend in certain literary circles has led critics toward a study of what they call "Jewish languages." By this, quite simply, they mean to highlight literary accomplishments by Jewish writers in Hebrew and Yiddish. In the case of the former, critics draw the reader's attention to developments in Israeli literature, while by focusing on Yiddish they examine a largely moribund eastern European literary tradition that existed for roughly a century and ceased in the mid-twentieth century. The most aggressive use of this frame of reference appears in Ruth Wisse's *The Modern Jewish Canon: A Journey Through Language and Culture*, where the one-time Yiddish lecturer at McGill makes use of the framework of "Jewish languages" to delimit her notion of what is in the modern Jewish canon and what is not. Wisse asserts that "modern Jewish literature tells the stories of the Jewish people in the twentieth century," and that a criticism associated with this literature must "establish criteria for Jewishness in the arts" by taking the measure of how contemporary identity is supported by an ongoing relationship between modern Hebrew and "the beginnings of modern Yiddish literature, although the resemblance has yet to be acknowledged or explored." More directly, Wisse writes:

[Neither] are there likely to be many great Jewish writers of the next century who are uninformed and uninspired by the spirit of Hebrew. Hebrew today is not only the language of Bible and liturgy, it is now also the language of the Jewish state where an increasing majority of the Jewish people resides. Hence, it is the crucible of the national fate. Individual genius may come wherever it comes and do whatever it does, but the Jew who has no access to the heart of the Jewish polity is ever less likely to generate a valuable literature of Jewish experience.[63]

These terms of reference put specific pressure on Jewish writers working in English, in particular figures like Cohen and Layton for whom neither Hebrew or Yiddish were important formative presences or linguistic frameworks. It should come as no surprise that Cohen and Layton do not receive a mention in Wisse's book, while Klein's novel *The Second Scroll* is examined for its portrait of a nascent Hebrew poetic tradition in Israel,[64] and is described, a little too heatedly, as an "exuberant response to the creation of Israel."[65] One finds in Wisse's approach an example of the dark territory a critic falls into when strictures are applied, however subtly, regarding whether a writer's output can be said to fall within or without a cultural tradition, based on a choice of language or particular stories. In such a case, a writer's oeuvre might be characterized in ways that have nothing to do with his or her stated identification and affiliation.

A related problem obscures our understanding of the role of Irving Layton and Leonard Cohen in the broader trends of English-language Quebec literature. From the earliest stages of their rise to prominence, both proved themselves too big and too singular to be subsumed into any imaginary local tradition. Critics, reviewers and anthologists have looked for ways to sequester their influence, in part by overstating the linkages between their work, and then by setting their contribution apart from the mainstream. This essay has highlighted critical moments at which their poetry has been set aside as *something else* (in the case of Farkas and Norris, the weird conglomeration "Jewish romantic lyricism,"[66] while Bowering looks, however lightheartedly, for the "Jewish mob".[67])These efforts clearly support the notion of firm lines of influence, and of a recognizable "Montreal School," the existence of which would allow the city's English-language poets to assert themselves as a prominent minority voice in Quebec. Cohen and

Layton have simply not proved useful in this ongoing project.

Both Layton and Cohen have remained remarkably distant from discussions related to the language issues and political infighting of post-1976 Quebec. Unlike Mordecai Richler, neither made such issues the focus of their work or public utterances. In a 1979 *Canadian Forum* article, Cohen is quoted in French, speaking unguardedly about the Quebec scene:

> Il y a un côté très messianique à la façon dont les gens gouvernent ici. On pense en fonction de sauver une race, d'ériger une nation. Je trouve cela un peu bizarre. Et puis nous autres, les Juifs, on a vu trop de drapeaux monter et descendre, et quand on sait qu'en fin de compte on se dirige tous vers la même chose, la tombe, on ne peut s'empêcher de trouver ces grandes théories et ces beaux idéaux un peu futiles.[68]

Layton, upon one of his numerous returns to the province, claimed that one of his goals was to reimmerse himself in the French Catholic milieu he had not taken seriously enough in the past.[69] In a quote that was picked up by the Canadian Press, and repeated in a Richler column in *Maclean's* magazine, Layton explains that if the "sad choice" of Quebec's separation comes, "I choose Quebec."[70] But such outbursts are too rare (might we even say too surreal?) to account for a deeper relationship between the Quebec political scene and Layton in late career. It is rare, too, for English-language critics to take account of the relationship between Cohen, Layton and local political and linguistic upheavals. One effort to do so appeared in a late-seventies issue of *Canadian Forum*, where A. D. Person wrote provocatively:

> But now Layton and Cohen have come back to Montreal, for their own good reasons I know. Their physical and spiritual repatriation is important for Quebec and Canada. Sun Life goes west, Layton comes back east. When independence comes will there be a line of poets waiting at the border to cross over into Quebec? I suspect there isn't time for the poets to teach us about the necessity for Canada of the independence of Quebec.[71]

Yet in the same article, whose *raison d'être* is in part a consideration of the anthology *Montreal: English Poetry of the Seventies*, Person neglects to mention the exclusion of Cohen and Layton by the anthology's editors. Farkas and Norris, sheepish themselves, make much in their introduction of these two writers' influence "upon the Montreal poets of the sixties," but they choose not to explain why such influence has become negligible to the point of irrelevance in the seventies.[72]

The absence of Layton and Cohen from an anthology like *Montreal: English Poetry of the Seventies* is on the one hand funny, for every reader will expect to see them, and on the other, bad business for the book publisher, since Layton and Cohen alone commanded a popular market; but more darkly, their absence bespeaks of an urgency by the editors to undertake a kind of utopian project (the engineering, let us say, of human souls) in which the contributions of Cohen and Layton to Montreal poetry are downgraded in favour of an effort to "make things new" or reorder the poetic playing field.

This essay might be seen as the beginning of a larger study toward an uncovering of the entanglement of Jewish, English and French Montreal in the best work of Leonard Cohen and Irving Layton. The imprint of both poets on the culture is a surprising blend of the personal, the local, and a range of traditional material broad enough to escape easy definition. Michael Harris celebrates Cohen's ability to strike an iconic pose on the Main, capable of inspiring poetry in others. Layton's iconic status has been debased, yet when talking with working poets, or surveying the history of Montreal literary life, his imprint is singular and inescapable. Both careers seem in danger of becoming obscured by myth, but one needs only to return to Belmont Avenue on a summer evening, or to St. Elisabeth Street under a hard snow, to recover a clearer view of the matters at hand.

A Walk in Montreal: Steps Through the Literary Politics of Contemporary English Quebec

DAVID McGIMPSEY

Mont Royal & Rivard

Depending on the weather, it's about a twenty-minute walk from where I live in Montreal's Mile-End district to the heart of the city's hip Plateau Mont-Royal. There, a couple of blocks away from the La Binerie (the classic Québécois restaurant memorialized in the novel and film *Le Matou*), on a brick wall overlooking a subway station park, is a public inscription of a poem called "Tango de Montreal":

Sept heures et demi du matin métro de Montréal
c'est plein d'immigrants
ça se lève de bonne heure
ce monde-là

le vieux coeur de la ville
battrait-il donc encore
grâce à eux

ce vieux coeur usé de la ville
avec ses spasmes
ses embolies
ses souffles au coeur
et tous ses défauts

et toutes les raisons du monde qu'il aurait
de s'arrêter
de renoncer[1]

Written in 1983 by Gérald Godin, the poem can still serve as a fair enough reminder to the people of Montreal. Whatever the political rumblings of the city, whatever its cultural shifts, the city continues; its citizens with more pressing demands than referendum debates or the public place of modern poetry, for that matter.

But the 1999 enshrinement of this particular poem was not just public works do-goodism—akin to initiatives that hang modern poetry on city busses so workaday travelers might read something besides ads that warn of a "new tuberculosis." This "public poem" and the re-naming the park space in honour of the poet is more specific to the ethno-linguistic chitter-chat of Montreal and the latest trends in separatist propaganda. Godin (1938-1994), after all, was Parti Québécois royalty: a political poet and journalist once detained under the War Measures Act, husband of beloved *chanteuse* Pauline Julien, member of René Lévesque's Cabinet where he once oversaw the enforcement of the province's controversial language laws. At the time of his appointment as top language cop, Godin's reputation as a warm and unprejudiced man was to give a new face to the Office de la langue française. He would be less the grim social engineer (that is, less like his *pur et dur* predecessor Camille Laurin), and more, as he put it, the cheerful "député des mots."[2] Similarly, when a Montreal city council chose "Tango de Montréal" as the representative Godin poem for this brand new space, it's easy to see how the poem's blessings could be used as civic redressment of Jacques Parizeau's infamous scapegoating of the 1995 referendum loss on "argent et la vote ethnique." Here was a poem, after all, by a separatist's separatist that offered "grace" to the ethnic vote—whether they liked it or not.

The placating gesture was certainly not ignored by the Union des écrivaines et des écrivains du Quebec (UNEQ) who wrote a letter to the city in protest over the chosen poem. UNEQ's president Denise Boucher complained that the poem was a weak example of Godin's art and, moreover, she felt the poem sent the wrong message: "il y a dans ce poème l'idée que ce sont eux autres qui se lèvent de bonne heure. Il n'y a pas juste des immigrants dans le métro, le matin."[3] Instead of choosing a poem so angled to "chercher le vote des immigrants," UNEQ's president suggested the city ought to have chose a more characteristic Godin piece. The union recommended "Portrait de mes amis,"—a wistful poem that makes metaphor of Lévesque's generation as smoldering embers, their great fires spent, but ever ready to spark the next conflagration of nationalist ardor.

So, rather than arguing against the sentimentalizing of immigrant labor, UNEQ declared a proprietary interest in the sentimentality itself. It was as if the Québécois must be the sole proletariat heroes of Montreal's literary landscape—and, so, an inspiring anger which remembers, as one partisan alleges, "l'époque où le francophone ordinaire devait se contenter d'une place comme coupeur de bois, porteur d'eau, ou personne invisible"[4] might still be maintained through Montreal's changing demography. Rather than questioning the interests behind this trope, "Tango de Montréal" self-consciously loans it to the city's immigrants. In effect, then, the connections Godin makes between unquestioning workers and the survival of the city aren't altogether different from ways in which a largely Francophone east end Montreal (which starts, in a way, with the Plateau) has been imagined and "valourized" by English Canadian writers. In Louis Dudek's poem "East of the City," for example, the lemon-sucking "haggard labourers" of the neighbourhood take refuge in "Maudlin" and "lager"[5] but, despite such faults, and like Godin's never-say-die immigrants, they are condescendingly applauded as "the wheel of society steel bright with the future."[6] In Al Purdy's homage to Maurice Richard, the Ahuntsic-born hockey player is exhalted in deference to poor "Montreal East kids with their ragged *Canadien* / sweaters ... out of work *pères* / and *mères* ... coughing their own smoke in Montreal East."[7]

Today, Montreal's east end is often met with the English-speaking Canadian's exotic reverence. Simultaneously percieved as a troubled, foreign place and as a place where one can lose touch with the dread conformities of the Americanized suburb—the *quartier* serves as poetic antidote to the repressive demands of the Wasp world. French *joie de vivre* is, after all, a traditional literary flourish used to expose the middlebrow hypocrisies of Anglo-American pursuits—and why go all the way to Paris? For the English Canadian artist then, working-class Montreal can be imaged as a Gallic frontier that questions his or her own ironic sense of middle class privilege and guilt. One can hear a sanctifying recognition of the ethnic and class sorrows of Montreal echo when middle-class Anglophones (of which I am one) celebrate Quebec as "Canada's smoking section" or extol the cholesterol levels of poutine as a virtue that an allegedly uptight Toronto couldn't possibly understand.

Though Godin could mock Quebec's "Louis Riels du dimanche" and the "molsonnutionnaires" of the taverns,[8] and talked of bringing to Quebec "une nationalisme beaucoup plus ouvert et beaucoup plus socieux de respecter les autres,"[9] he was very much a member of his party and his presence never made the Parti Québécois any more appealing to the province's "ethnic vote." As official *deputé des mots* it was in fact Godin's duty to make sure the avenue of Quebec's English-speakers (whetever their ethnicity) became more narrowly defined and looked after. "Tango," the public poem with the open hand, also subtly sees to the hope that the city's immigrants are no longer claimed by the Anglo-American mainstream—now that their honour has been so defended in the name of authentic Québécois culture. The enshrinement of the poem becomes a performance of Quebec's new-found "territorial nationalism," guiltily articulating hooray-for-us multi-ethnic Quebec all the while zealously asserting the immigrant's position beneath official state unilingualism. As Mario Dumont, leader of a "progressive youth party" would have it: "Every immigrant (to Quebec) signs a social contact with the State through which said immigrant promises to establish oneself, live and prosper in French."[10] Not exactly Emma Lazarus, but clear in its own terms.

From public poems to crossed-out English words on commercial signs to plaques dedicated to Charles DeGaulle, it's hard to walk (or drive) through Montreal without noticing the anxious political designs placed on the city space. How could one not notice, for example, the neo-colonialist implications behind a Parti Québécois announcement that they would build a new Francophone college in the city's largely Anglophone West Island and duly name it "CEGEP Gérald Godin"? How could an interested non-Francophone observer of the Quebec scene hear this funked-up Plateau toasted as a place "où se distillent une multitude d'influences culturelles et de modes de vie. L'individu y jouit d'une liberté de choix sans pareille"[11] without thinking about the state of linguistic liberty and choice in modern Quebec? It's nothing that could ruin a good long walk in the old city, but, as they often say about bad poetry, it's *interesting*.

134

St. Lawrence & Prince Arthur

It's about a twenty-minute walk from the Mont- Royal subway stop to the area around Prince Arthur and St. Lawrence streets (fifty if you stop by Schwartz's for a smoked meat sandwich)—the start of the Plateau, the heart of Montreal's legendary "Main." Traditionally, St. Lawrence street has been seen as a dividing line, "séparant caréement la ville en deux: les Anglais à l'ouest, les Francais à l'est."[12] While all geographic "two solitude" formulas painfully oversimplify Montreal's history, St. Lawrence Street is still noticeably more "English" than St. Denis Street which is just eight blocks to the east. Once the home of simpler ale houses, *St-Laurent* is now a meeting place for the desirable demographic; a bar scene for college-age drinkers, a romantic night spot for those who want balsamic vinegar at the table, our very own Queen Street.

Over the last twenty years, too, the locus of Montreal's English-language writing "scene" also has, I think, been increasingly centred on the Plateau and St. Lawrence street; metaphorically looking away from Montreal's traditionally English-speaking areas and towards the largely French-speaking east end. I recall how in the late 1980s, two new anthologies of English-language fiction from Quebec (*Souvenirs*, and *Montréal Mon Amour*) and an issue of *Canadian Fiction Magazine* all dramatically used traditional east end iconography (those streets, those wrought-iron stair cases) on their covers to promote this newness, while few (if any) of the writers in these collections were actually from the east end of the city. This embrace of Plateau Chic I would even go so far to say is now the defining characteristic of small press and coffee house literature from English-speaking Quebec. For many of the city's new English writers, this localizing also signals a slight shift from the cultural and political values associated with Montreal's downtown and west end. Where traditionally Anglophone areas could be imagined as the spiritual extension of the Toronto suburbs, the Plateau would be rhapso-dized as a "multicultural bohemia radiating out from every corner of Pine and St. Lawrence."[13] And for radiating so, the once low-rent area has become Montreal's hot cultural and low vacancy area—as one *Le Devoir* columnist put it: "Le Plateau est devenu le chic du chic, le boutte de toute."[14] Naturally, the Plateau's urban under-thirty hipness has also become a commodity worth pursuing for new writers understandably eager to assert difference in the Canadian literary marketplace.

As the English-Canadian intellectual has been prone to use the French-ness of Quebec as the spearhead in an otherwise-difficult-to-demonstrate claim that Canadians are different than Americans, the English Montreal intellectual may use the Frenchness of the Plateau as an argument against the West Island and against Toronto's centrality in Canadian literary culture. The completeness of Québécois culture, thought less contaminated by the likes of MTV, allows the English Canadian to imagine French Quebec as more authentic and more connected to the soul. Where the English Canadian is thought alienated—"never at / home in native space"[15] as Dennis Lee famously put it—French Quebec can "naturally" sing of itself. As *Globe and Mail* writer Ray Conlogue told *L'Actualité, (naturellement)*, "Aucun en tout cas qui chante Toronto comme Beau Dommage a chanté Montréal!"[16] In strategically locating Montreal as a fictioned escape from the hegemonies of Toronto U.S.A., this metaphorical Montréal (even for English writers) must be French—even Frencher than it actually is. The legendary Félix Leclerc understood this linguistic metaphor well, writing: "Toronto s'éloigne vers le sud dans une langue, Montréal grimpe vers le nord dans une autre."[17] So did poet Patrick Straram who saw parts of Montreal as "défiguré in english made in / U.S.A.,"[18] acknowledging a blemished purity that his love of the city must contend with.

Like Chicago and Detroit, Montreal and Toronto are natural civic rivals. Though the quality of literature can't be arrested in something as trivial as city affiliation, this civic rivalry is nevertheless spelled into important definitions of where the Canadian literary scene is today.[19] Toronto, the usual destination for the ex-pat Montrealer (*101 ou 401!* as one nationalist slogan elegantly puts it) and the cultural capital of English Canada, must be accounted for by Anglophones who continue to live and write in English in Montreal. Reactively, the English Montreal literary imagination often indulges in enumerating the Subaru-driving, "Kwee-beck"-saying sins of Hogtown. Admittedly, Toronto-bashing is second only to hockey among Canadian national pastimes and, considering The Barenaked Ladies and *Jonovision*, not entirely without reason. But in Montreal arts circles, the gesture can be more strategic: in casting aside the middle-class values of Upper Canada, the differences of Quebec can be co-opted as a sign of personal distance from the aesthetics of the English Canadian malls ("Hey, Brampton, look at me! I'm saying *dépanneur!*").

Not unlike the angry "Joe Canadian," who rants his desperate jingoism solely in contrast to America, more eloquent Anglo Montrealers also know what they're not and similarly embrace their regional marginality. In a good poem by Ruth Taylor, the province is briefly defined in terms of the Toronto-firster's arrogance: "The land of lys where Jean Baptiste / was born (as some believe) / is nothing but a crapaudière / thinks Joe Toronto."[20] Anything Toronto hates must be good. In distancing one's self from the prerogatives of Joe T.O., the English Montreal writer can claim a kind of exile from the bosom of Can Lit. As Montreal novelist Gail Scott told *Lettres Québécoises*, when asked if she thought of herself as a Canadian writer, "Je ne peux pas répondre que je suis une écrivaine canadienne. Je suis Anglo-Québécoise. Mais je me demande si je ne suis pas Montréalaise, tout simplement."[21]

I've heard Anglo writers who've come to Montreal from other parts of Canada romantically describe themselves as "double exiles." That is, exiled from Francophone culture in Quebec, exiled from the rest of Canada. This romance allows the Montrealer to ignore the obvious bonds of Anglo-American culture (nobody on this continent is truly exiled from the music of The Backstreet Boys, nobody is exiled from CNN), and to reify the experience of the Plateau as part of a more comprehensive anti-American identity. Using the same logic that lead Renault to market an American car called "le Car," the Frenchness of Quebec is used as a transformative device, something that makes the young lifestyle-consumer *better* and more *cultured*. Novelist David Homel translates the English Montreal artist's search for acceptance in Toronto almost as an episode from *Ma & Pa Kettle On the Town*: "Quand nous, les Anglo-Montréalais, arrivons à Toronto, il y a un malentendu culturel. Aucune identification n'est possible, il y a même une hostilité entre les deux villes. Pour tout dire, Toronto ne sait pas quoi faire de nous."[22] Thinking the Anglo-Montrealer as so misunderstood in Toronto is a confrontational fiction, a corollary to the Canadian hick who thinks a visit to Montreal must mean engagements with hostile, unilingual separatists. There is nothing to "do" with the Montrealer any more than there is something to "do" with the Winnipeger or the Haligonian in Toronto. If they can write in English, the market is all there. An actor can live and work in Sioux City, Iowa, but they ought not complain about how actors who live in California are just a drive away from the latest big film audition. Toronto-centrism exists, of course, and when it purports to represent the nation's interest it can be peculiarly noxious, however, it seems to me the condition that Montreal writers refer to as "double exile" is more properly known as "self pity".

A long time ago (1982?) I saw Margaret Atwood read at Concordia University and distinctly remember how one of my city's patriots stood up and asked Atwood why she always wrote about Toronto and never about Montreal. She dryly replied that she liked to write about places with "great pretension" so, maybe one day, she would "write about Montreal." Those in the audience who understood the dig, were naturally quite hissy about it. Even when dealing in truths, perceived slights to a fallen city's claims of pre-eminence rarely fail to arouse the ire of its citizens.[23]

Springfield, *c'est nous*.

Though Sherry Simon's bright and illuminating essay "Hybridité Culturelle" is more specifically about the Mile-End district, her thoughts on the Montreal "hybrid" sheds important light on how the Plateau dynamic is used to interpret Montreal's current cultural geography. In Simon's positive vision, Montreal is, above all, an exciting mix of cultures, where the backdrop of linguistic hostility actually makes the city more artistically exciting and, crucially, more "European." She writes: "à Montréal, la domination historique des anglophones, la nécessité de défendre le français face au pouvoir de l'anglais, ont créé de divisions profondes entre les deux groupes. Ce sont ces mêmes tensions qui animent des villes divisées comme Berlin, Jérusalem ou Trieste."[24] There is some truth in this, of course, but a truth that subtly exoticizes Montreal outside of its natural kinships. It's as if to be reminded that for many Montrealers, life in this city is actually way more like life in Pittsburgh or Cleveland or (gasp!) Toronto than it is to Berlin or Trieste is to give up a more glamorous theory that allows for a sense of European civic superiority. Who wants to write an essay about how any city is like Cleveland? What Montreal Anglophone would want to write anything literary about the West End's Cavendish Mall? Just as the Toronto literary scene is not exactly teeming with honest reflections on spring nights in Ajax, the literary imagination of Montreal also seeks exotic improvement. So, better "compare le cosmopolitisme montréalais au métissage culturel de l'Europe."[25]

Argumentations of Quebec's distinct status, despite good intentions, habitually enlist distrust of English speakers into the fold of a larger passion against the assimilative shadows of Anglo-American culture. Those who forget their real culture, Quebec poet Gaëtan Dostie writes, "s'abreuvent à la culture de l'occupant anglophone."[26] However couched in rationalized excuses of "c'est pas contre les Anglais ... / c't'une / question de respect /

Mes racines françaises,"[27] any philososphy of accepting Bill 101 must, at least, conceptualize Anglophone culture as invasive and unwelcome. Or, it's a free space, as long as the "necessity" to legislate against one scion of the hybrid culture (the bad one) is understood. This is not to deny the completeness, interestingness or specialness of Québécois culture, or to crawl back to the West Island burbs for cover: but to honestly recall that most Anglophones (and many Francophones too) do not feel deprived having grown up more with *Seinfeld* and Madonna than with *La Petite Vie* and *Vilain Pingouin* (who sing the lyrics about "respect" I just quoted). For Montreal Anglophones, to casually declare a primary cultural relationship with the continent around (to freely swim in the "English Sea" that allegedly imperils island Quebec) is almost to admit to a persistent nationalist critique of the city's English—namely, that the English won't "act like a minority" and, as one ideologue puts it, "Ils pouvaient continuer à y vivre comme si le Québec était une province anglophone et que le français n'existait pas."[28]

In Simon's celebration of the multicultural neighbourhood the attention is more cultural, with less attention paid to the role of gentrification and college education in making such a funky neighborhood. After all, the same multicultural "hybrid" areas Simon describes exist everywhere in North America (in Detroit's Hamtramck, in Brooklyn's Williamsburg, in Chicago's North Lakeside, in San Francisco's Mission District) but only the Montreal hybrid is refracted through the French language and the province's language laws. In the end, all these hip urban areas, these "latté towns" (as one cultural critic has dubbed them), are all about spending power. Other Montreal neighbourhoods are vibrantly multicultural and linguistically hybridized (Park Ex, Henri-Bourassa, Pointe St. Charles) but, unlike the Plateau or Mile-End, they are not neighbourhoods for college students and young professionals. The multicultural neighbourhood without the visibility and commerce of white yuppies is usually condemned as part of the "inner city." Manhattan's Lower East Side, once synonymous with impoverished immigrants, is now celebrated as perhaps *the* funky multicultural neighbourhood of the city, where rents are inaccessible to all but the most well off. Brooklyn's Flatbush, the area of Ebbett's Field, once the very symbol of the American multi-ethnic experience, is now often alluded to as a place you don't want to walk around late at night. In Montreal, the Plateau and the Mile End—once areas for working class Montrealers—are now giving way to higher rents, condo-mania, yuppie renewals, and, *grâce à eux*, educated yuppie respect for the multicultural.

If it weren't for the language issue there would be no difference between St. Lawrence and Queen streets. Montreal's polylingual credentials are certainly no more impressive than Toronto's or Vancouver's. Given the petty harrassment of immigrant shopkeepers by Quebec's language police, Montreal's reputation for tolerance is, in fact, worse. Furthermore, considering the effects separatist initiatives have had upon Montreal's English-speaking and ethnic communities, it's hard to consider literary rhetorics about polyethnic Montreal as a completely organic occurrence. What is being celebrated here? The mix of cultures, or *the right mix* of cultures? Does this "polylingualism" covertly celebrate the reviled program of Canadian *bi*lingualism or Canadian multiculturalism, without daring to speak its historical name? Or is it, even more daringly, a way of celebrating all other languages for their very un-Englishness? Welcoming the entire non-Anglo world into the cause against the language of Ronald McDonald? Cute as the lifestyle of the young may be, without serious questioning of how the Quebec government has styled and enforced immigration and language in Montreal, the idealized multi-ethnic paradigms of Plateau Mont-Royal and boulevard St-Laurent are as credible as the internationalism of Epcot Center.

Crescent & Saint Catherine

It may be a bit of a long walk along St. Catherine Street to get from the Main to Crescent Street downtown, but it's a walk most Montrealers have fared. In the 1950s, adored Québécois poet Gaston Miron once wrote about Montreal's big commercial drag as a kind of linguistic nightmare where "le Grande Saint Catherine Street galope et claque" garishly, in English, making the native Québécois feel "dépoétisé dans ma langue."[29] Among allegorizations of Anglophone power in Québécois culture, the Englishness of downtown is one of the most consistently provocative. Though St. Catherine Street is probably the most vigorously policed street by the Office de la langue française, with its American retail logos everywhere, its tourist-happy strip clubs, its longstanding locals full of native Anglophones, the English language is still vibrant in the street. So, "La Catherine" can always be counted on as an example of Montreal's failure to appear, as Camille Laurin wished, "as French as Toronto is English." In the year 2000, language watchdog Yves Hamel writes, incredibly, of this same westward walk in the entrenched terms

Miron counted on: "Dès le début de ma promenade ... on a commencé à toujours s'adresser moi en anglais d'abord. À aucun d'eux ne s'est-on d'abord adressé à moi en français. Il a toujours fallu que j'insiste, haussante le tone en disant 'pardon?', pour qu'on change pour le français ... le plus souvent avec un très difficile accent."[30] Furthermore, he illicits resonant terms of English bosses shaming French Canadian servants to describe an alleged encounter in a shoe store: "le gros idiot de service qui parlait français tradusait son boss anglophone et le faisant dans un charibia practiquement incompréhénsible. On comprend alors, ... que la plupart des francophones préfèrent se faire parler en anglais tellement ils doivent avoir honte!"[31]

Though the memento may say more about the baiting temper of the author, St. Catherine Street West actually does have the look and feel of Yonge or Robson streets and, by the time you get to Crescent, it may not be predominantly Anglophone, but there's a definite Montreal West accent. Crescent Street, like Rush Street in Chicago, is basically a tight enclave of bars and restaurants; moreover, Crescent (and the streets adjoining it) is generally thought to be a downtown "Anglo enclave." A few years ago there was some talk of renaming Crescent "Rue Nick" in commemoration of *Gazette* writer and former city councilman Nick auf der Maur, who had spent a good part of his career consulting with his constituents in the bars in the Crescent Street area. Rather than go that far, the city renamed an alleyway off Crescent (a "Ruelle" as opposed to an honest "Rue") in honour of this ardent lover of Montreal city life. For many, Auf der Maur's defense of the late night Montreal life, his championing the underdog, and his generous good cheer defined the kind of Montreal that made the city worth staying in. Where else could one live Nick's life? What would people say without the less-moralizing French terms *boulevardier* and *bon vivant*?

If literary Crescent street (as much as we could think of such a thing) starts with the spiritedness of Nick Auf der Maur it ends, in a way, with the achievement of Mordecai Richler. Richler, who often threw into his weekly *National Post* columns a mention of Ziggy's as a favorite watering hole and who started his non-fiction bestseller *Oh Canada! Oh Quebec! Requiem for a Divided Country* with a view to language cops outside Woody's, is arguably Montreal's best and certainly Montreal's most successful author. Though Richler became famous for writing about characters who grew up in immigrant communities in the now "hip" Mile-End he later became something of a reluctant oracle for Montreal's English-speaking community, largely following the controversy surrounding *Oh Canada! Oh Quebec!* And if Robert Majzels' *City of Forgetting* is Montreal's more Plateau-ready polylingual modernist classic, *Oh Canada! Oh Quebec!* is the city's cursed potboiler. A book actually read and debated about by people who did not go to college, a book frequently debated by those who've never read it. Others may artistically explore the "space between the languages" of Montreal but *Oh Canada! Oh Quebec!* actually found that space. The weaving style of this non-fiction essay is perhaps most befitting today's Montreal: turning from hilarious anecdote to what Richler calls "injustice collecting" at unpredictable turns—leaving the discussion of a shared history to the talk of a real community of peoples, not formalized abstractions which count on accepting marginality for the greater good.

The old news is that Richler, especially for ridiculing Quebec nationalism in the American press, has become a veritable synecdoche in French Quebec for the Bad Anglo.[32] And, though it would be pointless to recount the details and subsequent misinformations of the Richler controversy, perhaps the most potent confirmation of the timbre of *Oh Canada! Oh Quebec!* actually was the intensity of the reaction of separatist intellectuals to its publication. Richler's "Vu du Woody's Pub," wrote then *Le Devoir* editor Lise Bissonnette, was nothing less than open season on her people: "le Québec a rarement à souffrir de ce genre de diffamation collective."[33] Bloc Québécois leader Gilles Duceppe (then a backbencher) rose in the House of Commons to call on members of the English and Jewish communities to "denounce Richler's action" lest they be considered "his accomplices."[34] So whatever the vision of Quebec's born-again "territorial nationalism," the vision the enshrinement of "Tango de Montreal" looks to, when the *pays* has been slighted it's usually clear on what side of the collectivity you stand.

In fact, in one of Gérald Godin's last poems, "Les Mots," he warns his people to stand guard against a certain "carcajou à plumes" (which I'm dying to translate as the "the wingèd wolverine"). Enlisting some Native lore, Godin suggests his literary animal may be "le diable en personne" and, moreover, a surviving agent of "Lord Durham,"[35] out to mock and overrun the Québécois. This dangerous beast, Godin says, "invente une forme de mépris fondé sur la race et qu'il faut bien appeler l'antipeasoupisme, qui n'est pas plus tolérable que l'antisémitisme."[36] And, however dubious the comparative allegation, it's pretty clear just who and what Godin is talking about, so, he coyly ends the poem announcing that the most well-known example of the "carcajou à plumes" is, of course, "Mordecai Richler, écrivain estrien."[37]

It is indeed ironic to see the transformation of Richler from a novelist of St. Urbain Street to alleged Anglo establishment "antipeasoupiste", from the author of stories about sons from immigrant communities in Montreal to being cast by nouveau Plateau celebrants as "l'oppresseur ... le colonisateur,"[38] or as Godin's "écrivain estrien" comment suggests, not as a Montrealer but as English Loyalist Townships gentry. For the English literary community in today's Quebec, all this old news resonates: not because "we" all agree with the aim of Richler's satire (though I assume most Anglos do) but because Montreal Anglophones now live in Richler's world. When somebody here asks you what you think of Richler, it's generally not about the plot resolution in his Giller-prize winning book *Barney's Version*. And because the popular Québécois reaction to Richler was so intensely strong, it's not surprising that while many offer personal huzzahs, few will pop their heads up on Richler's side of the issue. The force of the reaction to Richler's fulminations sort of lets one know what awaits those who dare to criticize Québécois foundationalism. Because of its political implications, it was bracing, for example, to see how in two separate articles in the French press extolling the virtues of new English writing from Quebec, Richler's name was used as a totem, as something a new and improved "anglo-Québécoise" must transcend:

from *Lettres Québécoises:*

> Le discours de Richler ne tient plus pour la nouvelle génération", precis du reste Ellen Servinis, chroniqueure au *Montreal Review of Books* (MRB) ...
>
> Mordecai Richler c'est un extrême. Son antithèse pourrait par exemple s'appeler Gail Scott, qui vit autant en français qu'en anglais est très liée aux féministes québécoises. Ou Neil Bisoondath, pour qui "l'idee que les anglophones sont opprimés par la loi 101 constitue une aberration.[39]

from *Le Devoir:*

> Quand il est question de la littérature de langue anglaise au Québec, est-ce l'image de Mordecai Richler qui surgit en premier devant

vos yeux? Si c'est le cas, sérieux travail de rééducation vous attend. Plusieurs générations d'écrivains de langue anglaise ont eu le temps de s'ajouter à celle de Mordecai et de prendre des positions idéologique et esthétiques à milles lieues de celles de notre polémiste national.[40]

The new generation is allegedly "beyond" Richler, but somehow, someway, Richler's the first item on the menu. The English writer in contemporary Montreal can either follow in Richler's footsteps (at Crescent?) or be noted for how he or she is "miles away" from his "extreme" views (in the Plateau?). The allure of Richler as the one who must be answered is strong: a recent historical novel by Victor Teboul generously titled *Que Dieu vous garde de l'homme silencieux quand il se met soudain à parler*, about the struggle of a French-speaking Sephardic Jew to find his place in Montreal despite consistent misunderstandings from the city's English-speaking Ashkenazim, is ribboned with a red promotional banner proudly declaring the book as the "antithèse de Mordecai Richler."

In an episode of the unbelievably popular Québécois sitcom *Un Gars, Une Fille,* there's a skit where the protagonists of the show (Guy and Sylvie, an average middle-class Québécois couple) go out to dinner with their Anglophone counterparts. Sylvie is anxious to meet the Anglo woman, because Guy works with her and has admittted that she looks good, "pour une anglaise." Though the Anglo woman is bilingual and nice, her husband turns out to be more stereotypical matter, entering the scene complaining in loud English about a French cab driver who doesn't know the difference between Sherbrooke East and Sherbrooke West. When not embarrassing the savvy *gars* et *fille* by ordering ketchup with his meal and with his crass unilingualism, or by not brooking their despairing of Toronto as a "second-rate American city" with good grace, the Anglo also turns out to be obnoxiously eager to pin Guy on some "Canada is the best country in the world" cant. In the end, the men argue: the Anglophone dares Guy to name some English Canadian writers where Guy gamely comes up with Margaret Atwood and Robertson Davies. Emboldened, Guy holds out a twenty dollar bill and bets the Anglo that he could not name one single Québécois writer, to which the Anglophone calmly says "Mordecai Richler" and grabs the twenty. It's a rim shot scene, Guy foiled on a "technicality" that he is too politically correct to protest, yet still *pur laine* enough to feel burned by.

Inside Ziggy's (or at a cozy St. Denis Street counterpart) one's tempted to say that, in the end, it's all good. Everybody here seems nauseated with the national debate and, as Richler himself was quick to say, "this isn't Belfast." It's tempting to say that there are other paradigms which unite us all (loving the Habs, despairing construction on the Ville-Marie expressway) and, after all, no matter where you go everybody agrees: modern poetry stinks. But, whatever the promotional hoo-hah of the day, despite the presence of so many terrific authors, Montreal is not a particularly vibrant place for English-language writing today. Big deal. Some of this is trenched in the obvious: the English-language market here is about the size of the market of Saskatoon, and it's not getting bigger. What do you expect? But some of it is obviously political; the possibility of enjoying a wider audience in Montreal is often stalled by government designs, and by rhetorical strategies which hope to deny the diversity and continental potential of English writers from Quebec.

In a 1999 editorial, Yves Beauchemin, celebrated author of *Le Matou*, wrote:

Mais parler une langue, c'est aussi un geste politique. Parler anglais à New York, n'est-ce pas, d'une certaine façon, afficher son appartenance au bloc culturel américain? Parler kurde en Irak, catalan en Espagne, acadien au Nouveau-Brunswick, c'est affirmer un choix, exprimer une opinion, parfois prendes des risques.[41]

He is speaking of the linguistic politicization of the Québécois, of course, but to follow Beauchemin's logic then, to continue to speak and write in English in Quebec is also to affirm a choice, express an opinion and to take a risk. Sometimes it doesn't feel worth taking that risk. Given the threats associated with Englishness, arguing against the myths of Quebec is not a route to popularity here—or anywhere else, for that matter. In this way, all English-speaking Quebecers share the last breaths of the subject of Steven Heighton's poem "English Cemetery, Gaspésie":

a mute wind
hammering the walls.[42]

III. Sites and Scenes

The Vehicule Poets[1]

The Vehicule Poets and Second Generation Postmodernism

KEN NORRIS

The Vehicule Poets of Montreal were part of a second generation of postmodernists to emerge in Canada by the mid-1970s. In other parts of the country there were poets of a similar situation and orientation: Paul Dutton, Rafael Barreto-Rivera, Steve McCaffery, Bruce Whiteman, Chris Dewdney and Judith Fitzgerald in Ontario; Monty Reid, Erin Mouré, and Dennis Cooley on the Prairies; Sharon Thesen, Barry McKinnon and John Pass in British Columbia. Unlike the poets of the '60s—the first generation of Canadian postmodernists—these poets were very slow in becoming aware of one another's existence. This was a result of several different situational factors.

During the 1960s, Canadian nationalism was running very high, and the desire for a national literature to celebrate in time for Canada's centennial was palpable. By the 1970s, that high spirit of nationalism had given way to a burgeoning regionalism; in many ways, all of the second-generation postmodernist poets became regional writers to some varying degree. Although there were some strong regional elements in the work of first generation postmodernist poets like Cohen, Atwood, Newlove and Bowering, there was also a very strong nationalist tendency in their work. One thinks of poems like Cohen's "The Only Canadian Tourist In Havana Turns His Thoughts Homeward," Atwood's "The Animals In That Country" and "At The Tourist Centre In Boston," Newlove's "Samuel Hearne In Wintertime," and Bowering's ubiquitous "Grandfather."

All of these poems, in their own ways, are statements of nationalism. For the second generation postmodernists, "locale" proved to be more interesting, and less problematic, than "nation."

These poets' status as second-generation postmodernists also created certain terms of isolation. At a time when any number of Canadian poets were primarily interested in "putting the subject back into poetry" (a phrase taken from Stephen Spender's *The Thirties And After*), these poets were primarily interested in extending an avant-garde tradition that had begun with the early Modernists. All of these poets were the spiritual grandchildren of Pound and H. D. and Tzara, and the younger brothers and sisters of Atwood, Nichol and bissett.

Being in the second generation of anything always creates certain complications. If the first generation were the pioneers or the innovators, then what defines the second generation? Viewed unkindly, they are imitators; viewed with generosity and a sense of history, they can be seen as inheritors and extenders, the ones who further advance the possibilities of a new aesthetic. In popular music we have the example of The Beatles, who were second-generation rock and rollers. Elvis, Little Richard, Jerry Lee Lewis, Chuck Berry, and Carl Perkins were the breakthrough artists who invented a new kind of music. The Beatles advanced, amplified, extended, and improved that style of music. But early detractors could always view them as foreign guys with bad haircuts who were wildly derivative of their predecessors.

Now that we have seen at least three generations of postmodern Canadian poetry, I think it becomes much easier to understand what constitutes a particularly radical literary tradition. What all of these postmodern poets have shared is an appreciation of cutting edge Modernist art, and an understanding of their status and responsibility as postmodernist writers. They understand their place in literary history; that is, that they come "after Modernism." At the same time, coming "after Modernism" also creates the circumstances whereby their writing is different from Modernist writing. Although postmodern writing extends the advances of Modernist writing, it derives from a different set of social and aesthetic conditions. It is post-Modern, post-war, post-holocaust, post-atomic and, for more than a decade now, post-cold war. While embracing the Modern, these writers understand the necessity of being expressive of a post-Modern reality.

This was certainly true of the Vehicule Poets of Montreal, who were all interested in the radical advances of Modernist art and who were all committed to furthering those advances. In contrast to the earlier Tish poets (who, at least initially, all shared a common teacher, Robert Duncan, and a common textbook, Donald Allen's *The New American Poetry*), the Vehicule Poets were by no means monolithic in their early influences. This has led some to debate whether these poets actually had anything in common (with this debate sometimes taking placing among the Vehicule Poets themselves). It has certainly been argued more than once that they shared a moment more than they shared an aesthetic.

Looking at their influences, one can certainly see them as various. For example, Norris's great modernist poetic influence was William Carlos Williams, whereas Konyves's was Tristan Tzara. Similarly, they were all astute readers of postmodern American poetry, from which they chose to be influenced by different poets (Snyder and Corso for Farkas; Spicer and O'Hara for Gold; Ginsberg for Konyves; Waldman for Lapp; Whalen for McAuley; Eshleman for Morrissey; and Creeley for Norris). When turning to their immediate predecessors in Canada, we can again see them choosing to be influenced by different poets (Farkas by McFadden; Gold by Bowering and Lee; Konyves by Cohen; Lapp by Kiyooka; McAuley by Nichol; Morrissey by Dudek; and Norris by Cohen). Nevertheless, despite this diversity of specific influences, what the Vehicule Poets shared was a similar orientation: towards experimentalism and radical aesthetic innovation. This at a time when there was something of a conservative cultural swingback starting to take place in Canada (and mostly certainly in Montreal).

What is perhaps difficult to understand in the early years of the twenty-first century is that, by the mid-1970s, the social revolutions of the 1960s and the advances of postmodernism in art were in the process of being rejected. By many, both were proclaimed as failed revolutions, and a return to former social and artistic orders was being advocated. In the social sphere, various fundamentalisms began to emerge by the late 1970s. In art and poetry too, for a time, a new conservatism began to emerge.

Twenty-something years later this may be difficult to perceive, exactly *because* the social and artistic revolutions were ultimately won. The fact that we have now seen a third generation of postmodernist Canadian poets means that the postmodern tendency in art in Canada was not successfully nullified. Similarly, in society, we have moved on to a greater social and ethnic diversity, rather than back to traditional sexist, racist and homophobic formulations of society that were certainly being called for by various odd camps and their spokespersons in the late '70s and early '80s in both Canada and the United States.

What also needs to be understood is that by the mid-'70s, Canadian nationalism, in the form that it had taken, had become something of an unacceptable straitjacket. What had started out as a national pride in the '60s was, in some quarters, rapidly degenerating into cultural xenophobia. Poets like the Vehicle group found themselves being derided for having literary influences that were not "Canadian" (this had been true, as well, of the earlier *Tish* poets). Seen from our current globalized perspective, that form of criticism seems ludicrous. Nevertheless, at the time, it was offered in all seriousness. Similarly, within a regional context, the Vehicle Poets were criticized for being interested in poets who were not from Montreal, thus, somehow, betraying "the Montreal tradition."

At the time, these criticisms made no more sense to any of the Vehicle Poets than they do to a contemporary reader. Simply put, the people offering these criticisms were on the wrong side of history. They didn't understand art, and they didn't understand society. Wherever they were trying to drag art and society back to, art and society had no interest in going.

Here again we encounter a specific characteristic of a second generation of an artistic movement: to stick to the principles of the movement or aesthetic, knowing them to be right. The initial dismissal that any innovation in the arts faces manifests again later as a call for "a return to sanity," which then needs to be resisted and opposed by the second generation. By the time of the third generation the revolution has usually been won, and the victory is apparent. It is now an incontrovertible fact in Canada, as well as in most of the Western world, that an artistic period of modernism was followed by an artistic period of postmodernism. In the mid-1970s there were many arguing that this simply would not prove to be the case (interestingly, I just recently saw conservative columnist George Will declare on an American Sunday morning political show that September 11th had, rightfully and finally, brought an end "to what you could call postmodernism").

With hindsight, one can now look back and see that there was an entire generation of second-generation postmodernist poets spread out across Canada who constituted a formidable front. At the time, these writers had a very limited awareness of one another (it needs to be remembered that this was all taking place in a time before the proliferation of contemporary micro-technology). Perhaps the Vehicle Poets and The Four Horsemen[2] were most fortunate in having organized themselves into some forms of a collective. Otherwise, the maintaining of postmodernist principles in what was proving to be a rather anti-postmodernist time could get to be a lonely business. Certainly the Vehicle Poets initially banded together out of a sense of shared orientation, but also out of a need for mutual support. They all felt that there was an aesthetic war still to be won, and intuitively knew that there was strength in collective action.

"Vehicule"? Phooie!

ARTIE GOLD

I from the start resented this Vehicle Poets (Press, Gallery etc) seeing it as an affectation since every last soul among our group was 100% English (as opposed to 1 or more % French)…

I confess to a convergence sometime during those early 1970s for there we suddenly were, a bunch of us poets, in the same space at the same time—but who's to say there was just the one spider in Robert The Bruce's prison cell? Which is to say we were a "Petrified Forest", a "Bus-Stop" aggregate—a defaultive assembly—more the dregs who'd no recourse to the facilities of McGill & Sir George Williams (now Concordia) than a "first pressing."

I've said that all 25 years ago when asked by *Books in Canada* for several hundred words on the (then) current Montreal Poetry scene. I've since referred to it as my "disclaimer" vis-à-vis there being a Vehicle school—hell, had there been 40 spiders in with Bruce, they eventually might have turned out another Hamlet (—or would, after *Archie & Mehitabel, Cock-roaches* be more apt?) but that would make them neither *neo-Elizabethan playwrights* or '*throwbacks*'….And Hell again! Though we dregs were banned from Académe, our own efforts to be more expansive (often alas exhaustive!) did not preclude *our* inviting those very poets who sought to exclude us to come and read among us. We were not gastronomy but possessors of the common Montreal English language Soup Kettle and our efforts had too many ingredients in them for any succinct name. "Vehicule"? Phooie! This was "soup-bone" school at its basest.

***

(someone is still pulling my string):

"More words, Mr Gold! _ _"*You were there!*" O.K. O.K., "there" _ _
spirit of the place. Then (there) _ there *was a* certain spirit of place. . .

In the land of backbiters/the guile-less man, otherwise gregarious,
becomes egregious_ _ egad, whatta load of rhetoric!

Vehicule Poets scenario #? ? ?!

Solway falls on Harris who falls on Van Toorn who turns to krishna
(who dogs Solway?). Geddes. . .needs no man. Dudek, Layton, Gnarowski,
Siebrasse /are locked in a scrum. Richmond takes tickets for the *Montreal
Star* Literary page (7 1/5th of Canadian club=i dance).

Sweet Leonard Cohen has not the stomach for this Byzantine
excrescence _ _ nor in any case the *need*.

These left, some straggling, some struggling, to carry the ball down
through to the Muse's 5 yard line. . And they are. . .well, before you know it,
The *Vehicule* Poets; if not compatible with the label—at least comfortable
with each other's company.

The Early Years

STEPHEN MORRISSEY

The four years, 1969 to 1973, when I attended Sir George Williams (now
Concordia University) as an undergraduate were wonderful years for
me. It was a creative and expansive time, for me personally and for poetry
in Montreal. Two professors in the English Department organized a poetry
reading series and I tried to attend every reading they put on during my
undergraduate years. I heard American poets Robert Creeley, Jackson Mac
Low, Lawrence Ferlinghetti, Allen Ginsberg, Diane Wakoski, and many
others. Canadian poets who read their work included Alden Nowlan, David
McFadden, Patrick Anderson, Michael Ondaatje, Roy Kiyooka, George
Bowering, and Gerry Gilbert. Over at McGill University I heard W. H. Auden
read to a packed auditorium and met F. R. Scott at the McGill Faculty Club
after another reading.

While at Sir George Williams a high school friend asked me for some
poems for a chapbook. Another friend typed the poems on an IBM Selectric
typewriter and had the chapbook printed. Poems of mine had been
published in my high school's literary magazine and school yearbook. My

first chapbook, entitled *Poems of a Period*, was published in 1971. Around that time I also remember meeting Endre Farkas for the first time. I was impressed that he was already editing a magazine. Since then, Endre has become an integral and important part of the poetry community in Montreal.

I met Guy Birchard, a poet from Ottawa who later became a friend, at one of the readings at Sir George Williams. Guy introduced me to the poet Artie Gold. Artie was intelligent, intense, humourous, and dedicated to poetry. Artie's favourite poets were Jack Spicer and Frank O'Hara. Artie also led me to American poets that were new to me—James Schuyler, Bill Knott, and Larry Eigner come to mind—as well as to the music of Charles Ives, a composer whom he mentions in one of his poems. I particularly remember visiting Artie Gold at his flat on Lorne Crescent during the spring and late summer of 1974, the year I also spent six weeks in Europe. As soon as I met Artie, I felt he was an original poet and someone I wanted to know.

I also took Richard Sommer's creative writing class at Sir George Williams around 1972 and it was there I became good friends with Keitha MacIntosh. Later she published a little magazine, *Montreal Poems*. In 1973 I began my own magazine of experimental and concrete poetry, *what is*. Richard Sommer helped by giving me an extensive mailing list of poets, many of them in Vancouver, who might be interested in receiving *what is*. Those were the years that I was most interested in experimental poetry. My writing was influenced by William Burroughs's "cut-up technique" and John Cage's writings on Eastern philosophy and randomness as a way of making art. The readings I gave during those years reflected these interests.

By 1977 the concerns in my writing changed. I lost interest in both concrete and sound poetry. I felt that a good graphic artist could produce better visual poems than I was capable of creating. I remember Artie Gold commenting that there were so many concrete poems you could fill a room with them.

Convergences and the Collective /
Confessions of a Collaborator

ENDRE FARKAS

Let it be known at the outset, The Vehicule Poets were never a school, a movement or an aesthetic. At least not for me. The Vehicule Poets were a figment of other poets' imaginations. They made us up. We were a group of young writers who were beginning to hang around Véhicule Art Gallery. The Vehicule years were years of hanging out and learning the craft and learning that learning was not really done in schools but in moments shared. They were the times of getting into the same Véhicule for a ride to different destinations.

What did we do? It's been pretty well documented in *Vehicule Days* by Ken Norris.[3] Before we came on the scene there wasn't much. Occasional readings at Concordia, a book now and then, maybe. We made things happen on a regular basis. Readings every Sunday at Véhicule at two o'clock. In the winter you kept your coat and gloves on because the heat was off. Out of this came Véhicule Press. Once Ken and Artie & I became editors of Véhicule Press, books started to appear on a regular basis. We hung out together in different permutations and combinations at the gallery, at the El Dorado, at each other's places, though I don't remember ever going to Steve's. As a result of hanging out, we came up with plans for magazines, readings, books and events. It's good to be young and fearless and arrogant, to have a sense of humour and have people you can share with. I also hung out with dancers and painters and composers and performance artists (new concept then). So did Tom and Steve and John. This resulted in cross-pollination. Tom and I were the most involved in the collaborative process (maybe had something to do with the Hungarian socialist genes). I loved working with Contact Improvisational dancers. It was so physical and I got to (through them) make the text move! During this time, Tom made anti-art video-poems, Steve collaborated with Pat Walsh (visual artist) to make concrete (literally) haikus. John collaged and was cast (literally) into sculpture. Artie looked on bemused.

We got named the Vehicule Mafia. We became a force because we did things and because others made us powerful! I was having a gas. We started getting attention outside of Montreal. All this activity also made for more activity and not just by us. Others in reaction against us started magazines and publishing houses.

In the late seventies Véhicule Art Gallery split from the Press or vice versa (I don't remember which). The Gallery moved up the street to a bigger, more lavish space (which lasted only for another two or three years before going under). The Press also wandered about town. The Chinatown location was my favourite because it was in Chinatown—enough said.

***

In looking back, I realize that my performance collaborations were rarely with the Vehicule poets. Ken, the page-based poet, was the only one who participated in a couple of sound pieces. He can be heard on "*Er/words/ah*" *er*-ing, *ah*-ing, breathing hard and screaming on the LP "*Sounds Like*".

On the literary collaborative side, I was publishing. The Muses' mission was to publish new voices, like exiled Chilean poet Elias Letelier, Somalian poet Mohamud Siad Togane, queer/punk poet Ian Stephens and Ruth Taylor, who can not be labeled. The Muses was also now the publishing home for Ken Norris, Artie Gold, Tom Konyves and Cel (Claudia Lapp).

By the late Eighties, the formerly known "Vehicule Poets" were drifting off, physically and/or creatively, into their own solo spaces. In my solitary work, I was returning to the page using a "straight poetry" approach to deal with the mysteries of being human, of creating new life, and dealing with demons of forced exile. It was those Vehicule days that gave me, and continue to give me now, the freedom to explore the ways and means to push the limits of poetry, and that allowed me to share in the spirit of the times with others who were responsible for regenerating a decaying poetry scene globally and in Montreal locally. We opened the doors & windows to let in fresh air. I am glad to have been a part of it.

What Now?

CLAUDIA LAPP

In the end, maybe what it all came down to, this lucky convergence of seven young writers in Montreal in the early Seventies, was a "karmic" connection. Our affinities (and dissonances) created the Velcro which held us together for a brief while. We worked, clowned, taught, performed, collaborated on an LP (SOUNDS LIKE) and published more than a few books. We were friends of the same generation but were NOT united in a common Poetics at all, as Artie made clear in his Introduction to THE VEHICULE POETS.[4]

We anticipated the popular bumper sticker—HONOUR DIVERSITY. We witnessed each other in our individual expressive styles. We helped each other out, one interviewing, editing or reviewing another. We created a press and then others, as well as 'zines to launch ourselves into the world. We assembled around an open Space to give out what we had inside of us. We invited master poets to mentor and inspire. We were able to create a literary scene that was contemporary and relevant, a happening place in the community. This was our gift. We wrote love notes to each other, appeared in each others' dreams and now, we continue on separate creative paths, recalling the fortuitous, or maybe karmic ripening that made our paths cross with love and friendship and poetry.

I think the world of poetry is more visible and accessible to North Americans today than even twenty years ago, via poetry websites. (You can educate yourself this way. All I had to do was Google to find out about David McFadden's current books, read interviews and poems.) Photocopiers and colour Xerox have replaced malodorous mimeographs. PC printers have made it easier to send out neat copies from the home desk, or even publish right from home. Another "new" development is the Slam phenomenon, said to have originated in 1986 in a Chicago jazz club, and which has been gaining popularity since the early 1990s. Slam has its detractors, who point to it as a showcase for bad poetry. Yet Slam often brings relevancy and vigour to the scene, and really pulls in the young. Here in Eugene, Oregon, population 135,000, where I now live, there are monthly slams at Fool's Cap Books. A recent one drew about 150 people, most of whom appeared to be in their mid-twenties. Some of these kids are GOOD—their delivery makes the performance pieces we did at Vehicule seem tame and from a different world!

When I consider the entity we call "The Vehicle Poets", I find that, despite a desire for solidity, in fact, this construct no longer exists. The impermanence of VEHICULE is not changed by the fact that none of its erstwhile members have, as yet, left this incarnation. I am truly grateful to be able to reconnect with my former poetic companions, to rekindle friendship and stir the cauldron of memory. But I have no illusions as to the enduring importance of our small "team". This is not to deny that we made a contribution to the Montreal and even Canadian literary scene, or that all we did had great value for us as individual young writers. Yet I have no interest in making the Vehicle Poets into any kind of hype.

What feels important to me, now, twenty-five years later, is to ask:
WHAT ARE WE DOING *NOW* AS POETS THAT'S INTERESTING/ RELEVANT/ FRESH? WHAT CAN WE DO *NOW* WITH OUR LOVE OF LANGUAGE AND THE ARTICULATION OF LIFE EXPERIENCE? WHAT WILL HAPPEN WHEN WE MEET AGAIN, NO LONGER YOUNG, TO CREATE, SHARE, AND PERFORM? HOW CAN OUR DIVERSITY INTER-ACT TO CREATE SOMETHING OF INTEREST OR ASTONISHMENT FOR AUDIENCES WHICH MAY NOT KNOW US AT ALL? I DON'T WANT TO BE SENTIMENTAL ABOUT WHO WE WERE, BUT RATHER, ENGAGED IN WHAT WE HAVE BECOME AND HOW WE CAN POUR THAT OUT TO AN AUDIENCE.

For we have that in common—the love of giving out the words we discover, invent, recover.

The Effect on the Audience Was Not Meant to be Satisfying / The Avant-Garde Did Not Yet Exist

TOM KONYVES

We became friends, and our circle quickly grew to include the seven poets who eventually got tagged The Vehicle Poets—by Wynne Francis, an English professor at Concordia.[5] At first, the group's get-togethers were spent in talking about poetry and socializing. As we exulted in our camaraderie, I began to believe that the poems we wanted to read and hear, the poems we were all yearning for, had never been written; that all the master poets put together could not create the poems we needed, the poems we so yearned for—so *we* had to write them.

We agreed on some basic principles: that poetry should reflect the new (contemporary) in content and form; that experimentation should be encouraged; that conservatism and traditionalism should be dismissed and openly opposed; and that poetry should reach its audience in a more immediate way.

We watched our poems appear in public almost immediately after we wrote them – our first poetry magazine was the mimeographed *Mouse Eggs*. Poetry was alive, and Montreal was the right place to be a poet. I was feeling the freedom poetry is after. Experimenting with form could never have become so attractive in isolation; I was having serious fun! There were so many ways to express a poem that I began running, running until I ran off the page into visual performance, eventually video. And I kept asking, what has not yet been done?

The group was for the opposite of isolation; therefore it was inevitable that we would write collaborative poetry. As a matter of fact, the first night we really came together was when we followed a few beers with a blank sheet of paper which we passed around for a couple of lines.

What made the Vehicle Poets unique was this collaboration. Our *Collaborations* created *Partnerships*, at times a rare *Union*; there was a sense of *Solidarity*, we exulted in the *Camaraderie*, at the gallery meetings we displayed *Comradeship*, in our private lives we were *Close*, we were *Friends*.

***

The avant-garde did not yet exist. In the late sixties, the milieu was shared by two universities and a couple of bookstores: SGWU (Concordia) was spending on poetry readings by "name" poets while neighbouring McGill was fast becoming a steady publisher of young poets, through its *Literary Supplement* to the *Daily*. Two bookstores also sponsored readings and, located as they were on the perimeter of the universities, managed to mirror their respective styles: book launches were usually hosted by The Double Hook (its audience was ultra-Wasp Westmount mixed with Sir George hippies accompanying their profs), while The Word was an informal, intimate reading room (stacked from floor to ceiling with books, the small storefront room was quickly filled to capacity with McGill students). Of the cafés, the Kharma coffee-house put on some evenings of readings, and it was here that I encountered the living breathing poet in my Lit-Crit professor, Richard Sommer; here, under a spotlight directed at a simple red brick wall, less than a block away from the bureaucratic doublespeak of our institution, in an atmosphere of relative freedom and equality, he became a friend (and, for a short time, a genuine practitioner of experimental writing, even at the potential expense of being alienated from the Concordia English Department élite). His wife, Vicky Tansey, was a dancer, and he sometimes read his poems accompanied by Vicky, dancing.

The Department-sponsored readings at the University Hall could hold no real meaning for me, stamped as they were with institutional legitimacy, their all-too-civil decorum wafted in from the classrooms above. The English Department's agenda was clear: maintain a "conservative" policy of support-ing and protecting "mainstream poetry" while ignoring the rude post-modernists. No wonder some well-heeled profs later became the object of ridicule and a symbol of opposition to many of us.

In the early 1970s, the breakthrough for the experimental, the avant-garde, was realized with the sudden introduction of poetry to two of the new artist-run galleries, Powerhouse and Véhicule. Removed from the influence of the universities, Véhicule was also removed from the commercial influence of bookstores (although the gallery was occasionally used for book launches, primarily by small presses). Of our group, I became most intimately involved in the running of the gallery, at one point representing the poets on the board's executive.

My political involvement at Véhicule Art also strengthened my poetic "principles" (I can't help but think of Louis Dudek, who asked if we had "any" or did we "just churn it out") which, in view of the gallery's orientation to the experimental and the multi-disciplinary, I was in the process of formu-lating, as to what was or was not *avant-garde* poetry. These principles were based partly on my growing interest in Dada and Surrealism, but even more so on the visual art exhibitions and performance art I was witnessing at the gallery, works which ultimately inspired me to create what I called "video-poems" (1978) and to collaborate with other poets in performance poems like *Drummer Boy Raga, Red Light, Green Light* (1979). At the same time, most significantly, I learned to use the status of Véhicule Art as a non-profit organization to produce projects such as *Poésie en Mouvement/Poetry On the Buses* (1979), *Art Montreal,* the TV series (1979-1980), as well as an exhibition of *Concrete Poetry* (1981).[6] The precedent for these "gallery-sponsored" activities was already provided by Endre Farkas and Ken Norris, who had become editors of Véhicule Press while the press was still under the "umbrella" of the gallery, enabling all of us eventually to publish our books, thus creating an alternative publishing power to the established presses. (Ken Norris is the authority here.)

Two significant others: Opal L. Nations arrived from England and, almost immediately, collaborations and performances were happening. Steve McCaffery was part of The Four Horsemen, who performed sound-poetry, touring the parallel-gallery circuit, eventually arriving in Montreal, hosted by Véhicule.

For me, what defined the Vehicle Poets as a group (despite Gold's objections) was not simply *experimentation*, whether in structure or method on the page, in the subject matter of the poems or in their combination with other media; more unusual than these, not withstanding the *collaborations*, was the freedom expressed in our *joy of poetry* (and more transparent evidence of this cannot be found than on our faces for the cover photo of *The Vehicle Poets*), writing it, talking about it, sharing it, performing it, and when not up to our standards, dismissing it!

We ripped poetry out of the poetry books and the poetry readings and the universities and the poetry magazines and hurled them into the streets and the buses and the newspapers and the television sets, we pasted them on the walls of our galleries and the doors of our houses, we transformed our poems into visual experiences and we danced the poems and chanted them, we published them within days of writing them, we performed them with musicians, we read our poems together out loud, we cried them and sang them, we delivered them deadpan to the silence of a crowded room. We were the vehicle of the avant-garde, and the vehicle had arrived.

Postscript

JOHN McAULEY

My father was pretty skeptical about the poetry thing. He thought it was an excuse to stay on the pogey and smoke "funny cigarettes"—perhaps because I had written a Beat-like poem when I was ten, read it to parents and neighbours, and said I was dreaming of bathing in Chablis.

Maybe I should have been a little less naive. As Ken Norris somewhere wrote, "We live here and we've been part of trying to make things happen here & we want to continue to try to make things happen here & anywhere else we can get things going too." Maybe if I'd been more awake, I wouldn't always have been the last to find out what the boys were up to. Sometimes I'd get a phone call or it would be time for a love-in: "John, John!" Tom Konyves would begin with a conspiratorial smirk. Tom was the messenger. I always suspected Ken and Endre Farkas were up to something (with Artie Gold's okay). It's taken me until the twenty-first century to find out that there were no Vehicule poets, except maybe me in my own mind.

Endre (or Andre, his name in 1970) had more hair than a Hun when I first met him (before the Vehicule poets) in Henry Zemel's cinema class at Sir George. I was living in a commune in lower Westmount where writing poems was a challenge in the smoky atmosphere of seances and attempts to levitate the White House. My major influences were underground comic books, cheap art posters, and encyclopedias, though like many of my generation I dog-eared Donald Allen's *New American Poetry* and started trying my hand at concrete poetry after staring long and hard at Olson's essay on projective verse. My desk was a plywood board bolted to four wobbly legs. Being minorly dyslexic and majorly uncoordinated, I made a lot of typing errors pounding away on my old Royal portable typewriter, so I kept my poems short. Punctuation was something of a hazard too, but who really knew how to punctuate back then?

Around 1971 or '72, Endre and I went to a *Booster & Blaster* magazine meeting at Patrick Kelly Lane's place on Milton. Artie might have been there doing something or other for the magazine. About the same time, Endre took me somewhere in Côte-des-Neiges where we met Seymour Mayne, who was driving a VW van with Very Stone House, minus the "d," painted on its side. Endre and I had volunteered to collate an anthology of women poets. We danced the pages round and round a dining room table.

By 1975 I had also met Claudia Lapp. I remember her tripping onto the Park Avenue 80 bus wearing a long tight green skirt that made her look dangerous. Artie, too, impressed me because he'd been to the City Lights Bookstore on the West Coast and didn't have to hold down a job. He had an unsettling way of standing at the back of the room at any local poet's reading, frowning and relentlessly moving back and forth in the reader's line of sight. He could certainly make me flub my lines.

In late 1974, Michael Harris invited me to submit some work to the *10 Montreal Poets Reading at the CEGEPs* anthology, which also included poems by Artie, Endre, and Claudia. I gave Glen Siebrasse the name of a printer and took some flack from him for what he said was the printer's lousy job. All ten of us read at the CEGEPs. What I remember best is being ambushed at Champlain by the stutters. Poetry can be brutal.

In 1976, after I wrote Stephen Morrissey a fan letter commending him for publishing concrete poetry in his magazine *what is*, he generously sent me a copy of his mailing list to help me get started on *Maker* magazine. I was also designing concrete poetry kites, building a zoetrope with too few slits, and—my favourite—making concrete poetry slides for a stereoscope. *Maker* magazine lasted exactly three issues, the first photocopied, the other two offset printed at Véhicule Co-op in Chinatown. *Maker* went to poets and art centres in twenty-three countries. By the third issue, *Maker*'s layout had become an eclectic canvas for prose and poetry of varying lengths and types. Submissions came in every few weeks. South Americans sent a lot of political concrete poetry in Spanish. I loved the whole thing, but mailing out *Maker* got too expensive, so in 1979 I sent an obit to everyone and that was that.

By 1976, the Vehicule poets had been publicly named and Ken Norris had moved to Montreal. One (unspoken) rule of the Vehicules was to never criticize anything another Vehicule was doing. One time I put my foot in my mouth when I told Ken that he seemed to be writing a prose line. In return I got a public flogging in *The Tatooed Mouse*, where my work was mercilessly parodied. The piece began with a speaker offering "a ballantine across disneyland borders checkpointed by stars" and ended with a castigation of my "strange images" and "weird syntax." I (mentally) retaliated with who'd drink Ballantine anyway? Yet being a Vehicule poet was better than sitting on a mattress meditating.

In the summer of 1976, Trevor Goring and Chris Richmond engineered a takeover of the executive at Véhicule Art (Inc.), including the poets. Some tables and chairs were kicked around. Somehow I was appointed interim chairman and secretary of the gallery's executive. The latter position I held for two years. In 1976-77, with Bob Galvin and Stephen Morrissey, I also helped run Véhicule's poetry reading series. With sixteen individual or paired readings and one poetry-based performance, New Delta and Véhicule Press book launchings, an open reading, and a marathon, poetry became an integral part of the gallery's activities. The big splash in 1977 was *Montreal English Poetry of the Seventies* (with yet another ungainly title) edited by Ken and Endre. Endre helped himself to ten pages, Ken eleven, and I still have a hard time finding my work in the anthology. That year I became coordinator at Véhicule Art and worked at the job into June 1978, overseeing dozens of international, national, and local performances and exhibitions, and Véhicule's cross-Canada video tour.

Then publisher Simon Dardick decided to take Véhicule Press in a new direction, and Ken, Endre, and Artie were editors no longer. As usual, I wasn't privy to what actually happened; maybe Simon needed to earn a living. That's why Maker Press was established in late 1978. I did the layout for *The Vehicule Poets* anthology, a surprisingly smooth operation. Simon (my former library boss at Sir George) had taught me the art of putting a book together, and I enjoyed doing layout at the Co-op in Chinatown. But with only four other titles, Maker Press ended up an ephemeral venture.

The last collective reading by five of the Vehicule poets at Concordia on February 20, 1981, brought the curtain down. After this farewell performance, I suppose I went back to sleep.

Eating Our Own Words: Spoken Word in Montreal

COREY FROST

Since the mid-1990s, it has sometimes seemed that Montreal and spoken word were made for one another. In the winter 1998 issue of *Broken Pencil*, the Toronto magazine that bills itself as a "guide to alternative culture in Canada," the editors introduced an article about the city's spoken word scene by calling Montreal "the spoken word capital of North America."[1]

Nevertheless, as I outline the history and basic character of that scene, you can ask yourself this: is there something about Montreal that makes it a particularly energetic source of spoken word writing? And if the answer is yes, does that say something about Montreal writing in general? At the heart of this geographically specific question is a more fundamental one: what relationship does spoken word have to other writing? For some people, spoken word is culturally relevant because it is somehow more "real," more politically meaningful, than "academic" poetry. Others take the contrary view that it is a watered-down, popularized and commercialized facsimile of poetry. Is either of these things true, or are both? Can a distinction even be made between spoken word and other poetries? This last question can only be answered with a clumsy, incomplete and maybe redundant explanation of what spoken word *is*.

1

As a label, the term "spoken word" creates problems because it has the very broad and literal sense of spoken language as opposed to written language. When used by poets and artists over the last decade, though, it has usually meant something more specific: a performative artistic practice that incorporates multiple forms and techniques and is often defined chiefly by context. Partly, it is an extension of a tradition of poetry performance which can trace its roots back through the Black Mountain poets, the Beat poets, the Harlem Renaissance, and in fact all the way to the Homeric bards; other artistic phenomena have then converged on, or side-swiped, this tradition to produce a hybrid genre. It developed in tandem with the hip-hop culture of the '80s and '90s, and the invention of rap was an important source for the aesthetic of spoken word and a pre-condition for its current popularity. A parallel development is dub poetry, a mixture of Jamaican Creole speaking styles and rhythmic music that was developed in the '70s and usually deals with oppression, injustice, or poverty. Poetry slams, the most original and also the most vilified aspect of contemporary spoken word, grew out of the punk aesthetic of the late '70s and early '80s. The Chicago-style poetry slam, in which competing performers are rated by members of the audience, has become a carefully-regulated art-sport with specific rules and an international grand championship.[2] Another major component is sound poetry, as practiced by writer-performers such as the Dadaist Kurt Schwitters or The Four Horsemen (a quartet founded in 1970 by bpNichol, Steve McCaffery, Paul Dutton, and Rafael Barreto-Rivera). What is called spoken word today may be inspired by any of these traditions, or by performance art, theatre, jazz, story-telling, or stand-up comedy. In the '90s, spoken word started to produce a kind of subculture of its own, leading to the revalorization of a certain notion of poetry in the mainstream (at least for the sake of marketing to the profitable teens-and-twenties demographic). In practice, spoken word often seems to be only incidentally related to poetry. I would argue, though, that writing is the quiddity of the form, what makes it what it is.

Spoken word is first and foremost a kind of performance, but the performer is almost always the author of the work as well. It differs from a literary "reading" in that the work is usually written with performance in mind and performed from memory. Of course, sometimes the performer is not the author, or the work is not written for performance, or the performance is not memorized; the problem with defining spoken word is that there are exceptions to all of the defining characteristics. If we don't want to foreclose on any of the innovation and hybridity that are so important to the form, we have to leave the definition extremely vague: performed language. It is possible to define descriptively rather than prescriptively, though, in order to provide an idea of what spoken word usually is in real life.

The typical venue for spoken word is a single microphone on a stage in a bar or café. (It also happens in theatres, bookstores, lofts, parks, and bowling alleys, or it can be a recorded performance, whether "live" or mixed.) Usually the individual performance happens in a restrictive time frame: 15-20 minutes, or 3 minutes maximum in official slams. Usually, the emphasis is on performing *language* rather than personifying a character, so there is seldom reliance on costume or props. It can be dramatic, but it is not acting. On the other hand, the performance is sometimes accompanied by music, movement, or visuals. All of these factors affect the kind of work spoken word artists perform. The majority of spoken word is simple and accessible: the performer often tries to establish a direct connection with the audience and, to some extent, to entertain. The audience may not consist of people who read much poetry, and the work can sometimes be virulently anti-elitist or anti-academic. Often it is a vehicle for intensely-felt and bluntly-expressed political opinions, such as social criticism from a feminist or minority point of view. Of course, the style of the performance depends ultimately on the performer, and many performers produce subtle, abstract, quiet, difficult, experimental, theoretical, avant-garde or unpredictable work. Spoken word, though, is a form that clearly demonstrates how the division between low and high culture persists in these postmodern days. Performers who would rather not be associated with the "low" end of the genre may prefer the label "text-based performance art" to "spoken word."

2

The evolution of spoken word differs from city to city across North America, and the character of the individual scene depends on factors such as the history of writing and publishing in the city and its economic conditions. What follows is a brief outline of what happened to English spoken word in Montreal in the last decades of the twentieth century, and a list of some of the ingredients in its development.[3]

In the '70s and '80s, Montreal already had a significant history of poetry in performance. In the mid-'70s, the "Vehicle Poets" (a group of poets associated with the Véhicule Art Gallery and Véhicule Press that included Ken Norris, Artie Gold, Stephen Morrissey, Claudia Lapp, John McAuley, Tom Konyves, and Andre Farkas) involved themselves in readings as well as various poetry popularization schemes such as the placement of poem-posters on buses.[4] Through the '80s, several groups performed idiosyncratic concoctions of poetry and electric music, punk or jazz, such as Ian Stephens' band Wining Dining Drilling and Clifford Duffy's Nietzsche's Daughter. Ian Ferrier experimented with recording sound poetry from the '70s on, and Fortner Anderson documented the growing interest in spoken word in his zine *Brazen Auralities* and on his CKUT radio program "Dromostexte." But according to Ferrier, these activities were minimal and sporadic until 1994, when Montreal was infected by the new popularity of poetry performance engendered by poetry slams in the U.S., the strengthening impact of rap and hip-hop, the contagious early-'90s do-it-yourself zine culture, and a crossover of poetry to the pop music world (including poetry videos on MTV and Much Music). It was also a pop music event that was a major catalyst in producing a coherent spoken word scene in Montreal: Lollapalooza, the major pop/rock festival tour, came to Montreal for the first time in 1994 and featured a "spoken word stage" that would include local performers. The auditions for this event, which took place in June at the Phoenix Café on Boulevard St-Laurent, drew a large cast of curious writers, musicians, rappers, and spoken word enthusiasts. With such an array of performers assembled in one room to try out their various ideas, the enormous possibilities became evident, and organizers immediately put together a show at Le Bowling Bar the night before the main event, as well as an anthology chapbook, both called *Oralpalooza*.[5]

At around the same time, Ian Ferrier and Fortner Anderson, motivated by distress over the public's insignificant level of interest in poetry, began recording poetry performances to be played like songs on CKUT (Radio McGill). This initiative, called "Wired on Words," managed to put several poets in the top ten of the station's playlist, and a cassette was soon in the works. Also during that summer, the newly-formed performance quintet the Fluffy Pagan Echoes (Scott Duncan, Vincent Tinguely, Justin McGrail, Ran Elfassy and Victoria Stanton) started doing monthly shows, which were a big hit with the Phoenix Café crowd.[6] Ian Stephens launched a book with The Muses' Company Press that had obvious roots in spoken word; *Diary of a Trademark* is infused with the same mordant criticism of homophobia and complacency about AIDS that was central to Stephens' musical output.[7] Over the next year, these performers and others received a lot of attention from the city's press, both English and French. Poet Lee Gotham started a new series of events called *Enough Said* at Bistro 4 (also on St. Laurent, and like the Phoenix Café now defunct). Bistro 4 had previously been the venue for a regular reading series called Urban Wanderers, but the emphasis of Gotham's shows was on performance that attempted to do more than simply speak the words of a poem (hence the title), and so was perhaps the first conscious attempt to establish a regular venue for poetry performance as opposed to poetry reading. That winter, I took over the local magazine *index*, which had existed as a literary journal for a year, and, with the help of many people, it became a guide to and a forum for the emerging spoken word scene.[8]

Then, in the summer of 1995, Todd Swift, aided by Jasmine Châtelain and Dan Mitchell, introduced the poetry slam to Montreal in the form of Vox Hunt, a kind of carnivalesque poetry cabaret. Within a year, the Montreal team made a very popular debut at the International Slam in Ann Arbor, Michigan. That September, Jake Brown organized the first show of his *YAWP!* series, using a cabaret formula similar to that of Vox Hunt—a formula which became a nightlife phenomenon in Montreal—although the *YAWP!* style was more manic and rough around the edges, with Jake's shirtless, stage-diving antics contrasting sharply with Todd's bow-tied emcee act. *YAWP!* was followed by numerous other regular series: La Vache Enragée (an evenly bilingual show), the Funky-Ass Folk Babes series, Volume, Legba, The Devil's Voice, and Unusual Suspects, to name a few.

In the years just before and after the turn of the millennium, the spoken word scene underwent a few surges and lulls, notably the cessation of the popular *YAWP!* and Slam series (the latter had been sustained for several years by Alexis O'Hara), but a clear precedent had been established: spoken word would be taken seriously, and a new generation of writer-performers started appearing on the scene and starting their own performance events. Spoken word also began to productively mutate, splinter, and spread deeper into the French-speaking city. In February, 2002, due to the dedicated work of many people (especially Ian Ferrier, André Lemelin, and Victoria Stanton, who were succeeded by D Kimm), the annual Festival Voix d'Ameriques had its very successful inauguration, bringing together the several diverse streams of spoken word performance in Montreal, from traditional storytelling to rap to dub poetry to online poetry performance, in both English and French.

The fragment of time sketched above ended up producing an astonishing number of successful young writers and performers, including those I've mentioned as well as Catherine Kidd, Heather O'Neill, Golda Fried,

169

Julie Crysler, Trish Salah, Anne Stone, Jonathan Goldstein, Debbie Young, and Kaie Kellough, to name just a few. In 1998, Véhicule Press published an ambitious anthology of spoken word and "fusion poetry" in North America, *Poetry Nation*, containing works by twenty-one Montrealers (and over a hundred contributors in total); in 2002, Todd Swift, co-editor of that collection, followed it up with an even more ambitious project, a global anthology called *Short Fuse*, co-edited with Philip Norton and published by New York's Rattapallax Press, which contains at least seventeen Montrealers (or former Montrealers) in a field of some 175 poets doing performance-oriented work around the world.[9] Swift applies the term "fusion poetry" to this work, perhaps to get around the difficulty of defining a common practice among such a diverse group of writers. "Wired on Words" has continued to release Montreal spoken word recordings, including an anthology CD called *Millennium Cabaret* (1998), individual CDs by Fortner Anderson (1999) and Ian Ferrier (2000), an anthology of women performers called *Ribsauce* (2001), a CD by Tom Walsh and Todd Swift as Swifty Lazarus (2002), and a CD by Catherine Kidd with Jack Beetz, released together with a book from Conundrum Press (2002).[10] In the meantime, Planète Rebelle was producing spoken word CDs in French and the Vache Enragée CD anthologies in French and English.

For the moment, it seems that the popularity of spoken word events and their ability to attract talented writers have not diminished, although the quality and sophistication of the work fluctuates, partly due to the broad demographic range of the audiences and the constant turnover within the performing community. More than in any other Canadian city, spoken word in Montreal established a context and an audience for this kind of work. In comparison, while Toronto has many excellent writers who perform, it has never managed to support a sustained spoken word series with audiences that compare to those at, for instance, *YAWP!*, which at its height often drew 200-300 people. Vancouver is quickly developing its own reputation for spoken word in recent years, and the nascent Canadian Festival of Spoken Word, which will move from city to city, is encouraging more interaction between different scenes, but the explosive development of spoken word in Montreal and the sizeable audiences it has regularly attracted remain unique. What, then, are the reasons for Montreal's interest in and support for spoken word?

3

Montreal's English literary history is crowded with outspoken and enter-taining personalities such as Irving Layton and Leonard Cohen, a fact that has been often reiterated by poets of the last few decades attempting to establish a lineage. The present situation of the English-speaking community in Montreal, however, is not what it was in the '40s and '50s, when the city was largely controlled by the English-speaking population and was still a beacon of English culture in Canada. If English-speaking writers in Montreal today benefit from a flourishing creative community, it is not because of their cultural centrality but because of their marginality. It might be argued that the unique linguistic minorities-within-minorities situation makes simply reading poetry in public a political act, an affirmation of the possi-bilities of language, or of a language.

Furthermore, the typical elements of spoken word—accessibility, social critique, musical or theatrical performance—suit this city perfectly. Audiences for spoken word in Montreal seldom have a single first language in common, so non-verbal performance elements, such as sound poetry, are appealing. Le groupe de poésie moderne is a primarily Francophone sound poetry group which has been most popular among an Anglophone crowd. Politically, Montreal has a certain underdog status: impoverished, culturally marginalized by English Canada, and with a history of Québécois political insurrection. In practical terms, one of the ramifications of this marginality for English-speaking Montreal is that there are few publishers and few opportunities for local writers to publish. Many young writers there-fore turn to performance of their work as a way of reaching an audience.

For a few years in the mid-'90s there was a common perception that the English-speaking community of spoken word writers/performers in Montreal had established something that was lacking in the French-speaking community. In a 1998 interview in Broken Pencil (part of an article by Victoria Stanton and Vincent Tinguely which was the seed of their book Impure), Jasmine Châtelain mentions receiving a phone call from a journalist with La Presse who wanted to write an article on spoken word and who gushed, "Did you know that there's this thing, spoken word, that's happening? It's so amazing."[11] (Châtelain was at the time busy with Tongue Tied, a spoken word festival she organized along with Scott Duncan and others). The reaction was characteristic of the enthusiastic coverage by the Francophone press. Writer/zine publisher Jeremiah Wall, also quoted in the article, suggests a possible reason for this imbalance: "English is a renegade language in Quebec. That's why the French people think the English have a pretty dynamic scene. Because we make more noise than French culture does. French culture is all set up now in Quebec. But English society has to make itself wherever it can, set up the tents and do the circus, it's like the circus is in town."[12] This is an interesting statement, because the idea of a makeshift circus assembling and disassembling itself to create something in the interstices between established cultures is indicative of the strategic advantages that come from using a minority language, and it is also reminiscent of the impromptu atmosphere and irreverent spirit of spoken word itself. However, placing English in opposition to French neglects the fact that while French culture may be "set up" in Quebec, it is still a renegade culture in North America. If Anglophones are marginalized in Quebec, it has more to do with Toronto's centrality than any cultural hegemony imposed by French culture. In this way, French and English in Montreal could be seen as allies with a potential for innovation and subversion that comes from inhabiting the periphery.

4

I tend to regard spoken word performances and more "literary" readings as belonging to the same general category; both are performances, after all: dynamic interpretations of a text that create new, ephemeral works of art. Spoken word happens when the performer elects to take advantage of performance possibilities that are unavailable to a writer on the page. The absence of the page itself, although not strictly necessary, is important: it removes the artifact of the text from the scene and replaces it with a new artifact, the performance.[13] According to Catherine Kidd, the major difference between a reading and a performance is that, in a performance, "the text has been eaten, it's been sort of re-absorbed and I feel much more comfortable that way. Because if the words have sort of sunk down to gut-level and dispersed into the bloodstream, then I just have to plug into that and the piece leads me around by the nose."[14] This description suggests that there are two artistic moments involved: first the expulsion of words onto the page in writing, and then the re-absorption and re-expulsion of the words during performance. Two creative personas have worked on the text:

the writer and the performer. This suggests an affinity between spoken word performance and chapbook or writing-as-artifact publishing. The main similarity is that in each, the text is interpreted somehow after the writer is finished with it and before the audience receives it. The audiotext of a spoken word performance does not really exist until it is interpreted in this way; before that, it is only either a piece of writing on a page or a thought in the performer's head.

There is a profound metaphorical importance in eating the text. If the text has been incorporated into the body, the physical presence of the performer becomes the performance. When you watch a live spoken word performance what you see and hear is a text of sorts, but while it is a text—that entity which we have come to think of as authorless—it is a text embodied in the person of the writer herself, so in a sense the author is extremely present. We could say that spoken word skirts the displacement involved in writing, in a way that a simple reading cannot. Another Montreal writer, Heather O'Neill, says: "When I started performing my poetry, I thought I'd be more comfortable with it, because I'd done theatre for so long. But spoken word—all of a sudden, when I was first reading, I realized that I was there with myself. I was completely vulnerable and nervous."[15]

It is this directness—that is, the "un-theatrical" nature of the performance—that many audiences find so appealing in spoken word. Perhaps because of this, spoken word has often been used as a medium for explicit social critique and for confessional or accusatory writing. This quality of directness also provides something in the live performance that is not reproduced in the recording. Having said that, I want to point out that the idea of directness is a false lead: it would be naïve to suppose that spoken word artists provide a pure, unmediated glimpse of themselves when they perform. It is as if the popularity of spoken word is due to nostalgia for a mythical time when people could "tell it like it is," when our lives were not dominated by the virtual image, when there was still faith in the logocentric construct of the author as source of truth. People like to believe in the sincerity of speaking one's opinion, and they want to believe that the value of that act—its *truth*, even—somehow lies in that sincerity. Spoken word artist Fortner Anderson has said, "Spoken word is one of the only art forms that still allows people to communicate truth in a world destroyed by the filth, lies, and disease that pass for truth in our deeply sick society."[16] These harsh words have a certain ring of plausibility when one compares the raw irreverence of some spoken word with, say, television, but that longed-for ideal of "directness" and truth-based-in-sincerity is hardly realistic, or even desirable. (And furthermore, it becomes implausible to attribute to spoken word that elusive ability to speak truth when it collides with capitalism and is combined with television, as happened with MTV and Much Music's poetry videos and more recently with the HBO series "Def Poetry Jam.")

It's more likely that spoken word involves a kind of role-playing and that directness is one of the "effects" adopted by the performer. This would not mean that the performance is deceitful, but rather that various discourses are displayed for the audience in such a way that the constructed nature of those discourses is made obvious. In much spoken word the text is composed of a Barthesian tissue of pop cultural quotations: for example, the voice of a newscaster is used to convey incongruous emotional material, a snippet of pop melody is used as a refrain, and the metaphors used are drawn from TV shows and movies. This discourse collage is primarily a way of subverting the claim to "sincerity" of these pop sources. Spoken word of this variety could be seen as a kind of theatre that, rather than portraying *characters*, reproduces the interaction of *discourses*. Those performances that create a feeling of directness, on the other hand—this is especially true of the blunt, first-person forms of the poetry slam—focus on the discourse of a particular character that the performer inhabits.

Another symptom of the role-playing involved in spoken word is the tendency to foreground the writer's personality. Because author and performer are combined, and because the most personable writers tend to please audiences regardless of the quality of their writing, there is a large potential for the fetishization of the performer, a valourization of the aura of the artist rather than the work. In fact, it is impossible to separate the artist from the work. Those who desire to do so (to evaluate the writing separately from the delivery) may imagine a dichotomy between performance poetry, where the writing is supposed to be the substance of the show, and performance art, with its attention to the overall aesthetic. In "An Incomplete History of Slam," performance artist Anna Brown is quoted as saying, "A lot of performance poets are basically so happy to be reading their work in front of an audience that they tend to pander a little bit [in terms of the performance ...]. For the poets, the aesthetic is in the word." She continues, "Performance art is an extensive concept based in theoretical work, whereas to me a lot of the good performance poets have great theatric personalities and happen to be great writers."[17] What this means to me is that the poets Brown speaks of don't realize that they are engaged in performance art when on stage, that they *are* the show. This willed naïveté about performance is one of the most interesting aspects of the poetry slam, a sub-genre that was once the subject of endless conflict but that has now outlasted most of its criticism to become a cultural phenomenon in its own right.

Slams produce a certain kind of poetry, often sensationalist or humorous, known as slam poetry. The brevity of the form (3 minutes by the "official rules") and its reliance on lively, attention-grabbing presentation, owes a lot to television, but could just as easily be compared to many populist forms of live entertainment, from vaudeville to Shakespearean theatre in its day. To its credit, it provides a forum with a slightly more rigorous critical gaze than is typical of a traditional reading, and it has managed to entice large numbers of people who might otherwise never come in contact with poetry. But what is really interesting about the poetry slam is not the flashy tactics or the competition. In fact, although there is a certain prestige (and sometimes money) to be won, the competition could be seen as fundamentally artificial, a simulacrum, a dress-up show. The prestige of winning is mostly a badge of recognition for having performed a role well. In this way, the poetry slam veers off from the realm of literature and becomes its own sort of post-modern art happening, where the "rules of the slam" are in fact a guise for the underlying rules of the event as a performance. Criticizing the slam for somehow debasing poetry, therefore, misses the point that the entire event is theatre—another form of poetry, in a broader sense. This is how the slam was originally conceived at the Green Mill in Chicago: it was a performance art piece arranged by the "contestants" who were actually in cahoots—just like the "contestants" in a pro-wrestling bout—and who would wear costumes and play roles by adopting names or pretending, for example, to be famous dead poets.

It is paradoxical, then, that the participants in poetry slams today—unlike those first practitioners in Chicago and San Francisco—"compete" earnestly without always realizing their role in the *show* as opposed to the competition. Yet even if they don't consciously think of themselves as actors, their performance is still essentially a reproduction of the well-known character: the slam poet. The winners chosen by the audience tend to be those who are well-cast, who "work" as slam poets. In Montreal, such an assumption was made extremely evident when Alexis O'Hara introduced her series of "Sham Slams" which were supposed to be a contest to determine the *worst* slam poet in Montreal—that is, the one who could perform the most outrageous parody of a slam poet. It occurred to me that the skills required to "win" at the sham slam and those required for the "real" slam were not different in nature. Both events were in some sense a sham, a complicated postmodern conscious/un-conscious, sincere/ironic play. This sense of self-parody is common in spoken word in general, and particularly in Montreal it seems to have played an important role; for example, two popular performers in the mid-to-late '90s were Ed Fuller, whose act consisted of a lurid facsimile of a crooning lounge lizard, and Dayna McLeod, who was known for her routine dressed as a giant beaver, among other things.

This drag, burlesque-like performance may accomplish different things for different people, but two results stand out as relevant to literature. First, the carnival atmosphere of dress-up and attitude—the *posing*, if you like—creates a situation open to abrasiveness, conflict, confusion, humour, and all kinds of resistance, in a way that a more sedate, fixed-identity reading might not. It creates the possibility of risk. Secondly, it ensures accessibility. Because it is hip, lively and entertaining, the poetry slam manages to bring poetry to certain segments of the masses.

On the other hand, in the intermittent conflict between "traditional" poets and slam poets in particular, spoken word has been criticized for over-emphasizing accessibility. Slam poetry has focused on playing toward the audience, using colloquial speech and treating language as a more or less transparent medium. There has also been a certain resistance to publishing among slam poets, as if that would codify and defuse the work. This strategy has generated a great deal of interest among audiences who might not be willing to read poetry that is more subtle or experimental. The problem, the critics charge, is that packaging poems in short sound bites, like TV ads or music videos, is an evisceration of what is truly valuable about poetry. Poetry seldom survives an attempt to make it popular. In an article attacking National Poetry Month, Charles Bernstein says that promoting poetry as if it were an "easy listening" station "just reinforces the idea that poetry is culturally irrelevant and has done a disservice not only to poetry deemed too controversial or difficult to promote but also to the poetry it puts forward in this way."[18] Is "promoting poetry" a laudable enough goal that these aesthetic risks should be overlooked? Bernstein is critical of the very idea that poetry should be promoted: "The only reason that poetry matters is that it has something different to offer, something slower on the uptake, maybe, but more intense for all that, and also something necessarily smaller in scale in terms of audience. Not better than mass culture but a crucial alternative to it."[19] If you agree with this opinion—and I do—then you have to ask whether accessibility is one of the best things about spoken word events and poetry slams, or one of the worst.

Bernstein is himself a poet who performs and who has made major contributions to the study of poetry as an oral art form;[20] however, his personal preference is for performance of a minimalist kind. In the introduction to Close Listening, an anthology he edited on poetry performance, he describes the anti-expressivist style of poetry reading as one of "the least spectaclized events in our public culture"—valuable, therefore, because of its lack of drama and entertainment.[21] Critics of spoken word who suggest that ostentatious presentation necessarily implies a diminishment of the subversive value of poetry are often coming from an avant-garde perspective which holds that political subversion begins with linguistic subversion. Its defenders, on the other hand, are often more interested in using the genre as a kind of newsletter for the (political) revolution. Spoken word may attract audiences of young trend-conscious urbanites, but it is not neutral or bland; on the contrary, at its best it presents an ideological alternative to the slick banalities of mass culture. The intense anti-academic rhetoric found in some spoken word, though, tends to mistakenly see—or perhaps deliberately construct—"intellectual" writers as uniformly conservative. The debate between the academy and the slammers may in fact be a misunder-standing: each side fails to see the possibilities for subversion inherent in the other. I don't think the success of spoken word requires watering down the writing, aesthetically or intellectually, but it does involve a shift in the means of reaching an audience. The challenge for spoken word artists is to take advantage of the genre's anomalous popularity without allowing the art to be weakened by commodification, as difficult as that is in this late capitalist society.

The Montreal slam series that Alexis O'Hara took over from Todd Swift ended in 2000, but since then spoken word in Montreal has been more active and appreciated than ever. [The Kalmunity collective, for example, has grown rapidly in size and popularity, creating performance events that are a mix of musical improvisation and poetry; in 2007 they released a CD-book co-edited by longstanding poet-performers Kaie Kellough and Jason Selman.]

Every February the Festival Voix d'Ameriques draws capacity crowds (now more French than English) and invited performers from other cities to the Sala Rossa, an old dance hall on Boulevard St-Laurent Boulevard that has become a major venue, along with the Casa del Popolo across the street. At the autumn 2002 launch of *Short Fuse* in New York, the contingent of writer-performers from Montreal stood out as having a distinct style (granted, it's a style I'm particularly attuned to). Also, that Montreal style is often being exhibited in other places: writer-performer Catherine Kidd has taken her award-winning individual show *Sea Peach* to festivals in North America and Europe (including the Edinburgh Fringe Festival), Alexis O'Hara has toured North America, Europe, and Australia more than would seem humanly possible, and others from Montreal have toured in Canada and overseas, including Ian Ferrier, Victoria Stanton, and myself. For various reasons— economic freedom, linguistic diversity, cultural insularity—Montreal has provided an ideal incubator for this evolving genre. In the Montreal of the '80s and '90s, most young poets learned by necessity to subsist on a minimal diet—rice and lentils, or bagels and cream cheese—but little did we know that Catherine Kidd's technique of eating our own words would be so nourishing.

Zymergy: From the Neo-Ephemeral to the Odd Imbroglio

SONJA A. SKARSTEDT

> The little magazine is a form of semi-private publication which aims at
> public success and eventual victory over whatever is established in literary
> taste.
>
> –Louis Dudek and Michael Gnarowski[1]

The global clashes and thrusts of the 1980s—from recessions, AIDS and wars to Ethiopian famine—had as indelible an impact on Montreal's *Zymergy* as those societal factors that shaped literary magazines of the past. Leafing through the ten omnifarious issues I brought into existence between 1987 and 1991, I am struck by the incongruent harmony that still resonates from each volume. Fleeting though its existence was, and true to the traditions invoked by the concept of the "little magazine," *Zymergy* did manage to record the literary gist of its time and place to a burgeoning, if sometimes choc-a-bloc, degree.

During the fall of 1986, on the cusp between the "spoken word" movement and the unkempt typhoon of grassroots "zines" that would invade 1990s culture, I met with four or five Montreal writers to discuss a solution to the dearth of local literary magazines. Almost immediately the group fell into separate camps. It was pleasant enough to sit back in the candlelit comfort of the Café Prague, with its chess boards and Viennese pastries, and lob potshots at the city's existing magazines for being too academic *(Rubicon)*, too student-oriented *(Scrivener, The Moosehead Review, Matrix)*, or too small and infrequent *(Montreal Now)*. Everyone agreed that Montreal needed a magazine willing to provide an oxygenated forum for the bewildering gamut gestating in corners of the Main, St. Denis Street and west-end bookstores. Should the magazine be bilingual? Should there be graphics? Book reviews? Interviews? Special focus issues?

During the mid-1980s it seemed as though the last shreds of postmodernism were flying pell-mell, as if being driven by randomness for the sake of randomness itself. If there was a new literary "movement" afoot, it was composed of elements more in tune with that keystone of consumerism, disposability. Unlike Modernism and postmodernism, this brave new era had discarded all nineteenth-century nuances of destiny, its cataclysmic vastness barely held together by a momentous smattering of contradictory offshoots, ranging from academic adherence to tradition to ferocious experimentalism. I began to refer to this movement of movements as "neo-ephemeral": like its forerunners, the neo-ephemeral consisted of the need to break with once-gleaming, now outmoded ideals. At this juncture, it seemed that only inertia itself was capable of maintaining any sort of a momentum, its inculcations booming in the ongoing search for a semblance of destiny. If Modernism and postmodernism consisted of large-scale disillusionment propelling restless new visions, then the neo-ephemeral might be further defined via the outright embrace of the immediate, a dizzying vacillation between the contradiction of technological utopias and the elusive pastoral life.

According to Hubert H. Bancroft, the origins of North America's little magazine culture can be traced to the 1840s, when "in those days it was necessary for professional men of letters to adopt [...] the bread-winning employment of the newspaper. Literature as a profession did not really exist,"[2] and such immortals as Poe, Longfellow, Lowell, Hawthorne and the Cary sisters could at least secure the promise of an audience, despite the fact that the main attraction of magazines like Dennie's *Port Folio* and *Godey's Lady's Book* lay, for the most part, in their "colored fashion plates."[3]

A century later, the "little magazine" in Canada was taking "its inspiration from the experiments of F. R. Scott and A. J. M. Smith with the *McGill Fortnightly Review*."[4] Traces of its precursors flickered through *Zymergy*, from that groundbreaking Scott-Smith publication of the 1920s to Raymond Souster's and Louis Dudek's Contact Press, *CIV/n* and other literary envoys of the 1950s, as well as the more academically-inclined journals of the early 1980s. Cynthia Ozick has written that what "the small presses keep warm, and alive, are those very forms "the cultural situation" tends to submerge: essay, story, poem."[5] Does society instinctively obstruct these forms because they inherently challenge—thus ultimately endanger—the status quo? Dudek, ever the dissenter, wrote that *"Contemporary Verse* in Vancouver broke the ice"[6]—in setting the pace where hacking away at "deaf traditionalism" was concerned.[7] In other words, it was a literary magazine's duty to eschew the popular and rouse the establishment—confront stagnation—by welcoming those texts the established publishers deemed too risky.

North America's peak propagation period for literary publications was fuelled, like all undertakings of that period, by the post-World War II reconstruction tide of plenty. Yet the negatives comprising the groundswell beneath that prosperous tide—from turbulent human relationships to the nuclear knell—would continue to push their way up in the decades to follow, providing the raw irony for a dazzling number of creative achievements. If the harsh reality of the 1950s had "turned the attention of many [writers] away from their immediate social environment towards the more permanent world of archetypal forms and myths,"[8] then it was par for the course that the cultural milieu of the 1980s, long having come to terms with disillusionment, would expand upon the 1960s generation's preference for blunt reality, plotting a direct course for annihilation.

In 1986, Montreal was tight-roping its way across a deepening economic mire. North America's 1982 recession had slithered into Quebec on the heels of a massive, English-speaking, mostly middle-class exodus from the province, following the Parti Québécois' landslide election victory of 1976. The self-satisfied patina of post-World War II utopian fantasy was dissolving at an alarming pace. At the same time, an expanding global awareness was helping to scrape away the last vestiges of middle-class convictions. Ronald Reagan's family values agenda only highlighted the insane proportions of news from once unfathomable corners of the globe: incoming refugees relayed the first-hand horrors of Ethiopia's famine, Chile's "disappeared" and Somalia's civil war. Michael Callen summarized the '80s as "The AIDies."[9]

Technology aided and abetted the transmission of fact to an up-close and intimate degree. Estonian author Rein Raud, in Montreal for the 1989 PEN conference, related that the Communist government was no longer able to keep its secrets to itself because of the fax machine. Injustices could be communicated nearly at the very moment they were perpetrated. Across the ocean, Thatcherism complemented the United States' Republican agenda. The remnants of the '70s punk movement fermented in the youth consciousness of the early '80s, adding fire to the extended-teens, no-future existential clusters invading major North American cities. Cold-blooded new catchphrases such as "downsizing," "creative cost cutting measures" and "outsourcing" had wormed their way up through the daily vocabulary like noxious toadstools, heightening the new underdogs' response to the mainstream.

Montreal, unlike Toronto or Vancouver, offered a live-and-let-live environment for any "Anglo" nurturing literary aspirations, the bilingual city's lowly financial status being a primary inducement. The main arteries that defined this once-glittering "Paris of the North" were then pickled with *à louer* [for rent] signs whose accompanying high vacancy rates translated into a glut of cheap rents. All manner of affordable eateries and cafés proliferated: enter a reverse exodus of mostly twentysomethings, armed with university diplomas, joblessness and requisite manuscripts tucked in their backpacks, raring to party and thirsting for recognition. Bistro proprietors rolled out the welcome mats, encouraging their artsy post-punk patrons to settle in for hours on end (regardless of the single bowls of *au lait* that constituted the average order), wooing organizers of poetry readings and book launches. To the outside eye, Montreal appeared to have picked up where '60s hippie culture had left off: everyone shared a common cause—everyone could be a star. Let Bay Street obsess about money: life in this bilingual, ethnically-diverse hub demanded only the fullest expression of one's creative desire pulsating between palls of smoke, pitchers of beer, and the latest anarchic *raison d'être*.

The city's Latin tempo and multiethnic vibrancy offered a high-voltage locale, but could also prove a most daunting milieu when it came to achieving recognition. As Ken Norris wrote in 1978: "When he writes a poem, the Montreal poet knows of the limited access he has to an audience."[10] For the most part, the Québécois community maintained its own rather insular perspective, expressing about as much interest in what the Anglos had to say as the rest of Canada harboured toward Quebec. Montreal's Anglo writer therefore had to be prepared not only to accept these circumstances, but to derive his or her inspiration from the unpredictable tempo of life in this province, without being swept away by it. Given that the worldwide societal trend emphasized a breaking-away from the questionable safety nets of tradition, maybe the passionate, creatively inebriated metropolis of Montreal in the 1980s was the most logical place for an artist to be. On what seemed a daily basis, posters announcing the latest "Yawp" or "Vox Hunt" encrusted every available utility pole and boarded-up storefront. Across the city, minuscule yet fervid "extremist" factions blossomed and gathered to feast on every untapped Ideal of the Moment. Bombarded by decades of consumerist mores, the "discard" mentality had infiltrated even the street-level think-tank. Spray-painted slogans popped up in alleys and vacant lots, inviting the have-nots to, among other temptations, consume the rich.

In his preface to *Sounds New,* an anthology of new Montreal poets from the early 1990s, Peter Van Toorn acknowledged the influence of Irving Layton and others from preceding generations on the newcomers, but also observed that the younger poets were rediscovering and reestablishing a trust in spontaneity: "So it may well be that Canadian poets" are "treating the poet's chief method and instrument—the imagination—as a welcome ally, a partner in its quest, a source of insight and inspiration."[11] The work of these young writers also indicated their awareness of the need to re-adjust to oncoming fluctuations as they came to grips with a disaffecting, non-chartable age.

If Modernism and postmodernism shared one main attribute—i.e., preserving the very best of past cultural achievements, while simultaneously hacking away at the stasis incurred by adherence to aging cultural factions—there were indications at those bistro literary events of a growing determination to destroy the past, present and future. This nihilistic element was one defining characteristic of the neo-ephemeral: the society of the late twentieth century also seemed to be immersed in a global free-for-all. There were inevitable clashes between self-proclaimed Neoists and those whose incessant genuflections to the Beats and other past rebels were reflected in the tediously imitative product being churned out by "graduates" of the Bukowski school: drink hard, write fast, leave a beautiful corpse of a poem. Where one "spoken word" performer espoused the purity of the unrehearsed rant, another insisted on reciting a sonnet whose calcified contours would have been more at home in the Romantic age. Erupting like wary hot springs between revelations of middle-class hypocrisy, injustice and relationship angst, were entreaties by those who had fled life-threatening circumstances in their homelands. Could anything of lasting value emerge from such off-kilter cultural cross-hatchings?

At the same time, universities experienced a significant influx of students: creative writing programs flourished and their emerging graduates wondered where they fit, if at all, between academia and the street. On-campus readings could be claustrophobically formal, whereas bistro readings and "slams" were "in your face." Those university graduates who nurtured creative aspirations naturally veered toward checking out, if not necessarily participating in, the latest meltdown in progress. Sub-camps emerged and intermittently merged, and the resulting imbrications—post-feminist, pro-Beat, post-Bukowski, pro-anarchist, anti-Booker, pro-Buddhist, anti-Krishna—protruded like the warped spokes of a brassy circus wheel. As far as the public—mainstream and poet—was concerned, the status of the written word had become as palatable as an expired tin of Beluga caviar. Who in their right mind would start a literary magazine?

Within the next two months of the Café Prague gathering, my discovery of an antiquated Gestettner machine triggered a spark: visions of Contact Press glory danced in my head as the scarred oak stand was dragged into my apartment. By the time a repairman declared the machine a total write-off, I had already solicited enough material to put together a slender first issue. Murmurs of a new magazine had caused a small yet palpable anticipatory ripple within the literary community. My perception of the Montreal literary scene was further expanded by my participation in readings, personal correspondence and a growing library of international literary magazines. Ralph Gustafson had written that poetry was "in such a sorry state of neglect that to claim for the art the functions our civilization prizes is a heavy temptation."[12] Even if my as-yet unnamed journal didn't meet with worldwide acclaim, it might at least help block the dam. Poetry, after all, couldn't "wind clocks, but it [could] tell the time."[13]

When I mentioned my publishing plans to Louis Dudek, he graciously offered advice. Ever the mentor, he emphasized the importance of placing one's individual stamp on any literary venture. Based on my experiences working on student publications I had already decided that it would be more expedient to proceed on a solo basis. Deadlines would have a better chance of being met. My impetus was to avoid the blinkers of provincialism in order to maintain as international a focus as possible. There were also the examples set by predecessors. According to former curator David McKnight, curator of McGill's Rare Books and Special Collections Division, the 1980s journal *Rubicon* was "the most ambitious and most national in scope."[14] Although my goals did not deliberately include serving as an instrument of dissent against previous generations or literary schools of thought, I made it clear that the door was open to any and all articulate and innovative expressions of discord. *Zymergy* would primarily serve as a record of its time and place. I was determined to arrange the poems, stories, essays and graphics in such a way as to create a full faceted yet unified picture: a symphony evolved from a mass of diverse voices. I also decided to limit my own input to prefaces, pseudonymous book reviews and the occasional memorial poem.

Days later, Dudek handed me two poems and a subscription cheque. By this time I had requested a quote from a local printer. As desktop publishing had not yet become the norm, I purchased a new print wheel for my electronic typewriter. Although the all-caps font turned out to be the antithesis of aesthetic perfection, I wanted to avoid the grungy-typewritten aesthetic that pervaded the typical independent little magazine. There was also the matter of a suitable title. Having unsuccessfully run through a lineup of metaphorical catchphrases, flora, fauna and mythological figures, I finally leafed through a 1941 Webster's Dictionary until I came to the very last word: "Zy'mur-gy (zi'mûr'ji), no. [zym-+urgy.] Applied chemistry dealing with fermentation processes, as in brewing." This word—whose spelling I would alter, replacing the "u" with "e"—and its definition suitably expressed the intent and spirit of my journal-to-be: a potentially intoxicating, contemporary combination of voices. The première volume consisted of forty offset-printed pages within a glossy pale green cardstock cover; square, post-Deco neon-like caps comprised the logo set above Geof Isherwood's pen and ink drawing. For all its humble saddle stitching and "quirky chapbook" ambiance (as I would remark in the tenth issue's preface) the first issue of *Zymergy* did contain an impressive array of writing.

Editing and publishing a literary magazine would enable me to glean an eye-of-the-hurricane view of what was going on, not only in Montreal, but in the United States and abroad. Not unexpectedly, the first few issues of *Zymergy* contained a high ratio of material from Montreal and Toronto. There was poetry from Dudek, Mary Melfi, Raymond Filip, Laurence Hutchman, Gerald Doerksen, Anne Cimon and Charlotte Hussey; prose from Ann Diamond and Yeshim Ternar and two book reviews. Montreal artist Kris Pawelec's shadowy and figurative pencil drawings interspersed the texts with subtle aplomb.

Having no access to any distribution system, I happily delivered my precious cargo to consignment-friendly bookstores in Montreal and Toronto. Within weeks, offerings from the Maritimes, Northwest Territories, United States and Europe began trickling in. I also mailed letters of invitation to a number of established authors. That a certain number did not respond only enhanced the elation accompanying the arrival of poems from such luminaries as Phyllis Webb, bill bissett, Ralph Gustafson, Ted Joans, Shulamis Yelin, Lucien Francoeur, Claudine Bertrand and Robert Melançon.

By virtue of the material, each issue of *Zymergy* more or less guided its own momentum. Given the increasing number of submissions, the editorial challenge became more intricate with each issue: by my own estimation, about sixty percent of incoming texts could be classified as being emotionally resonant and soundly constructed. About fifteen percent consisted of religious or commercial evocations of love, nature and friendship. Twenty percent of poems could be perceived as above average, and less than five percent were what one might consider extraordinary.

As I mulled over the surplus of material in preparation for the second issue, I decided to query three Montreal authors about contributing their editorial insights. Poets Raymond Filip and Mohamud S. Togane and novelist Ann Diamond were not affiliated with any groups, movements, or organizations. Their individuality, I hoped, would provide some cohesive irony. Eschewing formal gatherings, I met with them separately, once or twice a month, to hear what each had to say and take note of other writers they recommended. Diamond, Filip and Togane would also be expected to contribute their own written work to the publication.

The second issue would set the definitive tone of *Zymergy*, in that it captured Montreal's quirky *joie-de-vie* and ethnic diversity—although that volume's burgundy-tinted interior pages and embossed cover art would be a one-time experiment. My acquisition of a fidgety, still-functional IBM Composer enabled me to switch to professional typesetting. The designated "double issue" (118 pages) marked a permanent departure: each issue to follow would consist of at least 110 pages. Its cover featured a storybook lion casting his quizzical upward gaze at a daydreaming woman whose arms were folded. Thanks to a chance meeting with Peter Van Toorn, I gained access to the poet's original manuscript for his critically-acclaimed book, *Mountain Tea*: Van Toorn had somehow managed to dismantle a spiral bound scrapbook onto whose liberated pages he typed his "Mountain" poems before reconstructing the book, coiling each page back inside the spine in such a way that the poems appeared to have been mysteriously transmuted therein. This bizarre artifact reminded me of poets' often-obsessive relationship with their calling.

Van Toorn's essay "Mountain Words" relayed the severe challenges faced by today's poets, particularly the feasibility of securing precious working time and space: "The poet finds the world a refuge for itself, a sanctuary of imagination, in words as they have been practiced from the beginning of time."[15] These words of wisdom served as a practical gel between poems like Raymond Filip's "Madonnari" (which, with its distinctive verve, classical references and characteristic alliteration, paid tribute to the poet Mary di Michele via the Montreal landscape); Ken Norris's characteristically low-key "Italia"; and Muriel Bédard's tender "Naya." New voices included poets M. L. Fabiani, Neil Henden, Stephen Brockwell, and Maxianne Berger, as well as experimental fiction by Peter Dubé (then known as Tei Tan 84). Mona Elaine Adilman's stark, shadowy "Gypsy Woman" and Shulamis Yelin's traditional ballads offered a contrasting medium for texts more in keeping with my "neo-ephemeral" classification, including work by Andre Farkas, Joan Ruvinsky and Mike Leneghan. One self-described "industrious and well-known underground publisher" contributed a manifesto entitled "THE underGROUND iS over," which protested Ontario's "Guardians for the Common Good," via the National Library of Canada's descent on participants in Toronto's 1987 Small Press Book Fair.

With the exception of refugees, Montreal's poets shared many of the same experiences as others across the continent. As Ken Norris pointed out in his introduction to *Canadian Poetry Now*, his anthology of twenty poets of the 1980s, "The exploration of the quotidian is a characteristic of much of this writing. These poets pay attention to the facts, conditions, and issues of living."[16] There was also the fact that, because women's rights had only been implemented recently, women were still confronting obstacles. As Norris remarks about the poets in his anthology: "All of their work has been affected by the feminist movement; something has clearly changed in male-female relations and many of these poets try to assess the shifts."[17] For all the positive changes, painful encumbrances continued to deliver their inflictions, as revealed through the sobering reflections within Robin Potter's poem "Miscarriage."

The "confessional" era continued to extend its apparently indefatigable shadow. Much like the material being featured in local readings, the majority of incoming poems tended to be autobiographical, centered on everyday life—from relationships to alienation, city vistas, naturescapes and political commentary. Readers could find themselves immersed in Claudine Bertrand's breathless, colloquially-teeming tribute to St. Denis Street, "La rue réclame sa propagande," in one moment, Stephen Brockwell's first-person exposé of "Pullet Carnivore," in the next, and then make the shift to knife wounds of a more surreal nature in Van Toorn's dream-walking "Mountain Ash."

The same phenomenon was unfolding in the world of Québécois *belles-lettres*. In 1996, Laurent Mailhot and Pierre Nepveu said of Québécois poetry: "The last twenty-five years have marked a return to the individual and to a cultural eclectic," also noting that "more than ever, Quebec is pluralistic and multi-ethnic."[18] Although I solicited material from the Francophone literary community, the number of responses was disappointing. Post-1976 angst hung in the air like smoke from a bitter *fête:* the province caught between a hangover from that first vote on separation and gathering steam for what would be the alarming close shave of the 1995 referendum. Nevertheless *Zymergy*'s "En Traduction" section was graced by some exquisite contributions, from Dwayne Perrault's polished interpretation of Patrick Lane to Jacques Marchand's *vif* version of Ray Filip's "Referendumb," as well as Louky Bersianik's manifesto "Mon engagement féministe" and new poems from Claudine Bertrand, Lucien Francoeur, Claude Beausoleil and Robert Melançon.

The fourth issue qualified *Zymergy* to apply for Canada Council funding. I proceeded with a black and white photo section highlighting Montreal literary events. It was my hope that this journal would be perceived as an equal among such publications as *Rubicon, The Scandinavian Review* and *The Antigonish Review,* without having to surrender its unconventional spark.

Zymergy's first controversy came in the form of an interview with Ann Diamond: "How I Became a Terrorist, Or Humour As a Terrorist Weapon." The author's "Terrorist Letters" comprised a series of poetic narratives exploring Canada's puritanical tendencies. In sending these "letters" Diamond hoped to call attention to "an organization based in Toronto which for some reason claims to represent poetry in this country."[19] In particular, Diamond was perturbed by the attitude of The League of Canadian Poets toward its "minority within a minority" Anglo-Quebec membership.[20] As well, she cited the do-gooder mentality inherent in the League's attitude towards Canadian books—i.e., that it was a patriotic duty to read them. The League did not take kindly to Diamond's tongue-in-cheek onslaught, aptly signed "the Voodoo Queen." Her "threats" included invading "their office disguised as a Macedonian bag lady," absconding "with their files" and creating "chaos by generating a lot of phony literary contests," giving "awards to non-existent poets" and staging a "hairspray demonstration" at the Annual General Meeting."[21] The League responded by calling in the Toronto Police and the RCMP, who informed the League that Diamond's "Letters" were "obviously a work of imagination" which in turn spurred Diamond to suggest that "the Toronto police have more literary judgment [than the League]."[22] If they didn't succeed in overturning League policy, the "Terrorist Letters" increased public awareness of the League of Canadian Poets, and impelled some provocative new poems.

Controversy of a distant nature presented itself in the memoir submitted by an elderly artist from England, which I immediately decided to include in the seventh issue. Trevor Thomas, Sylvia Plath's former downstairs neighbour, and the last person to see the poet alive, was in the process of being sued by Ted Hughes. Because of the resulting court order, I had no choice but to cut key paragraphs from the Thomas memoir. Despite the excisions, Thomas's text was a fascinating read, calling attention to the insurmountable barriers faced by a woman whose talent miraculously transcended her circumstances: "I had seen her angry before but this time there was something different, a note of desperation that went beyond the event itself. There was a kind of panic as if she was racing against time."[23] Perhaps Thomas's worst transgression was his portrayal of Plath in an all-too-human light: the public, after all, prefers to perceive its famous figures through a mysterious, majestic, and even deified haze.

By the fifth issue, the narrative-to-poetry ratio had achieved a healthier balance, featuring new fiction by Antanas Sileika, Kenneth Radu, Beverley Daurio, Jia Lin Peng, Martin Kevan and Robbie Newton-Drummond. The book reviews section was also thriving. A rustle of dissent followed my decision to use B.C. photographer Janosz Meissner's portrait of an upward-gazing man ("Birdman Fan") standing on a West Coast shoreline with cassette recorder tucked under his arm. Why promote the work of a B.C. resident on the cover of a Montreal publication? Aside from the fact that I considered this picture, with its aura of existential yet poetic perplexity, to be most suitable for that issue's cover, *Zymergy* was not interested in serving as a regional trumpet. In his day, Raymond Souster had also aimed for "a magazine that would break through national and provincial boundaries."[24] True to *Zymergy*'s propensity for the unexpected, the issue's very first page boasted Antanas Kmieliauskas' "Eye on the Apocalypse"—Saint George in the act of subduing a dragon as beams from a watchful orb divided the illustration into radiating segments.

As of the sixth issue, *Zymergy* began to feature interviews with prominent poets. I conducted some of these and learned in the process that poets can be as creatively compelling within a conversation as in their polished, published texts. For instance, my interview with Mary Melfi on "The Dangers of Poetry" provided a semi-analytical, yet imaginative interior view of the creative process: "Poets are as welcomed into our society as a squadron of battle-weary ghosts exhibiting themselves in the parking lot of some local mall."[25] Phyllis Webb offered her own enigmatic perspective on the interior process: "I have a line, an odd line, 'the mind doth know its own dictionary.' I'd inevitably look up these 'arriving words' and there would be such a skein of connection with what I'd written or that would come in to the writing [...] that the reason that word entered my head seemed to be a reason that connected with something I was doing."[26] Louise Schreier's interview with Louis Dudek ventured into the mysteries of the long poem, which "cannot be a digressive, expansive, boring exposition. It is really made of very sharp, Imagistic, quintessential poetic elements. Every rift, you know, is filled with ore."[27] Laurence Hutchman's interview with George Johnston detailed the intricacies of translation, the highly-respected poet and translator of traditional Nordic verse offering a *petit* provocation: "A knowledge of how an English sentence works or can work is something few contemporary Canadian poets have."[28]

At one point Chilean exile and Canadian poet Elias Letelier-Ruz announced that he was leaving for Managua, Nicaragua (a photograph of Ruz in full guerilla regalia appeared in the ninth issue) and asked whether I was interested in an interview with Ernesto Cardenal. During their meeting, Ruz had to make his way through a constant labyrinth of soldiers, students, bureaucrats, "workers requesting poetry readings for their unions" and "peasant women bringing him flowers."[29] To make matters more difficult, the renowned poet, priest, social activist and minister of Culture had an aversion to interviews. Nevertheless, the poet offered some forthright commentary on literature, politics and his fellow authors, including Gabriel García Márquez, who "is so stingy with his dialogues that he has even been accused of being totalitarian [...] because he won't let his characters speak."[30] On the causes of resentment between intellectuals he theorized that "so much arrogance and vanity cloisters them and they don't flower with all their interior richness like a creative artist."[31]

Jorge Etcheverry's essay, "Chilean Literature: Diaspora" added a painful perspective on life in Neruda's native country: "For the Chilean writer living abroad and cut off from a group of peers or a political organization, it is almost impossible to publish in Chile."[32] In his essay "Down But Not Out in Nicaragua," Gary Geddes's descriptions extended the sorrowful vista of everyday life in South and Central America: "Ahead of us, there's a cart containing a father and three sons being pulled by a horse so gaunt and diminutive it looks like a toy."[33] Steve Lehman's account of life as an outsider in Saudi Arabia was no less cautionary: "The scimitar whistles, and the heads of traitors, murderers, and rapists fall at midday on Fridays outside the Friday Mosque in Riyadh."[34] There were also reports from less tormented corners of the globe, including filmmaker Alan Collins's conversation with acerbic English novelist John Wain: "These chaps who go around American universities explaining how they write their poems, they might as well go around describing how they sleep with their wives."[35] Poems by Sweden's Heidi von Born, Lithuania's Antanas Kmieliauskas, and Hungary's Bari Kàroli offered a more classical than nihilistic literary perspective of life outside Canada and North America.

It was poet and essayist David Solway who would cause the greatest commotion through his essay "Fellatio, Depth-Analysis, and The Experience of the Surface." A discussion of textual analysis vis-à-vis pornography, the thinker warned of the dangers inherent within the too-facile swallowing, so to speak, of deconstructive reticence: "The act of perception which guarantees our experience of the world has been gradually reduced to the status of an *intention* which proposes to accomplish that which already exists."[36] A few readers cancelled their subscriptions solely on the basis of the essay's title. Others wrote letters denouncing the essay's "sexist overtones"—their outraged focus inadvertently revealing that they hadn't bothered to read the essay. However, it was Solway's commentary in regard to Margaret Atwood, during an interview I conducted with him in the sixth issue, that most rankled the public: "I think she's a second-rate, a very mediocre poet, who happened to be in the right place at the right time—in Toronto, during the media-onslaught of the Sixties."[37] As if this were not sufficiently sacrilegious, he added: "I must confess that I cannot read her novels. I find them so […] dull, predictable and derivative."[38] These comments earned *Zymergy* its first and only newspaper headline, in the Montreal

Gazette's Thomas Schnurmacher column, in which Schurmacher decried Solway's attack on "one of Canada's foremost contemporary authors" as "sour grapes."[39] Solway's comments regarding Canadian literature were no less searing: "You've got to publish a book a year, maybe a book every two years, if you want the League of Canadian Poets to remember you, if you want to get Canada Council grants, if you want to appear on CBC radio."[40] Numerous readers castigated Solway's arrogance and asked me why I had bothered to publish his comments. In that issue's editorial preface, I had asked, "Why not welcome dissension?" and made reference to the then-famous plight of Salman Rushdie. Ann Diamond was making valid criticisms about her country's tendency to perceive and treat its artists as entrepreneurs. David Solway was likewise stating his own opinion. It was the intention of both authors that the public be sufficiently awakened from its lassitude to question the system.

In addition to contributions from such established authors as Lucien Francoeur, John Asfour, George Ellenbogen, Peter Van Toorn, James Deahl, Phyllis Webb, Blaine Marchand, Barry Dempster, Yuki Hartman, Antonio D'Alfonso, Bruce Hunter, Claudine Bertrand, Michael Andre, Beverley Daurio, Bruce Taylor and others, *Zymergy* highlighted a plethora of new voices. Many, including Maggie Helwig, Bert Almon, Anne Cimon, Matt Santateresa, Stephen Henighan, Steven Heighton, Todd Swift, Lucille King-Edwards, Charlotte Hussey, David Manicom and Miriam Packer went on to full-fledged literary careers. Photographs of literary events, sculptures and illustrations from Mario Gross, Brendan Sanderson and Peter Flinsch lent a stimulating, even provocative visual edge. Much of each issue's contents were paradoxically juxtaposed to its rather formal appearance—reminiscent of author William Burroughs' wardrobe, more in keeping with Wall Street chic than Beat grunge—thus managing to encompass the volatile literary 1980s.

The tenth and final issue included over fifty contributors. In physical appearance and layout, the magazine had undergone a robust transformation since its humble inaugural issue—because of, or perhaps in spite of my "purposefully vague editorial policy."[41] From the pastoral emanations of George Ellenbogen's "Once in South Dakota" to the knife-like currents of rage driving Katharine Beeman's "Massacres"; from Barry Dempster's rapturous yet firmly-grounded "The Canadian Dream" to John Asfour's impassioned extravaganza, "Ben Hilali's Night of Revels"; from Stephen Brockwell's delicately melodic "Whale Teeth" to David McGimpsey's homages to pop culture—there was no singular pulse, but a series of individual heartbeats, some pummeling, some whispering, some coolly and some abruptly commandeering their way into a reader's consciousness.

After five years of intensive focus exacerbated by distribution gaps, feeble sales and a lack of publicity, I could now better appreciate the experiences of those whose devotion to publishing a literary magazine had also come full circle. Aileen Collins expressed it succinctly: "Looking back, I feel that the decision to forego mimeograph for print led to the demise of *CIV/n*; and as anyone associated with a little mag knows, the time and energy expended, the financial burden, and the decreasing enthusiasm slowly erode the burning faith in the cause."[42] Fifteen years later I am more acutely aware of the impermanence that delineates our existence as my eyes trace the names of those *Zymergists* who have passed on: Louis Dudek, Manuel Betanzos-Santos, Shulamis Yelin, Ted Joans, Mike Leneghan, Mona E. Adilman, William Davey, David Lawson, Ralph Gustafson, Gerald Doerksen and Muriel Bédard.

Twenty-odd years later, the neo-ephemeral shows signs of extending into the development of an even more precarious reality. Postmodernism has long run its course and the internet has caught up with an intensity matched only by its speed. Yet the little magazine continues to thrive; 1980s anarchy overkill seems to have whetted the creative appetite for more discipline and less destruction (for destruction's sake). Like *Zymergy*, these publications provide nascent confirmation that the word, written or spoken, will continue to be an essential component of human evolution. Despite the wars, the disease and the despair, we persist, our irrational hope perhaps best articulated by the creative sector's most eloquent affiliate—the poet.

The Decline and Fall of the Athens of the North: Literary Production in the Eastern Townships

MICHAEL BENAZON

During the previous century, English literary activity in the province of Quebec had two locales: the major centre in Montreal and a smaller, but by no means negligible, community in the Eastern Townships, which was at its creative height between 1963 and 1988. Ron Sutherland, who at the time was teaching at the Francophone Université de Sherbrooke, was one of several people who played an important role in concentrating the expression of that literature in the small town of North Hatley on the northern tip of Lake Massawippi. In an article designed to promote the merits of his adopted town, Sutherland picked up a phrase previously used by poet and critic A. J. M. Smith and ventured to call North Hatley "the Athens of the North."[1] For a time, North Hatley was indeed a meeting place for writers and artists from both the French and English communities of Quebec. The flowering of English-Quebec literature in the Townships during this twenty-five-year period was unusual, however, because the region's small, largely rural English population was in decline, and because prior to 1963, very few English-language writers lived in the area.

There were certain foundations. Bishop's University in Lennoxville had a small English department with a tradition of hiring poets to teach courses on poetry. Poet, writer, and literary translator John Glassco had been living near Knowlton since 1936, and A. J. M. Smith was accustomed to spending his summers in a family cottage at Drummond Point on Lake Memphremagog. A few years later, his friends and colleagues, poet F. R. Scott and novelist Hugh MacLennan acquired cottages in North Hatley, and it was there that they did much of their writing.

In 1961, poet Douglas Jones was hired to teach at Bishop's University. The same year, Ron Sutherland, who was engaged in setting up a Department of English at the Université de Sherbrooke, bought an old cottage on Houghton Street in North Hatley and proceeded to renovate it for year-round living. Sutherland was struck by the evident charm of North Hatley and the possibility of affordable and ample housing not far from his place of work.[2]

The Townships begin to emerge as a regional English literary centre around 1963, the year that Sutherland undertook to establish a Comparative Canadian Literature program at the Université de Sherbrooke. Since Douglas Jones's contract at Bishop's had not been renewed, Sutherland hired him to teach poetry courses at the Université de Sherbrooke. During that summer Jones and his first wife, Kim, bought the house on Houghton Street, North Hatley, next door to Sutherland. By coincidence, Ralph Gustafson, who was joining Bishop's University to replace Jones, bought a home on the same street but on the other side of Jones's house. Thus, the stage was set for Houghton Street to become the home of not one but two future winners of the Governor-General's Award for Poetry. Later the same year, John Glassco organized the Foster Poetry Conference, which was attended by Jones, Scott, Smith, and others, including Louis Dudek, Irving Layton and Leonard Cohen.

This nucleus of creative writers was created by the close proximity of three teaching institutions in Sherbrooke-Lennoxville. In the period under consideration, the English departments of the Université de Sherbrooke, Bishop's University and Champlain College all subscribed, consciously or unconsciously, to the notion that at least one and sometimes three or more staff members should be creative writers. Thus the presence of writers and poets Ralph Gustafson at Bishop's University; Douglas Jones, Ron Sutherland, Neil Tracy, and later Avrum Malus at the Université de Sherbrooke; and Michael Oliver, Robert Allen, Steve Luxton, Michael Harris, and Matthew von Baeyer at Champlain College is largely explained by hiring practices at those institutions.

Other writers were attracted to the delightful setting of North Hatley and by the prospect of acquiring an affordable and comfortable summer residence less than two hours' travel time from Montreal. Thus, Hugh MacLennan, F. R. Scott, and, later, such Francophone poets and singers as Roland Giguère, Gérald Godin, and Pauline Julien bought cottages in or near

North Hatley. Michel Garneau bought a summer residence near Bolton, and Louis Dudek acquired one in Way's Mills, just a few kilometres away. In 1975, Mordecai Richler purchased a winterized cottage on Lake Memphremagog. John Glassco and his friend, the CBC broadcaster and poet John Grenfell, Bernard Epps, Sara Nomberg-Przytyk, Don Bell, Richard Sommer, Louise Abbott, Réal Faucher, and Kathleen McHale also acquired year-round homes in the region.

The presence of these people attracted friends, colleagues, students, and protégés. Some of them—E. D. Blodgett, Michael Harris and Leonard Cohen, for example—were in the Townships for only a few months, but they shared in the literary production.[3] Ian Tait, Maria van Sundert, and Rod Willmot, graduates of the Université de Sherbrooke Comparative Canadian Literature program, remained in the region and began to write poetry during the period under discussion.

The first bilingual poetry reading in North Hatley took place in the large living room of local potter Mildred Beaudin, on August 8, 1968. It was organized by the recently-arrived Sheila Fischman and by Douglas Jones. The participants were A. J. M. Smith, Frank Scott, Douglas Jones, John Glassco, Roland Giguère, Pauline Julien, and Gérald Godin, all of whom were either living or summering in the Eastern Townships. The master of ceremonies was the fluently bilingual Ron Sutherland. According to some witnesses it turned into a rowdy, drunken carouse. Julien rattled Smith by interrupting him with taunts of "en français." Sheila Fischman was visibly upset that her attempt to bring two groups together was being challenged in this manner.[4] It seems that poetry readings, especially drunken ones, are not without their risks, but there is a certain fascination in watching a famous constitutional lawyer, civil libertarian, and poet stroke the leg of an equally famous Quebec singer as she dances in a pink miniskirt on the dining room table.[5] In fact, the evening seems to have ended happily enough with a boisterous party in Ron Sutherland's basement.

We should also note, as Sheila Fischman suggests in her amusing account of this key bilingual poetry reading, that, in the late 1960s, Anglophone intellectuals—imbued with the vision being set forth in the Laurendeau-Dunton Royal Commission on Bilingualism and Biculturalism—were looking for ways to build bridges between Francophones and Anglophones.[6] Frank Scott was well known for his experiments in arranging meetings between French and English Montreal intellectuals and writers.[7] It is understandable that the attempts to overcome political and linguistic differences would be continued in the Townships a few years later, after the passions of the October Crisis of 1970 had somewhat cooled.

The revival of local poetry readings occurred in the autumn of 1975 when a CBC-TV producer approached Université de Sherbrooke professor Avrum Malus. The producer wished to film the local literati in an informal setting. Malus consulted with his colleague, Douglas Jones, and together they came up with the idea of a poetry reading. The two spouses, Monique Martin and Monique Baril-Jones were enthusiastic, and so 7th Moon was born. It was not pure chance. Consider who the organizers were: Douglas Jones, an English-Canadian from Bancroft, Ontario; Monique Baril, a Francophone from Temiskaming; Avrum Malus from Montreal's Jewish community; and Monique Martin, a Francophone from Gaspésie. The women were fluently bilingual; the men only gradually learned to communicate in the language of their spouses. Three of them—Jones, Malus, and Baril—worked in language and literature at the Université de Sherbrooke, while Martin taught Psychology at nearby Champlain College. The 7th Moon readings were a natural outlet for their talents and interests, an extension of their professional lives and their close friendship.

The first reading was an extravaganza featuring six male poets—Robert Allen, Réal Faucher, Ralph Gustafson, Michael Harris, Avrum Malus, and Michael Oliver, together with one woman, Claudia Lapp, from Montreal. Scott had been invited to participate, but he was forced to cancel because of serious illness. Thus, in its early years, 7th Moon was a poetry fest—resolutely English, mainly male, and featuring local writers, though Ralph Gustafson was the only native Townshipper. The audience was largely composed of friends and family of the poets, teachers from the Université de Sherbrooke, Champlain College, and Bishop's University, their students, and a scattering of local artists. This was always the nucleus of the audience, but on that first night the glamour of the TV cameras raised the total to around 150—as reported in *Matrix* magazine.[8] These first participants were not paid for their services.

The annual readings soon became a local tradition. In the fall, the four organizers would meet over dinner to decide on the program. To increase the interest and novelty they tried to bring in new people every year. In 1978, organizers Philip Lanthier and Jan Draper (substituting for the usual foursome) heightened the excitement by inviting three Montreal poets to

197

participate. Variety was maintained over the next two years by juxtaposing local people with outsiders who were either visiting or living temporarily in the Townships.

The turning point came in 1981 when the original organizers invited four local Québécois poets to join in. It was a particularly tense reading as the organizers struggled to cope with a last-minute cancellation, a reader who went on for too long, and the need to give equal time to French and English introductions—all in an effort to maintain the interest of a mixed audience, not all of whom were bilingual.

Thus Frank Scott's vision of bringing Anglophone and Francophone writers together reasserted itself. The following 7th Moon readings all upheld the principle of bilingualism. The number of participants diminished, however, as the organizers found it increasingly burdensome to collect the funds necessary to cover the expenses of the often high-priced outside readers, together with all the other costs involved in mounting a ticklish enterprise. The readings were funded by the Canada Council, the Union des écrivaines et écrivains, the Université de Sherbrooke, Bishop's University, Champlain College, and local merchants. More than once, the organizers took money from their own pockets to defray the expenses. On two occasions between 1975 and 1990 there were no readings.

The annual 7th Moon readings were always at the end of October or beginning of November. However, Ken McLean at Bishop's University, together with a group of devoted faculty associated with *Matrix* and the *Moosehead Review* at Champlain College in Lennoxville, organized literary readings for students about four times a year and over a longer time period. These readings were mainly intended to interest students in the prose, poetry, and, sometimes, the plays of Canadian writers. Students were more than just encouraged to attend; usually the college teachers tied the readings to written assignments.

In addition, the editors of *Matrix* and the *Moosehead Review* used the occasion to solicit contributions for their journals. Usually these institutional readings were funded by the Canada Council. Some of the expenses, particularly if they involved local people, were covered by Champlain College. Occasionally, when a reader from outside the region was involved, Ken McLean used the Speakers' Fund of Bishop's University to pay the honoraria, travel, and accommodation costs.

The literary journals established in the Townships during this twenty-five-year period between 1963 and 1988 customarily mixed local authors with outside writers. The earliest, *Ellipse*, was founded in 1969 by Sheila Fischman, Douglas Jones, Joseph Bonenfant, and Richard Giguère of the Université de Sherbrooke as a translation journal. *Matrix* was founded in 1975 by Champlain instructors Philip Lanthier, Michael Oliver, Nigel Spencer, and Debby Seed to encourage new Canadian writing, but after 1981, *Matrix* began to specialize in Anglo-Quebec literature, which has remained a principal orientation ever since. The *Moosehead Review* was founded in 1977 by Champlain faculty—Robert Allen, Stephen Luxton and Jan Draper.

Thus a literary community developed in a small area of the Eastern Townships. As a result, the poets and writers came to know each other personally and were motivated to become the principal organizers and participants.

In summary, we can list the following achievements in the twenty-five year period: the production of a substantial body of literary work—publication of several novels, a scattering of stories, a number of important critical articles and books, voluminous translations, and reams of poetry—bringing acclaim and at times national attention to local writers. We have, moreover, the founding of four literary journals—*Ellipse, Matrix, Moosehead Review,* and *Samisdat*;[9] the establishment of two publishing houses—Burnt Lake Press by Rod Willmot from 1984 to 1990 and Pigwidgeon Press by John Mahoney in 1985; the creation of an audience—largely students, friends, colleagues, artists, but also including the general public; the organization of a program in Comparative Canadian Literature as well as translation courses at the Université de Sherbrooke; and the introduction of courses on translation and on Quebec writers at Champlain College and Bishop's University. Five films dealing with Townships life—*Mon Oncle Antoine* (1971), *The Pinnacle and the Poet* (1995), *F. R. Scott: Rhyme and Reason* (1983), *Winter Prophecies: The Poetry of Ralph Gustafson* (1989), and *The Eastern Townships, Quebec* (1993)—were fully or partly shot in this region. Four literary conferences were held. This area enjoyed an unparalleled number of readings by local and visiting writers, the promotion of English literary culture in the Townships, the promotion of Quebec English Literature in Canada, and the popularizing of that culture in the media.

However, the bloom on the literary flowering began to fade during the 1980s. Festival Lennoxville, the annual celebration of Canadian plays at Bishop's University, collapsed in 1982. The next year, the *Moosehead Review* left the Townships to be reconstituted in Montreal. In 1988, the editorial board of *Matrix* decided to transfer the journal to a collective based at John Abbott College in Montreal. The last of the annual 7th Moon readings took place in North Hatley on November 9, 1990. When Avrum Malus was diagnosed with an inoperable brain tumour, the other organizers lost their will to continue the annual tradition. The final 7th Moon reading occurred on November 4, 1995, in memory of Avrum Malus. Several of the former participants took part, and Avrum's son, Jacob, read from the work of his father. The spirit of 7th Moon has not entirely disappeared, but there is a tacit agreement not to use the name without the permission of the surviving organizers. Since then, Townships literary production has slowly declined because, as the writers have died, retired, or resigned from their teaching jobs, they have not, for the most part, been replaced.

There is no single factor that explains the literary plenitude of 1963 to 1988. It is the result of a propitious combination of people, institutions, and social circumstances, concentrated in a particular place. Today, the phenomenon appears to have exhausted itself. As Douglas Jones observes:

> What gets written, and the fact anything gets written at all, depends on the concatenation of individual, regional, and more large-scale events and conditions. The fact that various older writers had summer residences in the Townships, that several universities and colleges employed younger writers, that Quebec generally was engaged in a major change in the whole of the society, spearheaded in many ways by writers, especially poets and *chansonniers*, made the area and the province in the sixties and the early seventies an exciting place, even if one was not a "political" writer.[10]

Since these conditions do not exist today in the Townships, we no longer have the presence of a community of writers. It seems unlikely that this region will ever again be a major centre of literary production. Yet Douglas Jones continues to write poetry, Ron Sutherland produced a new novel in 2003, and the "Thirty-eight Sonnets from Jimmie Walker Swamp" that appear in Robert Allen's *Standing Wave* (Véhicule, 2005) are largely inspired by the environment of his Ayer's Cliff cabin.[11] A local literary magazine, *Flood Quarterly*, made a temporary appearance from 1999 to 2001; in 1999, two collections of Townships writing—*Taproot* and the *Anthology of 20th Century*

Poetry of the Eastern Townships—were launched. *Taproot* and *Black Cat Tales*, anthologies of Townships writing, appear annually. A new publishing house, Topeda Hill, based in Baldwin's Mill, was founded in 1993. Under the direction of Daniel Lewis, it published poetry collections by Université de Sherbrooke graduates Peter Harris and Maria Van Sundert; in 2002, it presented a collection of short stories by Gregory Reid. These developments suggest that a less spectacular, more indigenous literary production could continue in the Townships, but this literature no longer generates the interest and excitement it did in the past.

IV. Poets and Places

Creation, Re-Creation, Recreation: D. G. Jones and the Art of Translation

PHILIP LANTHIER

> "Without translation we would inhabit parishes bordering on silence."
> —George Steiner[1]

> "Basically, French and English are the same language."
> —D. G. Jones[1]

George Steiner has expressed the fear that "immersion in translation, the voyage out and back, can leave the translator unhoused," at home in neither his native tongue nor that mastered for translation.[3] So intimate is the task, so intricate and nuanced the grammatical and lexical operations that it would not be surprising to find translators wandering in a no-man's land between two linguistic encampments both equally enticing. Perhaps this is not entirely to be feared; it is becoming, in fact, the state of so many people, translators or not, who voluntarily or in desperation move from one part of the world to another, one language to another, and find themselves, for a period, in cultural transit and not necessarily the worse for it. Steiner's concern notwithstanding, there is a certain productive friction in living on the interface between two cultures even when one has not been displaced physically. There is, as most Anglo-Quebecers know, a strange kind of interlingual dance, often clumsy, sometimes amusing, which occurs on a daily basis. The translation of poetry—language in its extreme mode— is another matter. The impossibilities of finding poetic equivalencies are universally acknowledged and made painfully obvious when translation and original are presented on facing pages. There are the two houses occupying closely adjoining lots: home and a reconstruction using very different materials: home and not quite home. The experience may at times be quite uncanny, a word which translates the German *unheimlich*: not home.

D. G. Jones is not unhoused. He is one of the few Canadian poets who is able to move easily between the two official languages without any apparent feelings of dislocation. Not only has he undertaken the translations of a host of Quebec poets over the last thirty years, he has also imported French into many of his own poems and even composed a number of poems entirely in French. There is a sense, when reading both his poems and translations, that one is an extension of the other, that on occasion he has been able to create a hybrid form which brings the two languages and perceptions into the same neighbourhood. Taking a closer look at the creative interplay between French and English in his work shows an aspect of Jones which is often passed over. His poems are not always easily understandable; the presence of French in some of them may discourage certain readers. But taking the time to read on both linguistic frequencies will reward readers sufficiently acquainted with French to recognize how the languages illuminate each other, and more important, how imagining in two languages can enrich the experience of reading.

Jones's introduction to French poetry came when he was asked to teach a graduate course in the subject at the Université de Sherbrooke in the 1960s. It proved to be a rapid immersion in the language and provided him with the background needed to create, together with Sheila Fischman, Joseph Bonenfant and Richard Giguère, the first issue of *Ellipse* at the end of 1969. Four issues were published in the second year, three in the third, then one or two issues in subsequent years for a total of 66 before it was handed over to Jo-Ann Elder for publication out of Fredericton where it continues to flourish. It was, as a subsequent editor remarked, a pretty "haphazard and amateur" affair, guided by no particular theory, or at least none that was declared openly.[4] Perhaps the absence of "professional" constraints encouraged the many translators, some of them students, who set out on what is an often laborious task. Besides Philip Stratford and John Glassco, who provided a paternal and legitimizing presence in early issues, the journal attracted such French-to-English translators as Daniel Sloate, Judith Cowan, Kathy Mezie, Robert McGee, Sheila Fischman, and Fred Cogswell. The key editorial decision, from which there were occasional deviations over the years, was to present English and French poets in tandem each issue, original and translation appearing on facing pages. Thus, Michèle Lalonde and Margaret Atwood, Roland Giguère and Leonard Cohen, Paul-Marie Lapointe and Irving Layton, Michel Garneau and Al Purdy, Paul Chamberland and Allen Ginsberg, Rina Lasnier and Margaret Avison, Pierre Nepveu and Dionne Brand. There were also special issues devoted to love poetry, concrete poetry, Latino-Canadian poetry, and to poets of the Maritimes, the Eastern Townships, and Montreal. There was also an issue, edited by Colin Browne, presenting the results of a complicated exercise in which eight original poems, four in French and four in English, were translated into the opposite language, then translated back into the original from the translation until each poem had been passed from one language to another eight times. "I wanted to see what would persist," wrote Browne, and, surprisingly, four of the poems remained "curiously intact" while four others disappeared altogether.[5]

As one of the editors of *Ellipse* for much of its history, and certainly one of its guiding spirits throughout, Jones had ample opportunity to develop his creative touch as a translator of poets as diverse as Gaston Miron, Michel Garneau, Gérald Godin, Nicole Brossard, Gaétan Dostie, Michèle Lalonde, Paul-Marie Lapointe, Suzanne Jacob, and Serge Patrice Thibodeau. He also published in book form translations of Paul-Marie Lapointe, Gaston Miron, Émile Martel, and Normand de Bellefeuille. More recently he co-edited, with Louise Blouin and Bernard Pozier, a selection of late twentieth-century poetry from Quebec entitled *Esprit de Corps* in which he also appears as translator of poets such as Roger des Roches, Louis Jacob, Renaud Longchamps, Élise Turcotte, and the late Marie Uguay.[6] This amounts to an impressive output during a time when language issues dominated the political and social landscape in Quebec, when the act of translation into English could, in the eyes of the militant, be considered a form of capitulation to a dominant and repressive tongue. This, combined with what is usually considered a treasonous activity, and the anxieties of doing it no matter what the external circumstances might be, makes Jones' achievement all the more important.

Colin Browne, in commenting on the results of his experiment in translation, observed that there is "an air of madness" in changing word and idiom from source to target language while trying to ensure that the essence of the original remains the same. This is a contradiction, he says, which must not be overcome, but celebrated.[7] In a similar vein, Jones, in an earlier *Ellipse*, stated that though every act of translation may have a "touch of treason, it is equally true that we delight in sharing our most intimate secrets, that we must speak and be heard, listen and translate, or go mad."[8] Is translation, then, an act of madness to keep madness at bay? There is indeed a kind of heroic nuttiness in undertaking the translation of a poem, a form so thoroughly charged with implication, connotation, ironies and the complex and subtle use of diction, syntax and sound. In Quebec, the usual challenges of translation have been made more acute by the dramatic emergence from *le grand noirceur* of a whole culture. In the eyes of many this at first quiet then somewhat more vociferous revolution, accompanied by language laws, referendums and bombs, has indeed added a dimension of madness.

Born towards the end of the Quiet Revolution and one year before the October Crisis of 1970, the first issue of *Ellipse* declared its intention to narrow the gap between the two chief literatures of Canada, to provide "un vrai lieu d'échanges réciproques et un mobile circuit de communication."[9] A poem by Eugène Guillevic gave the journal its title and a logo, an ellipse being an oval figure which, in the original text and in Teo Savery's translation, has trouble keeping its equilibrium:

Tiraillé que tu es	**Pulled as your are**
Sur ton parcours entier	Throughout your whole course
Entre deux centres qui s'ignorent	Between two centres
Où qui s'en veulent	That don't know each other
	Or are fed up with each other.[10]

The dimensions of that ignorance and the degree to which the balance, such as it was (and is) could be maintained, were put to the test within a year by the events of October 1970 when a cell of the Front de Libération du Québec (FLQ) kidnapped James Cross, British High Commissioner in Montreal, and a second cell subsequently kidnapped and murdered Pierre Laporte, Quebec Minister of Labour. The FLQ had begun planting bombs in Montreal during the 1960s, and by the fall of 1970 their activities had claimed six lives. When Prime Minister Pierre Trudeau declared the War Measures Act on October 16, suspending civil liberties, police throughout Quebec rounded up nearly five hundred people suspected of having links to or sympathies with the FLQ and its call for the separation of Quebec from Canada by violent means. Among those incarcerated were members of the Quebec literary and cultural communities. Laporte's body was discovered in the trunk of car on the day following the invocation of the Act. Cross was released in December when police located the house where he was being held in Montreal, and his captors were given safe passage to Cuba.

But even before these events rendered the language gap more perilous and its bridging more urgent, Michèle Lalonde had expressed some of the anger which simmered throughout the Quiet Revolution. Her poem "Speak White" was translated by Jones in *Ellipse* 3 in the spring before the October crisis and for her the battleground was language:

> oui quelle admirable langue
> pour embaucher
> donner des ordres
> fixer l'heure de la mort à l'ouvrage

> yes, what a marvellous language
> for hiring and firing
> for giving orders
> for fixing the hour to be worked to death[11]

Jones has remarked that of all the poems he has translated this is the one most often solicited for copyright.[12] And indeed the poem remains relevant in the context of late twentieth-century globalization. Lalonde does not restrict her target to the English imposed on a workforce in Quebec. "White" may be Russian, it may be French, or it may be any language which is the instrument of repression and control:

> parlez un allemand impeccable
> une étoile jaune entre les dents
> parlez russe parlez rappel à l'ordre
>   parlez répression
> speak white
> c'est une langue universelle
> nous somme nés pour la comprendre

speak impeccable German
a yellow star between your teeth
speak Russian speak of the right
   to rule
            speak of repression
speak white
it's a universal language
we were born to understand it[13]

When, in the same issue, Jones asked Lalonde in an interview whether there could be a meaningful interaction between poets in Quebec and poets throughout the English-speaking world, her answer was one of qualified optimism:

> Offhand I would say certainly if only because we share the same continent. But our relationship to the English-speaking cultural "world" has been an unnatural one, forced upon us or distorted in many ways. Once our situation as a distinct cultural entity has been normalized, I feel sure we will discover it with greater objectivity and profit.[14]

Laws are one way of achieving normalcy. The creation of the Office de la langue française in 1960 was followed by a series of controversial laws intended to promote the French language in Quebec: Bill 63 in 1969, Bill 22 in 1974, and Bill 101 in 1977, all of which were founded on the principle of collective rights. As French gained ground in the workplace, the task of translation became increasingly a matter of practical necessity, but since the Quiet Revolution was partly driven by the passions of its singers, poets, novelists and essayists, literary translation in the eyes of its practitioners became a cultural obligation which did not need language laws to enforce it. *Ellipse* seldom referred to the political events which so dominated Quebec in the last decades of the twentieth century. "Politics," Colin Browne would later write when summarizing his experiment in translation, "has never once entered into our relationship; our interest in language has seemed to bind us together."[15] However, when the October Crisis broke and when a number of prominent cultural and political figures were detained, the language issue was suddenly made more dramatic and perilous by virtue of questions of censorship and violence. *Ellipse* reacted: "Un règne nouveau de la parole arrive" announced the unsigned "Avant-propos."[16] Before October, symbols were in search of reality; now, after October, reality has gone beyond symbol: "toute parole s'amplifie au point de retentir dans toutes les consciences, celles des vivants et celle de tous les morts de notre histoire."[17] "For words, not bullets, the whole arsenal of language is required to articulate a distinctive vision of life," said the also unsigned English editorial.[18]

Published six months after the Crisis and entitled simply "October," *Ellipse* 6 contained poems (originals and translations) by Yves Préfontaine, Michel Garneau, Nicole Brossard, Gaétan Dostie, and Paul Chamberland as well as a long poem by Raoul Duguay signed Raoul Luoar Yaugud Duguay. These poems, together with English work by Eli Mandel, Al Purdy, Joe Rosenblatt and David Helwig, struck a variety of positions regarding the imposition of the War Measures Act: anger, sadness, heavy irony, direct mockery, defiance, even hope. Duguay entered the fray with a mock Peace Measures Act replete with the rhetoric and typography of a manifesto: "LE PAROLE EST LE PAIN QUOTIDIEN DE L'HOMME. RAPATRIONS LA PAROLE .... Que l'Arme Suprême soit La Parole d'Amour."[19] "THE WORD IS MAN'S DAILY BREAD. LET US REPATRIATE THE WORD...Let the Ultimate Weapon be The Word of Love," translated Sheila Fischman.[20]

Michel Garneau, also tongue in cheek, called for a flood of maple syrup:

> quand notre pays sera pays et nos amours libres toujours
> quand cette câlice de prison sera poulailler modèle
> quand les vendus vendeurs travailleront pour les enfants
> quand il n'y aura plus de fripouille à occire
> quand nous n'aurons plus qu'à nous aimer
> en inondant le monde de sirop d'érable.[21]

Translated, by Ronald Sutherland, as:

> when our nation is a nation and our loves always free,
> when this goddamned prison is a model henhouse,
> when the salesman sell-outs are working for children,
> when there are no more rogues to get rid of,
> when we've no more to do than to love one another
> while flooding the world with maple syrup.[22]

However, the politicization of poetry, even when qualified with humour, worried Jones and probably the other editors of *Ellipse* as well. In an untranslated article entitled "La vraie révolution est celle de l'imagination"[23] which concluded *Ellipse* 6, Jones warned that recent Quebec poetry was tied too closely to political events, that although the liberation of Quebec had much to do with the liberation of its language, there was also a sense that "si rien ne bouge dans le domaine politique, rien ne bouge dans le domaine poétique."[24] A poetry based on continual "annunciation" becomes merely repetitive and stagnant, he argued.[25] Having destroyed the old structures, Quebec poetry needs to create new ones based on the human body as the unit of measure: "la découverte par le poète, de sa terre Québec est strictement et fondamentalement la découverte de son propre corps."[26] Jones finds this occurring already in the work of Chamberland, Duguay, Péloquin and Charlebois.

Jones seems to have found a voice to describe a new wind in the sails of the imagination in the work of intellectual guru Norman O. Brown whose *Life Against Death: The Psychoanalytical Meaning of History*, drawing heavily upon Freud, reminded its readers that man is a desiring (not thinking) animal, that art helps us overcome inhibitions, that language itself is a form of erotic play, and that we should seek the release of the body from repression into the polymorphous perverse, a state of Dionysiac consciousness which no longer negates and is no longer enslaved to the death instinct.[27] Jones endorses Brown's celebration of the imagination as a means of encompassing not only the liberated body but humankind as conceived in the image of the universe. This allegiance to a wider consciousness founded on a revaluation of the body not as something to be denied as the *corps d'amour* has remained a preoccupation of Jones throughout his career. In his introduction to the 1997 anthology of translations, *Esprit de Corps,* he suggests that the title might be rendered literally as bodily spirit or, with a small change to the preposition (esprit *du* corps) as the "spirit or consciousness of the body."[28] What links the poets in this collection, which includes writers from Anne Hébert to the present, is this body consciousness and the anxieties of desire and death now "confronted without the consolation of some conventional large faith or collective identity."[29] Quebec poetry, he says, has now joined the secular and fragmented society in which all North Americans live and where solidarity is with "ordinary living, and mortal, creatures."[30] The implication is clear: the individual body, with its

211

desires and decay, remains the site of poetry; the collective "body" is, however, less Québécois and more continental and international.

This evolution began back in the '60s and '70s when Quebec poets sought liberation from the confines of the Catholic Church and a closed culture by turning increasingly to the counter culture, particularly as voiced by such American poets Allen Ginsberg and Gregory Corso whose exuberant, angry, satiric lines in a free-wheeling, demotic idiom struck a responsive chord in the work of Garneau, Duguay, and Yves Préfontaine. Jones summed up Quebec poetry at the end of the 1950s in his introduction to *Butterfly on Rock* by remarking that it was "haunted by the sterility of an overly ascetic order resulting from a complete withdrawal from life."[31] The worlds which poets such as Nelligan, Grandbois, and Saint-Denys Garneau create, he went on to write, "may be a world of the past, either a collective past of the *ancien régime* or an individual past, the world of childhood. It may be a world of memory or of dream, of the religious or of the artistic vision, but it tends in any case to become an ever more enclosed and barren ideal."[32] More important now, in Jones's view, is the realization that the revolution of the imagination embraces all of North America, a nudge not only towards the larger world community of poetry, but also towards translation, which is one of the bridges to that wider world.

In 1977, Jones addressed the question of translation directly in an article entitled "Grounds for Translation" in which he acknowledges that although poetry, of all forms of utterance, resists translation, the world of civilized discourse demands translation.[33] We translate Quebec poetry "because, in a sense, we have been asked to. It is an immediate response to the cry to be heard, to be recognized, to be given existence in the eyes of others."[34] More fundamentally, Jones, recalling again Norman O. Brown, sees translation as analogous to sexual intercourse: "It may be an expense of spirit in a waste of shame, or it may be a kind of death and resurrection into a new and larger life":

> To write poems, to translate poems, is to engage ourselves in the kind of intercourse that is the essence of civilization—that is the bread and wine of our existence. I have said we translate so that we may exist, so that our particular identity may be recognized and reinforced in each other's eyes. But finally we do so so that we may cease to exist, so that we may say with the lovers in Jacques Brault's poem:

> You no longer exist I no longer exist we are
> We arrive together we are renewed [35]

The intimate, prolonged and intense engagement of translator with text is, for Jones, analogous to a love affair and to the sexual act itself. Translator Colin Browne, guest editor of *Ellipse* 29/30, proposes the term "transpiration" as way of describing what happens when the spirit or essence of an original is rendered from one textual context into another, a process which may involve a change of idiom, even a change of genre (for example, translating the *Odyssey* not as a poem but as a novel).[36] That a successful translation, "a transpiration", must be a successful poem, is a thought echoed at various times by both Jones and Fred Cogswell.

Both Browne and Jones claim a considerable degree of freedom for the poet-translator. Browne writes that "true fidelity lies in piercing through the surface into the universal source of the source text itself; Pound…had to become Ulysses in order to get his epic journey underway."[37] He also refers to Gabriel García Márquez, who found *One Hundred Years of Solitude* completely recreated in English by the intuitive genius of translator Gregory Rabassa. Jones goes further than Browne, however, in claiming a freedom to "play with what is given, to reverse what is given, to transform and recreate."[38] The poet/translator has the right to mistranslate. He cites Gladys Downes who, in translating André Major's love poem "Quel feuillage," titles it "Words" then, as Jones goes on to note, "takes the first verse, which in the original reads:

> ce que l'on dit enlacés
> saigne comme une mémoire
> et nous tient effarés dans un rêve trop beau

and she translates it as:

> When we lie together as leaves enfolded
> our words are sharply beautiful
> and hold us, shaken,
> in an amazing dream

She then takes the first line and, publishing a volume of translations and her own poems, entitles it *When We Lie Together*. Here in a nutshell lies the essential process and the raison d'être of both poem and translation.[39]

Clearly, this translation takes liberties: the title substitutes "words" for *feuillage* (leaves or foliage), turns *saigne* (bleeds) into "sharply" and *enlacés* into "enfolded," drops the idea of *mémoire*, and then takes *effarés* (alarmed) and divides it into "shaken" and "amazing." Finally, three lines are extended to four for rhythmical and rhetorical effect.

In his foreword to the fiftieth issue of *Ellipse*, published in 1993, Jones summarized the range of the translator's options, from word-by-word crib through to a "new text that assumes the freedom to improvise on what has been given in the source text," even to homophonic translations that "pay no attention to sense, only to sound."[40] *Ellipse* translators, he indicates, have attempted to stay fairly close to the source text. Marc Plourde, in his comment on translating Gaston Miron, has written that "any originality that appears in his (the translator's) work must seem to be an expression of the author's personality and talent, not his own,"[41] and Judith Cowan warns that the translation of a poem "should not be the writing of a completely different poem; it is the transformation of a poem as gracefully, as respectfully as possible from one language to another, and if the original is an honest and well-made poem then the translation has a better chance of being either graceful or respectful, or both."[42] Yet the genuine translation, as Steiner has remarked, discovers that the source text had "potentialities, elemental reserves as yet unrealized by itself."[43] There is always the impulse to re-create anew. "Every text," wrote Jones "is a pretext for another text."[44] This will often mean pulling some surprising English out of the French, and extending the phrasing of the original so that the English expresses what was implied or unsaid.

Gaston Miron was one of the first Quebec poets who Jones undertook to translate. On October 23, 1970, with Miron in jail because of the round-up under the *War Measures Act*, Jones gave a colloquium in French and English at the Université de Montréal in which he spoke of Miron's project of spiritual, psychological and mythological demolition. Like other Quebec poets, said Jones, Miron has recognized that he has an obligation "to free man from the prison of the unconsciousness, and from the possible prison of his own image of himself…. He has broken the mirrors. He has burned down the chateaux. He has placed a bomb in the brain to blow up the former structure of his sensibility."[45] The headlong intensity of Miron's passions find expression in an English which echoes Ginsberg's rhetorical energy.

Here is the concluding passage from "La marche à l'amour":

je marche à toi
je titube à toi
je meurs de toi jusqu'à la complète anémie
lentement je m'affale tout au long de ma hampe
je marche à toi, je titube à toi, je bois
à la gourde vide de sens de la vie
à ces pas semés dans les rues sans nord ni sud
à ces taloches de vent sans queue et sans tête
je n'ai plus de visage pour l'amour
je n'ai plus de visage pur rien de rien
parfois je m'assois par pitié de moi
j'ouvre mes bras à la croix des sommeils
mon corps est un dernier réseau de tics amoureux
avec à mes doigts les ficelles des souvenirs perdus
je m'attends pas à demain je t'attends
je n'attend pas à la fin du monde je t'attends
dégagé de la fausse auréole de ma vie

Jones translates these lines as:

I stride to you
reel to you
die for you even to the point of complete inanition
slowly I sink the whole length of my shaft
I stride to you, reel to you, drink
from the gourd empty of meaning
with these steps sown in the street without north or south
with these cuffs of the window without heads or tails
I have no more face for love
I have no more face for anything at all
sometimes I sit down out of kindness to myself
I open my arms to the cross of sleep
my body the last network of amorous tics

at my fingers threads of fond memories lost
I no longer wait for the end of the world, I wait for you
detached from the false halo of my life[46]

What Jones found in Miron's poetry of that time was a muscular, North American voice which challenged existing social, political and linguistic structures. "Mon Québec," is also "Compagnon des Amériques." Drawn as were so many Anglophone poets and intellectuals to the stirrings of Quebec nationalism, Jones is also interested in placing Miron in a larger context. In his short address to the 1970 colloquium at the Université de Montréal, Jones, citing Marshall McLuhan, welcomed Quebec writers into a global company of poets engaged in the "discovery of a new horizon, of new ways of perceiving the world."[47] "La marche à l'amour" fuses the impulse to love with the impulse to identify the act with the land of Quebec: "je roule en toi / tous les saguenays d'eau noire de ma vie" / "in you I roll / my Saguenays, all the black waters of my life."[48] It also celebrates the world altering powers of love:

tu seras heureuse fille heureuse
d'être la femme que tu es dans mes bras
le monde entier sera changé en toi et moi

you will rejoice my girl you will rejoice
to be the woman that you are in my arms
the world in us will be transformed[49]

In translating Miron, Jones was exploring the passionate and at times ecstatic new voice of Quebec poetry and bringing it vividly to the attention of English readers. Together with Marc Plourde, who translated other poems from *L' homme rapaillé* which are also included in *Embers and Earth,* Jones may not have found a poet whose verse resonated with his own technically, since Miron's lines—headlong, intense, unpunctuated, repetitive—are quite different from the shorter, more allusive and ironic lines which have characterized Jones's poetry from very early in his career. He did, however, respond to Miron's success in transforming the everyday language of Quebec into a powerful new means of expression. Plourde, in his cogent and helpful commentary "On Translating Miron," which concludes *Embers and Earth,* wrote that the challenge lay in the difficulty of finding English equivalents not only of Miron's extreme and changeable emotions but also of enacting his colloquial energy, his word-play and his musicality in English, without becoming too "general and abstract," the unique qualities of the verse disappearing into the "bland and conventional."[50] Both Jones and Plourde saw Miron's verse as a social act, the expression of the collective voice of previously inarticulate national aspirations. Miron, wrote Plourde, "turned the language of his people, *les Damned Canucks*, into poetry"[51]and Jones discovered a poet who, like other Canadian writers, had "found words for the obscure features of [his] own identity."[52]

In 1976, Jones published his translations of Paul-Marie Lapointe under the title *The Terror of the Snows: Selected Poems*. What he says about Lapointe's poems might well be applied to his own. He admires the "extreme speed and concision" of "Courtes Pailles" and also how the poems in general resist the logical and the linear. In a striking analogy, he describes how a Lapointe poem "is a series of luminous tracks that betray the invisible electrons startled from their atomic sleep."[53] The poem "Scene" provides a good example, says Jones, of how the "elliptical movement" of a Lapointe poem achieves its "mysterious coherence."[54] In translation, it looks and sounds not unlike a Jones poem:

heurté
le fourreau déploie ses lames

dans la biche la féminine
s'animent les sept langues de l'hydre

l'eau bouge
rapide effeuillaison du soleil

oubli double

au pied de l'étang
seul
un saule retient le vent

struck
the sheath unfolds its blades

in the doe the feminine
quickening the Hydra's seven tongues

the water stirs
rapid exfoliation of the sun

double oblivion

at the bottom of the pond
alone
a willow still holds the wind[55]

Here, for comparison, are the opening lines of "17/12/75" from Jones's original collection of poems, *Under the Thunder the Flowers Light up the Earth*:

Again
concretions of the snow-
filled air

the grey
fishers of the solstice
gulls

sweeping the sky
sweeping in silence over
the bare
selvage of orchard
ghosts of the deluge[56]

Treating a poem as a perpendicular construction, a tenuous spinal column with imagistic vertebrae, is a characteristic Jones technique, making for an elliptical and laconic form of notation. Reading and translating Lapointe must have sharpened this tendency or at least provided a flash of recognition, a form of poetic communion. When we observe the translation process, we can see how Jones plays with line lengths and sense, as if he were participating in a joint creation. For example, he makes subtle decisions in expanding or contracting many of Lapointe's original lines. For instance, in the poem

"Scene," cited above, although the English can't match the play of sound between *seul* and *saule*, it does succeed in creating overtones with "still," as in "continues to" and "not moving." "Still" also re-positions the multiple possibilities of *retient*: restrain, hold back, hold in position, withhold, etc. Similarly in his translation of Lapointe's "ICBM," Jones adds a strong verb, *flung*, where none exists in the original:

> sur les passerelles de nylon
> entre les mondes
> vacillent les tendres haunches des filles[57]

> on nylon catwalks flung
> between worlds
> sway the delicate haunches of girls[58]

A significantly different sort of challenge comes when Jones confronts a text in which the sentence and the paragraph are the controlling mechanism of the original. His translation of Normand de Bellefeuille's 1986 volume *Catégoriques un deux et trois* won him the Governor General's Award for Translation in 1993 and was followed in 1996 by a translation of *Pour orchestre et poète seul* by Émile Martel who had won the GG for poetry in French the previous year.[59] Both writers compose their works in prose "stanzas" or paragraphs with justified margins and in sequences which combine meditation and metaphor. Both works enact self-consciously their own process of creation, the verbal acts which lead them to paradox, enigma and discovery.

Bellefeuille's volume is by far the more challenging and complex of the two. In his afterword to *Categorics one, two & three,* Jones characterizes Bellefeuille's writing as occupying a "floating world of signs, of discourse, within which we live; it helps to generate the poem, at the edges of discourse; and yet it works to integrate in its net the immediate moments in an actual romance, moments of childhood, moments of everyday experience that may be both banal and poignant."[60] Hovering on the edges of sense, or at its beginning (hence the "one, two and three," as if counting up to the opening notes of a musical piece), elusive and surprising, Bellefeuille's sentences set the reader afloat through a verbal universe composing itself in sentences which are paradoxically categorical and lyrical. In such a discourse world, the dance is a dance of unpredictability, of delayed action:

La danse que j'imagine n'est ni du chiffre ni du sens, ni de dieu de foi de fils ou de mort heureuse ; plutôt tout à coup du quizz et de inimaginable écart ; car la danse que j'imagine bien sûr ne répond pas, car la danse que j'imagine n'est pas une science de la réponse.[61]

The dance I imagine is not a matter of numbers and codes, related to god or faith or the son or a happy death ; rather to the quick quiz and the unforeseeable swerve; for the dance I imagine certainly does not take steps to respond, for the dance I imagine is not a science of response.[62]

Je suis de ce retardement, de cette métaphore brisante à chaque coup brisante et incertaine, brisante et ne retenant que le tremblé de toute proposition sur le réel, je suis de ce retardement, je suis de la contre-danse et de sa politique, je suis de la contre danse et voilà: ça se paie ![63]

I side with this delayed action, this breaking metaphor, breaking and unpredictable with each step, breaking and retaining only the tremor of any proposition about reality, I side with the counter-dance and its politics, I side with the counter-dance and there it is: you must pay the price![64]

So language itself, despite the inescapability of the sentence, is unsettled, nomadic, carries with it a "powerful beauty of its uncertainty"[65]:

Je parle seul, à quelques-uns, puisque malgré les enduits, les pâtes et les vernis, on n'échappe pas à la phrase; catégorique, elle rafle jusqu'au rite, jusque'au frisson, catégorique, elle installe ses cercles et ses pâles, des univers de phrases dans la cité: n'en doutez plus, elle est la véritable opacité, elle est **l'unité de désastre.**[66]

I speak alone, to a few, since, despite pigments, varnish, grouts, there's no escaping the sentence; categorical, it rifles everything, even the rituals, even the lovely **frissons,** categorical, it installs its inner circles, its privileged pales, cosmologies of sentences in the heart of the city: there is no doubt about it, it is opacity itself, it is the **very currency and compass of disaster.**[67]

Divided into three sections, "Time" (music), "Steps" (dance) and "Brushstrokes" (painting), the sequence enacts and undermines the rationality implied by the title word *Catégoriques* rendering as an adjectives what is in both languages conventionally a noun, both words rooted in the Greek word *kategoria* which means "statement". The three classifications of the poem, however, do not clarify or rank; they subvert and baffle; the perceptions emerge by degrees and by the deft repetitions and variations of phrases, memories, and allusions, in effect what lyric poetry does but in this case compressed into the syntax of the sentence and sounding, from time to time, in English, like Gertrude Stein. This is discourse which comes from odd angles, which constantly readjusts perceptions and understanding. The epigraphs which precede many of his excursions hint at oblique thought processes: from Cioran: "what's the point of writing to say exactly what one had to say?" And from Alain Borer: "the illegible bits mark the moments when, as the Japanese say, one detects the **ah!** of things."

This weaving and dodging in and around meaning parallels Jones's quick and elusive movement towards the *ah!* of things by way of allusions, quotations, images, observations, memories, and languages. Where Bellefeuille compacts his off-centre insights into prose, Jones aerates his with line and stanza lengths and typography. Consider, for example the concluding poem from *The Floating Garden*, published three years after *Categorics*:

trees and snow in the clarity
of outer space, as cold
but with the added blue

Matisse arranging cut-outs for
la Gare du Nord

or an ad for *La Métropolitaine*
(insert photo and copy
                    Myriam Bédard

époustouflée en Norvège, avec
son petit fusil et ses skis mal accordés
à mi-chemin de la course
du biathlon[68]

moving art or active
meditation

once, in such a decor, I recall
the dog getting snow in its paws and stopping
again and again, to lick them (the flaw
that authenticates memory

a different dog
be brief—we'll soon be into the flip side
of winter
                is this the splendour of Ionian
white and gold
uh-uh, this is explicable
let's just call it a retirement gift: a snow garden
sunlit, with its small birds

enjoy it, like a child[69]

This is not a matter of influence since much of Jones' signature poetic techniques are demonstrated in this poem: the terse line, short stanzas, quotation (in this case from Eliot's *The Waste Land*), the quick leap from Matisse to Myriam Bédard, two brackets which open but mysteriously do not close. Although the poem is clearly different in effect from *Categorics*, one can see how, in Jones, Bellefeuille found his ideal translator, someone capable of handling asymmetrical thought processes and enigmatic language.

When Jones turned to the work of Émile Martel a year later, he found yet another poet engaged in a performance of the act of the mind. *Pour orchestre et poète seule*, a sequence of lyric paragraphs which ritually and at times comically assembles the components of orchestral performance in a celebration of the power of music to help us cast off from our moorings and "leap clear over the long stretch between the before-life and the afterlife."[70] The solo poet, somewhat in the manner of an elaborate karaoke performance, verbalizes the site, instruments, musicians and director, and the experience of creation itself. As the sequence draws to its conclusion, he is the director gesturing the music into existence:

> Ma paume s'est creusée, mes doigts son fortement, presque douloureusement collés ensemble. Vient un lieu dans la géographie de l'univers où ma main touche le zénith et tous les appels sont faits à la mélodie du temps, et chaque musicien sent que ses doigts ou ses cordes vocales, son souffle ou ses mains s'appliquent à démarrer aussi, ont trouvé le nom de l'île, ont identifié la couleur du désir et, dans un simple assentiment, tous, moi autant qu'eux – et je sais que je suis l'habitant de leur volonté comme ils sont les peuples de mes continents—nous fermons les yeux.[71]

> My palm is cupped, my fingers are tightly, almost painfully, fused. There comes a point in the geography of the universe where my hand touches the zenith and every appeal goes out to the melody of time, and each musician feels that fingers and vocal cords, breathing and hands are ready to cast off, that they have found the name of the island, have identified the colour of desire and, in a single accord, everyone, myself as the others—and I know I am a creature of their will even as they are the populace of my continents—we close our eyes.[72]

This is a concert for the end of the millennium, a "magical" music which, as the finale says, sends its cry into the silence in an attempt to free us from the various hells of living and "finally, finally, to exercise a certain control over simple ecstasy."[73] Jones, incidentally, adds a curious touch in his translation of the poem's final word *l'ivresse*; by inserting the qualifier "simple" that suggests an ordinariness which is not quite there in the French but which is an essential element in one of his own end-of-millennium poems.

In the same year that Martel published *Pour orchestre*, Jones published *The Floating Garden* which included a single prose poem, "Fin de Siècle Springtime Ramble." This too is an end-of-millennium meditation, but the music is much different. Martel marshals the elements of a symphony orchestra (with various chorales) to create an expansive and symbolic music whose powerful "thrust" will "carry them [the pessimistic, the hopeless] to the very threshold of heaven to free themselves from living and its various hells, to withdraw from the earth and the bondage to gravity, to leap clear over the long stretch between the before-life and the after-life."[74] Jones, however, sees the world very much from ground and lake level, a vision from lakeside in North Hatley of the refuse of twentieth-century culture:

> The world conceived as wreckage. The 20th century conceived as wreckage, the drifting remains of empires, economies, ideologies —bodies scattered on hillsides, washed over flood plains, stacked in the killing fields, hidden in boneyards, abandoned in parks or in parking lots, dumped in an alley. All part of the floating world, singed letters, sodden scripts, broken clichés—tablets, timbers, of temples and shrines, the law and the prophets—bibles, torahs, sutras, holy korans, handbooks of reason, catechisms of science— Newton's Principia, Kant's Critique—the colours leaching in the cartoon angels and devils, the lines softening in the crabbed anatomies, the forms of the papier-maché heroes and villains and architects of the universe swelling and dissolving.[75]

Against these observations, he sets the voice of the crow (a scavenger bird, appropriate for a world of detritus and bric-à-brac) which summons the persona of the poem to listen to the "song of a truck,"[76] presumably human-kind engaging in the mundane music of spring clean-up. This is one half of a musical conversation of which Martel is the other half. Both writers are seeking a moment of order amid general chaos and futility: "Faced with either total cacophony or complete silence," Martel collects himself, con-centrates, and then casts off into harmony, perhaps ecstasy.[77] Jones, on the other hand, seems very much the solo poet *sans orchestre*, listening for birdsong, listening even, as he says in one of his poems, "Singing up the New Century," to birds in the woods only "pondering songs."[78]

The gap between French and English poetry in Canada has, in Jones's view, narrowed somewhat. There is now, he has remarked, more "leakage" from one to the other as differences dissolve in a world of contemporary global culture.[79] To what extent this is measurable on a large scale is a matter for further investigation. What is striking about Jones's own poetry is its openness to natural and electronic atmospherics and to an extraordinary range of intertextuality and allusion, everything from Emmanuel Kant to Nancy Sinatra, Lady Di to Degas, North Hatley to the Van Allen Belt. What is also striking is the interplay and mutual illumination which takes place as Jones the translator moves between English and French verbal universes and the degree to which he invites French to enrich and colour his poetry, and to render it ironic. On one level, the presence of French lines, phrases and whole stanzas is perfectly understandable: French is inescapably and happily the prevailing verbal and cultural environment in Quebec, part of the climate. If the ice fisherman on Lake Massawippi says, "Viens icitte"("Come here") to the dog, then it goes into the lines, says Jones.[80] On another level, the frequency and astuteness with which French is employed reward more careful reading. Take, for example, "Words for the New Terrace" which appeared in *Under the Thunder the Flowers Light up the Earth* and is dedicated to Richard Giguère, a colleague of Jones at the Université de Sherbrooke and a fellow editor of *Ellipse*. Whatever the actual conversation going on here, words as conceived from a cosmic perspective ("bouncing / off the Van Allen belt"[81]) don't appear to mean very much, chiefly because the real conversation is occurring sub-vocally. There is the speaker (Jones?) and his friend (Giguère?), and there is "the girl," the word in Roman type, who says nothing, but who is turned into a ghost in italicized French:

> The girl
> *un peu de spectre, du front pâle, à la robe*
> *grise, portant*
> *de long bas gris, ses jambes*
> *vagues comme la fumée*
>
> *ne disait qu'un mot*[82]

She exists in French; she is silent. Is the conversation going on around her in French or in English? The Van Allen belt doesn't give a damn. The girl does not speak, but a bird does, yet *personne ne savait son nom* though it might be a chickadee in English, which in any case is simply a noise pretending to be a bird.[83] Later, when the terrace is silent, the speaker recalls the conversation and wonders whether the bird was underneath the girl's dress or "in her small / blurred mouth," whether yellow leaves, "*grande feuilles d'or*" were falling in her flesh, or whether, as was no doubt the case, she was simply falling into someone's bed. Words, then, don't mean much when birds speak and ghostly girls fall. Nature and sexuality, at least in this little scenario, prevail. Even the French, previously italicized as "different," gets typographically assimilated into Roman type in the second last line of the poem: "tombent-elles toujours dans sa chair pâle?"[84] Playing with fonts, with words, and with the silences which speak and do not speak, this poem enacts the ways in which the two languages touch or slide by each other, or blend. It is part of the artful dance. Or part of a delicate bilingual melody in which differences tend to get annihilated by more interesting sexual undercurrents.

In a latter poem, "Notes of Spring," the controlling metaphor is the fragile notes of coming spring overheard in a "winter-silent/house," an "air" in two senses of the word. The "notes" are both musical and lexical, the lines forming a series of brief and tantalizing notations, some in English, some in French, though French in this case has the last word, or strikes the last chord. It is an old refrain—*une vieille rengaine*—touching and *touchante*, and perhaps too late:

> no, no, I think that we shall die
> and someone will arrive belatedly to tinsel
> absence with an air, some shy
> filigree ...
>
>   *et quoi encore*[85]

In the poem "I annihilate," which appeared in *A Throw of Particles*, Jones again occupies the interface between the two linguistic regions but within the context of wider political and cultural concerns. The poem is worth quoting in its entirety:

> I annihilate the purple finch
> in the apple tree
>
> it is a winter dawn
>
> it is 'La Guerre' Henri Rousseau
> saw charging through the shattered space

of the Second Empire

it is a faint
raspberry
in the silent cosmos

c'est une tache
sur la page blanche

un cauchemar en rose

c'est le Québec
libre

a bird
c'est ça
un oiseau dans un pommier

it may fly off
but it won't go away

I neglected to mention the snow[86]

The poem is sparked by Andrew Marvell's "The Garden," in which the contemplative and poetic mind is an ocean wherein all phenomena find their resemblance and out of which "other worlds and other seas" can be created, "Annihilating all that's made / To a green thought in a green shade."[87] This is the paradoxical power of the imagination which can take the concrete, objective world and through the power of metaphor render it "nothing," which for Jones means variously a patch of purple on white snow, "*une tache / sur la page blanche*," (mere typographical marks on a white page) and, provocatively, "*c'est le Québec / libre*," Charles de Gaulle's notorious declaration which Jones "thought was a nice idea so [he] put it in."[88] Bird and de Gaulle may fly off but neither will go away. The bird leaves, the metaphor lingers. De Gaulle leaves, his phrase hangs out there over the crowd in front of Montreal's City Hall and then for years afterwards in the collective memory. But the poem is not, as Jones remarked to his interviewers, a "statement for the liberty of Québec one way or the other but rather a lyrical

227

version of politics."[89] The shifts from English to French, back to English, then to French and finally to English provide a kind of alternating linguistic current, key images and allusions introduced by parallel phrasing: "It is" / "C'est." There is the bird in the apple tree and there is winter suddenly recalled in the last line; there is the blank page; there is Henri Rousseau's apocalyptic painting of war riding a dark horse over dead bodies, and an incendiary political declaration. There is also a rose-coloured nightmare and a raspberry in the silent cosmos: all these particles are strung out on a tenuous track of association prompted by the finch and the Marvellian phrase. Rousseau and de Gaulle are, through the lyric fusion of the poem, ironically reduced to finch status. The poem also enacts a verbal pointing which takes place within a snowy winter dawn, and on the blank page of the poet's imagination, and within "the silent cosmos." Like a Lapointe poem, these words "make luminous tracks that betray the invisible electrons startled from their atomic sleep."[90]

Summoning up French is thus more than a matter of simple colouring. There are political and cultural implications sometimes in even the most innocent words and phrases, though in "Balthazar" some terms are clearly more ominous, and in another language: *Übermensch, Weissenschaft.* In this long poem, inspired by the nude and partly nude paintings of adolescent girls of the French-born, Polish-descended Balthazar Klossowski (1908-2001) otherwise known as Balthus, Jones explores the sinister interplay between eroticism and violence in the Europe of the 1930s and '40s, a society disinte-grating before the insidious incursions of brutality, eugenics, and mass extermination, in effect, the emergence of the barbarian from behind the bourgeois furniture. But he was also, as he announced in the version which first appeared in the *Moosehead Review* "exploring the range and possibilities of language."[91]The persona of the poem (not Balthus, Jones insisted in a note accompanying the poem) is an artist summoned to paint various ado-lescent girls of the German and French bourgeoisie. He is fed on condition that he remain a voyeur, though clearly he is fed also on a series of porno-graphic appetizers by maidens some of whom seem quite prepared to encourage his fantasies. The lines of the poem and its imagery also feed the reader details which tease with quick glimpses of the girls' anatomies, the half-seen, the spaces between:

> they were coming out of their clothes
> they wanted to. Their bodies
> didn't fit. They moved

like whores. The inky air
was pimp to the anatomy, a leg
a chalky rump, an armpit

With his eye, some days
brilliant, they composed a single
complex animal[92]

"Art," says the persona, "... avoids repletion ... Art postpones ... suspends / the machine of the real / to feed on the possible."[93] This might be an adroit observation on the nature of art, or it could be a description of the pornographic state of mind as it prowls restlessly through a phantasmagoric world of lust-inducing images, perpetually unsatisfied. In a cunning shift of pronoun from third person to first half way through the poem, the text nudges the reader closer to an identification with the speaker. The two are conjoined in the "Envoi": "He would be I."[94] The poem thus balances precariously between relishing its own images and mocking the pornographic sensibility which produces them. Achieving such an ambiguous high-wire act is a matter of employing various poetic techniques: a tight, three-line stanza, double entendre, oxymoron, puns, ironic juxtapositions, allusions to many of Balthus's paintings, and a deft switching from language to language, none of the "foreign" languages distinguished by italics. This is a cosmopolitan, multilingual world in which the slippage from one language to another can be quick and grimly comic:

Adieu
les filles de bonnes familles
It's finished, the family

business. Exit
Oedipus and Pussyfoot and the whole
cathouse. Oh

there will be progress
Eiffels of it, adult
professional, perfectly lethal

a sensation. Je suis
rétrograde. Ich gehe rückwärts
Do widzenia[95]

In this penultimate section of the poem, the pseudo-Balthus figure, blinded perhaps by too much overheated viewing, pussyfoots out of the European bourgeois brothel and the coming shambles. He decides to become *ein Landschaftsmaler*, a landscape painter, then backs out of the picture in three languages, the last line being Polish for goodbye. The "Envoi" which concludes the sequence evokes a number of Balthus' paintings, particularly *Nu devant la cheminée* (1955) and suggests that both persona and reader are part of the same porno-historical situation, "earth-walkers" apparently untouched by those forces which threaten "the fragile furniture / of Europe."[96] Just as Eliot's "hypocrite lecteur!—mon semblable,—mon frère!" in "The Waste Land," (a line borrowed from Baudelaire), is directed mockingly at the reader who thinks he is exempt from the spiritual aridity of the modern world, so also Jones suggests that the multilingual persona is all of Europe or, in fact, any reader with a lascivious eye for a Wilhelmina posed halfway over a table or Elsa and Isolde coming out of their clothing.

Informing "Balthazar" and acknowledged by Jones in his introduction to the *Moosehead* version of the poem is Michel Foucault's *The History of Sexuality* in which Foucault argues that beginning with eighteenth-century rationalism, sex became an "incitement" to analytical discourse: stocktaking, classification and specification. This was a discourse which has continued to be compulsive and verbose and which has created a complex set of mechanisms wherein "pleasure and power do not cancel or turn back against each other; they seek out, overlap, and reinforce one another."[97] But even with all this discourse, sex was still explored as a secret; there were authorized discourses which contained silences which were enforced by various forms of discretion. Against the sensibility which embraces sexuality through discourse, Foucault's included, Jones sets the promiscuous word, the language (and languages) of poetry. "Like the Word, we must be absolute / and empty or / shifty, promiscuous wholly / intertextual" he writes in a later poem.[98] If poets, like innumerable Adams and Eves in the Garden, re-enact creation, then they do so subversively and indiscriminately undermining both the ideologies of power, such as eugenics or rationalized sexuality, the walls protecting unilingual enclaves, or, as was the case in French Quebec,

230

communities stuck in a great darkness.

Translation is one way to overcome the abyss between linguistic jurisdictions. Appropriating the words themselves, placing them in the playful embrace of the mother tongue is another. In "Balthazar," the conjunction of languages carries with it a sinister cultural undertow; in poems set closer to home the interplay is more positive. Jones has referred to his use of French and English in the same poem as a form of gymnastics, and of any poem as a form of broken-field running in which "you keep going up and over and around. You negotiate all these things and to get there you also have to digest them. That's what people do in living. That's what the modern world keeps telling you to do. You don't settle down to anything. You keep your eyes open and watch what's coming up."[99] Though he may not be unhoused, D. G. Jones is certainly a man in motion who responds alertly to the unpredictable climate of the world around him, living in uncertainty, but capable of continual re-centering in poem after poem, and having a good time at it. In one of the last issues of *Ellipse* published in Sherbrooke, he quoted Wallace Stevens on the "gaiety of language":

> That surely is of the essence of poetry, attracting the reader—and the translator, even if it risks making him, or her, into a manic depressive, one minute high and the next minute stumped. Allowing language the freedom to play, discovering unexpected relations in assonance, in puns, spilled clichés, idioms exposed in unfamiliar contexts, words and phrases that wander from one paradigm to another—this is the liberation not only of language but of ourselves and the world, of perception and feeling.[100]

"At least in this country," wrote Jones in *Ellipse* 50, "an argument about poetry or its translation is not likely to produce tombstones."[101] Throughout his long and distinguished career as a creator of fine poems, as a re-creator of poems in translation, and as an artist delighted in the complex playfulness which characterizes good translation, D. G. Jones has given a new life to both English and French poetry in Canada. In lines rich with echoes, ironies, thefts, interruptions, idioms, asides, highlights, quotations, allusions, clichés, puns, French, German, Spanish, Latin and other verbal ingenuities, the gaiety and fertility of language has allowed him and his readers to discover, not tombstones, but "an order amid bright / fallen leaves."[102]

Michael Harris's Boo-Jhwah Appalachiana

CARMINE STARNINO

"It is the destiny of Montreal," wrote Louis Dudek, "to show the country from time to time what poetry is."[1] I hesitate opening with this quote as it seems perfectly designed to extend the nasty new habit of imagining Montreal as "a den of neo-con poets."[2] Yet Dudek's boast is a good example of the fealty that the city's English-language literary tradition inspires in its defenders. Ever since A. J. M. Smith and F. R. Scott led the Modernist intervention in the 1920s, a large subset of Montreal poets have felt themselves distinctly separate, and have shifted their sense of that separateness into idiosyncratic textures of language and feeling.

The result has been an identity without Canadian precedent; an identity, in fact, at war with any such cultural denominator. Predictably, this self-image—namely, as splinter stylists free of nativist traits—has made for poor flag-wavers. Few Montreal poets participated in the creation of a regulated Canadian sensibility during the 1960s and 1970s. Where Al Purdy won a Governor General's award for a collection called *The Cariboo Horses* (1965), Irving Layton got his for *A Red Carpet for the Sun* (1959).[3] The "Canadian-ness" of the two titles is telling: Purdy's is central and explicit whereas Layton's is incidental. And this ideal prized by Dudek, to which the whole country should aspire? That, too, emerges from the Purdy-Layton contrast. More comfortably than almost anyone else in Canada—though Atlantic poets have worked similar effects to advantage—Montreal wordsmiths have pioneered ways of using vernacular to hybridize traditional forms into deep and complex utterances (a high-water mark of this colloquially enriched prosody would be A.M. Klein's 1948 *The Rocking Chair and other poems*).[4]

Such a territorial aesthetic is not to all tastes (not all local tastes, even), but the superb poetry fashioned from it has marked the city indelibly on the map of our minds. Indeed you don't have to agree with Dudek to concede the phenomenon underwriting his words: a circle of poets who embraced an ideal so fervently, and gave it so enduring an expression, that they made Montreal not only a geographical omphalos but a geopsychical signpost in the progress of Canadian poetry.

Their legacy of independent-mindedness continues to exist, from its little corner in the canon, as an alternative world where unfashionable literary ideas (like the "well-made poem") are kept alive. From the perspective of a postmodern and peripatetic era, it might appear anachronistic to tie poets to place in this insistent way. Perverse, too, since it seems as if an historical circumstance (poets residing in the same milieu) is being forced to say more than it has any right to say. Yet I can think of poems by Montreal poets that do things other poems by Canadian poets don't, and often feel it is something about the experience of living in a bustlingly mixed and bilingual city—living, that is, in a hot zone of linguistic impurity—that gives one access to ambitions difficult to feel elsewhere. To satisfy those ambitions Montreal poets have had to evolve new structures of volubility, structures whose rush and bustle carry an undertone of defiance. Montreal poets, in other words, comprise a singing school not solely because of residency, but because their poems bushwhack an alternative path for readers and poets to follow. More specifically, Montreal poetry holds open a deracinated space in the national consciousness; a conjoining of terrain and tone that betokens a way of hovering, a way of placing the poetic self "in between"—close to Canada, but not touching it, alert to its ideological trappings, but free to escape.

Whatever the reason for this, it is clear that nowhere, outside Montreal, will you find anything comparable: poetry as a counter-force to the hollow forms of Canadian identity, poetry as a culturally sophisticated, captured-in-cadence opposition. Yet discussion of these Anglo-Quebec sentence-sounds occurs rarely in our criticism. Perhaps it's due, in part, to the many bargains such a thesis would need to strike with the stylistic differences among the poets. More likely the dearth of debate is a result of deep-standing anti-formalist prejudices (of which the "neo-con" jib is but one example). What this means is that, as a consequence, certain exemplary works by Montreal poets have failed to properly circulate. And in our case, it means many of you are probably in the predicament of never having read a poem by Michael Harris.

Harris, as I hope to soon show, is his own man. But he can best be understood by the company his poetry keeps, a coterie of poets whose ideas were forged in a line of development that has continued uninterrupted for nearly eight decades. A number of approximate analogies exist—the New York School of the 1950s, the postwar group of Rome's *terza generazione*—but Montreal's longevity as a verse nexus is exceptional. Across three generations we see an affection for words in experimental yet indigenously distinctive arrangements. And across three generations this liberating attempt to reaccent and realign language into what Klein called a "double-melodied vocabulaire" has left the *poète Anglais* outside the margins of Canadian poetry.

The sidelined—among them John Glassco, R. G. Everson, Robyn Sarah, Robert Allen and David Solway—form a distinguished society. They've created no socio-theatrical buzz (unlike the "Vehicle poets" who stole centre stage in the late 1970s with their rented-from-the-Beats bohemianness) and have shown no flair for the sort of platform dramatics that helped mark out Irving Layton's and Leonard Cohen's careers. Their of-a-pieceness is, instead, best seen on the page, where their virtuosity carries impact by encoding itself in open, accessible, undeceptive ingenuities. Ranging from temperamentally private to hot-blooded, from down-to-earth to magisterial, their poems accommodate innovation without visible strain. All practice reader-friendly risk-taking—nudging words in new directions, opening possibilities up—founded on the awareness that someone is going to read it and shaped by the determination to therefore make sense. Their most original poems (Klein's "Portrait of the Poet as Landscape," Glassco's "The Burden of Junk," Van Toorn's "In Guildenstern County" or Solway's "Stones in Water") prove that winning stylistic breakthroughs need not be gaped at uncomprehendingly.[5] Experiments can, instead, be consensual acts. The element of surprise can exist as a shared pleasure in the mind of the poet and reader. The ethic—if not the aesthetic—is one of courtesy: to set the poem ticking is to set the reader's imagination ticking too. It's an ethic, needless to say, that Harris shares.

Born in Scotland in 1943, Harris immigrated to Canada at the age of six. For most of his adult life, and until his retirement in 1997, he taught English literature at Dawson College. In 1970 he published his first book, the misconceived *Text for Nausikaa*, followed, in 1976, by the much-improved *Sparks*.[6] Not quite a trail-blazing beginning, but by the mid-eighties he was firmly established as an estimable local figure, and a favourite on the poetry-reading circuit with a national CBC prize to his name (awarded in 1985 for a long poem called "Turning out the Light"). If he is recognizable at all today it is likely for his twenty-five year tour of duty as founder and editor of Signal Editions, the poetry imprint of Véhicule Press (a post I now occupy).

Yet Harris has also written poems that rank with the best of his generation, a group that includes Robert Bringhurst, Tim Lilburn, Michael Ondaatje, and Don McKay. Interested readers can find this exceptional work in his last three books: *Grace* (1977), *In Transit* (1985), and *New and Selected Poems* (1992).[7] What it is about these collections that has warded off their deserved kudos is anybody's guess (though as early as 1986 we find David Manicom warning the situation was fast becoming "farcical").[8] Unaccountable neglect is, of course, a frequent theme in the lives of Montreal poets (a frustration beautifully captured in Klein's "Portrait of the Poet as Landscape"). But Harris also seems the sort of significant figure who would go unnoticed no matter where he lived. Quiet, unconnected to any literary movement, eschewing all fashions, his poems undoubtedly make dreary grist for the academic mill. He illustrates none of the trends (anti-colonial poetics, the evil egocentricity of the lyric voice, Heidegger-as-verse) running rampant in contemporary Canadian poetry. He has nothing to say on the subject of ecology, ontology, quantum physics, cultural politics or theology. Nor does his work call out for the kind of code-breaking that reviewers have lavished on glamorously difficult poets like A. F. Moritz, Tim Lilburn, Anne Carson, and Erin Mouré. That being said, Harris's poems *do* have a following, and there is no mystery about what causes his admirers to sit up and listen.

It begins—and ends—with his music. Everyone is praised for the musicality of their verse at some point or other. But of course, very few poets deserve the compliment. This is not unusual, since music in poetry is an event, an outcome that a poem builds deep into itself. We distinguish poetry from prose by the pause at the end of each line, yet the magic that music can bestow on an utterance—memorability, authority, verve— depends less on line-breaks than on an aptitude for tapping a deeper wildness and unpredictablity out of the words being used. I don't mean that line-breaks are unimportant in finding these qualities; merely that they are the least important. No poet can succeed for long without a good ear for breaking a line, but a line-break alone won't lead to a phrase that anybody will forever want to murmur to themselves.

Instead, music is about good line-*making*; about diction and syntax irreducibly fused, and the sound-signature enjambed into place. Music thus bodies forth from a poem's form, and form (or a decent definition of it, at least) is the structure that emerges when every line—run-on or end-stopped, short or long, dropped on a pile or stacked inside a stanza—is made to reciprocally amplify what surrounds it. Music, in short, is high-watt word-order. It does not so much deploy language as redeploy it, and redeploy it in directions that push vocabulary past its usual, commonsensical limits. The words we use, words depleted by the doldrums of daily conversation, stand apart in a poem because they're put in configurations that preserve their spokeness but suss out new mouth-filling nuances. Poets able to do this—thicken common speech into lyricism—are rare. The reason is that you need an ear able to ignore the consensual gist of a word and experience it as a dense bundle of acoustic meaning. But if music is so uncommon, what is it that we're so often praising? What we are praising—at least in Canada—are poets who codify sound as a trick of tone and personality (Al Purdy), or poets whose voices are the idiomatic equivalent of lip-synching (Margaret Atwood), or, as in this passage from Anne Michaels, poets who scent their lines with diction chosen solely for its implied sublimity:

> Time is like the painter's lie, no line
> around apple or along thigh, though apple
> aches to its sweet edge, strains
> to its skin, the seam
> of density. Invisible line
> closest to touch. Lines of wet grass
> on my arm, your tongue's
> wet line across my back.
>
> All the history in the bone-embedded hills
> of your body. Everything your mouth
> remembers. Your hands manipulate
> in the darkness, silver bromide
> of desire darkening skin with light.[9]

This sort of perfumed imprecision is, as Donald Davie once argued, nothing more than a smoke-screen to cover the getaway of a poet unwilling to stay behind to properly render what he or she has tried, unsuccessfully, to conjure. None of these lines find their pitch *as* lines—as scrupulously crafted sound-units of meaning—because none have been written with the ear. In fact, the words have been rushed through their aural implications so that they exist vacantly, in a kind of sonic disconnect from themselves. The collocation of syllables in "silver bromide / of desire darkening skin with light" doesn't draw its music from the living, blood-warm principle of natural speech; it is, instead, "poetic" phrasing trying to disguise as music what is really an artificial act of verbal creativity.

This is something of a trend in contemporary Canadian poetry, this tendency to regard words as cosmetic, useful for the simulation of sagacity, rather than as substances with their own weight and temperature. The poetry of Tom Wayman and Jan Zwicky (to name just two) is brittle for exactly this reason: it is made with language pillaged of its spoken density, language vampirized into adjectival intensifiers ("beautiful," "shining") and feeble abstractions ("dream," "love," "darkness"). Harris constructs his descriptive cadenzas the opposite way, not by embellishing ideas but by replenishing language: by giving language back its kinetic nutrients. Or, to use a line from Seamus Heaney, Harris writes poems that achieve the accuracy of words "founded clean on their own shapes."[10] We can see that accuracy helping to activate many of his metaphors: Emily Dickinson perceiving her blood as the "running red / foam of wheatfields at sundown"[11]; how surf is "the sea's / seemingly natural turns drawing curtain after curtain / on its own endless wash of applause"[12]; or couples "whose fingers thread jealousy together."[13] In each instance, the phonetic pith of the words (i.e., "running red," "endless wash of applause") has been absorbed into the image, creating a point-for-point matching of form to action. It is this copy-cat equivalency—where rather than evoked, assertions are enacted—that is responsible for Harris's most rewarding effects. Here is the start of "The Woods":

I know the mole's slow heart
troubles still with the mole's dull blood

and her glass eyes have filled
with dark. She lies made of mud

at the end of her burrowing,
still as sediment, a sludge.[14]

No word here takes up the menial task of merely "meaning." The message of these lines—a mole preparing to hibernate for the winter—is conveyed by the escalating heaviness of the details ("slow", "dull", "dark", "mud", "sediment", "sludge") and by the slowing heartbeat of each couplet. Notice how the speech rhythms, in their drowse of monosyllables and open vowels, begin decelerating from the first line, and then, by the end, how the entire thing culminates in the sluggishness-suggesting stresses in the last line, an effect heightened by that impeccably placed comma: "still as sediment, a sludge."

When attention is paid to things at this pitch of perception and vocabulary, especially when it is done with such casual legerdemain, the results are often construed as "well-crafted," a term that carries a faint condescension implying conservativism and lack of intensity. Language, we're told, should be practiced as an easy, even reckless, obligation; too much scrupulousness is stifling. Yet representations which, in their painstaking fitting-together of parts, try to stay true to the "realness" of an object are not a mark of compliance with normalcy; they are a mark of dissatisfaction. Any incidence of precision expresses a dilemma, not a solution: it is a rebellion against the unthinkingly assumed terms of a previous depiction. Take these opening lines from "The Hunting-Cabin in November": "Not a soul about / but the spinsterish / birches."[15] This sentence exemplifies the chief virtues of Harris's style: a plainspokenness that catches the full sense of every word and concentrates it, creating a vivid and believable snatch of voice. One notices the run of internal rhymes ("Not" with "about" with "but") and the liquidity of the phrasing ("spinsterish" sibilantly meshing with "birches"). Most masterful, however, is "spinsterish." Notice how it reinforces the feeling of isolation by metaphorically buttressing the description. But doesn't the word—and you need to simply repeat the lines to realize it—also have a kinesthetic allure, a visceral thrum that brushes against your senses? Such quiet marvels are the foundation of Harris's poetry. Again and again he gently pushes a word against the grain of its common usage, freeing loose a latent charge.

If Harris is more original from poem to poem than almost any contemporary Canadian poet I can think of, it is due to his habit of revising inattentively-nursed notions of words like "spinster." Which is to say that Harris represents the subtler experimental departures of Canadian poetry. You don't hear much about this group because our literary journalism expends its publicity on envelope-pushing that is far more brutally eccentric.

But to be frustrated by the limitations of diction is not always to move toward breaches of decorum; for some, like Harris, it means discreetly striving for a wider medley of aural possibilities. The genius of lines like "the glaze of the moon is a lighter liquid set loosely / on the mercury of water" or "the golden rain / of urine boiling its froth in the toiletbowl" or "a kiss / is just a cushioned push / of face" is that they appeal directly to the ear.[16] This means their persuasiveness is a listened-for property, the result of an alluring loading-up of monosyllables or the lovely tension between words combined for their alliterative and assonantal colour.

Many poets will fail to see anything daring about finding plausible and reliable ways of logging the physical world. They will appreciate bull's-eye formulations like "lighter liquid set loosely" or "boiling its froth" or "cushioned push" as casual felicities, and hunt elsewhere for their radical jolts. There are no such jolts in Harris's poetry. His innovations are instead maturely assimilated into the nouns and verbs that clinch his images in small but decisive ways. His poems, one could say, are a bold, shapely, and tightly orchestrated accumulation of countless of these tiny successes. The sophistication of Harris's technique is extraordinary, more so because his soundscapes do not need the services of a literary critic; he isn't a hard guy to keep up with. He writes aggressively but transparently, using a style that differs from ordinary speech only in its being more energetically economical, less vague, and more sonorous. The virtues of this sort of writing are not much remarked on these days. Made deaf with our large-gestured prosy pretensions, we belong to an era that has forgotten how difficult it is to write well:

> Metal-still   on the shed-roof tin
>   until it cocks its head
> to eye the world
>   which has begun to crack
> its own black shell
>
>   until its claws pull
> its body in
> with soft trigger-pressures   it's up
>   and up higher

all up in an arc wheeling down swooping
and screaming smoothly down dead
                on the twisting trail
                        of a dragonfly which turns
quickly in the silver
                signals of its wings
until the swallow takes that silver
                for treasure in its beak
and the beak's blunt scissor
                shuts down hard
and harder   then the bird pitches down
                the sheer cliffs of air
slipstreaming God
                to the shed-roof where it sits
and eats

and is
out again spinning
a thin blade turning
on a dotty moth dazed from every side by light
                and stoneblinded surely by
                this cararact of black

and is an air-ace barnstorming
                stealing the stomachs of the watchers
with its dolphin's bounce from an air to an air
and twists tricks turnings for the joy of it

and flies butterfly-fluttery
at all the edges of the sky

and there turns as quickly
as a liar in a lie[17]

Anyone who turns in this kind of writing is not a person who thinks lightly
of his task. Called "Barn Swallow," the poem does more than merely describe
one; it revises language into something abrupt and fast-moving, adapting it

to the conditions of avian life. Like Hopkins' "Windhover," which seems a clear influence, the artifice is all aural, with the accelerated vernacular ("it's up / and up higher / all up in an arc wheeling down swooping") served up to better air the mood of speed. Harris's success at creating such effects— and giving them the buzzing intimacy of direct speech—depends on a kind of fluency that achieves full flight from perfectly-weighed words.

It may seem an overstatement to suggest that such scrupulousness doomed his reputation, yet one cannot help but wonder if Harris's invisibility is due, in part, to a career that disappeared into its enthusiasm for precision, a precision whose greatest practical consequence—a slow, insight-marshalling method of composition—made him easier to ignore. Perfectionists are viewed dourly in Canada. We like our production Balzacian; recognition depends upon it (compare the three books Harris published between 1977 and 1985 to George Bowering's thirteen or Lane's six). In an essay called "Tradition and the Individual Talent of Charles Bruce" Richard C. Davis charges that our need to "celebrate a never-ending procession of new versifiers" has led to a publicity treadmill where "some other poet is in the ascendant and last year's darling recedes into anonymity."[18] If Davis is right, then Harris's judiciousness about what he allowed into his poems, and subsequently into print, brought about a veridical self-excision: he simply was not seen. After all, it isn't so much that Harris writes good poems, but that he writes the kind of good poetry—compacted, uncluttered—only very patient poets can carry off. Such unhurried artisanal industry works against the widespread notion that a poem is simply something you have had the luck to see or hear or taste, and that, awarded to you virtually complete, your only job is to punch up its straight-to-the-page transcription. We don't want to believe in words carefully sought and selected, we want our words thrown off with a flick of the wrist.

As long as enough of us believe that, then the slow producers and quiet operators like Harris will fare poorly. Of course, if he found himself behind the curve it didn't help that he looked at the world a little differently than his contemporaries. Everything I've quoted here comes from a spectacular collection—his third, published in 1977—called *Grace*, which was inspired by the few miles of green rusticity and wildness that hemmed a tiny farm he owned in North Hatley, in Quebec's Eastern Townships. Like the acrobatic barn swallow, the book did an end run around the Canadian poem as it then existed. It is difficult to imagine Patrick Lane or Susan Musgrave writing lines like "its dolphin's bounce from an air to an air/ and twists tricks turnings for the joy of it", or even of having such thoughts. Not to say the subject wouldn't have attracted their attention, but nothing in their poetry suggests they possessed a similarly astonishing ability to think themselves into the skin of a creature at once so tiny and fiercely alive. It bears remembering that, thanks to Tish, much of the country during this time was working within the shape and framework of the radically de-formalized poem. Homey gesturalism and low-key irresoluteness were *de rigueur*. (Montreal experienced Tish as the Vehicule poets.)

But for Harris, poetry meant something else. It meant walking the land, training his eyes, getting the measure of things right. For Harris, a poem was a device that caught, with mingled excitement and terror, observed details in the tactile suspension of stop-time. *Grace* made an excellent case for this sort of poetry, poetry whose descriptions existed in the music of their own happening. A few reviews sensed something ("a finely worked, accomplished volume"[19], "a technically dazzling blend of sound and dense imagery"[20], "Immediate authority, impeccable rhythms"[21], "real poetry, the kind that raises the hair on your neck"[22] but Canadian poetry never fully warmed to the book. It has yet to atone for that neglect, and, more specifically, for the neglect of the keen-eyed, robust, acoustically lively, reek-rich poems Harris wrote about the pigs, moles, frogs he grew to know so well—poems which leap these thirty years into sensory effects that still strike our ears as absolutely fresh. Here is the last seven stanzas of "The Gamekeeper":

...the gamekeeper's gone

whose crow's a tattoo
at the top of a tree, losing his grip
        at the too-thin tip
of the cold that is pricking him bare.
            He thinks war
and it's war though the summer's surrendered
        and raised its white flag
a million times over
and its snowing.

Now the waddling porcupine's swaying his quills
     all at sea in the swaddle
          of his winter fat;
he is slow in the sudden
     and no match at all
          for the silk and soft skins
of winter. He chews bark,
for the gamekeeper's gone

whose snakes took green with them
     and wove it in a bundle
          and buried it under a rock,
for the earth had stopped in tatters
    , and lay down dead-white,
          dead-skinned, belly-up
and not right. Then the wind coiled hugely,
     struck and coiled and shed its white
a million times over
and it's snowing.

Plump rats and grey weasels channel blindly
     their fright, clawing squealing
at their tunnels: to core them, seal them, escape
     from the light, from the ache
of a world wide with snow; but their black brains
are caught, are furnaced with the spark:
the gamekeeper's gone

whose starving, still hopeful, pure panic of deer
     tiptoe the brittle-twigged landscape to silence
to a deadhalt
at the appletree; and the appletree's victory stays
     stiff-necked, full of thrash
in its iron-bare head of black antler,
in the slow-moving barrens of its branches
     where the sky falls to pieces
sinking deeper and deeper

a million times over;

and it's snowing on the otter
whose eye is a film of ice.
It whispers blessing to the shivering field-mouse
whose heaven is black with snow.
It is snowing on the hare
whose fur is a layer of winter.
It falls against the houses,
against the drinkers in the bars,
a million times over. The gamekeeper's gone.

The fields harden fast
around their stone.[23]

Sound—as a series of heightenings and deepenings, intensifications and exaggerations—gives this poem its shape. Note the cascading sequences of internal rhyme, the smoothly slipping enjambment, the anaphoric bloom of imagery. Note, too, the stark final couplet, upon which all that flourish is suddenly snuffed, and how the lines get their power from the momentum still riding in from the rest of the poem.

But sound also gives "The Gamekeeper" its psychology: the poem *thinks* with it. This cognition-via-cadence is responsible for a great deal of the innovation in *Grace*; namely, Harris's attempt to connect Canadian speech to a more concretely sensuous music is an attempt to create new perceptions. Nothing necessarily unprecedented, mind you, but perceptions impossible to chime into existence using any other cluster of sounds. What made Harris so anti-zeitgeist in his penchants, in other words, was that instead of citing the physicality of a wintery landscape—*lots* of that in Canadian poetry—he improvised ways in which the landscape could give him the words it needed to utter itself. He didn't just describe an apple-tree, but devised the linguistic logic that let him see it as something "stiff-necked, full of thrash/ in its iron-bare head of black antler." Those lines are striking for their mimetic right-ness—a rightness largely monosyllabic, streaming with vowels, and made memorable by the jolt-awake energy of "thrash"—but also for the way they covet spoken rhythms. You can hear it in lines like "whose crow's a tattoo / at the top of a tree, losing his grip / at the too-thin tip / of the cold that is pricking him bare" or "the earth had stopped in tatters / and lay down dead-white, / dead-skinned, belly-up / and not right." Both examples have that intense, off-the-cuff precision of words that have been chanced upon rather than schemed. Harris gets his meaning across clearly and swiftly, but by compressing such shifts of pace and perspective into such a short space he also creates vivid moments of phrasing that stop readers short and force them to rethink language. A case in point would be the wonderful syntactic oddity of "he is slow in the sudden" or the fascinating verb-adverb joining of "channel blindly / their fright."

Harris stands alone. I can think of no other Canadian poet who so successfully turned ordinary English into a semaphore for sense impressions. There are many able to strengthen passages of description with a well-chosen word—itself no mean feat—but none who possess such unique onomato-poeic gifts. Speculating on why this is so brings us to a truth that, for many writers, has been too inconvenient to credit: the relative drabness of Canadian vernacular. Ken Babstock makes an interesting reference to this in an interview with Don McKay, how he finds himself drawn to breeds of English that are "more colourful and jagged and active."[24] Compared to other sorts of slang—the fast, festive accent of American, the roughened, rhythmical flurry of Australian—Canadians speak in rather unexceptional harmonies (not everywhere, of course: to spend some time in St. John's or Cape Breton is to understand the specific nervelessness of mainstream Ontario English). Is it any surprise, then, that surrounded by a diction without intrinsic music, music becomes barely a concern at the level of our style? Instead of extending our sentences to encompass the width, breadth, and depth of the English language, we've two-dimensionalized our ear, shrinking its sensitivities down to idea and intent. What is therefore interesting about Harris is his readiness to embark on a searching departure from this monotone norm, to repair the effects of its dullness by conjuring out of Canadian speech—using tiny touches, minimal modifications—a more interesting "English."

This, of course, also reflects the culturally synoptic condition of most Montreal poets, who are constantly forced, on a daily level, to shift between different registers and syntaxes and thus are more open to cross-influences than they might have been had they lived in Toronto or Vancouver or Calgary. The city itself lures our poems out of the verbal ghetto of what Solway has called "Standard Average Canadian."[25] An excellent example to set against the monolingual state of much Canadian poetry—reductionist, imprecise, inarticulate—is Robert Allen's long poem *The Encantatas* where Canadian language seems to reinvent itself with every line he writes. Allen (who described himself in the piece as "metabolizing with a pen stuck in the corner of my mouth"[26]) wasn't afraid of slang or shy of experiment, and, if he felt different, knew how to find new words for the changed state of his feelings.

Harris's refinement of this gift explains the eight-year hiatus between *Grace* and his fourth book, *In Transit*. The Anglo-Saxon speech-rhythms were recast into simpler felicities of expression. Seizing upon this more tender voice, and placing the emphasis on travel, coupledom, and family, Harris made (to use Lowell's famous line) a "breakthrough back into life." He now drew his words almost exclusively from the warp and weft of daily speech, and at his best—which would be a long elegy called "Turning Out the Light"[27] which episodically ledgers his brother's death from cancer—he spoke in a spare, unsentimental, easy-to-absorb vernacular. Indeed, one of the amazing things about Harris's new voice was the way it swiftly caught readers up in its effects:

> The morning drip
> eases red cells
> into the bloated arm
>
> which hangs from his body
> like some enormous slug
> feeding quietly at his shoulder.
>
> The nurse's fingers
> leave grooves in the underside,
> and a dent in the top
>
> where her thumb rests.
> Then fluid fills the arm
> and it is round again,
>
> leaking a little pink
> which pools on the sheet
> at his elbow. She uses that arm

until the vein is not available;
then she uses the other arm.
Twice a day,

on the column
by his head, his life
hangs, upended. (*IT*, 26)

These lines, taken from "Turning Out the Light," are intended, in their direct plainness, to act quickly on the emotions. They aren't meant to unseat perfection, or upset expectations: they are written out of an awareness of the response they will likely get. But this directness, too, is no less a formal experiment, no less an exploration of prosodic physics. True, in its conspicuous flatness and simple diction it may feel an inch away from prose. But what is poetry, after all, but a game of inches? And for a gifted poet even an inch is margin enough for ambitious acts of departure. Here Harris uses basic nouns, adjectives and verbs to help apply a defamiliarization to the scene. Everything is made new through perspective, giving us the expected —"the bloated arm"—in an unexpected way: "which hangs from his body / like some enormous slug / feeding quietly at his shoulder." The image is precise and alive, but the sound of its simplicity is also ripe with unsentimental intelligence. The problem with style is that despite its accuracies, it always revises things upwards: style is always happy. Harris's minimalism here is the mark of a style learning to subdue its grace-notes to a sad situation. You might say, then, that Harris discovered an *idiolect* for the experience: a tight, estranged-from voice, free of rhetorical add-ons. It is a kind of anti-style that illustrates what can be done with a plainspeaking argot. And for that reason it is important to acknowledge the resourcefulness coordinating each audio effect. Harris never leaves the ideal of poem-as-song very far behind. Beyond the lovely rhythmic balance between the tercets, his signature music-making can be seen in the way he doubles-down a six-syllable constant across two lines in "Then fluid fills the arm / and it is round again"; or how the soft alliterative bursts of "*leaking* a *little pink* / which *pools* on the sheet" are rounded off with the firmer cadence of "at his elbow"; or the piercing quick-trot precision of "Twice a day, / / on the column / by his head, his life / hangs, upended." As is often the case with Harris, the rhythms of ordinary speech undergo the most irreducible and refined modulations, in which shifting a single word can spill away half the poem's energy.

It doesn't always work. Harris sometimes seems to want to feel his own earnestness and pushes things, so that "every pore is a mouth / dumb with spent agony" (*IT*, 22) or daisies "scarcely veil / the sullen face / of the earth" (*IT*, 34). For the most part, though, his bewitchments are cannier. Language is pressed into disclosing perceptions so delicately stricken— "His fear is the house / where soundlessly the cancer / roots in the humid dark" (*IT*, 11)—they hardly seem to have required any pressure at all. There is no strain, no waste, no delay. Get going on some first lines—"He thinks his bones / are the stainless pipes / of the bedside table" (*IT*, 24)—and you enter their nakedness and fluency immediately. The secret is an unguardedness that seems found rather than made, giving us a poem that says extraordinary things while conveying the sense that these are things an ordinary person might actually say: "Evenings we watch / the darkness descend / in its needle // and the morphine / rise in the drowse / of his smile" (*IT*, 16), or "Your eyes were wide open / when the world fell away, / my lovely brother" (*IT*, 31).

Such limpidity, at once homely and elevated, brings Hardy to mind. A few frivolity-free notes also recall Lawrence and Frost; at other times, we even spot a Williams-like brevity. What Harris shares with these poets is a yen for poetry that gets its life-force by using distilled directness as a stay against the "literary": relax the concision-promoting strictures and the effect that snares the reader—the sense that language is drawing on firsthand rather than predigested experience—is lost. In other words, while the candor of Harris's voice is built with durable sounds and rhythms, it is not the candor, as such, that catches our attention. We believe what Harris says because he creates a plausible music for his statements. What seems an efficient way of telling a tale is actually artlessly mesmeric: an art that disguises its artfulness by dressing it in savoury and inventive speech. We can see this at work in a description like "the syringe's slim / savage jab" (*IT*, 21). The phrase hooks us precisely because it is slightly more agile and textured than one might find in real conversation, but it does not stretch credibility. Or here, where Harris's brother, a child in "schoolboy grey" (*IT*, 14) required to answer *Here, Sir* during roll call, begins to stutter:

> And the S began in a blush of trust,
> with a tearing sound
> as of long-ripping paper,

a valve not properly fitted,
as the lungs deflated slowly on and on
transfixing the master suddenly
charmed by this hissing serpentine sway,
the long consistent unstoppable sibilants,
esses upon esses and my brother almost
out of breath, eyes closed,
every muscle tense stepping out into
the sheerfall of accelerating seconds
tongue pressed aching relentlessly
against the incontinent buzz of his teeth—
until the throat stuck shut on its glottis
and his twisted face crimsoned
at the guttering ends of exhaustion— (*IT*, 15)

This passage, set inside a longer narrative, consists of ninety-eight perfectly ordinary English words spoken more or less every day in endless unremarkable combinations. Yet Harris yokes them into a particular arrangement and suddenly all cylinders are firing, every syllable hot-wired to life. It brings home, of course, the mystery of poetry, the ear-grabbing power than can be generated from certain words existing beside each other. But it also suggests the way in which Harris has kept a weather eye (and a diamond-stylus ear) on the English language, learning to fit its assonantal and alliterative effects to new functions. Let's not overlook, for example, how the "sheerfall" of his brother's stammering, perfectly tuned and turned, seems to take place in real time with the "unstoppable sibilants" that egg on each line transfixing the reader as it does the schoolteacher. "S began in a blush of trust" serves as an especially lovely mantra for Harris's evocation-as-enactment aesthetic—not to mention it is one of those phrases just begging to be remembered on its own. Sound not only serves sense, it helps Harris's lines linger in the mind.

But while the experience of having a crisp phrase forever force itself upon you is one of poetry's deepest satisfactions, there are subtler spells poetry can cast, and chief among them is what Clive James has called "sayability."[28] Harris poems demand to be read aloud. And to illustrate this you can do no better than the seventeen-line, single-sentence stanza above which, if recited, seduces your mouth into reliving a little boy's anguish.

Savouring each bouquet of "esses upon esses" becomes oddly cathartic as Harris transforms a remembered trauma into a triumph of form: a syntactically dynamic, forward-pushing aural simulacrum that traps our "tongue" and gives it back to us with his brother's breakthrough—"a deep, pure sob saying, *Sir, Sir!* and a last, / escaping, joyous, *I'm Here, Sir!*" (*IT*, 15). Speech running free on the joy of its hard-earned fluency is a rare triumph in "Turning Out the Light". Speech thwarted is the poem's major theme, speech defeated ("when they ask me what I want / I find that I can't speak" [*IT*, 38]) by the eloquence-smothering texture of grief. Like so:

> Lunch is a spoonful
> of raspberry Jello.
>
> Afternoons mean sleep
> or the introduction of long needles
> into the breast-bone or hip,
> or deep through the flesh of his back,
> for a plug of liver or an extract of marrow.
>
> The finger-pricks come twice a day.
> Even the sound of the softly opening door
> has him cry out and gag
> on the dregs of his vomit.
>
> Each day they
> change the soaking twist of sheet.
> They will continue this
> until they get it right,
> until the right one fits:
> it will be spotless,
> and dry, and neat. (*IT*, 20)

Throughout "Turning Out the Light", as his brother's dying is described and redescribed, Harris deftly catches his own anguish and awe at what he is seeing. Much of what makes the poem so moving is owed to these thumbnail portraits of decay. The unnerving "sound" of these portraits, the direct access they seem to give us to deep emotion, comes from wedding a certain sense of line with a certain turn of mind. We can see this in operation in the above excerpt, where Harris narrates his brother's suffering using the shorthand of hospital routines. An eye for detail is working alongside an ear that is able to heighten, through concision, the intensities inherent in unexceptional speech. The result is a catalog of expanding compressions. Confined to his brother's deathbed perspective, the narrative's tendency to stall, then reticently brood, on each specific incident ("Lunch is a spoonful / of raspberry Jello") amplifies what is not being said while staying clear of any prose-like coarsening into autobiography. Harris thus reminds us of the unresolved implications that can freight the choices we make in our vocabulary. We see this clearly in his manner of secreting a disquieting word in almost every line, from the gently unsettling ("introduction", "deep", "plug") to the near-provocations ("cry", "gag", "dregs", "soaking"). The sensitivity of Harris's ear—and for useful comparison one need only recall the poems in *Grace* where the phrase-making was ecstatic, startling and copious in its precisions—is overhauled and reconditioned. What Harris is after is a tonal truth, and buys off the banality of his terms using an auditory subtext thick with complication. His intonation is so complex and nuanced he has the Dickensonian ability to endow ho-hum words with severe particularity, making them crackle: "it will be spotless, / and dry, and neat." Those two lines—faultlessly punctuated, plangently emphatic—are pushed, unbearably, to the brink of their insinuation. Unsentimentality has been given gnashing exactitude and stinting economy of scale. Harris's success at inventing an exacter, plainer poetry to capture this effect is one of his finest achievements.

There is more. In fact, the delight of reading Harris, for those new to his poetry, will come from the salutary gratification of encountering work I have neglected to mention. The skylarking wordplay of "Death & Miss Emily"[29]; the knockabout wit of "A Visit to the Galleries"[30]; the intricate harmonics of "Dolphin"[31], the tender, tensile stride of "A View From the Kitchen"[32]; the ceremony and brio of "Epithalamion"[33]; the imagistic flexing of "Uncle Edward"[34]; the brisk élan of "Spring Descending."[35] To read these poems is to be struck by Harris's amplitude of thought and feeling—there is no prosy drift, only an urgency that makes the poems greater than the sum of their of lapidary parts. It is language made as clear and bright as it can ever get.

Appreciation is vital because in a time like ours, when immense-mystical modes are prized over even-tempered finesse, human voices like Harris's are at a disadvantage. They do not fit our notion of originality as repudiation, the cutting of ties. This is not to say talent like his attracts no admiration, but it is welcomed within limits. The poems are accepted as well-written; but because they are not a forecast of the future, they are seen as old news, a dead end. Yet Harris' ambition is perhaps the most ancient and most rarely attained: a natural speech. He gives poetry the real feel of talk, creating ingenious forms so colloquial in their syntax and sense-making that they rarely feel like experiments. No, Harris isn't the maker of an entirely new kind of poem, but he embodies what Wordsworth believed all poets should strive to become: "a man speaking to men."[36] Very few Canadian poets understand language's singing side, its vocal music, half as well as Harris, yet he burns through the specialism of his art and touches base with our own living accents even as he reinvents them. He can do this—assert his panache without appearing the least bit the poetry pro—because his poems make their first appeal on a level which demands from the reader no more than an ability to understand the language. And as if to gently remind us of that fact, there appeared, in the April 2002 issue of *Books in Canada*, a delightful bit of jabber called, appropriately, "Speech":

> When I had teeth, no accent at all
> was safe from me. I'd Irish
> groined and turd and tank-you
> Lard. I'd Scotch the ballads where
> those drowning lords were richt laith
> to weet their cork-heeled shoon.
> I'd do Canadian if I knew how,
> but settle now for American, its
> boo-jhwah Appalachiana
> that drawl y'all git from The Tee Vee.
> Still I'd like to report my love-life hasn't suffered.
> *In flagrante*, I moan like a heifer at stud,
> a moose with no teeth, a cleft-palate dog.
> Thank God I can croon the word Love.[37]

This—a sonnet in shape, if not intention—comes as close to seeming spoken as any poem I know. The quick and frequent changes of vocal angle, the near-delirium of its spiel, feels exquisitely homemade and points up the close-at-hand sounds Harris likes to use: the stylized patois of "I'd Irish / groined and turd and tank-you / Lard" or the mad amalgam of ad-libbed mannerisms in "American, its boo-jhwah Appalachiana / that drawl y'all git from The Tee Vee." Of course, these lines are also serious probings into idiom, and bespeaks a poet who conceives of his experiments not theoretically, but musically, and executes them with all the mischievous opting-out ("I'd do Canadian if I knew how") that characterizes his Anglo-Quebec mind-set.

I'm aware, of course, that many will regard my remarks about Montreal's poetic outsiderism as an irritant rather than a definition. But such irritants are useful reminders that there are always other interpretations, other hearings, other truths being held in check by the canon-compilers. We already see these subtle crowd-control tactics at work against distinctive poets like Richard Outram and George Johnston, who are exalted for their excellence and simultaneously excluded from serious literary debate. All the better, no doubt, to preserve the career convergences, the large-scale professional dress-ups—everyone doing the same thing, reading the same thing, until even readers are reconceived in the poet's own image. But for Montreal poets, readers are not an ideological idea. You might even say that Montreal poetry is defined, if not driven, by the knowledge that a real mind waits at the receiving end of the process, a mind with expectations of being interestingly addressed. This facing-the-reader voice—let's call it the "boo-jhwah Appalachiana"—belongs to a different sort of Canadian poetry: a poetry of one-offs and unpeggable sensibilities, a poetry of bona fide craftsmanship, solid sounds and language-refreshing surprises. As it happens, it is exactly the sort of poetry that is always the last to catch up in our march to the next prize-giving season. But the good news is that Harris's poems are in no hurry, and will wait for whomever can stop for them.

"Global/local"[1]: Montreal in the Poetry of Robyn Sarah, Mary di Michele and Erin Mouré[2]

LIANNE MOYES

Much was written in the 1980s and 1990s about the troubled cultural location of Anglo-Quebec writing and, in many ways, this body of writing—like others in Quebec—continues to dwell in the contradiction of its multiple affiliations.[3] Yet, if one considers a range of activities, from Erin Mouré's translation of Alberto Caeiro and Fernando Pessoa[4] to the 2004 Concordia University conference "New Readings of Yiddish Montreal" to Linda Leith's "Blue Metropolis International Literary Festival,"[5] it is possible to argue that Anglo-Quebec writing has begun to situate itself, on the level of the text as well as on the level of the literary institution, as part of a field of writing and intellectual work which is global as well as local.

To make such an argument and to focus more on global/local relations than on Francophone-Anglophone relations, is not to deny the importance of, indeed, the specificity of, interaction between French-language and English-language writing in Quebec. Indeed, my purpose is neither to eschew the complexities of the local in favour of the global (as if the two could be separated) nor to suggest that writing in English is in any way "more global" than writing in French. Rather, I am interested in exploring the engagement with the interface between "here" and "elsewhere" which I find in the texts of a number of Anglo-Montreal writers. If, as my reading of the latter texts suggests, "elsewhere" is in many ways constitutive of "here," then it is also important to recognize that this engagement with "here" and "elsewhere" takes forms particular to Montreal and to Quebec, forms which arise from the linguistic and cultural histories of "here." Insofar as global cultural processes are lived locally, a recognition of the global dimensions of Quebec culture—dimensions which are as present for Francophones as for Anglophones—contributes to an understanding of the specificity of Quebec culture.

The poems of Robyn Sarah, Mary di Michele and Erin Mouré which are the subject of this essay invite readers to conceive of Montreal as a global city. In the terms of Doreen Massey, they explore "a sense of place which is extraverted, which includes a consciousness of its links with the wider world."[6] As Massey goes on to explain, "Definition in this sense does not have to be through simple counterposition to the outside; it can come, in part, precisely through the particularity of linkage to that 'outside' which is therefore itself part of what constitutes the place."[7] In different ways, the poetry of each of these writers complicates the border between Quebec and the "wider world," and makes it difficult to discern something called the "outside." At the same time, there is in Mouré's poetry an attention to those subjects who are "held outside" the borders, who have no access to sites of power and privilege.

In a context where the globalization of culture is often equated with the homogenization of culture and where, in the words of Rob Wilson and Wimal Dissanayake, "locality becomes some backward-gazing fetish of purity to disguise how global, hybrid, compromised, and unprotected everyday identity already is,"[8] the poems of Sarah, di Michele and Mouré expose the heterogeneities, contradictions and uneven relations which subtend both the global and the local. Their writing explores what might be called the imaginary of the global/local, an imaginary structured, for example, by histories of migration and displacement, by the cultural networks and processes through which subjects generate a sense of home in Montreal, and by differentiations imposed by gender and by access to global mobility. Such histories, networks, processes and differentiations tend to be denied or oversimplified by discourses of globalism operating in the service of corporate transnationalization as well as by discourses of localism operating in the service of a mythic or exclusive notion of community.

If, as I have argued above, the texts of Sarah, di Michele and Mouré conceptualize Montreal as a global city, they do so in very different ways. These differences are, in some measure, evidence of Massey's argument from the perspective of a cultural geographer that "People's routes through the place, their favourite haunts within it, the connections they make (physically, or by phone or post, or in memory and imagination) between here and the rest of the world vary enormously."[9] However, such variations are also a function of the poetics of place at work in their texts and the different critical concepts those poetics entail. In fact, one of the purposes of this essay is to emphasize the heterogeneity of any corpus that might be drawn together under names such as "Anglo-Quebec poetry."

Sarah's 1998 collection *Questions About the Stars* constructs a sense of place through its engagement with the domestic and quotidian. The global is shown to inhabit the local through the disparate fragments of cultural belonging which the writing subject finds collaged in the streets and dwellings of Montreal and through the material traces of her family's own migrations. The text's refusal of museums as sites of authority, in conjunction with the writing subject's practice of "collecting," makes the work of Walter Benjamin an obvious point of reference. Benjamin's historical materialism, with its refusal of any view of the past as continuum, is especially helpful in reading those poems in Sarah's collection which offer an archaeology of the moment. Memory, in Sarah's writing, is part of the writing subject's experience of the present, part of the meanings she gives to the assemblage of objects or experiences she finds torn from earlier moments and other places. There is in Sarah's poetry a sense of nostalgia; yet this longing for home involves neither the idealization of the past nor the reconstruction of a homeland. Rather, nostalgia takes the form of recollections that are so partial, so idiosyncratic, and so anchored in a subject's experience of her immediate neighbourhood or domestic space, that they construct a compelling sense of home without idealizing or totalizing the local.

Whereas in Sarah's poems there are references to a family history of migration from place to place, in "Invitation to Read Wang Wei in a Montréal Snowstorm," a poem from di Michele's 1998 collection *Debriefing the Rose*, it is the place-name that migrates. In di Michele, *language* becomes the archaeological site and the point of exchange between local and global.[10] "Home," in "Invitation," is where the writing subject sits, feeling the fabric of the couch "rough against [her] calves."[11] Home is also a space in language which she explores through reading. Reading Wang Wei allows the writing subject to locate herself in the winter landscape outside her house, to see herself "wavering with winter trees, as if written in Chinese characters"; and it leads her to think about the fishermen she has seen at the Lachine rapids.[12] Through its interaction with other texts, di Michele's "Invitation" makes legible the "elsewhere" which is already "here." Intertextuality is an important critical concept in my reading of the poem, not simply in Julia Kristeva's sense of the text as a weave of other texts through which the subject speaks[13] but also in Yunte Huang's sense of the textually-mediated historical and material processes through which cultural meanings "travel."[14] In other words, the migrations of names are contingent upon, and made meaningful by, histories which are local as well as global, histories, for example, of spice trade, exploration of the Americas, colonization of indigenous peoples, settlement of New France, and fur trade.

Erin Mouré's poems examine the conceptual grids through which a sense of place is produced. In the "Seams" sequence from the 1992 collection *Sheepish Beauty, Civilian Love*, for example, floating grammatical and referential markers make it difficult for the reader to locate herself—or to locate the writing subject. This instability is compounded in *O Cidadán*, published in 2002, by shifts in voice and typography, and by the use of concrete forms such as charts, fractions and diagrams.[15] At the same time that the poems disorient, they generate an awareness of the *spatiality* of the page, that is, of the ways in which poetic practices organize and potentially open spaces. But language is not the only conceptual grid through which place is produced. The body, too, is key, both as "the locus and site of inscription for specific modes of subjectivity"[16] and as the subject's most unmistakeable locale—whether she travels intertextually, hypertextually or physically. In the terms of Mouré's *O Cidadán*, it is through the body, and not the nation-state, that the citizen negotiates a "relation-to-others-in-a-lieu."[17] The text reimagines the citizen as an internally heterogeneous border or seam, and citizenship, as the enactment of an ethical relationship to those historical subjects who fall outside the borders the nation draws around itself. In an effort to respond to the writing subject's concern not to invoke "transcendent 'citizens' as if Platonic 'ideas,'"[18] I draw more upon the theorists from cultural geography, cultural studies, feminist theory and political thought in my readings than upon the Continental philosophy with which the writing subject dialogues.

(Re)collecting Montreal

"The world is its own museum" suggest the poems which open and close Robyn Sarah's *Questions About the Stars*.[19] Sarah's poems make a point of turning attention away from sites of received order, value and significance, toward the immediacy of what the writing subject happens upon while walking in her neighbourhood, sitting in a restaurant, lifting the kitchen linoleum or digging out a new entranceway. The opening "proem," for example, describes an ageing poet named "*O*" who "*finds he has arrived at the Museum too early*" and who "*[i]nstead of waiting for the Museum to open, … decides to spend the whole day strolling in the sunshine.*" The catalysts in this decision are the sparrows he sees while he sits at a table in the deserted outdoor café, and the realization that "*poets are like sparrows, hopping around at the foot of café tables, waiting for crumbs.*"[20] This "proem" invites us to read *Questions* as a series of found poems, a collection of "crumbs" which the writing subject finds as she (like the ageing poet *O*) moves about the city of Montreal.

There is one poem in Sarah's collection, a poem entitled "A Brief History of Time: Digest and Subtext," which corresponds to a found poem in the conventional sense of an *objet trouvé*, especially a textual "objet trouvé." However, the poems which interest me most are those which "find" Montreal and, especially, neighborhoods like Mile End, through the process of writing. "When the Angels Leave," for example, speaks of writing in terms of:

> … touching
> pen to paper in that spirit
> of inquiry where you could find
> just about anything, a Yiddish newspaper
> from 1933 under the kitchen linoleum,
> chicken bones in the fixture
> of the chandelier.[21]

As the writing subject goes on to realize later in the poem, "all you need is to be / struck by the moment, to find it / momentous."[22] The "found poems" of *Questions* are very often "found experiences," experiences which pass by way of the senses and which are anchored in the materiality of the local and everyday. The local and everyday are made extraordinary, not through a claim of universality but rather through the speaker's apprehension of the layered histories and unexpected adjacencies which constitute them.

"Rue Jeanne Mance," for example, collages birds knocking snow from branches, two Hassidic Jews walking on the street, the bells of the Greek Orthodox church ringing and "arcs of breadcrumbs" thrown from a window.[23] I am reminded, here, not only of the story of *O* in the proem, but also of Sherry Simon's observation that Mile End's history is one of passage, of successive waves of immigrants, of languages written one on top of the next. Even where there is the appearance of continuity—as in the Yiddish newspaper available in the same corner store for over forty years—Simon suggests, one has to remember that the corner store was Jewish, then Greek, then Korean.[24] Sarah's "Rue Jeanne Mance" finds traces of Mile End's successive waves existing together in the same moment. Another poem, "Plateau Mont Royal: A Few Particulars, 8th of August" registers this layered simultaneity on the level of sound. As the writing subject listens to a "cor anglais" which "wobbles through the notes of a minor scale" and "wavers out of tune / to breaking," a church bell "makes its entry."[25] The poetic density of this poem is suggestive of what it means to hear more than one set of sounds at a time, to hear each set of sounds (whether one thinks of those sounds in religious or linguistic terms) as part of the music of the place. Sarah's Mile End poems participate in a new tendency which, as Simon points out, breaks with the neighbourhood's history of successive waves, a tendency toward taking up residence, finding a home, in heterogeneity.[26] The interest in Sarah's poems in catching the moment and in gathering bits and pieces of the past makes Walter Benjamin's work on collecting a valuable intertext. Although the *flâneur* is suggested by the strolling writing subject of poems such as "Grace," "Rue Jeanne Mance" and "To the Science Museum," the collector is the more pervasive figure in *Questions*, the figure who speaks most directly to the collection's concern with material memory and urban domestic space. "Collecting," writes Benjamin, "is a form of practical memory …."[27] For Benjamin, Michael P. Steinberg points out, the collector brings together practices of the nineteenth-century cultural historian and practices of the modernist "who lives and chronicles the transient, the fleeting, the contingent."[28] The writing subject of Sarah's poems is a collector insofar as she enacts "the desire of the present subject for self-understanding as well as for an understanding of the historical object-world" and insofar as her relationship with the world "is represented not as an all-encompassing totality but rather in terms of specific material and experiential constructions.[29] If, in *Questions*, the world can be said to be its own museum, this is because it furnishes, in an ongoing way, phenomena to be sensed and interpreted in terms of the writing subject's local archive. Temporary, haphazard, and focused on the work of memory in the present, Sarah's is a history of experience rather than a history of something called "the past." It resists a model of the past which marches toward and therefore justifies the present.

In the prose poem "Album Leaf," for example, the process of recollection counteracts the tendency of history to supersede memory and experience.[30] The poem begins with dried, pressed rose petals and maple leaves falling from between the pages of an Oxford dictionary, petals of roses from the sanatorium garden pressed in the 1930s while the writing subject's grandmother recovers from tuberculosis, and maple leaves pressed during the writing subject's childhood following the Second World War, which the grandmother's sister in Poland does not survive. Searching the dictionary for the word "stoic," the speaker and her grandmother notice the image of a swastika and are stunned to see it defined as an "emblem of good luck." Then they realize that "the dictionary was printed before the war." Juxtaposed as they are with the image of a swastika, the fragile pressings which fall from the dictionary enact the non-linear and potentially disruptive play of memory within history. Looking back, speaking retrospectively about how her grandmother almost returned to Poland when tuberculosis was first diagnosed, the writing subject nevertheless emphasizes the "now-ness" of her insights: "Strange to think now: *had she done so, I would not be.* For how could she, a sick woman, and her small-boned daughter, then five, have hoped to escape the ones who, even as she pressed those rose petals, were laying plans to destroy all of her kind under the banner of that 'emblem of good luck'?"[31] Writing the history of such disparate simultaneities, such disparate eventualities, Sarah's poem suggests, involves remembering them, allowing them to fall together in ways which will enable future understanding.[32]

As a city of memory as well as a city of modernity, the Montreal of Sarah's *Questions* is available to the reader in the form of overlapping fragments and debris, some of which speak of the past and some of which speak of the present but all of which gather significance in the moment of writing. Montreal, here, is rarely named and is never presented as a totality. We recognize it in references to "the alley," "the mountain,"[33] the Pam Pam Café, the Yiddish newspaper, "the *Monitrice*" and to Hassidim in the vicinity of "the Greek Orthodox church";[34] and we know it by names such as "La Ronde," "rue Jeanne Mance," "Outremont," "Plateau Mont Royal" and "Sherbrooke Street."[35] More precisely, Montreal surfaces in the unruly conjunction of all of these.

Intertextual Travel: Montreal-Lachine[36]

What Sarah's collection "finds" walking the streets of Montreal and putting pen to paper, di Michele's *Debriefing the Rose* finds in the process of reading. In one poem in particular, "Invitation to Read Wang Wei in a Montréal Snowstorm," questions of reading intersect with the topos of Montreal in ways that foreground the imbrication of "here" and "elsewhere." The poem participates in a practice which Yunte Huang, in a study of the migration of cultural meanings between Asia and the United States, calls "intertextual travel."[37] Di Michele's "Invitation" does not, at first, look like travel writing. Much of the poem takes place in semi-darkness on a couch in a "terra-cotta coloured cottage" somewhere in Montreal. The writing subject has un-plugged the telephone, given up on the television, and she hesitates before venturing outside during a snowstorm. Yet she does not close herself off from others. Her way of opening an interface with that which is outside herself is reading.

Intertextual travel is a practice of seeing other parts of the world without going there, a practice of reading on which ethnographers, translators and writers have often relied. One has only to think, for example, of Ezra Pound who, in Huang's words, "never stepped onto Asian soil."[38] Pound encountered Chinese culture through Chinese and Japanese painting in the British museum, particularly through the work of ethnographers such as Ernest Fenellosa, and through Japanese translations of Chinese poets such as Wang Wei. Di Michele's poem speaks of a similarly textual encounter with Chinese literature and language, and, in this sense, her poem is as susceptible to charges of Orientalism as is Pound's writing.[39] It is also possible to find in di Michele's poem a number of practices which trouble the dichotomies and dehistoricizations of Orientalist fantasies, and it is these which preoccupy me as I explore the different kinds of intertextual travel and the different postures toward Chinese intertexts which di Michele's poem performs.

Apart from the direct reference in the title, Montreal is present in this poem only obliquely: in the mediatized metropolis from which the writing subject retreats; in the "mauvais numéros" which—like Sarah's "cor anglais"—are inscribed in French in an English text and which remind us of the crossing of lines and languages; and in the image of fishermen by the Lachine rapids. It is this last reference and the unlikely connection the poem makes between reading Wang Wei and Montreal's "la Chine" which I address in this section of the essay. The "Wang Wei" text in question in di Michele's poem is a nature poem entitled "About Old Age, in Answer to a Poem by Subprefect Zhang."[40] Di Michele's writing subject responds to Wáng Wéi's "answer" with another set of questions:

> Wei, I have learned to excel through too much effort and a job in government service. Does it look like winning to you, the car in the driveway, the terra-cotta coloured cottage? When what I long for most is to sit and listen to song on your river estate? In the thick of the buzzing gnats of summer I have observed old men by the Lachine rapids drop worms from their lines. Though no fish were caught, the men snared clouds on their hooks.[41]

If Wang Wei's poem is a Taoist turn toward nature, di Michele's is a turn away from a regime organized according to success or failure. For di Michele's writing subject, hooking clouds instead of fish represents a departure from the logic of the practical and the material. Yet why does the poem need the words of Wang Wei to imagine this departure? In a sense, di Michele's "Invitation" draws upon a clichéd distinction between the material West and the spiritual East. This distinction is reinforced by the poem's construction of Wang Wei as ancient sage (albeit a sage who does not answer her questions) as well as by its focus on a pre-Revolutionary nature poet, a gesture which overlooks both contemporary China and the Chinese community in contemporary Montreal.

The pun on the place-name "Lachine," however, complicates this interpretation. The slippage between Lachine and "la Chine" prompts us to ask how a place on the southern shore of the island now known as Montreal came by this name. Historians explain that residents of Ville Marie gave the name "La Chine" to the village by the rapids in mockery of explorer Cavalier de LaSalle when he returned prematurely from a journey to the interior of the North American continent in search of China.[42] The Sulpician, François Dollier de Casson, who accompanied LaSalle, wrote playfully in his *Histoire de Montréal* of the "famous transmigration of China [Lachine] ... to these parts."[43] Dollier went on to observe that it would be "most cheering for those who may come to Mount Royal, to be told that they are only three leagues from China, and that they can live there without leaving this island which has the good fortune to contain it."[44] Unable to find a route to China, the French brought China to New France; the dream of the spice trade gave way to the network of the fur trade, in which Lachine became important as a point of departure and exchange.[45] In di Michele's poem, then, intertextual travel allows the writing subject not so much to "see China" as to revisit the city in which she lives. The ethnographic desire to know and to possess the other is thwarted by the mixing of foreign and familiar. Similarly, the poem's construction of Chinese culture as the spiritual counterpart of the material West is undercut by the fact that "la Chine" is also in Montreal.

"Lachine" is, of course, a complete misnomer, a term which signals just how far the European explorers and the poem's writing subject are from China. Indeed, it was the question of distance that made "Lachine" such an effective joke on LaSalle. Read in this light, "Lachine" suggests an awareness on the part of the writing subject of the limits of her knowledge of the languages and cultures of China and explains, perhaps, the absence of references in her poem to either contemporary China or the Chinese community of contemporary Montreal. Di Michele's poem addresses the Western text of China. If "Lachine" is a trace of the seventeenth- and eighteenth-century economic push among Europeans to discover a faster route to Asia and thereby to control the trade in spices, it is also the French-language name for China and a trace of Ville Marie, the French colony which preceded the English one.

As the example of "Lachine" illustrates, di Michele's poem dramatizes the migrations, preconceptions, and appropriations which Huang associates with "transpacific displacement"[46] as well as the superposition of "past upon present and Eastern culture on Western culture" which Zhaoming Qian associates with the poetry of writers such as Ezra Pound.[47] Pound is important to a reading of "Invitation" in the sense that he too wrote by way of an engagement with the texts of Chinese poets. In their introduction to *Laughing Lost in the Mountains: Poems of Wang Wei*, the English-language version of Wang Wei cited in di Michele's poem, Tony and Willis Barnstone explain that "[t]o learn how to render Wang Wei's lines we went to school, like so many translators of Chinese poetry, in the poetry of Ezra Pound."[48] Di Michele's writing subject, then, is reading an English translation of Chinese writer Wang Wei, a translation which was influenced by the poetry of Pound. Pound's poetry, in turn, was influenced by his practice of reading and translating Chinese writers such as Wang Wei.[49] This history of translations and borrowings makes legible the complex overlay of cultures and languages which constitute di Michele's poem and the intertextual networks through which her writing subject "travels."

Di Michele's "Invitation," insofar as it brings together and makes contemporary texts from several cultures and several historical moments,
participates in the projects of literary modernism associated with Pound.[50]
Yet di Michele's intertextual practice marks a certain departure from Pound's
"pancultural scheme."[51] Whereas Pound's juxtaposition of texts from different cultural traditions is, in Walter Benn Michaels's view, "a way of insisting
on their essential similarity," di Michele's introduces elements of difference
and distance.[52] When di Michele makes reference in a 1991 essay to "the
kind of dynamics that Ezra Pound believed were characteristic of culture
existing in translation," for example, she does so in order to emphasize the
extent to which "words from the foreign language . . . force themselves into,
and expand the boundaries of official-language literature."[53] When, in the
second stanza of "Invitation," the writing subject sees herself "Wavering with
winter trees, as if written in Chinese characters, black ink strokes on a white
and blowing page,"[54] this self-translation foregrounds the writing subject's
appropriation of the Chinese language. The image of "black ink strokes on
a white and blowing page," a somewhat predictable reference to Chinese
calligraphy, serves as a reminder that the writing subject does not read or
write Chinese, that her sense of the language is limited to what it looks like
on the page.

The image of self-enlightenment which concludes di Michele's
"Invitation"—"She who reads by her own light"[55]—is arrived at both through
reading Wang Wei and through reading Wallace Stevens, yet another
twentieth-century writer influenced by Chinese poetry and culture. What
is more, by inflecting the title of Stevens' "Phosphor Reading by His Own
Light," di Michele's poem makes visible the gender of its writing subject.
Whereas Pound is said to have "invented China,"[56] di Michele's poem shows
how an engagement with the literary culture of China allows the writing
subject to invent herself. In other words, "Invitation" cannot escape the terms
of intertextual travel, but it goes a certain distance toward making those
terms legible.

City of Seams

The relationship of poetry to the polis—and to broader spheres of political
engagement—is one of the central preoccupations of Erin Mouré's writing.
In the late 1980s, troubled by the focus in much feminist writing "on notions

of … the body as difference, as house of memory," Mouré writes essays attentive to "the bodily context: The City. Community, that elemental non-congruence"[57] and to "the edges, folds, contradictions, that feminism, radical feminism, blacks, lesbians, working class, the poor are talking about."[58] Opening the horizons of the term "citizen," the explicit project of *O Cidadán*, has roots in these essays as well as in *Sheepish Beauty, Civilian Love*. In *O Cidadán*, there is a transposition of the project of "civilian love" from the sphere of the city to that of the globe. This shift is not to be understood as a narrative of progress but rather as one of radical continuity. As is suggested by the sections in *O Cidadán* entitled "montréal papers," "roof papers, Rachel-Julien" and "parc Jeanne-Mance papers," Montreal is as crucial to *O Cidadán* as it is to *Sheepish*. Montreal is an important point of reference, for example, in the writing subject's exploration of the Galician city of Vigo on the northwest coast of Spain. Indeed, the edges, folds and contradictions which structure the "cidadan" are those of Vigo and of Montreal—and of Yorkshire, for that matter. These edges, folds and contradictions are also part of her body, part of the border between inside and outside which is her "corpo-reality."[59] As Elizabeth Grosz explains in her essay "Bodies-Cities": "the body is psychically, socially, sexually, and discursively or representationally produced, and … , in turn, bodies reinscribe and project themselves onto their socio-cultural environment."[60]

In the "Seams" series, this process of "turning *inside out* and *outside in*"[61] is brought to bear upon the distinction between the real and the fictional. The "Seams" poems interrogate the codes which regulate the way bodies occupy civic space and the sexualities that can and cannot be recognized within that space. In the poem "Meeting," for example, where one woman stands apart from another in a "room hot full of women," the seam is "folded and sewn shut between us"; it is "the space between the real & imagined meetings not to be broken."[62] At the same time that the poems interrogate prevailing codes, they also mobilize the unruliness of signifiers such as "seams." "What seems is not what is,"[63] says one woman to another, thereby opening a wrinkle in metaphor where lesbian representation might exist. Folding back the pages of the book and baring the seams,[64] the reader (like the writing subject) is both inside and outside the frame of representation. In other words, s/he cannot secure the border between "the real & imagined," the "unpresentable" and the "presentable."[65]

"Seams" makes a woman's desire for another woman legible in the streets of Montreal. One poem begins with a string of names of streets in the city's Mile End neighbourhood, "St. Viateur, Fairmount, Laurier, St-Joseph, Villeneuve," and offers the explanation, "When I can't think of you I think of the streets."[66] Each of the five streets listed above intersects with Jeanne-Mance, the street on which two women in the poem live. That one woman might conjure another by thinking of cross-streets is significant: it suggests that subjectivity is a movement between, a meeting or crossing. This "inter-subjectivity"[67] functions like a seam, bringing edges together and creating "a border that is not necessarily at the edge but in the middle. Wherein there are 'folds.' 'Seam' and 'seme.'"[68] In other words, the edges may be sewn together but the seam reveals the junction, the overlap, the strain on the fabric, and the work of the threads. The collectivity or community constructed by "Seams" is based not on a sense of common identity or sameness but on a "sense of 'non-congruity,'" a "sense of 'with'-ness, 'joint'-ness."[69]

O Cidadán draws upon this logic of non-congruity and adjacency in its deployment of terms such as "nation," "citizen" and "border." The nation, in these poems, is tentatively reformulated as an interface among several collectivities which traverse the subject or "cidadan": "What if 'nation' ceased to be pure given and were instead a nexus of differential topolities in the subject, who is formed partly by the coextensivity of subjects-around-her?"[70] With its combination of "topos" (a place) and "polity" (a form of political organization), the term "topolities" suggests a series of localized instances of civic practice and "civilian love." Mouré's "cidadan" is a point of transfer and exchange for these topolities, an enactment of the "'relation-to-others-in-a-lieu.'"[71] The cidadan is, of necessity, "localized" as a body[72] yet insofar as "bodies are junctive, insolvent across terrain,"[73] she is not localized by territory, by "soil's sovereignty."[74] *O Cidadán* opens a space, a conceptual, critical, political and erotic space, for a citizen whose sense of politics and of place are not circumscribed by the "*nation-state* and its 19th c. model of sovereignty."[75] The problem the writing subject faces is "how to articulate this without invoking 'transcendent "citizens" as if Platonic "ideas."[76] Indeed, the challenge of *O Cidadán* is to reimagine the citizen without subscribing to a view of transnationality that privileges those subjects who have access to metropolitan centres and global mobility at the expense of those who do not.[77]

As Caren Kaplan explains from a feminist perspective, "In a trans-national world where cultural asymmetries and linkages continue to be mystified by economic and political interests at multiple levels, feminists need detailed, historicized maps of the circuits of power."[78] One feels the need of such maps at certain moments in O Cidadán, especially when the text constructs the "cidadan" as "a product of migrations or emigrative qualities" and as "a seal or bond with *this world*, nothing to do with country or origin,"[79] or when the text imagines what it might mean "to dream a heterogeneity of borders, to speak a sororal idiom without that myth of forebears."[80] The transnationalism of the first example is a function of the desire of one woman for another and of the desire to create a genuinely "public space … where [they] are both signs."[81] The "sororal idiom" of the second example is posited in resistance to ideologies of ancestral blood and soil,[82] and in resistance to those who deny the assymetries of gender.[83] Both interventions are crucial in building alliances among feminist communities and among lesbian and gay communities across national borders. Yet the analysis of border politics offered elsewhere in Mouré's text might be brought to bear here in order to account for women who have no passport[84] and who know no "heterogeneity of borders."[85]

If Mouré's text seems at times to take for granted the world mobility, access to airports and cosmopolitanism of the "cidadan," it also draws attention to the various limits placed on border-crossing. Consider, for example, the gendering and sexualizing of "citizen," a gesture which simultaneously marks the border between masculine and feminine—and defies it. On the unnumbered page before the table of contents, for example, the writing subject sets out "To intersect a word: citizen" by inhabiting a word which "we recognize though we know not its language," a word which "seems inflected 'masculine'": "*cidadan*." Through a "move in discourse," the text displaces the border between feminine and masculine within the term "cidadan." In this way, the generic is denied its usual "transcendent value." The citizen, in Mouré's text, is "spoken from a 'minor' tongue" (the Galego of Galicia) by "a woman who bears—as a lesbian in a civic frame—a *policed sexuality*."[86] This uncanny relation between guest (a woman) and host (a word), this "in-/-corporation of the stranger, l'autrui"[87] which constitutes the "cidadan" is not limited to abstractions. It surfaces elsewhere in the text, for example, in the act of a Swiss border guard who in 1938 "altered 3600 passports to permit Austrian Jews entry to his country."[88] In other words, the crossing of borders that one might associate with world travel, is here presented in local terms. This border-crossing is only possible thanks to an extraordinary act of citizenship: "To make one's own inviolable seam permeable: this act a citizen's act."[89]

It is at the border that citizenship is both enacted and policed. *O Cidadán* is not, however, a call for a borderless world. In the words of Mouré's text: "But not to deny borders. For they mark a disruptive and unruly edge."[90] Mouré's poems work instead to make the borders legible. In so doing, they both expose the mechanisms by which borders are regulated and exploit the possibilities for unruliness, unruliness which takes many forms—from the possibility of thinking in one language and writing in another[91] to the non-coincidence of communities and territorial states.

"Bear[ing] a strange tongue (yet hegemonic)"[92]

In bringing together the poems of Sarah, di Michele and Mouré, this essay highlights some of the differences among the writings that constitute Anglo-Quebec literature. In the case of the three writers discussed here, these differences are evident in the poems' engagement with the local and the global, in their conception of urban space, in their construction of the writing subject, in the intertextual weave of their texts and in their approach to language.

The Montreal of Sarah's *Questions* is a heterogeneous assemblage of lived experiences, personal memories and disparate traces of cultural and religious belonging. Montreal is recognizable in *Questions* not only through references to familiar places and names but also through combinations like "Hassidim" and "Greek Orthodox church" which speak of specific neighbourhoods. If Sarah's lyric poems create a sense of home, it is a home pieced together from the remnants of places and cultural practices which have been "left behind"—both in the sense of remnants left behind by other tenants and in the sense of places and practices left behind by the writing subject's grandparents. Global migrations are, for the most part, situated in the past. It would be difficult to claim that Sarah's poems offer a substantial opening on a "wider world"[93] in the way that Mouré's do, for example. Sarah's poems are nonetheless interesting for their inquiry into the local and, specifically, into the status of the local as an interface rather than as an enclave, as an interface among cultures.

Although it would be fairly easy to read the city of Sarah's poems as English-speaking, there are occasional references, for example, to "Rue Jeanne Mance" or to the "*cor anglais*,"[94] which suggest that French is the language of the public sphere. The name "*cor anglais*" is thought to derive from the French "cor anglé" (a description of the instrument's curved shape) which was mis-transcribed by the English as "cor anglais" and therefore mis-translated as "English horn"[95] sometime during the eighteenth century. Insofar as Sarah's poem uses the French term for a horn which is "English" (although in name only), this figure also registers a certain irony and, perhaps, a certain resistance to attempts to legislate the "music" of the streets, that is, the movement from one language to another or the sound of several languages being spoken at once. The image of the "cor anglais" wobbling "through the notes of a minor scale" and wavering "out of tune / to breaking"[96] presents English in Quebec as a language in translation, as a language in a minor key. The text's attitude toward such "wobbling," "wavering" and "breaking" is left relatively ambiguous: the debates of the public sphere and the analysis of relations of power among languages are not part of the "everyday" of Sarah's poems.

Di Michele's "Invitation," too, constructs the local as an interface but an interface generated by layered histories more than by spatial adjacencies. Montreal is the metropolis from which di Michele's speaker retreats, the winter landscape she sees outside her house and, most significantly for my reading, the weave of words and names which includes "Lachine." Whereas Sarah's poems *use language* to create a sense of a locale, di Michele's "Invitation to Read Wang Wei in a Montréal Snowstorm" explores language itself as a locale, as a landscape which is linked to a given place yet which is also enmeshed in an intertextual network that moves across borders. In di Michele's poem, then, Montreal's links to the globe, like the city's internal linguistic borders, are presented primarily in textual terms. The use of the accent on "Montréal" in the English-language title of the poem, for example, is a way of signalling the specificity of a Québécois space, a space where languages meet but where French is recognized as the official language of the place. The poem's evocation of "Lachine," too, reminds readers of the French history of Montreal. Indeed, the place-name "Lachine" turns out to have more to do with "here" than with the "elsewhere" of Wang Wei's China. But it is nevertheless reading the Chinese poet Wang Wei which brings "Lachine" to the writing subject's mind. Indeed, the travels of the place-name "Lachine" from one side of the globe to the other are ongoing if one considers the intertextual processes of reading which animate di Michele's poem.

The Montreal of Mouré's *O Cidadán* is a site in which to rethink the citizen, a particularly auspicious site insofar as it allows the writing subject to imagine the "cidadan" as traversed by several languages as well as by several cultures. Mouré's poems, although written primarily in English, move frequently into other languages, thereby emphasizing not only the political and geographical borders the citizen traverses, but also those borders which structure her subjectivity. These internal folds and seams are enacted on the page through a geometry of disparate grammars, discursive frames, typographies, vectors, shapes and poetic forms. Indeed, the page becomes a space in which reading and writing subjects work to re-draw (in sculptural or architectural terms) the citizen and to re-direct public debate.

What the writing subject of *O Cidadán* finds in Montreal is not a "home" but rather the possibility of being a stranger, of bearing "a strange tongue" (English) and, at the same time, being "a part of the body politic."[97] Di Michele's writing subject finds the same possibility—the possibility of being a stranger if not that of bearing a strange tongue—in reading Wang Wei.[98] In Mouré's collection, Montreal serves as a site of "civilian love," a site in which subjects link themselves with those who might usually be seen as "other." Through the French word "autrui," *O Cidadán* explores citizenship as an ethics of "being-among,"[99] a concept which includes those one does not know but can *imagine* as part of the social, those who live, for example, outside the borders of Quebec. In Mouré's text, Quebec's relationship to the world is negotiated through French (and other languages) as well as through English. Substantially influenced by French-language culture and philosophy, Mouré's writing subject thinks in French (not to mention Spanish, Portugese and Galego) while writing primarily in English.[100] Montreal and, more broadly, Quebec make this internal border crossing possible for Mouré.

Such crossings exist in the writing of Sarah and di Michele but they are not as explicit, as politicized or as disruptive in formal terms. Puns such as "*cor anglais*" and "Lachine," for example, are richly suggestive of the overlay of languages and cultures one finds in Montreal; and French words such as "rue" and "Montréal" effectively interrupt the English text but none of them involve French as an everyday discursive practice or as a medium through which to organize thought. The allusion in di Michele's title to Baudelaire's prose poem "Invitation au voyage" speaks of an intertextual relationship with French-language culture akin to that of Mouré. Indeed, the affinity between the writing of di Michele and that of Mouré is clear from the shared interest in intertextuality and in language as space or locale. However, one of the many differences lies in the fact that when di Michele's writing engages with "elsewhere," that engagement is heavily mediated by *literary* intertexts. Nonetheless, in the case of all three writers, French inhabits their poetry in ways which reinforce my argument that "elsewhere" is constitutive of "here" and that the relationship between "here" and "elsewhere" is mediated by the specificity of linguistic and cultural practices in Quebec. In other words, the local orients and organizes the traffic and travel of the global.

Fugitive Places: Anne Carson and the Unlost

DEAN IRVINE

Where is here?

> World as it is when I am not there.
> —Anne Carson[1]

For the special millennial issue of *Essays on Canadian Writing* (2000), editors Robert Lecker and Kevin Flynn recast Northrop Frye's infamous riddle ("Where is here?") in the conclusion to *The Literary History of Canada*.[2] Posing the question "Where Is Here Now?" to "scholars, writers, and editors," Flynn and Lecker solicited formal and informal essays in response and collected them as a "field report" on the state of Canadian literature at the end of the millennium.[3] David McGimpsey's essay in the issue, "A Walk in Montreal: Wayward Steps through the Literary Politics of Contemporary English Quebec," takes us on a tour from Montreal's Mile End district to Crescent Street, providing peripatetic commentary on the city's English-language urban culture. According to his final report, "despite the presence of so many terrific authors, Montreal is not a particularly vibrant place for English-language writing today.... Some of this is entrenched in the obvious: the English-language market here is about the size of Saskatoon, and it's not getting bigger."[4] Yet the example McGimpsey makes of the late Montreal celebrity and bestseller Mordecai Richler should indicate the limited reach of his essay's localized argument, for neither literary celebrity nor literary markets are restricted to a specific locality. The question "Where is here?" is no longer a local, regional, or even a national concern but one loaded with global implications.

If the absence of Anne Carson from McGimpsey's millennial tour of literary Montreal is symptomatic of her belated celebrity in Canada, her subsequent honours—the Griffin Poetry Prize and nomination for the Governor General's Award for Poetry in 2001, the publication of *Canadian Literature*'s special issue on Carson in 2003, and her appointment to the Order of Canada in 2005—swiftly confirmed her status as a nationally celebrated writer. At the same time, the appearance of a series of essays in 2001–02 by Sherry Simon affirmed Carson's largely unacknowledged presence as a "quintessential" and "emblematic" Montreal writer.[5] These acts of national and local definition, which raise questions about the "Canadianness" of her work[6] and about the linguistic hybridity of Montreal and her writing's affinities to the multilingual city's "translational sensibility,"[7] are indicative of the critical tendency in Canada since the turn of the millennium to reclaim Carson's internationally acclaimed oeuvre as a distinguished contribution to Canadian and Quebec literatures and thereby gain purchase on her celebrity.

Carson's rise to literary celebrity coincided with her tenure as a professor of Classics at McGill University from 1988 to 2003. Although an English-language author living in Quebec, she had little reason to be concerned with Montreal's limited Anglophone audience. If she ever shared David Solway's anxieties about being a "double exile"[8]—at once exiled from Francophone Quebec, and exiled from the rest of Anglophone Canada—her early critical success in the United States and concomitant penetration of international markets must have helped to assuage any concerns by enabling her to transcend limitations imposed by locality and nationality. After the London, Ontario small press Brick Books brought out her first poetry collection *Short Talks* in 1992, she rapidly secured an international following through publication by major American presses (New Directions and Alfred A. Knopf). To say that Carson has achieved a kind of literary celebrity unbounded by civic, provincial, or national borders is to state the obvious. As accruals of symbolic capital, neither her celebrity nor the status of her work derives from local or national recognition; this is the cultural logic of literary values transacted in an era of late capitalism. Carson trades her capital on a transnational English-language market, where the materiality of civic and national markets is liquidated under the pressure of late capitalism's push toward globalization. Di Brandt, another contributor to the "Where Is Here Now?" issue, similarly acknowledges Carson's globalized market value. Brandt's essay "Going Global" includes Carson among a clutch of Canadian authors who lately "cracked the international market," authors who see themselves "as successful entrepreneurs with valuable cultural capital to trade."[9] While McGimpsey searches for answers to the question "Where is here?" and locates Montreal authors in a civic market, Brandt contends that Carson and other Canadian authors are more inclined to ask "Where is there?" and finds them seeking answers in a globalized literary marketplace.[10] This tendency toward the internationalization of Canadian literature was already prominent among Canada's late nineteenth- and early twentieth-century expatriate authors. As Nick Mount's *When Canadian Literature Moved to New York* attests, and as Eva Hemmungs Wirtén remarks, "we can understand the emerging internationalization taking place more than a century ago as a thing apart from, yet also reminiscent of, what we will encounter in globalization."[11]

The chief opponent to the rapid inflation of Carson's market value is David Solway, a Montreal poet and scholar who finds her celebrity nothing less than scandalous.[12] His polemical essay "The Trouble with Annie" is perhaps too easily dismissed as an *ad hominem* attack, but he does manage to mix ineffectual invective with incisive analysis of the media and institutional machines responsible for manufacturing Carson's celebrity: "Sometimes I find myself inadvertently thinking that Carson doesn't exist but is rather the creation of a couple heavyweight critics and a swarm of quailing lightweights straggling along in their wake." Later he surmises that "A major reason for her surging popularity may have something to do with the current obsession with fragments and simulacra?"[13] The trouble with Solway is that his propensity for diatribe clouds his insights into the simulationist logic that operates under the economy of late capitalism. If he's been reading his Baudrillard, he may continue to believe that "Carson doesn't exist," that she is the product of institutions and media that replicate the "fragments and simulacra" of late-capitalist culture, and that her celebrity is just as unreal as he wishes *her* to be.

Solway's last-ditch attempt to sabotage Carson's international success is to draw attention to the way in which one of her publishers (and to some extent Carson herself) markets her books.[14] With reference to the back-cover flap of her recent titles with Alfred A. Knopf (*Autobiography of Red: A Novel in Verse* [1998], *Men in the Off Hours* [2000], and *The Beauty of the Husband* [2001], *If Not, Winter: Fragments of Sappho* [2002]), he quotes the laconic biographical statement: "Anne Carson lives in Canada." "The implication," he says, "is that Canada is fortunate for being put on the map by virtue of its association with Anne Carson."[15] Yet the statement takes on significations other than an American publisher's condescension to Canadian nationalist pride. Consider that these books are published in the United States. Knopf has marketed her as an author positioned in between nations: living in Canada, but publishing for an international audience in the United States. For her publisher to announce "Anne Carson lives in Canada" is to situate her not "here" but "there." Being both "there" (living in Canada) and "here" (publishing in the United States), she occupies a transnational position in the book industry. Richard Cavell's explication of the Frygian riddle in the "Where Is Here Now" issue is pertinent to Knopf's location of Carson not "here" but "there": "If Frye's 'Where is here?' was supposed to articulate our identity in terms of place, then what the question mark pointed toward was a *Canadasein* (to use Avital Ronell's felicitous coinage[16]) whose 'being there' was always somewhere else."[17] For Carson, "living in Canada" is that state of *Canadasein*—"being there" in Canada, not "being here." In a globalized economy, the transnational state of *Canadasein* is always somewhere else, in transition, in between.

The Life of Towns

> I went travelling to a wreck of a place.
> —Anne Carson[18]

Montreal is alluded to only once in Carson's books. In a section of "The Anthropology of Water" in *Plainwater*, the travelogue is divided into entries with geographical headings—the majority of which are towns and interstates across the United States, but five of which are Lachine, Quebec. One of the Lachine entries includes an allusion to the massacre of fourteen women at L'École Polytechnique in Montreal on December 6, 1989: "Tonight as we drive down Route 15, the evening news on the radio brings a story from my hometown, where a man with a hunting rifle walked into a schoolroom and shot fourteen girls dead."[19] The L'École Polytechnique massacre is an event that immediately recalls its location in the narrator's hometown of Montreal and, at the same time, exceeds its locality. That the narrator and her companion ("the emperor") are driving on Route 15 places them in Quebec, heading south from Montreal to the U.S. border. The news broadcast of the l'École Polytechnique massacre presents a trauma narrative that radiates beyond the civic limits of Montreal—like the narrator and the emperor, crossing international borders. Although the entry is headed "Lachine, Quebec," the narrator speaks of the "story from my hometown" as if it were somewhere else: Montreal is always elsewhere in her narrative, a hometown where she is never at home.

Montreal maintains a low profile in "The Anthropology of Water," but the generic figure of the town is prominent elsewhere in *Plainwater*. Yet the "towns" in *Plainwater* are not really towns at all. "The Life of Towns" is a sequence of thirty-six poems, none of which refer to actual civic spaces. Carson opens the prose introduction to the sequence with the definition of a "town" and her narrator's relationship to it:

> Towns are the illusion that things hang together somehow ....
>
> I am a scholar of towns, let God commend that. To explain what I do is simple enough. A scholar is someone who takes a position. From which position, certain lines become visible. You will at first think I am painting the lines myself; it's not so. I merely know where to stand to see the lines that are there. And the mysterious thing, it is a very mysterious thing, is how these lines do paint themselves .... Well, let's not get carried away with exegesis. A scholar is someone who knows how to limit himself to the matter at hand.
>
> Matter which has painted itself within lines constitutes a town.[20]

Carson's definitions bespeak a certain resistance to location. Her poet-scholar takes a position, but never reveals a location. These towns she studies are everywhere and nowhere at once. They are simply the "matter" of poetry demarcated by the "lines that are there." As the *OED* reminds us, the modern usage of "town" derives from an Old English word meaning an "enclosed space." Carson's towns are textual spaces bounded typographically by the limit of the poetic line; each line is punctuated with a period, a perceptual and rhythmic break foregrounding the spatial limits of "the matter at hand" and the materiality of the language. The textual "matter" of the poems consists of sentence fragments, textual rubble—or, to materialize the metaphor, walls of towns that "hang together somehow." To reformulate Carson's opening and closing definitions of a town, one might say: (1) sentences are the illusion that language hangs together somehow; (2) language which has painted itself within lines constitutes a poem. Her punctuation in "The Life of Towns" calls attention to the position of the poet-scholar in relation to the poem: it reveals the edges of her perception, the limits of where she stands to see the poem. Language is always already there; it's a matter of the poet-scholar positioning herself in relation to it and seeing it, like a town, as an enclosed space.

The materiality of the "town" as a poetic form is related to Carson's thinking about the fragment. When asked in interview about her predilection for writing and translating fragments, she replied:

> I think two things: the fact that it has an unreal border, that is, it's broken off something that was bigger or intended to be bigger, and when I describe a fragment that way I'm thinking of the ones that I study in Greek or Latin manuscripts which are literally just shreds or something that was originally a bigger text. So that border which for us is a border of space or silence and quite unnatural gives an immediate defamiliarization, and also a framing which strengthens the content of whatever's left there on the page, or on the fragment, on the shred.[21]

The process of defamiliarization is inscribed at every line break of "The Life of Towns." Each punctuated line reveals the "unnatural" frame of white space around the lines that "paint themselves." These textualized towns at once mark the limit of the familiar and the unfamiliar, the natural and the unnatural. The illusion that towns "hang together somehow" as a whole is predicated upon a conception of the town as a familiar and natural dwelling space, but the fracturing of that illusion through the punctuated fragmentation of the wholeness of each poem effects the defamiliarization of the town and its revelation as an unnatural space assembled by means of *bricolage*.

As Carson puts it, "What I am writing in my own text is not a fragment, and I have to artificially create angles and fragmentation to make it more like those ancient pieces."[22] "The Life of Towns" is built upon the artifice of the fragment as an aesthetic unit of composition: it gestures toward wholes greater than the parts represented in the poems. As in the case of Greek or Latin manuscripts, fragments at once point toward the lost text that surrounds them and signify that which has been salvaged from libraries, archives, ruins, and middens. These towns are constructed in relation to that loss beyond the punctuation mark; they are poems that she would call "unlost"— that is, borrowing from Paul Celan, "*unverloren*," what is kept or saved or remembered, what is paradoxically not lost and yet always permeated by loss.[23] The white space of the right-hand margin signifies a lacuna, the unlost text beyond the sentence fragments of "The Life of Towns," which is not the same as the lacunae of an ancient manuscript or papyrus scroll. Even so, Carson's text playfully suggests the artifactual quality of textual fragments and towns. The punctuation at the right margin signals the modernity of these fragments, their typographically marked distinction from unpunctuated ancient manuscripts and papyri. These are, after all, ersatz fragments; their deliberate artifice produces an almost absurdist collection of textual fragments, texts in which arbitrary punctuation of otherwise perfectly legible sentences serves a visual rather than grammatical function. This punctuation manufactures the aura of an original text or town of which only fragments remain, even though there is no original. While "The Life of Towns" is obviously not an authentic collection of textual fragments, it is the simulation of one. The text purveys a simulationist logic: there is no original whole which has been lost, but rather the image of its loss marked by the wall of punctuation at the edge of a textualized town. Carson cultivates the appearance of the unlost text as a "mysterious thing," a material object invested with cultural capital normally accorded to unique artifacts and their reproductions. The mystery lies in what is lost, what cannot be represented by the semiotics of the text.

The unlost text is not just an aesthetic object, one that embodies a restricted economy of language, but one that circulates in a gift economy as a form of symbolic capital. According to Carson, a "poem yields surplus value"; it gives "a gift that for once is not a debt. Dismantling the axiom of exchange that says there is no such thing as grace in economics."[24] The surplus value of the unlost text lies in its lacunae, its silences. For Carson, "the economy of the unlost always involves gratuity. Whether you call it a waste of words or an act of grace depends on you."[25] The lacuna is the consummate gift: it wastes nothing, not a word. When Carson asks in her introduction to "The Life of Towns," "Can you punctuate yourself as silence?" she speaks to the ways in which the punctuation at the edge of the text become the "walls" of the town that "stand by in silence."[26] Not even a word, a mark of punctuation stands between the text and a place where "You will see the edges cut away from you, back into a world of another kind—back into real emptiness, some would say."[27] The wall of silence that separates the textual world from absolute negation is *not nothing*. It is, rather, a notation of the unlost.

In her edition of the fragments of Sappho, Carson chooses to foreground what is lost through the typographic arrangement of the fragments. Writing under the heading "On Marks and Lacks" in her introduction to *If Not, Winter: Fragments of Sappho*, she comments on her use of open-ended square brackets (] [)in her transcription to indicate the loss or illegibility of the original text:

> Brackets are an aesthetic gesture toward the papyrological event rather than an accurate record of it.... I emphasize the distinction between brackets and no brackets because it will affect your reading experience, if you allow it. Brackets are exciting. Even though you are reading Sappho in translation, that is no reason you should miss the drama of trying to read a papyrus torn in half or riddled with holes or smaller than a postage stamp—brackets imply a free space of imaginal adventure.[28]

Carson's distinction between the citation of Sapphic fragments in the works of ancient authors and the extant fragments preserved on papyri returns to the consideration of the fragment as an aesthetic object. The open brackets perform a function similar to the punctuation in "The Life of Towns" in that they gesture toward a lost text. Yet Carson suggests that the brackets create the possibility for the reclamation of the lost text through the "imaginal adventure" of reading. Her open brackets point toward another species of unlost text, one that the reader can pursue through an act of imagination. No amount of imagining will ever reconstitute the original. Rather, the "imaginal adventure" of navigating the open spaces of the unlost text is analogous to the early-modern explorer's interpretation of maps whose edges are bordered by *terra incognita*. Like the illuminated edges of explorer's maps that signify unexplored areas of the globe, Carson's invitation to "imaginal adventure" tempts the reader's eye to venture into unmapped territories, to participate in the romance of reading, to make meaning of a perpetually lost world that the romantic imagination translated into one inhabited by whales, dragons, and monsters and that modern-day readers of Sappho populate with the gods and heroic figures of Greek mythology, the denizens of her hometown Mytilene, and the honey-hued landscapes of her native Lesbos. This is less true of the citations of fragments from ancient authors, the interpretation of which serves to fix the fragment (and its lost context) in a given reading. But the unlost text surrounding the papyri fragments is intractable, resistant to hermeneutic mastery. It remains *terra incognita*. The undiscovered text is perpetually nowhere.

Where is Erytheia?

> "In the middle of nowhere."
> Where.
> Would that be?
> —Anne Carson[29]

Autobiography of Red is a book that Carson might have called "Red Town." Just as "The Life of Towns" innovates the genre of a town's biography, so *Autobiography of Red* relates in part the narrative of an island called Erytheia. The island's name (which she translates as "The Red Place"[30]) derives from the ancient Greek poet Stesichoros's lyric account of the tenth labour of Herakles. Only fragments of the lyric survive under the name "*Geryoneis* ('The Geryon Matter')."[31] According to Carson's proem ("Red Meat: What Difference Did Stesichoros Make?"), the fragments "tell of a strange winged red monster [Geryon] who lived on an island called Erytheia (which is an adjective simply meaning 'The Red Place') quietly tending a herd of magical red cattle, until one day the hero Herakles came across the sea and killed him to get the cattle."[32] The second section of the book ("Red Meat: Fragments of Stesichoros") consists of Carson's translation of "The Geryon Matter," another series of her variations on the form and content of fragments. Two appendices follow the translation, prior to the central section of the book, "Autobiography of Red: A Romance." The romance is a verse narrative in which the mythologically named main characters Geryon and Herakles meet by chance at a bus station on the island of Erytheia.

The first half of the romance takes place on Erytheia, revolving around the childhood and adolescence of Geryon, a wingèd red boy. Upon Herakles' arrival on the island from New Mexico, the two adolescents become entwined in an erotic affair. The island narrative culminates in a road trip to "Herakles' hometown of Hades / [which] lay at the other end of the island about four hours by car." Hades is "a town of moderate size and little importance /

except for one thing," it has an active volcano.[33] Rather than setting Erytheia in a particular geography, Carson resists its location.[34] Erytheia remains a mythical island, its location symbolic of the region of death that in ancient Greek myth lies in the far west. That Hades should be located on the island confirms its association with the symbolic *topos* of Greek myth. Erytheia is not an island found on ancient maps; nor is it an island in the mouth of the St. Lawrence River. As the pre-adolescent winged red boy writes in his notebook (his "*Autobiography*") under the heading "Total Facts Known About Geryon," "Geryon lived on an island in the Atlantic called the Red Place."[35] It is significant that the island is known only by the ancient Greek adjective for "red place." This is not a fixed place, but a colour; not a proper noun, but an adjective. Adjectives are relational parts of speech: they take a position in relation to a noun; they qualify the kind of place the noun occupies and names. As Carson says, "Nouns name the world. Verbs activate the names. Adjectives come from somewhere else."[36] Erytheia is not a fixed location, but always "somewhere else."

Carson's so-called *auto*biography begins with a *bio*graphy of Stesichoros, about whom we apparently know very little, and a history of the language of "The Geryon Matter." The probably apocryphal story of Stesichoros's life for which he is most famous—his blinding at the hands of Helen of Troy for having written about her unfavourably, and his subsequent restoration of vision after writing a renunciation—is contained in the three appendices following the first poetic section of the text ("Red Meat: Fragments of Steisichoros"). In juxtaposition to the apocrypha, Carson's biography of Steisichoros places emphasis on the cultural location of his writing and the sources of his language. According to this biography, he "lived among refugees who spoke a mixed dialect of Chalcidian and Doric. A refugee population is hungry for language and aware that anything can happen." These details, which situate the author of "The Geryon Matter" among refugees, speak to the innovative character of language in his lyric sequence, particularly adjectives, as in part responsive to changes introduced by the refugees' "mixed dialect." As Carson notes, "The word *adjective* (*epitheton* in Greek) is itself an adjective meaning 'placed on top,' 'added,' 'appended,' 'imported,' 'foreign.'"[37] Adjectives, so it seems, are "imported" and "foreign" parts of speech analogous to "a refugee population." For Carson, as for Steisichoros, adjectives are the refugees of language.

So, too, is the "Red Place" a fugitive place. In "Autobiography of Red: A Romance," Geryon names the island the "Red Place,"[38] but its name is never revealed outside the text of his *Autobiography*. The island is unnamed but permeated by redness in "Red Meat: Fragments of Stesichoros." Carson's translation of "The Geryon Matter" covers the fragments with a red wash, allowing its colour to penetrate the surfaces of everything on the island. The adjectival profusion of "red" throughout her version of "The Geryon Matter" is unique among translations of Stesichoros. The flood of red liberates Carson from the strictures of literal translation; her adjectives "come from somewhere else" and allow her to translate "The Geryon Matter" to a location that is not Stesichoros's "Red Place" but elsewhere. Her translation produces a sequence of fragments saturated with their location in a "red world."[39] Yet their location remains unnamed and fluid. Rather than fixing the island's location with nouns that "name the world," she employs adjectives which in the Homeric tradition "are in charge of attaching everything in the world to its place in particularity"[40] but which in Stesichoros are released from their fixity.

The fragmentary state of Stesichoros's text invites Carson to take an "imaginal adventure"[41] in the translation: she interpolates the "matter" of the modern world ("ticking red taxi," "Coil of the hot plate," "glass-bottomed boat," "the bar," "the police," "the blind Atlantic morning"[42]) into the "matter" of ancient fragments. These anachronisms displace Stesichoros's fragments from their original chronotopic frame into another temporal and spatial location. The lacunae in "The Geryon Matter" present Carson with what she calls a "free space"[43] in the translation, a space in which her interpolated anachronisms dislocate the original into a new matrix of spatial and temporal relations. In a 1997 interview, Carson anticipates the disorientations effected by her Stesichoros translation: "What I'm trying to do is to describe an object or event that could never exist, or more dimensions than are possible, or more angle division than a person could take. So that the fictional rises up through the factual and adds angles that go off into dotted lines because there are not real lines there."[44] This compositional practice differs from her poet-scholar's perspective on the "matter" of towns. Her translation of Stesichoros veers from the "lines that are there," inserts lines that "could never exist," and thus multiplies the angles and dimensions of the fragments.

The angles she creates in "Fragments of Stesichoros" do not lead directly back to an original; there is no linear trajectory connecting source and target text, original and translation. Carson's translation frequently follows the trajectories of "dotted lines" into the lacunae that surround the extant text. "Fragments of Stesichoros" also incorporates contextual commentary ("Old scholia say that Stesichoros says that"[45]), absorbing the ways in which some fragments have been preserved as quotations within the works of ancient authors into the body of the translation. Describing the state of the surviving originals, she notes that "the fragments of the *Geryoneis* itself read as if Stesichoros had composed a substantial narrative poem then ripped it to pieces and buried the pieces in a box with some song lyrics and lecture notes and scraps of meat. The fragment numbers tell you roughly how the pieces fell out of the box. You can of course keep shaking the box."[46] Her invitation to "keep shaking the box" is not to suggest that the original order could somehow be arrived at by chance, but to say that the method of her translation is to accept the randomness of the text. The selection and arrangement of some of the "principal fragments"[47] embraces the random character of the extant original, using its textual instability and corruption as points of departure for her shifting representations of Stesichoros's "Red Place."

Moving from the translation of Stesichoros to the central romance narrative, Carson leads us beyond the "free space" around "Fragments of Stesichoros." The genre of romance is ideally suited to an "imaginal adventure" into the peripheries of "The Geryon Matter." "Autobiography of Red: A Romance" follows a narrative vector—not unlike the romances of ancient and early-modern times that spin out of epics and sacred texts. There is only a tangential relationship between the original fragments and Carson's romance narrative: it consists of lines that "could never exist" and heads outward from the "The Geryon Matter" in the direction of "dotted lines because there are not real lines there." Instead of interpolating into the extant fragments, the romance extrapolates from the fragments. Carson's romance is another species of unlost text, a narrative that builds upon the matter imported into "Fragments of Stesichoros" from "somewhere else." There is, of course, no lost original of her romance; it is predicated upon the "economy of loss"[48] that pervades "The Geryon Matter." Her unlost text is analogous to the posthumous stories that Carson identifies, in her introduction to her translation of Sappho, "at the inside edge where her words go missing, a sort of antipoem that condenses everything you every wanted her to write."[49] These unlost texts are the stories of ancient poets that circulate around fragments but never deliver the fragments themselves, the apocryphal stories that accumulate for centuries and become the matter of romance.

Autobiography of Red is situated between verse and prose, poem and antipoem, text and context. Like the island of Erytheia, its genre evades the fixity of singular location. It incorporates an introductory essay, three appendices (prose testimonia, verse palinode, and prose syllogism), a verse translation, a verse romance, and an interview. It advertises itself as an autobiography, yet none of its multiplicity of genres resembles auto-biography. The accumulated parts of the text run into a generic surplus, but its totality shows a generic lack. Even as the text's economy of genre tends toward excess, its surplus is negated by the evident absence of conventional autobiography.

Even so, we encounter the multiple versions of Geryon's unconventional autobiography throughout the romance section of the text—as sculpture (a tomato with a shredded ten-dollar bill for hair),[50] as juvenilia (an early "notebook" version of "Red Meat: Fragments of Stesochoros"),[51] and as photographic essay.[52] These autobiographies conclude, significantly, with an absent photograph of the interior of a volcano: "It is a photograph he never took, no one here took it."[53] This unlost photograph, whose title ("The Only Secret People Keep") is taken from the Emily Dickinson poem (#1748) that serves as the epigraph to the section, captures the flight of Geryon's "imaginal adventure" into a romance narrative that transcends the fixity and closure of his death as told in "The Geryon Matter." Instead of taking his camera on his flight into the volcano, Geryon takes the tape recorder with which Herakles and Ancash record volcanoes for their "*documentary on Emily Dickinson.*"[54] At the moment when the "ancient eye" of the volcano is transformed into a "camera" that takes the image of his immortality, Geryon prefaces his recording of the volcano with a dedication: "*This is for Ancash.*"[55] Rather than conclude his autobiography with a closing photo-graph, Geryon offers the recording as a gift. This act of grace is a sign of his autobiography's economy: its gratuity, its surplus, its gift that is not a debt.

Autobiography of the Unlost

> This thing, language, remained unlost, yes, in spite of everything.
> –Paul Celan[56]

Not unlike the ways in which *Autobiography of Red* transacts an economy of negation, Carson seeks to negate her own autobiography. This act of negation is an attempt to depersonalize her art, to remove herself from the spotlight of celebrity into the shadows of anonymity. Journalists and interviewers have repeatedly called attention to Carson's resistance to disclosing autobiographical detail and to her frustration of their demand. As an interviewee Carson has always been anti-autobiographical—a tendency that extends to the mock interviews she stages in her poetry—but in conjunction with the rise of her celebrity she has taken refuge in the idea of anonymity. Speaking in interview, she reflects upon her preference for the anonymity of the ancient poets: "We have no idea what Homer looked like, and the only description that exists from antiquity of Sappho is that she was short, dark, and ugly ...: So I'm happy to be thought short, dark and ugly!"[57] Carson's desire to purvey the image of her own anonymity is a counter-reaction to the consumption of her celebrity. Anonymity is a negation of celebrity, a mode of resistance to consumption. It operates in a negative economy, where celebrity is exchanged for the sign of anonymity.

Celebrity subscribes to the mode of consumption to which Carson refers in the introduction to *Autobiography of Red*. "Consumption is not a passion for substances but a passion for the code," she quotes from Baudrillard. Stesichoros, she claims, had a "passion for substances" which compelled him to release adjectives from their fixed Homeric codes and to reclaim the materiality of language as "substance."[58] The code of Carson's literary celebrity is similarly fixed, tied to her publisher's marketing strategies—from biographical statements to blurbs from high-profile authors such as Alice Munro, Susan Sontag, Michael Ondaatje, and Michael Cunningham. Carson's attempts to unfix the code are evident in her aggressive critique of the packaging and marketing of her books by Knopf: "They think you care—they quote marketing statistics at me. But I'm working to subvert this system from within, ... along with the whole economy.... This is my present aspiration next time: to have a blank book: just a title, author (smaller), publisher—nothing else."[59] This anticonsumerist project has not so far been realized. Her desire to undermine the economy of the book industry would likely fall on deaf ears at Knopf. Were Carson to pitch her plan to an avant-garde press, she might actually see the book in production.[60]

In any event, the implications of her blank book are considerable, if only as a theoretical text. Its marketability would depend entirely upon Carson's literary celebrity, so that consumers would purchase a text entirely on the basis of their willingness to invest in a code without receiving anything of actual substance (except a blank book in which they could perhaps write their own autobiographies). In that consumers would receive a material object, they would obtain something in exchange, but they would essentially be wasting their money in order to own a piece of Carson's symbolic capital. As an avant-garde provocation of the narrowly economic interests of the publishing industry, her book would exist only as a material object—a kind of anti-book that directs our attention only to its materiality and its resistance to consumption as a commodity. As a text, the blank book would be comparable to a volume consisting of only the spaces that surround fragments, an artificially produced version of lost text. Its title would be analogous to those vanished books whose titles still survive in citations. Yet it would be the epitome of all *un*lost texts—a text in which not a word is wasted, nothing lost. Even to speak of a book that does not exist (nor, in all likelihood, ever will exist) is already to participate in its negative economy, for Carson's blank book can be cited but never quoted from—even if it were released by a publisher. It could, therefore, effectively advance a critique of the consumerist impulse to expend capital on nothing but the code of celebrity. And it would, after all, be the final word in anti-celebrity—an anti-autobiography.

Carson's critique of literary celebrity returns us in ironic counterpoint to David Solway. When he considers the possibility that "Carson doesn't exist," that her celebrity is a fabrication and that she is a "literary impostor,"[61] he identifies the code of consumption whereby the author ceases to exist except as a sign to be exchanged for symbolic capital. While Roland Barthes famously identified the modern fixation on the "'person' of the author" with "capitalist ideology,"[62] more recently, Pierre Bourdieu has positioned the author as the agent of a capitalist-bourgeois ideology that is predicated upon the "collective disavowal of commercial interests and profits."[63] According to Bourdieu, the author's "practical *negations*" or disavowals of economic capital are "reconverted into symbolic capital,"[64] which accrues around the name of the author. "For the author …," he argues, "the only legitimate accumulation consists in making a name for oneself, a known, recognized name."[65] As a critique of the capitalist-bourgeois economy and celebrity-oriented book industry, Carson's blank book would efface the "person" of the author, presenting herself only as a nominal sign without exchange value. Her authorial sign would preside over a text that discloses nothing of the "person" behind the name. Frustrating the tendency to identify the content of the book with the author, Carson would reveal that the author has been emptied of signification. The blank book thus approaches her ideal of authorial anonymity. Under the sign of authorship, she would inhabit a textual position in relation to the book, but evade location as a "person."[66]

The trajectory in Carson's work that leads from *Plainwater*, to *Autobiography of Red*, to *If Not, Winter*, to the blank book describes an arc that moves from textualized space outward to what she calls "free space." But what and where is free space in a globalized market economy? One possibility can be found in Carson's poetics of the unlost, her economy of negation. The textualization of these unlost spaces in *Plainwater*, *Autobiography of Red*, and *If Not, Winter* anticipates the unrealized, utopian free space embodied by the blank book. This antibook is, in a way, a companion text to *Economy of the Unlost*, where Carson writes about Simonides of Keos and Paul Celan and their practice of the poetics and economics of negation.[67] "There is too much self in my writing,"[68] she begins, and proceeds "to talk about two men at once. They keep each other from settling. Moving and not settling, they are side by side in a conversation and yet no conversation takes place."[69] Carson is the third in the conversation, but she wants to write herself out of her own writing; she inhabits a medial space between two authors, which prevents her from "settling" or writing about herself. However, by shuttling back and forth between the ancient and the modern and by inscribing her own mediality, Carson effectively re-enacts her own poetic practice, which enables her to mediate the conversation between Simonides and Celan and, at the same time, express her own interest in the poetics and economics of negation. As a gesture toward her own writing, *Economy of the Unlost* is shadowed by its author contemplating her own text of absolute negation and perfect economy—a blank book, an anti-autobiography, a free space.

Carson's most recent text isn't a blank book, but it does pursue a poetics of the unlost and its negative economy to different ends. *Decreation* (2005), another multigeneric collection, which culminates in an eponymous essay ("Decreation: How Women Like Sappho, Marguerite Porete, and Simone Weil Tell God") and opera ("Decreation: An Opera in Three Parts"), reiterates Carson's preoccupation with "getting the self out of the way."[70] Adopting the program Simone Weil called "decreation," Carson embarks in her essay to elaborate the ways in which certain women have sought to decentre the self in their writing and, instead, "create a sort of dream of distance in which the self is displaced from the centre of the work and the teller disappears

287

into the telling."[71] Although Carson is not explicitly writing about herself, we may infer that the strategies of "decreation" that she identifies in Weil's work are active in Carson's as well. Given her tendency in the essay to offer broad pronouncements on the conditions of being a writer, her decision not to speak of her own writing seems a deliberate strategy at once to deflect attention away from herself and to reflect upon her own situation as an author: "To be a writer is to construct a big, shiny centre of self from which the writing is given voice and any claim to be intent on annihilating this self while still continuing to write and give voice to writing must involve the writer in some important acts of subterfuge or contradiction."[72] As should be apparent from her musings on the blank book, her anti-autobiographical interviews, as well as her essays and criticism, Carson's penchant for subterfuge and delight in contradiction may well be among the defining attributes of her continued efforts to decreate herself in the very act of writing—or, in the idiom of her "Decreation" essay, "telling"—her self out of the way.

Among the self-reflexive acts of decreation in her most recent book is her evident success in persuading Knopf to divest her book of the most conspicuous codes of literary celebrity. Instead of back-cover copy on the book jacket—conventionally the space reserved for the publisher's promotion of the author's works—there is only a bronze colour field with the mandatory UPC barcode and ISBN number at the foot, which flies in the face of her publishers' past practice of packing her dust jackets with compendia of praise and acclaim by literary luminaries. Even so, the laconic "Note about the Author" that had appeared in the back pages and on the jacket flap of her previous Knopf titles ("Anne Carson lives in Canada") has been replaced by a lengthy list of her awards and accomplishments:

> Anne Carson was twice a finalist for the National Book Critics Circle Award; was honored with the 1996 Lannan Award and the 1997 Pushcart Prize, both for poetry; and was named MacArthur Fellow in 2000. In 2001 she received the T.S. Eliot Prize for Poetry—the first woman to do so; the Griffin Poetry Prize; and the Los Angeles Times Book Prize. She currently teaches at the University of Michigan.

Her "biography" is almost entirely comprised of prizes and awards, punctuated by the announcement of a new change of address: she no longer "lives in Canada."

Rather than the former pose of pseudo-anonymity ("Anne Carson lives in Canada"), her new identity has become one and the same as the resumé of awards and prizes that signify her celebrity. This is, in effect, an act of decreation—a strategy of "getting the self out of the way" that employs both contradiction and subterfuge. Carson's biography is represented by an encyclopedic list of accolades that distracts us from the fact that we no longer know anything of substance about the person of the author, except that she is a consecrated name. Her name is no longer a cipher of self, but a signifier of celebrity. Where she lives has ceased to matter. What matters—at least to her publisher—is her accelerated accumulation of symbolic capital, her literary value that is substituted as a negation of her economic value. Because her name now sells itself, independent of plaudits from the literati, Knopf can afford to grant Carson a "free space" on the back of *Decreation*—no, not a blank book, but a space in which the author (in collaboration with jacket designer Carol Devine Carson) abstains from marketing her literary celebrity, and in doing so makes a cunning, albeit lacunal, statement of anti-celebrity. Because this is a free space that is exchanged for the surplus value of her celebrity, it isn't really "free" at all, but rather the simulation of a gift, an economy of loss afforded by and indebted to an economy of celebrity. Whether we call it a waste of space or an act of grace depends on our disposition toward the economy of Carson's book, its simultaneous negations and accruals of capital, its subterfuges and contradictions.

Jabbed with Plenty: Peter Van Toorn and the Canadian Condition

ZACHARIAH WELLS

Our national foundation myths tell us that when European settlers first arrived in Canada, they found a vast empty land. If it was full of anything in the eyes of these pioneers, it was the raw potential of resources—and the anxiety-causing potential of failure and death. As schematic syntheses like Margaret Atwood's *Survival* demonstrate, much of our literature has been obsessed with making sense of the putative vacuum, with recording the ways in which we have attempted to fill the void and with negotiating our psychological sense of inferiority or victimhood, wedged as we are between the mute rock of northern nature on the one hand and the intimidating cultural hard places of Great Britain and the U.S.A. on the other. Atwood's wary approach to a theory of Canadian Literature is in fact uncannily similar to early settlers' notions of their new found land. She tells us that her assumption prior to beginning *Survival* was that there was no such thing as Canadian Literature, that it was a dearth, a shapeless scatter of texts bound together by no single theme or myth. Even if there was a pattern to be discerned—and not merely one to be superimposed, as David Solway maintains[1]—perhaps we would be better off now if Atwood had pretended otherwise, for despite her repeated disclaimers that she does not consider *Survival* to be the final word in delineating a Canadian literature, any such attempt at a critical meta-narrative inevitably involves the fixing of perimeters and parameters, establishing not-so-ghostly demarcations between what is "literature written by Canada" and what is not.

This is the theoretical equivalent to clearing brush and woodland to build a homestead. Atwood says that the Canadian pioneer:

> ... is a square man in a round whole; he faces the problem of trying to fit a straight line into a curved space. Of course, the *necessity* for

the straight lines is not in Nature but in his own head; he might have had a happier time if he'd tried to fit himself into Nature, not the other way round.[2]

That Atwood's pioneering study is such a neat analogue for the literal breaking of ground by main force is the central irony of *Survival*. It is hard not to see her as Paul Bunyan and her book as Babe the Blue Ox, bound and determined to pull the bows out of the laughing Mississippi of literature. Her book gives handy thematic shortcuts to academic specialists and to writers seeking to curry the favour of a university audience, but the straight line it takes elides the essential curviness of the literary enterprise and thereby excludes much undomesticated writing that doesn't fit into the established paradigm—whilst promoting less accomplished, but thematically correct, texts to canonical status.[3] *Edible plants inside, weeds outside*: a tautology that renders anything that grows on one side of the fence foison and anything on the other side poison, so that if one comes across an unidentifiable plant in one's wanderings beyond the well-hoed rows of the garden, one will be automatically suspicious of it, though it be the most delectable fruit in the forest. The problem with a literature based on themes of survival and victimhood is a Maslovian one.[4] When the basic requirements of staying alive occupy the mind, the higher functions of self-actualization—including aesthetic pleasure and grace, including the manic elation of inspiration—go unfulfilled. Can there be a greater failing for an artist than this? The dogged cultivation of stunted crops in soil and weather ill-suited to their growth is stupid—tragically so—when richer nourishment hangs ripe and ignored on the bough.

Several critics have objected to the bare-bones, unadorned survivalist ethic in recent decades. In 1985, thirteen years after the publication of *Survival*, M. Travis Lane wrote in a review of George Elliott Clarke's *Saltwater Spirituals and Deeper Blues*, that:

Many of our contemporary Canadian poets have adopted for their verse a deliberately plain style, whose lack of ornamentation, allusion, and musical grace is intended, in most cases, to portray a sense of newness, of emptiness—what they perceive as the linguistic and cultural barrenness of the Canadian "landscape," the Canadian experience. This style conveys a sense of cultural de-racination, but, sometimes, also a kind of cultural inhibition—as if a turn of speech natural to an educated mind might be somehow un-Canadian. At its best (Atwood, Kroetsch) this style of heightened simplicity can be powerful, but, as in the comparable paintings of Colville, it is not so much a representation of reality as it is *an artificial conventionalization of reality*. The adoption of this plain style may have helped our poetry sever its colonial roots, and, as practiced by its masters, it need never be rejected. But a mature literature needs to use the whole of its inheritance.[5]

Lane here points out the central fallacy of the Canadian plain style: that it is somehow more natural and native than showy imports using meter, metaphorical flourishes and patterns of rhyme. Most prosodists, in fact, insist that metrical verse is less artificial and synthetic than prose, which evolved as a literary form along with other sophisticated technological developments, such as the printing press. Thus, the deliberate prosiness of Canadian poetry, far from being aligned with the "barren emptiness" of Canadian nature, is the kissing cousin of Western industrialization, of mankind's alienation from the earth's natural rhythms and patterns.

Another writer taking issue with orthodox Canadian poetics in the 1980s was Peter Van Toorn, whose seminal work *Mountain Tea* was published in 1984. The critical neglect of Van Toorn's poetry is perhaps the grossest instance of the literary establishment's blind husbandry and bad diet. On the surface, at least according to Survivalist logic, Van Toorn is the most un-Canadian of poets. Whereas the pioneer poet has a puritanical suspicion of "superfluous" ornamentation, Van Toorn deploys a "baroque artillery" of catholic technique.[6] Whereas Canadian settlers seem to lack the vocabulary to identify the elements of their environment, Van Toorn's improvisatory and often inventorial poems are overbrimming fonts of aboriginal nomenclature.[7] Whereas *Survival* poets focus on the here and now, Van Toorn is a cosmopolite who ranges widely and travels in time by translating poems from other eras and by adapting classical forms into his own unique idiom. In short, it's no small temptation to see Van Toorn as an alien in a strange land. Certainly, he seems to have been perceived as such, if the grudging praise and dismissive skepticism of *Mountain Tea*'s early reviews and the subsequent critical silence are anything to go by.[8] But it is my contention that the superabundance of his verse, his proclivities for catalogue and neologism, are the formal answer to a land that is not in fact harsh and empty, but bountiful and populous. His globetrotting and time-travelling quests for antecedents do not so much constitute a negation of Canadian identity as a mature awareness that our collective character is not singular but prismatically various; that we are not at the awkward early stages of history rising out of primeval mud, but the heirs of a wide range of traditions—traditions which ought not to be rejected as foreign baggage, but sifted through and borrowed from as a great trove of treasure. The brash swagger of Van Toorn's virtuoso technique does not reflect a hubristic failure to recognize the meanness of our colonial condition, but is proof that this status is more psychological affliction—an internalized victim complex—than objective reality.

Early reviews of *Mountain Tea* give the distinct impression that the reviewers don't quite know what to make of Van Toorn's writing. Tom Marshall, who finds Van Toorn "impressive even when he is most irritating," advises that "one has to get used to his style, his unusual and rich diction" and that "diction and rhythmic shape are foregrounded, 'content' somewhat submerged."[9] Similarly, John Tucker observes that "images ... do not resolve themselves. The landscapes that are his frequent subject remain elusive. Sonic gain ... seems to entail semantic loss."[10] Tucker finds in *Mountain Tea* a "singleness of style"[11] and Marshall feels the book does not contain "a particularly compelling vision of life."[12] What is most interesting about these baffled and bemused readings is the extent to which they echo the settler's responses to the foreign landscapes and cultures he encounters upon arrival in the Canadian wilderness: the need to adapt, to "get used to" strange new surroundings; the absence or non-disclosure of significance; the overwhelming sameness; the dearth of coherent culture, of "vision." In their efforts to make sense of *Mountain Tea*, Marshall and Tucker attempt to plough straight furrows through knotty, "bouldershot",[13] "taiga/full of elbow holes/and timber."[14] The strain shows.

The beautiful irony here is the extent to which Van Toorn anticipates such square-peg criticism. "In Guildenstern County" and "Epic Talk," the two sequences framing the first section of *Mountain Tea*, are, besides being catalogues of, and meditations on, Canadian landscapes, reproaches to the "bad brush"[15] of Canadian poets and the "orthodox trajectories/of historians/ /whose assymptotes [sic]/never meet"[16]—to artists and thinkers who have failed to do justice to their surroundings. Wind, linked through breath to inspiration, is a unifying motif of the book as a whole and blows especially fiercely through "In Guildenstern County":

> In guildenstern county
> where there's hardly any wind
> to go by
> you can smell the poem in a thing for miles
> when wind wins.
> Wins,
> handsdown, right out of nowhere: given
> good grass out front,
> bad brush behind.
> Even so,
> not counting wind in the pines,
> wind in the brakeslams,
> there's hardly any
> to go by. Go
> by, put arms around, smoke on, ride off, bounce
> on a blanket about. Just
> miles and miles
> to crash
> and keep crashing through.[17]

A passage like this could be interpreted as an orthodox settler perspective, with nothing but "miles and miles" of empty space to crash through and the poet clearing "bad brush" to plant "good grass." But if you look more closely, you see that Van Toorn has turned these tropes on their heads. There is "no wind" (inspiration) *except* "in the pines" and "brakeslams"; it's official Canadian culture (as represented by "guildenstern cojunct county") that's lacking in wind; when it does blow, it "carries ... bluster,"[18] not beauty. There's "So much to trip out on" in nature, full of the "honkiest names."[19] What "suck[s] your eyes out" is not the landscape's curviness, but the straight lines of "trackpoles and lineside" and "Dewline"[20] cutting through it.

In case he hasn't made his point sufficiently clear through the oblique jazz riffs of "In Guildenstern County," Van Toorn is more explicit in "Epic Talk." In "Bee's Eye," the fourth poem of the sequence, George, a "guide" (someone therefore with intimate knowledge of the wilderness), leads a "vip's wife" into the bush,

with her old man
complaining

of the humid subzero sting
and snowy

blindmaking
of this damned climate

it was as if you were
walking

in a ping pong ball
she said

and George he nodded
and smiled

as the wind removed
a right pawfull

of snow
off the trees and slammed

it like snowthoughts
on the ground

on she complained
about

the winter air's
prickle

and never noticed how
something

sound of drumskin
on fire

the lemon sparkle in
the eyes

the old pride
at seeing

not a missing of
moisture

but a firing
of that same moisture

into diamondiest flakes
a trout sparkle

it took an eye
his eye

compound
as a bee's eye

to grasp a wealth
instead

of a relative
vacuum[21]

I'm reminded here of Marshall's inability to see any "compelling vision" in Van Toorn's poems. A poem like this one—and many others in which eyes and tropes of vision appear—reveals that it is critics like Marshall, dazzled by the "blindmaking" surface of *Mountain Tea* and hobbled by received conventional wisdom, who, too caught up in their talk, lack the vision required to see clearly. It takes a true local like George (a stand-in here for the seeing and naming poet) to perceive the "wealth" of his supposedly blank surroundings. If Marshall and others fail to detect *a* vision, it's because Van Toorn does not restrict himself to any single focal point. Note the third- and fourth-last couplets quoted above, in which three of four lines end with "eye" and the odd line out with "compound." Always true to the details, Van Toorn has created a small picture in words of a bee's eye to reinforce the visionary theme of the poem. This trio of eyes should also be read as a trinity of "I's": ever the protean conjurer, Van Toorn, who "can tell nothing about me" does not confine himself to a singular identity.[22]

At the risk of setting off alarm bells in the headquarters of the politically correct, I would call Van Toorn's techniques of seeing and naming aboriginal. By this I don't mean that he uses native themes or figures symbolically, a trait of Canadian Literature identified and explicated by Atwood in Chapter Four of *Survival* and lambasted by Solway in "The Flight from Canada."[23] Nor do I mean that he attempts to speak in an Authentic Native Voice in the manner that has been with no small justice called the "appropriation of voice." Unlike many an achingly righteous liberal, Van Toorn does not claim special access to the spiritual life or cultural plight of dispossessed Native Canadians. Rather, Van Toorn's relationships to landscape and language exist in a fluent comfort zone that runs *parallel* to aboriginal peoples' symbiotic rapport with the extra-human natural world—prior to European colonization and interference.

The aboriginality of *Mountain Tea* is most obviously embodied in its author's use of language. In part, this involves his adoption of words from various native idioms, especially "wawa," the windy theme of "In Guildenstern County's" jazz variations. More to the point, however, aboriginality inheres in Van Toorn's insistence on "iconic" instead of "referential"[24] language.[25] Van Toorn sees much contemporary poetry as having been impoverished by reliance on the sort of stripped down "blandly referential" "utility prose" appropriate to survival and rational analysis, but not to fulfillment and spiritual ecstasy:

> In utility prose words "go public" and have the inertia and com-
> placency of conventionalized life. Their function is so referential
> that their value is mainly utilitarian: the reader notes the point

they make and dispenses with them. The iconic qualities of language are absent from utility prose—rhythm, sound word play, metaphor, idiom, etc.—so that the reader or listener feels no ripple in his consciousness at these very things being described. Utility prose describes the mechanism of a goose pimple, even how it feels, but it cannot make you feel it.[26]

Rather, "Poetry, whose units of sound, image, significance and spiritual flow are aboriginally tiny, condenses as it slows down or accelerates into a time whose locus it shares with song and dance."[27] Occasionally, this means that Van Toorn appears to put down words for the pure play of sound, as in "Mountain Boogie," an anaphoric—and euphoric—litany of sensory delight:

> O peppermint moon behind the loud running clouds!
> O aspirin violets!
> O the cue to look up splickering out there in the U-sphere!
> O aspirin ivories!
> O nick nock of madder smoosh!
> O the sparks when she peels her sweater in the dark!
> O sepia blush!
> O pink pink: the fingers' rinks winking with quick![28]

And so on for 46 more lines. This poem, for all its non-linear elements, does have formal antecedents in public prayer and ritual chant. Its title announces that it will be more dance than essay, eschewing analysis in favour of apostrophe, enumeration and celebration. Presumably it's this sort of writing that leads critics like Tucker and Marshall to complain of sense subordinated to sound, of "semantic loss" and the absence of "a compelling vision."[29] Leaving aside the fact that such thoroughgoing absorption in 'pure sound' is far from Van Toorn's only, or even usual method, the inability to perceive the transcendent sense of a poem like "Mountain Boogie" signals a singular failure of the imagination on the part of *Mountain Tea*'s reviewers. As Douglas Burnet Smith writes of another of Van Toorn's catalogue poems, "The Cattle," "the rhetorical and the figurative represent one another coming to life as each description is added to the next to make an accumulated epiphany."[30] Again, Smith has it right when he says of "Mountain Boogie" that for Van Toorn, "the bombastic is the vessel of the subtle."[31] By downplaying the referential function of language and stepping up its iconic quotient, by refusing to pander to the Canadian reader's expectations, Van Toorn sidesteps the decidedly unsubtle options of exposition, analysis and declaration. He thereby comes closer than almost any modern era poet (with the possible exceptions of Clare and Hopkins) to defying Wittgenstein by bridging the gap between language and the world it is supposed to represent, and to fulfilling Archibald MacLeish's axiom that

A poem should be equal to:
Not true.

For all the history of grief
An empty doorway and a maple leaf.

For love
The leaning grasses and two lights above the sea—

A poem should not mean
But be.[32]

Through the rhythmic accumulation of minute particulars (lists of all sorts abound in *Mountain Tea*), Peter Van Toorn broaches the cosmic. He makes the reader *see* differently.

He accomplishes this transport not only through linguistic play, but also through precise observation, in which mode his language downshifts from the outright "bombastic" to the minutely rigorous. Consider this passage, describing the courtship rituals of dragonflies:

…Those wings
and spiny forelegs must have been battered stiff
by every kind of twist in wind on deck,
while she slipped her steering end into U-curves
under the floating fabric; and battered stiff
from trying out so long, racing for solid
hours between beds, often landing just to check
and take off again. Nine times out of ten
something in the bed blocked the way solid.

She'd arch and strain her whole fuselage
dipping it under again and again
(sometimes rocking the fabric apart, stage
by stage: water splashing up all around her
and priming the air with a rainbow)
trying to up and around where his began.
And he'd be doing a standstill solo
in the air, wings pitched at fortyfive degrees
from her lock-in sockets, and doing ninety
to keep the whole thing balanced. Then off again
when it wouldn't work. She with her sounder
ochre butt, he with a longer, more pliable
end of sorts.[33]

As with the best nature poems of John Clare ("The Nightingale's Nest" comes to mind), the sharp focus zoom of the vision and inobtrusive colloquial fitness of the diction create the illusion that there is no text mediating between the reader and the event described. The writing, in fact, does not so much *describe* as *inscribe* and enact the aerial flirtation and fornication of the two insects, as though the poet had hitched a ride on one of their backs, hanging on for dear life and taking notes with his free hand.

Van Toorn extends such tactics radically in his remarkable sonnet, "Mountain Leaf":

A bird pushes a leaf on a red roof,
aiming for ground, so it falls—not the roof,
but the leaf a bird pushes; and the more
it pushes (crisp beak and twig toes), the more
it pushes a still bronze leaf, all curled up
in a cone (showing a beak all curled up
in a cone too, aiming a bronze baked leaf)
for grounds that roll the curls out of a leaf,
grounds which, though rolling round a huger sound,
nevertheless snap twigs in leaf's own sound,
so that, round on round, the red roof, while not
waiting for a leaf to fall, is still not
tongue-tied either, but stands by, push for push,
ready for leafy bird's stiff, crisp, bronze push.[34]

On one level, this poem is a piece of virtuoso stuntwork. The diction is Frostian in the extreme: the sonnet's 140 syllables are deployed in 123 words, only fifteen of which have more than one syllable (counting "tongue-tied" as a single word). It is the intricate patterns of repetition Van Toorn builds out of this sparse language that make this poem a dizzying bit of crafts-manship. Most obviously, this repetition takes the form of the identically rhymed couplets, an unusual strategy to see employed once in a poem, never mind seven consecutive times. This alone goes against all conventional workshop wisdom. But that's not all. Of the 123 total words Van Toorn uses, only twenty-three occur uniquely; the other one hundred are repetitions of thirty-two other words. Whole phrases ("a bird pushes"; "red roof") get recycled; and just look at the enjambments in lines three through six: "the more/it pushes"; "all curled up/in a cone." It is also interesting to note the way in which the poem unfurls. In the first six lines, we find only two of the uniquely occurring words, whereas twenty-one appear in the following eight lines, giving the sense of a movement out of sheer neurotic repetition into more confidently purposeful—if still without obvious reason—activity, beyond the mere pushing of boundaries into the realm of art. Chief among the repetitions of single words is "push," which makes seven appearances; also notable is eight instances of words ending in "ound" (sound, round, ground). In a poem so intentionally and tightly structured, it can hardly be accidental that these specific reiterations stand out: Van Toorn is pushing the limits of sense and sound, just as the bird is pushing the leaf across the roof, and likewise just for the sheer perverse pleasure of the labour, the end result of which, for both bird and poet, is a "stiff, crisp, bronze push."

Van Toorn's capacity for identification with his subjects in a manner that is at once spontaneous and highly wrought is one of the most sophisti-cated examples I've seen in recent poetry of Keatsian negative capability.[35] Van Toorn is keenly aware of what he's doing, as he quotes Keats's famous remark ("If a sparrow comes before my window, I ... pick about the gravel.") as an epigraph to "Mountain Rain," a poem in which the poet follows the path of rain "washing cracks/in worms' backs."[36] In "Mountain Maple" there is a perfect reversal of subject and object as the poet literally enters the eponymous tree, which speaks the poem to the poet:

On me you scratch and blot your bitter ink.
I make the matches, handles, and boxes

you burn me, cut me, and bury me with.
I am a cross between man and grass, and
grow in the thought of him from the ground up.
Is it for cutting me down for no use,
for letting too many of us go, till
everything's up to the nostrils in snow,
that you sing and cry and write down this thing?[37]

This fluid plasticity of identity I would call shamanic. As anthropologist Hugh Brody explains, "shaman" is a word used by the Tungus of Siberia "to denote a person who has the power to cross from the human to the spirit world, and to make journeys in a disembodied form."[38] "Shamans are the people whose special skills and techniques allow them to move from the practical realm to the spiritual, from the everyday to the metaphysical."[39] Note the emphasis here on "special skills and techniques" and recall Marshall's opinion that Van Toorn's technique is "often gratuitous and a little empty."[40] Many Canadian poets espouse a shamanistic ethos and strike a shamanistic pose,[41] but with very few exceptions, the reader is not allowed to forget that they are reading a poet shamming at being a shaman because their visions lack the immediacy and verbal authenticity required to make their cartoonish caricatures of medicine men credible. As we have already seen above, Van Toorn, through improvisatory language, imaginative leaps and precise observation—in short, through *technique*—is a poet who seems able to cross the porous "boundaries around the human world"[42] effortlessly and at will, becoming possessed by the life energy of insects, birds, foxes, trees and other men.

Brody also tells us that "all those who rely on shamans believe it is possible for especially gifted men and women to visit places beyond the reach of ordinary travel; they also believe that shamans can make journeys to other times."[43] Van Toorn performs such transit in two different, but related, ways. The first way is highly metaphysical and can be seen in a handful of oneiric, hallucinatory poems, such as "Russia Home," "The Snow Remover is Coming," "Kora's High," "Baudelaire," and "Mountain Tea." These are poems in which the poet taps into the subconscious, often with the help of mind-altering drugs, as is made explicit in "Baudelaire" (who was himself, of course, a notorious experimenter with narcotics), with its "black and gold logic."[44] Significant also that pride of place is given to "Mountain Tea"—

tea being a slang term for cannabis—a sonnet in which the subject of the poem, addressed in the second person but probably the shaman-self of the poet, literally loses his head and goes

> …falling a few planets deep,
> and deeper, where nothing warns you straight out,
> a pair of hands, pulled by the pull of sleep,
> won't meet, to pour mountain tea out, without
> fire that air, earth that water, dreams that sleep
> pour out deeper than a few planets deep.[45]

John Tucker, with the defensive unease of the unsettled settler, finds it "puzzling" that this poem, which "successfully defends its obscurities from the probings of the 'utility prose' intellect," should share its title with the book.[46] But the strange imagery of poems like this one are only "obscure" to Joe Friday minds resolutely dedicated to the dichotomies of fact and fantasy, reality and dream. In contrast, as Brody tells us, there are for people with faith in shamanic wisdom "facts about things and facts about spirits. And the wall between these two kinds of entity is not solid."[47]

> [D]reaming … allows a form of knowledge that in effect processes
> all other knowledge. … Dreams take the dreamer not to some
> surreal universe in which the natural order is transcended or
> reversed, not to a land of fantasy, but to the place and creatures he
> or she knows best. … By escaping mere facts, [hunter-gatherers]
> discover the most important facts of all.[48]

This statement from a renowned anthropologist could easily be a prose paraphrase for "dreams that sleep/pour out deeper than a few planets deep." It's not much of a stretch to say that Van Toorn is primarily concerned, as artist and thinker, with opposing the "merely factual"—which, as Solway says, is "[i]n poetry … merely factitious"[49]—with dream journeying. Consider a few choice quotations from *Mountain Tea*. In "Pigeon Feeder," the eponymous character (as is the case with the guide, George, a poet figure) is surrounded by "dumb and cruel" birds (surrogates for poetasters or blind critics) who "Peck peck, crabbing for *facts*/those spic and span beaks knurly with cancers."[50] Their empty talk, their "peckerblab hangs [in the air] like a neurosis."[51] The association of "spic and span" beaks[52] with "cancers" and "neurosis" is no accident: the neat and tidy straight line of utility prose leads us mentally and physically astray from profounder insights into our psyches and environment and into pathological disorders and physical illness. In "Metaphor," the sixth poem in the "Epic Talk" sequence, Van Toorn praises the poet who provides "an//endless/chain of mysteries,"[53] as opposed to those who have on offer "mere barbarities."[54] In case you think I'm stretching Van Toorn's poems in a procrustean manner to accommodate pet theories, consider the poet's plain prose assertion that "[a]n age prone to stichic assimilation in verse betrays a predilection for reason over rhyme, statement over suggestion, definition over rune, and confession over apostrophe."[55] The title of *Mountain Tea*'s prefatory poem is "Rune," in which Van Toorn lays out his poetic principles in opposition to contemporary convention. He describes the "rumour that starts like a rune/in the earth" as a "heresy." The rumour is further associated with nature and music ("like a frog, a bird, a song/or a stone"), dreams and negative capability ("it's a walk/in somebody's bones"). It is both precise and spontaneous ("runs like a clock/ but keeps changing time"), prismatic ("In a poem it boasts all colours of the sun."), and finally independent and defiant ("Like a bronze pope, it salutes no one.").[56] Clearly, Van Toorn is on the warpath against the predominant trends in contemporary—and particularly contemporary Canadian—poetry and poetics. In this programmatic poem, as in his prose writings, he insists on the primacy of icon over reference, of outward attention and address— as in "The Cattle" and "Mountain Boogie"—over inward self-examination, the extraordinary and miraculous over the banal and quotidian.[57]

Waldo Frank, in an essay on Hart Crane (one of Van Toorn's exemplars) writes that "Whitman's challenge was not widely accepted; the plain-minded folk, the fact-minded poets of his time and ours resisted him. Hart Crane shares Whitman's fate."[58] So, too, does Peter Van Toorn. Consider Atwood's assertion that:

> ... a reader must *face the fact* that Canadian literature is undeniably sombre and negative, and that this to a large extent is both a reflection and a chosen definition of the national sensibility. ... in Canadian literature, a character who does much more than survive stands out almost as an anomaly, whereas in other literatures ... his presence would be unremarkable.[59]

Atwood earlier mixes praise and complaint when she observes that:

> The really positive virtue is the insistence ... on *facing the facts*, grim though they may be. Romanticism and idealism are usually slapped down fairly hard ... What one misses, though, is joy. After a few of these books you start wanting someone, sometime, to find something worth celebrating. Or at least to have fun.[60]

Note the reiterated emphasis on the settler virtue of facing the perceived facts. The problem is of course that Atwood begs the question of factuality. She and so many others are caught in an unimaginative dichotomous thought-system which sees only the polar opposites of "facts" and "romantic ideals." Small wonder that a character such as Van Toorn, who "does so much more than survive," gets, if not "slapped down pretty hard," widely ignored by his contemporaries. If there is insufficient joy to be found in Atwood's reading, as she complains, her thesis does nothing to remedy the *fact*.

Van Toorn's war is also against the parochial inwardness and self-referentiality of most Canadian verse, which brings us to the other principal means employed by him to travel through space and time: translation. The poet returns from his shamanic wanderings with news that stays news from Ancient Rome, Medieval France, Renaissance Germany and nineteenth-century Japan, to name but a few of his plunders. Thirty-eight of *Mountain Tea*'s eighty-six poems are versions of pieces written originally in a language other than English. Other poems, such as "Baudelaire," "Icarus Like Crane" and "Swinburne's Garden," are significant tributes to, and engagements with, the work of past masters. Whereas pioneer poets are obsessed with forging an original Canadian style and identity, Van Toorn writes of becoming through translation "unencumbered by the burden of originality."[61] Although he loves his "Snoweyes country,/surly over flag debates,"[62] he knows that a poet's true north strong and free has no fixed boundaries because it is poetry itself. And he knows that to have a proper perspective on his here and now, the poet must be steeped in past and elsewhere. As he puts it "A translation can provide the poet with a perspective lacking in his culturally inherited situation ... it can allow him elbow room for interpretation of values which his native culture will only allow if sanctioned by exotic sources."[63] He likens translation's capacity for imaginative expansion to travelling in time and draws distinctions between "literal translation," which involves "travelling backward in time" and "original and innovative translation" which moves old poems "forward in time."[64] Van Toorn's translations are of the "original and innovative" variety. In resolutely un-Canadian fashion, he "approaches the celebrated poet of the past as an equal," as John Tucker puts it. Tucker's evaluation, tainted by settler prejudice, is not praiseful. He calls Van Toorn's adaptations "as much acts of defiance as acts of homage" and wonders what the authors of the originals would make of his "melodies from different periods played on the saxophone."[65] Because the default Canadian position being deference, assertions of creative will, speeches made from a position of strength, are seen as artistically and ethically suspect.

In Atwood's terminology, most if not all of the poetry in *Mountain Tea* should be categorized under "Position Four" in the hierarchy of "Basic Victim Positions": "a position not for victims but for those who have never been victims at all, or for ex-victims." For the non-victim, "creative activity of all kinds becomes possible"[66] and nature "exists as a living process which includes opposites: life and death, 'gentleness' and 'hostility.'" Van Toorn is not, as discussed above alienated by or from his surroundings or his sexuality, he sees himself, in Atwood's terms "as part of the process."[67] The catch of course is that, although such moments are "imaginable and therefore possible," they "are few in Canadian poetry,"[68] obsessed as it is—or at least as its critics are—with victimization and oppression. The emergence of a Position Four poet—of an artist perfectly at ease in his skin[69] and environ- ment: Bloom's "strong poet", or Nietzsche's *übermensch*—in a too-human culture syllogistically preoccupied with its imagined victim status on the one hand and its oppression of other cultures on the other, is bound to be mistaken for something less than it is, or even resented, much as a country boy who makes good in the big city comes to be seen as "too big for his britches" back home.

The clarity of Van Toorn's perspective on Canada no doubt has much to do with the fact that, as an emigrant from the Netherlands, he is not burdened by prior generations of inward-focused Canuck roots-seeking, nation-building and meaning-making. He glosses this in the penultimate poem of "Epic Talk":

a people's genius
emerges

from a black felt hat
upside down

not when a rack is placed
for its hanging

but when a violence
of metaphor

a soil's flower
dragged up by the roots

hangs fire
on the lapel of an outsider

whose unique ability
to yank

more than mere barbarities
from the hat

gives him an insider's right
to wear that hat

a people's genius
emerges

when an outsider can wear
a felt hat

inside out
ably yanking from it an

endless
chain of mysteries

that grow on them
as

flowers grow
on a woman's breast

or pollen rubs off on
the bee's leg[70]

The self-confidence implicit in writing like this is alone sufficient to brand
Van Toorn as un-Canadian. It is precisely his "outsider" status, however, his
turning inside-out of what is commonly held to be Canadian—as embodied
by the straight-line "rack"—that makes him the ideal Canadian citizen and
artist. "Genius" here has a triple connotation: it encompasses "exceptional
creative power" as well as "the tutelary spirit of a place" and "the prevalent
feeling or associations etc. of a nation, age, etc."[71] Poetic genius and the
spirit of the land are one.[72] And it is important to note that Van Toorn does
not restrict the spirit of the land to "the deep country," but locates it also in
"urban/spaces."[73] Like his Montreal pigeon feeder, Van Toorn wears both
the "overalls" of the hick rural bard and the "black beret" of the hip urban
poet.[74] I doubt that anyone has limned the simultaneous beauty and *laideur*
of a Montreal winter—"Snowbound/in a stolen newness, swaggering in
goo"—as memorably as in his lines in the first section of "Icarus Like
Crane."[75] As with the virtuoso description of dragonfly sex this kind of scene
painting is highly innovative, but is not, *pace* Marshall, "gratuitous."[76] Rather,
Van Toorn's virtuosity serves to bridge the gap between reader and scene, to
collapse the boundary between language and objective reality; one hardly
needs to have experienced a Montreal winter to get a vivid picture and feel
for it when reading this poem—which is crucial for communicating Canadian reality and not merely warped tomographs of the "Canadian" psyche
to the world outside our borders.

Canada is a staggeringly diverse mix of geographies and peoples. Most
of the literature that has been identified as characteristically Canadian has
not been equal to the formidable challenge of representing that diversity.
Small wonder if we have, as is often complained, produced no Yeats. Too
often what we get—what we settle for—is a grainy Polaroid of our own
intimidation in the face of that challenge. This is not to say that the settler

perspective is invalid, but that as a paradigm Survivalism is inadequate and constricting. Now, though Alden Nowlan's observation that "this is a country/ where a man can die/simply from being/caught outside" is still accurate, it is hardly reflective of daily life for the vast majority of our citizens.[77] Rather, statements like Nowlan's, in all their no-nonsense, stripped down prosiness, do little more than convey a stray thought that happened to pass through the poet's mind as he was walking home to his heated flat after work. To restrict oneself to a narrow range of subjects and styles is to remain in the garrison. It takes a more innovative vocabulary, a greater attention to form, a broader frame of geographic, historical and literary reference, a comfort within—but also an ability to step out of—one's own skin and skull, to *embody* the "genius" of the Canadian people. This heady mix is just what we have had under our noses since 1984, when *Mountain Tea* was first published. David Solway puts it perfectly in describing Peter Van Toorn as "an archi-tectonic magpie gathering his materials from everywhere and arranging them in the best, most startling and yet wholly appropriate order."[78] He demon-strates in poem after poem that he is at once profoundly spiritual and wittily urbane; that he is rigorously disciplined and wildly freewheeling; that he is attuned to the value of both innovation and tradition; that he is both indigene and immigrant; that he is a poet of Nature as well as a poet of Society; that his verse embodies, in short, the kernel of what Canada has been, can be and should be, with all the chaff left on the threshing floor. My hope (on better days, my belief) is that we are at last—or at least— approaching the level of cultural maturity and self-confidence required to move beyond mere survival and our preoccupation with identity, to recognize that Van Toorn and other singular talents have already done much to define our culture without delimiting it, and not to dismiss their superior skill and vision as alien because they refuse to conform to easily commodified package concepts of Canada.

An Appetite Abroad: or, David McGimpsey's Burgerworld and the Map of Contemporary Poetry[1]

NICK LOLORDO

begin with the opening lines of a poem entitled "Burger on Yeats' Grave":

> At dawn, near Dun Aengus on Inishmore
> I had a vision:
> I would put a hamburger on W. B. Yeats' grave.
>
> A vision of opening up wax paper
> in front of a sharp tombstone;
> meaty and simple,
> the unpretentious burger.[2]

In what follows, the vision becomes reality: a "ground beef odyssey" commences. Burger from a generic "Fast Food" shack in hand, the poet arrives at the grave, where he fulfills his Irish precursor's injunction—but not before adding a little extra: "I left the still warm prayer and passed by." Then he departs for Dublin on a night train full of schoolkids in uniform "reciting lines from their favorite shows."[3]

McGimpsey's burger gesture playfully signifies on Yeats; and on what sociologists have recently called the "McDonaldization" of society.[4] Emblematizing an age in which the contemporary incarnations of Yeats' school children take their guidance from the transmissions of the American tube, McGimpsey brings the burger, king of Yankee commodities, to the grave of the staunch lyric individualist, whose own *A Vision* involved an arcane anti–modern symbolism. This seems a pointedly aggressive gesture.

Yet consider Yeats' famous injunction in "Under Ben Bulben": "Irish poets learn your trade / Sing whatever is well made."[5] "[M]eaty and simple, / the unpretentious burger": McGimpsey's lines propose the unlikely ground beef sandwich as just such an object. And they foretell the title sequence of *Hamburger Valley, California*, in which the (Irish-Canadian) poet David McGimpsey sings the hamburger.[6]

Travel, as we know, broadens; TV rots the mind. Yet the touristic attitude and the stance—or slouch—of the television viewer must be understood together: for this conjunction enables McGimpsey's poetics.[7] Two cultural positions characterize his work. The poet is both contemporary commodity consumer, located in a media-saturated everywhere that is nowhere in *particular* and pop-cultural tourist who stubbornly persists in thinking these mass-produced relics worth a pilgrimage.[8] (McGimpsey, as it were, takes his task from Theseus in *A Midsummer Night's Dream*, Act 5, Scene 1: as commodity culture "bodies forth / The forms of things unknown, the poet's pen / Turns them to shapes, and gives to airy nothing / A local habitation and a name.") The touristic role, then, itself proves double: McGimpsey can be both the ambassador of the commodity (as in "Burger on Yeats' Grave") and a pilgrim in search of its holy sites of origin, descending into "Hamburger Valley, California." If—as I will propose in what follows—this latter sequence most fully embodies the dual sources of McGimpsey's poetics, this is so because commodity culture itself is inherently dual: it exists simultaneously as (symbolically, archeologically) American and (in the terms of contemporary economic logic) multinational.

Another Dublin poem, "Kentucky Fried Dublin," clarifies this logic. Chatting with a local, the poet is told that "Dublin's KFC / was voted the best KFC in Europe"; he counter-boasts with an example from the myth-repository of what I will call commodity authenticity: "I had no idea they had elections, / but told him a story of somebody / who once met Colonel Sanders himself."[9] National differences are measured on the yardstick of American/global commodity culture. The delicate misuse of the term "election" here is evocative of that shift of priorities I have already mentioned, in which democratic prerogatives are absorbed by the sphere of consumption. Indeed, in Kentucky Fried Dublin, the hoary clichés of the "typical" national subject are rearticulated within this global system:[10] "I told the guy [...] in Canada / there was no extra-crispy or tea biscuits," recounts the poet, "so that at least in chicken-frying technology / the Republic was well ahead."[11]

Ohh... Canada? (America's forgotten market.) The subject position at this instant is *echt*-Canadian. But these are not the outraged tones of anyone ever handed American money by an oblivious tourist. Rather, we hear a voice alive to the subtle refinements of the commodity even while understanding the ridiculousness of its transformation into an index of national difference. Ultimately, I will suggest, McGimpsey is a poet of the local and the specific—which can mean Quinpool Rd. in Halifax or Sullivan's Tap Room in Boston; the Montreal suburb of Ville D'Anjou or the Olympic Stadium.[12] He is this poet precisely to the extent that he *refuses* to sing the larger geopolitical entities (Quebec, but equally Canada)—which for him lack force when compared to the transnational, intangible nonentity that characterizes postmodern consumer society.[13] "Canadian content"—Can-Con—in McGimpsey's work is typically deployed for the purposes of self-mockery and auto-critique.[14] The coordinates of the poet's world are succinctly indicated in the (hardly promising) title "Taco Bell in Kingston." The names of this placeless realm, of course, are legion; Fredric Jameson has famously called it "the cultural logic of late capitalism."[15] For McGimpsey, as I shall argue in what follows, the "world"—that abstract phrase so often mobilized to generate post-nationalist master-narratives—is simply the Burgerworld.

1

McGimpsey's poetry has always been concerned with the alluring promises of self-transformation that consumer culture offers—and with the letdowns that so often follow. In his first two volumes, *Lardcake* (1996) and *Dogboy* (1998), McGimpsey served up versions of the self as junk-food cyborg—whether the eponymous Lardcake, figure of fun, or the still more literal dogboy, a kind of centaur figure, half-man, half-frank. *Lardcake* presents such figures as a woman with a "case of hamburger disease" and a man who promises to "be your Mayor McCheese;"[16] in a poem entitled "Roger Clintonesqueria," McGimpsey condemns the brothers of the famous to a mild hell of disappointment he calls "Burgerworld."[17] The coexistence of self-indulgence and self-criticism is continued in *Dogboy*, perhaps most notably by a succession of sixteen-line "chubby" sonnets in which the desire for fame, the fact of obscurity, and the limitless availability of junk food conspire to produce a succession of comic nightmares. Presenting the self as always already composed of the sort of detritus which a purer poetics might overlook altogether, McGimpsey's speaker avoids the pathos of the confessional mode, replacing it with the more abstract and democratic pathos of the commodity form itself.[18]

For a Canadian involved in the culture industry, to travel to America is to open oneself to a certain insinuation: a litany awaits recitation, the names of those who left and then stayed away, whose national identities are now hardly perceptible, known only to experts (which is to say, to all Canadians). America, the voice of Canadian identity tells us, seeks to erase difference. Charles Bernstein has meditated on the logic of *absorption* in terms that suggestively associate fleshy bodies and bodies politic:

> Canada does not wish to be absorbed into the U. S.
> cultural orbit any more than Quebec wishes to be
> absorbed by Canada; but then Quebec feminists may not
> want to be absorbed by a male-dominated "free" Quebec.
> Identity seems to involve the refusal to be absorbed
> in a larger identity, yet the identity formed as
> a result of an antiabsorptive autonomism
> threatens to absorb differential groupings
> within it [...][19]

Acts of cultural refusal, of the kind mapped by Bernstein, occur throughout McGimpsey's poetry. An early poem entitled "O Coconut," spoken from Halifax, N. S., dares to refer flippantly to CanLit's most famous mandarin—and by association to "national" culture, imposed as if by commissars from Toronto down. The poet enlists weather in an unequal battle against Culture: "Once the snow was so deep / you almost couldn't hear Margaret Atwood."[20] Official Canadian metaphorics nervously disavows conflict at such levels, gesturing toward the "cultural mosaic" and in so doing necessarily invoking its source, the "melting pot," celebratory American meta-phor of absorption *par excellence*. The truly Canadian writer ought not to engage in internal squabbles: preservation of national difference against the monolith to the south takes priority.[21]

Does McGimpsey travel to "Hamburger Valley, California" *as a Canadian poet?* To begin to answer this question, we first need to untangle the interwoven strands of commodity culture and American culture. The absorptive powers of America have long been understood to precede the political: American social space itself consumes the individual who consumes its blandishments. We are what we eat, goes the common sense account: commodity culture denationalizes us from the inside out—absorbing, we are absorbed. At the same time, the relation of the burger to American culture cannot simply be reduced to an equation between burger and commodity; for even as the former serves that synechdochic function, it functions at the same time as a figure for American freedom. To understand McGimpsey's quest, we must flesh out this skeletal equation.

We might begin by "reading" the ground-beef patty, noticing, perhaps, its formal abstraction, so characteristic of American poetics since Walt Whitman. A figure of passive absorption, it also resonates with important American themes of mobility, both social and literal. McGimpsey's epithet—" the unpretentious burger"—captures the former sense; one might equally say, "the democratic burger."[22] The burger is the perfect American abstraction produced through the process of grinding down distinctions. Indeed, McGimpsey is hardly the first to offer the ubiquitous burger as a meaty metonymy of American culture. Sketching the urban American landscape with a few brief strokes, Richard Rodriguez resorts to the burger as locale of the American essence: "America exists everywhere in the city—on billboards; frankly in the smell of burgers and French fries...in the slouch of the crowd, the pacing of traffic lights, the assertions of neon, the cry of freedom overriding the nineteenth-century melodic line."[23] The implicit association of "freedom" and consumer society (burgers and billboards) found here is one fundamental to specifically American accounts of modernity. The catalog offers not a symbolic substitute by which we might somehow grasp the whole of America, but a series of metonymies encountered in a process of movement that does not merely discover but enacts what is "American." At the same time the passage evokes a subject who takes in the scene via a visual and pedestrian process of consumption: one classically identified with the *flâneur*, that European figure synonymous with Walter Benjamin's Baudelaire (though also—as we'll see—with Whitman's loafer).

The particular historical timetable of North American modernization dictates that in its more recent incarnation, the American *flâneur* is essentially an Eastern figure: the urban artist with more taste than money. (Frank O'Hara, to name a figure, stands as the exemplary *flâneur* of mid-century New York.) Against this backdrop, the defining qualities of *Hamburger Valley, California*'s protagonist are apparent—qualities which mark him as a *post-*

modern revision of the *flâneur*. He travels by automobile, rather than by foot, and his consumer activity is both metaphorical and relentlessly literal. All American literary accounts of the road are foreshadowed by the Whitman of *Leaves of Grass*. In "Song of Myself" the poet assumes, as part of his democratic prerogative, an uncheckable mobility ("I rise extatic through all, and sweep with the true gravitation."[24] A century and a half later, McGimpsey is powered almost exclusively by car. *Hamburger Valley, California* also includes a short sequence, "The Inaugural Poem of the Los Angeles Subway System." The poem contains moments of freedom, even what looks like a moment of pedestrian bliss: "love can prove a congested drive–thru, / but the way around town / is smooth, / just like the theme music from *Barnaby Jones*."[25] But the imaginary soundtrack in the head quickly turns dissonant: "NOTE TO SELF: *get started / on plan to publish world's stupidest book, / titled,* The Walking Tour of L. A."[26] This stands as the poem's sardonic commentary on Los Angeles' recent move towards a revitalized downtown.

The symbiosis of burger and car developed in post-war Southern California, as the population tripled over the twenty-year period from 1920 to 1940, a time when the automobile had become affordable for the middle classes. The rapid post-war economic growth that followed saw the flowering of car culture: among global firsts was the world's first drive-through. One early drive-through baron proclaimed that "People with cars are so lazy they don't want to get out of them to eat!"[27] Putting his money where his mouth was, he called his chain the "Pig Stand." Car and burger, then, are themselves part of a larger, closed system, part of the peculiar ecology of Southern California: one eats so that one can drive, one drives in order to eat. But my equation here leaves out an important third term in the historical nexus I am describing: sex. Evoking the world of the early roadside burger joint, Schlosser comments further that the combination of "girls and cars and ... food" was a potent one. Alone in his car, fueled by fast food and a (presumably meager) Canada Council grant, the Canadian poet abroad is simultaneously commodity tourist and victim: research, for him, becomes reenactment.[28]

2

The conjunction of burger, car, and sex that defines "Hamburger Valley, California" is established by the snapshot that introduces the poem:[29] a sign for "In-N-Out Burger."[30] Alluding to the desire for a speedy return to the road, the duplicitous words none-too-subtly suggest the congruence of all desires for the flesh, even as the sign's neon arrow points upwards, as if to hint at the possibility of some burger-fueled apotheosis. The restaurant's name returns as the beginning of a gigantic phallic compound fantasy burger-name in "God Bless Los Angeles": the poet orders the "In-N-Out Quarter Pound Big King Classic."[31]

Moreover, McGimpsey positions the poem's speaker as the consequence of this particular historical nexus. The apostrophe of its opening lines is at the same time a kind of testimony:

> Hamburger, hamburger,
> the desert valley lights—
> San Bernardino opens out,
> my great neon drink
> bubbling its icy pinks and turquoises,
> satisfying the near–summer night.[32]

San Bernardino: the site of the drive–in, owned by Maurice and Richard McDonald, visited in July 1954 by soon-to-be-founder of McDonalds Ray Kroc—the site, we might say, of the single greatest epiphany in the history of burgerdom. But this speaker is no Ray Kroc. We hear not the voice of an innovator but of one near the end of the line: alone, enraptured in the "near–summer night" by the vision of hamburger as fantasy: "Hamburger, hamburger, / my last little dream, / my last promise to myself."[33] Kroc, by contrast, saw the San Bernardino restaurant at day, with the clear vision of Keats' Cortez gazing upon the new world. His memoir provides eloquent testimony: "In a bright yellow convertible sat a strawberry blonde who looked like she had lost her way to the Brown Derby or the Paramount cafeteria... it was not her sex appeal but the obvious relish with which she devoured the hamburger that made my pulse hammer with excitement."[34] Invoking the overtly sexual only to disavow it, then relocating desire everywhere in the landscape—from the woman's "obvious relish" to his own "hammering" entrepreneurial pulse—Kroc's narrative-of-origin suggests, with charming literalness, a certain displacement. But in any case, his perhaps only retrospective clarity is exemplary, for this focused "excitement" is precisely the opposite of the confusion upon which commodity culture depends: that is, a confusion of desire in which one might ask "How can we tell the burger from the blonde?"[35] Or as McGimpsey puts it in a section headed: "Burger-lotion, burgerlinament":

> burger combo with lengthy nap and sex-fantasy to go [...]
> the one who said it was the best in the country,
> the hottest in the sack,
> the biggest fly freshest[36]

Two constants, then, all but define Hamburger Valley: the presence of Burger, and the absence of Woman. One eats to drive, then drives so that one can eat again. The freeway system thus takes on a cyclical quality; along it, the poet is driven by desire. McGimpsey's relationship to the hamburger is not exhausted by the need for sustenance which the hamburger satisfies: it is a phantasmatic relationship, structured by the burger's commodity form. And thus it is inevitably conflicted, as Jean Baudrillard tells us: "in the process of consumption internal conflicts or 'deep drives' are mobilized and alien-ated."[37] The poet's odes *to* the burger exemplify their relationship. "The Ham-burger Song" confronts the commodity fetish directly:[38] "O Hamburger, you're more than a sandwich to me."[39] More than a sandwich, which is to say, more than "a material ... object of need and satisfaction" the burger is a *commodity*.[40] Part of a system of signs, the burger/commodity, as if by tran-substantiation, makes human relations available for consumption, while at the same time consummating—which is to say concluding, finishing off—this sociality. As Baudrillard explains the logic of this economy of signs: "*[I]t is the idea of the relation* that is consumed in the series of objects which manifests it. This is no longer a lived relation: it is abstracted and annulled in the object-sign where it is consumed."[41]

Such an endemic condition of failed relationality is by no means exclu-sive to Baudrillard's conception of post-modernity. In order to help us maintain the association of commodity and sexual desire, we might recall here Lacan's reminder that "There is no sexual relation."[42] Indeed, a reading of consumption as the (impossible) effort to obtain a *relation* is dramatized in "The Hamburger Song." McGimpsey fantasizes a conversation with the burger, whose potency is blatantly contrasted with the poet's own weakness:

> But you could see I was tired, hamburger,
> and you took a look into my eyes;
> you said "Pull over, Dave, you fat bastard,
> and just let me drive"[43]

Lonely in Hamburger Valley, the poet finds his only society to be that of the burger—the commodity—itself; and the above moment is only the clearest example of such a dynamic in a sequence of passages utterly emptied of human social relations. The (fetishized) burger stands not "with its feet on the ground"—to borrow from Marx's *Capital*—but with its hands on the wheel, driving McGimpsey, at the poem's conclusion, to Circus Liquor; where, presumably, it'll be the whiskey talking.[44]

In the next poem, a failed conversation between lover and burger (shades of "The Waste Land" and the woman whose "nerves are bad tonight"[45]) dramatizes the entropy that the Burgerworld seeks to deny: "O jingle burger, / were the song true, / the kiss in the rain ... would have lasted forever."[46] All the songs of "Hamburger Valley, California" are so many cover versions of what McGimpsey calls the song of "the burger's dark delight", the undersong of mortality that persists: "Murmur burgertotenlieder in perfect weather."[47] The poet sings these songs. The allusion to "kindertotenlieder" (Mahler's songs for "lost" children) allows us—in invoking the death that flickers throughout this poem—to return once more to the central structuring image of the "drive." Moved through greater Los Angeles by desire, by a lethal cocktail of Eros and Thanatos that we might, half-seriously, call Burgeros, the poet seeks sustenance, in vain. "[Y]ou need not commodify these deferrals," the poet pleads—but the twin logics of commodification and deferral, the motors of the Burgerworld, are precisely what drives him back and forth, in and out.[48]

3

Passing through layers of sedimented fast-food history, McGimpsey's tour of Burger Valley thus serves as a kind of implicit archeology. It suggests that the logic of fast-food production is itself visible in the experience of the individual consumer. The pressure for constant redefinition that (as scholars have argued) characterizes the fast-food industry reinforces a similar pressure that modern consumer culture exerts upon the subject. The consumer, as Baudrillard reminds us, is "obliged to be happy ...to be in love ... to be dynamic."[49] He elaborates: "Consumption is a collective and active behavior, a constraint, a morality, and an institution ... a complete system of values."[50] As such it transcends the "private" sphere of personal freedom (the sphere in which a poetry more traditionally lyrical than McGimpsey's might exist unthreatened). The possibilities of consumption are inexhaustible—and therefore exhausting—responsibilities.

One crucial question remains to be answered: what resources of resistance are possessed by the (Canadian) subject? I have already suggested that McGimpsey's two poetic roles, commodity consumer and pop-cultural tourist, are fused in "Hamburger Valley, California." On the one hand, in his constant invocation of death, the poem's subject might be thought to perform the function of a kind of commodity Christ. But such gestures can never be sustained: "I'm dying" becomes, three lines later, "I am dying for just a bit more."[51] For all his outsize desires, a Whitmanesque absorptive power is denied the poet: no larger than anyone else, he is not dying for us but alongside us.

Nor is McGimpsey's stance as pop-cultural tourist ultimately liberatory. Imaginary narratives of the self collide with pre-packaged images of the Canadian abroad, and the poet, victim of a "sack of belly bombs," dreams of a generic fate (in "La La Burger"): "another Ugly Canadian swoons USA, / leaves a signature on a HMO deal."[52] The pathos of socialized medicine is here deployed in a manner typical of McGimpseyan CanCon. Even the dying "Ugly Canadian" is Canadian only as an inversion of a prepackaged American cultural narrative. The tourist can ally himself with pop-cultural sources of strength, as when McGimpsey speaks with the voice of Elvis—better, the voice of "Dead Elvis": "So ring out the Taco Bell, / tell Wendy to grease up the griddle, / Santa Claus is back in town."[53] But all too often, a burger fails to be "more than a sandwich"; sometimes—as Freud might have wearily observed—a burger is "just a burger."[54] Such a formulation expresses the dark side of the eating cycle: the lethargy, disillusionment, and nausea that always return. "O! Unhappy!" exclaims a Homer(Simpson)esque voice.[55] And with this return of the real, a return that inevitably follows the dissipation of glossy fantasy images, comes the relentless, greasy substance of the burger *qua* burger—the final fact we must consider.

"All this I swallow and it tastes good .... I like it well, and it becomes mine."[56] In his "Song of Myself" Whitman poses a challenge that few American poets have met—indeed, one from which American poetry might be said to have turned squeamishly away. The poem leaves no doubt that Whitman's omnivorous powers of consumption are matched by an equally fabulous digestive capacity. Yet for this the poet pays a certain price: the line just cited is immediately followed by one of the poem's most quoted

319

assertions: "I am the man .... I suffered .... I was there."[57] McGimpsey, too—
as we shall see—will suffer: as he writes, late in the sequence: "today, I pay
for the meaty thrill...."[58] (The poem from which this line is drawn is entitled,
succinctly, "I fucked up.") Nor does McGimpsey project that famously
imperial Whitmanian self capable of annexing the experience of others;
rather, he is alienated from even his own experience. A commodity tourist
and a Canadian self, he has already been doubly swallowed. What he devours
does not become his—rather, *he* becomes *its*: "The weekends have piled up,
Wimpy / and I am, Jughead, just another cartoon face."[59] McGimpsey might
well ask the question that Walt Whitman poses in "Song of Myself": "How
is it I extract strength from the beef that I eat?"[60] Whitman's question is
rhetorical: the absorptive capacities manifest throughout his voraciously
inclusive poem are simply demonstrated yet again by his ability to digest
this suitably manly sustenance. McGimpsey, by contrast, seeks not only to
scarf down burgers but also to find sustenance in the commodity form itself.

Hamburger Valley is where Whitman's America meets Baudrillard's
society of consumption: It is composed of floating signifiers that inexhaust-
ibly incite desire—even, or especially, the desire that *knows better*: what
McGimpsey calls "middle-aged desire .... up for no good reason / but up all
the same."[61] The photographs of signs placed throughout the book as
illustrations all but literalize this metaphor. These grainy black-&-white snaps
evoke the photos in *Learning from Las Vegas* in a manner which hints at a
debt to Venturi et al's groundbreaking (and very Baudrillardian) semiotic
analysis of the Las Vegas landscape.[62] McGimpsey drives in a closed car, unlike
the blonde's "convertible"—and he does not have even the fantasy of a "real
landscape" to traverse. As he remarks at the beginning of "La La Burger,"
"it's all just names and place names now:"[63] all, that is, signs (preeminent
among which are the billboards and drive-ins that reduce material form
itself to signifying space). Baudrillard's distinction between modern and
postmodern experience of the automobile in "The Ecstasy of Communication" is pertinent here: "No more fantasies of power, speed and appropriation linked to the object itself, but instead ... [t]he vehicle now becomes a
kind of capsule, its dashboard the brain, the surrounding landscape
unfolding like a televised screen."[64] Against the materiality of beef (and its
devastatingly tangible effects on the body), the poet seeks to ally himself
with the untouchable, abstract commodity form, to escape into the realm
of "glossy impossible blues" and "orange bounties": "You can't touch me

when I've gone Hollywood."[65] But ultimately such efforts are in vain. The hamburger respects no national boundaries. Its material ground(beef)endness is coextensive with its immaterial reach. There is nothing outside the bun.

A late section of the poem entitled "Fritous!" shifts to a Quebec City McDonald's, presenting "a pinewood carving / in traditional French-Canadian style, / a two foot tall figure of a dauntless fry cook."[66] But the logic of authenticity quickly yields to that of equivalence—"I said I wanted it 'to go.' / Pour apporter"—and a catalog translates the hamburger form around the globe, from the "Tiltburger on Hochelega" to "the hamburger placed on W. B. Yeats' grave." Just as there is no catching up (as we've already seen), "there is no getting away."[67] The effort to escape is finally dramatized near the conclusion of the sequence. Here, in a comic nightmare of distorted scale, what Bernstein calls "the biological senses / of absorption and excretion: the body's narration" are linked with the condition of the (post-national) subject as always already a victim of cultural absorption.[68]

Squeezing past
the gunnery ranges of the Chocolate Mountains
and the retirement homes of Twenty Nine Palms
all the rumblings of escape are equalized [...][69]

Retreating in the direction of Phoenix, the bloated bard can barely fit down I-10.

In the extended counterpoint passage that follows, the Big Mac becomes the perfect icon of exchange value.

Upper Peninsula pastes, Big Mac;
Texas brisket, Big Mac;
Nebraska runzas, Big Mac;
Manhattan pastrami, Big Mac [...][70]

The Big Mac becomes a kind of digestive version of the car stereo's graphic equalizer; stomach rumbles fade and McGimpsey moves to an abstract catalog in which everything is equal to one Big Mac. In the showdown between local delicacies and the universal Burger, the true Equalizer is revealed to be the commodity form itself. Even "Montreal poutine" and "homemade," the final two terms in the list, meet their McMatch. And if death seems for a moment to stand alone (here we might think of Baudrillard's contention that only death escapes the logic of equivalence), even this singularity is undermined by this poem's entirely logical conclusion:

And death too

my bad (my Big Mac).[71]

"What I Do Best, What I Do Now": Robert Allen's Twice-deepened Poetry[1]

TODD SWIFT

> Everything is all here. The chipmunk is here, the stars are
> here, and all these actions take place.
> —A.R. Ammons[2]

"So full of contradictions"

The subject-matter of Robert Allen's poetry is beautifully varied.[3] It is also variously beautiful, though not unafraid to stray into less seemly territory. Allen is a conscious voyager into undiscovered realms, able to write of a closely observed newt, cannibalism after an air disaster, the Magellenic cloud, the beauty of a North Hatley winter and Errol Flynn's cock. Everything is all here. There is the romantic sense of a man looking out at the world— as Wordsworth writes, contrasting nature and books, "with a heart/ that watches and receives."[4]

Allen has several times used the term "Magellan's clouds" in his poetry. It is a perfect trope for him, since it combines two of his main interests, terrestrial and space exploration, with a third and fourth figure, that of the voyaging heart (or lover) and writing itself as voyage. Indeed, in Allen's global lyric vision, he is able to merge the most complex of scientific discoveries, derived from physics, astronomy, zoology and so on, with their correlatives in human emotion. He is, in short, a romantic modern, who sees the writing of the self in terms of how it impinges on the very limits or horizons of feeling, knowledge, life and death. The beauty is half in the moving forward, unmapped.

Allen is no disoriented magpie, though he does wear many different, sometimes eclectic, suits, in his various celebrations of Science, Art *and* Nature—a *very* late romantic, then. He selects his subjects carefully, with a diverse and curious eye. He does so as both an intellectual—he is a university professor—and something of a free-ranging maverick (he is a fan of country and western bands like Kinky Friedman and The Texas Jewboys, after all).

Allen, whose writing often explores the idea of doubles, doppelgangers and personal identity, is a many-sided, even divided, writer. This may make him quintessentially a Canadian writer, as well. Carmine Starnino, discussing W. P. Wilgar's idea of the divided mind in Canadian verse, and the promise of future Canadian poetry, writes: "We are a new method of conservation or recovery and revitalization. And what allows us such a unique, richly faceted dialogue with the entirety of English lyric tradition is that (unlike the British poets) we are freed from having to write inside that tradition, but (unlike the American poets) are able to stay outside even when we do enter it. This is because we enter the language by a process of division, a double attitude as heir and progenitor. And this conflict-ridden, conflict-reconciling thinking—and the twice-deepened lyricism it produces—continues to be the creative rubric for our best poets."[5] Allen's lyric work is often twice-deepened.

One of his earliest collections of poetry contains the lines, from the aptly-titled "Fetishists": "The world is so full of contradictions/ we are forced to fall back on the assumption / of private lives."[6] Aptly-titled because Allen often observes (and diagnoses) the condition of the world in language derived from psychoanalysis, a favoured discourse of his. Freud has figured not only unconsciously in Allen's poetry but as a real presence. Allen writes in the prose poem in *Magellan's Clouds*, "Events in the childhood of Freud": "All thoughts of home were driven from his mind by the clouds of acrid steam and the terrible iron clatter of the wheels. Small blue and white flames burned in the gas jets, and their doubles burned in the burnished wood of the coach."[7]

Time and again, certain images resurface in Allen's writing, such as: *clouds, steam, flames, doubles*. Most significantly, the absence and presence of home is a central concern for Allen, who left Bristol young, and has long made Quebec his new home; a problematic, uncanny home in some ways, and one which Allen associates with the travails of literary precursors of his, such as Melville.

His *unheimlich* attempts to place himself in his wintry home, Quebec, lead over time to the verbal and imaginative hybridity of his later writing, which evolves to become increasingly and purposively far-flung and outlandish, turning the tables, as it were, on the very ideas central to Wordsworthian romanticism, between the public and private self, between the world and the person. Allen *does* divide his time between the country and the city, and this pastoral-cosmopolitan tension is played out in the ways the writing is also divided, at times, between prose and poetry, between different and multiple poetic traditions, and his often-opposed themes of high and low culture, woods and the boulevard, love and desire, humour and melancholy.

"Not all quite anywhere"

Allen is a major Canadian poet, both in terms of his written achievement and his value as mentor figure to other poets that come after him in the Anglo-Quebec literary tradition he has done so much to help encourage over the past thirty years. He manages to find a synthesis of the many poetic traditions that converge in his bilingual multicultural home province, thereby resolving, in exemplary fashion, the problem of "double exile"; this he does by never being provincial, and yet always keeping one eye on the strategies of a local-voiced regionalist, (the other on the open, unbounded options of the unfettered internationalist).

In this struggle to find a place and voice that can be heard in Quebec's often cold, uninviting landscape, Allen is not alone.[8] He has collaborated with many poets, particularly Stephen Luxton and Mark Teicher. He has edited many more, for Allen is also an active editor, of *The Moosehead Review* series, of the long-running *Matrix*[9], and the DC Books New Writers Series.

Allen, Luxton and Teicher—friends and long-time associates—banded together in 1980 to publish a collaboration of poems, *Late Romantics* (suggested by the project of Wordsworth/Coleridge's *Lyrical Ballads)*. From the back of the Moosehead Press book we learn that Allen was "born in Bristol, England in 1946"; Luxton "was born in Coventry, England, in 1946" and Teicher in Poland, in 1948.[10] Almost exact contemporaries, the three poets are all landed immigrants, part of the post-war Canadian experience of coming to the new world, with old world baggage, both personal and aesthetic.

Late Romantics arises from a desire to share and create a co-extensive poetic context, not just for reasons of "critical familiarity with one another's work" as the cover says but in order to struggle with the cold facts of recognition, and its sometime lack. It is no coincidence that a recurring motif in Allen's work is snow-bound survivors, whether of crashes, or love affairs gone off-course. In "Hazard", a poem concerned with surviving in winter, from his 1986 collection, *One Night At The Indigo Hotel*, Allen writes: "We hazard with our one and only heart, whirled / this winter in tumbling, tumultuous skies. / Shifts of weather set the heart on edge."[11]

It sometimes seems as if all of Anglo-Quebec poetry has become "lost" after an air crash, left wandering in the wilds, wintering an indifferent audience (the local French, the rest-of-Canada, and then the world).[12] Quebec (though often confronting fascinating and complex political and socio-linguistic tensions throughout the 1970s and into the present) has rarely been able to muster much international interest. Anglo-Quebec poetry, though it "boasts" poets like A. M. Klein, Irving Layton and Leonard Cohen, has yet to be taken entirely seriously abroad.[13]

As Mordecai Richler wrote in 1970 in London, England, "We remain the English-speaking world's elected squares.... I do not subscribe, *pace* too many embittered Canadian small talents, to the wildly self-flattering theory that there is an anti-Canadian cultural cabal common to London and New York. What I do believe is even more depressing. The sour truth is just about everybody outside of Canada finds us boring. Immensely boring."[14] As a Canadian writer based in the same city more than thirty years later, let me add this seems to remain sadly accurate.

Such lack of cultural and critical attention from the wider world, the sense of being a sort of poetic cul-de-sac, has not been a total disaster though. Allen, Luxton and Teicher turned this absence of any extended exterior interest to their relative advantage. Their poetry is often kick-started by the isolation of Quebec's (and Canada's) vast natural environment; the ironic penalties and rewards of writing itself, figured in such isolation—and poetry's powerful, if often ill-fated, attempts to address the gap between nature, reader, and writing.

Luxton's poem "Letter from Exile" for instance, imagines a post-apocalyptic world where things are "Getting better. But still not all quite anywhere."[15] The fragmented syntax highlights a telling dislocation, not just in space or time, but language-meaning, and being. For Luxton, the ontological work is tied to the struggle to clear—in fact, identify—a place that, far from being utopian, is barely placed on the map. This austere cultural location, whose coordinates are not quite anywhere, can inspire a pioneering linguistic style, such as is found in Dorn's *Gunslinger*.[16]

Such a "cowboy" persona—flippant, free-wheeling, and refreshingly unhinged—emerges in the texts of the poets being read here. In Allen this is often a cowboy, or sailor figure—in Luxton, more a contemporary woodsman, a twenty-first-century *voyageur*, setting off in to the brush to wryly rediscover the new world.[17] These nature-based personas are usually juxtaposed with the paradoxes of urban, if not universal, life (including lust and death). Notably, Teicher has written wintry lyric poems on Eros and Thanatos, such as "I Sat with a Rose."[18]

Allen's ambitious, stylistically voyaging writing, expresses this desire to spread and flow beyond the usual set and limited formal borders that British and Irish poetry tends currently to occupy, but which more open-form contemporary American poetry explores with pleasure.

Allen and Luxton, though British-born, in a way both begin their poetic lives as American poets, aware of and influenced by the ecological poetry of Whitman, Snyder, and especially A. R. Ammons. They do so, somewhat paradoxically, while maintaining a sensibility which negotiates the hostile Quebec landscape (cultural and environmental) by contrasting it with a freedom underwritten by learning, an enthusiasm for nature, and a dandyism, whose urban, urbane style includes references to high and popular culture.

It is at the later stages of Allen's and Luxton's writing, in their more recent collections especially, that this merger of ecological sincerity and downtown wit achieves a stable condition; and becomes their best, least borrowed voice—even as it plays off of developments in recent poetry written by their younger Montreal-based peers.

"Mutteringly mad, and the snow"

Robert Allen is a novelist as well as a poet, and his two major works of fiction, cult classic two-volume novel *The Hawryliw Process* (Porcupine's Quill Press, 1979 & 1980), and *Napoleon's Retreat* (DC Books, 1997) are to some readers his major linguistically innovative achievements. Arguably, he is even more fascinating as a poet in the way his writing intersects with so many streams of poetic tradition.

Allen has published many collections of poems, beginning thirty-five years ago, in 1971, with *Valhalla at the OK*, and then *Blues & Ballads*, in 1974, both published by Ithaca House Press, in America; through to his major early collection (which contains half a dozen of his finest poems) *The Assumption of Private Lives* (New Delta, 1977), to *Wintergarden*

(Quadrant, 1984) which introduces "The Encantadas" beyond to his *Magellan's Clouds, New and Selected Poems* (Véhicule Press, 1990).

His decade-long poetic silence of the '90s was broken by *Ricky Ricardo Suites* (DC Books, 2000), containing the middle third section of "The Encantadas", then followed five years later by *Standing Wave* (Véhicule Press, 2005) and *The Encantadas* (Conundrum Press, 2006).

Allen has three strong literary precursors which he has recently acknowledged in a note contained in *Standing Wave*: Herman Melville, Wallace Stevens and A. R. Ammons. Aside from their literary similarities, these three American master-stylists all share aspects of Allen's own personal biography: Melville worked diligently in semi-obscurity for many years on his major work; Stevens, an unassuming professional man, achieved his greatest, more quiet work in later life, focused on imagined American landscapes, eschewing the European scene except by reference; Ammons, by all accounts modest and affable, kept a relatively low profile, while nonetheless commanding the respect of his peers, and wrote with precisely scientific observational clarity of the natural, swerving course of things, without giving up on a colloquial sense of humour or his urge to deviate towards experiment and wordplay.

These stoic, almost-private heroic figures, help to locate one aspect of both Allen the person and the writer, as well as Allen's texts. In *Wintergarden*, Allen's four-part poem "Melville" addresses his thoughts, not only on solitary, long writing in a wintry, unforgiving environment (after all the opening line is simply "Melville, wintering") but also the difficulty for any writer of maintaining relationships with themselves, their loved ones, and the wider world. The following section is in the voice of Melville's wife:

> Lately the silence drives him
> mutteringly mad, and the snow
> blinds him. I don't know how many times
>
> I've knelt on the floor beside him
> with a compress for his eyes . . . ."
> His wife—who suffered
>
> winter with him, bore and took care
> of his children, where is her book?
> It was Herman who ate all the voices

from the wind, made them talk
his words: a novel, written largely
from a landlocked ship....[19]

His exceptionally inventive long poem *The Encantadas* is such a Melvillian text, "written largely" with many ("all") of the voices made to talk by Allen. The long poetic sequence consists of 158 sections, in a form "derived from poets like Wallace Stevens and A. R. Ammons"[20]—three-stanza, nine-line sections. It has finally been collected and published in a revised edition, gathering sections heretofore scattered across a variety of different collections and anthologies.

"more exciting than the sea-surfaces"

"The Encantadas" is a major Canadian long poem, vastly imaginative and ambitious, deserving of its own, in-depth study. Still, now that it is possible to read the work as Allen intended, and with his revisions, some immediate commentary is both desirable and timely.

Readers of Allen will not be surprised to find that the first word of *The Encantadas* is snow, or that he begins his epic poem with a quote from Gilbert White (1720-1793), England's first ecologist: "All nature is so full, that that produces / the most variety that is most examined."[21] There is a sense in which Allen's writing has always been a Darwinian variety show, generously exploring and presenting the many freaks (such as tap-dancing turtles), wonders and untold elements of the natural (and unnatural) world as it and the writing evolve.

As such, there is a fascinating sub-textual discourse which runs through the poem, on the nature of poetry and poetry's relation to nature, which can be figured as the debate between the poet-critics Yvor Winters and John Crowe Ransom—or more to the point, Winter's critique of Ransom; it is only slightly fanciful to note how the allusive Allen enjoys having both winter and Winters in his work.

Allen, who taught at Kenyon College, the legendary home of the New Criticism and Ransom, is pleased to relate his own work (in both reality and fantasy) to the New Critic and author of, among others, the poem "Captain Carpenter" (a poem alluded to in *The Encantadas* in section 64 with its "Clack! Clack!"[22]). In a recent interview he says: "[I spent] my year at Kenyon living next door to Ransom, who could be seen, wrapped in a blanket, in the blue light of the television. I never saw him but that way, and read about his death the following summer while I was in Oregon. When I am in a tall-tale-spinning mode, I often say that I replaced John Crowe Ransom as Creative Writing Professor at Kenyon."[23] *The Encantadas* is such a mode, and Ransom is part of the tall tale.

In the essay "John Crowe Ransom or Thunder Without God", Winters takes Ransom to task for his new critical approach that leads him "at times to make curiously insensitive remarks" such as, in comparing poems by Wallace Stevens and Allen Tate: "The deaths of little boys are more exciting than the sea-surfaces"—a remark Winters writes "which seems worthy of a perfumed and elderly cannibal."[24] Allen, who has written at least one poem about cannibalism, and whose *The Encantadas* enjoys, in full Wallace Stevens mode, the surface (and depths) of the sea as well as explorations of death and dying, seeks to play with such tensions.

In part 1, section 30, the poem presents *both* a dead child (a daughter)—strongly echoing Ransom's poem "Bells for John Whiteside's Daughter"—and the "stormy Pacific, just / euphoric and light. He might as well rise to his feet, follow those / lightshafts home."[25]

This passage is extraordinary for how it manages to wittily yoke together the various excitements proposed by Ransom and Winters, and suggest a textual resolution in the form of *The Encantadas* itself. In Part I, section 38, Allen supplies more mischievous textual fuel for this esoteric key to the text (that is, the agon of mid-century American poetic debate, resolved by the poetics of Ammons as exhibited in *Garbage*, say, or *Sphere*[26]). Line three begins with the word "crows" and line five, of thirteen words, has, as its central word, "winters".[27] At such times, it is good to remember that Allen has always been an exceptionally playful, and complex, post-modern writer, who cut his teeth on Joyce, Nabokov and Pynchon. His texts are multi-layered and rich with meanings.

The sources of the John Crowe Ransom-Yvor Winters clash are several, but at heart is the question of evil in poetry—particularly evil in Baudelaire (an important poet for Allen as well as for modern poetry in general). In Part 1, section 2: "he writes / of a shadow of shadows, with all his bright skill"[28] is almost a poetic paraphrase of Winters' celebration of Baudelaire's ethical response to darkness: "He dealt with the problem of evil in the terms in which he had met it, the terms of the romantic view of life; and it was because of these terms that he was able to embody the universal principles of evil in the experiences of his own age and evaluate that experience."[29]

This idea of objectively evaluating experience (and also doing so with one eye on the romantic view of life) greatly appeals to the natural scientist in Allen. In "Jack", Part I, "He lines up a knothole in the barn / with the falling evening star"[30]—and such a radical alignment presents both the moral and visual perspective of the poet as scientist. This is the perspective often used by Allen's most direct precursor, Ammons—a poet whose long poetic sequences and poems *The Encantadas* is often modelled on and with whom Allen studied as a graduate student at Cornell University.

In an interview with Steven P. Schneider, Ammons discusses the innovative form of his poem *Tape for the turn of the year*, begun at Cornell at around the time Allen would have studied there. Speaking of its "Ulysses theme" (and the sense of coming home, strong in *The Encantadas* too) Ammons says of his critics: "But they never seemed to have gotten that it could be like a novel, with a beginning, a middle, and an end."[31] *The Encantadas* are presented in a volume with the following back blurb: "The poem weaves together three main narrative threads, and in fact has all the twists and turns of an adventure novel." Allen writes, echoing and expanding this, in *Standing Wave*, "A Note on *The Encantadas*":

> The poem contains three main narrative threads, corresponding roughly to the three thirds of the poem. Sections 1-60 tell the tale of Jack, an oceanographer who undergoes rapture of the deep in the Pacific Ocean and returns to a family farm in Quebec's Eastern Townships, where he begins to come to terms with his past and with his avoidance of it. [...] Sections 61-100 [...] mainly involve Jack's *body double*, "The Antediluvian Vaudevillian", Teddy the tap-dancing turtle, through whose oceanic voyages Jack's fears and doubts are further acted out. In the poem's last third ... Jack is back on the seas, sung onward by his muse, as he smuggles *wine* from Corfu to the English coast, re-enacting the path of Dionysius in bringing Mediterranean wine to Northern Europe.[32]

This is a poem with an eclectic, inclusive design—to borrow from Ammons, it is arguably shaped by "the curve that includes everything"[33] (a motto that Allen could surely make his own). And it is a poem further shaped by Ammons's idea of a rhetoric where "you pretend that you are creating 'a spontaneous flow' that imitates the mind."

The Encantadas is the flow of a mind, a mind able to take in the curve of everything—especially "the odd shapes in the world that carry mean-ing"[34]—the "flow and process of the long poem" able to bear along traditional poetic forms in new ways, or more radically, "dissolve such a small, little perfect configuration of things."[35]

In Part One, section 53, "in the rigging, flapping in the flow, for all the world / like sails"[36] the text offers a strong symbol for the mind in such a creative process—the sailor (Jack). As Ammons' poetic proposes to do away with forms except in motion and reorder the lyric tradition, so too does Allen borrow and build on such an adventure.

Building on a reading of *The Encantadas* which navigates its form and signifying play in relation to American literary modernism and new critical texts, it is fascinating to turn to Part 1, Section 45, which sees the enraptured (romantic figure) of Jack in Mexico and its jungles. The middle of line 5 reads: "X marks nothing, as the jungle knows." This sounds like Winters again, namely, his essay "The Significance of *The Bridge*, by Hart Crane or What Are We To Think of Professor X." In this once-infamous essay, Winters, a one-time friend of Crane, blames the Emerson-Whitman poetic tradition for destroying the young romantic-modernist poet; and also examines, and finds major structural fault with, Crane's ambitious long poem, *The Bridge*, meant to extend and even supplant the work laid down by T. S. Eliot in *The Waste Land*, and in the process create a new myth for America.[37]

It could be argued that Allen's *The Encantadas* is nothing less than a furthering, by other means, of Crane's own grandiose attempt to build up an epic poem on contemporary themes. Crane is certainly never far from Allen's poem, especially in section 45, Crane having also died in the sea he loved by drowning after leaping off a boat bound from Mexico.[38]

Professor X is a sentimentalist, who fails to recognize the dangerous power of poetry and ideas, if taken to their logical (or irrational limit).[39] Allen descends from the Emerson-Whitman-Ammons line that is queried in Winters' essay. His poem struggles to engage with the enrapturing and narcotic powers of the poetic. Allen's long poem is an exploration of the risks and rewards entailed by any romantic or scientific voyage of discovery; but, given that it is a poem grounded in the texts of the greatest naturalist of all, it is also surely a balancing (or tap-dancing) act between reason and *enchantment* (the source of the title) to be found in Nature Poetry.

Hence the relevance, finally, of Allen's thinking through of the Professor X position (a position which, while granting that poetry may be *magic* in a vaudeville sense, does not admit that it might be *supernatural* in a more profound way). Allen's poem finally stakes its claim to being a major poem about these issues, and about imagination itself. It is an epic about the way poetry enchants. This ambition is well expressed in section 54: "A flood is in my eye, an epic. I must go like Gilgamesh, still an undrowned / hero..."[40]— undrowned unlike Crane.

The last three lines, perhaps the most lyrically sustained and beautiful of Allen's long career, spell out his method, his fluid and versatile *ars poetica*:

> But moving in space is what I do best, what I do now. The whole
> air of earth can be thought of as a sea, to move side to side, up and
> down, back and forward in. / & half on purpose he fell in, circled once,
>
> *Was gone.*[41]

Standing Wave

Allen's *Standing Wave* is one of his most significant books of poetry and the clearest statement yet of his divided, fascinating relationship to the many poetic traditions that both bind and release him. Hence the elegant multiple meanings of the title. The collection is formally complex, too, beginning with his long sonnet sequence, and ending with the last third of "The Encantadas"—becoming in the process perhaps his most pronounced tussle with poetic form and language.

Like a wilder Wallace Stevens in Florida, "Thirty-eight Sonnets from Jimmie Walker Swamp" begins with an invocation to that popular muse, the grape: "The declined summer seemed to call for white wine" before uttering what could be his credo: "The map went to the edge, then kept going, to the wild."[42]

In these hazy auroras of late summer creation, Allen is also the follower of Ammons. In sonnet "35" he writes, "I have read // other things: science, cosmology, evolution."[43] In sonnet "16" he observes the heavens, as if twice-deepening Ammons' clear, sharp eye: "Without much in my head tonight, I nevertheless / think fleetingly of Mars, closer than in sixty thousand years" and moves on to say "Without weather I would be lost. It drives me / to poetry."[44]

In "23" Stevens combines with Allen's own concerns: "A peaceful, rising moon: warm bullets / of stars: a spray of them over Key West"[45]—we get the American Allen. That is, a poet allowing the shape of his loosely-metered lines to flow like speech within the sonnet, like small model ships allowed to sail in under glass, to be bottled, their full rigging only raised once slipped in to the form.

Allen is, as was said earlier, a various poet, one with his own built-in shadow, his own Acme Instant Doppelganger. He is, like all good Montréalais, as much European (say it: French) as he is North American, or English. How else to explain his counter-rational confession, in sonnet "31": "Rimbaud and Baudelaire and Mallarmé made me / into the poet I am. They trespassed on the order / I saw all around."[46]

This is Allen thinking through ideas regarding a pure poetry of the mind, an abstract poetry of beauty and ideas, forever entangled with its origins in the linguistic, experiential diabolism at the core of modernist, nineteenth-century French poetry, à la Baudelaire and Rimbaud (Allen intriguingly inverts their historical progression to assert the pre-eminence of the younger poet). To locate Allen's allegiance to this "decadent" undercurrent of countervailing stylists, we need to read of Allen's other cast of precursor-protagonists, which include "edgarpo, frank ohara" and "humbert,"[47] from his previous collection, *Ricky Ricardo Suites*, also a twenty-first-century work, and, to my way of reading, equally significant.

Edgar *Allan* Poe (note how Allen subtracts himself—his own name-sake—from the equation above, as it were); Frank O'Hara, and Vladimir Nabokov (Humbert Humbert's creator) are all representatives, though deliciously different, of a high style, one in many ways derived from, as well as influential on, European letters—Poe most obviously through translation back into French, by Charles Baudelaire, O'Hara, whose studies of French writers led to his best-known "New York School" poems of the city, Eros and visual representation; and Nabokov, as the classic arch-postmodernist academic wit turned American satirist in *Lolita* (a founding text for Allen, as can be seen in his provocative portrait in the *Montreal Review of Books*, summer 2006, where Allen poses with his shades in front of a brick wall stencilled over dozens of times with the word "Lolita").

The cover of *Ricky Ricardo Suites* features another striking, even transgressive image of a shark-finned American automobile knocking a woman down (from *Life*, April 6, 1953); is this a reference to Mrs. Haze's (Lolita's mother) accidental and all-too-convenient vehicular death? No doubt. In this collection Allen's own many-styled textual and linguistic zaniness approaches that of the inventiveness of the character Clare Quilty as played by

334

Peter Sellers in the film version directed by Stanley Kubrick in 1962.[48]

Allen, by 2000, had presumably tired of his earlier short, lyric poetry in part because it did not afford him the same release as he found in his longer forms of writing. The earlier poems (often more traditional—in terms of form and subject-matter—a few of his best appear in the mid-period *Wintergarden*) had never been as polysemous as his novels, which benefit from being able to sustain more character development and wacky, surreal or parodic situations.

Allen learned from the many younger poets at work in Montreal in the 1990s, such as David McGimpsey, Jason Camlot and Heather O'Neill, all of whom write a hip, funny, post-modern poetry (inspired in part, say, by David Trinidad or late Ashbery). Allen also appears to have taken special sustenance from the upsurge of interest in the popular underground cabaret poetry "scene" at the time, as well, which he often appeared at, performing his own work in cowboy boots and tinted glasses; indeed, Allen has said, "I believe that from the early '90s to the present I flourished as a writer mostly because of the force and ferment of the Montreal scene."[49]

In the title poem, in the first section, he writes: "My friends and I are sitcom ciphers", and then further explores Ricardo's marginal status as an other, an outsider. In part iii of the same poem he writes: "Like Ricky Ricardo's country mine never made it on television."[50] This at once raises the spectre of the identity crisis (or crisis of reception) for Anglo-Quebec writers, and also the hipster textual focus of influential peers, especially McGimpsey, who in some ways defined the televisual-sublime as a new sub-genre in Canadian poetry.

Allen's resurgent work here becomes more brazen, more itself—fully merging his many alternative and various interests. In 2000, or just beforehand (some of the *Ricardo* poems were composed in the 1990s) Allen seems to find a fusion that works, and simply erupts into his late, present period, where the poetry, and the prose, both find their expression in a new cross-genre exuberance.

In his TV-inspired title (Ricky Ricardo / Desi Arnaz being a sort of perennial insider-outsider figure, at once dapper and hapless, married to Lucy / Lucille Ball) Allen signals a turn to what has always really driven him—pop culture, sex, a love of musical and poetic figures across the whole high-to-low spectrum. Mozart, Stravinsky, Jim Morrison, Paul Bowles, Biggie Smalls and Billie Holiday are mentioned—Holiday in two poems—as if to out-Holiday O'Hara.

Allen seems to be presenting himself here as the ultimate poetic insider-outsider—the European-in-America, able to master the North American vernacular, and its parochial as well as sprawling concerns, while never abandoning his sophisticated, cosmopolitan roots in French modernism and decadent dandyism. In the prose poem "Boulevard" this bohemian *flâneur* role is captured in the opening line: "In a warm bar full of lovers, coats and smoke."[51] Allen is able to locate his own nineteenth-century Paris in *fin-de-siècle* Montreal.

The Stravinsky appearance is perhaps most striking. Twenty years after *Late Romantics*, Allen returns to his old stomping grounds, bolstering this belated romanticism with a quote as frontispiece to the collection, from the modernist-pioneer-turned-Hollywood-conductor[52], whose own career trajectory from Europe to America, in some ways mirrors Allen's, Nabokov's *and* Ricardo's: "Those others, they're still romantics—I'm already a romantic."[53]

This twisted linguistic logic plays on the difference between "still" being and "already" being—the difference, that is, between "hanging on" as it were, or simply, being "one of the first". In terms of romanticism, Allen seems to be saying he is not really late at all—the party started by about the time he got there.

It is a wonderful moment of late-career braggadocio, this lifting of Stravinsky, worthy of a rap artist, laying down his street cred, and indeed, Allen writes, in "The History of Western Music From Mozart to Biggie Smalls" of a transmission of all Western culture (and Western in both senses, since Allen's first book takes its title from the OK Coral gunslinger showdown): "On the top floor stereo, Mozart K 45, / downstairs its bitches and hos" and then, in the facing poem, "My son, to me" replies "Rap is love and violence without history."[54]

Whether that is a fair estimate of rap, Allen's own poetry is, as he says in "Cock Ale" "molten in the mouth"[55]—that is, his poetry *is* a history, a cultural history, of love and violence. The violence that obsessive love (we're talking Nabokov, Poe and Ricardo, here) of culture (art, music, and writing) does, self-reflexively, to itself or at least, sometimes, its practitioners (one recalls, again, Crane's doomed life here). Allen thus serves notice that his oeuvre is molten, potent and destructive as Stravinsky's *Fire Bird* or O'Hara's *Fire Island* (another vehicular tragedy).

Allen has long treasured the trope, derived from astronomy as well as early popular musicians, such as Jerry Lee Lewis, of fire as a destructive personal element. Perhaps this fuses in the body of one Sam Phillips, of Sun Records. In one of his signature poems, "Magellan's Clouds", first collected in *Wintergarden*, he writes: "I used to think I was a ball of fire/ brighter the faster I burned."[56]

All of this extraordinary expenditure of energy and display comes to a head in the bawdy prose poem "Tosltoi Station" from *Ricky Ricardo Suites*, one of Allen's most innovative (and best) mid-length poems. The rollicking jouissance of the text has much in common with *Napoleon's Retreat* (with its set-piece lists and Sterne-like digressions).[57]

Section 2 of the poem is titled "a greater glory than you guess: carré Baudelaire"; section 3, alluding to *Don Quixote*, the first (and still one of the most subversive) novels, suddenly gives us the rather less-than-Cervantean "your daughter's diary speaks of sex with a band called the cranberries. you wistfully fucked her yourself. she is *another*…."[58]

Section 4 is titled "for edgarpo and frank o'hara: fire island sky" and features "The motel where lo and humbert stayed has finally changed the sheets / take out an ad, america: *shoulders wide enough for the world, and stirred, not shaken, American loins!*"[59] in what must be the first pastiche of Ginsberg's, Fleming's *and* Nabokov's varieties of writing on, about, or in, American cultural, political post-war hegemony.

Speaking of post-war 1950s America, the back of this collection, not to be outdone, features an anti-McCarthy CBS radio broadcast by Edward R. Murrow, in-studio and on-air (also in 1953); Allen was only seven then, and no doubt, endlessly formed by the sort of 50s events which these sensational Beat-Bond-*Lolita* references lovingly, if vicariously, valorise.

The last section of this emblematic poem is titled "at the conclusion of her orgasm the sensitive chambermaid bit my shoulder."[60] In phrases reminiscent of Leonard Cohen, he terminates the poem, abruptly, as follows: "love, I have taken all words for granted. i have misread marx and nostradamus. i have dreamt of the aegean, from cockeyed sky. the earth blows steam / like a braking train."[61]

Allen's grand tour of Western history, from Homer's Aegean, through Nostradamus's middle-aged apocalyptic pronouncements, through Marx's steam-driven run-away engine, blows hot and cold, terminating in steamy words, clouds of Magellan.

V. Appendices

Anglo-Quebec Poetry Periodicals, c1976-2006

JASON CAMLOT

The following annotated bibliography is not exhaustive in its coverage of English-language poetry magazines from Quebec, and its descriptions aim at highlighting what the bibliographer has found interesting and worth mentioning, rather than at thoroughness for its own sake. Some of the magazines listed could not be consulted despite my knowledge of their existence. These appear with very limited or no descriptions and are marked in the titles list with an asterisk. For useful coverage of some of the little poetry magazines that appeared just prior to those of the period covered here I recommend chapter nine of Ken Norris's *The Little Magazine in Canada 1925-1980* (Toronto: ECW Press, 1984), pp. 154-172. Among the earlier periodicals discussed there, but not here, are: *Cataract* (edited in the early 1960s by Seymour Mayne, K. V. Hertz, and Leonard Angel), *Catapult* (which continued *Cataract* for a couple of years), *Yes* (edited by Michael Gnarowski and Glen Seibrasse. 1956-1970), *Moment* (published by Al Purdy and Milton Acorn in Montreal between 1959-1961), and Louis Dudek's personal magazine *Delta* (1957-1966). Karen Emily Suurtamm's groundwork on this bibliography was formidable, and so I acknowledge her again here.

Journal Titles in Order of First Appearance

1970	*Ingluvin*
1971	*Jaw Breaker*
1972	*Booster & Blaster*
	Le Chien D'Or/The Golden Dog
	Moongoose
	*The Wrecker's Ball**
1973	*Bruises*
	*Davinci**
	Feminist Communication Collective
	*What is**
1974	*The Alchemist*
	Montreal Poems
	*Samisdat**
1975	*Cross Country: A Magazine of Canadian-U.S. Poetry*

	Los (Concordia University)
	Matrix
	Process
1976	*Cyan Line*
	Hobbyhorse (Hh)
	Mouse Eggs
	Solitude-Inflexion
	Versus
1977	*Arcady: The Dawson College Literary Magazine*
	Maker
1978	*Atropos*
	Locus
	*Montreal Journal of Poetics (MJP)**
	Montreal Poems / Poésie de Montréal
	Montreal Writers' Forum
1979	*Athanor*
	Loomings
1980	*Scrivener: Journal of Creative Writing*
1981	*Disabled Writers' Quarterly: The International Literary Magazine of Physically Disabled Writers*
	Tobacco Shop
1982	*Four by Four*
	Short Poems
1983	*Hejira*
	Rubicon
1984	*Lucky Jim's*
	Montreal Now!
	Raw Verse
	Xero
1987	*Alpha Beat Soup*
	Kola: A Black Literary Magazine
	New Canadian Review
	Revue ex-it Press
	Seen: A Literary and Visual Arts Magazine
	Zymergy
1988	*The Moosehead Anthology*
1989	*Dis-ease: A New Strain of Verse*
	Skylark
1990	*Pawn to Infinity*
1991	*Echoes: A Literary Review*

1992	Errata: Independent Arts Montreal
1993	Poet's Podium
1994	Broke
	Corridors
	Index: The Montreal Literary Calendar
1996	Agent: broken word manual ·
1998	Headlight Anthology
	Soliloquies
1999	Flood Quarterly*
2001	(Ex) cite: Journal of Contemporary Writing
	Slingshot
	Vallum: Contemporary Poetry

Agent: broken word manual, 1996

Two issues of this 28 page, staple-bound and grey cardstock covered chapbook litzine were circulated (Summer and Winter 1996). Simple in design and production (Winter 1996, the only issue consulted has a black and white close-up photo of a giraffe's face on the cover, and a simple centered list of contributors on the back), *Agent* carried the best and most exciting Anglo writers of the Montreal scene for that year. Published by Vox Hunt Press, and serving in part as a print vehicle for the key impresarios involved in producing the Vox Hunt reading series—Dan Mitchell (coordinating editor), Jake Brown (editor-at-large), and Todd Swift (poetry editor)—*Agent* featured such writers and artists as Anne Stone, American poet Regie Cabico, Fortner Anderson, Golda Fried, Jake Brown, Derek Webster, Heather O'Neill, Jonathan Goldstein, Andy Brown, Robert Allen, Jason Camlot, Billy Mavreas and bill bissett (who was featured reader at the *Agent* launch, Saturday, December 7, 1996 at Gallery Isart, 263 St. Antoine West). The theme of the Winter 1996 issue was "Poetry is Agency", and a brief editorial statement on the masthead page states that "Agent is a quarterly broken-word manual for the Montréal writing life." It was "Available exclusively at Danger!" (a bookstore on boul. St-Laurent). Published by Vox Hunt Press, submissions sent to Agent, 5167 St-André, Montreal, Quebec, H2J 3A6 or email booter@accent.net. Cost: $3.50.

The Alchemist, 1974-1990

Edited primarily by Marco Fraticelli, *The Alchemist* appeared nearly annually from 1974 to 1990 in a variety of formats, from perfect binding to stapled to wrapped loose cards to the 1984 (3.1) Floppy Disk issue (in a cardboard envelope). An average of 200-300 copies were published up until the early 1980s when 500 copies where produced for several years in a row. After the first few issues, an editorial statement of mandate appears indicating that "the Alchemist will include a haiku section and a Québécois poet in translation, as well as its regular features of prose, poetry, and graphic art." In addition to its haiku and translation mandate, it was also very interested in concrete poetry, collage graphics and block printing. Publisher: Alchemist, P.O. Box 123, Lasalle, Quebec, H8R 2Z4. Cost ranged from $4/4 issues in 1974, to $12/4 issues in 1990.

Alpha Beat Soup, 1987-1990

The editorial mandate states, "Alpha Beat soup is an international literary magazine featuring Beat and post-Beat independent and modern writings published twice a year." Edited by Dave Christy, this inconsistently biannual serial publishes short essays, anecdotes and poems about the Beat era. The 50-75 pages that appear on folded legal sized sheets, between stapled cardstock covers are usually split fifty-fifty between poetry and prose, with the issue contents listed in the back. Carl Solomon writes a column at the start of every issue—about being someone once associated with the "Beatnick" culture in the age of *Reagan*! There are dispatches from others on the scene during that era, correcting or corroborating mythic anecdotes (as when Dylan and Ginsberg first met) in short prose pieces, or letters to Dave Christy. Poets that appear here include Burroughs, Ferlinghetti, Kerouac, Ginsberg, Snyder, Gregory Corso, Michael McClure, Anne Waldman, and Charles Bukowski. Published by Alpha Beat Press, 5110 Adam St., Montreal, Quebec, H1V 1W8. Cost: $3 per issue/$5 per year.

Anthol, 1972-1974

Edited by Robert Morrison and Diane Keating, the editors state that "*Anthol* has been conceived as a bi-annual publication providing an outlet for young Montreal artists. The editors wish, as well, to help foster a poetic community here in Montreal, and urge anyone with similar interests to contact them.... We have in mind the engendering of informal meetings, poetry readings, critical sessions, etc." This poetry journal of anywhere between 25 and 93 pages was perfect-bound between thick textured cardstock colored green, blue, orange, and other colors, a new one for each issue. While it was intended as a biannual publication, the reality is it appeared just "fairly" annually, as a venue for the work of such Montreal poets as Michael Harris, Diane Keating, Tom Konyves, Bob McGee, Anne McLean, Robert Morrison, Sharon Nelson, Glen Siebrasse (the editor of Delta), Richard Sommer, John McAuley, Andre Farkas, and Stephen Morrissey (mostly shape and art poems). The list suggests that *Anthol* was a pre-Vehicle publication which brought some West Island poets together, plus a few from downtown—like Harris and Sommer. Of interest in Issue 4 (1975) is Louis Dudek's review of four 1974 Da Vinci Press poetry books: *From Yr Lover Like an Orchestra* by Ian Ferrier, *Arctic Char In Grecian Waters* by Tom Ezzy, *Szerbusz* by André Farkas, *Dakini* by Claudia Lapp. *Anthol* was published by R. Morrison/Anthol Press, 71 Pardo #208, Point Claire, Quebec. Cost: 1 (50 cents); 2-3 ($1); 4 ($2).

Arcady: The Dawson College Literary Magazine, 1977-1978

The consulting editor of this college journal was Gabriel Safdie. It consisted of seventy-two pages of poetry and some prose, stapled between a black and white cardstock cover. Some names of interest to appear here are Robbie Newton Drummond, Ann Rothman, and Tom Konyves as well as a selection of poems by Brian Trehearne, the scholar of Montreal poetry of the Forties. Trehearne is also thanked for his help on the production of *Arcady* at every stage. Published at Dawson College. Price unknown.

Athanor, 1979-1980

The name is a combination of Greek words: thanatos = death, athanato = immortality, and the long introduction to the first issue states that "[t]he poet is both alchemist and anthanor. Life is the nigredo, or raw material from which he draws the substance of his poems. This raw material is subjected to the discipline of the furnace: the fires of passion transform it while the fires of intellect shape and perfect it." This journal of "Canadian poetry & Inter/views", edited primarily by Kathleen C. Moore and Russell Thornton seems to have been associated with Concordia University, the first issue (100 printed) having been sponsored by the Arts Students Association of that university. Issues include poems by, among others, F. R. Scott (poet in residence at Concordia), Patrick Lane, John Barton, Gary Geddes, Henry Beissel and Mona Elaine Adilman (these last three teaching at Concordia at the time), Irving Layton, Dorothy Livesay, Gwendolyn MacEwen, Seymour Mayne, Al Purdy and interviews with Scott, Layton, Lane and Mayne. Numbers 1-3 were stapled cardstock and ran to about 40 pages. Number 4 was perfect bound and 85 pages. Published by *Athanor*, P.O. Box 562, Victoria Station, Westmount, Quebec, H3Z 2Y6. Cost: n.1-3 were $1/each, n.4 cost $2.

Atropos, 1978

Intended as a semi-annual, this perfect-bound journal with glossy finish on baby blue cover and black lettering (looking much like the *Partisan Review* or *Salmagundi* in its design) seems to have appeared only once. Its 93 pages of content (plus ten pages of advertisements from Montreal stores) consisted of poetry, essays, interviews and fiction. An editorial stance is gleaned from the page before the table of contents in 1.1: "The existence of many of the 'literary' magazines is a sort of superfetation: they've grown excessively flabby, biased and archaic. In short, they're largely irrelevant to the state of the arts today. This is the first number of a magazine committed to the gathering together of a body of quality literature for *now*." The contents—mainly English, with some French—included poetry by George Woodcock, Robert Creely, Denise Levertov, Andrei Codrescu, Mary Melfi, Jack Hannan, and Anne Waldman and an interview with Creeley. Advertisements indicate some of the happening bookstores at the time: ATHANOR bookshop, 2985 St. Denis (see the magazine *Athanor*), Mansfield Book Mart, Graduate Society of McGill U,. Botrees Occult Bookshop (Decelles), Metamorphoses Books, Telid Sub-Rosa Inc. (St. Marc) specializing in the occult, discomanie, Multimags, The Word, Old McGill '78, Academic Book Shop. Co-edited and published by James D. Campbell and Zsolt S. Alapi with the aid of assistant editor Carl H. Snyder. Atropos Publishing, Enrg., 325 Prince Edward Avenue, Otterburn Heights, Quebec J3H 1W1. Printed in Montreal by Coopérative d'Imprimerie Véhicule. Price: $2.50

Booster & Blaster, 1972

Bryan McCarthy's editorial essay of the first number explains its perception of the present writing scene, and how *Booster & Blaster* hopes to alter that situation: "During the Forties, Fifties and Sixties, poets in Montreal were in the habit of getting together, reading each other's work, criticizing it frankly, even ruthlessly, and publishing it in local mags. A sense of community survived until the early Sixties. What happened after that cannot be easily summed up.... The sense of community was lost. Poets worked either in total isolation, or incestuously in cliques, not caring much about the world outside.... A number of poets have told me that they are fed up with this situation.... I believe that this magazine with its hospitable editorial policy will help bring about this joyous state of affairs, to the great benefit of Montreal poets and poetry.... How will this magazine attempt to knit our fragmented community together? ... To begin with, poets of *all* tendencies will be made VISIBLE to each other and to the general public. Our magazine is uniquely (some would say insanely) open. Cooperatively run by the participants, it has no editor in the sense of someone who rejects material on grounds of quality. It's FREE in every sense except the financial one. A poet publishes his work... because *he thinks they should be published*—and is prepared to pay his share of the costs ($2.00 per page) and do his share of the work involved....Does this mean that BOOSTER & BLASTER is a cooperative Vanity Press? If it is, the genre is new. A participant has the right to criticize the work of any other contributor, in the SAME issue of the magazine, in any way he please s...[It] is an invitation to Montreal poets to come out INTO THE OPEN and make some sort of public stand." Among the twenty-five poets to chip in their $2 for the cause of a poetry community were Avi Boxer, Louis Dudek, Michael Gnarowski, Seymour Mayne, Marc Plourde, Peter Van Toorn and Glen Siebrasse. This first number consists of 65 letter-size pages stapled three times between orange and beige cardstock covers. At the back Bryan McCarthy prints his "GENERAL ASSESSMENT OF THE POETRY IN THIS ISSUE",

346

assessment categories ranging from Very Good, Good, Worth Reading, to Poems I Do Not Understand, and then Mediocre or Bad. Comments by some contributors upon the work of others also appear at the end. The second number (December 1972) has some interesting concrete poetry by Richard Sommer, and a note from Leonard Russo on the last page announcing the demise of *Jaw Breaker* and the founding of *The Wrecker's Ball*. "Published cooperatively six times a year. 6580 MacDonald, Montreal, 254. Phone: 861-6635." Cost $0.50 Canada, $0.65 USA.

Broke: A Literary Magazine, 1994

This glossy cardstock-covered, stapled, and nearly square-shaped journal of poetry and prose fiction was edited with humor and style by Andrea Strudensky. Her sense of humour comes through in the editorial remarks of the second number: "Once there was a magazine called The Little Review, a small private press that printed the likes of Salinger, Joyce, Lewis, Pound, Hemingway, etc… and even faced obscenity charges for publishing the Nausicaa portion of Ulysses. From that press grew another magazine which is sold throughout North America. That is not the story of this mag." The story of this mag seems to be that it was more obscure, and shorter lived, but not completely forgotten. The poetry contributors to the second number (the only one consulted) are Darius V. Snieckus, Bryan Sentes, Kathryn Mockler and George Slobodzian. The magazine was independently financed, with clean and avant-garde graphic design by Mark Lawrence Silverstone. The cover was printed by Style Printing, 120 Louvain, Montreal. The magazine was published by *Broke*, 5145 Cote St. Luc Rd., Suite 1, Montreal, Quebec, H3W 2H5. Cost: $1.

Bruises: Another Literary Magazine, 1973

The brown cardstock cover of this perfect-bound journal bears a somewhat psychedelic drawing of a tree growing out of a head with a mountainous landscape in the background, but nothing indicating the name of the magazine. Turn the first of the one hundred brown pages and you learn that *Bruises* is a publication of the John Abbott College Literary Society, with an editorial board of eight students. The contents consist of poems, fiction and articles, including work by David Sorensen, Peter Tower, Thomas Kinsella, Brian Bartlett, and Denis Donoghue! (an essay on Yeats). Published by the Literary Society of John Abbott College, Ste. Anne-de-Bellevue, Que. Cost: $1.

Corridors, 1994

Perfect bound with a blue cardstock cover bearing a handsome red ink drawing of fancy shoes with untied laces placed on the armrests of a carved wood chair, *Corridors* was a Concordia University anthology which marked the first publication of "Downtown Press" which was intended "to begin a series of annual anthologies at Concordia" and which contained the work of "faculty and students from Concordia's creative writing program, other departments and universities, as well as reputed Montreal writers." The stated goal of this anthology series is to reveal "propensities particular to Concordia's place in Montreal, and ensure that its vivacity continues to be heard." John Asfour served as the anthology's editorial consultant, and Eric Williamson was its editor and Alexis Diamond associate editor. Consisting of some prose, but mostly poetry, the verse contributors appearing within the 128 pages of the 1994 issue (the only one consulted) included Henry Beissel, Sonja Skarstedt, Alexis Diamond, Todd Swift, George Piggford, Richard Sommer, Golda Fried, Catherine Kidd, Gary Geddes, John Asfour, and Denise Roig. Published by *Corridors*, c/o Downtown Press, 1455 de Maisonneuve Blvd. W., Suite 637, Montréal, Québec, H3G 1M8. Cost: $6.95.

CrossCountry: A Magazine of Canadian-U.S. Poetry, 1975-1979
"In recent years poetry has evolved along national lines—this has led to a renaissance in North American poetry and the recognition of an individual poetic heritage in Canada. For the most part, this new Canadian-U.S. poetry has attracted only native readers. WE feel it is time for a crossing of the borders. For too long schools of poetry have emphasized national differences and played down the similarities of our North American experience. With CROSS COUNTRY we hope to provide a forum for the cross-germination needed to stimulate this continent's poetic explorations and to bring them a common audience." Edited by Ken Norris (Montreal) and Jim Mele (New York), this journal of poetry (mainly), reviews, interviews and some fiction appeared tri-annually, bi-annually and annually, stapled, wrapped, and (mostly) perfect bound, depending on the year. Names to appear included: George Bowering, Ken Norris, Andre Farkas, George Woodcock, Allen Ginsberg, Louis Dudek, John Glassco, Artie Gold, Nicole Brossard (in French), Ralph Gustafson, Al Purdy, Steve McCaffery and bp Nichol. The 1975 volume (numbers 3-4) was bilingual, co-edited with Marcel Hébert, and printed with the assistance of Véhicule Press. Number 10 was a special postcard issue, the postcards designed and hand-composed at Dreadnaught (24 Sussex Avenue, Toronto), each card with a short poem on it—including poems by Margaret Atwood, George Bowering, and Peter Van Toorn. Published by Cross Country Press (Montreal and New York): nos. 1-4: 1935 Tupper Street Apt. 14, Montreal Quebec; 5-7: 2365 Hampton Ave., Montreal Quebec, H4A 2K5, and, 3553 Aylmer St.; No. 6: Montreal Quebec, Canada (an indication, perhaps, of where Ken Norris lived during these years). Cost: 1975 ($6 for individual and $8 institutions for 2 years); 1977 ($9 individual and $12 institution for 2 years); 1979 ($4/each individual, $6/each institution).

Cyan Line: A Literary Magazine From McGill, 1976

Cyan Line is a perfect bound, handsomely produced anthology-style literary review of 46 pages "representing various young writers round Montreal and Canada." Among the poets identified as Montreal-based to be published in the second number (Fall 1976, the only one consulted) are Carole TenBrink, Jeremy Walker, Jean Cribb, Carol Leckner. Marsha Barber, Star Smith, and perhaps most importantly, John Lavery. An extensive ten-page interview by Tessa and John Lavery with F.R. Scott also appears in this number under the title, "An Afternoon With F.R. Scott." Edited by Kathryn Esplin with C. Abbot Conway serving as McGill staff advisor. Published by Cyan Line, McGill University Arts Building, P.O. Box 6070, Station A, Montreal, Quebec, Canada. The journal was typeset by Student Society's Typesetting, printed by Véhicule Press. Cost: unknown.

Davinci, 1973-1979

Only *Davinci* 5 (autumn 1977) has been consulted. This elegantly designed 5½ by 7½ inch periodical of about forty pages was printed on Véhicule Press off-cuts, paper left over from paying customers. Consequently, the kind of paper used changed from issue to issue, but the size of the magazine always stayed the same. Artist Allan Bealy, the editor and designer of this literary magazine, was a member of Véhicule Art Inc.,—Montreal's first artist-run gallery—and produced a visually beautiful periodical with the assistance of publishers Simon Dardick and Guy Lavoie (designer of the Véhicule Press logo of horse and rider in a half circle). Poems and visuals appeared seamlessly together. As Simon Dardick puts it, "the artworks weren't used as room dividers; the verbal and visual were integrated into a whole gestalt." Some highlights from number 5 include an experimental "text" (which is formatted somewhat like a david antin poem) by Frank Kuenstler, collage concrete poems by John McAuley, typewriter concrete poetry by Ian Kreiger, and "automobiles in bondage" drawings by Guy Lavoie, including a Ford Ltd. with "wipers taped over" and a Triumph TRD "in a muzzle". Published by Véhicule Press, PO Box 125, Station G, Montreal, QC, H2W 2M9. Single issue $2, subscriptions (3 issues), $6 individuals, $8 institutions.

Disabled Writers' Quarterly: The International Literary Magazine of Physically Disabled Writers, 1981

Editor Samuel Miller (Montreal) states in his editorial preface: "[I]t is my hope that Disabled Writers' Quarterly will challenge our small satisfactions, prod our waning ambitions, and inspire us to go deeper into the human condition, as well as instill in the able-bodied reader an intimate comprehension of 'disabled life.'" This glossy covered, perfect-bound journal of about 110 pages was an internationally organized project from the get go, with its editor Samuel Miller in

Montreal, and Associate editors in the U.S., U.K., Australia. It doesn't seem to have run beyond the first two numbers. Published by Disabled Writers' Quarterly, 2495 Major St., St. Laurent, Montreal Quebec, H4M 1E5.

Dis-ease: A New Strain of Verse, 1989-1990

This short-lived, stapled journal of about 45 pages, edited Frank Manley, Claude Paradox, James Whittall, claimed to be "[t]he only literary magazine of its kind in Canada with a clearly defined editorial policy." The policy states 1) that it will "refuse to publish anything having to do with postmodernism or other kinds of trendy 'isms' which employ facile verbal tricks or technical acrobatics to draw the reader's attention away from the fact that the author has nothing relevant to impart," 2) that it believes "that satire, irony and parody are well within the poet's domain...and can be used creatively to counter the good fellowship and bad writing", 3) that literary magazines should not be funded by the state, and 4) that Dis-ease (unlike Poetry Toronto) will not outlive its natural lifespan, and survive in glossy format on government life support. This journal took every opportunity to criticize trends in the current literary scene, usually through satire and parody, whether it be Erin Mouré, "The best in British-style opinion in Toronto", or "MAPRIX, writers worth beating." The intention was to make Dis-ease a bi or tri-annual, but only two issues are to be found at the National Library. Given the journal is published from 777 Walker Avenue, Montreal Quebec, H4C 2H5, it may have been a Concordia University venture. It cost $7 per year and was on sale at the Word bookstore.

Echoes: A Literary Review, 1991

Two numbers of this student journal of about 50 pages (stapled between cardstock covers decorated with cutesy pictures of tulips and such) were issued in the Spring and Winter of 1991. A note at the start of each number states: "Echos [sic] is a publication of Collège Marie-Victorin English Adult Ed. Center. All articles have been submitted by students and selected for publication by the editorial board." Lillian Shoub. Program Coordinator says, "'Echoes', a literary review, is a mosaic of poetry stories, articles, critiques and art that portrays images of life experiences, fantasy, nostalgia and love." Published: College Marie-Victorin, English Adult Education Centre, 7000 Marie-Victorin St., Montreal Quebec, H1G 2J6, or, 500 rue Sherbrooke, Montreal Quebec, H2H 1B9. Cost: AMICUS, the National Library Catalogue says "limited free distribution", but the hard-copy issues say $4.

Errata: Independent Arts Montreal, 1992-1994

Errata dubbed itself "Montreal's only independent English arts bi-monthly" and may have had in mind something along the lines of what Derek Webster's

Maisonneuve Magazine has become. It was stapled at the spine like a magazine, had glossy covers with photography on the back. It consisted mostly of fiction, but always had poems and poetry related articles in it, including, in 1.3 (1992), poems by Buffy Rhodenizer-Childerhose, Michael Harris, Julie Bruck, and an essay by David Solway on teaching Erin Mouré in his CEGEP class and boldly stating "she's a boring and frankly a bad poet." Stephen Evans was the publisher, Keith Marchand the editor in chief, Carmine Starnino the poetry editor, and Rupert Bottenberg the illustration assistant. Published by Mile-End Press, Montreal, 26 Bernard St. E., Montreal Quebec, H2T 1A3. Cost: $4 per issue.

(Ex) cite: Journal of Contemporary Writing, 2001

The editors, Rossana Coriandoli and Mary Gurekas, introduced *(Ex) cite* as "A new journal on the Canadian literary landscape." Originally it was going to be a magazine for women only, but the editors changed their minds. Still, they decided, it would be sensitive to women's writing and issues regardless of gender, etc. of the author. Diversity was another key term in their self-conception as a journal. As the editors put it: "(EX) CITE will strive to remain current, quirky and (un)balanced. It will seek voices that aren't bound by convention, but faithful to their own truth. (EX)CITE isn't interested in boundaries. Let us fray a little at the edges. WE want to hear moans and whispers, roars and whimpers. We want ranting and raving, story-telling and poetry of the finest you can produce." This perfect bound, glossy full-colour covered journal of about 75 pages consisted of half poetry and half prose. Published by Morgaine House, P.O. Box 267, Pointe-Claire, Quebec, H9R 4N9. Cost: $7 per number.

Feminist Communication Collective, 1973-1977

This journal of varied frequency, printed by the Women's Press, was first issued, prior to Oct./Nov. 1973, as a section of the journal *Logos* (edited by Robert Karniol and Mona Forrest, and published by the Montreal Community Press, P.O. Box 455, Montreal, Quebec). Its 25-30 photocopied pages of 8 1/2 x 11 paper, stapled together, carried articles on feminism, announcements of meetings, and 5-10 pages of poems at the back. The editors—Mona Forrest, Hilary Dickson, Beth Blackmore, and Jackie Manthorne—called for "[c]ontributions from women of articles, poems, graphics, information, letters, reviews, and what-have-you are welcome." Published by Asylum (Montreal) and the Feminist Communication Collective, P.O. Box 1238, Place d'Armes, Montreal Quebec, H2Y 3K2, it cost 35 cents per issue.

Four by Four, 1982-1985

The editors—Fred Louder, Robyn Sarah and Jack Hannan—had an idea for a small poetry journal that offered four poems by four poets in each issue. It is small for financial reasons, but also because, the editors say, it is time to be selective: "The enormous mass of poetry published in the past twenty years begins to seem a eutrophic growth. In the mid-seventies one enthusiast seriously declared that there were 187 'major poets' writing in English. Is that a renaissance – or a bloom in still water? It is time to be selective" (this unsigned statement from the first number). The editors also insist on having four poems for each poet because they feel one cannot judge someone's ability on less than four poems. As far as the selection criteria go, the editors "admit a certain bias in favour of poets whose work is strongly individual; readers should expect some startling contrasts. This does not, however, rule out occasional issues representing groups or schools of poets" (1.1). Five numbers were published over four years. The poets published were: no.1 (1982)- Peter Van Toorn, Lucille King-Edwards, Noah Zacharin, August Kleinzahler; no.2 (1983)- George Evans, Michael Cameron, Raymond Filip, A.F. Moritz; no.3 (1983)- Erin Mouré, Brent MacKay, Ruth Taylor, Jack Hannan; no.4 (1984) Bruce Taylor, Guy Birchard, Roo Borson, Brian Swann; no.5 (1984)- Ronald Reichertz, James Graham, Cathy Matyas, Stephen Brockwell. Each number ran to about 30 pages, and had a nice simple design of letter-sized newsprint folded in half, stapled at the spine, with cardstock covers. Published by Villeneuve Publications, 4647 Hutchinson St., Montreal, Quebec, H2V 4A2. Cost: $1.50 each.

Headlight Anthology, 1998-ongoing
This is a Concordia student journal with a twist: "*Headlight Anthology* is open to submission by all current and former Concordia University students." The result is a consistently impressive annual with the work of undergraduate and graduate students appearing alongside the occasional alumnus. Cover, guts and always stunning advertising poster designed by a different fine arts student each year, the nine extant issues of this perfect-bound journal are all interesting both visually, and for the poetry and prose they contain. Past editors and board members have included Joshua Knelman, Sarah Steinberg, April Ford, and Sascha Jackson. Some issues include a forward written by a more established writer, so, Carmine Starnino introduces *Headlight* 1, and George Elliot Clarke introduces and contributes to *Headlight* 8. Poetry contributions have come from such (at the time) young up-and-comers as Alex Porco, Emily Evans, Sara Peters, Ryan Arnold, Adrienne Ho, Jon Paul Fiorentino, Melissa Thompson, Angela Sczcepaniak, Corey Frost, oana avasilichioaei, Andy Brown, Erin Robinsong, Barrie Sherwood, Ibi Kaslik, and Jonathan Goldstein. Located at and mostly funded by Concordia University, issues usually cost $5, and are most easily obtained at the annual launch reading. This journal also has a neatly designed website: < http://errant.gryphonsoft.com/headlight/>.

Hejira: A Woman's Monthly Creative Journal, 1983
The editorial note on the cover page states that "*Hejira* is a search for a more accurate presentation of women, one which is affirmed through our own pens." The editorial collective consisted of nine McGill students, and Professor Maggie Berg is mentioned as the faculty advisor for the joual. The first issue is 28 pages, folded and held by staples between a beige cardstock cover. The first issue consists mostly of poems and pen and ink graphics, some of the poetry contributors being Lucille King-Edwards, Catherine Jensen, Anne McLean, and multiple pieces by Ruth Taylor. Published by *Hejira* c/o/ M. Berg, Porter's Office, Art's Building, McGill University, 844-4697. Cost: $1.

Hobbyhorse (Hh), 1976
Made of 11x17 unstapled sheets folded in half, the single number of *Hh* or *Hobbyhorse* ran to about fifteen with no pagination, is an avant-garde type journal with concrete, collage and other TISH-like poetry (all hobby horses of *Hh*'s editor Tom Konnyves at the time). Most pages include words running diagonally along, that read like cut-ups (quite random). In addition to collages, there is art by Owen Johnson and experimental poetry by Andre Farkas, Ken Norris, and Artie Gold. It also contains the "[CAN]NADA Manifesto, which is a kind of nihilistic manifesto punning on Canada and DADA. (by James T. Kirk, March 11]. Published by Asylum Publishing Co., 2572 Bedford Rd., Montreal, Quebec, with thanks to Ken Norris, Véhicule Press. Whether it had a price attached to it, or even was sold, is unknown.

Index: The Montreal Literary Calendar, 1994-1996
This is a title that had two completely different manifestations within a three-year period. In its first incarnation (March 1994 to February 1995), it was a stapled journal of about forty pages containing poetry, fiction and interviews of Montreal writers, and included an extensive, twenty-page Listings section, announcing readings, lectures, and launches. An editorial statement from this period reads: "A magazine like ours holds certain assumptions about the vigour and tenacity of this city's literary scene. Indeed, our monthly presence is a steady challenge to all those who think that talent in this city, and support for that talent, is evaporating. At INDEX, we believe that Montreal is marked by some extraordinary writers (both established and new). Not only is the rest of the country beginning to realize this, but, most importantly, we as a city are too. Through the efforts of magazines like errata, and the newer Perhaps? and Broke... we are coming to terms with what this city's most seasoned literary veterans have always known: that Montreal is one of the most important creative matrices in this country." Stephanie Blanshay was the editor for this first year, with Carmine Starnino serving as the journal's poetry editor. In vol. 1, no. 3, Starnino interviews Mark Abley and Anne Carson, and

a selection of poetry by each (including Anne Carson's "Hero") appears. In March 1995 Blansay stepped down as editor, and the FEWQ (Federation of English-Language Writers of Quebec, an early version of the Quebec Writers' Federation), which funded the venture for a short while, contacted Corey Frost (who was running ga press at the time) to take it over. Frost, Trish Salah, Dana Bath and Laura Killam changed the format and contents of *Index* drastically to a free newsprint zine that focused more on the St. Laurent spoken word scene than it had before. It was distributed to cafés and bookstores around town, and delivered by hand to subscribers' addresses. In that format, it ran for over a year, until the July/Aug issue of 1996, or 14 issues in all (it was monthly except for August and January). Other people who came and went on the editorial board during this second phase: Andy Brown (present publisher of Conundrum Press), Tracy Bohan, and Taien Ng-Chan as well as Bradd Colbourne, Buffy Childerhose, Peter Dubé and Daegan Frykland. In addition to listings, the new *Index* published interviews and reviews of books, fiction and poetry in every issue, including work by Todd Swift, Ian Stephens, Zoë Whittal, Adeena Karasick, Jean-Sebastien Huot, Vincent Tinguely, Anne Stone, Lydia Eugene, Robert Majzels, and Ibi Kaslik. It also published short theoretical pieces by the likes of Eve Kosofsky Sedgwick and Arthur and Marie Louise Kroker. In its second phase it was self-consciously irreverent, and even antithetical to what its earlier manifestation stood for. As Frost states in his first editorial from the April 1995 issue: "Are these indices. In fact it's been over a year, and this issue is the constant re-incarnation that subtly affects everything around it. Some rapid change in the (Montreal) (English) (literature) (writing) community, this re-incarnation, is the constant issue: the swell in popularity of readings and non-readings, and new publications—so this is a zine/chapbook?—who deny the creation myth of corporate publishing by evolving absolutely independently. This is an index. Have vandals got into the chemistry lab and are they trying to find a universal solvent for a calcified establishment that needs dissolution. Real small publishing seeks to mess up the formula so that the results are unpredictable. And of what is this indicative. Would you have succeeded if it weren't for those meddlesome kids. Is it a plot to abolish the question mark. This is another of the indices. More paren-thetical elements made apparent. (Many) more paren(theses). Mix metaphors to the point of saturation by selecting any old body's metaphor if it appeals to you, and make it precipitate...." In 1994 owned and published by Stephanie Blanshay and Index: The Montreal Literary Calendar, 266 Fairmount W., Montreal, P.Q. H2V 2G3, cost: $3.25; from April 1995 to August 1996 edited by the collective, including Corey Frost, Trish Salah, Dana Bath, Laura Killam, Tracey Bohan and Andy Brown, 4068 St. Laurent, PO Box 42082 Montreal, Quebec, H2W 2T3, cost: "free around Montreal with a suggested $1 donation."

Ingluvin, 1970-1971

The first page of the first number of *Ingluvin* prints an article expressing the editors' disappointment that Milton Acorn did not win the Governor General's Award. It complains further that an "increasing preoccupation with American styles and concerns, and neglect of the Canadian tradition are obfuscating our past." This was a short-lived, tiny-format magazine that subtitled itself, in the second number, "The Magazine of Canadian Writing." Managing and fiction editor Kenneth V. Hertz and poetry editor Seymour Mayne clearly had in mind a journal that would combat the recent influence of Black Mountain poetry from the U.S.A. In a year or so, Montreal will begin to see a new crop of Black Mountain and TISH inspired little magazines appear. The first number of *Ingluvin* has a neat design. Its thirty pages stapled between glossy covers were ten inches tall and only four inches wide, making it very friendly to the shape of verse. Among the poets to appear in the first number were Kenneth Hertz, Harvey Mayne, John Glassco, Seymour Mayne and Peter Huse. The second number (1971) was perfect-bound, 88 pages long, still four inches wide, but now only six inches tall. Leonard Cohen, Sylvia Barnard, Bryan McCarthy, Hertz, Glassco, Alan Pearson, Irving Layton, Robin Mathews and Seymour Mayne appeared in the second number. Published by INGLUVIN, #41, 5355 Walkley Avenue, Montreal 265, Quebec, Canada. The intended cost was 6 issues for $3. No. 2 cost $0.75.

Jaw Breaker, 1971-1972

"A little magazine of poetry, fiction & literary opinion", *Jaw Breaker* consisted of ten or so photo-offset printed sheets (usually coloured paper) stapled between cardstock covers. Three numbers of *Jaw Breaker* were produced by its publisher and editor, Leonard Russo and printed by Precis Instant Printing. The paper and printing details are provided for the last two numbers, no. 2 printed on 20lb. Carnaby Bond (Torrid Orange) and typeset on a Royal 970 typewriter, and no. 3 on Mod Bond (Midi Blu) paper and typeset on an IBM selectric. No. 1 (1971) consisted primarily of a profile of Glen Seibrasse, including a brief profile of his work, and five pages (half the total in this number) of his poems. No. 2 (1971) has a similar profile of Darl Hine, and prints letters from Ralph Gustafson, Denis Lee and Hugh MacLennan, commending Russo on the first number of *Jaw Breaker*. No. 3 (1972) is a special issue on "Black Poetry" with a five-page essay of that title by Russo, and three poems by Montreal poet Sharron Lee Smith. At the back of the December 1972 issue of *Booster & Blaster*, Russo writes "to announce the end of JAW BREAKER, the little magazine I founded and edited. I see no real difference between Jaw Breaker and such publications as BOOKS IN CANADA, CANADIAN LITERATURE, TAMARACK REVIEW…the books put out by DELTA CANADA, WEED/FLOWER, COACH HOUSE PRESS, INGLUVIN, ETC. They are all part of

CanLit Inc. They are what you might expect. Public Relations Image consciousness. Names. Titles. Government stamp of approval. I see no reason to continue this. Something altogether different is needed. In view of this, I have joined with Bryan McCarthy, who feels as I do, in founding THE WRECKER'S BALL, to cope somehow with this situation. See me or Bryan if you have something to say." Published by JAW BREAKER, P.O. Box 545 Westmount Station, Westmount 215, P.Q., Canada. The newsstand price was $0.35.

Kola: A Black Literary Magazine, 1987-2000
The title is taken from kola nut—a symbol of hospitality in West African society. There are many international authors (from America, Africa, Caribbean), especially in the earlier issues of this literary journal which began as a humble stapled magazine run c/o the Negro Community Center (2035 Coursol St., Montreal Quebec, H3J 1C3), and moved increasingly towards an academic literary journal with Ph.D. advisory editors. It was a tri-quarterly periodical of stories, poems and critical writing. As stated in 5.1 (Winter 1991/92), "Kola was launched in 1987 to meet the needs of creative artists who have an interest in publicizing any work that reflects the Black experience in Africa and the diaspora." It ran from about forty pages early on to 150 pages in later years, and alternated between stapled and perfect binding. Editorial staff varied, but the most recurrent names include Horace I. Goddard, H. Nigel Thomas, Shirley Small, Anthony Joyette, Pamela Edmonds and Nalini Warriar. 1.1 features an essay on Dianne Brand. Among the poets to appear in *Kola* are Bob McNeil, Leonard A. Slade Junior, Bernadette Charles, Debbie Young and, across many years, George Elliot Clarke. While the first issues of *Kola* were published care of the Negro Community Center, middle issues are listed as KOLA, P.O. Box 1602, Place Bonaventure, Montreal, Quebec, H5A 1H6, and later issues as Kola, 2689 Place Vermandere, Saint-Laurent, Quebec, H4R 2H8. Cost ranged from $2.50 per number in the first year to $8 in the last.

Le Chien D'or / The Golden Dog, 1972-1974
Carlo Fonda (Modern Languages Dept., Loyola [Concordia University]) and Michael Gnarowski (English Dept., Sir George Williams [Concordia]) published four numbers of this journal of criticism and poetry between 1972 and 1974, none as beautifully produced as the first perfect-bound number which appears between thick golden cardstock covers and uses coloured inks, op-art graphic dividers and wide margins for the prose pieces to give it a Bauhaus feel. This first number was designed by André Goulet and produced in collaboration with Les Editions d'Orphée, Montreal. Each issue has at least one extended piece (often poetry) by a Franco-phone author, including Louis Geoffroy's "L'Homomythe" (no. 1 1972), Paul Toupin's essay, "Montréal Cosmopolite" (no. 3 1974) and Gustave Labbé's poem

"Borduas" (no. 4 1974). Other pieces to appear in the first number are an essay titled "Language and the NEW Culture" by Neil Compton, a poem—"Erotic Tropes" by Louis Dudek—printed in purple ink, an interview with Irving Layton, an essay on Leo Kennedy and "Educating the Critics", an article by Louis Dudek. The journal seems to have lost much of its financial resources after the first number as it becomes a mimeographed journal by no. 2 without any of the exciting design of the inaugural issue, and is bound with tape by no. 4. It is an interesting example of a journal that mixes academic criticism by new faculty that has arrived at Montreal's universities with literary journalism and poetry. The first number opens with a cryptic editorial, in French verse, spoken in the voice of the golden dog who says he is reposing now, but warns that a time will come when he will bite the one who has bitten him. *Le Chien D'or* seems to represent an venue for thinking about the future of local writing, but pursues this thinking often by looking back to the heyday of Canadian modernist writing in the city. Published by Modern Languages Department, Loyola of Montreal, 7141 Sherbrooke Street West, Montreal, Quebec, H4B 1R6. Cost: no. 4 indicates that an annual subscription cost $6, but no price indicated on individual numbers.

Locus, 1978

Edited by Claire Sargeant, this journal (possibly by McGill students) of 24 pages was stapled between blue cardstock contained mostly poetry (by the likes of R. De Smit, Neil Henden, Hilary Maus, Guy McLoughlin, and Sonja Skarstedt) and photos by Ben Soo. The poetry here is mostly sparse, imagistic free verse. (*Locus* Vol. 1, No. 3 has been the only number consulted.) Typeset at the "Info Office". Cost: $3.95?

Loomings, 1979

Published by the Student Literary Association of Concordia University, the editors of this perfect bound journal of 77 pages, sporting a simple all white cardstock cover with the journal title in large bold black letters on the front cover, and nothing on the back cover, were John Bourgeois, Marina Devine, Lise-Anne Forand, Alan Hefits and Mary Rimmer. Their editorial preface states: "Our aim is to make *Loomings* a forum for students' creative and critical work, and each year to present a cross-section of the current literary productions of the Concordia student community." There seems to have been only one issue, but that is not confirmed. Vol. 1, no. 1, the only issue consulted, has poetry by Steven Rosenstein, Gisela Dessner, Paukl Serralheiro, Robert Nadon, and three poems by Ian Stephens ("Jack", "May Rome '79" and "He casts no glint"). Printed by Concordia University Printing Services, submissions were sent to *Loomings*, c/o Department of English, 1455 de Maissoneuve Blvd. W., Montreal, Québec, H3G 1M8. Cost not indicated.

Los (Concordia University), 1975-1985, 1989.
This undergraduate journal, computer-printed and published annually by the students of the Concordia University Loyola Campus averaged about 30 pages in its early numbers which were stapled between cardstock with simple black ink images on the covers, and then was perfect bound between a glossy cardstock cover for its final few issues, from number 8 on, when it became an English department journal serving both the Loyola and downtown campuses. The founding editors were Ian Ferrier, along with Dr. Patrick Holland and David Skyrie. Later editors included Robert Elkin, Peggy Curran, Michael Donovan, and Jennifer Boire. Skyrie, in his introduction to the first number, identified this journal as one that "focuses mainly on writers based in and around the Loyola community" but which welcomes "manuscripts from promising writers in other parts of the city, country or universe." The contents of some issues show that *Los* reached out beyond Loyola. Names to appear here included Naomi Guttman, Hugh Hazelton, Ross Leckie, Richard Sommer, Pier Giorgio Di Cicco, A. F. Moritz, Vincento Albanese, Ken Norris, Joseph Rogel, April Bulmer, Anne Cimon, and Irving Layton. *Los* 1 includes a review by Patrick Holland of four books from Davinci Press (books by Tom Ezzy, Andre Farkas, Ian Ferrier and Claudia Lapp). Note that Louis Dudek reviewed the same four books in *Anthol* 4 (1975). Reviews are less common in other issues of *Los* which sometimes mix poetry and fiction, and sometimes are poetry-only. Funding for this journal came initially through the Loyola English Students' Association, and later from Concordia University Students' Association (CUSA). Published by *LOS* c/o the English Department, Hingston Hall, Third Floor, Loyola College, 7141 Sherbrooke Street West, Montreal, Quebec. Cost unknown.

Lucky Jim's: Journal of Strangely Neglected Topics, 1984-1986
Now this is something really special. I have only been able to consult four issues (2, 3, 5, and the hand-painted corrugated cardboard covered issue of 1984). As the editorial statement notes, this is "a non-profit venture. The price of each issue will depend upon the cost of production." The production of each issue differs drastically: Issue 3 (number 13 of the 170 copies made) has a stamped, ink drawn and green-painted cover with tiny macaroni numbers and letters glued to it. Issue 5 (number 109 of 225 copies) has a detailed cartoon drawing by Bernie Mireault of a bearded cowboy with a swastika armband saying with bubble caption reading "Similacra!!...The Ancients must be preserved!" And the aforementioned cardboard cover issue (number 20 of 55 copies) has a spray-painted stencil image of what might be Plato with a harp (in blue, white, black and grey). The contents chosen by editors Gary Clariman, Michael Granatstein and William Hall are equally quirky, fun and interesting, with lots of poetry by, among others, Zsolt Alapi, Ronald Reichertz, J. Dixon, Mike Lenaghan, Steve Petipas, and David McGimpsey (including

an Elvis sonnet in Issue 2, and a selection of his Batman sonnets in Issue 3). *Lucky Jim's* started at this Montreal address: 6860 Hutchison Ave., Montreal, Quebec H2V4C1, but moved in later issues to various addresses in Ontario. Cost varied, but was usually about $1.50.

Maker, 1977-1979
The editorial header reads: "MAKER will be published periodically according to your response." The response was good enough to result in a handful of numbers across three years. The literary aesthetic is decidedly experimental and playful and the production aesthetic shows a designer's touch and appears avant-garde in its use of its home-made, mimeograph medium. The (usually) 8 pages of poetry and graphic art were 11 x 16 sheets folded in half, sometimes stapled, sometimes not. It included anything that was of interest to the *bricoleur*-editor, and was mailed out internationally for free, which is the likely explanation as to why it did not continue for more than a few years. The editor is John McAuley, and the publisher, Maker, 1206 Seymour Ave. Montreal, Quebec, H3H 2A5.

Matrix, 1975-ongoing
Matrix has a website: <http://alcor.concordia.ca/~matrix/>.
Founded at Champlain College in Lennoxville, and run out of the English Department of Concordia University since 1995, *Matrix* is presently one of the most important literary arts journals in Canada. It has persistently held a cosmopolitan purview, publishing work from across Canada, the U.S., and the world. The list of names to appear in *Matrix* over the years is far too long to give in full, but includes: Nicole Brossard, D.G. Jones, Anne Carson, Gilbert Sorrentino, David Trinidad, Mikhail Iossel, Ricardo Sternberg, Irving Layton, Steve McCaffrey and Al Purdy. Early editors included Phil Lanthier, Robert Allen, Marjorie Retzleff and Steve Luxton. Some of the middle-years' editors include Linda Leith (now organizer of Montreal's Blue Metropolis festival) and Terence Byrnes. The editor-in-chief up until his death in November 2006 was one of its founding participants, Robert Allen, with Jon Paul Fiorentino serving as managing editor. *Matrix* has gone through a great variety of formats from stapled glossy magazine, to quarto sized perfect-bound journal, to the recent graphics oriented, full-color perfect bound magazine format. Its first publishing address was Box 510, Lennoxville QC, J0B 1Z0, and the most recent head office is 5607 Ave de l'Esplanade, Montreal, Quebec, H2T 2Z9. The cost has ranged from $1 for the earliest numbers, to its present newsstand price of $8.

Montreal Journal of Poetics (MJP), 1978-1985
Stephen Morrisey edited this stapled, double-sided letter-sized photocopied pamphlet, and bpNichol, Ken Norris and Richard Sommer are listed as contributing

editors. Not a poetry journal, *per se*, but a venue for essays about poetry and poetics, the purpose of *MJP*, as Morrisey writes on the first page of issue 2.1 fall-winter 1982 (the only paper copy consulted) is to allow for "a free and open discussion of poetics. This is obviously not an academic journal (thank god!) and there is no prestige in being published in it; however, because of this one has the freedom to try out new ideas, to explore areas of poetics not acceptable to the more traditional-minded small magazine." With this specific sixteen-page issue Morrissey instituted the second series of his magazine, and changed its title to the letters MJP. This issue contains "Rhythm: A Few Observations" by George Johnston, an essay on the creative process by Guy Birchard, and two short essays by Ken Norris. Other issues, as described in the listing of the Stephen Morrissey papers held by the McGill Library, carried essays by Louis Dudek, Andre Farkas, Gerry Gilbert, Tom Konyves, Claudia Lapp, John McAuley, letters to the editor by bpNichol, and dialogues about poetry, as with the dialogue between Norris and McAuley in Issue 3 (spring-summer 1980). Published by Stephen Morrissey, 4359 Route 138, RR #2, Huntingdon, Quebec, J0S 1H0. Subscriptions: individuals $2 per copy, institutions $5 per copy.

Montreal Now, 1984-1985

Edited by Endre Farkas, Lucien Francoeur, Ken Norris, Ruth Taylor, and (in 1985 only) Claudine Bertrand, this thirty-page stapled journal had no explicit editorial policy, but one might be gleaned from a D. G. Jones quote that appears on the back cover of no. 3 (1984): "I've been waiting for fifteen years to see what might happen when the two language groups get together to make poetry." The poetry to appear the glossy covers (each issue printed in a different coloured ink—blue, green, red, purple, turquoise, orange, blue, dark blue, etc.) is half in French, half in English, and thus makes *Montreal Now*, along with D. G. Jones's *ellipse*, one of the few truly bilingual poetry journals published in Quebec during this period. Some names to appear here (indicating the 50-50 French-English mix) include: Michel Beaulieu, Claudine Bertrand, Francois Charron, Antonio D'Alfonso, Denis Desautels, Endre Farkas, Lucien Francoeur, Anne McLean, Ken Norris, Robyn Sarah, Ruth Taylor, Nicole Brossard, Peter Van Toorn, Yolande Villemaire, Jean-Paul Daoust, Louise Desjardins, Louis Dudek, Bill Furey, Mary Melfi, André Roy, Elise Turcotte, Irving Layton, Michèle Pontbriant, Noah Zacharin and Lorna Crozier, Publisher: The Muses' Company, 1A St-Etienne, Ste Anne de Bellevue, Quebec, H9X 1E8. It cost $2 per number.

Montreal Poems, 1974-1976

This hand-stitched, irregular annual of about forty pages run by Richard and Susan Hull was initially sponsored by the Concordia University Council on Student Life, and is continued by *Poésie de Montréal Poems* (see next entry). As an editorial statement, the magazine quotes Concordia University Canadian Literature Professor Wynne Francis: "The 'little magazine,' striking at the roots of the prevailing culture, spends some of its energy attacking the rhetoric of that culture and the rest in exploring the untapped resources of language, and the potential of other media of communication in the hope of discovering new values and new idioms in which to express them." It included shape/art poems by Stephen Morrissey, and other concrete poetry, as well as poems by Richard Sommer, George Bowering, Artie Gold, Mona Adilman, Louis Dudek, Ray Filip, Sheila Martindale, Mary Melfi, Ken Norris, Al Purdy, Shulamis Yelin and Brian Bartlett. A poem in no. 1 (1974) entitled "October in Quebec, 1973" by Jim Nucci ends with the lines, "You were never pregnant/ Quebec/ You were only expecting." No. 2 (1975) has a preface by Louis Dudek, and a review of *Dk: Some Letters of Ezra Pound* (DC Books, 1974) by Seymour Mayne and Keitha K. MacIntosh. This review is interesting for the direct parallel it makes between Pound's supportive activities of young poets, and similar activities on the part of Dudek. Published by Sunken Forum Press (Keitha K. MacIntosh), 1050 Riverview Ave., Verdun, Quebec, H4H 2C2. It cost $3.50 per number.

Montreal Poems / Poésie de Montréal, 1978-81

Continued from *Montreal Poems* (see above), this semi-gloss, perfect-bound journal of about 75 pages was edited by Keitha MacIntosh, Mattie Falworth, Steve Luxton and Grace Millman. Despite the addition of "Poésie" to the title, the journal continued to be primarily English, with a couple of French poems per issue. Contributors over the years included: Mona Adilman, Gaston Miron. Claudia Lapp, Mary Melfi, Stephen Morrissey, Henry Beissel, Mattie Falworth, Ray Filip, Gary Geddes, Michael Harris, Jim Joyce, Ross Leckie, Steve Luxton, Sharon H. Nelson, and Marc Plourde. An editorial in no. 5 (1981) asks: "Why does so much poetry come from Montréal? Is it because of our divided heritage, our deep and diverse attachments to this city, that nurture and sustain us who live here?....[T]he divisions are here. The perplexing anglo-franco relationship lies at the base of the present binational crisis. The dilemma, with its accompanying fears, conflicts and yearnings for compromise, creates a layered and evocative ambience." Published by Sunken Forum Press, Old Log House, Dewittville Quebec, J0S 1C0, and cost $3 per number.

Montreal Writers' Forum, 1978-1979

This little poetry magazine was made of 11 x 16 sheets folded in half, was simple stitched with one signature, and had thin cardstock covers, with the following statement printed on the inside of each one: "Montreal Writers' Forum is a literary \magazine with the purpose of displaying the work of new and established writers presently working in Montreal. With our monthly format and low price we intend the magazine to be both current and accessible. The magazine will consist of poetry, short stories, sections of novel or drama, satire, essays, and reviews. We will also have an information section bringing you news of the upcoming readings in town and new books of Montreal writers soon to be published." The editors were Ross Leckie, Louise Burns, George Agetees, Mary Jane Brennan and Kate MacNeill. Some of the poets who appeared here include Artie Gold, August Kleinzahler, Raymond Filip, Gaston Miron (translated by Marc Plourde), Fraser Sutherland, André Farkas, Kenneth Radu, and Jack Hannan. In 1.7 (1979), Richard Sommer reviews Tom Konyves's book of poetry, *No Parking* (Véhicule Press, 1978). This is the earliest review I have found in which the poetry of these poets (the Vehicules, in this case) are referred to as "Anglophone." Sommer writes of "the progress of anglophone poetry toward an openness and size adequate to fulfill the implications of its being written here." Advertisements inside give a sense of some cultural landmarks of the time. They include ads from The Word, and "Books and Things" (a country bookshop in Morin Heights), as well as music clubs Yakkitty-Yak (rock and roll live band), The Lancer Pub (sing a long), FM (the club with a difference, live entertainment), CKBUK livres & disques d'occasion (24 Prince Arthur O.), and the Double Hook bookstore in Westmount. Published by the Montreal Writers' Forum, Box 333, Morin Heights, Quebec, J0R 1H0. Cost: $5.50/12 issues, 50 cents each.

Moongoose, 1972

Mimeograph stenciled on the brown letter sized envelopes that held the loose pages of *Moongoose* was the sillouette of a Flamingo-like bird looking upwards (howling at the moon?) and the notice that this envelope held "A Fanciful Little Package of the Graphic Arts, Poetry & Fiction & Other Delightful Little Pieces of Creativity Especially Useful for Whiling Away Extra Hours on Sunless Days." It seems to have appeared at least three times in the spring and summer of 1972. It was published out of James Lyng High School, where the managing editor, Ralph Alfonso, was a student. Other conspirators listed at the back of no. 2 (1972) include V. Peter Bilodeau, Frank Cianciullo (editor of *Moongoose,* head of the Disposable Paper Press and the Writers' Workshop and a teacher at James Lyng), Louis Dudek, Ray Fraser, Frank Scott (of McGill) and Bob Gibbs (editor of the *Fiddlehead*). Other names to appear in no. 3 include Brian Bartlett and Marc Plourde. This is a magazine that materializes when a high school writing teacher who knows some established poets has access to free (multicoloured) paper and cheap printing in the form of a high school mimeograph machine. The result is a neat, eclectic and uneven array of free-verse and concrete poetry and graphics. It is especially interesting as an example of how the theme of Canadian unity was integrated into writing classes at the high school level, many of the poems and graphics carrying the message (to cite one example from no. 2): "The Future is in Our Hands. Canada. Stand together. Understand together." Published by *Moongoose*, Frank Cianciullo, 5440 Notre Dame West, Montreal, Quebec. Cost: $0.30.

Mouse Eggs, 1975-1981

A folio sized, mimeographed pamphlet published by Artie Gold and Ken Norris on white or colored paper, with purple or brown ink, this 25 or so page, occasional publication consisted of all poetry and some drawings, the cover art usually done by Artie Gold. I have examined three separate numbers. The "Valentine's Day, 1976" issue, printed on pink paper, stapled back to front with a couple drawings (of mice) by Marc Nerenberg and poems by Artie Gold, Andre Farkas, Harland Snodgrass, Ken Norris, T. Konyves, Arnold Snardon and Stephen Morrissey. was probably distributed at a Véhicule Gallery Valentine's Day reading, and was also the original venue of John McAuley's poem, "I Am Sending You a Valentine." The "Baker's Dozen" 22 June 1977 contained poems by Vehicule poets, prose by Opal L. Nations, and a neat cover drawing in brown ink of a mouse chef cooking a cat, the drawing most likely by Artie Gold, as he was usually responsible for the cover art. An issue from 1981 (50 cents) has Vehicule poets plus poems by Peter Van Toorn and Jim Mele. The exclamation "GRASS-ROOTS FOREVER" appears at the back of this 1981 issue. The motto "Typos copyright the author" appears on the first or last page of each of the three *Mouse Eggs* pamphlets I examined. Published by Cross Country, 2365 Hampton Ave. Apt. 7, N.D.G., Montreal. Cost: 35 cents, later 50 cents.

The Moosehead Anthology, 1988-ongoing

An irregular annual published since 1988 by Livres DC Books, usually organized by a guest editor or editorial collective, but always under the attention of the editors in chief, Robert Allen and Stephen Luxton. It is consistently perfect bound with a glossy cover, elegantly produced, and usually runs to between 100 and 150 pages. While some issues have been devoted to fiction, it has had a strong poetry mandate, with an internationalist leaning, and has published, over the years such names as: Lorna Crozier, Irving Layton, Todd Swift, Njabulo S. Ndebele, José Maria Sison, Edgar Maranan, Servando Machanua, Martin Mooney, Leonard Cohen, Shie Min, Alexander Hutchinson, Mark Cochrane, Anne Stone, and in a recent edition (no. 10, 2005), David Wevill, Sina Queyras, Raymond Hsu, Robert Minhinnick, Jon Paul Fiorentino, David Prater, J. R. Carpenter, and David McGimpsey. Cost ranges from $6.95 in 1988 to $15 in 2006. The publisher also once promised a "lifetime subscription" for $50, but it is unclear whether or not that still holds.

The Moosehead Review, 1977-1981, 1983-1986

Founding editors Robert Allen, Jan Draper, and Stephen Luxton started this very interesting, internationalist and irregular bi-annual in the Eastern Townships where they lived and taught at Champlain College. In 1986 it followed Rob Allen down to Concordia University in Montreal. At that time it announced it would become an annual, and then ceased publication altogether, but was unofficially continued in 1988 by the looser *Moosehead Anthology* (see above). *The Moosehead Review* was an elegantly designed, perfect bound journal with alternating glossy and textured cardstock covers. Issues usually consisted of a couple of articles, 15-25 poems in English plus about four translated poems, two or three short stories, and several photos or graphics. Reviews also appeared on occasion. The first number has an essay by John Berger on Gabriel Garcia Marquez, and poetry by Ralph Gustafson and Richard Jorgensen. Later numbers have work by Pablo Neruda, Roch Carrier, Gary Geddes, Roo Borson, Pier Giorgio de Cicco, Al Purdy and Peter Van Toorn. Issue 2.1 (1979) is exceptional in that nearly half of the copy in this issue consists of reviews. A blurb at the end of 2.2 (1979) announces the first book published by the Moosehead Review Press, *Late Romantics*, a collaborative collection of poems and prose by Robert Allen, Stephen Luxton and Mark Teicher (see Todd Swift's essay in this current book for more discussion of the collaborative collection).

The moose logo (appearing on or inside all issues of the *Review*, and then later on all volumes of the *Moosehead Anthology*) is by Margaret Matson. The original publishing information was Moosehead Review, P.O. Box 169, Ayer's Cliff, Quebec, J0B 1C0. It cost $3 per number.

New Canadian Review, 1987-1991

The aesthetic of this perfect-bound, glossy review of about 125 pages was very explicitly motivated by a Trudeau-inspired conception of multiculturalism. Editors Lino Leitão, Michael Spillane (associate), Rosemary Leaver (assistant), and Raquel Torres (assistant) open every number with the same epigraph from F. R. Scott: "The World is my country/ The human race is my race/ The spirit of man is my God/ The future of man is my heaven." In the first number they state: "We are Proud to present "NEW CANADIAN REVIEW" to Canada and the World. Canada is a very fortunate country, fortunate to have peoples from all parts of the globe. Peoples with diverse cultures, peoples belonging to different religions and peoples of all shapes and colours have made Canada their home. There are the peoples who left their native lands for one reason or another. Accepted in Canada, all these peoples now live in relative harmony. "THE NEW CANADIAN REVIEW", through the medium of literature, would like to bring awareness of these cultures to all Canadians. If multiculturalism is to be a vibrant expression in Canada, it is essential that all Canadians should share these cultures. Such an understanding will strengthen the existing bond of harmony among all Canadians and the peoples of the World." A clarification of their submission policy is made in 1.3/4 (1988-89) due to confusion arising from the prospectus just cited: "Some individuals have mistakenly assumed that *New Canadian Review* is a literary journal whose contributors consist solely of new Canadians, born in other countries. That is not so." The editorial in issue 2.3 (1990-01) mentions the Oka crisis, the resurgence of racism that accompanied it, and notes again the goal of the periodical towards reconciliation and understanding. Published from P.O. Box 717, Pointe-Claire-Dorval Quebec, H9R 4S8. It cost $8 per number.

Pawn to Infinity, 1990-1991

The managing editor was "M. D. Généreux" with an editorial collective too long to list, but which included Michael Roy, Sean Fortier, Infrid Phaneuf, Heather MacDonald and Lee Gotham. Issues 1.2 and 1.3 have the subtitle "a tri-annual magazine of extraordinary poetry, fiction, art and voices," but it doesn't seem to have appeared tri-annually. *Pawn to Infinity* (size 28 cm) was printed on quality paper and had a stapled cardstock binding. It ran between 32 and 46 pages. Issue 1 (1990) has a decidedly post-feminism feminist stance to it, with poems about love and lust from a female perspective, an article, "Feminism, Poetry and Men: A Sense of Safety in the World" by Taylor Jane Green, and another titled, "Oh, the Joy of Having Your Child All to Yourself" written and translated from the French by Claude Fortin; and a poem by Cornelia Hoogland titled "Towards a Feminist Theory". This feminist concern continues in subsequent issues with articles on domestic violence, and other topics. Very interestingly for graphic Zine enthusiasts: each issue has a graphic story insert (8½ x 11 sheets folded in half) stapled into the middle. The first is a panel story about sex ending in a gothic abortion called "Wild Love." In vol. 2 it's "Sky Fishing" by David Abu Bacha. Vol. 3 has poems by Rob McLennan and Buffy Rhodenizer-Childerhose and an article by Todd Swift, "Poets, Leagues, and a Tale of Two Cities: Memoirs of the Main", in which the following assessment of Anglo-Quebec poetry appears: "It must be understood that I am not an expert on the subject of francophone poetry in Québec, but when in Paris last I read a remarkable anthology of French Canadian verse representing a force of intention and commitment, a describing into being of community, alien to the English in Québec and especially Montréal; theirs unlike ours is a very lively solitude indeed. The English scene was, to pun, unheard of. Instead, anglophone poets in Montréal, like personalities in Norman Bates, had all kinds of splits to choose from, but no act of union to war for or against." Published by Pawn to Infinity, c/o M. D. Généreux, Box 33, 2050 Claremont Ave., Montreal, Quebec, H3Z 2P8. Cost: vol. 1 $2.50, vol. 2 $3.50, vol. 3 $5.00.

Poets' Podium 1993-ongoing

This quarterly journal is designed as a venue in which poetry can be celebrated at the grassroots level by amateurs. It functions as a participatory, poetry-*Reader's Digest* with features like "Bits & Pieces" by Aurora Leigh and Ken's Kwickie Kwiz, asking questions like, what does the G. J. stand for in G. J. Pratt? "Bits & Pieces" provides information like, "According to the *Guinness Book of World Records* the earliest birth date of anyone's whose voice was recorded is Tennyson." On the first page, there is a special "profile" article on a famous poet. *Poet's Podium* started in Montreal (1993-1999), moved to Cornwall, Ontario in 1999, and then to its present home base of Hawkesbury, Ontario in March 2000. Editors involved throught this time have been Kenneth Elliot, Robert Piquette, Harry P. Fox (founder), and more recently, Catherine Barrowcliffe. Each number is twelve pages long (three colour, legal-sized sheets folded in half and stapled at the spine) and printed at photocopy shops (the first issues from the COPY EXPRESS in Chomedy, Laval). In 3.4 (1996) There is a special profile on "The Concordia Writer's Group" which congregates every Thursday afternoon "at the University's Loyola campus....[E]ncouragement is offered to all and valuable ideas exchanged, thereby providing the members with a much needed support group." Issue 4.3 (1997) introduces the new feature of "Poet's Podium Reviews." The reviews are gentle, but also offer suggestions for improvement. Here, *Poets' Podium* also begins publishing its own chapbooks (of past contributors) and having other contributors/readers review them for the magazine. They also issued an anthology of its contributors called *Whispers* ($5.00). The original publisher location was *Poet's Podium*, Suite 211, 2525-C Havre-des-Îles, Laval, Quebec, H7W 4C6. Cost was and continues to be $2.50 per single issue.

Process, 1975-1979

Four numbers of this perfect bound, professionally designed all-poetry journal were published. Edited by Matt Tolland and Richard Sommer for the first two numbers (and then by Sommer and Matt Santateresa for the last two), the editor's note inside the orange cardstock cover of no. 1 states that "PROCESS is concerned with the craft of poetry. Poems of any style or persuasion are acceptable. Manuscripts will be given personal attention..." The editor's note inside the glossy white cover of no. 2 reads: "PROCESS is a magazine for the poetry people, by the poetry people of Concordia University and the Montreal CEGEPs. Montreal poets are in painful isolation. However, that situation is changing and we hope that PROCESS will contribute to that change." The first number has only sixteen pages of poetry by five poets (John McAuley, Stephen Morrisey, Andre Farkas and the two editors). Charlotte Hussey, Anne McLean, Michael Harris, Keitha MacIntosh, Ian Ferrier, and Pier Giorgio Di Cicco are some of the poets to appear in the next three issues. For nos. 1-2, the magazine's address was: *Process*, c/o Matt Tolland,

400 Mt. Pleasant Ave. Montrel, Quebec, H3G 3Y8. For nos. 3-4 it was: *Process*, c/o Matt Santateresa, 3445 Ridgewood Ave., Apt. 104, Montreal, Québec, H3V 1B7. Cost unknown.

Raw Verse, 1984

Editor Jésus Cardozo writes on the first page of the first number: "RAW VERSE is the need to take chances. It is for the lines that seem too personally dangerous, the experiments we hesitate to try. It is for the stories that come closest to the truth, and because of that, never quite get written the way we'd like." Published in a limited press run of 200 copies, the mimeo-printed 28 pages are stapled between a thick cardstock cover with a blurry (punk or pornographic?) image of a woman with bleached hair upside down on a sofa with what may be a thick collar around her neck. The first issue comes complete with "a centerfold: a limited edition poem personally signed by the poet and suitable for framing." The centerfold poem is "Roxanne II" by Brian Millward, a poem addressing a prostitute, ending with the line, "I am the perfect man fit for destruction." Other contributors include Clifford Duffy, Joan Dow, and a prose piece, "The Haida Medicine Man" by Ian Ferrier. Published by *Raw Verse* c/o Les Éditions Blue Night, 125 Mount Royal W., Suite #22, Montreal, Quebec H2T 2S9. Cost: "One Buck and A Half."

Revue ex-it Press, 1987-1988

Revue ex-it Press "is created to present the works of all peoples of the art milieu, especially those of Quebec, as non-discriminatingly as possible, to the public consciousness." The editor, Serge LeBel, invites people to layout their own works— in handwriting, if they wish—and he will reproduce them in facsimile. This is an amateur, contributor-friendly journal. In no. 1 (1987) the following statement indicates that the journal is for writing in both French and English: "To all writers; this is a bilingual magazine, in the sense that we print your work in the language you send in. We do not translate, nor do we alter the text of any piece of writing." It seems to have been intended as a quarterly. The two issues examined consisted of about 85 stapled sheets, half artwork and half writing, the latter mostly poetry. The poetry is of high school yearbook quality, and the graphics often consist of partial nudes. Published by *Revue ex-it Press,* P.O. Box 5259 Station B, Montreal, Quebec, H3B 4B5. Cost unspecified.

Rubicon, 1983-1988

Rubicon superseded the *McGill Literary Journal* and produced its first, perfect bound, professional-looking number in 1983. Funded by the Arts and Science Under-graduate Society of McGill University, and initially printed by McGill printing services, this was not a typical student journal, but a national publishing venture run by McGill students, with the guidance of local mentors like Adrian and Lucille King-Edwards and Robert Lecker. The editor of all issues was T. Peter O'Brien. Editorial assistants varied somewhat over the years, but included most consistently, Barbara Leckie, Stephen Brockwell and David Manicom. Editorial staff revolved from number to number. While the first two numbers had cardstock covers and ran to 150 pages, from 1984 on *Rubicon* became a glossy literary arts journal similar in look to *Descant* or *The Malahat Review*, and typically contained 250 pages of artwork (beautifully reproduced on glossy pages), interviews, fiction, translation, and a lot of poetry. Poets to appear here over the years include Diana Brebner, John Barton, Erin Mouré, Robyn Sarah, Julie Bruck, David McGimpsey, Peter Van Toorn, bp Nichol, Christopher Dewdney, Margaret Christakos, Mary di Michele, Seymour Mayne, Robert Kroetsch, John Steffler, as well as poetry features, such as "The New Montreal Poetry" (edited by Ken Norris, no. 2 1983-84) and "New Poems from Australia" (no. 8 1987). Poets interviewed here included Mouré, Van Toorn, Dewdney, Margaret Atwood, Roo Borson, and Nicole Brossard. Published by *Rubicon*, McGill University, 853, rue Sherbrooke Ouest, Montreal, QC, H3A 2T6. Cost: $4 for a single issue in 1983, $6 in 1987.

Scrivener: Journal of Creative Writing, 1980-ongoing

Scrivener has a website: <http://www.arts.mcgill.ca/programs/english/scrivener/> Usually an annual (but in some years a bi-annual), *Scrivener* is "published by the students of McGill University under the auspices of the English Literature Association." The editorial staff is revolving depending on the student body in any given year. Ranging between 32 and 50 pages, an issue usually consists of at least one-third poetry. Its editorial vision for the most part adhered to that stated in the first issue: "*Scrivener* is a creative journal which publishes all kinds of creative writing, literary journalism, art work and photography. Our purpose is to provide a creative, critical, and practical outlet for university students. Though it enjoys the support of professional advice, the magazine is funded, edited, and produced entirely by students. Our staff felt it beneficial to creative students to have their work set along-side that of established Canadian writers and artists." The result is often very interesting, and the magazine has produced some wonderful issues due to McGill's ability to attract established writers to campus for readings, and the enthusiasm and talent of McGill undergraduates. Louis Dudek was a mentor of the earliest issues which feature poetry by F. R. Scott, Sonja A. Skarstedt ("a second-year English student at McGill"), Ken Norris ("currently a doctoral candidate at McGill U."), George Elliot Clarke, Peter Van Toorn and Leonard Cohen, and interviews with Margaret Laurence, Cohen, Seamus Heaney, Lawrence Ferlinghetti, Nadine Gordimer and Margaret Atwood. The balance of later numbers tips more towards student writing, with less "established Canadian writers" appearing.

Published by *Scrivener* c/o English Literature Association, Room B20, Arts Building, McGill University, 845 Sherbrooke St., Montreal, Quebec, H3A 2T6. It cost $1.50 in 1980, $5 in 1989, and $8 in 2005.

Seen: A Literary and Visual Arts Magazine, 1987

Edited by Dawson students Lisa Vinebaum, Susan Briscoe, Scott Hout and Susan Duncan, *Seen* was a fifty page stapled journal with cardstock cover, produced on a computer, and filled in good part with the works of its editors. The combination of visual works with poetry makes both more interesting than they would have been on their own. Editor Lisa Vinebaum's closing photograph, a distorted negative of a Montreal walkup with trees (sandwiched between two of her written pieces) is particularly powerful. Cost unknown.

Short Poems, 1982

Offset printed in blue ink (the cover) and black ink (the contents) on coarse eggshell sheets of uneven sized paper, and stitched together with blue thread, the title of this 24 page, square shaped journal describes its contents. The contributors of the short pieces (not all haiku, mind you) are Robyn Sarah, Endre Farkas (who is thanked by editors Greg Lamontagne and Stephen Brockwell for "The Press"), Peter Van Toorn, Noah Zacharin, Edie Robinson, Ken Norris, Mona Fertig, Neil Henden, Ben Soo, and both editors. The editorial policy can be summed up as such: "We welcome manuscripts of poems around 20 lines in length." There doesn't seem to be a poem longer than twelve lines in the first number. Published by SHORT POEMS, 691 Victoria Dr., Baie D'Urfe, Que., H9X 2K3. Cost: $1.50.

Skylark, 1989-1991

About fourteen numbers of this eclectic magazine appeared, all under the editorship of Suzanne Fortin, and consisting almost entirely of poems. Each number ran to about 25 pages, and was stapled in thin coluor cardstock covers. A few issues have book reviews. No discernible aesthetic seems to govern the editorial selections. *Skylark* seems to have published anything that came its way. Published by *Skylark* c/o Suzanne Fortin, Apt. 8, 2130 Charleroi, Beauport, Quebec, G1E 3S1. Cost: $2 per number.

Slingshot, 2001-ongoing

Founding editor Andrea Ryder's background in the visual arts has set the *Slingshot* mandate: "to bind unconventional and compelling visual and literary arts in a way that has complicity, intelligence, and life. The writing must be visual, and the visuals, a good read." (From the *Slingshot* web site: <http://www.slingshotmagazine.org/>). Writers who have appeared in this perfect bound, visually colourful magazine include Robert Allen, Oana Avasilichioaei, Stephanie Bolster, Louis Dudek, Bill

Furey, Adrienne Ho, Yann Martel, Robyn Sarah, and George Slobodzian. *Slingshot* has never had a stable mailing address, but has an email address: editors@slingshotmagazine.org

Soliloquies, 1998-ongoing

This is a student-run annual published with the help of the Concordia Association of Students in English (CASE). Having published nine issues to date, it accepts undergraduate poetry, short fiction and drama submissions from Concordia students, and publishes in March as part of the Art Matters festival organized at Concordia. As their recent statement on the Concordia English Department website says: "Our mission is to publish new and exciting voices who don't yet have access to other channels of publication, and to develop the community of young writers at Concordia and in Montreal." Published by CASE, 1455 de Maisonneuve Blvd. West, Montréal, QC, H3G 1M8. Price has varied, depending on the year, from $5 for *Soliloquies* 5 (2002), to $15 for *Soliloquies* 6 (2003).

Solitude-Inflexion, 1976-1977

The editor, Guy Maheux, wants to use his magazine so that people can work on their writing with him as mentor. Each subscriber gets five poems published a year, if she is willing to work with Maheux and his English co-editors (Rachel Clarke and Peter Osborne) on her craft. Maheux says he is looking for poems with some of the following qualities: 1) appeal to the senses 2) rhythm 3) patterns of grammar 4) metaphor, simile, etc. 5) syntax 6) tension 7) emotional integrity 8) communication 9) visual integrity. It publishes established poets alongside the subscriber poets. The poems that appeared on the twenty or so pages, stapled between paper covers, were in a different coluor ink each issue. So, the poems of Patricia Ewins, Ari Snyder, Antoine D'Alfonso, Sheila Martindale and Sholem Stern to appear in no. 1.1 (1976) were printed in brown ink, and later issues were printed in green, orange, purple, etc. The poems of the amateur subscriber-poets often appear along with self-written profiles that introduce the poet to the world, and with a photo of the author. The photos are very interesting as a record of aspiring poets in the city, mostly women. This bilingual periodical was superseded by *L'Esplumoir* (French only). The claim was that *S-I* would appear ten times a year, but it seems to be quarterly. The back pages have a lot of advertising by tailors and jewelers. Published by the Société des Belles-Lettres, Guy Maheux, Suite 101, 7705 de l'Acadie Blvd., Montreal, Quebec, H3N 2W1 (in collaboration with Montreal Poet's Information Exchange). Each issue cost $1.25.

Tobacco Shop, 1981

This very simply, yet elegantly produced magazine (about twenty letter-sized sheets printed on one side only and stapled between two separate cardstock boards) was edited by Ross Leckie. *Tabacco Shop* takes its name, the editor tells us, from Fernando Pessoa's poem of that title, but is "also meant to conjure the mood of the many little tobacco shops in Montreal which seem to be the heart of the city's print trade. Among the poets to appear in no. 1 (the only number consulted) are Hugh Hazelton, Martin Reyto, Jim Smith, Ronn Silverstein, Lucille King-Edwards, Tom Convey, and the editor. Mostly free verse lyrical poetry. Published by Tobacco Shop, Ross Leckie, 30-48th Ave. Lachine, Quebec, H8T 2R6. Cost: $2.

Vallum: Contemporary Poetry, 2001-ongoing

Vallum has a website: < http://www.inperspective.ca/vallummag/homepage.html> This perfect-bound, glossy bi-annual with extra-wide pages to accommodate poems without forcing unwanted line-breaks was launched with great success at Montreal's Casa Del Popolo (a popular venue for poetry performance) in 2001. Edited by poets Joshua Auerbach and Eleni Zisimatos Auerbach, *Vallum* publishes art, essays, reviews and, above all, poems. It publishes an eclectic selection of excellent poetry and has become a venue for some of the best poets in Canada and abroad. Some contributors since its inception include: Andrew Motion, Paul Muldoon, Les Murray, Stephen Dunn, George Eliott Clarke, Norm Sibum, Erin Mouée, Nicole Brossard, Charles Bernstein, Anne Simpson, bill bissett, Stephanie Bolster and D. G. Jones. Published by the Vallum Society for Arts & Letters Education, P.O. Box 48003, 5678 du Parc, Montréal, QC H2V 4S8. Cost: $14 per issue.

Versus, 1976-1978

"*Versus* is an unperiodical literary review," the byline says. Edited and designed by Fred Louder and Robyn Sarah, they send out the following message to potential contributors in the first issue: "We are looking for good writing, in whatever shape or form we find it, wherever it comes from. We are not confining ourselves to Canadian writers, nor to Canadian content. We would like to provide an outlet for unknown and lesser-known writers, but we do not preclude writers whose names are already familiar to readers...[F]or the time being we are eschewing a critical program of our own....[T]he choice of the name VERSUS in no way reflects our stance vis-à-vis other small magazines. We see it, rather, as reflecting the position of literature today in general....[T]hough the newspapers this year were full of articles decrying the spread of illiteracy, the public show no sign of relaxing their embrace of the audio-visual media for entertainment, information, and communication...[T]o engage an audience, writing must now be better than ever: it must have something unique to offer and must offer it in an idiom unique to itself; it must, above all, be *readable*. VERSUS is a statement of faith in the validity of good writing, and awareness of its predicament." It was made of 8½ x 11 sheets folded in half and stapled between cardstock covers of various colours. Numbers also included a hand-set broad-sheet of one poem per issue as an off-print. The first broadsheet no. 1 (1976) was "The Poem Becomes Canadian" by Pier Giorgio di Cicco and the second "Mountain Stick" by Peter Van Toorn. Othe poets to appear in this magazine include August Kleinzahler, Raymond Filip, Mary Melfi, David Solway, Barry Dempster, A. F. Moritz and Fraser Sutherland. In no. 4 (1979) we find ballads of Itzik Manger translated by eminent Harvard Professor, historian of American literature (and ex-Montrealer), Sacvan Bercovitch. Published by Villeneuve Publications, P.O. Box 503, Outremont Station, Montreal, Quebec, H2V 4N4. Cost: $1.50 per number.

what is, 1973-1976

The first seven issues of this monthly little magazine made by Stephen Morrissey consisted of only one legal sized sheet of paper. *what is* was mailed without cost to names on a subscription list that was (according to the description of the Stephen Morrisey papers held at McGill University Library) "largely compiled with the help of Richard Sommer, one of Morrissey's professors at Sir George Williams University (Concordia University since 1974)." The first six issues of *what is* (April to September 1973) consist only of work by Morrissey, one sound poem and five concrete poems, including a poem about John Cage, and an homage to Salvador Allende. The magazine becomes less regular after that. Issue #7 (January 1974) has concrete poetry by Morrissey and Artie Gold. The remaining seven issues that appeared sporadically between April 1974 and January 1976 consisted of anywhere between one and four legal sized sheets, and offered text-based and visual poetry by Guy Birchard, Andre Farkas, Claudia Lapp, Gerry Gilbert, Davi Det Hompson, John McAuley, bpNichol, Pat Walsh, Allan Bealy, Don Druick, Edwin Varney, and Martine and Roy Arenella. Published by Stephen Morrissey. Free.

Xero, 1984

"*Xero* is a collective publication, both self-financed and self-managed" is what it says on the inside of the back dark green matte cardstock cover, without actually naming names. One can only assume that Micheline Parent (graphics and layout), Joy Glidden (cover design), and some of the poetry contributors (Clifford Duffy, Thomas Renix, Anne Marie Marko, and Luli Zinc) were a part of this collective. The poetry appearing on the twenty-four pages of the one number examined is mostly free verse, with the odd photograph separating the poems. Contributing patrons who advertised at the back included Véhicule Press, No Exit Bookshop, and a bunch of records stores (Cheap Thrills, Déja Vu, Dutchy's). Published by *Xero,* 2002 rue St. Dominique, Montréal, QC, H2T 2X1. Telephone: 514-288-8184. Cost $1.50.

Zymergy, 1987-1991

This glossy perfect-bound biannual (the first number was stapled) was an important venue for Montreal poetry during the period of its existence. As the editor, Sonja Skarstedt notes in an early editorial, the magazine "endeavours to serve as a voice for both new and established writers, particularly poets." Issues usually ran to between 100 and 150 pages, and as of no. 3.1 (1989) included about ten author-photographs per issue, giving faces to the names of local writers. For a more detailed account of this magazine, its purpose and contents, see Sonja Skarstedt's essay in the present volume. Published by S. A. Skarstedt, P.O. Box 1746 Place du Parc, Montreal Quebec, H2W 2R7. Cost: no. 1 $2.95 per copy, no. 7 $6 per copy, no. 10 $7 per copy.

Anglo-Quebec Poetry Publishers c1976-2006

I. Active. Established Poetry Publishers

Conundrum Press
PO Box 55003, CSP Fairmount
Montreal, QC H2T 3E2
email conpress@ican.net
website home.ican.net/~conpress

Cumulus Press
PO Box 5205, Station B
Montreal, QC H3B 4B5
phone 514.522.5404
email cumulus@cumuluspress.com
website www.cumuluspress.com

DC Books Canada
Box 662, 950 Decarie
Ville St. Laurent, QC H4L 4V9
phone 514-843-8130
fax 514-939-0569
email dcbooks@videotron.ca
website www.dcbooks.ca

Empyreal Press
P.O. Box 1746 Place du Parc
Montreal, QC H2X 4A7
email skarwood@progression.net
website http://web.netrevolution.com/prma1753/EMPYREALPRESS.htm

McGill-Queen's University Press
3430 McTavish Street
Montreal, QC H3A 1X9
Phone 514-398-3750
fax 514-398-4333
email mqup@mcgill.ca
website http://www.mqup.mcgill.ca/

Snare Books
784 Laurier Ave E
Montreal, QC H2J 1G1
website www.snarebooks.wordpress.com

Véhicule Press and Signal Editions
C.P. 125, Succ. Place du Parc
Montreal, QC H2W 2M9
phone 514-844-6073
fax 514-844-7543
email vp@vehiculepress.com
website www.vehiculepress.com

II. Micro, Defunct and Relocated Poetry Publishers

Alithea Press. Published two books in 1975.

Aviv Press. Published one book in 1993.

B'nai B'rith Hillel Foundation at McGill University. Published about four poetry titles between 1967-1973.

Books for Looks. Published one book in 2006.

Bowering. Published books by Victor Coleman, David McFadden, Gladys Hindmarch and George Bowering between 1967-1970

Concordia Poetry Workshop. Registered by Irving Layton, it published one title, *Rawprint* (1989), an anthology of work from a poetry workshop Layton taught at Concordia that year.

CrossCountry Press. Published about ten titles by the likes of Ken Norris, Jim Mele, Paul Metcalf, John McAuley, Larry Zirlin, Murphre Roos, and Artie Gold between 1976-1980.

Delirium Press. Has published over ten hand-stitched and artistically designed poetry chapbooks by Canadian and American poets since 2004.

Dromos. Published two books Clifford Duffey's *Blue Dog Plus* (1984), and *Schizotexte* (1986) by John Rieger, Michael Toppings, Anne Marie Weiss-Armush.

Douglas Press. Published one book in 1972.

Éditions Ming. Published one anthology of poetry in 2002.

Editions d'Orphée. A handful of poetry books, and a couple of reprints have been published under this edition beginning in 1961, and most recently in 1999.

Egg Sandwich Press = Editions Sandwich aux Oeufs. Some ten or so titles have been published by this press between 1994 and 2005, mostly the work of Vince Tinguely and Victoria Stanton, but also a title by Justin McGrail in 2000.

Ga Press. Published five titles in 1994. Work by Fortner Anderson, Judy MacInnes, Patchen Barss, Colin Christie, Stephen Edgar, and Corey Frost.

Guernica Editions. Established by Antonio D'Alfonso, still editor-in-chief of the press, Guernica Editions published some 130 titles, poetry and otherwise from its Montreal offices before moving to Toronto in the early 1990s. Guernica has published many notable Anglo-Quebec poets, and French Canadian poets in English translation, over the years.

House of Sesum. Published one anthology (1972) and one book (1976).

Ingluvin Publications. Published seven or so titles between 1970 and 1976, including the work of Partrick Lane, Raymond Fraser, Marquita Crevier, Kenneth V. Hertz, Marya Fiamengo, and an anthology of Canadian women poets edited by Dorothy Livesay and Seymour Mayne.

Ink/Inc. Published one book in 1969.

Jawbone Press. Published one book in 1989.

Jet Copy House. Published one book, *Free, Accept One* by Randy Lake in 1975.

Laureson Press. Has published about five poetry titles between 1995 and 2005.

Les Éditions du CIDIHCA. One poetry title and about ten other fiction and non-fiction titles by this Haitian-concerned press.

Llewellyn & Sons. One poetry anthology in 1970.

Nuage Editions [Also, Nu-Age Editions. Continued as Signature Editions]. From 1986-1997 this Montreal-based press published some thirty-five titles, including several books of poetry by the likes of Richard Sommer and Andre Farkas. Since relocating to Winnipeg, it has continued to publish Montreal-based authors such as Caroliyne Marie-Souaid, Susan Gillis, and Jon Paul Fiorentino.

Maker Press. Published about seven titles from 1979-1985, including works by John McAuley, Ken Norris, and the 1979 anthology, *The Vehicule Poets.*

Matthias Claudius Press. Published one book, *Indigo* by Matthew Von Baeyer (1980), and one poetry CD, *Melopoiesis* (1998).

Mémoire d'Encrier. Published three poetry titles between 2003-2005.

Mercutio Press. Has published some fifteen poetry chapbook titles between 1997 and 2006.

Metonymy Productions. Published one title, *Packaging: The Purim Papers* by Sharon H. Nelson in 2000.

Midlands Margin Press. Published one title in 1998.

Mondiale Publishers. Published four titles 1970-1975.

Montreal Poets' Information Exchange. Published the *Montreal Poets' Information Exchange Sampler* in 1976.

[Montreal] Writers' Cooperative. Published about ten titles, fiction and poetry between 1972-1976.

The Muses' Co. In 1995, Gordon Shillingford bought this Quebec poetry press that had been operational since 1980. The Muses' Co. published over thirty important poetry titles and anthologies during its Montreal period, and continues to publish Montreal-rooted authors like Ken Norris, Erin Mouré and Nicole Brossard from its new offices of J. Gordon Shillingford Publishing, Winnipeg, Manitoba.

Nbj/Writing. Published one title, *Character* by Daphne Marlatt and Nicole Brossard, 1987.

New Tomorrow Pub. Published *New Life Poets: An Anthology* in 1994.

Orange Monad Editions. Has published one poetry title by Paul Hartal.

Pages Noires. Published two audio recordings and one book between 1987-1995.

PeaFart Press. Published one title in 1974.

Planète Rebelle. An established French-language publisher, PR has published one English language title to date, Ian Ferrier's *Exploding Head Man: A CD Book*, 2000.

Poetry Elite. Published one title, *A 1985 Anthology of Canadian Poetry*.

Poets' Podium. Has published some 20 poetry chapbooks and anthologies, 1997-1999.

RevWord Press. Published *The N'X step : Hochelaga and the Diasporic African Poets: A Collection of Performance Poetry by a Montreal-Based Black Writers Group*, edited by Anthony Bansfield in 1995.

SCW Books. Published two books and a journal from 2001-2004.

Société de Belles-Lettres Guy Maheux. Published seven poetry titles, including Sheila Martindale's *Darkness on the Face of the Deep: Poems* and the journal *Solitude-Inflexion* from 1976-1977.

Sunken Forum Press. Between 1974 and 1983, Sunken Forum published four poetry titles, including titles by Stephen Morrisey and Sharon H. Nelson, as well as the periodicals, *Montreal Poems* and *Poésie de Montréal-Montreal Poems*.

Trans-Verse Productions. Published one book in 1988.

Triptyque. Has published two anthologies one a collection of English Canadian poets in French, edited by Pierre DesRuisseaux and Mona Elaine Adilman in 1996, and an anthology of Eastern Townships poetry (published in coordination with Véhicule Press, 1999).

Villeneuve Publications. Between 1977 and 1984 Villeneuve published nine poetry titles by authors such as Robyn Sarah, Jack Hannan, Bruce Taylor, August Kleinzahler, Brian Bartlett and A. F. Moritz, as well as the poetry journals *Four by Four* and *Versus*.

Vox Hunt Press. Published Todd Swift's chapbook, *Top Twenty* in 1997.

White Drawf Editions. Published two books by Hugh Hazelton in 1982, and one title in 1997.

Wildtext Press. Published one title in 1997.

Wired on words. Produces poetry publications in audio format, including Ian Stephens's *Diary of a Trademark* on cassette in 1995, and the audio anthology *Millennium Cabaret* in 1998.

Work Study Institute's Black Writers' Workshop. One title in 1973.

Woodley & Watts. Published one poetry title in 2003, and about six titles in other genres since 1998.

Zaman Promotion Institute. Published one poetry title in 1988.

QWF Poetry Prize Winners, 1988-2006

The Quebec Writer's Federation was founded in 1988 as the Quebec Society for the Promotion of English Language and Literature (QSPELL), and has continued to promote English-language writing in Quebec through activities and programs that include writing workshops, mentorship programs, the sponsorship of readings in high-schools and CEGEPs, and its annual awards ceremony. The QWF prize for best book of poetry by an Anglo-Quebec writer based in Quebec has been known, since 1992, as the A. M. Klein Prize for Poetry. Below is a list of past finalists for the award, with the winner's name appearing at the top of the list for each year. The QWF has a website: < http://www.qwf.org/>.

2006   Susan Elmslie, *I, Nadja and Other Poems* (Brick Books)
          Jon Paul Fiorentino, *The Theory of the Loser Class* (Coach House)
          Lazar Sarna, *He Claims He is the Direct Heir* (Porcupine's Quill)

2005   Erin Mouré, *Little Theatres* (House of Anansi)
          Mark Abley, *The Silver Palace Restaurant* (McGill-Queen's)
          Sherwin Tija, *The World is a Heartbreaker* (Coach House)

2004   Carmine Starnino, *With English Subtitles* (Gaspereau)
          David Solway, *Franklin's Passage* (McGill-Queen's)
          Robyn Sarah, *A Day's Grace* (Porcupine's Quill)

2003   Susan Gillis, *Volta* (Signature Editions)
          Carolyn Marie Souaid, *Snow Formations* (Signature Editions)
          Caroline Zonailo, *The Goddess in the Garden* (Ekstasis)

2002   Norm Sibum, *Girls and Handsome Dogs* (Porcupine's Quill)
          Erin Moure, *O Cidadán* (House of Anansi)
          Portlin Cochise, *A Bulldog's Guide to Small Engine Repair* (Woodley & Watts)

2001   Anne Carson, *The Beauty of the Husband* (Alfred A. Knopf)
          Jason Camlot, *The Animal Library* (DC Books)
          Andrew Steinmetz, *Histories* (Véhicule)

2000   Rachel Rose, *Giving My Body to Science* (McGill-Queen's)
          Faizal Deen, *Land Without Chocolate* (Wolsak & Wynn)

Carolyne Marie Souaid, *October* (Signature Editions)

1999 Bruce Taylor, *Facts* (Véhicule)
D. G. Jones, *Grounding Light* (Empyreal)
Erin Mouré, *A Frame of the Book* (House of Anansi)

1998 Anne Carson, *Autobiography of Red* (Alfred A. Knopf)
David Manicom, *The Older Graces* (Oolichan)
Mary di Michele, *Debriefing the Rose* (House of Anansi)

1997 Ralph Gustafson (d.1995), *Visions Fugitive* (Véhicule)
Stephen Schechter, *David and Jonathan* (Robert Davies)
Carmine Starnino, *The New World* (Véhicule, Signal Editions)

1996 Anne Carson, *Glass, Irony and God* (New Directions)
Carolyn Marie Souaid, *Swimming Into the Light* (Signature Editions)
Erin Mouré, *Search Procedures* (House of Anansi)

1995 D. G. Jones, *The Floating Garden* (Coach House)
Mark Abley, *Glasburyon* (Quarry)

1994 Julie Bruck, *The Woman Downstairs* (Brick Books) / Raymond Filip, *Flowers in Magnetic Fields* (Guernica)
Ruth Taylor, *The Dragon Papers* (The Muse's Co.)
Erin Mouré, *Sheepish Beauty / Civilian Love* (Véhicule)

1993 Ralph Gustafson, *Configurations at Midnight* (ECW)
Anne Carson, *Short Talks* (Brick)
Eric Ormsby, *Coastlines* (ECW)

1992 Naomi Guttman, *Reasons for Winter* (Brick)
Louis Dudek, *Small Perfect Things* (DC Books)
Sharon H. Nelson, *The Work of Our Hands* (The Muse's Co.)

1991 Eric Ormsby, *Bavarian Shrine and Other Poems* (ECW)
Charlotte Hussey, *Rue Sainte Famille* (Véhicule, Signal Editions)
Patty Webb, *Woman Listening* (Merlin)

1990 Erin Mouré, *WSW (West South West)* (Véhicule)

Bruce Taylor, *Cold Rubber Feet* (Cormorant)

1989   D.G. Jones, *Balthazar and Other Poems* (Coach House)
       Mark Abley, *Blue Sand, Blue Moon* (Cormorant)
       Louis Dudek, *Infinite Worlds* (Véhicule)

1988   David Solway, *Modern Marriage* (Véhicule)
       Ralph Gustafson, *Winter Prophecies* (McClelland & Stewart)
       Endre Farkas, *How To* (The Muse's Co.)
       Erin Mouré, *Furious* (House of Anansi)

Concordia University M.A. Poetry Theses, 1974 - 2006

1974   John McAuley (1947-), Three Relics / 66 leaves.

1976   Andre Farkas (1948-), Szerbusz / 69 leaves.

1978   Michael Harris, Poems, 1976-1978 / 66 leaves.

1979   Carole H. Leckner (1947-), The Mountain in the City / 69 leaves.

1981   Jim Barclay, The High Price of Oil / 200 leaves.

        Hugh Hazelton (1946-), Crossing the Chaco / 74 leaves.

        Ronn David Silverstein (1950-) Notes on Insufficient Laughter / 69 leaves.

        Donna Steinberg, Don't Pack Me a Sandwich / 285 leaves.

        James Wesley Smith, Circuits / 80 leaves.

1982   Thomas C. Fodor, Fodor's Guide to Crocodilium / 187 leaves.

        Ross Leckie (1953-), The sound in a forest / 71 leaves.

        Matthew Santateresa, Notes from an Island / 55 leaves.

        Mohamud Togane, The Bottle and the Bushman / 80 leaves.

1983   Thomas P. Convey, Tuning Inner Radio / 64 leaves.

        Charlotte Sheasby-Coleman, The Movement of Clouds / 118.

        Michael Whatling, From Unsettling Dreams / 221 leaves.

1984   Angelo Salvatore Clemente, The Seasons of an Immigrant / 116 leaves.

        P. Scott Lawrence, The Malory Arms Stories / 175 leaves.

        Ian Stephens (1954-), Two Plays / 73 leaves.

1985   Jennifer Clark (1947-), Raspberry Vinegar / 73 leaves.

        Mylene Lise Pepin, Silent Stone / 67 leaves.

1986   Cedric Speyer, How to Answer the Question "How Are You?" / 63 leaves.

1987   Joanne Stanbridge (1960-), How Tomorrow Sounds : A New Voice for Samuel / 86 leaves.

1988   Keith Bellamy, Patrick White's Flesh/Spirit Balance / 160 leaves.

        Su Croll (1961-), More Great Dinners from Life / 67 leaves.

1989   Carolyn Gammon (1959-), I : Lesbian / 90 leaves.

        Peggy Hoffman, All Songs on That Theme : A Collection of Lyric Poems / 64 leaves.

        Bryan Sentes, In the Way of Knowledge / 104 leaves.

1990   Patty Archer, Where the Tongue Roots Lie / 75 leaves.

Alan Bourassa, Quantum Song : A Collection of Poems and Prose Poems / 73 leaves.

April Bulmer (1963-), A Salve for Every Sore / 68 leaves.

David McGimpsey (1962-), 4 Poems / 88 leaves.

1991   Mark Cochrane (1965-), Three Years from Long Beach / 63 leaves.

Richard Harrison (1957-), Recovering the Naked Man / 91 leaves.

Janet Madsen, The Body Land / 112 leaves.

Jennifer L. Price, Still Lives : [Poems] / 64 leaves.

Esther Ross (1951-), Renovations in the Ghetto / 61 leaves.

Ruth Taylor (1961-2006), The Dragon Papers / 80 leaves.

1992   Karen Elizabeth Massey, Soundings / 74 leaves.

1993   Douglas Isaac, Past Present, Tense—and Selected Poems / 77 leaves.

Lazer Lederhendler, The Inner City Exhibits / 65 leaves.

1994   Jennifer Boire (1954-), Dreaming Our Mothers / 105 leaves.

1995   Sina Queyras (1963-), Someone from the Hollow / 82 leaves.

Carolyn Marie Souaid (1959-), Hollow Grass / 73 leaves.

1996   Maxianne Berger, References and Their Uses : Intertexts in the Critical Carpet / 114 leaves.

1996   Shaun Leggett, Cro's Cabin / 79 leaves.

Aurelia R. Pontes , Before We Were Born / 157 leaves.

1997   William H. Ford (1951-), Transparencies / 96 leaves.

Matt Holland, Taking Place / 217 leaves.

1998   Melanie Frances, Independence and Other Poems / 73 leaves.

Catherine Kidd, Bestial Rooms : A Work of Prose Fiction / 160 leaves.

W. Taien Ng, The Maps of Our Bodies and the Borders We Have Agreed Upon / 71 leaves.

Juliet Waters, El Nino / 96 leaves.

1999   Jonathan Goldstein (1969-), I Found Your Address in a Fortune Cookie : A Novel / 152 leaves.

Lee Gotham, The Festive Wound : L'anormale and El Quemado : Twin Fictions / 45 leaves.

Frances Mary Maika, Lifesaving / 64 leaves.

2000   Lance Blomgren (1970-), Walkups : Documentaries and Commentary : A Series of Prose Poems / 73 leaves.

Susan Kernohan, This All Works Well up to a Point / 65 leaves.

Adam Lock, Fragments of a Previous, Grander, Project / 110, [2] leaves.

Carmine Starnino, What Do You Call This? / 52 leaves.

David N. Wright, Machine / 89 leaves.

2001   Melissa Weinstein, Some Geographies / 83 leaves.

2002   Oana Avasilichioaei, Abandon / 60.

Joshua A. Auerbach, Natural Exile / 73 leaves.

Jon Paul Fiorentino, Hello Serotonin : Poems / 60 leaves.

Susan Gillis (1959-), Intersection : Poems and Permutations / 69 leaves.

Jack Illingworth, Panography / 73 leaves.

Helen Zisimatos (1964-), Oracular / 61 leaves.

2003   Beth Barnyock, Meat and Bone / 64 leaves.

Suzanne Buffam, Plenty / 51 leaves.

Angela Hibbs, Water Street / 71 leaves.

Meaghan Strimas, Body and Blood : Poems / 63 leaves.

2004   Angela Carr, Ropewalk / 53 leaves.

Moberley Luger, Ragtime for Beginners / 54 leaves.

Jeannette Lorito, What's Lost Already / 73 leaves.

Susan Briscoe, Minor Arcana / 103 leaves.

2005   Alessandro Porco, The Jill Kelly Poems / 64 leaves.

Christine Murray, The Dying Art of Conversation/ 122 leaves.

2006   Beth Cote, Near Here/ 59 leaves.

Katia Grubisik, What if Red Ran Out?/ 66 leaves.

Alexandra Pasian, Every Day/ 72 leaves.

Elizabeth Marshall, Letters from a Young Poet/ 48 leaves.

Sachiko Murakami, The Invisibility Exhibit/ 58 leaves.

Kate Hall, The Certainty Dream/ 64 leaves.

Notes

Introduction / Camlot

[1] John Glassco, "Preface," *English Poetry in Quebec: Proceedings of the Foster Poetry Conference, October 12-14, 1963*, ed. John Glassco (Montreal: McGill University Press, 1965), pp. 6-7.

[2] Louis Dudek, "The Montreal Poets," *Culture* 8 (1957): 149. This article is reprinted in its entirety in the present collection.

[3] The phrase "language events" is borrowed from Richard Bouhis's "Introduction and Overview of Language Events in Canada," *International Journal of the Sociology of Language* 105/106 (1994): 5-36. The J. L. Austin text I have in mind is *How To Do Things With Words* (Cambridge, Massachusetts: Harvard University Press, 1975).

[4] Alexander Norris, "The New Anglo," *Gazette* [Montreal] (29 May 1999): A1.

[5] Norris, "Rallying Anglos: Signs and Battles of the Anglo-Rights Movement Resonate Less with Younger English Quebecers," *Gazette* [Montreal] (5 June 1999): A1.

[6] Josée Blanchette, "L'Anglo tout nouveau, tout beau," *Le Devoir* [Montréal] (2 juin 1999): B1. The original passage reads: "Les querelles ataviques de naguère sont plutôt le fait commun de l'ancienne generation de péquistes et de fédéralists qui règlent leurs comptes avec l'histoire tandis que la réalité emprunte de chemins de traverse." All translations in this essay are my own.

[7] David Solway, "Double Exile and Montreal English-Language Poetry," *Books in Canada* 31 (Winter 2002): 26.

[8] Solway, "Introduction," *4 Montreal Poets* (Fiddlehead: New Brunswick, 1973), p. 8. The four poets are Peter Van Toorn, Marc Plourde, Arty Gold, Richard Sommer.

[9] Ibid., p. 11.

[10] A. M. Klein, "Portrait of the Poet as Landscape," in *The Rocking Chair and Other Poems* (Toronto: Ryerson Press, 1948), p. 51

[11] Solway, "Introduction," p. 8. It is worth noting that this argument has had some play in the French press. When Solway won the Prix littéraire de la ville de Montréal in 2004 for his book, *Franklin's Passage* (McGill-Queen's University Press, 2003), *Le Devoir* published an article about him—with the headline, "David Solway, un poète en exil"—in which Solway was quoted as saying: «Pour moi comme pour d'autres écrivains anglophones du Québec [précise-t-il dans un très bon français], la barrière linguistique a souvent été un obstacle. Nous vivons un double exil, d'abord par l'intermédiaire de la langue anglaise, mais aussi face aux poètes du Canada anglais qui s'acharne à défendre la cause canadienne. Ce prix vient briser, d'une certaine façon, le mur qui existe entre les deux solitudes au Québec.» Translation: For me, as for other Anglophone writers of Quebec (he explains in a very good French), the linguistic barrier was often an obstacle. We live a double exile, first of all by the intermediary of the English language, but also in relation to Anglo-Canadian poets who fiercely defend the Canadian cause. This prize comes to break, in a certain way, the wall that exists between the two solitudes in Quebec.

(David Cantin, "David Solway, un poète en exil," *Le Devoir* [Montréal] [samedi 18 décembre 2004]: F8.)

[12] See Solway, "Double Exile and Montreal English-Language Poetry," reprinted in the present collection. Again, it should be said that this argument has circulated in French circles, as well. For example, in an article Yves Boisvert published in *La Presse* about Martha Radice's sociological study, *Feeling Comfortable? - les Anglo-Montréalais et leur ville* (Presses de l'Université Laval, 2000), Boisvert summarizes Radice's argument in the following way:

Radice en vient à dire que Montréal est une "cité-république" aux yeux de bien des anglophones. D'abord, parce que graduellement, les Anglo-Montréalais se sont détachés du reste du Québec, largement francophone. En même temps, ils répugnent à s'identifier culturellement au Canada, s'estimant plus sophistiqués que les gens de l'Ouest, par exemple, et croyant avoir acquis de leur fréquentation des francophones cette supposée "joie de vivre" et des tournures de phrase qui les rendraient différents de tous les Anglo-Canadiens—à l'exception des liens politiques.

Translation: Radice comes to say that Montreal is an "urban-republic" in the eyes of many Anglophones. First, because gradually Anglo-Montrealers came to be detached from the rest of Quebec, which is largely Francophone. At the same time, they resist cultural identification with the rest of Canada, considering themselves more sophisticated than Westerners, for example, and believe that they have acquired by their frequent contact with Francophones that supposed "joie de vivre" and turns of phrase that render them different from all other Anglo-Canadians—except in the area of politics. (Yves Boisvert, "Anthropologie de l'Anglo-Montréalais." *La Presse* [Montréal] [5 juin 2000]: A5.)

[13] Michael Harris, "A Note About This Collection," *Poetry Readings: 10 Montreal Poets at the CEGEPS* (Montreal: Delta, 1975), n.p.

[14] Ibid.

[15] The ten poets included in this anthology and reading tour were: Peter Van Toorn, John McAuley, Richard Sommer, Michael Harris, Bob McGee, Artie Gold, Andre Farkas, David Solway, Claudia Lapp, and Marc Plourde.

[16] Arguably, it now *does* hold true for American and British poets writing at the present time. Louis Dudek, "Academic Literature" (1944), *The Making of Modern Poetry in Canada*, ed. Louis Dudek and Michael Gnarowski (Toronto: The Ryerson Press, 1967), p. 104.

[17] Ibid., p. 105.

[18] Andre Farkas and Ken Norris, "Introduction," *Montreal English Poetry of the Seventies* (Montréal: Véhicule Press, 1978), p. ix. The Farkas and Norris introduction is reprinted in the present book.

[19] See appendix, "Concordia University M.A. Poetry Theses, 1974-2006," for a list of poets who have graduated from that program over the past forty years.

[20] This assertion must be qualified, somewhat, by acknowledging the importance of readings organized by institutions like the Atwater, Fraser-Hickson and Jewish Public Libraries, by the Blue Metropolis Festival's sponsorship of readings by local poets, and by the fact of the great variety of reading series, cabarets, and spoken word events that have continued to exist from the mid-1970s, onwards,

not all of which are wholly dependent upon students for their audiences. See Corey Frost's article in the present collection for some examples of these latter venues.

[21]The poets included in *Montreal: English Quebec Poetry of the Seventies* are: Van Toorn, Anne McLean, Fraser Sutherland, Guy Bichard, Sommer, Raymond Gordy, McAuley, Joan Thornton-McLeod, Harris, Stephen Morrissey, Artie Gold, Carole Ten Brink, McGee, Ritchie Carson, Plourde, Marquita Crevier, Solway, Farkas, Laurence Hutchman, Lapp and Konyves.

[22]Louis Dudek, *Epigrams* (Montreal: DC Books, 1975), p. 30.

[23]Farkas and Norris, "Introduction," p. ix.

[24]Ibid., p. ix.

[25]Ibid., p. xi.

[26]Peter Van Toorn, "Introduction," *Cross/cut: Contemporary English Quebec Poetry*, ed. Peter Van Toorn and Ken Norris (Montréal: Véhicule Press, 1982), p. 21.

[27]Gilles Marcotte, "Le double exil d'Octave Crémazie" (1955), in *Une litterature qui se fait* (Montréal: Les Éditions HMH, 1962), pp. 74-75. Original passage: d'Ancien Régime, tout nourri de regrets, de nostalgias. On vit au Canada, on va y rester, on lui appartient; mais en meme temps on ne cesse de rêver de la France comme d'une patrie perdue.

[28]Ibid., p. 81.

[29]Ibid., p. 82. The original passage: il manquait le minimum d'unité intérieure indispensable à la creation poétique.

[30]T.S. Eliot, "The Metaphysical Poets" (1921), in *Selected Essays* (London: Faber & Faber, 1951), p. 288.

[31]Pierre Nepveu, *L'écologie du réel: Mort et naissance de la literature Québécoise contemporaine* (Montréal: Boréal, 1988), p. 48. The original passage reads: étrangeté à la vie, absence au monde, alienation intérieure.

[32]This bill made French the only official language of the legislature, the courts, statutes and regulations. It made it the legal right of Francophones to communicate in French when dealing with provincial administrative services, health and social services, as well as business and retail firms. Quebec Francophones now had the legal right to work in French exclusively, and businesses with more than fifty employees were required to adopt French as the official language of work. Public signs and commercial advertising were now to be in French only and all immigrant children not registered in English schools as of 1977 would have to attend French schools. See Bouhis, p. 25.

[33]This latter idea—that of the development of a pluralist citizenship through the medium of French has been stressed by the Parti Québécois since the second referendum in 1995, as a kind of corrective to Jacques Parizeau's statement in his concession speech that the referendum was lost to "Money and ethnic votes," and the more Jacobin (if not purely ethnic) brand of nationalism promoted by the hardcore wing of the PQ.

The following passage from an advisory document presented to the Quebec "minister des Relations avec les citoyens et de l'immigration" entitled, *Un Québec pour tous ses citoyens* (Montreal: Conseil des Relations interculturelles, 1996) is representative of this notion: "La diversité des apports culturels n'est l'occasion d'enrichissement pour tous que dans la mesure où tous les groupes ont la capacité de communiquer entre eux au moyen d'une langue commune. Le français doit être considéré comme un instrument privilégié pour entretenir le dialogue intercultural et l'accent doit être mis sur son rôle intégrateur" (p. 13). Translation: The diversity of cultural contributions and participation is only an opportunity for widespread, mutual enrichment to the degree that all groups have the capacity to communicate to each other by means of a common language. French must be considered as a privileged instrument by which to foster intercultural dialogue, and the accent must be put on its role as a tool for integration.

For an interesting interpretation of Parizeau's 1995 concession speech as having more to do with a Québécois version of Jacobin nationalism than with ethnic nationalism, see Dimitrios Karmis, "Pluralism and National Identity(ies) in Contemporary Québec: Conceptual Clarifications, Typology, and Discourse Analysis," trans. Mélanie Maisonneuve, *Québec: State and Society*, Third Edition, ed. Alain-G. Gagnon (Peterborough: Broadview Press, 2004), pp. 88-90.

[34]Reed Scowen, *A Different Vision: The English in Quebec in the 1990s* (Don Mills: Maxwell Macmillan Canada, 1991), p. 25.

[35]Ibid., p. 25.

[36]Ibid., p. 25.

[37]Ibid., p. 150.

[38]Ibid., p. 153.

[39]Ibid., p. 151.

[40]Scowen quotes Salman Rushdie when stressing this last point: "Could we all possibly become a little more relaxed about our need for linguistic and cultural distinctiveness and celebrate, in the words of Salman Rushdie, the 'inevitable polyglot world' of 'hybridity, impurity, intermingling, the transformation that comes of new and unexpected combinations of human beings, cultures, ideas, politics, movies, songs,' rejoice in 'mongrelization' and fear 'the absolutism of the Pure'? In other words, might Quebec not now join the immediate future, and do it better than many more homogeneous societies that only know one way of life?" (p. 153)

[41]Josée Legault, *L'Invention d'une minorité: Les Anglo-Québécois* (Québec: Boréal, 1992), p. 160. The original passage runs as follows: "Il vise à convaincre les francophones que les Anglophones sont une minorité 'comme les autres', que leur langue, parlée par près de 300 millions de Nord-Américains, est en danger, qu'ils sont menacés et maltraités, et surtout, que leurs 'droits' doivent être élargis, et non consolidés. Il vise également à faire croire qu'une communauté Anglophone ne pourrait vivre dans un Québec don't la principale langue de communication ne serait pas la sienne. Il vise enfin à obtenir le 'maximum', soit le bilinguisme, dans un Québec independent, ou non. Cette dualité vouée à l'échec au Canada, serait ainsi transposée dans un Québec 'reborn'."

[42]Ibid., p. 189.

[43]As Legault points out, Scowen's vision for the future of Quebec echoes many of the sentiments articulated by Trudeau's vision of multiculturalism. Sentiments like those expressed in the following excerpts from Trudeau's speech on Canadian

multiculturalism delivered to the House of Commons, 8 October 1971: "[A]lthough there are two official languages, there is no official culture, nor does any ethnic group take precedence over any other. No citizen or group of citizens is other than Canadian, and all should be treated fairly....[A]dherence to one's ethnic group is influenced not so much by one's origin or mother tongue as by one's sense of belonging to the group, and by what the commission calls the group's "collective will to exist."...The individual's freedom would be hampered if he were locked for life within a particular cultural compartment by the accident of birth or language. It is vital, therefore, that every Canadian, whatever his ethnic origin, be given a chance to learn at least one of the two languages in which his country conducts its official business and its politics. A policy of multiculturalism within a bilingual framework...should help break down discriminatory attitudes and cultural jealousies. National unity if it is to mean anything in the deeply personal sense, must be founded on confidence in one's own individual identity; out of this can grow respect for that of others and a willingness to share ideas, attitudes and assumptions. A vigorous policy of multiculturalism will help create this initial confidence. It can form the base of a society which is based on fair play for all." (Pierre Elliot Trudeau, "Multiculturalism [with Government Response to Volume 4 of the report of the Royal Commission on Bilingualism and Biculturalism, Commissioners André Laurendeau and Davidson Dunton]." Speech delivered to the House of Commons, 8 October 1971. <http://www.canadahistory.com/ sections/ documents/ trudeau_-_on_multiculturalism.htm> [22 July 2005].)

[44]Gouvernement du Québec, Ministère des Communautés culturelles et de L'Immigration, *Au Québec. Pour bâtir ensemble. Énoncé de politique en matière d'immigration et d'intégration* (Québec: Gouvernement du Québec, 1998), p. 16. Cited in Karmis, p. 87.

[45]Karmis, pp. 79-80.

[46]Sherry Simon, *Hybridité Culturelle* (Montréal: L'Île de la Tortue, 1999), p. 56. Simon's original text: "Ce sont les artistes, autant que les politicians, qui trouveront une réponse à ces questions."

[47]Simon, *Hybridité Culturelle*, pp. 45-54.

[48]Klein, *The Rocking Chair*, pp. 29-30.

[49]Van Toorn, *Mountain Tea* (Montréal: Véhicule, 2003).

[50]Gilles Deleuze and Félix Guattari, *Kafka: Toward a Minor Literature*, trans. Dana Polan (Minneapolis: University of Minnesota Press, 1986), p. 16.

[51]Erín Mouré, *O Cidadán* (Toronto: House of Anansi, 2002), n.p.

[52]Ibid., p. 42.

[53]Carmine Starnino, *With English Subtitles* (Kentville, Nova Scotia: Gaspereau Press, 2005), pp. 26-27.

[54]Adult Italian slang for the pejorative expletive designating someone as a boorish, ill-mannered person.

[55]Starnino, *With English Subtitles*, p. 25.

[56]Marc Shell uses and defines these terms in the following passage from his essay, "Language Wars": "All too often in human history the motives for 'linguicide' (destroying a language) and 'glottophagie' (absorbing or consuming a language),

verge on the terrible purposes of 'genocide' (destroying all the individuals of a culture)." (Marc Shell, "Language Wars," *The New Centennial Review* 1.2 [2001]: 3.)

[57]This area is now the Montreal borough called Ahuntsic-Cartierville, which includes the following five districts: Ahuntsic, L'Acadie, Cartierville, Sault-au-Récollet and St. Sulpice.

[58]William Wordsworth, "To the Cuckoo." *Wordsworth: Poems* (London: Penguin Books, 1988), p. 32.

[59]Shell, "Babel in America; or, The Politics of Language Diversity in the United States," *Critical Inquiry* 20 (Autumn 1993): 118.

[60]What happened for many years in Quebec is that they were designated either one or the other, according to a sometimes random legal fiction about the identities of those whose mother tongue was other. In l968 one specific thing that happened ("to these 'immigrants' to Québec") in the case of the Italian-speaking ones of St. Léonard in Montreal is that they found themselves facing a slate of Catholic School Commission candidates who were set on channeling all the children of "immigrants" (in this case, mostly children whose mother tongue was Italian) into French schools. The public and legal protests launched by the Italian community were vehement and the protests prompted a variety of statements from prominent figures in Quebec. Premier Daniel Johnson "promised that English-speaking Quebecers will never be forced to integrate their schools with those of French-speaking Catholics" (Unsigned, "Premier Promises No Forced French," *Gazette* [Montreal] [13 June 1968]: A1). Dr. Wilder Penfield, renowned McGill University neuro-surgeon, in his comments "on the suburban St. Leonard controversy over bilingual schools" remarked that "the 'bilingual brain' is a superior instrument and all Canadian parents have the right to demand bilingual education for their children" (Unsigned, "'Bilingual Brain' Superior—Penfield." *Gazette* [Montreal] [15 June 1968]: A3). René Lévesque—then leader of the Mouvement Souvérainété-Association and Independent MNA for Laurier—declared that the "rights of English speaking residents should be respected," but "the government should declare that, starting at some future date, Quebec will provide funds to support only French-language schools for immigrants" ("Lévesque Jumps Into School Controversy." *Gazette* [Montreal], [14 June 1968]: A4). As a Montreal *Gazette* editorial pointed out, the real question raised by the St. Leonard controversy "is whether it is to be official and government policy to remove from New Canadians who have settled in the province...their freedom of choice in the education of their children" ("Test Case in St. Leonard," [Editorial] *Gazette* [Montreal] [12 June 1968]: A7).

New provincial laws on language education were developed in response to this crisis. The short-term result of this education controversy was Bill 63—The Law to Promote the French Language in Québec, passed after a lame duck session by the Union National government of Jean-Jacques Bertrand in the fall of 1969. This bill was intended to ensure that English-speaking children learn French, but it gave the freedom of choice over the language of study to parents, and consequently it was firmly opposed by Québec nationalists who felt it compromised the future of French in Québec. Widespread discontent with this bill, combined with the findings of the Gerondon Commission report, eventually led to the passing of Bill 22, and finally Bill 101, which went very far in prohibiting immigrant children from attending English schools. As Donat J. Taddeo and Raymond C. Taras state, the St. Leonard crisis is what first pushed the government to establish laws about language education (*Le Débat Linguistique au Québec: La Communauté Italienne et La Langue d'Enseignement* [Montréal: Les Presses de l'Université de Montréal, 1987], p. 97). For more detailed accounts of the St. Leonard language crisis within the context of Quebec language and education debates, see: Linda Kahn, *Schooling, Jobs, and Cultural Identity: Minority Education in Quebec* (New York and London: Garland, 1992), pp. 93-96; and Andrée Dufour, *Histoire de l'éducation au Québec* (Québec: Boréal, 1997), pp. 95-97.

[61]Starnino, *With English Subtitles*, p. 25.

[62]"The Greek term barbarian suggests enemy and stutterer, but it comes down to its older meaning: 'a people who cannot speak 'our' language 'properly' or who cannot speak any language without accent, like the still growing number of immigrants and stateless persons in the world today who may be or represent a real problem of international peace and security" (Shell, "Language Wars", p. 3).

[63]The English language meaning of the term appears in the *Oxford English Dictionary*: "Cafone, *n.*" 2. *slang*. Esp. in Italian-American usage: a coarse-mannered person; a low-life, a lout. According to this same *OED* entry, the etymology of this term is in dispute, but seems, from its earliest usage to be associated with a lack of education: ["Italian *cafone* peasant (1861 as *caffone*; 1882 as adjective in sense 'uneducated'), now also 'boor, lout'; further etymology uncertain and disputed." In form *gavone* representing Italian regional pronunciation. In plural form *cafoni* after the Italian plural form.]

[64]Starnino, *With English Subtitles*, pp. 28-29. The poem later explains: "(And *futtiti*? It means ef-you-see-kay-e-dee)." p. 29.

[65]Alan Liu, *Wordsworth: The Sense of History* (Stanford, California: Stanford University Press, 1898), p. 467.

[66]Ibid., p. 29.

[67]Ibid., p. 26.

[68]Carolyn Marie Souaid, *October* (Winnipeg: Nuage Editions, 1999), p. 67.

[69]Actually, information from later in the poem suggests it is most likely the federalist French paper, *La Presse* that is being read here:

I do not need a subscription to *Le Devoir*
    to make me an enlightened anglo
In Quebec. I do not need a subscription to *The Gazette*
    to make me an enlightened anglo in Quebec. (Souaid, *October*, p. 68)

[70] David McGimpsey, *Hamburger Valley, California* (Toronto: ECW Press, 2001), p. 18.

[71]Ibid., p. 15. A further, local reference that might be relevant here: These kinds of "macaroni salutes" to Quebec from Anglo-Canada were particularly pronounced in the summer of 1990 as the June 23 deadline for ratification of the Meech Lake Accord grew near. As Ed Bantey, a separatist columnist who was hired by the Montreal *Gazette* to raise the ire of its readers on a weekly basis, quotes in one of

his goading columns:

> La Presse devoted almost an entire page of love letters from British Columbia, from Ontario, from Nova Scotia, proclaiming, "Nous vous aimons, ne partez pas!" ("We love you, don't leave us!")

> That gave birth to what I shall modestly call the Bantey Principle: distance, not absence, makes the heart grow fonder.

Bantey then proceeds to cite passages from the hate mail he says he receives on a regular basis, the purpose of which is summed up in the headline of his column: "Letters from cowardly anglos full of hate and racism" (*Gazette* [Montreal] [3 June 1990]: A2). This column is relevant, not merely because McGimpsey's poem depicts a local version of the kind of effusion that the "Bantey Principal" attributes only to Anglos far away, but because McGimpsey felt compelled to respond to this particular column with a letter to the editor, taking special offence to the characterization of Anglo-Quebecers as hateful and racist:

> I read Ed Bantey's tendentious and aggressive column every Sunday. It rarely fails to give me a charge. Perhaps this charge is not dissimilar to the kind of perverse pleasure Mr. Bantey receives when he goes to Murray's [restaurant] hoping to be censured for speaking in French.

> Regardless, I must say that his June 3 column was simply journalism gone berserk. Publishing his personal hate mail is, first of all, a vainglorious waste of ink. But to categorize these sophomonic, ignorant, intolerant letters as in any way representative of English-speaking Quebecers is both unfair and insulting. (David McGimpsey, "Hate mail published," *Gazette* [Montreal] [13 June 1990]: B2.)

[72]In the library, the detention-serving student of McGimpsey's poem is "pretending to learn the Greek alphabet—/ never quite knowing "ελληνικος from τουρκος" (i.e. Ellinikos [Greek] from Tourkikos [Turk]) (p. 16). David Solway, in his poem, "On Learning Greek" also uses this ancient language as a synecdoche for the cultural barriers that language can entail: "Language is the longest wall in the world and the strongest" (Endre Farkas, ed., *The Other Language: English Poetry of Montreal* [Dorion, Québec: The Muses' Co., 1989.], p. 36).

[73]McGimpsey, *Hamburger Valley, California*, pp. 17-18.

[74]Ibid., pp. 19-20.

[75]Leah Marcus, *Puzzling Shakespeare: Local Reading and Its Discontents* (Berkeley: University of California Press, 1988), p. 213.

[76]Liu, "Local Transcendence: Cultural Criticism, Postmodernism, and the Romanticism of Detail," *Representations* 32 (1990): 82.

[77]See the entry for the little magazine *Ingluvin* (1971) in my annotated bibliography of "Anglo-Quebec Poetry Periodicals, c1976-2006" for more on this kind of stance.

[78]For a book of essays about Solway, see Carmine Starnino's edited collection, *David Solway: Essays on His Work* (Toronto: Guernica, 2001).

I. Foundational Polemics and Self-Assessments

The Montreal Poets / Dudek

[1]Reprinted from *Culture: A Quarterly Review* 18 (1957): 149-154.

Introduction to *Montreal: English Poetry of the Seventies* / Farkas and Norris

[1]Reprinted from *Montreal: English Poetry of the Seventies*, (Montréal: Véhicule Press, 1977), pp. ix-xii.

[2]Louis Dudek, *Epigrams* (Montréal: DC Books, 1975), p. 30.

Introduction to Cross/cut / Van Toorn

[1]Reprinted from *Cross/cut: Contemporary English Quebec Poetry*, ed. Peter Van Toorn and Ken Norris (Montréal: Véhicule Press, 1982), pp. 19-37.

[2]Chateaugué finds him handsome, says he has fiery hair, the nose of a lion and eyes as soft as butterfly wings. The photograph we stole depicts him with a lavallière tie around his neck. The photo could just as easily have captured him with a lavallière around his forehead. Then he would have had a fertile air about him. His intense hair, eyes of a woman, nose of a beast, soft lips, hard mouth; he is just as we imagined: that is what struck us most when we met him between two pages…[Translations in this essay by Jason Camlot.]

[3]The essay referred to is Paul West's "Ethos and Epic: Aspects of Contemporary Canadian Poetry," *Canadian Literature* 4 (1960): 7-17. [Editor's Note.]

What Now, Montreal? / Hancock

[1]Reprinted from *Matrix* 20 (1985): pp. 5-15.

[2]David O'Rourke, "A Second Look at English Poetry in Montreal," *CVII* (spring 1980): 24-27

[3]The correct title of this little magazine is *Booster & Blaster*. [Editor's Note.]

Double Exile and Montreal English-Language Poetry / Solway

[1]This article first appeared in *Books in Canada* 31 (Winter 2002): pp. 25-26.

[2]The Maritime provinces might also make a strong case for themselves as a center of genuine poetic creativity—what with poets like Brent MacLaine, Ross Leckie, John Steffler and Mary Dalton—but I leave it to others to account for the reasons.

[3]I cannot resist customizing the first part of a celebrated Wordsworth poem to suggest what the city at a privileged period in its literary history has given us:

Great men have been among us: hands that penned
And tongues that uttered wisdom—better none:
The early Dudek, Klein and Sutherland,
Young Cohen, and others who called Layton friend.

Louis Dudek and the Question of Quebec / Tremblay

[1]Louis Dudek, "Louis Dudek 1918 - ," *Contemporary Authors Autobiography Series*, vol. 14, ed. Joyce Nakamura (Detroit: Gale, 1991), p. 123.

[2]Dudek, *1941 Diary*, ed. Aileen Collins (Montréal: Empyreal, 1996), p. 33.

[3]Dudek, "On Getting to Know Nelligan," *Open Letter* 4 (Spring/Summer 1981): 306.

[4]Ibid., p. 305.

[5]Ibid., p. 307.

[6]Dudek, *East of the City* (Toronto: Ryerson, 1946), p. 45.

[7]Ibid., p. 46.

[8]Dudek, "Louis Dudek 1918 -," p. 126.

[9]John Nause and Michael Heenan, eds, "An Interview with Louis Dudek," *Tamarack Review* 69 (Summer 1976): p. 31.

[10]Dudek, "Geography, Politics, and Poetry," *Open Letter* 4 (Spring/Summer 1981): p. 142.

[11]Dudek, "Autobiographical Sketch 1951," *Open Letter* 4 (Spring/Summer 1981): p. 313.

[12]Dudek, "Louis Dudek 1918 -," p. 130.

[13]E. Fuller Torrey, *The Roots of Treason: Ezra Pound and the Secret of St. Elizabeths* (New York: McGraw-Hill, 1984), p. 217.

[14]Humphrey Carpenter, *A Serious Character: The Life of Ezra Pound* (New York: Delta, 1988), p. 800.

[15]Ezra Pound, "Provincialism the Enemy," *Selected Prose 1909-1965* (New York: New Directions, 1973), p. 189.

[16]Ibid., p. 190.

[17]Ibid., p. 199.

[18]Ibid., p. 199.

[19]Ibid., p. 202.

[20]Laurence Hutchman, "An Interview with Louis Dudek," *The River Review* 1 (1995): p. 64.

[21]Dudek, "Louis Dudek 1918 -," p. 132.

[22]Dudek, "Patterns of Recent Canadian Poetry," *Selected Essays and Criticism* (Ottawa: Tecumseh, 1978), p. 109.

[23]Dudek, "The Transition in Canadian Poetry," *Selected Essays and Criticism*, p. 135.

[24]Dudek, "Introduction," *Some Poems of Jean Narrache* (unpublished manuscript, 1999), n.p.

[25]Dudek, "The Two Traditions—Literature and the ferment in Quebec," *Selected Essays and Criticism*, p. 158.

[26]Ibid., p. 163.

[27]Ibid., p. 158.

[28]Ibid., p. v.

[29]Ibid., p. 158.

[30]Ibid., p. 159.

[31]Ibid., pp. 162-63.

[32]Ibid., p. 164.

[33]Pound, *ABC of Reading* (New York: New Directions, 1987), p. 73.

[34]Dudek, "The Two Traditions," p. 164.

[35]Dudek, "Fusing Our Two Literatures," *In Defence of Art: Critical Essays & Reviews*, ed. Aileen Collins (Kingston: Quarry, 1988), p. 155.

[36]Dudek, "Robitaille's Exhilarating Work," *In Defence of Art*, ed. Collins, p. 188.

[37]Dudek, "Gilles Vigneault: Poet of Natashquan," *In Defence of Art*, ed. Collins, p. 191.

[38]Dudek, "The Critical Essays of Jean Ethier-Blais—A Notable Literary Contribution," *In Defence of Art*, ed. Collins, p. 205.

[39]Dudek, "Anne Hébert Translated: Some Thoughts on Dual Literature in Canada," *In Defence of Art*, ed. Collins, p. 208.

[40]Dudek, "Those Damned Visionary Poets (Les Poètes Maudits Visionnaires)," *Selected Essays and Criticism*, p. 166.

[41]Ibid., p. 166.

[42]Ibid., p. 167.

[43]Dudek, "Translations Enrich French-English Literature," *In Defence of Art*, ed. Collins, pp. 198, 200.

[44]Dudek, "The New Oxford Book of Canadian Verse in English," *In Defence of Art*, ed. Collins, p. 245.

[45]Hutchman, "An Interview with Louis Dudek," p. 74.

[46]Bronwyn Chester, "Small Magazines, Big Influence," *McGill Reporter*, 11 Mar. 1999, n.p.

[47]Dudek, "Aquin's *Prochain Épisode* is Nearer Poetry than Prose," *In Defence of Art*, ed. Collins, p. 195.

[48]Ibid.

[49]Quoted in Hutchman, "An Interview with Louis Dudek," p. 73.

[50]Dudek, "Committed to Excellence," interview in *Books in Canada* 22 (November 1993): 12.

[51]Dudek, *Dk/ Some Letters of Ezra Pound* (Montréal: DC Books, 1974), p. 77.

[52]Dudek, "Anne Hébert Translated," p. 209.

[53]Dudek, "Too Many Controls Spoil the Show," *In Defence of Art*, ed. Collins, p. 74.

[54]Ibid., pp. 74-75.

[55]Dudek, "Introduction," *Some Poems of Jean Narrache*, unpublished manuscript, 1999, n.p.

[56]Ibid.

[57]Dudek, "Louis Dudek 1918 -," p. 124.

[58]Dudek, "A Real Good Goosin': Talking Poetics," *An Unorthodox History of Montreal's Vehicle Poets*, ed. Ken Norris (Montréal: Nuage, 1993), p. 62.

[59]Ibid., p. 79.

[60]David Solway, "Louis Dudek Made Poetry Irresistible," *Quill & Quire* 67 (May 2001): 10.

[61]Frank Davey, *Louis Dudek & Raymond Souster*, (Vancouver: Douglas & McIntyre, 1980), p. 37.

[62]Brian Trehearne, *The Montreal Forties: Modernist Poetry in Transition* (Toronto: University of Toronto, 1999), p. 318-19.

[63]Dudek, *Epigrams* (Montréal: DC Books, 1975), p. 11.

[1]Leonard Cohen, *The Favorite Game* (New York: Viking, 1963), pp. 68-9.

[2]Cohen, *The Favorite Game*, p. 24.

[3]Irving Layton, *Waiting for the Messiah: A Memoir* (Toronto: McClelland & Stewart, 1985), p. 21.

[4]A. M. Klein, "Review of *Here and Now* by Irving Layton," *Literary Essays and Reviews*, ed. U. Caplan and M. W. Steinberg (Toronto: University of Toronto, 1987), p. 215.

[5]Layton, *Waiting for the Messiah*, p. 136.

[6]Ibid., p. 160.

[7]Ibid., p. 224.

[8]Emphasis in original. Michael Harris, "Leonard Cohen: The Poet as Hero— 2," *Saturday Night* 84.6 (June 1969): p. 27.

[9]Aileen Collins, ed., *CIV/n: A Literary Magazine of the 50's* (Montréal: Véhicule, 1983), p. 126.

[10]Layton, *For My Brother Jesus* (Toronto: McClelland & Stewart, 1976), p. xvi.

[11]Mordecai Richler, "Be it ever so (increasingly) humble, there's no place like home," *Maclean's Magazine* 91 (1 August 1978): 54.

[12]Ira Nadel, *Various Positions: A Life of Leonard Cohen* (Toronto: Random House, 1996), p. 27.

[13]Tom Waits, *Big Time* (New York, Island Records, 1990).

[14]Eli Mandel, *Irving Layton* (Toronto: Forum House, 1969), p. 16.

[15]William Carlos Williams, "A Note on Layton," in Irving Layton, *The Improved Binoculars* (Highlands, North Carolina: J. Williams, 1956), pp. 9-10 [page numbers not marked].

[16]Mandel, *Irving Layton*, p. 16.

[17]Seymour Mayne, "Introduction," *Irving Layton: The Poet and His Critics* (Toronto: McGraw-Hill Ryerson, 1978), pp. 2-3.

[18]Ibid., pp. 5, 10.

[19]Harris, "Leonard Cohen: The Poet as Hero - 2," pp. 27, 30.

[20]Ibid., p. 28.

[21]Ibid., p. 30.

[22]Collins, *CIV/n: A Literary Magazine of the 50's*, p. 211.

[23]Ibid., p. 231.

[24]Ibid., p. 185.

[25]Nadel, *Various Positions: A Life of Leonard Cohen*, p. 62.

[26]Ibid., p. 63.

[27]George Bowering, "On Not Teaching the Vehicle Poets," in *Vehicule Days: An Unorthodox History of Montreal's Vehicle Poets*, ed. Ken Norris (Montréal: Nuage, 1993), p. 115.

[28]There is an argument to be made for the wide-ranging influence of American poets and novelists on Leonard Cohen. One fruitful but unstudied connection might be between Cohen's pop persona and that of Allen Ginsberg. A Cohenesque confusion of poet and singer/musician appears in Ginsberg's *First Blues: Rags, Ballads & Harmonium Songs 1971-74*, where poems are accompanied by musical

notation, including guitar chords, while poems with titles like "Walking Blues" receive rhythmic descriptions: "(andante)." To round out the interplay between American popular music and literature, the frontispiece of *First Blues* is a photograph of Ginsberg and a guitar-strumming Bob Dylan seated before the Massachusetts grave of "'Ti Jean' John Kerouac." Allen Ginsberg, *First Blues: Rags, Ballads & Harmonium Songs 1971-74* (New York: Full Court, 1975), p. 11.

[29]Andre Farkas and Ken Norris, eds., *Montreal: English Poetry of the Seventies* (Montréal: Véhicule, 1977), p. x.

[30]Ibid., p. xi.

[31]Cohen and Layton reappear in the 1982 anthology *Cross/cut: Contemporary English Quebec Poetry*, edited by Peter Van Toorn and Ken Norris. The introduction to this volume is notably attentive to American influence and to political concerns. Klein's "meteoric" career is said to have been interrupted by "twenty years of silence," and there is passing mention of Cohen. But the Anglo-Jewish dichotomy is no longer in play; rather, Jewishness is seen to be subsumed in the "pluralist mosaic of Canadian poetry," whose Quebec version Van Toorn depicts as a kind of wedding banquet of Arab, Italian, Scots, Welsh, Irish, Asian and Jewish offerings, all of which are apparently invited in order to consummate "[c]ontact with French civilization." Peter Van Toorn, "Introduction," *Cross/cut: Contemporary English Quebec Poetry* (Montréal: Véhicule, 1982), pp. 28, 36.

[32]Michael Harris, personal interview, 14 August 2005.

[33]Ibid.

[34]Farkas and Norris, *Montreal: English Poetry of the Seventies*, p. ix. This quote originally from Louis Dudek's *Epigrams* (Montreal: DC Books, 1975), p. 30.

[35]Harris, personal interview.

[36]Ibid.

[37]Ibid.

[38]Ibid.

[39]Irving Layton, letter to Keith Garebian, 5 Feb. 1978, in *Wild Gooseberries: The Selected Letters of Irving Layton*, ed. Francis Mansbridge (Toronto: Macmillan, 1989), p. 306.

[40]Michael Benazon, "Irving Layton and the Montreal Poets," *Matrix* 20 (Spring 1985): 16.

[41]Layton, letter to Ken Sherman, 29 Apr. 1984, in *Wild Gooseberries: The Selected Letters of Irving Layton*, ed. Mansbridge, pp. 352-53.

[42]Sherman, "Five Pieces for Irving Layton," *Books In Canada* 30 (Sep./Oct. 2001): p. 25.

[43]Sherman, email correspondence, 9 Aug. 2005.

[44]Ibid.

[45]Solway, "Framing Layton," *Random Walk: Essays in Elective Criticism* (Montréal/Kingston: McGill-Queen's University Press, 1997), p. 86.

[46]Ibid.

[47]Solway, personal interview, 16 Nov. 1999.

[48]Ibid.

[49]Solway, "*TDR* Interview: David Solway," <http://www.danforthreview.com>

(18 Aug. 2005). This characterization of the poet's role comes up again and again in Layton's forewords to his own books, as well as in interviews. From a 1975 interview: "It was necessary to kick the door in, smash a few windows, and let some fresh air in.... I enjoyed having fights with librarians, with school principals, and with booksellers. I enjoyed writing letters to publishers and to newspaper editors, because I felt that what I was doing was a good thing, that it had to be done, and that, eventually, my point of view would prevail." Sara D'Agostino, "The War Goes On: A Conversation with Irving Layton," *Acta Victoriana*, vol. 100, no. 1 (Fall 1975), pp. 9, 13.

[50]Sherman, "Five Pieces for Irving Layton," p. 25.

[51]Lazer Lederhendler, email correspondence, 1 Dec. 2005.

[52]Sherman, "Five Pieces for Irving Layton," p. 25.

[53]Osterlund writes: "I had no doubts about Layton—through and through he was a poet. Let him storm and rage, be contradictory or wonderfully ridiculous, a buffoon or a warrior. Critics demanded an objective, cool-headed Layton....I wanted the artist and the man—subjective, sensitive, riddled with holes." Steven Osterlund, "Fumigator: An Outsider's View of Irving Layton," in *Irving Layton: The Poet and His Critics*, ed. Mayne, p. 264.

[54]Jack Batten, "Leonard Cohen: The Poet as Hero," *Saturday Night* 84 (June 1969): p. 25.

[55]One anecdote in Nadel's biography signals a rare case when Cohen's literary output had a direct impact on the musical scene. The story's background is Cohen's infatuation with the singer Nico, who "made it clear that nothing would happen between her and Cohen." In the meantime, she introduced Cohen to her collaborator, Lou Reed, arguably the most important songwriter of the New York underground of the late 1960s: "Reed had a copy of *Flowers for Hitler*, which he asked Cohen to sign, and was an early reader of *Beautiful Losers*. Cohen confided, 'In those days I guess he [Reed] wasn't getting very many compliments for his work and I certainly wasn't. So we told each other how good we were.'" Nadel, *Various Positions: A Life of Leonard Cohen*, pp. 147-48.

[56]Ibid., p. 223.

[57]Stephen Scobie, "Introduction," *Essays on Canadian Writing* 69 (Winter 1999): 3.

[58]Asa Boxer, personal interview, 22 August 2005.

[59]Ibid.

[60]Ibid.

[61]Jason Camlot, personal interview, 1 Nov. 2005.

[62]Ibid.

[63]Ruth Wisse, *The Modern Jewish Canon: A Journey Through Language and Culture* (New York: Free Press, 2000), pp. 10, 15, 28-9.

[64]Ibid., pp. 26-7.

[65]Ibid., p. 260.

[66]Farkas and Norris, *Montreal: English Poetry of the Seventies*, p. x.

[67]Bowering, "On Not Teaching the Vehicle Poets," p. 115.

[68]A. D. Person, "The poets were péquistes when Lévesque was a Liberal," *Canadian Forum* 59 (April 1979): 16. Translation: "There is a very messianic

dimension to the way people govern here. One thinks in terms of serving to save a race, of setting up a nation. I find this a bit bizarre. And further, we 'others', the Jews, we have seen too many flags rise and fall, and when one knows that in the end we are all headed towards the same thing, the tomb, one can't help but find these big theories and beautiful ideals a bit futile. [Translation by Jason Camlot]

[69]In an article for the *Thursday Report*, Concordia University's faculty newspaper, Layton is said to be "coming home" "to discover the 'ties that bind'; he also is demonstrating for the first time a genuine interest in Catholic humanism and "French-Canadian Catholicism." Beverly Smith, "The Gospel According to Irving Layton," *Thursday Report* 2 (26 Oct. 1978): p. 5.

[70]Richler, "Be it ever so (increasingly) humble, there's no place like home," p. 54.

[71]Person, "The poets were pequistes when Lévesque was a Liberal," p. 15.

[72]Farkas and Norris, *Montreal: English Poetry of the Seventies*, p. x.

A Walk in Montreal.... / McGimpsey
[1]"Montreal Tango"

Montreal metro, 7:30am
it's full of immigrants
they're early-risers
these people

The city's old heart
beats still
thanks to them

this old worn-out heart of the city
with its spasms
its embolisms
its heart tremors
and all its irregularities

and with all the reasons in the world
to stop
to give up
[Translation by Jason Camlot.]

[2]Jean Royer, "Les Poètes du Québec," *Le Québec en Poèéie*, ed. Jean Royer (Paris: Gallimard Jeunesse, 1995), p. 133.

[3]Stéphane Baillargeon, "Le mur des lamentations," *Le Devoir* [Montréal] (14 septembre 1999): B8. Translation: There is in this poem the idea that it is *they* who wake up early. It's not just immigrants in the metro, in the morning. [Translations for this article are by Jason Camlot.]

[4]Jean-Paul Marchand, *Conspiration? Les anglophones veulent-ils éliminer le français du Canada?* (Montréal: Stanké, 1997), p. 78. Translation: The era where

the ordinary francophone had to content himself with the position of woodcutter, water-bearer, or invisible person.

[5]Louis Dudek, "East of the City," *Quebec Suite: Poems for and About Quebec,* ed. Andre Farkas (Montréal: The Muses Company, 1995), p. 49

[6]Ibid., p. 50.

[7]Al Purdy, "Hommage To Ree-shard," *Thru the Smoky End Boards: Canadian Poetry About Sports & Games,* ed. Kevin Brooks and Sean Brooks (Vancouver: Polestar, 1996), p. 60.

[8]Gérald Godin, *Les Cantouques* (Montréal: Éditions Parti Pris, 1967), p. 26

[9]Arlindo Viera, "Les immigrants sont des poèmes," in *Gerald Godin: Un Poète en Politique,* ed. Lucille Beaudy, Robert Comeau and Guy Lachapelle (Montréal: l'Hexagone, 2000), p. 133. Translation: a nationalism much more open and much more careful of respecting the others.

[10]Eric Grenier, "Hello Pot? It's the Kettle," *Hour Magazine* (24 Feb.-3 Mar. 2000): p. 8.

[11]Christian Monnin, "Présentation: Un espace du possible," *Liberté* 42.1 (2000): pp. 4-5. Translation: where a multitude of cultural influences and modes of living are distilled. The individual enjoys, here, a freedom of choice without parallel.

[12]Victor Teboul, *Que dieu vous garde de l'homme silencieux quand il se met soudain à parler* (Montréal: Les Intouchables, 1999), p. 31. Translation: firmly splitting the city into two; the English to the west, the French to the east.

[13]Linda Leith, "Conjugations: New English Writing from Quebec," *Canadian Fiction Magazine* 63 (1988): 5. The bohemian *esprit* of Montreal's Plateau has inspired the most noticeable new dynamic of Montreal's lit-scene: interest in so-called "spoken word" events. As local writer and musician Jeremiah Wall says, there isn't "a large commercial publication presence here", so local talent has put its energy into stage appearances or into public reading series. "In Montreal, readings, slams and litzines sprout like weeds in unfertile ground." Victoria Stanton and Vincent Tinguely, "Reinventing the Word: The Montreal Poetry Scene Speaks for Itself," *Broken Pencil* 6 (Winter 1998): 13.

[14]Jean Dion, "Puerto Plateau," *Le Devoir* [Montréal] (6 avril 2000): A3.

[15]Dennis Lee, "Civil Elegies,"*Civil Elegies and Other Poems* (Toronto: Anansi, 1972), p. 33.

[16]Carole Beaulieu, "C'est la culture … Stupid!" *L'Actualité* (15 mars 1997): p. 56. Translation: No one ever sang Toronto the way Beau Dommage sang Montreal.

[17] Leclerc, Félix, *Rêves à Vendre* (Montréal: Nouvelles Editions de l'Arc, 1984), p. 60. Translation: Toronto moves further and further south in one language, Montreal climbs towards the north in another.

[18]Patrick Staram,. "Ville 1," *Ellipse* 56 (1996): p. 40.

[19]P. Scott Lawrence, introducing new English fiction from Quebec, starts: "the best writing rarely deals with place in terms so narrowly circumscribed." Foreword, *Souvenirs: New English Fiction from Quebec,* ed. P. Scott Lawrence (Dunvegan, Ont.: Cormorant, 1987), p. 5.

[20]Ruth Taylor, "Une Québécoise Errante (Referendum 2010),"*Quebec Suite: Poems for and About Quebec,* ed. Farkas, p. 133.

²¹Quoted in Françine Bordeleau, "La Révolution anglaise," *Lettres Québécoises* 93 (Spring 1999): 18. Translation: I cannot answer that I am a Canadian writer. I am an Anglo-Quebecer. But I wonder if I'm not just, quite simply, a Montrealer.

²²Ibid., p. 20. Translation: When we, the Anglo-Montrealers, arrive in Toronto, there is a cultural misunderstanding. No identification is possible, there is even a hostility between the two cities. In short, Toronto doesn't know what to do with us.

²³Recently, critic Dana Gioia offended the literary community of San Francisco by suggesting that the Bay Area had "lost it" as a major literary center. Defining literary as an overlapping, interdependant "ecosystem of newspapers, magazines, publishers and theaters," Gioia declared that without such a system, authors were doomed to careers without any national influence. Richard Silberg, "On 'Fallen Western Star': Dana Gioia Stirs It Up," *Poetry Flash* 285 (May/June 2000): p. 48. Interestingly, the predicatable *but what about Michael McLure?* outrages of San Francisco's defenders mirrored the bohemian ethic of Montreal. Rather than take the city to task for not being one of the "broadcast capitals like New York and Los Angeles" (as Canada's Toronto is), San Francisco was to be applauded as a credible center for anti-establishment forms (as Montreal might be for its "slams and litzines").

²⁴Sherry Simon, *Hybridité Culturelle* (Montréal: l'Île de la tortue, 1999), p. 25. Translation: In Montreal, the historical domination of the Anglophones, the need to defend French agains the power of English, created divisions between the two groups. It is these same tensions that animate divided cities like Berlin, Jerusalem or Trieste.

²⁵Ibid., p. 60. Montreal's "European" flair, a tourist guide standby, further inspires the city to import Parisian custom and retroactively claim it as its own. The phrase "as Montreal as a two-cheeked kiss" is one of those backformations, now "enforced" in the streets—much to the dismay of old-school handshakers. Translation: Compare Montreal's cosmopolitanism to the cultural cross-breeding of Europe.

²⁶Quoted in Émile Roberge, *Sur la Place Publique* (extraits). Montréal: de la Paix, 1995. <www.multimania.com/poetesse/souvreine/roberge>. Translation: Quench their thirst on the culture of the Anglo occupier.

²⁷Rudy Caya, "Je Me Souviens," *Vilain Pingouin-Y'é quelle heure?* [Sound Recording] (Montreal: Audiogram, 1998). Translation: It's nothing against the English…/ it's a / question of respect / for my French roots.

²⁸Jean-Paul Marchand, *Conspiration? Les anglophones veulent-ils éliminer le français du Canada?* (Montréal: Stanké, 1997), p. 77. Translation: They could continue to live here as if Quebec was an Anglophone province and French didn't exist at all.

²⁹Gaston Miron, *L'Homme Rapaillé* (Montréal: Éditions Typo, 1996), p. 93.

³⁰Yves Hamel, "Question linguistique à Montréal: Sur la Catherine, vente trottoir ou garage sale?" *Le Devoir* [Montréal] (20 juillet 2000): A7. "Translation: From the beginning of my walk…they started talking to me always in English first. Not one of them ever first addressed me in French. It was always necessary for me to insist, raising my voice as I said, 'Excuse me?', for them to shift to French…and

then most often with a laborious accent.

[31]Ibid., p. A7. Translation: The idiotic French server who spoke French translated his Anglo boss and did so in a nonsensical speech that was practically incomprehensible. So we understand…that the majority of francophones must be so ashamed that they prefer to be made to speak English.

[32]Richler's status in the French Press is often indicated by the informality of how he is usually adressed. "Il était normal de s'addresser à Mordecai Richler en applelant 'Mordecai' ou 'Monsieur Mordecai'. Imagine-t-on recevoir Anne Hébert à la télévision d'État et l'interpeller d'un 'Anne' ou d'un 'Madame Anne'"? Benoît Melançon, "Sept minutes de honte," *Le Devoir* [Montréal] (28 octobre 1997): A7.

[33]Lise Bissonnette, "Vu du Woody's Pub," *Le Devoir* [Montréal] (18 septembre 1991): A8. Translation: Quebec has rarely suffered such wholesale slander.

[34]Qtd. in Richler, "My life as a racist," *The Globe & Mail* (16 Feb. 1993): A18.

[35]Gérald Godon, *Sarazènes* (Montréal: Écrits des Forges, 1983), p. 15.

[36]Ibid., p. 15. Translation: invents a kind of racial contempt that we are well to call antipeasoupism, which is no better than antisemitism.

[37]Ibid., p. 16.

[38]Jean-Yves Durocher, "Mordecai—l'oppresseur opprimé," *Le Devoir* [Montréal] (10 octobre 1999): B8.

[39]Quoted in Bordeleau, p. 19. Translation: "Richler's discourse doesn't hold for the new generation," is the assessment of Helen Servinis, reporter for the *Montreal Review of Books* (MRB)…

Mordecai Richler is an extreme example. His antithesis might, for example, be called Gail Scott, who lives as much in French as in English and is closly allied with Quebec feminists. Or Neil Bisoondath, for whom 'the idea that Anglophones are oppressed by Bill 101 constitutes a misconception.'"

[40]Simon, *Les Solitudes*, p. D1. Translation: When it's a question of English-language literature in Quebec, is it the image of Mordecai Richler that rises first before your eyes? If that' the case, you have some serious reeducation work ahead of you. Several generations of English-language writers have had the time to add to that of Mordecai, and to take idealogical and aesthetic positions to a thousand places other than those of our national polemicist.

[41]Yves Beauchemin, "Parler français, pour combien de temps?" *Le Devoir* [Montréal] (9 mars 1999): A7. Translation: But to speak a language, that's also a political gesture. To speak English in New York, doesn't that, in a certain way, signal one's belonging to the American cultural mainstream? To speak Kurdish in Iraq, Catalan in Spain, Acadian in New-Brunswick, is to affirm a choice, to express an opinion, sometimes to take risks.

[42] Steven Heighton, "English Cemetery, Gaspésie," *Quebec Suite: Poems for and About Quebec*, ed. Farkas, p. 98.

III. Sites and Scenes

The Vehicule Poets / Farkas, Gold, Konyves, Lapp, McAuley, Morrissey, Norris

[1]This collective essay is an edited and abridged version of a longer article composed jointly by the Vehicule Poets. The longer piece will be made available at the online journal <poetics.ca>.

[2]The Four Horsemen: bpNichol, Steve McCaffery, Paul Dutton, and Rafael Barreto-Rivera.

[3]Ken Norris, ed., *Vehicule Days* (Winnipeg: Signature Editions, 1993). [This and all subsequent notes to this essay have been added by the editors.]

[4]Endre Farkas, Artie Gold, Tom Konyves, Claudia Lapp, John McAuley, Stephen Morrissey, Ken Norris, *The Vehicule Poets* (Montreal: Maker Press, 1979).

[5]Wynne Francis was the author of *Irving Layton and His Work* (Toronto: ECW Press, 1984), and editor of Layton's *Selected Poems* (Toronto: McClelland & Stewart, 1969). She started teaching at Sir George Williams in 1942 and retired from Concordia University in 1991. (Laura Groening, "In Memoriam: Wynne Francis," *Thursday Report* [Sept. 28, 2000]: 22.)

[6]Some of these performances are documented in Tom Konyves, *Poetry in Performance* (Ste. Anne de Bellevue, Québec: The Muses Co., 1982).

Eating Our Own Words... / Frost

[1]Victoria Stanton and Vincent Tinguely, "Reinventing the Word: The Montreal Poetry Scene Speaks for Itself," *Broken Pencil* 6 (Winter 1998): p. 1.

[2]A detailed account of the genesis of the poetry slam can be found in Kurt Heintz, "An Incomplete History of Slam: A Biography of an Evolving Poetry Movement," *e-poet's online library* (1994, 1996, 2000) <http://www.e-poets.net/library/slam/> (11 November 2006).

[3]For a much more in-depth history of this community, the definitive resource is Victoria Stanton and Vincent Tinguely's *Impure: Reinventing the Word: The Theory, Practice and oral History of Spoken Word in Montreal* (Montréal: Conundrum, 2001), a compendium of quotations from the participants in the scene that documents, as the subtitle puts it, "the theory, practice, and oral history of 'spoken word' in Montreal"; while it does not present a coherent theory of spoken word, it makes up in polyphonic richness what it lacks in unity.

[4]Ken Norris produced a documentary book called *Vehicule Days* (Winnipeg: Signature Editions, 1993), which is a good source for more on the Vehicule poets.

[5] Fortner Anderson, et al., *Oralpalooza 94 Montreal* (Montréal: ga Press, 1994).

[6]Ian Ferrier and Fortner Anderson, eds., *Wired on Words*. [Audio Cassette and Chapbook] (Montréal: Wired on Words and ga Press, 1994).

[7]Stephens, who was HIV-positive at the time, died of AIDS two years later in 1996. Ian Stephens, *Diary of a Trademark* (Ste. Anne de Bellevue, Québec: The Muses Co., 1994).

[8]Trish Salah, Dana Bath, Laura Killam and Corey Frost formed the original collective, later joined by Andy Brown, Tracy Bohan, and Taien Ng-Chan, among

others.

⁹Todd Swift and Regie Cabico, eds., *Poetry Nation: The North American Anthology of Fusion Poetry* (Montreal: Véhicule Press, 1998); Todd Swift and Philip Norton, eds., *Short Fuse: The Global Anthology of New Fusion Poetry* (New York: Rattapallax Press, 2002).

¹⁰Ian Ferrier, ed., *Wired on Words: Millenium Cabaret* [Audio CD] (Montreal: Wired on Words, 1998); Fortner Anderson, *Sometimes I Think* [Audio CD] (Montreal: Wired on Words, 1999); Ian Ferrier, *Exploding Head Man* [Audio CD and Book] (Montreal: Planète Rebelle, 2000); Alex Boutros, Taien Ng-Chan and Karla Sundström, eds., *Ribsauce: a CD/Anthology of Words by Women* [Audio CD and Book] (Montreal: Véhicule Press, 2001); Todd Swift and Tom Walsh, *The Envelope, Please* [Audio CD] (Montréal: Wired on Words, 2002); Catherine Kidd and Jack Beetz, *Sea Peach: Halocynthia Auranthium* [Audio CD and Book] (Montréal: Conundrum Press, 2002).

¹¹Stanton, "Reinventing the Word," p. 15.

¹²Ibid., p. 15.

¹³One of the major differences between spoken word in English and in French in Montreal is that French performers are much more reluctant to abandon the page while performing. In English spoken word, memorization is the norm, but in the French scene many writer-performers—but not all—see the page as symbolically important in distinguishing their work as literature, not theatre, and themselves as writers, not actors.

¹⁴Stanton, "Reinventing the Word," p. 14.

¹⁵Quoted in Stanton, "Reinventing the Word," p. 16.

¹⁶Quoted in Juliet Waters, "Wordmakers: A Guide to Montreal's Noisy Spoken-Word Scene," *Montreal Mirror* (5 Jan. 1995): 14.

¹⁷Heintz, "An Incomplete History of Slam," n.p.

¹⁸Charles Bernstein, "Against National Poetry Month As Such," (1999) <http://www.press.uchicago.edu/Misc/Chicago/044106.html> (11 November 2006).

¹⁹Ibid.

²⁰Bernstein is co-director, for example, of PennSound, a website that presents a warehouse of valuable poetry sound recordings.

²¹Charles Bernstein, *Close Listening: Poetry and the Performed Word* (New York; Oxford: Oxford University Press, 1998), p. 10.

Zymergy... / Skarstedt

¹Louis Dudek and Michael Gnarowski, eds., *The Making of Modern Literature in Canada: Essential Articles on Contemporary Canadian Poetry in English* (Toronto: Ryerson Press, 1967), p. 203

²Hubert H. Bancroft, ed., *The Great Republic by the Master Historians* <http://www.humanitiesweb.org/human.php?s=n&p=l&a=i&ID=18> (11 November 2006).

³Ibid., p. 7.

⁴Dudek and Gnarowski, *The Making of Modern Literature in Canada*, p. 203.

[5]Cynthia Ozick, "The Function of the Small Press," *Metaphor & Memory* (New York: Alfred A. Knopf, 1989), p. 123.

[6]Dudek, *The Making of Modern Literature in Canada*, p. 123.

[7]Ibid., p. 208.

[8]Desmond Pacey, *Creative Writing in Canada* (Toronto: Ryerson Press, 1967), p. 231.

[9]Michael Callen, "Local Health Services: Crisis on the Front Line," American Public Health Association Annual Meeting, Las Vegas, Nevada, Wednesday, October 2, 1986, <http://www.humanitiesweb.org/human.php?s=s&p=h&ID=1011>.

[10]Ken Norris, "Montreal English Poetry in the Seventies," *CVII* 3:3 (January 1978). Reprinted in Ken Norris, *Véhicule Days* (Montreal: Nuage Editions, 1993), p. 11.

[11]Peter Van Toorn, *Sounds New* (Montréal: The Muses Co., 1990), p. vi.

[12]Ralph Gustafson, *Plummets* (Vancouver: Sono Nis Press, 1987), p. 13.

[13]Ibid.

[14]Bronwyn Chester, "Small Magazines, Big Influence," *McGill Reporter* (11 March, 1999): front page.

[15]Van Toorn, "Mountain Words," *Zymergy* 1.2-3 (Autumn 1987): 21.

[16]Norris, ed., *Canadian Poetry Now: 20 Poets of the '80s* (Toronto: House of Anansi Press, 1984), p. 13.

[17]Ibid., p. 13.

[18]Laurent Mailhot and Pierre Nepveu, eds., *La Poésie Québécoise (des origines à nos jours)* (Montréal: Éditions Typo, 1996), p. 34.

[19]Ann Diamond, "How I Became a Terrorist, Or: Humour As a Terrorist Weapon," *Zymergy* 2 (Autumn 1988): 45.

[20]Ibid., p. 46.

[21]Ibid., p. 46.

[22]Ibid., p. 46.

[23]Trevor Thomas, "Sylvia Plath: Last Encounters," *Zymergy* 7 (Spring 1990): 46.

[24]Norris, "The Significance of Contact and *CIV/n*," in *CIV/n: A Literary Magazine of the 50's*, ed. Aileen Collins with Simon Dardick (Montréal: Véhicule, 1983), p. 259.

[25]Mary Melfi, "An Interview with Mary Melfi: The Dangers of Poetry," *Zymergy* 7 (Spring 1990): 121.

[26]Sonja Skarstedt, "Hanging Fire: Interview with Phyllis Webb," *Zymergy* 9 (Spring 1991): 40.

[27]Louise Schrier, "The Breathless Adventure: An Interview With Louis Dudek on the Long Poem," *Zymergy* 8 (Autumn 1990): 43.

[28]Laurence Hutchman, "An Interview With George Johnston," *Zymergy* 10 (Autumn 1991): 56.

[29] Elias Letelier-Ruz, "An Interview With Ernesto Cardenal," *Zymergy* 9 (Spring 1991): 58.

[30]Ibid., p. 62.

[31]Ibid., p. 62,

[32]Jorge Etcheverry, "Chilean Literature: Diaspora," *Zymergy* 7 (Spring 1990): 70.

[33]Gary Geddes, "Down But Not Out in Nicaragua," *Zymergy* 8 (Autumn 1990): 10.

[34]Steve Lehman, "Arabian Recollections: The First Day," *Zymergy* 10 (Autumn 1991): p. 64.

[35]Alan Collins, "A Conversation with Novelist John Wain," *Zymergy* 9, (Spring 1991): p. 113.

[36]David Solway, "Fellatio, Depth-Analysis, and The Experience of the Surface," *Zymergy* 10 (Autumn 1991): 16.

[37]Skarstedt, "From *Modern Marriage* to Quebec's Literary Renaissance: An Interview With David Solway," *Zymergy* 6 (Autumn 1989): 55.

[38]Ibid., p. 55.

[39]Thomas Schnurmacher, "Montreal Poet Solway Finds Atwood a Dull Read," *Montreal Gazette* (2 Oct., 1989): B5.

[40]Skarstedt, "From *Modern Marriage* to Quebec's Literary Renaissance," p. 55.

[41]Skarstedt, "Editor's Note," *Zymergy* 10 (Autumn 1991): p. 5.

[42]Aileen Collins, *CIV/n: A Literary Magazine of the 50's* (Montréal: Véhicule Press, 1983), p. 10.

The Decline and Fall of the Athens of the North... / Benazon

[1]Ron Sutherland, "The Athens of the North," *Les Cantons de l'Est*, ed. Jean-Marie Dubois (Sherbrooke: Université de Sherbrooke, 1989), p. 266.

[2]Ron Sutherland, personal interviews, 10 Dec. 1994 and 8 Apr. 2000.

[3]Leonard Cohen wrote much of the manuscript of *The Spice-Box of Earth* in the summer of 1960, while staying in a cabin belonging to the Scott family on Lake Massawippi. His poem, "Summer Haiku," was engraved on a stone in the garden of Scott's cottage in North Hatley.

[4]Sheila Fischman, "A Night in August," *Matrix* 22 (Spring 1986): pp. 23-27; Dean Mullavey, interview, Oct. 1995; Sutherland, personal interview, 8 Apr. 2000.

[5]Fischman, "A Night in August," p. 25.

[6]Ibid., pp. 23-7.

[7]Sandra Djwa, *The Politics of the Imagination* (Toronto: McClelland & Stewart, 1987), pp. 320-21, 371-374.

[8]Robert Allen, "The Seventh Moon," *Matrix* 2 (Fall 1975): 17A.

[9]*Samisdat,* edited by Merritt Clifton, continued the *Berkeley Samisdat Review* [1973-1974], and was published from Brigham, Quebec and from its official publishing address in Richford, Vermont.

[10]Douglas Jones, personal interview, 1 Nov., 1995.

[11]Robert Allen, *Standing Wave* (Montréal: Véhicule, 2005).

IV. Poets and Places

Creation, Re-Creation, Recreation... / Lanthier

[1]George Steiner, *Errata, An Examined Life* (New Haven, Conn.: Yale University Press, 1998), p. 107.

[2]D. G. Jones, "Two Windows: An Interview with D.G. Jones," *Poetry Canada Review* 8 (Spring 1987): p. 4.

[3]Steiner, *Errata*, p. 111.

[4]Larry Shouldice, "Forward," *Ellipse* 27-28 (1981): p. 7.

[5]Colin Browne, "Introductory Notes," *Ellipse* 29-30 (1982): 15.

[6]Louise Blouin, Bernard Pozier and D. G. Jones, eds., *Esprit de Corps, Québec Poetry of the Late Twentieth Century in Translation* (Winnipeg: The Muses Company, 1997).

[7]Browne, "Introductory Notes," *Ellipse* 29-30 (1982): p. 12.

[8]Jones, ""Grounds for Translation," *Ellipse* 21(1977): p. 74.

[9]Eugène Guillevic, "Avant-propos," *Ellipse* 1 (Fall 1969): p. 4. Translation: a real place for exchange and an open line of communication.

[10]Guillevic, "Ellipse," trans. Teo Savery, *Ellipse* 1 (Fall 1969): p. 3.

[11]Michèle Lalonde, "Speak White," trans. D.G. Jones, *Ellipse* 3 (Spring 1970): 26.

[12]Jones, personal interview, 24 Sept., 2003.

[13]Lalonde, "Speak White," p. 29.

[14]Lalonde, "An Interview with Michèle Lalonde," interview conducted by D. G. Jones, *Ellipse* 3 (Spring 1970): p. 41.

[15]Browne, "Introductory Notes," *Ellipse* 29-30 (1982): 17.

[16]Unsigned, "Avant-propos," *Ellipse* 6 (Winter 1971): 4. Translation: A new reign of the word has arrived.

[17]Ibid., p. 5. Translation: Every word amplifies itself, echoing within the consciousness of all the living and all the dead of our history.

[18]Unsigned, "Editorial," *Ellipse* 6 (Winter 1971): p. 6.

[19]Raoul Duguay [Luoar Yaugud], "Lettre d'amour à Toulmonde," *Ellipse* 6 (Winter 1971): 34.

[20]Ibid., p. 35.

[21]Michel Garneau, "A G – (aile gauche)," *Ellipse* 6 (Winter 1971): p. 14.

[22]Garneau, "L W (Leftwing)," trans. Ronald Sutherland, *Ellipse* 6 (Winter 1971): p. 15.

[23]Translation: The real revolution is that of the imagination.

[24]Jones, "La vraie révolution est celle de l'imagination," *Ellipse* 6 (Winter 1971): 91. Translation: If there's no movement in the political sphere, there's no movement in the poetic sphere.

[25]Ibid., p. 91.

[25]Ibid., p. 93. Translation: The poet's discovery of his native land is strictly and fundamentally the discovery of his own body.

[27]Norman O. Brown, *Life Against Death: The Psychoanalytical Meaning of History*. (London: Routledge, 1959).

[28]Jones, "Introduction," *Esprit de Corps, Québec Poetry of the Late Twentieth Century in Translation*, ed. Louise Blouin, Bernard Pozier and D. G. Jones (Winnipeg: The Muses Company, 1997), p. 10.

[29]Ibid., p. 10.

[30]Ibid., p. 11.

[31]Jones, "Introduction," *Butterfly on Rock* (Toronto: University of Toronto Press, 1970), p. 9.

[32]Ibid., p. 9.

[33]Jones, "Grounds for Translation," p. 74.

[34]Ibid., p. 78.

[35]Ibid., p. 84.

[36]Colin Browne, "Introductory Notes," pp. 8-13.

[37]Ibid., p. 13.

[38]Jones, "Grounds for Translation," p. 86.

[39]Ibid., p. 88.

[40]Jones, "Foreword," *Ellipse* 50 (1993): p. 7.

[41]Marc Plourde, "On Translating Miron," in Gaston Miron, *Embers and Earth (Selected Poems)*, trans. D. G. Jones and Marc Plourde (Montréal: Guernica, 1984), p. 113.

[42]Judith Cowan, "The Translation of Poetry," *Ellipse* 21 (1977), p. 104.

[43]George Steiner, *After Babel, Aspects of Language and Translation* (Toronto: Oxford University Press, 1998), p. 318.

[44]Jones, "Forward," *Ellipse* 50 (1993): p. 8.

[45]Jones, "Gaston Miron: A Testimony," *Ellipse* 5 (Autumn 1970): 55-56.

[46]Gaston Miron, *Embers and Earth (Selected Poems)*, trans. D. G. Jones and Marc Plourde (Montréal: Guernica, 1984), pp. 76-77.

[47]Jones, "Gaston Miron: A Testimony," p. 56.

[48]Gaston Miron, "La marche à l'amour," trans. D. G. Jones, *Embers and Earth*, p. 68.

[49]Ibid., pp. 66-67.

[50]Marc Plourde, "On Translating Miron," p. 119.

[51]Ibid., p. 122.

[52]Jones, *Butterfly on Rock* (Toronto: University of Toronto Press, 1970), p. 183.

[53]Paul-Marie Lapointe, *The Terror of the Snows: Selected Poems*, trans. D. G. Jones (Pittsburgh: University of Pittsburgh Press, 1976), pp. xiv, xv.

[54]Ibid., p. xv.

[55]Lapointe, *The Terror of the Snows*, pp. 2-3.

[56]Jones, *Under the Thunder the Flowers Light up the Earth* (Toronto, Coach House, 1977), p. 64.

[57]Lapointe, "ICBM (Intercontinental Ballistic Missile)," *Le réel absolu, poèmes 1948-1965* (Montréal: L'Hexagone, 1971), p. 259.

[58]Lapointe, *The Terror of the Snows*, p. 56.

[59]Both these translations were dedicated to Jones's wife Monique Grandmangin, identified in the dedication to the Normand de Bellefeuille translation as his "Ariadne amid the maze of French syntax and semantic turns" and in the Martel translation as helping him avoid "gratuitous dissonance" in his rendition of the original's music. Grandmangin, an excellent translator in her own right, was active as an *Ellipse* editor for most of its years at the Université de Sherbrooke.

[60]Jones, "Afterward," in Normand de Bellefeuille, *Categorics one, two & three*, trans. D. G. Jones (Toronto: Coach House, 1993), p. 76.

[61]de Bellefeuille, "À chaque Jambe, L'inimaginable écart," *Catégoriques un deux*

et trios (Trois Rivières: Écrit des Forges, 1986), p. 35.

[62]de Bellefeuille, "With Each Leg, The Unforseeable Swerve," *Categorics one, two & three*, p. 33.

[63]de Bellefeuille, "Dans l'éclaircie et la gaieté," *Catégoriques un deux et trios*, p. 51.

[64]de Bellefeuille, "Amid Clearing and Gaiety," *Categorics one, two & three*, p. 49.

[65]de Bellefeuille, "With All the Precision Required," *Categorics one, two & three*, p. 72.

[66]de Bellefeuille, "Sur fond de figures diverses," *Catégoriques un deux et trios*, p. 71. Words and phrases in bold print appear as such in the original texts.

[67]de Bellefeuille, "Against a Background of Diverse Figures," *Categorics one, two & three*, p. 69.

[68]Translation: Myriam Bedard / amazing in Norway, with / her little rifle and her skis askew / halfway through the biathlon.

[69]Jones, "Like Fishing in Winter," *The Floating Garden* (Toronto: Coach House, 1995), p. 105.

[70]Émile Martel, *For Orchestra and Solo Poet*, trans. D. G. Jones (Winnipeg: J. Gordon Shillingford, 1996), p. 70.

[71]Martel, *Para Orquestra y Poeta Solo*, edición bilingüe, trans. Mónica Mansour (Trois Rivières: Écrits des Forges, 1999), p. 130.

[72]Martel, *For Orchestra and Solo Poet*, p. 68.

[73]Ibid., p. 70.

[74]Ibid., p. 70.

[75]Jones, "Fin de Siècle Springtime Ramble," *The Floating Garden*, p. 58.

[76]Ibid., p. 59.

[77]Martel, *For Orchestra and Solo Poet*, p. 65.

[78]Jones, "Singing Up The New Century," *Wild Asterisks in Cloud* (Montreal, Empyreal Press, 1997), p. 9.

[79]Jones, personal interview, 24 Sept., 2003.

[80]Ibid.

[81]Jones, "Words for the New Terrace," *Under the Thunder the Flowers Light up the Earth*, p. 28.

[82]Ibid., p. 28. Translation: something of ghost, with a pale brow, in a grey dress / with long grey stockings, her legs / as indistinct as smoke / didn't say a word.

[83]Translation: Nobody knows what it's called.

[84]Jones, "Words for the New Terrace," *Under the Thunder the Flowers Light up the Earth*, p. 29. Translation: Do they always fall on her pale skin?

[85]Jones, "Notes of Spring," *Grounding Sight* (Montréal: Empyreal Press, 1999), p. 78. Translation: and now what.

[86]Jones, "I Annihilate," *A Throw of Particles, the New and Selected Poetry of D. G. Jones* (Toronto: General, 1983), p. 60.

[87]Andrew Marvell, "The Garden," *The Complete Poems*, ed. Elizabeth Story Donno (Harmondsworth: Penguin, 1972), p. 101.

[88]Jones, "Two Windows: An Interview with D. G. Jones," *Poetry Canada Review* 8 (Spring 1987): 4.

[89]Ibid., p. 4.

[90]Jones, "Introduction," in Paul-Marie Lapointe, *The Terror of the Snows*, p. xv.

[91]Jones, "Note" to "Balthazar: The Real Thing," *Moosehead Review* 8 (1983): p. 25.

[92]Jones, *Balthazar and Other Poems*, (Toronto: Coach House, 1988), p. 12.

[93]Ibid., p. 18.

[94]Ibid., p. 30.

[95]Ibid., p. 29. Translation: I'm a reactionary / I go backwards / Goodbye.

[96]Ibid., p. 11.

[97]Michel Foucault, *The History of Sexuality, Volume 1, An Introduction*, trans. Robert Hurley (New York: Vintage Books, 1980), p. 48.

[98]Jones, "Christmas / going on," *The Floating Garden*, p. 23.

[99]Jones, "The *Matrix* Interview," *Matrix* 50 (1997): p. 16.

[100]Jones, "Foreword," *Ellipse* 60 (1999): p. 6.

[101]Ibid., p. 8.

[102]Jones, "Soon, Yes," *A Throw of Particles*, p. 94.

Michael Harris's Boo-Jhwah Appalachiana / Starnino

[1]Louis Dudek, *Epigrams* (Montreal: DC Books, 1975), p. 30.

[2]George Bowering, "Introduction," *The Vehicle Poets Now*, ed. Tom Knoyves and Stephen Morrissey (Winnipeg: The Muses' Company, 2004), p. 4.

[3]Al Purdy, *The Cariboo Horses* (Toronto: McClelland & Stewart, 1965); Irving Layton, *A Red Carpet for the Sun* (Toronto: McClelland & Stewart, 1959).

[4]A. M. Klein, *The Rocking Chair and other poems* (Toronto: Ryerson Press, 1948).

[5]Klein, "Portrait of the Poet as Landscape," *The Collected Poems* (Toronto: McGraw Hill Ryerson, 1974), pp. 330-335; John Glassco, "The Burden of Junk," *Selected Poems* (Toronto: Oxford University Press, 1971), pp. 25-27; Peter Van Toorn, "In Guidenstern County," *Mountain Tea* (Montreal: Véhicule Press, 2003), pp. 21-28; David Solway, "Stones in Water," *Bedrock* (Montréal: Véhicule Press, 1993), pp. 88-90.

[6]Michael Harris, *Text for Nausikaa* (Montreal: Delta Canada, 1970); *Sparks* (Lasalle, Québec: New Delta, 1976).

[7]Harris, *Grace* (Montréal: Delta, 1977); *In Transit* (Montreal: Véhicule Press, 1985); *New and Selected Poems* (Montreal: Véhicule Press, 1992).

[8]David Manicom, Review of *In Transit* by Michael Harris. *Rubicon* 8 (Spring 1987): p. 173.

[9]Anne Michaels, "Last Night's Moon," *Skin Divers* (Toronto: McClelland & Stewart, 1999), pp. 18-19.

[10]Seamus Heaney, *Opened Ground: Poems 1966-1996* (London: Faber & Faber, 1998), p. 21.

[11]Harris, *Grace*, p. 63.

[12]Harris, *New and Selected Poems*, p. 47.

[13]Ibid., p. 93.

[14]Harris, *Grace*, p. 20.

[15]Ibid., p. 42.

[16]Ibid., pp. 73, 34, and 27, respectively.

[17]Harris, *Grace*, pp. 22-23.

[18]Richard C. Davis, "Tradition and the Individual Talent of Charles Bruce," *The Dalhousie Review* 59 (Autumn 1979): p. 443.

[19]Libby Scheier, "Grace That Comes with Death," *Contemporary Verse II*, 4 (Spring 1980): pp. 32-33.

[20]David S. West, "Graceful Kindlings," *Fiddlehead* 121 (Spring 1979): 157-160

[21]Michael Hornyansky, "Poetry," *University of Toronto Quarterly* 47 (Spring/Summer 1979): p. 352.

[22]Kurt Van Wilt, "Gods of Order, Gods of Death," *Matrix* 9 (Spring/Summer 1979): 67.

[23]Harris, *Grace*, pp. 14-15.

[24]Ken Babstock. "The Appropriate Gesture, or Regular Dumb-Ass Guy Looks at Bird" [interview with Don McKay], *Where The Words Come From: Canadian Poets in Conversation*, ed. Tim Bowling (Roberts Creek, BC: Nightwood Editions, 2002), p. 47.

[25]David Solway, "Standard Average Canadian," *Directors Cut* (Erin, Ontario: Porcupine's Quill, 2003), pp. 87-100.

[26]Robert Allen, *The Encantadas* (Montréal: Conundrum Press, 2006), p. 125.

[27]Harris, *In Transit*, pp. 11-39. References for discussion of this poem shall appear as *IT* and page number, in my text.

[28]Clive James, "Somewhere Becoming Rain," *Reliable Essays: The Best of Clive James* (London: Picador, 2001), p. 34.

[29]Harris, *Grace*, pp. 53-78.

[30]Harris, *New and Selected Poems*, pp. 89-100.

[31]Harris, *In Transit*, p. 104.

[32]Ibid., p. 68.

[33]Harris, *New and Selected Poems*, p. 45.

[34]Harris, *Grace*, p. 34.

[35]Harris, *New and Selected Poems*, p. 15.

[36]William Wordsworth, "Preface" to the *Lyrical Ballads*. 1802. S.T. Coleridge and William Wordsworth, *Lyrical Ballads*, ed. W. J. B. Owen (Oxford: Oxford University Press, 1998), p. 165.

[37]Harris, "Speech," *Books in Canada* 31 (April 2002): p. 28.

"Global/local"... / Moyes

[1]I borrow this configuration of the relationship between the local and the global from the work of Rob Wilson and Wimal Dissanayake.

[2]This essay was first published as "'Global / local,' Montréal dans la poésie de Robyn Sarah, Mary di Michele et Erin Mouré," trans. Catherine Leclerc, *Voix et images* 90 (spring 2005), pp. 113-132. I would like to thank Jason Camlot, Wendy Eberle-Sinatra, Bennett Fu, Heike Härting, Marie-Claire Huot, Catherine Leclerc, Robert Majzels and Andrew Miller for their dialogue during the writing of this essay. Research for the project, enabled by funding from the Social Sciences and Humanities Research Council of Canada, was carried out with the assistance of

411

Najla Bahri and Richard Cassidy.

[3]See, for example: Michael Benazon, "Senses of Insecurity: Montreal Writers View their City," *Tangence* 48 (1995): pp. 97-115; Geoff Hancock, "What Now Montreal?" *Matrix* 20 (Spring 1985): pp. 5-15; Catherine Leclerc and Sherry Simon, "Zones de contacts. Nouveux regards sur la littérature anglo-québécoise," *Voix et images* 90 (Spring 2005): pp. 15-29; Linda Leith, "Quebec Fiction in English During the 1980s: A Case Study in Marginality," *Quebec Studies* 9 (Fall 1989/Winter 1990): 95-110; Lianne Moyes, ed., "Écrire en anglais au Québec: un devenir minoritaire?" *Quebec Studies* 26 (Fall 1998/Winter 1999): pp. 3-37; Gregory Reid, "Is There an Anglo-Québécois Literature?" *Essays on Canadian Writing* 84 (Winter 2005): forthcoming; and Sherry Simon, "L'anglophonie éclatée," *Spirale* 34 (1983): pp. 14-15.

[4]Erin Mouré, *Sheep's Vigil by a Fervent Person: A TransElation* [sic] *of Alberto Caeiro/Fernando Pessoa's O guardador de rebanhos* (Toronto: Anansi, 2001).

[5]The international frame of Metropolis bleu/Blue Metropolis is also suggested by the proliferation of words "bleu, blue, blau, blauw, azzurro, azul, kék."

[6]Doreen Massey, "A Global Sense of Place," *Marxism Today* (June 1991): p. 28.

[7]Ibid., p. 29.

[8]Rob Wilson and Wimal Dissanayake, "Tracking the Global/Local," *Global/Local: Cultural Production and the Transnational Imaginary* (Durham: Duke University Press, 1996), p. 5.

[9]Massey, "A Global Sense of Place," p. 28.

[10]Mary di Michele, *Stranger in You: Selected Poems & New* (Toronto: Oxford University Press, 1995.), p. 83.

[11]di Michele, "Invitation to Read Wang Wei in a Montréal Snowstorm," *Debriefing the Rose* (Toronto: Anansi, 1998), p. 27.

[12]Ibid., p. 27.

[13]Margaret Waller, "An Interview with Julia Kristeva," trans. Richard Macksey, *Intertextuality and Contemporary American Fiction*, ed. Patrick O'Donnell and Robert Con Davis (Baltimore: Johns Hopkins University Press, 1989), pp. 281-282.

[14]Yunte Huang, *Ethnography, Translation, and Transpacific Displacement: Intertextual Travel in Twentieth-Century American Literature* (Berkeley: University of California Press, 2002), p. 3.

[15]*O Cidadán* is signed by Erín Moure who, the back cover tells us, is "also known as Erin Mouré." This gesture of allowing accents to migrate is crucial; it not only destabilizes our sense of the coherence of "the writer" through time but also signals a shift in that writer's attention to her roots in Galicia in north-western Spain. Given that I cite several of her texts, some published under the name "Erin Mouré," I have chosen to use the later configuration throughout this essay.

[16]Elizabeth Grosz, "Bodies-Cities," *Sexuality and Space*, ed. Beatriz Colomina (New York: Princeton Architectural Press, 1992), p. 241.

[17]Mouré, *O Cidadán* (Toronto: Anansi, 2002), p. 47.

[18]Ibid., p. 42.

[19]Robyn Sarah, *Questions About the Stars* (London, Ont.: Brick, 1998), pp. 69, 108.

[20]Ibid., p. 11.

[21]Ibid., p. 88.

[22]Ibid., p. 91.

[23]Ibid., p. 37.

[24]Simon, "Entre les langues: l'écriture juive contemporaine à Montréal," *Montréal: l'invention juive*, ed. Groupe de Recherche Montréal Imaginaire (Montréal: Département d'études françaises, Université de Montréal, 1991.), p. 87.

[25]Sarah, *Questions About the Stars*, p. 61.

[26]Simon, "Entre les langues," pp. 88-89.

[27]Walter Benjamin, "Convolute H [The Collector]," *The Arcades Project*, trans. Howard Eiland and Kevin McLaughlin, (Cambridge, Mass.: Harvard University Press, 1999), p. 205.

[28]Michael P. Steinberg, "The Collector as Allegorist," *Walter Benjamin and the Demands of History*, ed. Michael P. Steinberg (Ithaca, NY: Cornell University Press, 1996), p. 89.

[29]Steinberg, "The Collector as Allegorist," pp. 92-93.

[30]See Esther Leslie, "Souvenirs and Forgetting: Walter Benjamin's Memory-work," *Material Memories: Design and Evocation*, eds. Marius Kwint, Christopher Breward and Jeremy Aynsley (New York: Berg, 1999), p. 109.

[31]Sarah, *Questions About the Stars*, p. 36.

[32]See the words of Benjamin in his notes on the "dialectical image": "Only the future has at its disposal a developer strong enough to let the image appear in all its details." Esther Leslie, "Souvenirs and Forgetting: Walter Benjamin's Memory-work." *Material Memories: Design and Evocation*, ed. Marius Kwint, Christopher Breward and Jeremy Aynsley (New York: Berg, 1999), p. 109.

[33]Sarah, *Questions About the Stars*, p. 61.

[34]Ibid., pp. 87, 88, 92 and 37, respectively.

[35]Sarah, *Questions About the Stars*, pp. 31, 37, 47, 61, 71.

[36]A preliminary version of this section of the essay, given as a conference paper in Rouen at the 2003 meeting of the Association française d'études canadiennes appeared in *Études canadiennes / Canadian Studies* 55 (Winter 2003): pp. 85-97.

[37]Huang, *Ethnography, Translation, and Transpacific Displacement* , pp. 1-7.

[38]Ibid., p. 65.

[39]The term "Orientalism," introduced into critical discourse by Edward Said, is further explored in Zhaoming Qian, *Orientalism and Modernism: The Legacy of China in Pound and Williams* (Durham: Duke University Press, 1995), pp. 1-6; and Yunte Huang, *Ethnography, Translation, and Transpacific Displacement*, pp. 6, 11, 68. Huang, for example, suggests that Pound's Imagistic principles create "a body of ethnographic discourse that fashions an image of the Orient projected largely through linguistic traits" (p. 11).

[40]"In old age I ask for peace / and don't care about things of this world. / I've found no good way to live / and brood about getting lost in my old forests. / The wind blowing in the pines loosens my belt, / the mountain moon is my lamp while I tinkle / my lute. You ask, / how do you succeed or fail in life? / A fisherman's song is deep in the river." Wang Wei, *Laughing Lost in the Mountains*, trans., Tony Barnstone, Willis Barnstone and Xu Haixin (Hanover: University Press of New

England, 1991), p. 22.

[41]di Michele, *Debriefing the Rose*, p. 27.

[42]See Denis Gravel, *Une approche historique et économique de la société Lachinoise, 1667-1767* (LaSalle: Société historique Cavelier-de-LaSalle, 1993), p. 8; and Normand Moussette, *En ces lieux que l'on nomma 'La Chine': Premiers volets d'une recherche touchant plus de trois siècles d'histoire* (Ville de Lachine, 1978), p. 21.

[43]François Dollier de Casson, *A History of Montreal, 1640-1672*, trans. Ralph Flenley (New York: E. P. Dutton, 1928), p. 327.

[44]Ibid., p. 327.

[45]Normand Moussette *En ces lieux que l'on nomma 'La Chine,'* p. 20; and Marcel Trudel, *The Beginnings of New France, 1524-1663*, trans. Patricia Claxton (Toronto: McClelland & Stewart, 1999), p. 99.

[46]Huang, *Ethnography, Translation, and Transpacific Displacement* , pp. 3-5.

[47]Qian, *Orientalism and Modernism*, p.109.

[48]Tony Barnstone and Willis Barnstone, "Introduction: The Ecstasy of Stillness," *Laughing Lost in the Mountains: Poems of Wang Wei* (Hanover: University Press of New England, 1991), p. ixx.

[49]Qian, *Orientalism and Modernism*, p. 88-109.

[50]Pound wrote in "Praefatio ad Lectorem Electum," for example, that "All ages are contemporaneous." Ezra Pound, "Praefatio ad lectorem Electum," *The Spirit of Romance* (New York: New Directions 1968), p. 5.

[51]Huang, *Ethnography, Translation, and Transpacific Displacement*, p. 5.

[52]Walter Benn Michaels, *Our America: Nativism, Modernism, and Pluralism* (Durham: Duke University Press, 1995), p. 108.

[53]di Michele, "Notes towards Reconstructing Orpheus: The Language of Desire," *Essays on Canadian Writing* 43 (Spring 1991): p. 21.

[54]di Michele, *Debriefing the Rose*, p. 27.

[55]Ibid., p. 28.

[56]T. S. Eliot credits Pound with the "invention of China." Marjorie Perloff, "The Contemporary of Our Grandchildren: Ezra Pound and the Question of Influence," *Poetic Licence: Essays on Modernist and Postmodernist Lyrics* (Evanston, Ill.: Northwestern University Press, 1990), p. 131.

[57]Mouré, "Poetry, Memory and the Polis," *Language in her Eye: Views on Writing and Gender by Canadian Women Writing in English*, eds. Libby Sheier, Sarah Sheard and Eleanor Wachtel (Toronto: Coach House, 1990), p. 205.

[58]Mouré, "The Anti-Anaesthetic," *Open Letter* 9 (1995): p. 21.

[59]Mouré, *O Cidadán*, p. 87.

[60]Grosz, "Bodies-Cities," p. 242.

[61]Ibid., p. 242.

[62]Mouré, *O Cidadán*, p. 51.

[63]Ibid., p. 50.

[64]Ibid., p. 52.

[65]Ibid., pp. 51, 53, 59, respectively.

[66]Ibid., p. 53.

[67]Lisa Dickson, "Signals Across Boundaries": Non-Congruence and Erin Mouré's *Sheepish Beauty, Civilian Love*," *Canadian Literature* 155 (Winter 1997): pp. 18-19.

[68]Mouré, "The Anti-Anaesthetic," p. 13.

[69]Mouré, "Poetry, Memory and the Polis," p. 203

[70]Mouré, *O Cidadán* , p. 39.

[71]Ibid., p. 47.

[72]Ibid., p. 47.

[73]Ibid., p. 63.

[74]Ibid., p. 63.

[75]Ibid., p. 42.

[76]Ibid., p. 42.

[77]Massey, "A Global Sense of Place," pp. 24-26; Pheng Cheah, "Given Culture: Rethinking Cosmopolitical Freedom in Transnationalism," *Cosmopolitics: Thinking and Feeling Beyond the Nation* (Minneapolis: University of Minnesota Press, 1998), pp. 296-297, 302.

[78]Caren Kaplan, "The Politics of Location as Transnational Feminist Critical Practice," *Scattered Hegemonies: Postmodernity and Transnational Feminist Practices*, eds. Inderpal Grewal and Caren Kaplan (Minneapolis: University of Minnesota Press, 1994), p. 148.

[79]Mouré, *O Cidadán*, p. 9. My emphasis.

[80]Ibid., p. 132.

[81]Ibid., p. 9.

[82]Ibid., pp. 63, 132.

[83]Ibid., p. 133.

[84]Ibid., p. 94.

[85]Ibid., p. 132.

[86]Ibid., n.p.

[87]Ibid., p. 87.

[88]Ibid., p. 42.

[89]Ibid.

[90]Ibid., p. 112.

[91]Ibid., p. 75.

[92]Ibid., p. 82.

[93]Massey, "A Global Sense of Place," p. 28.

[94]Sarah, *Questions About the Stars*, p. 61.

[95]"Cor anglais," *Wikipédia, l'encyclopédie gratuite et libre* <http: // fr.wikipedia.org/wiki/Cor_anglais>.

[96]Sarah, *Questions About the Stars*, p. 61.

[97]Mouré, *O Cidadán*, p. 82.

[98]It is worth noting that, writing in English, di Michele is herself already writing in a strange tongue. She does not need to come to Quebec to be a stranger; she is already one in Toronto. "What does it mean," asks di Michele" "to write in a language not your own?" The implications of such a practice, di Michele's essay suggests, are simultaneously enabling and alienating. Mary di Michele, "Notes towards

Reconstructing Orpheus: The Language of Desire," *Essays on Canadian Writing*, no. 43 (spring 1991), p. 14.

[99]Mouré, *O Cidadán*, p. 72.

[100]Ibid., p. 75.

Fugitive Places... / Irvine

[1]Anne Carson, "Decreation Aria," *Decreation: Poetry, Essays, Opera* (New York: Knopf, 2005), pp. 235.

[2]Northrop Frye, conclusion, *Literary History of Canada: Canadian Literature in English*, ed. Carl F. Klinck (Toronto: University of Toronto Press, 1965), p. 826.

[3]Kevin Flynn, "Introduction: Here We Are," *Essays on Canadian Writing* 71 (2000): pp. 2, 3.

[4]David McGimpsey, "A Walk in Montreal: Wayward Steps through the Literary Politics of Contemporary English Quebec," *Essays on Canadian Writing* 71 (2000): 165.

[5]Sherry Simon, "A Single Brushstroke: Writing through Translation: Anne Carson," *Journal of Contemporary Thought* 15 (2002): 90; "Crossing Town: Montreal in Translation," *Profession* (2002): p. 23. I would like to thank Ian Rae for drawing my attention to Sherry Simon's essays on Carson and translation theory and for sharing with me his forthcoming essay, "'Verglas': 'The Glass Essay' by Anne Carson," *Autres voix du dedans: la littérature anglo-québécoise*, ed. Catherine Leclerc (Québec: Nota Bene, forthcoming).

[6]Anne Carson, "Gifts and Questions: An Interview with Anne Carson," int. Kevin McNeilly, *Canadian Literature* 176 (2003): 13.

[7]Simon, "Crossing Town," p. 23; see also "Hybrid Montreal: The Shadows of Language," *Sites: The Journal of 20ʰh-Century/Contemporary French Studies* 5.2 (2001): pp. 315-330.

[8]David Solway, *Director's Cut* (Erin, Ont.: Porcupine's Quill, 2003), p. 60.

[9]Di Brandt, "Going Global," *Essays on Canadian Writing* 71 (2000): 106, 107.

[10]Ibid., p. 107.

[11]Nick Mount discusses the globalization of literature in *When Canadian Literature Moved to New York* (Toronto: University of Toronto Press, 2005), p. 162. The citation is from Eva Hemmungs Wirtén, *No Trespassing: Authorship, Intellectual Property Rights, and the Boundaries of Globalization* (Toronto: University of Toronto Press, 2005), p. 5.

[12]For an extensive analysis of Solway's critique of Carson, see Ian Rae, "Anne Carson and the Solway Hoaxes," *Canadian Literature* 176 (2003): pp. 45-65. For an encore of Solway's denunciations, see Carmine Starnino, "Eight Short Views," *A Lover's Quarrel: Essays and Reviews* (Erin, Ont.: Porcupine's Quill, 2004), pp. 247-65.

[13]David Solway, "The Trouble with Annie," *Books in Canada* 30 (July 2001): p. 25.

[14]Speaking in response to Kevin McNeilly's query about her minimalist bio-blurbs, Carson suggests that she does exert "control ... to keep [her] photography, biography, and blurbs off the cover." Carson, "Gifts and Questions," p. 24.

[15]Solway, "The Trouble with Annie," p. 26.

[16]Avital Ronell, *The Telephone Book: Technology—Schizophrenia—Electric Speech* (Lincoln: University of Nebraska Press, 1989), p. 321.

[17]Richard Cavell, "Here is Where Now," *Essays on Canadian Writing*, vol. 71 (2000), p. 196. Cavell's reference to "*Canadasein*" is taken from a chapter title in Avital Ronell's *The Telephone Book: Technology—Schizophrenia—Electric Speech*, p. 321.

[18]Anne Carson, "Short Talk on Where to Travel," *Short Talks* (London, Ont.: Brick Books, 1992), p. 21.

[19]Anne Carson, "The Anthropology of Water," *Plainwater* (New York: Knopf, 1995), p. 232.

[20]Carson, "The Life of Towns," *Plainwater*, p. 93.

[21]Anne Carson, "Dialogue without Sokrates: An Interview with Anne Carson," int. Dean Irvine, *Scrivener* 21 (1997): 83.

[22]Ibid., p. 83.

[23]Quoted in Anne Carson, *Economy of the Unlost (Reading Simonides of Keos with Paul Celan)* (Princeton: Princeton University Press, 1999), p. 29.

[24]Ibid., p. 10.

[25]Ibid., p. 129.

[26]Carson, *Plainwater*, p. 94.

[27]Ibid., p. 94.

[28]Anne Carson, trans., *If Not, Winter: Fragments of Sappho* (New York: Knopf, 2002), p. xi.

[29]Carson, "A Town I Have Heard Of," *Plainwater*, p. 105.

[30]Anne Carson, *Autobiography of Red: A Novel in Verse* (New York: Knopf, 1998), p. 5.

[31]Ibid., p. 5.

[32]Ibid., p. 5.

[33]Ibid., p. 46.

[34]Ian Rae suggests that Carson's Erytheia is "a combination of Stesichoros's mythic 'Red Place' and contemporary Montreal." "Erytheia," he elaborates, "is a North American island where older brothers play hockey (p. 34), where baby-sitters read from 'the loon book' (p. 32), where an American dollar bill is a 'novelty' (p. 29), and where schoolchildren examine 'beluga whales newly captured / from the upper rapids of the Churchill River' (p. 90)." (Ian Rae, "'Dazzling Hybrids': The Poetry of Anne Carson," *Canadian Literature*, vol. 166 (2000), p. 39 n6; Rae's citations from Carson, *Autobiography of Red*.) In addition, the presence of the unnamed volcano on the island suggests the faint traces of Montreal in Carson's island narrative: one of the persistent urban myths that circulates in Montreal guidebooks is that Mount Royal, the topographical centre of the city, is an extinct volcano. This is a myth, but one that adds to Carson's layering of mythological narratives in *Autobiography of Red*.

[35]Carson, *Autobiography of Red*, p. 37.

[36]Ibid., p. 4.

[37]Ibid., p. 4.

[38]Ibid., p. 37.

[39]Ibid., p. 14.

[40]Ibid., p. 4.

[41]Carson, *If Not, Winter*, p. xi.

[42]Ibid., pp. 10, 10, 11, 11, 12, 13, respectively.

[43]Ibid., p. xi.

[44]Carson, "Dialogue without Sokrates," pp. 83–84.

[45]Carson, *If Not, Winter*, p. 14.

[46]Ibid., pp. 6–7.

[47]Ibid., p. 6.

[48]Carson, *Economy of the Unlost*, p. 10.

[49]Carson, *If Not, Winter*, p. xiii.

[50]Carson, *Autobiography of Red*, p. 35.

[51]Ibid., pp. 37–38.

[52]Ibid., p. 60ff.

[53]Ibid., p. 145.

[54]Ibid., p. 108.

[55]Ibid., p. 145.

[56]Paul Celan (qtd. in Carson, *Economy of the Unlost*, p. 29).

[57]Anne Carson, "Interview with Anne Carson," int. Ken Chen, *Satellite Magazine* 1.1 (October 1999), http://www.readsatellite.com/culture/1.3/carson.chen.1.3.1.htm.

[58]Carson, *Autobiography of Red*, pp. 4, 5.

[59]Carson, "Interview with Anne Carson."

[60]Carson's blank book recalls a 1916 issue of Margaret Anderson and Jane Heap's avant-garde magazine, *The Little Review*, in which they printed only an editorial, protesting the dearth of quality submissions, and a cartoon, and left twelve pages blank.

[61]Rae, "Anne Carson and the Solway Hoaxes," p. 49.

[62]Roland Barthes, "The Death of the Author," *Image—Music—Text*, trans. Stephen Heath (Glasgow: Fontana/Collins, 1977), p. 142.

[63]Pierre Bourdieu, *The Field of Cultural Production: Essays on Art and Literature*, ed. Randal Johnson (New York: Columbia University Press, 1993), p. 75.

[64]Ibid., pp. 74, 75; emphasis in original.

[65]Ibid., p. 75.

[66]Another way in which Carson practices her "subversion of the whole marketing rigmarole" has been to produce hand-made books that resist publication. These books consist of "drawings, writing, photographs glued in, stapled" (Anne Carson, qtd. in Sarah Hampson, "The Unbearable Lightness of Anne Carson," *Globe and Mail* [14 September, 2000]: R1.) These books, according to Ian Rae, "she compiles by hand and distributes among friends."(Rae, "Anne Carson [1950–]," *The Literary Encyclopedia*, <http://www.litencyc.com/php/speople.php?rec=true&UID=758> (20 October 2006).

[67]Carson, *Economy of the Unlost*, (see esp. pp. 100–119).

[68]Ibid., p. vii.

[69]Ibid., p. viii.

[70]Carson, *Decreation*, p. 167.
[71]Ibid., p. 173.
[72]Ibid., p. 171.

Jabbed with Plenty... / Wells

[1]David Solway, *Director's Cut* (Erin, Ont.: The Porcupine's Quill), p. 25.

[2]Margaret Atwood, *Survival* (Toronto: House of Anansi, 1972), p. 120.

[3]As Solway says, "What begins to unite us is not so much the search [for roots] but the recognition that the search is good business. It helps politicians get elected, enables merchants to peddle their wares, provides media and university jobs, and hands over to the poets a ready-made subject ..." (David Solway, *Director's Cut*, p. 25.) This is of course not a new argument, as it was voiced by A. J. M. Smith, in very similar terms, as long ago as 1928.

[4]It is worth noting in this context that Maslow developed his theory of human motivation as a reaction to orthodox behaviourism and psychoanalysis, dominant procedural modes which he deemed to have an unhealthy preoccupation with pathology, in much the same way that orthodox approaches to Canadian literature—if not the bulk of the literature itself, as Atwood diagnoses it—have a morbid obsession with survival and victimhood, precluding the achievement of full human potential.

[5]M. Travis Lane, "An Unimpoverished Style: The Poetry of George Elliott Clarke," *Canadian Poetry* 16 (1985): pp. 1-20. Italics added.

[6]Peter Van Toorn, "Swinburne's Garden," *Mountain Tea* (Montréal: Véhicule Press, 2003), p. 60.

[7]As Atwood says, "In a lot of early Canadian poetry you find this desire to *name* struggling against a terminology which is foreign and completely inadequate to describe what is actually being seen. Part of the delight of reading Canadian poetry chronologically is watching the gradual emergence of a language appropriate to its objects" (Margaret Atwood, *Survival*, p. 62). This is to me a rather dubious assertion of literary evolution that begs the question of teleological progress and makes excuses for studying what would otherwise be dismissed as bad poetry.

[8]With the exception of one essay, by Douglas Burnet Smith, "Hyperbole in Peter Van Toorn's *Mountain Tea and Other Poems*," *Essays on Canadian Writing* 43 (Spring 1991): pp. 23-36.

[9]Tom Marshall, "Virtuoso Turns," *Canadian Literature* 103 (Winter 1984): 98.

[10]John Tucker, "Peter Van Toorn, *Mountain Tea and Other Poems*," *Journal of Canadian Poetry* 1 (1986): p. 109.

[11]Ibid., p. 112.

[12]Marshall, "Virtuoso Turns," p. 98.

[13]Van Toorn, "Mountain Stick," *Mountain Tea*, p. 92.

[14]Van Toorn, "In Guildenstern County," *Mountain Tea*, p. 25.

[15]Ibid., p. 21 ff.

[16]Van Toorn, "Epic Talk," *Mountain Tea*, p. 72.

[17]Van Toorn, "In Guildenstern County," *Mountain Tea*, p. 21.

[18]Ibid., 26.

[19]Ibid., 24

[20]This is an especially Canadian reference. The DEW (Distant Early Warning) Line is a string of radar sites in remote northern regions, established by the U.S. government to detect a possible Soviet attack on North America from the north. When Van Toorn writes of "radar caught up in the Queen's fuddy lace," he encapsulates the *Survival* theme of Canada caught between the USA and the U.K. Unlike Atwood and others, however, he dismisses this situation as "Nothing to get stung up about" (Van Toorn, "In Guildenstern County," *Mountain Tea*, p. 24)—probably an allusion to the Beatles' song "Strawberry Fields" in which "nothing is real, and nothing to get hung about."

[21]Van Toorn, "Epic Talk," *Mountain Tea*, pp. 80-2.

[22]Van Toorn, "Mountain Dragon," *Mountain Tea*, p. 114

[23]I concede that the "crone Huron on Bear / Island" in part three of "Epic Talk" could be construed as a symbol. It seems to me, however, that Van Toorn's portrait of the old man is imbued with a degree of disillusioned realism that makes him a credible character. At any rate, this instance, whether symbolic or not, is not strictly related to Van Toorn's Native fluency as I intend to define and describe it.

[24]Van Toorn, "Babel," *Mountain Tea*, p. 100.

[25]For my ideas about Van Toorn's aboriginality of idiom, I am in part indebted to Milton Acorn's notion of "Ojibway" as a universal language of poetry, as articulated in "On Speaking Ojibway":

> In speaking Ojibway you've got to watch the clouds
> turning, twisting, raising their heads
> to look at each other and you.
> You've got to have their thoughts for them
> and thoughts there'll be which would never
> exist had there been no clouds.
>
> Best speak in the woods beside a lake
> getting in time with the watersounds.
> Let vibrations of waves sing right through you
> and always be alert for the next word
> which will be yours but also the water's.
>
> No beast or bird gives a call
> which can't be translated into Ojibway.
> Therefore be sure Ojibway lives.
> There's no bending or breaking in the wind
> no egg hatching, no seed spring
> that isn't part of Ojibway.
> Therefore be sure Ojibway lives.
> The stars at night, their winking signals;

the dawn long coming; the first
thin cut of the sun at the horizon.
Words always steeped in memory
and hope that makes sure
by action that it's more than hope,
That's Ojibway, which you can speak in any language.
(Milton Acorn, "Minago," *The Island Means Minago* [Toronto: NC Press, 1975],
p. 110.)

As with many *ars poetica* statements in verse, Acorn's is, paradoxically, more
about how to "speak Ojibway" than it is an example of same (much as Archibald
MacLeish's famous poem, when it says that "A poem should not mean / But be,"
[Archibald MacLeish, " Title," *Collected Poems 1917-1982* {Boston: Houghton
Mifflin, 1985}, p. 107] contradicts itself). Many instances in Van Toorn's poetry, by
contrast, could be construed as statements of purpose, but he makes most of his
statements analogically rather than didactically, as in, for instance, "Mountain Leaf,"
discussed below. Generally, Van Toorn is more inclined to make overt statements
of poetics in prose essays.

[26]Van Toorn, "Babel," *Mountain Tea*, p. 100.

[27]Van Toorn, "A Goose in the Caboose: Ideas on the Sonnet," *Poetics.ca* 3 (Fall
2003), unpaginated. <http://www.poetics.ca/poetics03/03pvt.html> (23 December
2005).

[28]Van Toorn, "Mountain Boogie," *Mountain Tea*, p. 164.

[29]There is a compelling historical parallel to this kind of critical failure of eye
and ear to perceive the value and validity of "unorthodox" means of communication.
In the 1980s, in Gitxsan land claims hearings in Smithers, British Columbia, Chief
Justice Allen McEachern deemed inadmissible hundreds of hours of testimony in
the form of Gitxsan oral history and song. In his excellent book *The Other Side of
Eden: Hunters, Farmers, and the Shaping of the World*, anthropologist Hugh Brody
reproduces part of the courtroom transcript from the case, in which an elder, Mary
Johnson, wishes to include a traditional song as part of her testimony. McEachern's
response is: "I have a tin ear ... It's not going to do any good to sing to me. ... I
don't think that this is the way this part of the trial should be conducted. I just
don't think it's necessary. I think it is not the right way to present the case." (Hugh
Brody, *The Other Side of Eden: Hunters, Farmers, and the Shaping of the World* [New
York: North Point Press, 2001], p. 202.) Brody writes much as Atwood does about
the straight-line, square-peg mentality of European agriculturalists in Canada and
about the incompatibility of such approaches with aboriginal hunter-gatherer
mores and with nature itself.

[30]Douglas Burnet Smith, "Hyperbole in Peter Van Toorn's *Mountain Tea and
Other Poems*," p. 28.

[31]Ibid., p. 33.

[32]MacLeish, "Ars Poetica," *Collected Poems 1917-1952* (Cambridge, Mass.:
Houghton Mifflin, 1952), p. 41.

[33]Van Toorn, "Dragonflies, Those Bluejays of the Water," *Mountain Tea*, pp.
30-31.

[34]Van Toorn, "Mountain Leaf," *Mountain Tea*, p. 106.

[35]Solway has said of Van Toorn that he is "what we might call a *natural* poet, at one with the concrete world around him, and yet at the same time the most rigorous of verbal disciplinarians, one who still remembers how to gaffle a line." David Solway, *Director's Cut*, p. 103.

[36]Van Toorn, "Mountain Rain," *Mountain Tea*, p. 131.

[37]Van Toorn, "Mountain Maple," *Mountain Tea*, p. 144.

[38]Brody, *The Other Side of Eden: Hunters, Farmers, and the Shaping of the World*, p. 233.

[39]Ibid., p. 128.

[40]Marshall, "Virtuoso Turns," p. 98.

[41]For example: Susan Musgrave, of whom Carmine Starnino has said that "few Canadian poets have written poetry that boasts such a full quotient of shamanistic glamour." Carmen Starnino, *A Lover's Quarrel* (Erin: The Porcupine's Quill, 2004), p.173.

[42]Brody, *The Other Side of Eden: Hunters, Farmers, and the Shaping of the World*, p. 233.

[43]Ibid., p. 128.

[44]Van Toorn, "Beaudelaire," *Mountain Tea*, p. 53.

[45]Van Toorn, "Mountain Tea," *Mountain Tea*, p. 94.

[46]Tucker, "Peter Van Toorn," p. 111.

[47]Brody, *The Other Side of Eden: Hunters, Farmers, and the Shaping of the World*, p. 233.

[48]Ibid., pp. 248-9.

[49]Solway, *Director's Cut*, p. 27.

[50]Van Toorn, "Pigeon Feeder," *Mountain Tea*, p. 35. Italics added.

[51]Ibid., p. 36.

[52]It is noteworthy that Marshall praises the George Bowering's language, in contrast to Van Toorn's, for its cleanness. Marshall, "Virtuoso Turns," p. 98.

[53]Van Toorn, "Epic Talk," p. 86.

[54]Ibid., p. 85.

[55]Van Toorn, "A Goose in the Caboose: Ideas on the Sonnet," n.p.

[56]Van Toorn, "Rune," *Mountain Tea*, p. 17.

[57]For contemporary poems that exemplify what Van Toorn opposes, see Sharon Thesen's "Mean Drunk Poem" and "Hello Goodbye." In the former, Thesen writes "I get drunk // to lubricate my brain & all that comes out / of my Gap / is more bloody writing"; in the latter, "Helpless, / I yearn for this one or that one / happy in their houses or unhappy / as the case may be" (Sharon Thesen, "Mean Drunk Poem" & "Hello Goodbye," *The Broadview Anthology of Poetry*, ed. Herbert Rosengarten and Amanda Goldrick-Jones [Peterborough: Broadview Press, 1993], pp. 874-875). Thesen is, admittedly, an arbitrary choice; one could pick any number of poems from the 1980s preserved in any number of anthologies to illustrate the case that what poets like Van Toorn and M. Travis Lane were objecting to was ubiquitous and is still prevalent and valued by many critics.

[58]Waldo Frank, "Hart Crane," *The Complete Poems and Selected Letters and*

Prose of Hart Crane, ed. Brom Weber (Garden City: Anchor Books, 1966), p. 270.

[59]Atwood, *Survival*, p. 245. Italics added.

[60]Ibid., italics added.

[61]Van Toorn, "Babel," *Mountain Tea*, p. 101.

[62]Van Toorn, "Ode" *Mountain Tea*, p. 43.

[63]Van Toorn, "Babel," *Mountain Tea*, p. 101.

[64]Ibid., pp. 102-3.

[65]Tucker, "Peter Van Toorn," pp. 110-111.

[66]Atwood, *Survival*, p. 38.

[67]Ibid., p. 63.

[68]Ibid., p. 63.

[69]Sex and the erotic in *Mountain Tea* would make a rich topic for future discussion. Among Canadian poets, Irving Layton and Milton Acorn are perhaps Van Toorn's only rivals for sheer gusto of writing on the subject. When he digresses to comment on his own performance of dragonfly sex, it's not hard to read it as a playful jab at Acorn's "The Natural History of Elephants":

> ... As a whole
> much more truly quotable,
> more strictly independent and severe
> (though less essential, and with more art)
> than an elephant with one-storey shoulders
> and bouldering mind, swinging
> a rubber boom.
>
> (Van Toorn, "Dragonflies, Those Bluejays of the Water," *Mountain Tea*, p. 32.)

[70]Van Toorn, "Epic Talk" *Mountain Tea*, pp. 85-6.

[71]Katherine Barber, ed., *The Canadian Oxford Dictionary*, 2nd edition (Toronto: Oxford University Press, 2004), p. 583.

[72]The word "spirit" is often poo-pooed in this ironic and pragmatic age as a mystical vagary, but it bears remembering that the word's origins are by no means metaphysical. Rather, spirit is etymologically related to inspiration, and hence to breath, or "wind" in Van Toorn's symbological universe.

[73]Van Toorn, "Epic Talk" *Mountain Tea*, p. 84.

[74]Van Toorn, "Pigeon Feeder" *Mountain Tea*, p. 35.

[75]Van Toorn, "Icarus Like Crane" *Mountain Tea*, p. 65.

[76]Marshall, "Virtuoso Turns," p. 98.

[77]Nowlan, *Selected Poems*, p. 77.

[78]Solway, *Director's Cut*, p. 104.

An Appetite Abroad... / LoLordo

[1]Thanks to Jason Camlot, my editor, for slapping a couple extra slices of cheese on my theoretical burger.

[2]David McGimpsey, *Dogboy* (Toronto: ECW Press, 1998), p. 112.

[3]Ibid., p. 112.

[4]See George Ritzer, *The McDonaldization of Society* (Thousand Oaks, CA.: Pine

Forge Press, 1996), and Mark Alfino, John S. Caputo and Robin Wynyard, *McDonaldization Revisited: Critical Essays on Consumer Culture* (Westport, CT: Praeger, 1998).

[5]McGimpsey, *Dogboy*, p. 122.

[6]In the recent volume McGimpsey lists this originary gesture, referring, in a catalog of burgers, to "the hamburger placed on W. B. Yeats' grave" David McGimpsey, *Hamburger Valley, California* (Toronto: ECW Press, 2000), p. 9.

[7]This latter role has been persuasively analyzed by Jason Camlot, who sums up the persona of the early *Lardcake* poems with the unsurpassable epithet "couch poetato." My own account is indebted to Camlot's consideration of the peculiarly McGimpseyan pathos. In watching TV, McGimpsey exposes himself to "the delivery system of commodity life" (Jerry Mander, *Four Arguments for the Elimination of Television* [New York: Morrow, 1978], quoted in Camlot, "The Couch Poetatoe: Poetry and Television in David McGimpsey's *Lardcake*," *Postmodern Culture* 9.2 [January 1999]); in "Hamburger Valley", he engages in a nostalgic commodity tourism.

[8]This is also a specifically Canadian position. As Geoff Pevere and Greg Dymond argue in *Mondo Canuck*, our experience dispersed along the northern edge of the U. S. in a sparsely-populated, media-saturated, predominantly suburban environment has shaped a peculiar contemporary Canadian subjectivity: the dish-assisted snowbound cable junkie. See Pevere and Dymond, *Mondo Canuck: A Canadian Pop-Cultural Odyssey* (Toronto: Prentice Hall, 1996).

[9]David McGimpsey, *Lardcake* (Toronto: ECW, 1996), p. 77.

[10]Compare internal folk debates over which county's Guinness, which state's Coke, prevails. Such debates might be seen as a form of the "resistance" so beloved of cultural studies scholars, as a rewriting of the logic of advertising, in which brand abstraction underlies and enables the *global* debate between, say, *all* Coke and *all* Pepsi.

[11]McGimpsey, *Lardcake*, p. 77.

[12]This footnote honours the Montreal Expos, translated to Washington by the forces of monopoly capital since the initial drafting of this article.

[13]To reiterate, this is not to say that McGimpsey views the local as a privileged source of authenticity. The latter quality, rather, becomes just another marketing signifier, as in these lines, the climax of a bizarre ballade of Cajun romance: "'Would you like some pie?', Lou said to Ms. Lafitte / 'It's made of bog and sod and authentic Irish peat.'" (McGimpsey, *Dogboy*, p.38.)

[14]Of course such suspicion of the "Canadian" is without doubt a deeply Canadian attitude; one might compare McGimpsey's sensibility with that of Chris Woods, whose paintings might be characterized as minimally Canadian in their "content" while at the same time infused with a peculiarly Canadian attitude towards multinationals and their ubiquitous signifiers.

[15]Fredric Jameson, *Postmodernism, or, The Cultural Logic of Late Capitalism* (Durham: Duke University Press, 1991).

[16]McGimpsey, *Lardcake*, pp. 11, 95.

[17]Ibid, p. 17.

[18]This is not, of course, to praise the poetry for "impersonality," as if the ubiquitous burger were some beefy objective correlative.

[19]Charles Bernstein, *A Poetics* (Cambridge, Massachusetts and London, England: Harvard University Press, 1992), p. 20.

[20]McGimpsey, *Lardcake*, p. 96.

[21]For a classic example of the rhetoric of subversion and treachery in Canadian poetry polemics, see Keith Richardson's *Poetry and the Colonized Mind: Tish* (Oakville and Ottawa, Ontario: Mosaic Press, 1976).

[22]The contemporary burger, of course, has class-specific associations (compare the steak, "meat of the élite"), as can be seen in the title of Ray Kroc's (ghosted) memoir, *Grinding it Out*—a title which also carries a disturbing reminder of the burger's nature as *ground*-beef patty. Evidently memories of Upton Sinclair's *The Jungle* no longer resonated in 1970s America. (The full citation for Kroc is *Grinding it Out: The Making of McDonald's*, New York: Berkeley, 1977).

[23]Richard Rodriguez, *Days of Obligation: An Argument with My Mexican Father* (New York: Penguin, 1992), p. 158.

[24]Walt Whitman, *Leaves of Grass. The First (1855) Edition*, (New York: Penguin, 1976), p. 68.

[25]McGimpsey, *Hamburger Valley, California*, p. 34.

[26]Ibid, p. 35.

[27]Eric Schlosser, *Fast Food Nation: The Dark Side of the All-American Meal* (New York: HarperCollins, 2002), p. 17.

[28]He refers to this funding in "The Hamburger Song" (75), thus invoking, however briefly, the classic "Canadian in America" narrative (itself perhaps best seen as a belated, ironically self-aware variation on the American "innocent abroad" motif). Robert von Hallberg's chapter on "Tourists" astutely reads a similar dynamic, the self-definition of American poets in Europe on Fulbrights during the 1950s (von Hallberg, *American Poetry and Culture, 1945-1980*, [Cambridge, Mass. and London, England: Harvard University Press, 1985], pp. 62-92).

[29]In-N-Out is one of the older surviving burger chains, and a California original, having been founded in Irvine in 1948 (as the information display inside the In-N-Out down the street from my office informs me).

[30]McGimpsey, *Hamburger Valley, California*, p. 69.

[31]Ibid, p. 79.

[32]Ibid., p. 71.

[33]Ibid., p. 71.

[34]Kroc, *Grinding it Out*, pp. 7-8. Quoted in John A. Jakle and Keith A. Sculle, *Fast Food: Roadside Restaurants in the Automobile Age* (Baltimore: The Johns Hopkins University Press, 1999), p. 148.

[35]Kroc's McDonald's, as it developed, was noted for its refusal to hire young female staff. In this sense its family-oriented vision was a development from the traditionally male-oriented drive-in world. The metonymic associative moment of Kroc's originary myth thus leads to a full-fledged substitution: burger replaces blonde.

[36]McGimpsey, *Hamburger Valley, California*, p. 73.

425

[37]Jean Baudrillard, *Selected Writings*, ed. Mark Poster (Stanford: Stanford University Press, 1988), p. 19.

[38]While I first heard these lines in an imagined Bee Gees' falsetto ("more than a woman to me"), I have since learned from Jason Camlot that McGimpsey has in fact recorded a cover version of this particular track. In any case, the allusion, I'd argue, lays bare the dynamic that drives "Hamburger Valley." McGimpsey's scenario echoes the foundational process enacted by Kroc: ontogeny, we might say, recapitulates phylogeny. Again, burger *replaces* woman.

[39]McGimpsey, *Hamburger Valley, California*, p. 76.

[40]Baudrillard, *Selected Writings*, p. 21.

[41]Ibid, p. 22.

[42]Lacan here describes the problem of heterosexuality. Charles Shepherdson explicates the Lacanian distinction between the object of need and the object of demand, "the first being necessary to biological life, the second designating an object that belongs to the field of the Other." Eros "emerges *in the difference between need and demand*," and so its object cannot be attained through biological satisfaction (Charles Shepherdson, "The Elements of the Drive," *UMBR(a)* 1 [1997]: 139). We might say that the demand acting on the protagonist of "Hamburger Valley, California," is a demand that belongs to *the field of the Burger*.

[43]McGimpsey, *Hamburger Valley, California*, p. 75.

[44]Karl Marx, *Capital: A Critique of Political* Economy, Vol. 1, trans. Samuel Moor and Edward Aveling (New York: International Publishers, 1967), p.71.

[45]T. S. Eliot, *Collected Poems 1909-1962* (London: Faber & Faber, 2002), p. 57.

[46]McGimpsey, *Hamburger Valley, California*, p. 78.

[47]Ibid., pp. 80, 79.

[48]Ibid., p. 102.

[49]Baudrillard, *Selected Writings*, p. 48.

[50]Ibid, p. 49.

[51]McGimpsey, *Hamburger Valley, California*, p. 73.

[53]Ibid., p. 72. Here I cite the title of Greil Marcus' study, in which "dead" refers precisely to the uncanny afterlife of Elvis as a voice (body, etc.) that can be appropriated, potentially retaining a certain counter-hegemonic or anarchic force. Elsewhere in the poem Elvis is sung, the protagonist of a losing battle: "Hungry Presley Agonistes / fought the burger's dark delight" only to end up asking for one "real well-done" (McGimpsey, *Hamburger Valley, California*, p. 81).

[54]A famous exchange from *Hamlet* (IV, II, 17-19) springs to mind here (for "body," we might read "burger"):

Ham. The body is with the King, but the King is not with the body. The King is a thing—

Guil. A thing, my lord!

Ham. Of nothing.

[55]McGimpsey, *Hamburger Valley, California*, p. 88.

[56]Ibid., p. 62.

[57]Ibid., p. 62.

[58]Ibid., p. 95.

[59]Ibid., p. 102.

[60]Walt Whitman, *Leaves of Grass. The First (1855) Edition*, ed. Malcolm Cowley (New York: Viking, 1973), p. 43.

[61]McGimpsey, *Hamburger Valley, California,* p. 83.

[62]For Venturi and Scott Brown, Las Vegas was the definitive post-modern landscape, existing as a linear array of signs and parking spaces, and incomprehensible in terms of sculptural modernist paradigms of architectural space.

[63]McGimpsey, *Hamburger Valley, California*, p. 82.

[64]Baudrillard, "The Ecstasy of Communication" in *The Anti-Aesthetic*, ed. Hal Foster (Port Townsend, WA: The Bay Press, 1983), p.127.

[65]McGimpsey, *Hamburger Valley, California*, p. 92.

[66]Ibid., p. 99.

[67]Ibid., p. 99.

[68]Bernstein, p. 21.

[69]McGimpsey, *Hamburger Valley, California*, p. 96.

[70]Ibid., p. 96.

[71]Ibid., p. 97.

"What I Do Best, What I Do Now"... / Swift

[1]This essay was written before and just after Robert Allen's death, at the age of 60, on November 3, 2006, from cancer. No attempt has been made in the light of this sad event to change the tone of the article, to force a too-immediate sort of summing up. It remains the first comprehensive overview of an exceptional poet in early-late career.

[2]Ammons in interview: Steven P. Schneider, "Part IV: from The Wind To The Earth: An Interview With A. R. Ammons," *Complexities of Motion: New Essays On A.R. Ammons's Long Poems*, ed. Steven P. Schneider (Cranbury: Associated University Presses, 1999), p. 329.

[3]As Randall Jarrell once said of John Crowe Ransom's poetry. Randall Jarrell, "John Ransom's Poetry," *Poetry and The Age* (New York: Vintage Books, 1955), p. 87.

[4]William Wordsworth, "The Tables Turned," *Poems Selected by Seamus Heaney* (London: Faber & Faber, 2001), pp. 32-33.

[5]Carmine Starnino, *A Lover's Quarrel* (Erin: The Porcupine's Quill, 2004), p. 84.

[6]Robert Allen, "Fetishists," *The Assumption of Private Lives* (LaSalle: New Delta, 1977), p. 56.

[7]Allen, "Events in the Childhood of Freud," *Magellan's Clouds: Poems 1971-1986* (Montréal: Véhicule Press, 1987), pp. 33-34.

[8]Anglo-Quebec poetry has proven more wintry and unforgiving for some than others. Take the case of the tragically isolated poet, broadcaster John Bishopric (stage name John Grenfell), friend to John Glassco among other Eastern Townships-based literary figures, whose superb voice interpreted poems on CBC radio programmes for many years, but whose own difficult, long modernist works, such as "The Cosmosis Odes" (grandly opening, after a quote from Pound, "Earth/ - spun / topspun / prone / the sound sleeper / stirs") remain mainly unheard,

unpublished, unduly neglected and still waiting for their apt advocate. Bishopric's poetry is not as obscure as his current reputation which was partially due to his own reluctance to submit work during his life, which ended in 1996. In an icy climate, poets do not always find an adequate handhold.

[9]*Matrix* is Quebec's longest-running English-language literary journal.

[10]Robert Allen, Stephen Luxton and Mark Teicher, *Late Romantics* (Ayer's Cliff: The Moosehead Press, 1980). From the back cover.

[11]Allen, *One Night At The Indigo Hotel* (Dunvegan: Cormorant Books, 1986), p.17.

[12]"But what seems hard to refute is that after two centuries of striving, and three decades after the first organized push in the 1970s to track down, encourage and anthologize representative poets, we have yet to serve up a single career able to excite—as A.D. Hope and Les Murray have for Australia—worldwide attention for our verse. Who has introduced our aesthetic into the maps of English poetry?" (Carmine Starnino, *A Lover's Quarrel*, p. 34.).

[13]Klein, Layton and Cohen's collected or selected works are not currently in print in the United Kingdom; and, the latest American anthology of Canadian Poetry, edited by Sina Queyras, *Open Field* (New York: Persea Books, 2005) was, as unlikely as it sounds, the first such American survey in more than thirty years.

[14]Mordecai Richler, *Canadian Writing Today* (Middlesex: Penguin Books, 1970).

[15]Allen, Luxton, Teicher, *Late Romantics*, p. 21.

[16]Arguably, Luxton's and Allen's work is most British when inspired by certain American post-Beat poets like Dorn or O'Hara, key figures to many poets in the contemporary British avant-garde.

[17]Several poem's in Luxton's third full collection, *Luna Moth and other poems* (Montreal: DC Books, 2004) present his version of the new urban-pastoral hybrid genre I am suggesting here, such as "The Angler Re-connects", "Boreal Phantasmagoria" and "September Campfire on the Gouin Reserve".

[18]Allen, Luxton, Teicher, *Late Romantics*, pp. 15-16.

[19]Allen, *Wintergarden* (Dunvegan: Quadrant Editions, 1984), p. 39.

[20]Allen, *Standing Wave* (Montreal: Véhicule Press, 2005), p. 51.

[21]Allen, *The Encantadas* (Montreal: Conundrum Press, 2006), title page.

[22]Allen, *The Encantadas*, section 64 (the book is not paginated but the sections are each a page long and correspond, more or less, to a standard pagination system).

[23]Bert Almon, "Song of the Sea," interview with Robert Allen, *Montreal Review of Books* 9.4 (Summer 2006): 9.

[24]Yvor Winters, *On Modern Poets* (New York: Meridian Books, 1959), p. 86.

[25]Allen, *The Encantadas*, section 34.

[26]A.R. Ammons, *Sphere: The Form of a Motion* (New York: W.W. Norton and Company, 1974) and *Garbage* (New York: W.W. Norton and Company, 1993).

[27]Allen, *The Encantadas*, section 38.

[28]Ibid., section 2

[29]Winters, *On Modern Poets*, p. 77.

[30]Allen, *The Encantadas*, section 4.

[31]Schneider, p. 334.

[32]Allen, *Standing Wave*, p. 51.

[33]Schneider, p. 329.

[34]Ibid., p. 342.

[35]Ibid., p. 343.

[36]Allen, *The Encantadas*, section 53.

[37]Winters, *On Modern Poets* (New York: Meridian Books, 1959), pp. 120-143.

[38]Allen, *The Encantadas*, section 45; "Buzzards of death emerge" from this Mexican sojourn, as they did for Crane.

[39]Winters, *On Modern Poets*, p. 141.

[40]Allen, *The Encantadas*, section 54.

[41]Ibid., sections 54 and 55.

[42]Allen, *Standing Wave*, p. 11.

[43]Ibid., p. 41.

[44]Ibid., p. 26.

[45]Ibid., p. 33.

[46]Ibid., p. 31.

[47]Allen, *Ricky Ricardo Suites* (Montreal: DC Books, 2000), p. 23.

[48]This sort of darkly comic cinematic virtuosity is par for the course—Allen is a master impersonator, whose James Mason (Kubrick's Humbert Humbert) is dead-on.

[49]Almon, p. 13.

[50]Allen, *Ricky Ricardo Suites*, p. 21.

[51]Ibid., p. 75.

[52]Stravinsky was no stranger himself to doomed, late-night poets, having written *In memoriam Dylan Thomas*.

[53]Allen, *Ricky Ricardo Suites*, frontispiece.

[54]Ibid., pp. 24, 25.

[55]Ibid., p. 26.

[56]Robert Allen, "Magellan's Clouds," *Wintergarden*, p. 20.

[57]Robert Allen, *Napoleon's Retreat* (Montreal: DC Books, 1997). See for instance "Book Seven: Adventures of a Girl Gone Bad" with its tour-de-force listing of place names, starting with "Where would you fetch up?" and ending with "Aix on Wye", pp. 287-295.

[58]Allen, *Ricky Ricardo Suites*, p. 23. Italics in the original text.

[59]Ibid., p. 23.

[60] Ibid., p. 23.

[61]Ibid., p. 23.

Bibliography

Acorn, Milton. *The Island Means Minago*. Toronto: NC Press, 1975.

Alfino, Mark, John S. Caputo and Robin Wynyard. *McDonaldization Revisited: Critical Essays on Consumer Culture*. Westport, Connecticut: Praeger, 1998.

Allen, Robert. *The Assumption of Private Lives*. Montreal: New Delta, 1977.

_____. *Blues & Ballads*. Ithaca: Ithaca House Press, 1974.

_____. *The Encantadas*. Montréal: Conundrum Press, 2006.

_____. *The Hawryliw Process*. Erin: Porcupine's Quill Press, 1979 & 1980.

_____. *Magellan's Clouds: Poems 1971-1986*. Montreal: Véhicule Press, 1987.

_____. *Napoleon's Retreat*. Montréal: DC Books, 1997.

_____. *One Night At The Indigo Hotel*. Dunvegan: Cormorant Books, 1986.

_____. *Ricky Ricardo Suites*. Montréal: DC Books, 2000.

_____. "The Seventh Moon." *Matrix* 2 (Fall 1975): 17A-24H.

_____. *Standing Wave*. Montréal: Véhicule Press, 2005.

_____. *Valhalla at the OK*. Ithaca: Ithaca House Press, 1971.

_____. *Wintergarden*. Dunvegan: Quadrant Editions, 1984.

Allen, Robert, Stephen Luxton and Mark Teicher. *Late Romantics*. Ayer's Cliff: The Moosehead Press, 1980.

Almon, Bert. "Song of the Sea." Interview with Robert Allen. *Montreal Review of Books* 9.4 (Summer 2006): 8-9. 13.

Ammons, A. R. *Garbage* New York: W. W. Norton and Company, 1993.

_____. *Sphere: The Form of a Motion*. New York: W. W. Norton and Company, 1974.

Anderson, Fortner. *Sometimes I Think*. Audio CD. Montreal: Wired on Words, 1999.

Anderson, Fortner, et al. *Oralpalooza 94 Montreal*. Audio CD. Montreal: ga Press, 1994.

Anderson, Fortner and Ian Ferrier. *Wired on Words*. Audio Cassette and Chapbook. Montréal: Wired on Words and ga press, 1994.

Atwood, Margaret. *Survival*. Toronto: House of Anansi Press, 1972.

Austin, J. L. *How to Do Things with Words*. 1962. Cambridge, Massachusetts: Harvard University Press, 1975.

Babstock, Ken. "The Appropriate Gesture, or Regular Dumb-Ass Guy Looks at Bird." Interview with Don McKay. *Where The Words Come From: Canadian Poets in Conversation*. Ed. Tim Bowling. Roberts Creek, BC:

Nightwood Editions, 2002: 44-61.

Baillargeon, Stéphane. "Le mur des lamentations." *Le Devoir* [Montréal]. (14 sep. 1999), B8.

Bancroft, Hubert H., ed. *The Great Republic by the Master Historians*, Vol. 1. <http://www.humanitiesweb.org/human.php?s=n&p=l&a=i&ID=18> (11 November 2006).

Bantey, Ed. "Letters from cowardly anglos full of hate and racism." *Gazette* [Montreal] (3 June 1990): A2.

Barber, Katherine, ed. *The Canadian Oxford Dictionary*. Second Edition. Toronto: Oxford University Press, 2004.

Barnstone, Tony, Willis Barnstone and Xu Haixin, trans. *Laughing Lost in the Mountains: Poems of Wang Wei*. Hanover: University Press of New England, 1991.

Barthes, Roland. "The Death of the Author." *Image–Music–Text*. Trans. Stephen Heath. Glasgow: Fontana/Collins, 1977.

Batten, Jack. "Leonard Cohen: The Poet as Hero." *Saturday Night* 84 (June 1969): 23-26.

Baudrillard, Jean. *Selected Writings*. Ed. Mark Poster. Stanford: Stanford University Press, 1988.

_____. "The Ecstasy of Communication." *The Anti-Aesthetic*. Ed. Hal Foster. Port Townsend, Wash.: The Bay Press, 1983. 126-133.

Beauchemin, Yves. "Parler français, pour combien de temps?" *Le Devoir* [Montréal] (9 Mar. 1999): A7.

Beaulieu, Carole. "C'est la culture … Stupid!" *L'Actualité* (15 Mar. 1997): 56-59.

Benazon, Michael. "Irving Layton and the Montréal Poets." *Matrix* 20 (Spring 1985): 16-20.

_____. "Senses of Insecurity: Montreal Writers View their City." *Tangence* 48 (1995): 97-115.

Benjamin, Walter. "Convolute H [The Collector]." *The Arcades Project*. Trans. Howard Eiland and Kevin McLaughlin. Cambridge, Mass.: Harvard University Press, 1999. 203-211.

Benn Michaels, Walter. *Our America: Nativism, Modernism, and Pluralism*. Durham: Duke University Press, 1995.

Bernstein, Charles. "Against National Poetry Month As Such." <http://www.press. uchicago.edu/Misc/Chicago/044106.html> (26 April 1999).

_____. *A Poetics*. Cambridge, Massachusetts: Harvard University Press, 1992.

_____. "Introduction." *Close Listening: Poetry and the Performed Word*. Ed. Charles Bernstein. New York: Oxford University Press, 1998: 3-26.

Bernstein, Charles, ed. *Close Listening: Poetry and the Performed Word*. New York: Oxford University Press, 1998.

Bissonnette, Lise. "Vu du Woody's Pub." *Le Devoir* [Montréal] (18 Sep. 1991): A8.

Blanchette, Josée. "L'Anglo tout nouveau, tout beau." *Le Devoir* [Montréal] (2 June 1999): B1.

Blodgett, E. D. *D. G. Jones and His Works*. Toronto: ECW Press, 1984.

_____. "*Transfiguring* Transfiguration." *Ellipse* 64 (2000): 16-23.

Blouin, Louise, and Bernard Pozier, eds. *Anthologie poètes québécois*. Trois Rivières: Écrits des Forges, 2001.

Blouin, Louise, Bernard Pozier and D.G Jones, eds. *Esprit de corps: Québec Poetry of the Late Twentieth Century in Translation*. Winnipeg: The Muses' Company, 1997.

Boisvert, Yves. "Anthropologie de l'Anglo-Montréalais." *La Presse* [Montréal] (5 June 2000): A5.

Bordeleau, Françine. "La Révolution anglaise." *Lettres Québécoises* 93 (Spring 1999): 17-21.

_____. Littérature anglo-québécoise: une minorité fort." Lettres Québécoises 124 (Hiver 2006): 16-18.

Bouhis, Richard. "Introduction and Overview of Language Events in Canada." *International Journal of the Sociology of Language* 105/106 (1994): 5-36.

Bourdieu, Pierre. *The Field of Cultural Production: Essays on Art and Literature*. Ed. Randal Johnson. New York: Columbia University Press, 1993.

Boutros, Alex, Taien Ng-Chan and Karla Sundström, eds. *Ribsauce: a CD/Anthology of Words by Women*. Audio CD and Book. Montréal: Véhicule Press, 2001.

Bowering, George. "Introduction." *The Vehicle Poets Now*. Ed. Tom Knoyves and Stephen Morrissey. Winnipeg: The Muses' Co., 2004: 1-6.

_____. "On Not Teaching the Vehicle Poets." *Vehicule Days: An Unorthodox History of Montreal's Vehicle Poets*. Ed. Ken Norris. Montréal: Nuage, 1993. 115-117.

Brandt, Di. "Going Global." *Essays on Canadian Writing* 71 (2000): 106–113.

Brody, Hugh. *The Other Side of Eden: Hunters, Farmers, and the Shaping of the World*. New York: North Point Press, 2001.

Brown, Norman O. *Life Against Death: The Psychoanalytical Meaning of History*. London: Routledge, 1959.

Browne, Colin. "Introductory Notes." *Ellipse* 29/30 (1982): 6-17.

Cabico, Regie and Todd Swift, eds. *Poetry Nation*. Montréal: Véhicule Press, 1998.

Camlot, Jason. "The Couch Poetato: Poetry and Television in David McGimpsey's *Lardcake*." *Postmodern Culture* 9.2 (January 1999): n.p.

Cantin, David. "David Solway, un poète en exil." *Le Devoir* [Montréal] (18 déc. 2004): F8.

Carpenter, Humphrey. *A Serious Character: The Life of Ezra Pound*. New York:

Delta, 1988.

Carson, Anne. *Autobiography of Red: A Novel in Verse*. New York: Knopf, 1998.

_____. *Decreation: Poetry, Essays, Opera*. New York: Knopf, 2005.

_____. "Dialogue without Sokrates: An Interview with Anne Carson." Interviewed by Dean Irvine. *Scrivener* 21 (1997): 80–87.

_____. *Economy of the Unlost (Reading Simonides of Keos with Paul Celan)*. Princeton: Princeton University Press, 1999.

_____. "Gifts and Questions: An Interview with Anne Carson." Interviewed by Kevin McNeilly. *Canadian Literature* 176 (2003): 12–25.

_____. "Interview with Anne Carson." Interviewed by Ken Chen. *Satellite Magazine* 1.1 (October 1999). <http://www.readsatellite.com/culture/1.3/carson.chen.1.3.1.htm>

_____. *Plainwater*. New York: Knopf, 1995.

_____. *Short Talks*. London, Ontario: Brick Books, 1992.

Carson, Anne, trans. *If Not, Winter: Fragments of Sappho*. New York: Knopf, 2002.

Cavell, Richard. "Here Is Where Now." *Essays on Canadian Writing* 71 (2000): 195–202.

Caya, Rudy. "Je Me Souviens." *Vilain Pingouin-Y'é quelle heure?* Sound Recording. Montréal: Audiogram, 1998.

Cheah, Pheng. "Given Culture: Rethinking Cosmopolitical Freedom in Transnationalism." *Cosmopolitics: Thinking and Feeling Beyond the Nation*. Minneapolis: University of Minnesota Press, 1998: 290-328.

Chester, Bronwyn. "Small Magazines, Big Influence." *McGill Reporter* (11 March 1999): front page. <http://ww2.mcgill.ca/uro/Rep/r3112/literary.html>.

Cogswell, Fred, ed. and trans. *The Poetry of Modern Quebec: An Anthology*. Montréal: Harvest House, 1976.

Cohen, Leonard. *The Favorite Game*. New York: Viking, 1963.

Collins, Aileen, ed. *CIV/n: A Literary Magazine of the 50's*. Montréal: Véhicule, 1983.

_____, ed. *In Defence of Art: Critical Essays & Reviews*. Kingston: Quarry, 1988.

Collins, Alan. "A Conversation with Novelist John Wain." *Zymergy* 9 (Spring 1991): 107-113.

Cowan, Judith. "The Translation of Poetry." *Ellipse* 21 (1977): 102-104.

D'Agostino, Sara. "The War Goes On: A Conversation with Irving Layton." *Acta Victoriana* 100 (Fall 1975): 9-16.

Davey, Frank. *Louis Dudek & Raymond Souster*. Vancouver: Douglas & McIntyre, 1980.

Davey, Frank and bp Nichol, eds. *Open Letter* 4 (Spring/Summer 1981).

Davis, Richard C. "Tradition and the Individual Talent of Charles Bruce." *Dalhousie Review* 59 (Autumn 1979): 443-451.

de Bellefeuille, Normand. *Catégoriques un deux et trois*. Trois Rivières: Écrit des

Forges, 1986.

_____. *Categorics 1, 2 & 3*. Trans. D. G. Jones. Toronto: Coach House, 1993.

Deleuze, Gilles and Félix Guattari. *Kafka: Toward a Minor Literature*. Trans. Dana Polan. Minneapolis: University of Minnesota Press, 1986.

Dickson, Lisa. "Signals Across Boundaries": Non-Congruence and Erin Mouré's *Sheepish Beauty, Civilian Love*." *Canadian Literature* 155 (Winter 1997): 16-37.

Diamond, Ann. "How I Became a Terrorist, Or: Humour As a Terrorist Weapon." *Zymergy* 2.2 (Autumn 1988): 53-56.

di Michele, Mary. "Invitation to Read Wang Wei in a Montréal Snowstorm." *Debriefing the Rose: Poems*. Toronto: Anansi, 1998: 27-28.

_____. "Notes towards Reconstructing Orpheus: The Language of Desire." *Essays on Canadian Writing* 43 (Spring 1991): 14-22.

_____. *Stranger in You: Selected Poems & New*. Toronto: Oxford University Press, 1995.

Dion, Jean. "Puerto Plateau." *Le Devoir* [Montréal] (6 Apr. 2000): A3.

Djwa, Sandra. *The Politics of the Imagination*. Toronto: McClelland & Stewart, 1987.

Dollier de Casson, François. *A History of Montreal, 1640-1672*. Trans. Ralph Flenley. New York: E. P. Dutton, 1928.

Dudek, Louis. *1941 Diary*. Ed. Aileen Collins. Montreal: Empyreal, 1996.

_____. "Academic Literature." 1944. *The Making of Modern Poetry in Canada*. Ed. Louis Dudek and Michael Gnarowski. Toronto: The Ryerson Press, 1967: 104-106.

_____. "Anne Hébert Translated: Some Thoughts on Dual Literature in Canada." *In Defence of Art: Critical Essays & Reviews*. Ed. Aileen Collins. Kingston: Quarry, 1988: 207-09.

_____. "Aquin's *Prochain Épisode* is Nearer Poetry than Prose." *In Defence of Art: Critical Essays & Reviews*. Ed. Aileen Collins. Kingston: Quarry, 1988. 194-95.

_____. "A Real Good Goosin': Talking Poetics." *An Unorthodox History of Montreal's Vehicle Poets*. Ed. Ken Norris. Montréal: Nuage, 1993: 57-79.

_____. "Autobiographical Sketch 1951." *Open Letter* 4 (Spring/Summer 1981): 309-15.

_____. "Committed to Excellence." Interview. *Books in Canada* 22 (November 1993): 7-12.

_____. "The Critical Essays of Jean Éthier-Blais—A Notable Literary Contribution." *In Defence of Art: Critical Essays & Reviews*. Ed. Aileen Collins. Kingston: Quarry: 1988. 205-07.

_____. *Dk/ Some Letters of Ezra Pound*. Montreal: DC Books, 1974.

_____. *East of the City*. Toronto: Ryerson, 1946.

435

_____. *Epigrams*. Montreal: DC Books, 1975.

_____. "Fusing Our Two Literatures." *In Defence of Art: Critical Essays & Reviews*. Ed. Aileen Collins. Kingston: Quarry, 1988: 155-57.

_____. "F.R. Scott and the Modern Poets." *Selected Essays and Criticism*. Ottawa: Tecumseh, 1978: 11-23.

_____. "Geography, Politics, and Poetry." *Open Letter* 4 (Spring/Summer 1981): 141-42.

_____. "Gilles Vigneault: Poet of Natashquan." *In Defence of Art: Critical Essays & Reviews*. Ed. Aileen Collins. Kingston: Quarry, 1988: 191-93.

_____. "Introduction." *Some Poems of Jean Narrache*. Unpublished manuscript, 1999.

_____. *Dudek, l'essentiel*. Trans. Pierre DesRuisseaux. Montréal: Les éditions Triptyque, 1997.

_____. "Louis Dudek 1918 - ." *Contemporary Authors Autobiography Series*. Vol. 14. Ed. Joyce Nakamura. Detroit: Gale, 1991: 121-42.

_____. "The Montreal Poets." *Culture: A Quarterly Review* 18 (1957): 149-154.

_____. "The Montreal Poets." *Selected Essays and Criticism*. Ottawa: Tecumseh, 1978: 59-64.

_____. "The Monument." *In Defence of Art: Critical Essays & Reviews*. Ed. Aileen Collins. Kingston: Quarry, 1988. 176-79.

_____. "The New Oxford Book of Canadian Verse in English." *In Defence of Art: Critical Essays & Reviews*. Ed. Aileen Collins. Kingston: Quarry, 1988: 244-47.

_____. "On Getting to Know Nelligan." *Open Letter* 4 (Spring/Summer 1981): 305-07.

_____. "Patterns of Recent Canadian Poetry." *Selected Essays and Criticism*. Ottawa: Tecumseh, 1978: 94-110.

_____. "Robitaille's Exhilarating Work." *In Defence of Art: Critical Essays & Reviews*. Ed. Aileen Collins. Kingston: Quarry, 1988: 188.

_____. *Selected Essays and Criticism*. Ottawa: Tecumseh, 1978.

_____. "The State of Canadian Poetry: 1954." *Selected Essays and Criticism*. Ottawa: Tecumseh, 1978: 45-51.

_____. "Those Damned Visionary Poets (Les Poètes Maudits Visionnaires)." *Selected Essays and Criticism*. Ottawa: Tecumseh, 1978: 166-67.

_____. "Too Many Controls Spoil the Show." *In Defence of Art: Critical Essays & Reviews*. Ed. Aileen Collins. Kingston: Quarry, 1988: 74-75.

_____. "The Transition in Canadian Poetry." *Selected Essays and Criticism*. Ottawa: Tecumseh, 1978: 122-35.

_____. "Translations Enrich French-English Literature." *In Defence of Art: Critical Essays & Reviews*. Ed. Aileen Collins. Kingston: Quarry, 1988. 198-200.

_____. "The Two Traditions—Literature and the Ferment in Quebec." *Selected Essays and Criticism*. Ottawa: Tecumseh, 1978: 157-65.

_____. Unpublished letters to Ezra Pound. Copyright © 2001 by Louis Dudek. Used by permission of Louis Dudek.

_____. Unpublished letter to John Sutherland. Copyright © 2001 by Louis Dudek. Used by permission of Louis Dudek.

Dudek, Louis and Michael Gnarowski, eds. *The Making of Modern Literature in Canada: Essential Articles on Contemporary Canadian Poetry in English*. Toronto: Ryerson Press, 1967.

Dufour, Andrée. *Histoire de l'éducation au Québec*. Québec: Boréal, 1997.

Duguay, Raoul [Luoar Yaugud]. "Lettre d'amour à Toulmonde." *Ellipse* 6 (Winter 1971): 32-47.

Durocher, Jean-Yves. "*Mordecai—l'oppresseur opprimé*." *Le Devoir* [Montréal] (10 Oct. 1999): B8.

Eliot, T. S. *Collected Poems 1909-1935*. London: Faber & Faber, 1936.

_____. *Collected Poems 1909-1962*. London: Faber & Faber, 2002.

_____. "The Metaphysical Poets." 1921. In *Selected Essays*. London: Faber & Faber, 1951: 281-291.

Etcheverry, Jorge. "Chilean Literature: Diaspora." *Zymergy* 7 (Spring 1990): 67-70.

Farkas, Endre, and Ken Norris. "Introduction." *Montreal English Poetry of the Seventies*. Montreal: Véhicule Press, 1978: ix-xii.

Farkas, Endre, ed. *The Other Language: English Poetry of Montreal*. Dorion, Québec: The Muses' Co., 1987.

_____, ed. *Quebec Suite: Poems For and About Quebec*. Montréal: The Muses' Co., 1995.

Farkas, Endre, ed., and Émile Martel, trans. *Passeport: La poésie moderne de langue anglaise au Canada*. Winnipeg: J. Gordon Shillingford, 1998.

Farkas, Endre and Ken Norris, eds. *Montreal: English Poetry of the Seventies*. Montréal: Véhicule, 1977.

Farkas, Endre, Artie Gold, Tom Konyves, Claudia Lapp, John McAuley, Stephen Morrissey, and Ken Norris. *The Vehicule Poets*. Montréal: Maker Press, 1979.

Ferrier, Ian. *Exploding Head Man*. Audio CD and Book. Montréal: Planète Rebelle, 2000.

Ferrier, Ian, prod. *Millenium Cabaret*. Audio CD. Montréal: Wired on Words, 1998.

Fischman, Sheila. "A Night in August." *Matrix* 22 (Spring 1986): 23-27.

Flynn, Kevin. "Introduction: Here We Are." *Essays on Canadian Writing* 71 (2000): 1-5.

Foucault, Michel. *The History of Sexuality, Volume 1, An Introduction*. Trans. Robert Hurley, New York: Vintage Books, 1980.

Francis, Wynne. *Irving Layton and His Work*. Toronto: ECW Press, 1984.

Frank, Waldo. "Hart Crane." *The Complete Poems and Selected Letters and Prose of Hart Crane*. Ed. Brom Weber. Garden City: Anchor Books, 1966. 269-273.

Frye, Northrop. "Conclusion." *Literary History of Canada: Canadian Literature in English*. Ed. Carl F. Klinck. Toronto: Toronto University Press, 1965. 821–49.

Garneau, Michel. "A G – (aile gauche)." *Ellipse* 6 (Winter 1971): 12-15.

_____. "L W (Leftwing)." Trans. Ronald Sutherland. *Ellipse* 6 (Winter 1971): 12-15.

Geddes, Gary. "Down But Not Out in Nicaragua." *Zymergy* 8 (Autumn 1990): 9-14.

Gilloch, Graeme. *Walter Benjamin: Critical Constellations*. Cambridge, UK: Polity, 2002.

Ginsberg, Allen. *First Blues: Rags, Ballads & Harmonium Songs 1971-74*. New York: Full Court, 1975.

Glassco, John. *Selected Poems*. Toronto: Oxford University Press, 1971.

Glassco, John, ed. *English Poetry in Quebec: Proceedings of the Foster Poetry Conference, October 12-14, 1963*. Montréal: McGill University Press, 1965.

_____. *The Poetry of French Canada in Translation*. Toronto: Oxford University Press, 1970.

Godin, Gérald. *Les Botterlots*. Montréal: l'Hexagone, 1993.

_____. *Les Cantouques*. Montréal: Éditions Parti Pris, 1967.

_____. *Sarazènes*. Montréal: Écrits des Forges, 1983.

Gouvernement du Québec, Ministère des communautés culturelles et de l'immigration. *Au Québec. Pour Bâtir ensemble. Énoncé de politique en matière d'immigration et d'intégration*. Québec: Gouvernement du Quebec, 1998.

Gravel, Denis. *Une approche historique et économique de la société Lachinoise, 1667-1767*. LaSalle: Société historique Cavelier-de-LaSalle, 1993.

Grenier, Eric. "Hello Pot? It's the Kettle." *Hour Magazine* (24 Feb. - 3 Mar. 2000): 8.

Groening, Laura. "In Memoriam: Wynne Francis." *Thursday Report* (28 Sept. 2000): 22.

Grosz, Elizabeth. "Bodies-Cities." *Sexuality and Space*. Ed. Beatriz Colomina. New York: Princeton Architectural Press, 1992: 241-253.

Guillevic, Eugène. "Avant-propos." *Ellipse* 1 (1969): 4.

_____. "Ellipse." Trans. Teo Savery. *Ellipse* 1 (1969): 3.

Gustafson, Ralph. *Plummets*. Vancouver: Sono Nis Press, 1987.

Hamel, Yves. "Question linguistique à Montréal: Sur la Catherine, vente trottoir ou *garage sale*?" *Le Devoir* [Montréal] (20 jul. 2000): A7.

Hampson, Sarah. "The Unbearable Lightness of Anne Carson." *Globe & Mail* (14 Sep. 2000): R1.

Hancock, Geoff. "What Now Montreal?" *Matrix* 20 (Spring 1985): 5-15.

Harris, Michael. "A Note About This Collection." *Poetry Readings: 10 Montreal*

Poets at the CEGEPS. Ed. Michael Harris. Montréal: Delta, 1975. n.p.

_____. *Grace*. Montréal: Delta, 1977.

_____. *In Transit*. Montréal: Véhicule Press, 1985.

_____. "Leonard Cohen: The Poet as Hero – 2." *Saturday Night* 84 (June 1969): 26-31.

_____. *New and Selected Poems*. Montréal: Véhicule Press, 1992.

_____. *Sparks*. LaSalle, Québec: New Delta, 1976.

_____. "Speech." *Books in Canada* 31 (April 2002): 28.

_____. *Text for Nausikaa*. Montréal: Delta Canada, 1970.

Harris, Michael, ed. *Poetry Readings: 10 Montreal Poets at the CEGEPS*. Montréal: Delta, 1975.

Heaney, Seamus. *Opened Ground: Poems 1966-1996*. London: Faber & Faber, 1998.

Heighton, Steven. "English Cemetery, Gaspésie." *Quebec Suite: Poems for and About Quebec*. Ed. Andre Farkas. Montréal: The Muses' Co., 1995: 97-98.

Heintz, Kurt. "An Incomplete History of Slam: A Biography of an Evolving Poetry Movement." *e-poet's online library* (1994, 1996, 2000) <http:// www.e-poets.net/library/slam/> (11 November 2006)

Hornyansky, Michael. "Poetry." *University of Toronto Quarterly* 47 (Spring/Summer 1979): 339-353.

Huang, Yunte. *Ethnography, Translation, and Transpacific Displacement: Intertextual Travel in Twentieth-Century American Literature*. Berkeley: University of California Press, 2002.

Hutchman, Laurence. "An Interview With George Johnston." *Zymergy* 10 (Autumn 1991): 45-57.

_____. "An Interview with Louis Dudek." *The River Review* 1 (1995): 63-79.

Jakle, John A. and Keith A. Sculle. *Fast Food: Roadside Restaurants in the Automobile Age*. Baltimore: Johns Hopkins University Press, 1999.

James, Clive. "Somewhere Becoming Rain." *Reliable Essays: The Best of Clive James*. London: Picador, 2001: 25-35.

Jameson, Fredric. *Postmodernism, or, the Cultural Logic of Late Capitalism*. Durham, N.C.: Duke Universtiy Press, 1991.

Jarrell, Randall. *Poetry and The Age*. New York: Vintage Books, 1955.

Jones, D. G. *A Throw of Particles, the New and Selected Poetry of D. G. Jones*. Toronto: General, 1983.

_____. "Afterword." In Normand de Bellefeuille, *Categorics 1, 2 & 3*. Trans. D. G. Jones. Toronto: Coach House Press, 1992: 76-77.

_____. *Balthazar and Other Poems*. Toronto: Coach House, 1988.

_____. *Butterfly on Rock*. Toronto: University of Toronto Press, 1970.

_____. *The Floating Garden*. Toronto: Coach House, 1995.

_____. "Foreword." *Ellipse* 60 (1999): 6-9.

_____. "Foreword." *Ellipse* 50 (1993): 6-8.

_____. "Gaston Miron: A Testimony." *Ellipse* 5 (Autumn 1970): 55-57.

_____. *Grounding Sight.* Montréal Empyreal Press, 1999.

_____. "Grounds for Translation." *Ellipse* 21 (1977): 58-91.

_____. "Introduction." *Esprit du corps: Quebec Poetry of the Late Twentieth Century in Translation.* Ed. Louse Blouin, Bernard Pozier, and D. G. Jones. Winnipeg: The Muses' Co., 1997: 9-11.

_____. "Introduction." In Paul-Marie Lapointe, *The Terror of the Snows, Selected Poems.* Trans. D. G. Jones. Pittsburgh: University of Pittsburgh Press, 1976: xi-xv.

_____. "The Matrix Interview" *Matrix* 50 (1997): 8-16.

_____. "Note" to "Balthazar: The Real Thing." *Moosehead Review* 8 (1983): 25.

_____. "Two Windows: An Interview with D.G. Jones." *Poetry Canada Review* 8 (Spring 1987): 3-5.

_____. *Under the Thunder the Flowers Light Up the Earth.* Toronto: Coach House, 1977.

_____. "La vraie révolution est celle de l'imagination." *Ellipse* 6 (Winter 1971): 91-97.

_____. *Wild Asterisks in Cloud.* Montréal: Empyreal Press, 1997.

Kahn, Linda. *Schooling, Jobs, and Cultural Identity: Minority Education in Quebec.* New York and London: Garland, 1992.

Kaplan, Caren. "The Politics of Location as Transnational Feminist Critical Practice." *Scattered Hegemonies: Postmodernity and Transnational Feminist Practices.* Ed. Inderpal Grewal and Caren Kaplan. Minneapolis: University of Minnesota Press, 1994: 137-152.

Karmis, Dimitrios. "Pluralism and National Identity(ies) in Contemporary Quebec Conceptual Clarifications, Typology, and Discourse Analysis." Trans. Mélanie Maisonneuve. In *Québec: State and Society.* Ed. Alain-G. Gagnon. Peterborough: Broadview Press, 2004: 69-96.

Kidd, Catherine, with music by Jack Beetz. *Sea Peach: Halocynthia Auranthium.* Audio CD and Book. Montréal: Conundrum Press, 2002.

Klein, A. M. *The Collected Poems.* Toronto: McGraw Hill Ryerson, 1974.

_____. "Review of *Here and Now* by Irving Layton." *Literary Essays and Reviews.* Ed. U. Caplan and M. W. Steinberg. Toronto: University of Toronto, 1987: 212-215.

_____. *The Rocking Chair and Other Poems.* Toronto: Ryerson Press, 1948.

Konyves, Tom. *Poetry in Performance.* Ste. Anne de Bellevue, Québec: The Muses' Co., 1982.

Kristeva, Julia. "An Interview with Julia Kristeva." Interviewed by Margaret Waller.

Trans. Richard Macksey. *Intertextuality and Contemporary American Fiction*. Ed. Patrick O'Donnell and Robert Con Davis. Baltimore: Johns Hopkins University Press, 1989: 280-293.

Kroc, Ray. *Grinding it Out: The Making of McDonald's*. New York: Berkeley, 1977.

Lalonde, Michèle. "An Interview with Michele Lalonde." Interview by D. G. Jones. *Ellipse* 3 (Spring 1970): 33-41.

_____. "Speak White." Trans. D.G. Jones. *Ellipse* 3 (Spring 1970): 24-31.

Lane, M. Travis. "An Unimpoverished Style: the Poetry of George Elliott Clarke." *Canadian Poetry* 16 (1985): 1-20.

Lapointe, Paul-Marie. *Pour les âmes précédé de choix de poèmes/Arbres*. Montréal: Éditions Typo, 1993.

_____. *Le réel absolu, poèmes 1948-1965*. Montréal: L'Hexagone, 1971.

_____. *The Terror of the Snows, Selected Poems*. Trans. D.G. Jones. Pittsburgh: University of Pittsburgh Press, 1976.

Larouche, Jean-Sébastien. *Rose et rasoir*. Outremont: Lanctôt Éditeur, 1998.

Lawrence, P. Scott, ed. *Souvenirs: New English Fiction from Quebec*. Dunvegan, Ont.: Cormorant Books, 1987.

Layton, Irving. *For My Brother Jesus*. Toronto: McClelland & Stewart, 1976.

_____. *The Improved Binoculars*. Highlands, North Carolina: J. Williams, 1956.

_____. *A Red Carpet for the Sun*. McClelland & Stewart, 1959.

_____. *Selected Poems*. Ed. Wynne Francis. Toronto: McClelland & Stewart, 1969.

_____. *Waiting for the Messiah: A Memoir*. Toronto: McClelland & Stewart, 1985.

Lecker, Robert. "Where Is Here Now?" *Essays on Canadian Writing* 71 (2000): 6-13.

Leslie, Esther. "Souvenirs and Forgetting: Walter Benjamin's Memory-Work." *Material Memories: Design and Evocation*. Ed. Marius Kwint, Christopher Breward and Jeremy Aynsley. New York: Berg, 1999: 107-122.

Letelier-Ruz, Elias. "An Interview With Ernesto Cardenal." *Zymergy* 9 (Spring 1991): 57-70.

"Lévesque Jumps into School Controversy." *Gazette* [Montreal] (14 June 1968): A4.

Liu, Alan. "Local Transcendence: Cultural Criticism, Postmodernism, and the Romanticism of Detail." *Representations* 32 (1990): 75-113.

_____. *Wordsworth: The Sense of History*. Stanford, California: Stanford University Press, 1998.

Luxton, Steve. *The Hills That Pass By*. Montréal: DC Books, 1987.

_____. *Iridium*. Montreal: DC Books, 1993.

_____. *Luna Moth and Other Poems*. Montreal: DC Books, 2004.

MacLeish, Archibald. "Ars Poetica." *Collected Poems 1917-1952*. Cambridge, Massachusetts: Houghton Mifflin, 1952.

Mailhot, Laurent and Pierre Nepveu, eds. *La Poésie Québécoise (des origines à nos jours.)* Montréal: Éditions Typo, 1996.

Mandel, Eli. *Irving Layton*. Toronto: Forum House, 1969.

Mander, Jerry. *Four Arguments for the Elimination of Television*. New York: Morrow, 1978.

Manicom, David. Review of *In Transit* by Michael Harris. *Rubicon* 8 (Spring 1987): 173-6.

Mansbridge, Francis, ed. *Wild Gooseberries: The Selected Letters of Irving Layton*. Toronto: Macmillan, 1989.

Marchand, Jean-Paul. *Conspiration? Les anglophones veulent-ils éliminer le français du Canada?* Montreal: Stanké, 1997.

Marcotte, Gilles. "Le double exil d'Octave Cremazie." 1955. *Une literature qui se fait*. Montréal: Les Éditions HMH, 1962: 71-83.

Marcus, Greil. *Dead Elvis: A Chronicle of a Cultural Obsession*. New York: Doubleday, 1991.

Marcus, Leah. *Puzzling Shakespeare: Local Reading and Its Discontents*. Berkeley: University of California Press, 1988.

Marshall, Tom. "Virtuoso Turns." *Canadian Literature* 103 (Winter 1984): 97-8.

Martel, Émile. *Para Orquesta y Poeta Solo*. Edición bilingüe. Trans. Mónica Mansour. Trois Rivières: Écrits des Forges, 1999.

———. *For Orchestra and Solo Poet*. Trans. D. G. Jones. Winnipeg: J. Gordon Shillingford, 1996.

Marvell, Andrew. *Andrew Marvell, The Complete Poems*. Ed. Elizabeth Story Donno. Harmondsworth: Penguin, 1972.

Marx, Karl. *Capital: A Critique of Political Economy*. Vol. 1. Trans. Samuel Moor and Edward Aveling. New York: International Publishers, 1967.

Massey, Doreen. "A Global Sense of Place." *Marxism Today* (June 1991): 24-9.

Mayne, Seymour. "Introduction." *Irving Layton: The Poet and His Critics*. Ed. Seymour Mayne. Toronto: McGraw-Hill Ryerson, 1978: 1-22.

McGimpsey, David. *Dogboy*. Toronto: ECW Press, 1998.

———. *Hamburger Valley, California*. ECW Press, 2001.

———. "Hate mail published." *Gazette* [Montreal] (13 June 1990): B2.

———. *Lardcake*. Toronto: ECW Press, 1996.

———. "A Walk in Montreal: Wayward Steps through the Literary Politics of Contemporary English Quebec." *Essays on Canadian Writing* 71 (2000): 150–68.

Melançon, Benoît. "Sept minutes de honte." *Le Devoir* [Montréal] (28 oct. 1997): A7.

Melfi, Mary. "An Interview with Mary Melfi: The Dangers of Poetry." *Zymergy* 7 (Spring 1990): 118-129.

Michaels, Anne. "Last Night's Moon." *Skin Divers*. Toronto: McClelland & Stewart, 1999: 17-25.

Miron, Gaston. *L'Homme Rapaillé*. Montréal: Éditions Typo, 1996.

_____. *Embers and Earth (Selected Poems)*. Trans. D.G. Jones and Marc Plourde. With translator's commentary by Marc Plourde. Montréal: Guernica, 1984.

Monnin, Christian. "Presentation: Un espace du possible." *Liberté* 42.1 (2000): 3-5.

Mount, Nick. *When Canadian Literature Moved to New York*. Toronto: University of Toronto Press, 2005.

Mouré, Erin. "The Anti-Anaesthetic." *Open Letter* 9.3 (1995): 13-24.

_____. *O Cidadán*. Toronto: Anansi, 2002.

_____. "Poetry, Memory and the Polis." *Language in Her Eye: Views on Writing and Gender by Canadian Women Writing in English*. Ed. Libby Scheier, Sarah Sheard and Eleanor Wachtel. Toronto: Coach House, 1990: 201-208.

_____. *Sheepish Beauty, Civilian Love*. Montreal: Véhicule Press, 1992.

_____. *Sheep's Vigil by a Fervent Person: A TransElation of Alberto Caeiro / Fernando Pessoa's O Guardador de Rebanhos*. Toronto: Anansi, 2001.

Moussette, Normand. *En ces lieux que l'on nomma 'La Chine': Premiers volets d'une recherche touchant plus de trois siècles d'histoire*. Ville de Lachine, 1978.

Moyes, Lianne. "Ecrire en anglais au Québec: un devenir minoritaire?" *Quebec Studies* 26 (Fall 1998/Winter 1999): 26-37.

_____. "Intertextual Travel in the Writing of Gail Scott and Mary di Michele." *Études canadiennes / Canadian Studies* 55 (Winter 2003): 85-97.

_____. "'Global / local'. Montréal dans la poésie de Robyn Sarah, Mary di Michele et Erin Mouré." *Voix et images* 90 (Spring 2005): 113-132.

Nause, John and Michael Heenan, eds. "An Interview with Louis Dudek." *Tamarack Review* 69 (Summer 1976): 30-43.

Nepveu, Pierre. *L'écologie du real: Mort et naissance de la literature Québécoise contemporaine*. Montréal: Boréal, 1988.

Norris, Alexander. "The New Anglo." *Gazette* [Montreal] (29 May 1999): A1.

_____. "Rallying Anglos: Signs and Battles of the Anglo-Rights Movement Resonate Less with Younger English Quebecers." *Gazette* [Montreal] (5 June 1999): A1.

Norris, Ken. "The Significance of Contact and *CIV/n*." *CIV/n: A Literary Magazine of the 50's*. Ed. Aileen Collins. Montréal: Véhicule, 1983: 253-267.

Norris, Ken, ed., *Canadian Poetry Now: 20 Poets of the '80s*. Toronto: House of Anansi Press, 1984.

_____, ed. *An Unorthodox History of Montreal's Vehicle Poets*. Montreal: Nuage, 1993.

_____, ed. *Vehicle Days*. Winnipeg: Signature Editions, 1993.

Norton, Philip and Todd Swift, eds. *Short Fuse*. New York: Rattapallax, 2002.

443

Nowlan, Alden. *Selected Poems*. Ed. Patrick Lane and Lorna Crozier. Concord: Anansi, 1996.

O'Rourke, David. "A Second Look at English Poetry in Montreal." CV/II 4 (Spring 1980): 24-27.

Osterlund, Steven. "Fumigator: An Outsider's View of Irving Layton." *Irving Layton: The Poet and His Critics*. Ed. Seymour Mayne. Toronto: McGraw-Hill Ryerson, 1978: 260-271.

Ozick, Cynthia. "The Function of the Small Press." *Metaphor & Memory*. New York: Alfred A. Knopf, 1989.

Pacey, Desmond. *Creative Writing in Canada*. Toronto: Ryerson Press, 1967.

Perloff, Marjorie. "The Contemporary of Our Grandchildren: Ezra Pound and the Question of Influence." *Poetic Licence: Essays on Modernist and Postmodernist Lyrics*. Evanston, Illinois: Northwestern University Press: 119-144.

Person, A. D. "The poets were pequistes when Lévesque was a Liberal." *Canadian Forum* 59 (April 1979): 13-17.

Pevere, Geoff and Greg Dymond. *Mondo Canuck: A Canadian Pop-Cultural Odyssey*. Toronto: Prentice Hall, 1996.

Plourde, Marc. "On Translating Miron." In Gaston Miron, *Embers and Earth (Selected Poems)*. Trans. D. G. Jones and Marc Plourde. Montréal: Guernica, 1984: 113-122.

Pound, Ezra. *ABC of Reading*. 1934. New York: New Directions, 1987.

_____. "Praefatio ad lectorem Electum." *The Spirit of Romance*. New York: New Directions 1968: 5-8.

_____. "Provincialism the Enemy." *Selected Prose 1909-1965*. 1950. New York: New Directions, 1973: 189-203.

Purdy, Al. *The Cariboo Horses*. McClelland & Stewart, 1965.

_____. "Hommage To Ree-shard." *Thru the Smoky End Boards: Canadian Poetry About Sports & Games*. Ed. Kevin Brooks and Sean Brooks. Vancouver: Polestar, 1996: 59-61.

Qian, Zhaoming. *Orientalism and Modernism: The Legacy of China in Pound and Williams*. Durham: Duke University Press, 1995.

Queyras, Sina, ed. *Open Field*. New York: Persea Books, 2005.

Rae, Ian. "Anne Carson (1950–)." *The Literary Encyclopedia*. <http://www.litencyc. com/php/speople.php?rec=true&UID=758> (20 October 2006).

_____. "Anne Carson and the Solway Hoaxes." *Canadian Literature* 176 (2003): 45–65.

_____. "'Dazzling Hybrids': The Poetry of Anne Carson." *Canadian Literature* 166 (2000): 17–41.

Reid, Gregory. "Is There an Anglo-Québécois Literature?" *Essays on Canadian*

Writing. Forthcoming.

Richardson, Keith. *Poetry and the Colonized Mind: Tish*. Oakville and Ottawa, Ont: Mosaic Press, 1976.

Richler, Mordecai. "Be it ever so (increasingly) humble, there's no place like home." *Maclean's Magazine* 91 (1 Aug. 1978): 54.

_____. *Canadian Writing Today*. Middlesex: Penguin, 1970.

_____. "My life as a racist." *Globe & Mail* (16 Feb. 1993): A18.

_____. *Oh Canada! Oh Quebec! Requiem for a Divided Country*. Toronto: Penguin, 1992.

Ritzer, George. *The McDonaldization of Society*. Thousand Oaks, Cal.: Pine Forge Press, 1996.

Richard Rodriguez, *Days of Obligation: An Argument with My Mexican Father*. New York: Penguin, 1992.

Roberge, Émile. *Sur la Place Publique* (extraits). Montréal: de la Paix, 1995. <www.multimania.com/poetesse/souvreine/roberge> (15 June 2000).

Ronell, Avital. *The Telephone Book: Technology—Schizophrenia—Electric Speech*. Lincoln: University of Nebraska Press, 1989.

Roy, G. R., ed. and trans. *Twelve Modern French Canadian Poets/Douze poètes modernes du Canada français*. Toronto: Ryerson, 1958.

Royer, Jean. "Les Poètes du Québec." *Le Québec en Poèsie*. Ed. Jean Royer. Paris: Gallimard Jeunesse, 1995.

Said, Edward. *Orientalism*. New York: Random House, 1978.

Sarah, Robyn. *Questions About the Stars*. London, Ont.: Brick, 1998.

Schlosser, Eric. *Fast Food Nation: The Dark Side of the All-American Meal*. New York: HarperCollins, 2002.

Schnurmacher, Thomas. "Montreal Poet Solway Finds Atwood a Dull Read." *Gazette* Montreal] (2 Oct. 1989): B5.

Scheier, Libby. "Grace That Comes with Death." *Contemporary Verse II* 4 (Spring 1980): 32-33.

Schrier, Louise. "The Breathless Adventure: An Interview With Louis Dudek on the Long Poem." *Zymergy* 8 (Autumn 1990): 39-53.

Scobie, Stephen. "Introduction." *Essays on Canadian Writing* (Winter 1999): 3-4.

Scowen, Reed. *A Different Vision: The English in Quebec in the 1990s*. Don Mills: Maxwell Macmillan Canada, 1991.

Schneider, Stephen P., ed. "Part IV: From The Wind To The Earth: An Interview With A. R. Ammons." *Complexities of Motion: New Essays On A.R. Ammons's Long Poems*. Cranbury: Associated University Presses, 1999: 325-349.

Shell Marc. "Babel in America; or, The Politics of Language Diversity in the United States." *Critical Inquiry* 20 (Autumn 1993): 103-127.

_____. "Language Wars." *The New Centennial Review* 1.2 (2001): 1-17.

Shepherdson, Charles. "The Elements of the Drive." *UMBR(a)* 1 (1997): 131-145.

Sherman, Ken. "Five Pieces for Irving Layton." *Books In Canada* 30 (Sept./Oct. 2001): 24-25.

Shouldice, Larry. "Foreword." *Ellipse* 27/28 (1981): 6-7.

Silberg, Richard. "On 'Fallen Western Star': Dana Gioia Stirs It Up." *Poetry Flash* 285 (May/June 2000): 48.

Simon, Sherry. "L'anglophonie éclatée." *Spirale* 34 (1983): 14-15.

_____. "Crossing Town: Montreal in Translation." *Profession* (2002): 15–24.

_____. "Entre les langues: l'écriture juive contemporaine à Montréal." *Montréal: l'invention juive*. Ed. Groupe de Recherche Montréal Imaginaire. Montréal: Dép. d'études françaises, Université de Montréal, 1991: 87-102.

_____. "Hybrid Montreal: The Shadows of Language." *Sites: The Journal of 20th-Century/Contemporary French Studies* 5.2 (2001): 315–330.

_____. *Hybridité Culturelle*. Montréal: l'Île de la tortue, 1999.

_____. "A Single Brushstroke: Writing through Translation: Anne Carson." *Journal of Contemporary Thought* 15 (2002): 37–47. Reprinted in *In Translation: Reflections, Refractions, Transformations*. Ed. Paul St-Pierre and Prafulla C. Kar. New Delhi: Pencraft International, 2005: 90–98.

_____. "Les solitudes abolies." *Le Devoir* [Montréal] (27 nov. 1999): D1-D2.

Skarstedt, Sonja A. "Editor's Note." *Zymergy* 10 (Autumn 1991): 5.

_____. "From *Modern Marriage* to Quebec's Literary Renaissance: An Interview With David Solway." *Zymergy* 6 (Autumn 1989): 47-64.

_____. "Hanging Fire: Interview with Phyllis Webb," *Zymergy* 9 (Spring 1991): 35-49.

_____. "Towards Redemption: The Poetry of Pierre DesRuisseaux." In Pierre DesRuisseaux, *Graffiti: New Poems in Translation*. Trans. Louis Dudek, et al., Ed. Sonja Skarstedt. Montreal: DC Books, 2002. 73-80.

Smith, Beverly. "The Gospel According to Irving Layton." *Thursday Report* 2.10 (26 October 1978): 1, 5.

Smith, Douglas Burnet. "Hyperbole in Peter Van Toorn's *Mountain Tea and Other Poems*." *Essays on Canadian Writing* 43 (Spring 1991): 23-36.

Solway, David. *Bedrock*. Montreal: Véhicule Press, 1993.

_____. *Director's Cut*. Erin, Ont.: Porcupine's Quill, 2003.

_____. "Double Exile and Montreal English-Language Poetry." *Books in Canada* 31 (Winter 2002): 25-26.

_____. "Fellatio, Depth-Analysis, and The Experience of the Surface." *Zymergy* 10 (Autumn 1991): 7-21.

_____. "Framing Layton." *Random Walks: Essays in Elective Criticism*. Montreal/Kingston: McGill-Queens, 1997: 86-103.

_____. *Franklin's Passage*. McGill-Queen's University Press: 2003.

_____. "Louis Dudek Made Poetry Irresistible." *Quill & Quire* 67 (May 2001): 10.

_____. "Standard Canadian Average." *Director's Cut*. Erin, Ont.: Porcupine's Quill, 2003: 87-100.

_____. "*TDR* Interview: David Solway." *The Danforth Review* <http://www.danforthreview.com/features/interviews/solway/david_solway.htm> (18 August 2005)

_____. "The Trouble with Annie." *Books in Canada* 30.1 (2001): 24–26. Revised and reprinted in Solway, *Director's Cut*. Erin, Ont.: Porcupine's Quill, 2003: 39–58.

Solway, David, ed. *4 Montreal Poets*. New Brunswick: Fiddlehead, 1973.

Souaid, Carolyn Marie. *October*. Winnipeg: Nuage Editions, 1999.

Stanton, Victoria and Vincent Tinguely. "Reinventing the Word: The Montreal Poetry Scene Speaks for Itself." *Broken Pencil* 6 (Winter 1998): 13-17.

_____. *Impure: Reinventing the Word: The Theory, Practice and Oral History of Spoken Word in Montreal*. Montréal: Conundrum Press, 2001.

Starnino, Carmine. *A Lover's Quarrel*. Erin, Ont.: The Porcupine's Quill, 2004.

_____. *With English Subtitles*. Kentville. Nova Scotia: Gaspereau Press, 2005.

Starnino, Carmine, ed. *David Solway: Essays on His Works*. Toronto: Guernica, 2001.

Steinberg, Michael P. "The Collector as Allegorist." *Walter Benjamin and the Demands of History*. Ed. Michael P. Steinberg. Ithaca, NY: Cornell University Press, 1996. 88-118.

Steiner, George. *After Babel, Aspects of Language and Translation*. Third Edition. Toronto: Oxford University Press, 1998.

_____. *Errata, An Examined Life*. New Haven: Yale University Press, 1998.

Stephens, Ian. *Diary of a Trademark*. Montreal: Muses' Co., 1994.

Stevens, Wallace. "Phosphor Reading by His Own Light." *The Collected Poems of Wallace Stevens*. 1954. New York: Vintage, 1990: 267.

Straram, Patrick. "Ville 1." *Ellipse* 56 (1996): 40-41.

Sutherland, Ron. "The Athens of the North." *Les Cantons de l'Est*. Ed. Jean-Marie Dubois. Sherbrooke: Université de Sherbrooke, 1989: 265-271.

Swift, Todd, with music by Tom Walsh. *The Envelope, Please*. Audio CD. Montréal: Wired on Words, 2002.

Taddeo, Donat J. and Raymond C. Taras. *Le débat linguistique au Québec: La communauté Italienne et la langue d'enseignement*. Montréal: Les Presses de l'Université de Montréal, 1987.

Teboul, Victor. *Que Dieu vous garde de l'homme silencieux quand il se met soudain à parler*. Montréal: Les Intouchables, 1999.

"Test Case in St. Leonard." Editorial. *Gazette* [Montreal] (12 June 1968): A7.

Thesen, Sharon. "Mean Drunk Poem" & "Hello Goodbye." *The Broadview Anthology of Poetry*. Ed. Herbert Rosengarten and Amanda Goldrick-Jones. Peterborough: Broadview Press, 1993: 874-875.

Thomas, Trevor. "Sylvia Plath: Last Encounters." *Zymergy* 7 (Spring 1990): 41-54.

Torrey, E. Fuller. *The Roots of Treason: Ezra Pound and the Secret of St. Elizabeths*. New York: McGraw-Hill Book Company, 1984.

Trehearne, Brian. *The Montreal Forties: Modernist Poetry in Transition*. Toronto: University of Toronto, 1999.

Trudeau, Pierre Elliott. "Multiculturalism (with Government Response to Volume 4 of the report of the Royal Commission on Bilingualism and Biculturalism, Commissioners André Laurendeau and Davidson Dunton)." Speech delivered to the House of Commons, October 8, 1971. <http://www.canadahistory.com/ sections/documents/ trudeau_on multiculturalism.htm> (22 July 2005).

_____. "New Treason of the Intellectuals." *Federalism and the French Canadians*. Toronto: Macmillan, 1968. 151-181.

Trudel, Marcel. *The Beginnings of New France, 1524-1663*. Trans. Patricia Claxton. Toronto: McClelland & Stewart, 1973.

Tucker, John. "Peter Van Toorn, *Mountain Tea and Other Poems*." *Journal of Canadian Poetry* 1 (1986): 108-12.

Un Québec pour tous ses citoyens. Montréal: Conseil des relations interculturelles, 1986.

Unsigned. "Avant-propos." *Ellipse* 6 (Winter 1971): 4-5.

Unsigned. "'Bilingual Brain' Superior—Penfield." *Gazette* [Montreal] (15 June 1968): A3.

Unsigned. "Editorial." *Ellipse*, 6 (Winter 1971): 6-7.

Unsigned. "Premier Promises No Forced French." *Gazette* [Montreal] (13 June 1968): A1.

Van Toorn, Peter. "A Goose in the Caboose: Ideas on the Sonnet." *Poetics.ca* 3 (Fall 2003): n.p. <http://www.poetics.ca/poetics03/03pvt.html> (23 December 2005).

_____. "Introduction." *Cross/cut: Contemporary English Quebec Poetry*. Montréal: Véhicule Press, 1982: 19-37.

_____. *Mountain Tea*. Montréal: Véhicule Press, 2003.

_____. "Mountain Words." *Zymergy* 1.2-3 (Autumn 1987): 18-21.

_____. "The Pain of Babel." *The Antigonish Review* 53 (Spring 1983): 99-107.

_____. *Sounds New*. Montreal: The Muses' Co., 1990.

Van Wilt, Kurt. "Gods of Order, Gods of Death." *Matrix* 9 (Spring/Summer 1979): 67-71.

Venturi, Robert, Denise Scott Brown and Steven Izenour. *Learning from Las Vegas*.

Revised Edition. Cambridge, Massachusetts: The MIT Press, 1997.

Viera, Arlindo. "Les immigrants sont des poèmes." *Gerald Godin: Un poète en politique.* Ed. Lucille Beaudy, Robert Comeau and Guy Lachapelle. Montréal: l'Hexagone, 2000: 129-134.

Von Hallberg, Robert. *American Poetry and Culture, 1945-1980.* Cambridge, Massachusetts: Harvard University Press, 1985.

Waits, Tom. *Big Time.* Audio CD. New York: Island, 1990.

Waters, Juliet. "Wordmakers: A Guide to Montreal's Noisy Spoken-word Scene." *Montreal Mirror* (5 Jan. 1995): 14.

West, David S. "Graceful Kindlings." *Fiddlehead* 121 (Spring 1979): 157-160.

West, Paul. "Ethos and Epic: Aspects of Contemporary Canadian Poetry." *Canadian Literature* 4 (1960): 7-17.

Whitman, Walt. *Leaves of Grass: The First (1855) Edition.* Ed. Malcolm Cowley. New York: Viking, 1973.

Williams, William Carlos. "A Note on Layton." In Irving Layton, *The Improved Binoculars.* Highlands, North Carolina: J. Williams, 1956: 9-10.

Wilson, Rob and Wimal Dissanayake. "Introduction: Tracking the Global/Local." *Global/Local: Cultural Production and the Transnational Imaginary.* Durham: Duke University Press, 1996: 1-18.

Winters, Yvor. *On Modern Poets.* New York: Meridian Books, 1959.

Wirtén, Eva Hemmungs. *No Trespassing: Authorship, Intellectual Property Rights, and the Boundaries of Globalization.* Toronto: University of Toronto Press, 2005.

Wisse, Ruth. *The Modern Jewish Canon: A Journey Through Language and Culture.* New York: Free Press, 2000.

Wordsworth, William. "Preface" to the *Lyrical Ballads.* 1802. In S. T. Coleridge and William Wordsworth, *Lyrical Ballads.* Ed. W. J. B. Owen. Oxford: Oxford University Press, 1998: 153-179.

_____. *Wordsworth: Poems.* London: Penguin Books, 1988.

Yeats, William Butler. *Yeats' Poetry, Drama, and Prose.* Ed. James Pethica. New York and London: W.W. Norton & Co., 2000.

Contributors

Michael Benazon taught at Champlain Regional College, Lennoxville, Quebec, and published and presented papers in the fields of Quebec literature and Jewish studies. He received his Ph.D. from McMaster University in 1975, writing his doctoral thesis on the fiction of Thomas Hardy. He is the editor of *Montreal Mon Amour: Short Stories from Montreal* (Deneau, 1989), and the author of a memoir, *The Wandering Josephs: A Biographical Family History* (1996). He died in late 2006.

Jason Camlot is a Montreal-born poet and critic. He is author of two collections of poetry, *The Animal Library* and *Attention All Typewriters*. His poems and critical essays have appeared widely in journals and anthologies including *New American Writing*, *Postmodern Culture* and *English Literary History*. He received his Ph.D. from Stanford and teaches literature at Concordia University.

Louis Dudek was born in Montreal's East End in 1918 and died in 2001. He is often considered the father of contemporary Anglo-Quebec poetry. He received a B.A. from McGill University. From 1943-1951, he lived in New York City, where he graduated with a Ph.D. from Columbia, and then taught English at (the) City College of New York. His friends at this period included Cid Corman and Ezra Pound. In 1951 he joined McGill's English Department, and lectured there until his death. He pioneered the role and significance of small press publishing in Canada, particularly in the 1950s, 60s and 70s, through his work as contributing editor to *First Statement*, his little magazine *Delta* (founded in 1957), and the founding of Contact Press in 1952. He was later the editor and publisher of Delta Canada Press (now DC Books), which published the work of R.G. Everson and F.R. Scott, among others. Dudek was also instrumental, through the McGill Poetry Series, in publishing Leonard Cohen at the start of his career. Dudek's own poetry was published over a span of six decades. His major books include *East of the City* (Ryerson, 1946), *Europe* (Laocoon, 1955), *Atlantis* (Delta Canada, 1967), *Continuation* (Véhicule, 1981) and *The Caged Tiger* (Empyreal,1997).

Endre Farkas (known as Andre Farkas until the mid-1970s) was born in Hungary and has lived in Montreal since 1956. He was a member of the Vehicle poets in the 1970s, founded the Muses' Company press in 1980, one of the original founders of QSPELL and the Quebec Writers Federation (QWF), and a former president of the Quebec English Language Publishers' Association (AELAQ). Farkas has published nine books of poetry, including *In The Worshipful Company of Skinners* (The Muses' Co., 2003). He has edited a number of anthologies including *Canadian Poetry Now* (Anansi, 1984) and (with Ken Norris) *Montreal: English Poetry of the Seventies* (Véhicule, 1977).

Corey Frost is the author of the short-story collections *My Own Devices* (Conundrum, 2002) and *My Own Devices: Airport Version* (Conundrum, 2006), as well as *The Worthwhile Flux* (Conundrum, 2004), a collection of performance texts. Born in Summerside, P.E.I. in 1972, he moved to Montreal in the early nineties and became involved in small press publishing and spoken word performance. Since 2002 he has lived in New York City, where he is a Ph.D. candidate at the CUNY Graduate Center and a Writing Fellow at Brooklyn College.

Artie Gold was born in Brockville, Ontario in 1947, grew up in Outremont, Quebec, and became a Montreal poetry legend. His work came to prominence in the early 1970s when he was published in *4 Montreal Poets* (1973), and then with his first full collection, *City Flowers* (Delta, 1974). His work was regularly included in key anthologies of the period. *The Beautiful Chemical Waltz: New & Selected Poems* (J. Gordon Shillingford) was published in 1992. He died on Valentine's Day, 2007.

Geoff Hancock received his M.F.A. from the University of British Columbia in 1975, the same year he took over the editorship of *Canadian Fiction Magazine*, a position he held until it folded in 1998. During his tenure at *CFM*, Hancock published the work of some of Canada's best-known writers, including Margaret Atwood, Matt Cohen, Mavis Gallant, Alice Munro, Leon Rooke, Josef Skvorecký, Jane Urquhart, and Miriam Waddington. Hancock is the editor of numerous anthologies of short fiction, including *Metavisions* (Quadrant, 1983), *Invisible Fictions: Contemporary Stories from Quebec* (Anansi, 1987), and *Singularities* (Black Moss, 1990), and a collection of his interviews, *Canadian Writer's At Work* (Oxford UP, 1987).

Dean Irvine is an Associate Professor in the Department of English at Dalhousie University. He is the editor of *Archive for Our Times: Previously Uncollected and Unpublished Poems of Dorothy Livesay* (Arsenal Pulp, 1998), *Heresies: The Complete Poems of Anne Wilkinson, 1924-1961* (Véhicule, 2003), and *The Canadian Modernists Meet* (University of Ottawa Press, 2005), and author of *Editing Modernity: Women and Little-Magazine Cultures in Canada, 1916-1956* (University of Toronto Press, 2007). Since 2004 he has been the director and English-language general editor of the Canadian Literature Collection/La collection de la littérature canadienne at the University of Ottawa Press.

Tom Konyves is currently an English/Visual Arts instructor at University College of the Fraser Valley, residing in White Rock, BC. *Sleepwalking Among the Camels: Selected Poems* (Muses' Company) was published in 1995. His most recent work, *Out Of Sight, Out Of Mind (OOSOOM)*, a surreal novella, was published by BookThug, 2007. In 1978, he coined the term "videopoetry" to describe his multimedia work, and is considered to be one of the original pioneers of the form.

Philip Lanthier's interview with D.G. Jones can be found in *The Matrix Interviews* published by DC Books. He was the editor of the English selection of poems which appeared in the *Anthologie de la poésie des Cantons de l'Est au 20e siècle/Anthology of 20th Century Poetry of the Eastern Townships* published by Triptyque/Véhicule. Retired from Champlain College, Lennoxville, he now teaches English part-time at Bishop's University in Knowlton. He lives in Bolton Ouest.

Claudia Lapp's poetry publications include *Dakini* (Davinci, 1974), *Honey* (Véhicule/CrossCountry, 1977), *Horses* (Véhicule Art, 1977), and *Cloud Gate* (Muses' Company, 1985). She continues to be an active poet and poetry organizer in Eugene, Oregon.

Nicholas LoLordo is Assistant Professor of English at the University of Nevada, Las Vegas, where he teaches courses in modernism and twentieth-century English-language poetry and poetics. He has published articles in *The Wallace Stevens Journal, Contemporary Literature,* and *Postmodern Culture,* and is currently completing a manuscript on the 'notorious difficulty' of American poetry since modernism.

John McAuley was born in Montreal. He is the author of *Nothing Ever Happens in Pointe-Claire* (Véhicule, 1977), *Hazardous Renaissance, Mattress Testing* (CrossCountry, 1978), and *What Henry Hudson Found* (Véhicule, 1979). His most recent work has appeared in *Matrix* and *The Vehicle Poets Now.* He teaches in the Department of English at Concordia University.

David McGimpsey is a writer of fiction, poetry and cultural criticism. A Ph.D. in Literature, he is the author of the award-winning study *Imagining Baseball: America's Pastime and Popular Culture* (Indiana, 2000). His travel writing is frequently featured in *The Globe and Mail* as well as in a regular column for *EnRoute* magazine. A new book, his fourth collection of poems, will be released in the fall of 2007 by Coach House Books. David McGimpsey currently lives in Montreal and teaches at Concordia University.

Stephen Morrissey was born and lives in Montreal. He has published seven books of poetry, including *Mapping the Soul, Selected Poems 1978-1998* (Muses' Company, 1998). He was one of the original Vehicle Poets and has edited two experimental literary magazines, *what is* and *The Montreal Journal of Poetics.* With Carolyn Zonailo he publishes online poetry chapbooks at www.coraclepress.com. He teaches literature at Champlain College, in St-Lambert, Québec. Morrissey's literary papers are held at the McLennan Library, McGill University.

Lianne Moyes teaches Canadian and Québécois literature in the Department of English Studies at Université de Montréal. She is editor of *Gail Scott: Essays on Her Works* (2002) and co-editor of *Adjacencies: Minority Writing in Canada* (2004), both with Guernica. From 1993 to 2003, she was co-editor of the bilingual, feminist journal *Tessera*. Her work in the field of Montreal writing has appeared recently in *Études canadiennes*, *Voix et images* and *Canadian Literature* as well as in the collections *Un certain genre malgré tout*. *Pour une réflexion sur la différence sexuelle à l'oeuvre dans l'écriture* (Nota Bene) and *Trans.Can.Lit* (Wilfred Laurier UP). Born in Scotland, she now lives in St-André-d'Argenteuil.

Ken Norris was born in New York City and emigrated to Canada in the early seventies, where he quickly became one of Montreal's Vehicule Poets. He became a Canadian citizen in 1985. Norris teaches Canadian Literature and Creative Writing at the University of Maine. He currently divides his time between Canada and Maine. He is the author of many books of poetry and the editor of eight anthologies. Two of his books have been translated into French: *La Route Des Limbes* (*Limbo Road*, Écrits Des Forges) and *Hotel Montréal* (Éditions Du Noroît). *Hotel Montreal: New and Selected Poems* (Talonbooks) was published in 2001.

Norman Ravvin's books include two novels, *Lola by Night* (paperplates, 2003) and *Cafe des Westens* (Red Deer, 1991), and the story collection *Sex, Skyscrapers and Standard Yiddish* (paperplates, 1997). His essays on Canadian and American literature are collected in *A House of Words: Jewish Writing, Identity and Memory*. He is also the co-editor with Richard Menkis of *The Canadian Jewish Studies Reader*. His work has received the Canadian Jewish Book Award as well as the Ontario Arts Council K. M. Hunter Emerging Artist Award. He is Chair of the Concordia University Institute for Canadian Jewish Studies.

Sonja Skarstedt is a Montreal-born editor, painter and the founder of Empyreal Press. Her essays, short stories and poetry have appeared in numerous anthologies and periodicals. She is the author of four poetry collections including *In the House of the Sun* (2005) and a play, *St Francis of Esplanade* (2001). She is currently working on *Abundances* (poetry, Coracle Press, 2007) and a children's novel, *Ogden and the Erc.*

David Solway's most recent book of poetry is *Reaching for Clear* (Véhicule Press, Signal Editions, 2007). *Franklin's Passage* (McGill-Queen's, 2004), was awarded *Le Grand Prix du Livre de Montréal*. A political study, *The Big Lie: On Terror, Antisemitism and Identity*, appeared in 2007 with Lester, Mason & Begg/Random House. Appointed poet-in-residence at Concordia University for 1999-2000, he is currently an associate editor with *Books in Canada*.

Carmine Starnino has published three volumes of poetry, for which he has won numerous awards, including the A. M. Klein Prize and the F. G. Bressani Prize for his most recent book *With English Subtitles* (Gaspereau Press, 2004). He is the author of *A Lover's Quarrel* (Porcupine's Quill, 2004), a collection of essays on Canadian poetry, and the editor of *The New Canon: An Anthology of Canadian Poetry*

(Véhicule, 2005). He lives in Montreal, where he works as an associate editor for *Maisonneuve* and *Books in Canada*.

Todd Swift is the Montreal-born author of three collections of poetry, *Budavox*, *Cafe Alibi*, and *Rue du Regard*. He is the editor of numerous international poetry anthologies such as *Poetry Nation* and *100 Poets Against the War*. In 2005 he edited a special section, "The New Canadian Poetry", for New American Writing. His poems and reviews have appeared widely in journals and anthologies including *Books in Canada*, *The Globe and Mail*, The New Canon and *Poetry Review*. He has been Oxfam Great Britain's Poet-in-residence since 2004.

Tony Tremblay is Professor of Canadian and Cultural Studies at St. Thomas University. His articles have appeared in publications such as *English Studies in Canada*, *Studies in Canadian Literature,* and *Essays on Canadian Writing,*and in a number of book-length scholarly collections on Atlantic and Canadian modernism. He has also edited three collections of essays. His critical biography, *David Adams Richards of the Miramichi*, is forthcoming in 2007. His current research involves two archival projects: one on New Brunswick's pioneering modernists (A.G. Bailey and Desmond Pacey) and one editing the *Selected Letters of Louis Dudek*.

Peter Van Toorn was born in Holland in 1944 and raised in Montreal. He attended McGill University and taught for nearly thirty years at John Abbott College in Ste Anne de Bellevue, where he still lives. He is the author of *Leeway Grass* (1970), *In Guildenstern County* (1973), and *Mountain Tea and other Poems* (which was nominated for the Governor General's Award in 1984 and reissued by Véhicule Press in 2003). He co-edited (with Ken Norris) *Cross/cut: Contemporary English Quebec Poetry* (1982) and *The Insecurity of Art: Essays on Poetics* (1982).

Zachariah Wells is the author of *Unsettled* and Reviews Editor for *Canadian Notes & Queries*. His poems and critical prose have been published widely. Originally from Prince Edward Island and formerly resident in Ottawa, Halifax, Iqaluit, Montreal and Resolute Bay, he now lives in Vancouver and works for Via Rail. A children's book, co-written with Rachel Lebowitz and illustrated by Eric Orchard, is due for publication late 2007.

Index

100%